Collective Creativity for Responsible and Sustainable Business Practice

Ziska Fields
University of KwaZulu-Natal, South Africa

A volume in the Advances in Business Strategy and Competitive Advantage (ABSCA) Book Series

IGI GLOBAL
DISSEMINATOR OF KNOWLEDGE
www.igi-global.com

Published in the United States of America by
IGI Global
Business Science Reference (an imprint of IGI Global)
701 E. Chocolate Avenue
Hershey PA, USA 17033
Tel: 717-533-8845
Fax: 717-533-8661
E-mail: cust@igi-global.com
Web site: http://www.igi-global.com

Library of Congress Cataloging-in-Publication Data

Names: Fields, Ziska, 1970- editor.
Title: Collective creativity for responsible and sustainable business practice / Ziska Fields, editor.
Description: Hershey : Business Science Reference, [2017] | Series: Advances in business strategy and competitive advantage | Includes bibliographical references and index.
Identifiers: LCCN 2016044128| ISBN 9781522518235 (hardcover) | ISBN 9781522518242 (ebook)
Subjects: LCSH: Cooperative societies. | Sustainable development. | Social marketing.
Classification: LCC HD2963 .C65 2017 | DDC 658.4/08--dc23 LC record available at https://lccn.loc.gov/2016044128

This book is published in the IGI Global book series Advances in Business Strategy and Competitive Advantage (ABSCA) (ISSN: 2327-3429; eISSN: 2327-3437)

British Cataloguing in Publication Data
A Cataloguing in Publication record for this book is available from the British Library.

Advances in Business Strategy and Competitive Advantage (ABSCA) Book Series

Patricia Ordóñez de Pablos
Universidad de Oviedo, Spain

ISSN:2327-3429
EISSN:2327-3437

Mission

Business entities are constantly seeking new ways through which to gain advantage over their competitors and strengthen their position within the business environment. With competition at an all-time high due to technological advancements allowing for competition on a global scale, firms continue to seek new ways through which to improve and strengthen their business processes, procedures, and profitability.

The **Advances in Business Strategy and Competitive Advantage (ABSCA) Book Series** is a timely series responding to the high demand for state-of-the-art research on how business strategies are created, implemented and re-designed to meet the demands of globalized competitive markets. With a focus on local and global challenges, business opportunities and the needs of society, the **ABSCA** encourages scientific discourse on doing business and managing information technologies for the creation of sustainable competitive advantage.

Coverage

- Joint Ventures
- Foreign Investment Decision Process
- Strategy Performance Management
- Value Creation
- Business Models
- Tacit Knowledge
- Strategic management
- Ethics and Business Strategy
- Adaptive Enterprise
- Co-operative Strategies

IGI Global is currently accepting manuscripts for publication within this series. To submit a proposal for a volume in this series, please contact our Acquisition Editors at Acquisitions@igi-global.com or visit: http://www.igi-global.com/publish/.

The Advances in Business Strategy and Competitive Advantage (ABSCA) Book Series (ISSN 2327-3429) is published by IGI Global, 701 E. Chocolate Avenue, Hershey, PA 17033-1240, USA, www.igi-global.com. This series is composed of titles available for purchase individually; each title is edited to be contextually exclusive from any other title within the series. For pricing and ordering information please visit http://www.igi-global.com/book-series/advances-business-strategy-competitive-advantage/73672. Postmaster: Send all address changes to above address.

Titles in this Series

For a list of additional titles in this series, please visit: www.igi-global.com

Applying Neuroscience to Business Practice
Manuel Alonso Dos Santos (Universidad Católica de la Santísima Concepción, Chile)
Business Science Reference • copyright 2017 • 332pp • H/C (ISBN: 9781522510284) • US $200.00 (our price)

Handbook of Research on Fuzzy and Rough Set Theory in Organizational Decision Making
Arun Kumar Sangaiah (VIT University, India) Xiao-Zhi Gao (Aalto University, Finland) and Ajith Abraham (Machine Intelligence Research Labs, USA)
Business Science Reference • copyright 2017 • 474pp • H/C (ISBN: 9781522510086) • US $275.00 (our price)

Digital Entrepreneurship and Global Innovation
Ioan Hosu (Babeş-Bolyai University, Romania) and Ioana Iancu (Babeş-Bolyai University, Romania)
Business Science Reference • copyright 2017 • 301pp • H/C (ISBN: 9781522509530) • US $195.00 (our price)

Factors Affecting Firm Competitiveness and Performance in the Modern Business World
Aspasia Vlachvei (Western Macedonia University of Applied Sciences, Greece) Ourania Notta (Alexander Technological Educational Institute of Thessaloniki, Greece) Kostas Karantininis (Swedish University of Agricultural Sciences, Sweden) and Nicholas Tsounis (Western Macedonia University of Applied Sciences, Greece)
Business Science Reference • copyright 2017 • 359pp • H/C (ISBN: 9781522508434) • US $195.00 (our price)

Case Studies as a Teaching Tool in Management Education
Dominika Latusek (Kozminski University, Poland)
Business Science Reference • copyright 2017 • 326pp • H/C (ISBN: 9781522507703) • US $190.00 (our price)

Analyzing the Relationship between Corporate Social Responsibility and Foreign Direct Investment
Marianne Ojo (North West University, South Africa)
Business Science Reference • copyright 2016 • 322pp • H/C (ISBN: 9781522503057) • US $185.00 (our price)

Comparative Perspectives on Global Corporate Social Responsibility
Dima Jamali (American University of Beirut, Lebanon)
Business Science Reference • copyright 2017 • 367pp • H/C (ISBN: 9781522507208) • US $215.00 (our price)

Crowdfunding for Sustainable Entrepreneurship and Innovation
Walter Vassallo (MC Shareable, Monaco)
Business Science Reference • copyright 2017 • 336pp • H/C (ISBN: 9781522505686) • US $205.00 (our price)

Editorial Advisory Board

Table of Contents

Detailed Table of Contents

collective creativity and innovation, and influences sustainability for business organizations competing in an environment that is in a permanent state of flux. This chapter trails a series of concepts to find the relationship between the concept of bisociation, collective creativity and sustainable business practices. The aim is to show how consistent creative thinking and exploration of information in different spaces of thought can proffer innovative solutions organizations require for their long term survival and prosperity.

Information technology is rapidly increasing and evolving all the time in pursuit for better solutions and products for the digitized world. Technology advancement and greater connectivity has moved organizations to better economic markets for sustainability. Together with better technology and greater connectivity, cybercrime is swiftly growing on par with these developments. This chapter focuses on the cyber security landscape and threats faced by organizations. The growth and sophistication of cybercrime is stressed. Cyber security creative approaches security risk assessment, cloud collaboration and data analytics are provided. This chapter ends with propositions that security creative approaches should be used as a method of managing cybercrime and ensuring that the organization's sustainability and governance are improved.

The traditional view of problem solving is that experts are best addressed to solve complex but narrow problems. Intelligent novices, who have broad backgrounds and the motivation to learn and propose unique solutions, is an untapped source of experience. People increasingly want to take ownership of their lives and address problems that range from the routine (e.g., financial planning, healthcare, education) to the catastrophic (e.g., natural disasters, pandemics, terrorism). Features of human societies and traits of problem solving in humans are discussed. Examples of international problem solving are provided. The chapter describes three approaches to community problem solving, including problem solving groups, community decision support systems, and portals.

This chapter examines the concept of collective creativity in the work environment and in particular the manufacturing sector in Gweru, Zimbabwe. The chapter analyzes the role of a leader in fostering a work climate that cultivates collaborative efforts by followers in creating new ideas and for the sustainability of business operations. Literature relating to leadership role in enhancing sustainable and responsible collective creativity is reviewed. The chapter adopted a quantitative approach in which a survey questionnaire was pilot tested to assess the clarity of the questions on the questionnaire and test the internal consistency of the questions. A pilot test of the situational outlook questionnaire (SOQ) was conducted on 20 respondents in the manufacturing industry to assess the questions for clarity and internal consistency. The final survey questionnaire was distributed to 60 employees in the manufacturing sector in Gweru, Zimbabwe. The items on the questionnaire were rated on a 5 point Likert scale. Data was analysed using SPSS version 23. Data was analysed to determine the correlations between the independent variables and dependent variables. Transformational leadership constructs, namely idealised influence, intellectual stimulation, inspirational motivation and individualised consideration constituted leadership independent variables. Analysis of research data reveals that high performance is related to sustainable business practices such as the creation of environmentally friendly and affordable products. Unethical business practices are found to be negatively related to business performance and collective creativity. Analysis of the data revealed a positive correlation between individualised consideration construct of transformational leadership and ideal support ($r=.527$, $p=.001$) and a positive correlation between individualised consideration and openness ($r=.343$, $p<.001$), and a positive correlation between individualised consideration and involvement ($r=.123$, $p<.001$) This means that when a leader displays support through taking into consideration the individual needs of his or her followers, subordinates feel that the leader is encouraging them to participate in company activity and increase their perception of an involving climate. Acts of leadership support also stimulate subordinate views of an open forum where they can contribute to collective creativity within the organisation.

Co-engagement of organisation leadership in collective decision-making is recognised as a key modality for encouragement of collective creativity as well as responsible and sustainable business practices. In cases of public enterprise (PE) collective decision-making regarding organisational policy is necessary for organisation leadership to co-engage with key decision-makers in government to ensure responsible and sustainable execution of policy. Often policy-making and implementation allows little scope for innovation and creativity, in other words, for flexibility, with direct consequences for success or failure of collaboration. This chapter explores key inferences such as the need for creative strategic intent; need for co-engagement; need for responsible and sustainable business practices to build morale and the need for innovate approach to policy-making.

Since the dawn of civilisation, human communities have collectively allowed for the creation, and regularly taken advantage, of concepts, social arrangements and simple as well as complex tools aimed at fulfilling life-enabling ends for their members, under remarkably diverse circumstances. Natural and artificial languages, food recipes, universal health plans, urban sewers, open paths in the countryside, sports and games, pollution controls, old-age pensions, and regulated maximum working hours and minimum wages have all been tokens of "civil commons", a term coined in the 1990s by Canadian value theorist John McMurtry, meaning the "social constructs which enable universal access to life goods". In this chapter, McMurtry's axiology is presented, explained and applied, so as to highlight its implications for responsible and sustainable business practice.

Establishing a sustainable energy future can justifiably be considered the next frontier in global sustainable development under the agenda laid out in the Sustainable Development Goals (SDGs). The newly adopted Paris Agreement which seeks to hold global average temperature increase to "well below 2°C" above pre-industrial levels inserts additional urgency into this agenda. To realize the commitments outlined in the agreement, implementation of innovative sustainable business models capable of producing strong mitigation and adaptation outcomes is required 'on the ground' and needs to be available for subsequent diffusion across different countries, contexts and domains. This chapter explores the value of polycentric climate change governance through an investigation of sustainable business model innovation. An example of a sustainable business model, called the Sustainable Energy Utility (SEU), is evaluated and an assessment of United Nations-based programming to aid future diffusion of such business models is conducted.

Due to pressures of globalization and competition, the quality of corporate leadership has come under great scrutiny as questions are being raised worldwide regarding the ability of leaders to deliver long term growth on a sustainable basis. This can be referred to as the "sustainability leadership cavity." The chapter attempts to explore: what are the evolving challenges companies faces, what are the implications on demands placed on leaders and what new leadership competencies are required to ensure sustainability goals are achieved. It also intends to provide cases of successful sustainability leadership. Through grounded theory, in-depth literature review and contextual analysis the core of this chapter is to understand the organizational elements, structure, challenges and competencies crucial and critical for sustainability leadership.

This chapter focuses on responsible and sustainable management practices in business based on the 10 principles of the United Nations Global Compact (UNGC). The UNGC has been named the world's largest corporate sustainability initiative and it has already made a significant contribution to the entrenchment of globally acceptable business ethics. The UNGC identifies ethical leadership as an important organisational asset, which has also contributed to the implementation of key responsible and sustainable practices, such as anti-corruption seminars and corporate social responsibility, among others. A comparative analysis of responsible and sustainable management practices of businesses in Nigeria and the United Kingdom revealed that some practices, such as corporate social responsibility, are being practiced in both business environments, among other findings.

Foreword

This text is truly a timely and very appropriate publication to address the concerns of societies and nations regarding the manner in which business and governmental entities function on a global scale. The premise is that there are real indicators and trends pointing to the fact that in many countries, existing actions of corporates and governments, are slowly and systematically destroying the planet, and that humans are the most critical contributors to this growing threat.

This text starts by addressing the growing concern among scholars and practitioners of another 'melt down' – or destruction of the existing social, economic and physical systems as we know them. The consequential effects of poor practices and approaches to management lead to many other dire consequences, and sometimes unforeseen consequences such as the phenomenon referred to by some scholars as the Holocene extinction.

The editor and the authors of this book offer scholars and practitioners insight into the possibility of utilising the power of collective creativity to resolve some of these vexing problems. Several new and novel thoughts are offered, such as 'whole brain thinking', creative problem solving techniques, exploring the Bisociation Concept, building and managing collaborative networks, and fully utilising appropriate technologies.

The authors also weave into the text the important role of the United Nations endeavours such as the Global Compact, Global Sustainability Goals, and Principles for Responsible Management Education (PRME), ISO Standards, and Corporate Governance Principles as guiding precepts to and frameworks for guiding us towards resolving this dilemma.

Added into the mix, is the role of Green Marketing, comprehensive environmental consciousness in advertising and the responsible application of social media in achieving long term sustainability in the way in which we plan and execute executive business objectives.

This text serves as a valuable guide to business and governmental and NGO actors, in policy-making and achieving the desired outcome of being much more responsible in every action that will affect the future sustainability of the planet. The proposed case studies and examples will ensure a well-rounded text for both students and practitioners by illustrating several real world issues and solutions.

This is a welcome contribution to the much needed literature in this field.

Henry Wissink
University of KwaZulu-Natal (UKZN), South Africa

Preface

We rich nations, for that is what we are, have an obligation not only to the poor nations, but to all the grandchildren of the world, rich and poor. We have not inherited this earth from our parents to do with it what we will. We have borrowed it from our children and we must be careful to use it in their interests as well as our own. (Moss Cass)

Mankind, however is realizing that the world has changed drastically and the planet is in crisis (King, 2012). Emmott (2013) explains that "our cleverness, our inventiveness and our activities have modified almost every part of our planet. In fact, we are having a profound impact on it. Indeed, our cleverness, our inventiveness and our activities are now the drivers of every global problem we face". This is a scary thought, because our abilities which makes us different from other species are being used for our own selfish satisfaction and needs, rather than to use it wisely for the benefit of the planet we call home.

Kolbert (2014) agrees with Emmott when she wrote in her book *The Sixth Extinction* that human qualities like mankind's restlessness, creativity, the ability to cooperate, to solve problems, and complete complicated tasks are leading mankind to change the world so rapidly and profoundly that other species cannot keep up, are either extinct or are headed towards oblivion. In addition, the normal process of evolution cannot take place due to the accelerated die-off rate of species due to humans' unmindful living (Vince, 2012) and irresponsible business practices are causing melting glaciers, resource depletion, ocean acidification, and deforestation.

Some of the causes of environmental degradation are greenhouse gas emissions, deforestation, and water pollution and other forms of industrial wastes which are the result of human progress and irresponsible business practices. Even "new" technology (cell phones, laptops, iPads) is causing white waste and mankind does not have the answers to get rid of the daily waste being produced in an individual, business, country and world level. Kolberg (2014) stated that a Holocene extinction is imminent due to mankind's indifference and even cruelty to other life on the planet in its pursuit of money and progress.

The financial crises, climate change, ecological overshoot, population growth, water and food shortages and greater expectations of shareholders are causing people and business to rethink human- and business activity. New and better ways are explored in an attempt to not harm the environment by a few concerned environmentalists. However, the world is still faced with more greed than concern, which are not taking the care for the planet seriously enough to make a significant difference. What is clear however is that a conducive natural environment is important for healthy living and the sustainability of all creatures.

Deterioration of the global environment creates risks and opportunities for firms operating in the 21st century. Competencies in creativity, problem-solving and formulating competitive and environmental management strategies becomes crucial in building sustainable business practices. The UN's Global Compact and the Principles of Responsible Education (PRME) also aim to focus the attention of business leaders and educators on responsible and sustainable business practices in an effort to minimize the harm humans are causing the planet.

The only way forward, if we are going to improve the quality of the environment, is to get everybody involved. (Richard Rogers)

This book explores how collective creativity can be used to find novel solutions to the problems caused by mankind and to develop responsible and sustainable business practices specifically in an effort to prevent and minimize a Holocene extinction. It is evident that mankind needs to work together and that everyone should play their part in decreasing the negative impact they make on a daily basis.

This comprehensive and timely publication aims to be an essential reference source, building on the available literature and expertise in the field of creativity and responsible and sustainable management practices in developing and developed countries, while providing for further research opportunities in this dynamic field. It is hoped that this text will provide a resource that governments, nonprofit and for-profit organizations, business leaders and managers, universities and academics as well as community members and leaders can use to encourage collective creativity to develop responsible and sustainable business practice. It is also hoped that the book will play a role in creating greater awareness and action to make a real difference.

Saving our planet, lifting people out of poverty, advancing economic growth ... these are one and the same fight. We must connect the dots between climate change, water scarcity, energy shortages, global health, food security and women's empowerment. Solutions to one problem must be solutions for all. (Ban Ki-Moon)

The concept of responsible and sustainable business practices has been given considerable attention in recent years. The link to collective green creativity and eco-innovation has not been as strongly investigated. It is the view of the contributors of the book chapters that collective creativity can indeed help to find better solutions and create a sustainable planet for all, because creativity leads to new discoveries and new opportunities.

Capital isn't so important in business. Experience isn't so important. You can get both these things. What is important is ideas. If you have ideas, you have the main asset you need, and there isn't any limit to what you can do with your business and your life. (Harvey Firestone)

This book is divided into four sections.

Section 1 in the text focuses on collective creativity and the link to sustainable business practices. This section consists of six chapters focusing on collective green creativity and eco-innovation as key drivers of sustainable business solutions in the organization, Bisociation, the need for Cyber Security Creativity, the empowerment of communities to address impossible problems, the role of leadership in cultivating a responsible collective creative work environment and the co-engagement of organizational leadership in collective decision-making looking at a public enterprise.

Section 2 focuses on strategies and leadership for responsible and sustainable business practice. This section consists of five chapters focusing on the collective creation of Civil Commons, sustainable business model Innovation by using Polycentric and Creative Climate Change Governance, corporate leadership, responsible and sustainable management practices, developing and developed business environments, as well as a systemic approach towards responsible and sustainable economic development focusing on entrepreneurship, systems theory and socioeconomic momentum.

Section 3 in the text focuses on responsible management education and consists of two chapters. The first chapter explores the principles of Responsible Management Education (PRME) specifically and the second chapter in this section discusses educational and business co-operatives as channels of collective creativity and entrepreneurial teams.

Section 4 in the text focuses on social marketing for a sustainable future and consists of three chapters, namely social marketing to achieve sustainability, the use of social media and online petitions to achieve collective change for a sustainable future and finally using successful cases to promote environmental sustainability.

This book is a contribution to help inspire mankind to work with Mother Nature in sustainable, responsible, caring and creative ways to prevent the destruction of this wonderful and amazing planet we live in. All that is left is to make a stand and make a difference.

John W. Gardner (2015) once said, "When Alexander the Great visited Diogenes and asked whether he could do anything for the famed teacher, Diogenes replied: 'Only stand out of my light.' Perhaps someday we shall know how to heighten creativity. Until then, one of the best things we can do for creative men and women is to stand out of their light" because our planet's survival depends on creative men and women.

The book is dedicated to the future of everything living on this planet, we call home.

Ziska Fields
University of KwaZulu-Natal, South Africa

REFERENCES

Emmott, S. (2013). Humans: the real threat to life on Earth. *The Guardian*. Retrieved June 15, 2016 from https://www.theguardian.com/environment/2013/jun/30/stephen-emmott-ten-billion

Gardner, J. W. (2015). *Quotation #2458*. Retrieved July 8, 2016 from http://www.quotationspage.com/quote/2458.html

King, E. (2012). *King report on corporate governance in SA*. Retrieved June 15, 2016 from http://www.iodsa.co.za/?kingIII

Kolberg, E. (2014). *The sixth extinction: an unnatural history*. New York: Henry Holt and Company, LLC.

Vince, C. (2012). *A looming mass extinction caused by humans*. Retrieved August 20, 2016, from http://www.bbc.com/future/story/20121101-a-looming-mass-extinction

Acknowledgment

The editors would like to acknowledge the help of all the people involved in this project and, more specifically, to the authors and reviewers that took part in the review process. Without their support, this book would not have become a reality.

First, the editors would like to thank each one of the authors for their contributions. Our sincere gratitude goes to the chapter's authors who contributed their time and expertise to this book.

Second, the editors wish to acknowledge the valuable contributions of the reviewers regarding the improvement of quality, coherence, and content presentation of chapters. Most of the authors also served as referees; we highly appreciate their double task.

Ziska Fields
University of KwaZulu-Natal, South Africa

Section 1
Collective Creativity

Chapter 1

Collective Green Creativity and Eco-Innovation as Key Drivers of Sustainable Business Solutions in Organizations

Ziska Fields
University of KwaZulu-Natal, South Africa

Sulaiman Olusegun Atiku
University of KwaZulu-Natal, South Africa

ABSTRACT

The main objective of this chapter was to explore if collective green creativity and eco-innovation can create novel and sustainable business and management practices. A literature review approach was conducted on the link between collective creativity, innovation, and sustainable business practices. It was found that collective green creativity and eco-innovation can create sustainable business practices. The process starts with the creative individual which needs creative thinking skills, creative motivation, green mindfulness and green self-efficacy. A creative collective is then created using their creative intelligence and creative exchange to create a shared green vision. The creative collective requires green transformational leadership with access to green dynamic capabilities and resources to be effective in the business environment. This creative collective follows the six-step creative problem-solving process which enables the collective to create eco-innovation using an additional four steps. The end result is novel and sustainable business practices and solutions.

INTRODUCTION

King (2012) stated that the world has changed and that the planet is in crisis. Holthaus (2015, p.1) wrote that "we have reached the point of no return: climate change nightmares are already here". The climate has visibly changed and more species are dying out at disastrous rates. Dell'Amore (2014) reports that mankind is busy causing the rapid loss of species estimated by experts to be between 1,000 and 10,000

DOI: 10.4018/978-1-5225-1823-5.ch001

times higher than the natural extinction rate. For example, *because scientists do not know how many different species there are on the planet yet*, if there are around 2 million different species on the planet, then between 200 and 2,000 extinctions occur every year. If there are 100 million different species, then between 10,000 and 100,000 species are becoming extinct each year.

Mankind are faced with serious challenges due to human overexploitation of resources and unsustainable living. If this habit and mind-set are not changed very quickly by everyone on the planet, the unsustainable living and destruction of the incredible biodiversity on this planet, which is essential for mankind's survival, can lead to the so-called sixth extinction as identified by Kolberg (2014).

Traditional business and management practices have been blamed for the crises of the planet specifically. Issues like ecological overshoot, population growth, water and food shortages, financial crises, greed and corruption, as well as greater expectations of shareholders are however causing the rethink and transformation of business practices and other unsustainable human activity. An ever-increasing number of businesses are realizing that their long-term profitability is now dependent on social justice and protecting the environment (Global Sustainability Standards Board (GSSB), 2015). These expectations will intensify as businesses, financiers, customers and other stakeholders become more aware of the critical need for a sustainable economy (GSSB, 2015). This book and chapter, aims to play a role in creating more awareness to enable people and business to change and transform to protect the planet and life on it, because mankind have not been and still are not sustainable.

The main objective of this chapter was to explore whether collective creativity and eco-innovation in organizations can create novel and sustainable business and management practices. The secondary objectives were to

1. Explain the concept of collective creativity, green creativity and eco-innovation in business,
2. Identify the barriers to collaborative creativity and eco-innovation,
3. Discuss the determinants for successful organizational, collective creativity and eco-innovation with a view to enhance collaboration, and
4. Show how collaborative green creativity and eco-innovation can be used to solve 'wicked problems' and to create sustainable business practices.

The chapter starts off by providing the background to the chapter. This will be followed by a discussion on collaborative creativity and eco-innovation in organizations and how it can be used to create sustainable solutions, practices and strategies in an effort to minimize damage caused to the planet. Recommendations will also be made to enhance collaborative creativity and eco-innovation at organizational level in contemporary and future organizations.

BACKGROUND

The planet experienced five extinction events. The next extinction, the Holocene extinction, also called the sixth extinction, started at the end of the last Ice Age. Vince (2012) predicts that in the next 300 years, a total of 75% mammal species will disappear due to a human-caused extinction. Mankind's attributes and intelligence are responsible for the biological success and advancement as a specie, however mankind's successes also altered the climate and reduced animal species. Kolbert (2014) chronicles that man's indifference (cruelty) to other life on the planet and unmindful living makes every human a partner in these die-offs.

Unheeded warnings and mankind's reactive mindset are evident throughout history. There will always be people that disagree, those that prefer to ignore warning signs and then action will only be taken after a disastrous event occurred that could have been prevented if proactive action was taken. This is called the Cassandra syndrome or complex.

In Greek mythology, as cited in Greek Myths and Greek Mythology (2016), Cassandra was one of the princesses of Troy, daughter of Priam and Hecuba, who had a gift and a curse of foreseeing the future. There are several different versions explaining the gift and curse of Cassandra. The most popular one is that Apollo fell in love with her and gave her the gift of prophecy as a token of his love. When Cassandra rejected his advances, he placed a curse on her that no one will believe her predictions – even though her premonitions were always accurate. Based on the myth of Cassandra, the French Philosopher Gaston Bachelard, identified the Cassandra syndrome or complex in 1949, which is applied in cases where people would have valid alarms, visions, or dreams about upcoming events, which are disbelieved (Elgueta, 2014), often with disastrous consequences.

In 2000, a small group of leaders from the United Nations (UN) and business created the United Nations Global Impact. The aim of the UN is to build a sustainable, inclusive global community that can thrive within the environmental limits of the planet by creating an inclusive global economy that delivers lasting benefits to all people, communities and markets. The UN tries to inspire, guide and support companies to do business responsibly and take action for a more sustainable future by using the ten principles: Human rights (principles 1-2); Labour (principles 3-6); Environment (principles 7-9) and Anti-corruption (principle 10). However, deep-seated business paradigms and the expectations of societies caused high profile clashes between various organizations and societies (United Nations Global Compact Report, 2015). The Cassandra syndrome became evident from criticism against the UN Global Compact and the future it is trying to prevent, if nothing is done. For example, to name a few, some people view it as a superficial contribution to development; a PR tool; not in line with the traditional position of the UN on issues of economic policy. The UN seems like a less reliable partner for NGOs and other partners particularly in developing countries; and the initiative is seen as "global corporatism" (Bandi, 2007). Despite the criticism and Cassandra syndrome being evident, the goal of the UN is to make sure that mankind does not reap benefits at the expense of the environment and future generations (United Nations Global Compact Report, 2015), which remains a noble and very important one.

A documentary film in 2006, *An Inconvenient Truth*, was an effort by former US vice-president Al Gore to educate citizens about global warming and to reenergize the environmental movement. Gore discussed the present, future effects and consequences of global warming if human-generated greenhouse gases are not significantly reduced. The theme song "I need to wake up" by Melissa Etheridge encouraged viewers and listeners to realize the impact and effect of global warming. In the music video, some alarming facts are highlighted, for example that 70 million tons of CO_2 is released into the atmosphere every single day and that there is more CO_2 in the atmosphere now than in 650 000 years. Al Gore ended the film with the words:

Each one of us is a cause of global warming, but each one of us can make choices to change that with the things we buy, the electricity we use, the cars we drive; we can make choices to bring our individual carbon emissions to zero. The solutions are in our hands, we just have to have the determination to make it happen. We have everything that we need to reduce carbon emissions, everything but political will. But in America, the will to act is a renewable resource.

As with Cassandra, Al Gore's message was criticized by the President of the United States and certain Senators. There was also global criticism. The Prime Minister John Howard for example refused to meet with Al Gore or agree to Kyoto, because he said that he does not take policy advice from films. Even today, the Cassandra syndrome is evident across the world regarding climate change. Current president candidate for the Republican Party in 2016 Donald Trump said that he would "cancel the Paris Climate Agreement and stop all payments of U.S. tax dollars to UN global warming programs" because "the concept of global warming was created by and for the Chinese in order to make U.S. manufacturing non-competitive" (Jacobson, 2016, p. 1). There is a website called the GlobalClimateScam.com and here Beauregard (2015, p.1) reported on the site that climate change is a hoax; 31,000 scientists have signed a petition saying they do not believe in 'Catastrophic Man-Made Global Warming'; and that NASA found that most of the CO2 in the atmosphere was not coming from the industrialized northern hemisphere, but from the rainforests in South America, Africa and China. However, on 'NASA's Global Climate Change – vital signs of the planet' website, it is reported that the "current warming trend is of particular significance because most of it is very likely human-induced and proceeding at a rate that is unprecedented in the past 1,300 years" and that "evidence for rapid climate change is compelling" (NASA Global Climate Change, 2016, p.1). Even with criticism, there were positive responses to the film and the film became a memorable effort to create sustainable solutions for the planet

Vaidyanathan (2016) indicated what happened 10 years after An Inconvenient Truth and stated that scientists that the planet is now in the Anthropocene time, meaning that humans have surpassed nature and that humans are the primary shapers and directors of the planet story. Elizabeth Kolbert wrote a book called, 'The Sixth Extinction: An Unnatural History' which was published in 2014. This is seen as an important book about the future of the world as it predicts the most devastating extinction event since the asteroid impact that wiped out the dinosaurs and confirms Vaidyanathan's statement. Kolbert's book is based on the work of researchers in half a dozen disciplines (for example geologists, botanists, marine biologists) and she accompanied many of them into the field. Kolberg cited in Gore (2014) explains that extinction is a relatively new idea in the scientific community, because most scientists could not imagine a planetary force powerful enough to wipe out forms of life. People in general also find it unthinkable that mankind can destroy the planet's ecology (Gore 2014). Kolberg (2014) however predicts that the sixth extinction is likely to be mankind's most lasting legacy. Kolbert (2014) wrote that:

the qualities that made us human to begin with: our restlessness, our creativity, our ability to cooperate, to solve problems and complete complicated tasks are leading us to change the world so rapidly and profoundly that other species cannot keep up.

Muhammad (2015, p.1) indicates that Kolberg however discusses *"why humanity is wreaking such havoc, with no consideration of the crucial role that capitalism's relentless search for growth and accumulation has played."* This is an important aspect to consider in addition to the issues that are now grouped under the heading of 'sustainability'. These issues are ranging from stopping global warming to saving ecosystems, changing economics and ending global poverty. These issues can be referred to as 'wicked problems'. The concept of a 'wicked problem' was identified by Rittel and Webber (1973) cited in Jackson (2013, p.5) as "a problem that is essentially unique, the search for solutions will never stop, it can be seen as a symptom of another problem and is often intertwined with other problems; it involves many stakeholders, and it generates unexpected consequences over time". It is evident that issues around the sixth extinction, climate change, unsustainable living, to name a few, are complex and not easy to resolve due to the intertwined nature of it and the involvement of a lot of different stakeholders. Another challenge, adding to the wicked problem, is that history has demonstrated that humans often do not listen to warnings about the future, even when warnings were justified. There is still time to listen and to do something about it.

It is important that organizations realize that no business can be prosperous in an environment faced with catastrophic climate change, rampant unemployment and social conflict. The only way to create a prosperous business environment, stable societies and a healthy planet, is for organizations to ensure that the benefits and profits that they reap today, are not at the expense of the environment or future generations. This chapter therefore focuses on organizations specifically as we search for ways to create sustainability.

The question is, what can organizations do to transform themselves to become more responsible and sustainable and can eco-creativity and eco-innovation, as a collaborative effort, help to create novel and sustainable business practices?

COLLECTIVE GREEN CREATIVITY AND ECO-INNOVATION

Organizations can no longer continue on the same path and repeat the old and unsustainable business practices of the past. An overhaul of the traditional and dominant worldviews about resource management and the negative impact of business practices on societies and the environment are necessary and imperative. Creative and innovative thinking and problem-solving can offer sustainable ways to conduct business now and in the future, even if Kolberg (2014) explained that our creativity, our ability to co-operate and to solve problems is changing the world rapidly and profoundly. This ability can be used to improve the world and find ways to assist species to keep up with changes made by mankind.

It is important however to first explain what creativity and innovation mean before it can be explored from an ecological perspective as a possible way to create and enhance sustainable business practices.

Creativity

Cropley (2016) supports the view of Plucker, Beghetto and Dow (2004) when he explains that creativity is like a system with four interacting elements namely the person (which refers to the interaction among aptitude), press (which refers to the process and environment), product (which refers to a novel and useful product) and the social context. Cropley (2016, p. 63) further explains that

Creativity is about solving problems and satisfying needs by developing novel and useful solutions—in other words, creativity is all about the aptitudes, processes, and environmental factors that help us to generate new and useful products.

Vygotsky (2004) states that a creative act is any human act that leads to either a new physical object or some mental or emotional construct that lives within the person who created it. Creativity is also explained as a mental and social process which involves the discovery of novel ideas by combining ideas or seeing new relationships among ideas and discarding preconceived assumptions, in an attempt to come up with a new approach (Afolabi, Dionne & Lewis, 2009, p. 2). Creativity, according to Boden (2004), is the ability to generate ideas that are new, surprising, and valuable. Creativity occurs on the right side of the brain when ideas are sparked. To make creativity useful requires both divergent thinking (generating many unique ideas) (Runco, 2007) and convergent thinking (combining those ideas into the best result). Creativity, according to Groenewald (2013) involves lateral thinking, decision-making and problem-solving.

Cropley and Cropley (2010) explain that creativity is the generation of effective novelty and the National Advisory Committee on Creative and Cultural Education (NACCCE) (1999) agrees and adds that novelty can be identified in three possible ways: individual creativity (also referred to as personal creativity); relative creativity (refers to originality in relation to a person's peer group); and historic creativity (refers to an original previous output). Boden (2004, p. 2) identifies it a bit differently by stating that "psychological" creativity (P-creativity) "involves coming up with a surprising, valuable idea that is new to the person who comes up with it, no matter how many people have had that idea before"; and historical" creativity (H-creativity), "involves an idea that no-one else has had before and seems to appear for the first time in human history".

Parjanen (2012) indicates that there are two different types of creativity namely individual creativity and collaborative creativity. This links to NACCCE's personal and relative creativity as ways to add novelty. According to Parjanen (2012), p. 2)

A collective creativity system becomes a co-creation between the founders of the system and the crowd members, who both design the products and contribute to the design of the system. Out of this comes a kind of system that benefits society through its creative outputs and benefits participants through the mastery they attain.

For this book and chapter, the focus is on collective creativity, because the idea of a lone creative genius will not be useful in the search for the higher potential source of creativity to create novel and sustainable business practices. A collective of creative people working as a team can create better ideas and solutions for unsustainable business practices and living than one individual. In sustainability, the nature of the output of collective creativity can be aggregated which refers to the collection of each participant's work or emergent which refers to something new and novel. Emergent outputs are developed through discovery where the participants find something never seen before or through combination where the participants' work are combined and integrated to produce something novel (Yu et al., 2012).

This is also a valuable view of creativity, which will also be valuable for this chapter, because it shows that creativity can be seen as a concept of growth or development where the human will is the central cause of action, is the view of Rank (cited in De Sousa, Pellissier & Monteiro, 2012), that

Each individual is unique and carries within him or her the potentiality of creating something new, different and unexpected out of past experience (via the human capacity to internalize experiences of the outer environment and making it a part of the self).

From the above explanation, creativity and specifically, collective creativity, seems to be an important phenomenon to consider in the search for sustainable business practices because it creates novel solutions, it can enhance human development and is linked to the human will to make a difference.

Sherwin (2011) wrote in an article that the missing link in sustainable ideas is creativity and agree that creativity needs to play a bigger role in finding better sustainable solutions and business practices. This type of creativity can possibly be linked to eco-creativity and green creativity. Eco-creativity is described as the combination of creativity and art; the marriage of reusing, recycling and creativity (Lapia & Knight, 2011), as well as eco-design where creativity, brainstorming, imagination and trash materials are used. Green creativity was highlighted by Chen and Chang (2013) as part of green product development. They stated that for green creativity and green product development to be successful, green dynamic capabilities and green transformational leadership are required. Chen, Chang, Yeh and Cheng (2015) added that a green shared vision, green mindfulness and green self-efficacy are needed to enhance green creativity. The concept of green creativity therefore can be seen as the most suitable concept that can be used to link creativity to sustainable ideas presently. Green creativity is valuable because it involves a whole-brain activity, linking divergent and convergent thinking, as well as leadership, capabilities, vision, mindfulness and self-efficacy to create novel green solutions to "wicked" unsustainable practices and environmental problems. There are, however, barriers to creativity and bad habits that should be identified and overcome to ensure that any creative endeavor can succeed.

Barriers to Creativity

There are various barriers that can prevent individuals and teams from using creativity and these are, for example, not believing you are creative; acceptance of the status quo; having no creative role-models; narrow-mindedness; feeling silly; red tape, procedure and group-process constraints; conformance pressure; and being too busy.

Hiam (2003) identified nine bad habits that can prevent creativity which are still relevant today and these are:

1. **Failure to Ask Questions:** Creativity requires a lot of why questions to be asked to create creative insight. Not asking questions cannot lead to creative ideas.
2. **Failure to Record Ideas:** If ideas are not recorded, similar ideas can be generated over and over again without having more efficient and productive ideations sessions, where previous ideas can be built upon on linked together to find better ideas.
3. **Failure to Revisit Ideas:** If this is done, old ideas are not given a second chance and old assumptions are not identified.
4. **Failure to Express Ideas:** This is normally done through self-censorship and trying to have an orderly mind which prevents one from figuring out if an idea is worthwhile and novel.
5. **Failure to Think in New Ways:** If a person or team cannot focus on thinking differently and use a variety of structured creative thinking techniques, new and novel ideas cannot be generated.
6. **Failure to Wish for More:** Creativity is about making the impossible seem possible and finding a better way to improve the current status quo. If one does not wish for more and better things, the creative process cannot be successful as only "possible" ideas will be generated.
7. **Failure to Try Being Creative:** Many people still think that creativity is a special and rare gift and that they can never be creative, which prevents them from being willing to be part of the creative process and participate in creative thinking.

8. **Failure to Keep Trying:** Creativity requires continuous effort, because brilliant novel ideas are not usually created with the first try and it is very easy to abandon a possible idea prematurely and then missing out on a creative discovery.
9. **Failure to Tolerate Creative Behaviour:** When people are being creative, their behaviour might seem weird to others and this should be tolerated to ensure that the creative thinking process leads to useable and novel ideas.

From the discussion in this section it seems that there are a great deal of different barriers and behaviours that can hamper creativity. It is therefore important to be aware of it and to find ways to overcome these barriers and behaviours to be able to solve "wicked" problems and to profit from creative thinking. Some ways to overcome the barriers and bad behaviours for example are to behave in ways that you are creative, behave in ways to generate many fresh ideas, offering ideas to others, applying ideas in the specific context, using divergent and convergent thinking (the whole-brain approach), experimenting with creative thinking processes and techniques as well as breaking boundaries to become an independent thinker/team. It is also helpful to use the five stages of the creative process and creative problem-solving.

The Creative Process and Creative Problem-Solving (CPS)

The creative process consists of five stages and is not a linear process according to Von Oech (cited in Groenewald 2013). The five stage are:

1. Preparation when the problem is defined, information is gathered and creative questions about the problem is formulated;
2. Frustration where the creative questions does not guarantee immediate or effective solutions;
3. Incubation where one steps away from the problem to allow the subconscious to come up with new insights;
4. Illumination where the answer is identified which might need further refinement to create a novel idea and solution; and
5. Elaboration where the idea is refined to develop further through innovation.

Creative problem-solving (CPS) aims to solve specific problems and the process was developed by Alex Osborn and Sydney Parnes (Groenewald, 2013). The process consists of five steps where the problem is defined and the objective is determined, followed by fact finding, idea finding, evaluating and prioritizing ideas and developing and implementing the plan to solve the problem. Various creative techniques can also be used in each of the five steps, for example in step one, the 5Ws/H method can be used when one is uncertain about what the problem really is; in step two, the bug list technique can be used to focus on finding fault with things around us that can lead to corrective action being taken; in step three, brainstorming can be used; in step four, the advantage-disadvantage technique or the reverse brainstorming technique can be used; and in step five, CPS techniques can be used and an action plan developed.

The process of green creativity and green creative problem-solving need to include specific focus areas to make it successful as identified by Chen and Chang (2013) and Chen et al. (2015). The collective (can be an organization/s or team/s for example) gathered to generate novel ideas, need to share a green vision created by green transformational leadership, which are supported by green dynamic capabilities.

The collective, as individuals, should also possess green mindfulness and green self-efficacy. Collective green creativity will follow the same steps as discussed in this section and the focus will be on achieving new and novel environmentally friendly and sustainable business ideas.

Innovation

Innovation is crucial to the economy and the performance of organizations (Groenewald, 2013). It also involves a variety of approaches like technological innovation, product-market innovation, innovative marketing strategies and management innovation like new organizational systems and techniques according to Groenewald (2013).

The processes of innovation and creativity overlap although these processes are different. Creativity is seen as the cognitive process of development of ideas, which normally takes place first, while innovation occurs when these ideas are applied and turned into something of value, for example, a new product or a new process. Florida (2002) expresses that creativity drives the innovation process which basically means that creativity is the key in generating new business opportunities – the start of any innovative idea. Innovation is the ability to apply creative solutions to enhance or enrich the lives of people according to Scarborough and Cornwall (2015).

Jones and George (2014, p. 23) defines innovation as "the process of creating new or improved goods and services that customers want or developing better ways to produce or provide goods and services". The authors identify two kinds of innovation:

1. Quantum product innovation, and
2. Incremental innovation.

Quantum product innovation is the development of new or radically different kinds of goods and services due to technology and the possibilities of pioneering discoveries. Incremental product innovation takes place when gradual improvements to existing products are made due to existing technologies being perfected. Groenewald (2013) explains that innovation can be divided into radical (similar to quantum production innovation), incremental (similar to incremental product innovation) and modular innovation. Modular innovation which involves the change of some of the components to new or significantly adapted components as per Groenewald (2013).

Hamel and Breen (2007) cited in Groenewald (2013) created a hierarchy of innovation which consists of five different levels. The lowest level, operational innovation, involves innovations to make organizations faster and better by focusing, for example, on the manufacturing processes and the development of online transactions. The second level, product and service innovation, is the most visible one as it involves for example completely new products, line extensions or product repositioning. The third level, business model innovation, focusses on value creation and value capture to enhance the profitability of the organization. The fourth level, architectural innovation, which implies a redesign or reconfigured system and industry. Level five, management innovation, which refers to strategic planning, project management, knowledge management and performance management, for example. Management innovation ensures the long-term success and competitive advantage of organizations (Hamel and Breen, 2007).

Martins (2002) explains that innovation is the implementation of a new and problem-solving idea, practice or artifact through which change is brought about. In addition, Puccio and Cabra (2010, p. 149) stress that *"innovation comes about as the result of the interaction among people, the processes they engage in, and the environment in which they work"*. Rothwell and Zegveld in Conway and Steward (2009, p. 9 & 10) define innovation as *"the commercialization of technological change"*. Innovation concerns "novelty" (as with creativity), and is a process that embraces various activities to ensure that the actual discovery is commercialized.

These different views are important for this chapter as it explains that innovation is the result of interaction among people and it creates something new that enhances or enriches lives and leads to change.

Eco-Innovation

Innovation is therefore important for sustainable business practices and can be referred to as eco-innovation, which requires collaboration to make it successful. Eco-innovation is explained as

the production, assimilation or exploitation of a novelty in products, production processes, services or in management and business methods, which aims, throughout its lifecycle, to prevent or substantially reduce environmental risk, pollution and other negative impacts of resource use (including energy) (OECD, 2009, p. 6).

Three aspects are important in eco-innovation as per OECD (2009) namely:

1. The target which refers to products, processes which tend to rely on technology, marketing, organizations and institutions. The target can be technological or non-technological.
2. The mechanism which refers to the method by which the target is changed and can either be possible through modification, redesign, alternatives or creation.
3. The impact which refers to the potential environmental impact due to the target, mechanism and their interaction with the socio-technical surroundings.

Part of eco-innovation is to look at the environmental effects across value chains and product lifecycles. Biomimicry specifically can be very helpful to create eco-innovation. Here innovation comes from nature's best ideas in terms of natural systems and its success in nature. Nature's ideas are then imitated to provide innovative and sustainable solutions (Benyus, 2006). The nine basic laws of biomimicry are also important for eco-innovation because it identifies the key working principles needed for ideas, namely:

1. *Nature runs on sunlight;*
2. *Nature uses only the energy it needs;*
3. *Nature fits form to function;*
4. *Nature recycles everything;*
5. *Nature rewards cooperation;*
6. *Nature banks on diversity;*
7. *Nature demands local expertise;*
8. *Nature curbs excesses from within; and*
9. *Nature taps the power of limits (Benysus, 2006 , p. 129).*

The Biomimicry Guild, for example, aims to help businesses to become more sustainable by focusing on the transfer and application of biological knowledge, developing business model innovation as it integrates this biological knowledge into the business focus and strategy, and ensuring that progress are monitored (The Biomimicry Institute, 2015). However, as with creativity, there are barriers to innovation that need to be addressed to make the innovation process successful.

Barriers to Innovation

Innovation is viewed form a number of perspectives which can make the innovation process challenging. As a management process, the focus is on the organization and management; as a social process, the focus is on the importance of social interaction during the innovation process; as political process, the focus is on the use of resources and between alternative solutions; and as emotional process, the focus is on psychological safety in allowing people to challenge the status quo according to Conway and Steward (2009, p. 12). If leadership cannot drive innovation and if the business culture does not support innovation, employees will not be innovative. Barriers are created when leaders, managers and employees do not have the required skills, are not aware of the latest trends and technology, do not have the passion to be innovative, or are afraid of risk taking and the cost involved in failure. The different activities that are necessary for innovation can cause tension and barriers as well. Dougherty (1996, p. 431) cited in Conway and Steward (2009) identifies four tensions due to contradictory practices which are identified in Table 1.

The Innovation Process

The innovation process consists of three phases according to Smith (2010). Phase one is the invention stage where a new idea, product, service, method or process is created. This phase is not yet innovation and can be linked to the creative process discussed earlier in the chapter. The viability of the invention should first be determined by ensuring that it can create a competitive advantage (unique selling proposition), it is aligned with the business strategy and objectives, it creates business value, customer needs

Table 1. The tensions between contradictory practices and capacities to restore the balance

Activity	Tension	Problem of Normal Functioning that Disrupts Tension	Capacities to Restore Balance in the Tension
Market-technology	Outside versus inside	Keeping operations efficient	Generate and maintain an identity based on the value provided to customers
Organizing for creative problem solving	New versus old	Managing complexity	See work of organization in terms of process, focusing on relationships among parts, and changes
Evaluating and monitoring innovation	Determined versus emergent	Controlling multiple activities	Situated judgement, collective ability to be engaged in details of work but also appreciate unstructured problems
Developing commitment to innovation	Freedom versus responsibility	Accounting for work, results	Collective accountability, accept and share responsibility, legitimize innovation and inclusion

Source: Dougherty (1996, p. 431) cited in Conway and Steward (2009)

Figure 1. Fields's collective green creativity and eco-innovation process framework
Source: Own compilation

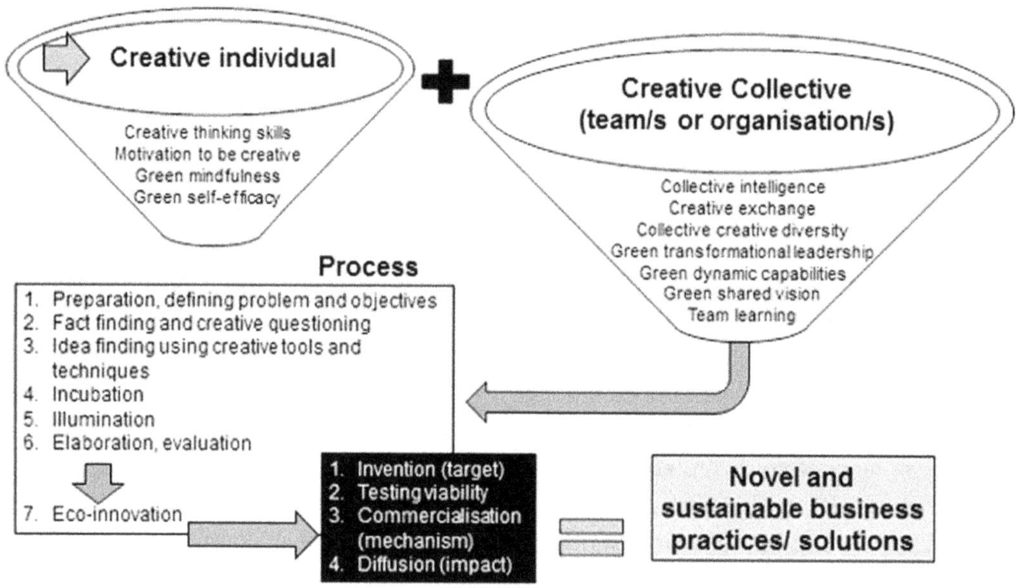

are taken into consideration and the invention is successfully executed. This will then lead to phase two, commercialization of the invention, due to value creation and value capture to create demand and profits. Phase three is the final phase and is referred to as diffusion which refers to the adoption rate of consumers which can be fast or slow. Consumers need to familiarize themselves with the innovation first, so diffusion is normally slow. Figure 1 shows the link between collective green creativity and eco-innovation.

The process starts with the creative individual which needs creative thinking skills, creative motivation, green mindfulness and green self-efficacy. A creative collective (team or organization for example) is then created consisting of a diverse mix of these creative individuals who will use their creative intelligence and creative exchange to create a shared green vision. The creative collective will need green transformational leadership with access to green dynamic capabilities and resources to be effective in the business environment as well as the other determinants to make the process successful. This creative collective will then follow the six step creative problem-solving process which will enable the creative collective to create eco-innovation using an additional four steps. The end result will be novel and sustainable business practices and solutions.

Managing the Creative Collective and Creative Intelligence in Organizations

Collective green creativity and eco-innovation can be seen as creative exchange as identified by Flieschmann and Hutchinson (2012) although the practice of creative exchange was developed for the tertiary education environment. This method however fits into the development of sustainable business practices as well, because it is important to get multi-disciplinary and multi-industry perspectives to generate green creative and eco-innovative ideas. Creative exchange is helpful due to the fact that it fosters debate and dialogue amongst stakeholders, support expertise from various disciplines, acknowledges the differences in culture, communities and industries. In addition, creative exchange supports and develops individual and team development and examines debates and contemporary issues. It seems therefore that creative exchange can play a key role in collective green creativity and eco-innovation.

Parjanen (2012) defines collective creativity as social interactions between individuals due to new interpretations and new discoveries that the individuals involved could not have generated by themselves. Collective creativity is not simply the sum of individual creativities (Parjanen, 2012), but is greater than the sum of individual creativities, because it intensifies and multiplies due to the level of the problem and common concerns experienced about the problem. Creativity and innovation is a collaborative process and teams and people from various fields contribute to implementing new ideas. Therefore, managing collective green creativity and eco-innovation is critical for sustainable business practices in business organizations.

According to Parjanen (2012), four key elements are fundamental in managing collective creativity and innovation in business organizations. The first element is strategy. Collective creativity flourishes in an organization where policies are in support of team learning and free flow of productive ideas leading to new products or services (Anderson, Potočnik & Zhou, 2014; Marquardt, 2011; Parjanen, 2012). The second element is the usefulness in enhancing cognitive ideas and innovation is leadership (Parjanen, 2012). The leadership structure that supports collective creativity in developing new products or services will embraces comment from all stakeholders irrespective of their status in the organization (Zhang, Tsui & Wang, 2011). Thirdly, the methods or approaches adopted in collecting and distribution of information within the system will determine the success or failure of creative ideas at the implementation stage (Bissola & Imperatori, 2011; Parjanen, 2012). For example, superior ideas can be generated through informal interactions or interpersonal relationships with the subordinates. This example shows that collective creativity and innovation in organizations are not limited to formal discussions/interactions, or team learning (Parjanen, 2012). The last but not the least element according to Parjanen (2012), is organizational culture. The fourth element relates to a set of core values or management principles that supports continuous learning and knowledge sharing at all levels within the organization (Anderson, Potočnik & Zhou, 2014). Superiors and subordinates are open minded, but thorough in their habits of challenging the status quo. A proper alignment of strategic goals, leadership structures, approaches to interactions and shared values within an organization is necessary for collective green creativity in developing eco-friendly products or services (Chen & Chang, 2013; Parjanen, 2012).

Management support for team learning and knowledge sharing through brainstorming are efforts toward collective creativity. Collective creativity could be enhanced through task experiences, personal and team development. Gino, Argote, Miron-Spektor, and Todorova, (2010) found that teams who acquired direct task experiences are more creative compared to teams who acquired experience through feelings or actions of another person. Empirically, the study found that task experience has a direct positive influence on collective creativity. Therefore, eco-innovation can be enhanced through direct or indirect task experiences either acquired or shared within a group. Statistically, Sung and Choi (2012) found that team experience management and transfer are positively associated with collective creativity and sustainable business outcomes. Through horizontal and vertical communication individual creativity can easily be transformed into collective creativity, provided that policies and programmes are in support of the exchange process (Bissola & Imperatori, 2011; Gong, Kim, Lee & Zhu, 2013). For instance, team activity, storage and retrieval (Decuyper, Dochy & Van den Bossche, 2010) are some of the important elements in building team creativity and innovation. Findings from Bissola and Imperatori, (2011), informed that collective creativity and innovation is a function of individual innovative ideas, group dynamics and managerial resolutions. That is, developing sustainable business practices requires well harnessed individuals, teams and managerial creative capabilities. A learning culture that supports knowledge exchange through interactions within or between work groups is crucial in generating collective ideas and building sustainable business outcomes in the knowledge economy (Martins & Terblanche, 2003; Yoon, Song, Lim & Joo, 2010). Also, corporate entrepreneurial orientations such as creativity, innovation, and competitive aggressiveness of individuals and teams could be regarded as collective efforts in building sustainable business outcomes.

The concept eco-innovation for business organizations is an add-on to Corporate Social Responsibility (CSR), which also stands against profit maximization from the classical point of view (Carroll & Shabana, 2010). This chapter submits that collective green creativity and eco-innovation are essential in developing sustainable business models for the interest of all stakeholders in the 21st century. The reason is that, global warming, for instance, is a global issue confronting all stakeholders.

Another interesting emphasis for sustainable business practices in this chapter is the role of technology in collective creativity and team learning. Kirkman, Rosen, Tesluk and Gibson (2004) put it that improvements in information technology (IT) played a significant role in sharing knowledge situated in distance locations across the global with teams. Team members can be linked up using IT, which points to the importance of technology in generating collaborative intelligence. Also, distance is no longer a barrier in the global environment. Collaborative ideas could be easily generated, shared and improved on using online platforms, especially among work groups that are geographically dispersed (Faraj, Jarvenpaa & Majchrzak, 2011). Contemporary work organizations may find the IT based learning platforms valuable in advancing collaborative ideas and developing sustainable business models. Studies conducted by Hill, Brandeau, Truelove and Lineback (2014), reveal that *collaborative problem solving, discovery-driven learning* and *integrated decision-making* were instrumental in attaining *collective genius* at selected world leading IT firms. Collaborative problem solving starts with the documentation of interchange content and objectives; by verifying customers' current/future needs, and developing sustainable models in line with the global requirements (Aarikka-Stenroos & Jaakkola, 2012; Kirschner, Buckingham-Shum & Carr, 2012). Collective problem solving sets the pace for teams' discovery-driven learning in the act of creating collective intelligence (Hill, Brandeau, Truelove & Lineback, 2014), which is key to new products or services development. A discovery-driven learning is an action plan to arrive at more efficient, but sustainable business models through continuous update of skills and experiences at team levels (Chesbrough, 2010; McGrath, 2010). A discovery-driven learning in this context, could be enhanced using information and communication technologies in disseminating information among members. An integrated decision-making process in the knowledge economy is more advanced with the use of IT in consultation with all stakeholders or based on green IT balanced scorecard (Bhattacharya et al., 2014; Wati & Koo, 2011). Collaborative intelligence drawn from integrated decision-making process in advancing eco-innovation through green IT balanced scorecard could be regarded as efforts in the right direction toward sustainable business practices of the 21st century. The next section provides explanations regarding the merits of collective creativity and innovation.

Advantages of Collective Creativity and Innovation

Creativity could be referred to as one of the greatest potential sources of competitive advantage in the 21st century (Amabile, 2011). Survival of business organizations in the modern economy is largely dependent on creative capabilities of individuals, teams and management boards. The reason is not far-fetched, state-of-the-art products and services one can count on today emerged from collaborative creativity. According to Articles (n.d.) the following are advantages of collective creativity to business organizations:

- **Better Teamwork and Team Bonding:** Collaborative creativity enhances interpersonal relationships within groups. Organizations that generate ideas through the practice of collective culture stand to experience team efficiency.
- **Increased Workplace Engagement and Interaction:** Generally, collaborative brainstorming improves communication and employee involvement in decision making process both at groups and organizational levels.
- **Improved Ability to Attract and Retain Quality Employees:** The sensitive issue of employee retention can be overcome by recognition of creative ideas of competent employees. This gives a sense of belonging and boosts employees' level of engagement and creativity.
- **Increased Staff Morale, Fun and Happiness:** Collective intelligence could be used a motivational tool to improve employees level of productivity, in terms of quality and quantity of units produced or quality of service delivery.
- **Increased Workplace Problem Solving and Productivity:** Involvement of stakeholders in diagnosing and problem solving process puts an organization ahead its competitors. Particularly, when such information are well coordinated, the result; which is collective genius is far rewarding compared to individual intelligence (Hill, Brandeau, Truelove, & Lineback, 2014).

Therefore, this chapter submits that collective creativity and innovation will impact more on organizational productivity and competitive advantage; when the processes are well managed at all level in an organization. In addition, collective green creativity and eco-innovation in organizations and amongst various organizations and industries can create novel sustainable ideas and solutions that mankind has never thought about that can prevent or decrease the 6th extinction to allow mankind to save the planet and all life on it. It is clear that we cannot save the planet with the same kind of thinking used when we are busy destroying it. Mankind still have a long way to go, but we have creative and innovative intelligence that can change the current fate of the planet.

Disadvantages of Organizational Creativity and Innovation

There are however a negative side to creativity and innovation, specifically in the 21st century. It is one of the reasons why our planet is in distress in the first place. Mankind only focused on the ideas and novel innovations without considering the consequences on the planet. In the 21st century, "*an excess of creativity can lead to a breakdown between the phases of the innovation process with detrimental consequences*" (Del-Corte-Lora, Vallet-Bellmunt & Molina-Morales, 2015, p. 4). Accordingly, an overflow of collaborative ideas may cause an adverse effect on organizational productivity, due to issues of absorptive capacity and timing problem. The authors are supporting the positive side of collective creativity and innovation to business organizations, but are aware that excessive creativity may leads to confusion or business failure if not managed properly and sustainably as well. For example, when a creativity idea failed to materialised into desired outcomes after huge investments at the implementation stage. This kind of result may cause a serious setback to an organization, if no provision was made for such circumstance.

Technological innovations around the world created dependency on technology for daily survival (Belcher, n.d.). As such, technological breakdown often disabled humans until the problem is fixed. Another shortcoming of digital automation is that it contributes to the high rate of unemployment, by continuously putting less value in human capital (Belcher, n.d.; Rotman, 2013). Rotman (2013), reports that the service industry contributed 79.7% to the United States (US) Gross Domestic Product (GDP) in 2013, as a result of automation in the US service industry. Automation has taken over jobs meant for employees around the world, for example, the use of electronic banking applications (Automated Teller Machine (ATM), online banking, and mobile banking have displace human resources worldwide in the banking industry. Similarly, Nisen (2013) alerts that advances in artificial intelligence could cause up to 75% unemployment rate in the global environment. This is a projection that requires all hands on deck in developing collective green ideas and eco-innovation to savage employment generation in the knowledge economy. The paradigm shift from collective genius (Hill, Brandeau, Truelove & Lineback, 2014) to artificial intelligence (Gurkaynak, Yilmaz & Haksever, 2016; Rodríguez, Soria & Campo, 2016) is another shortcoming of creativity and innovation, considering its negative influence on humans. The greatest danger is that artificial intelligence might subdue human intelligence in the nearest future (Gurkaynak, Yilmaz & Haksever, 2016). The following are some of the shortcomings of technological innovations in the manufacturing industry, according to Payne (2013):

- **Less Versatility:** Advances and adoption technological innovations in the manufacturing plants displace the human element in an unprecedented proportion.
- **More Pollution:** The use of machines in factories has negative impact on human environment (Melville, 2010). The practice of corporate social responsibility as a compensation is often not commensurate with the amount of damages done to the natural environment (Carroll & Shabana, 2010; Melville, 2010).
- **Large Initial Investment:** It requires huge amounts of money for purchase of automated machines and huge investment are usually made regarding technical know-how and costs of maintenance.
- **Increase in Unemployment:** The high rates of unemployment recorded in the global environment could be traced to utilization of digital automation in workplaces around the world (Nisen, 2013; Rotman, 2013). Therefore, collective efforts are required in building green business models and eco-innovations for the sake of sustainability in the global business environment. The next section unveils the determinants for effective collective green creativity and eco-friendly innovations in modern organizations.

Determinants for Successful Organizational Creativity and Innovation

This chapter submits that collective green creativity and eco-innovations are essential requirements for sustainable business models/practices. One of the basic determinants for sustainable business practices is a corporate culture that supports collaborative ideas and green products development (Chen & Chang, 2013; Im, Montoya & Workman, 2013; Martins & Terblanche, 2003). A cultural pattern that embraces team learning, free flow of information, and shapes attitudes as well as behavioural patterns is effective in stimulating collective creativity and organizational innovation (Martins & Terblanche, 2003; Yoon, Song, Lim & Joo, 2010). Such cultural values are usually aligned with the organizational strategy, structures and objectives. Knowledge management could be regarded as a key determinant for effective collaborative creativity and new products development (Lee, Leong, Hew & Ooi, 2013). Knowledge management at individual, team and organizational levels need to be well planned, delivered and transferred into outstanding discovery and innovation.

Apart from culture and knowledge management that supports collective creativity, superior capability in managing team dynamics is also crucial in building sustainable business models in the 21st century. For instance, Im et al. (2013), found that managing team dynamics and interpersonal relationships are a forerunner to generating collective intelligence, thereby resulting into new products development. The question of newly developed products meeting the global requirements in reducing the issue of global warming is at the centre stage of sustainable business models. Work groups in the 21st century need *green dynamic capabilities*, and *green creativity* in accordance with the global demand for eco-innovation (Chen & Chang, 2013). Accordingly, green dynamic capabilities is the ability of an organization to exploit current resources and collective intelligences to rejuvenate or enhance its business models in responding to business demands in the 21st century. Chen et al. (2015) submit that green creativity is more essential for business organizations operating under the context of eco-innovation and sustainable business practices.

Green transformational leadership is another determinant for sustainable business models and eco-innovation in the global economy (Chen & Chang, 2013; Gumusluoglu & Ilsev, 2009). Green transformational leadership could be referred to as a set of behavioural patterns of business leaders in motivating their organizational members to generate eco-friendly creative ideas and inspire teams to surpass the requirements of eco-innovation (Chen & Chang, 2013). Personality traits of leaders in business organizations can either support or demean collective intelligence in developing new products. For example, transformational leaders could assist in creating new ideas by providing a vision and boosting followers' morals toward development of innovative products or services.

Risk-taking capabilities and willingness to finance creative ideas is a powerful determinant for successful organizational creativity and innovation (Stanley, 2016). Organizations are sometimes sceptical in exploring new products development due the level of risk involved. The fact remains that no creative idea can materialise in new products or services without adequate investments of both financial and non-financial resources (Leachman, 2014). Financial analysis of risk and uncertainty is a key factor to consider in new product development (Mazzucato, 2013). Such analysis would help in making decisions about calculated risk and uncertainty. Rather than treating each determinant for effective organizational creative and innovation in isolation, Parjanen (2012), submits that all determinants should be logically aligned to arrive at expected outcomes. That is, the organizational vision and mission statements should be logically aligned with the corporate/business strategies, organizational culture, structure and leadership, methods of managing team dynamics, knowledge sharing capabilities and approaches of financing innovation.

RECOMMENDATIONS

The threat of the 6th extinction is real and should be treated as such. Organizations can no longer continue on the same path and repeat the old and unsustainable business practices of the past. It is important that organizations understand their impact on the planet and not remain indifferent due to the Cassandra syndrome, and that the various stakeholders of these organizations ensure that organizations behave ethically and sustainably. Various organizational watchdogs should be set up that support the United Nations Global Compact initiative and communities should use their collective power to force organizations to behave responsibly towards the environment and their communities.

Creativity is often seen as a rare gift only given to a selected few. Greater awareness is needed to develop the understanding that creativity is a skill that everyone is born with and this skill can be developed through training and development. Organizations specifically should not only see innovation as an important aspect in business to ensure a competitive advantage, but realise that innovation starts with creativity at an individual level which are then enhanced through collaborative problem solving, discovery-driven learning and integrated decision making to attain collective genius (collective green creativity and eco-innovation for example) in organizations. Organizations need to incorporate creativity and innovation awareness programmes in the training and workshops of all employees at all the various levels in the organization, focusing on individual and collective creativity and innovation.

Organizations should manage creativity and innovation from a strategic perspective by incorporating it in the shared vision, strategic goals and policies. Green creativity and eco-innovation should specifically be focused on to create sustainable business practices and problem-solving. This also calls for organizational intrapreneurship to create strategic renewal, sustained regeneration and pioneering strategies. Leadership should be aligned to the green shared vision and transformational leadership should be developed to encourage team learning, team development and the development of an organizational culture that supports creative and innovative thinking. This may sound easy, however some organizations might struggle to change the current organizational culture that supports unsustainable business practices and where unethical behaviour is rife. It is critical that the top management understands and supports green creativity and eco-innovation before transformation of an organization can start.

Technology will be an important and critical key component to initiate, drive and implement collective green creativity and eco-innovation. Ideas will need to be captured and evaluated using technology. Collective activities should be documented to ensure that a record is kept of all the ideas and innovations to not generate similar ideas and waste time, but rather to encourage building on ideas already identified previously but not implemented. People sharing ideas need to feel that their efforts are not a waste of time and that it is evaluated fairly. A reward system can be an important driver in the process.

There are various recommendations which cannot all be provided in this chapter. It is the hope of the authors that readers will also consider the recommendations provided in other chapters and then to develop a unique and creative strategy for their specific organization.

FUTURE RESEARCH DIRECTIONS

The Fields collective green creativity and eco-innovation framework needs to be empirically tested in various organizations in various countries to specifically focus on the outcome (for example, green and eco-friendly products, services, processes, business practices) and its impact on sustained sustainability for organizations, communities and the planet.

Concepts like green mindfulness, green self-efficacy, collective intelligence and collective exchange in sustainable businesses development should be explored in more detail. Specific processes and techniques should then be developed to enable organizations to implement collective green creativity and eco-innovation in their organizations

CONCLUSION

'Believing Cassandra' is the only way to avoid a predicted disaster of a sixth extinction. Mankind need to take corrective action to ensure that the Cassandra syndrome is recognized and that predictions and warnings are taken seriously. Business organizations also have active and important roles to play in safe--guarding the natural environment. Rather than just considering the customers' needs, technology, investments and profitability, the environmental impacts of new products and services should be taken seriously in the 21st century. The environmental impact, points to the importance of collective green creativity and eco-innovation to develop sustainable business practices in the global economy. Industrial organizations could utilised collective creative intelligences in creating green creativity to solve business and environmental problems, such as; melting glaciers, resource depletion, ocean acidification, and deforestation. This implies that an organization can be conscious of its environment in formulating competitive strategies and design of new products and services. An organization could achieve eco-innovation and sustainable business practices by tapping into the collective creative genius of its members through green mindfulness, green self-efficacy and shared vision, green transformational leadership, and green creativity. Therefore, collective green creativity and eco-innovation can offer novel solutions to the 'wicked problem' we are faced with of unsustainability and the possibility of a global extinction event caused by mankind.

REFERENCES

Aarikka-Stenroos, L., & Jaakkola, E. (2012). Value co-creation in knowledge intensive business services: A dyadic perspective on the joint problem solving process. *Industrial Marketing Management*, *41*(1), 15–26. doi:10.1016/j.indmarman.2011.11.008

Afolabi, M. O., Dionne, S., & Lewis, H. (2009). *Are we there yet? A Review of Creativity Methodologies*. Retrieved May 19, 2015, http://www.cs.cornell.edu/Conferences/ASEE2006/ASEE%20Papers/Session%204/ASEE%20Final%20vs%203_Afolabi.pdf

Amabile, T. M. (2011). How to kill creativity. In S. Johnson (Ed.), *The innovator's cookbook: Essentials for inventing what is next* (pp. 38–63). New York, NY: RiverheadBooks.

Anderson, N., Potočnik, K., & Zhou, J. (2014). Innovation and creativity in organizations a state-of-the-science review, prospective commentary, and guiding framework. *Journal of Management*, *40*(5), 1297–1333. doi:10.1177/0149206314527128

Articles. (n.d.). *The benefits of creative workplace*. Retrieved August 18, 2016, from http://www.bestpracticeconsulting.com.au/_blog/Articles/post/Fostering_creativity_in_the_workplace/

Bandi, N. (2007). *United Nations Global Compact: impact and its critics*. Retrieved May 25, 2016, from http://www.ethicalquote.com/docs/UnitedNationsGlobalCompact.pdf

Beauregard, E. (2015). *Top Ten Reasons Climate Change is a Hoax*. Retrieved May 25, 2016, from http://www.globalclimatescam.com/opinion/top-ten-reasons-climate-change-is-a-hoax/

Belcher, L. M. (n.d.). *Advantages and Disadvantages of Technology Advances*. Retrieved August 19, 2016, from http://smallbusiness.chron.com/advantages-disadvantages-technology-advances-12579.html

Benyus, J. M. (2002). *Biomimicry: Innovation Inspired by Nature*. New York, NY: Perennial.

Bhattacharya, A., Mohapatra, P., Kumar, V., Dey, P. K., Brady, M., Tiwari, M. K., & Nudurupati, S. S. (2014). Green supply chain performance measurement using fuzzy ANP-based balanced scorecard: A collaborative decision-making approach. *Production Planning and Control*, *25*(8), 698–714. doi:10.1080/09537287.2013.798088

Bissola, R., & Imperatori, B. (2011). Organizing individual and collective creativity: Flying in the face of creativity clichés. *Creativity and Innovation Management*, *20*(2), 77–89. doi:10.1111/j.1467-8691.2011.00597.x

Boden, M. A. (2004). *The Creative Mind: Myths and Mechanisms*. London: Routledge.

Carroll, A. B., & Shabana, K. M. (2010). The business case for corporate social responsibility: A review of concepts, research and practice. *International Journal of Management Reviews*, *12*(1), 85–105. doi:10.1111/j.1468-2370.2009.00275.x

Chen, Y. S., & Chang, C. H. (2013). The determinants of green product development performance: Green dynamic capabilities, green transformational leadership, and green creativity. *Journal of Business Ethics*, *116*(1), 107–119. doi:10.1007/s10551-012-1452-x

Chen, Y. S., Chang, C. H., Yeh, S. L., & Cheng, H. I. (2015). Green shared vision and green creativity: The mediation roles of green mindfulness and green self-efficacy. *Quality & Quantity*, *49*(3), 1169–1184. doi:10.1007/s11135-014-0041-8

Chesbrough, H. (2010). Business model innovation: Opportunities and barriers. *Long Range Planning*, *43*(2), 354–363. doi:10.1016/j.lrp.2009.07.010

Conway, S., & Steward, F. (2009). *Managing and shaping innovation*. New York, NY: Oxford University.

Cropley, D. H. (2016). Creative products: Defining and measuring novel solutions. In J. Plucker (Ed.), *Creativity and Innovation: Theory, Research, and Practice* (pp. 61–74). Austin, TX: Prufrock.

Cropley, D. H., & Cropley, A. J. (2010). Functional Creativity: Products and the generation of effective novelty. In J. C. Kaufman & R. J. Sternberg (Eds.), *Cambridge Handbook of Creativity* (pp. 301–320). New York, NY: Cambridge University. doi:10.1017/CBO9780511763205.019

De Sousa, F. C., Pellissier, R., & Monteiro, I. P. (2012). Creativity, Innovation and Collaborative Organizations. *The International Journal of Organizational Innovation*, *5*(1), 26–64.

Decuyper, S., Dochy, F., & Van den Bossche, P. (2010). Grasping the dynamic complexity of team learning: An integrative model for effective team learning in organisations. *Educational Research Review*, *5*(2), 111–133. doi:10.1016/j.edurev.2010.02.002

Del-Corte-Lora, V., Vallet-Bellmunt, T., & Molina-Morales, F. X. (2015). Be creative but not so much. Decreasing benefits of creativity in clustered firms. *Entrepreneurship & Regional Development*, *27*(1-2), 1–27. doi:10.1080/08985626.2014.995722

Dell'Amore, C. (2014). *Species Extinction Happening 1,000 Times Faster Because of Humans? National Geographic Reports*. Retrieved May 25, 2016, from http://news.nationalgeographic.com/news/2014/05/140529-conservation-science-animals-species-endangered-extinction/

Elgueta, D. (2014). *The Cassandra Syndrome - Ancient Greek Myth*. Retrieved May 25, 2016, from http://www.pseudoparanormal.com/2014/02/the-cassandra-syndrome-ancient-greek.html

Faraj, S., Jarvenpaa, S. L., & Majchrzak, A. (2011). Knowledge collaboration in online communities. *Organization Science*, *22*(5), 1224–1239. doi:10.1287/orsc.1100.0614

Flieschmann, K., & Hutchinson, C. (2012). Creative exchange: An evolving model of multidisciplinary collaboration. *Journal of Learning Design*, *5*(1), 23–31.

Florida, R. (2002). *The rise of the creative class and how it's transforming work, life, community and everyday life*. New York, NY: Basic Books.

Gino, F., Argote, L., Miron-Spektor, E., & Todorova, G. (2010). First, get your feet wet: The effects of learning from direct and indirect experience on team creativity. *Organizational Behavior and Human Decision Processes*, *111*(2), 102–115. doi:10.1016/j.obhdp.2009.11.002

Global, N. A. S. A. Climate Change. (2016). *Climate change: how do we know*. Retrieved June 19, 2016, from http://climate.nasa.gov/evidence/

Global Sustainability Standards Board (GSSB). (2015). *G4 Sustainability reporting guidelines. Global reporting initiative*. Retrieved June 1, 2016, from https://www.globalreporting.org/standards/g4/Pages/default.aspx

Gong, Y., Kim, T. Y., Lee, D. R., & Zhu, J. (2013). A multilevel model of team goal orientation, information exchange, and creativity. *Academy of Management Journal*, *56*(3), 827–851. doi:10.5465/amj.2011.0177

Gore, A. (2014). Without a Trace. *The New York Times*. Retrieved June 2, 2016, from http://www.nytimes.com/2014/02/16/books/review/the-sixth-extinction-by-elizabeth-kolbert.html?_r=0

Greek Myths & Greek Mythology. (2016). *The Myth of Cassandra*. Retrieved June 2, 2016, from http://www.greekmyths-greekmythology.com/the-myth-of-cassandra/

Groenwald, D. (Ed.). (2013). *Contemporary Management Aspects*. Cape Town: Juta.

Gumusluoglu, L., & Ilsev, A. (2009). Transformational Leadership, Creativity, and Organizational Innovation. *Journal of Business Research*, *62*(4), 461–473. doi:10.1016/j.jbusres.2007.07.032

Gurkaynak, G., Yilmaz, I., & Haksever, G. (2016). Stifling artificial Intelligence: Human perils. *Computer Law & Security Review*. Retrieved June 2, 2016, from http://www.elig.com/docs/0bc70-stifling-artificial-intelligence-human-perils.pdf

Haim, A. (2003). *The Manager's Pocket Guide to Creativity*. Mumbai: Sanman.

Hamel, G., & Breen, B. (2007). *The future of management*. Boston, MA: Harvard Business School Publishing.

Hill, L. A., Brandeau, G., Truelove, E., & Lineback, K. (2014). Collective genius. *Harvard Business Review*, *92*(6), 94–102. PMID:25051858

Holthaus. (2015). The point of no return: climate change nightmares are already here. *Rolling Stone*. Retrieved June 15, 2016 from http://www.rollingstone.com/politics/news/the-point-of-no-return-climate-change-nightmares-are-already-here-20150805

Im, S., Montoya, M. M., & Workman, J. P. Jr. (2013). Antecedents and consequences of creativity in product innovation teams. *Journal of Product Innovation Management*, *30*(1), 170–185. doi:10.1111/j.1540-5885.2012.00887.x

Jackson, N. (2006). Creativity in Higher Education – creating tipping points for cultural change. *SCEPTrE Scholarly Paper*, *3*, 25.

Jacobson, L. (2016). *Yes, Donald Trump did call climate change a Chinese hoax*. Retrieved June 15, 2016 from http://www.politifact.com/truth-o-meter/statements/2016/jun/03/hillary-clinton/yes-donald-trump-did-call-climate-change-chinese-h/

Jones, G. R., & George, J. M. (2012). *King Report on Corporate Governance in SA*. Retrieved June 15, 2016 from http://www.iodsa.co.za/?kingIII

Kirkman, B. L., Rosen, B., Tesluk, P. E., & Gibson, C. B. (2004). The impact of team empowerment on virtual team performance: The moderating role of face-to-face interaction. *Academy of Management Journal*, *47*(2), 175–192. doi:10.2307/20159571

Kirschner, P. A., Buckingham-Shum, S. J., & Carr, C. S. (2012). *Visualizing argumentation: Software tools for collaborative and educational sense-making*. Berlin: Springer Science & Business Media.

Kolberg, E. (2014). *The sixth extinction: an unnatural history*. New York: Henry Holt and Company, LLC.

Lapia, R., & Knight, L. (2011). *Recycle, reuse, design: eco-creativity in Rome*. Retrieved August 20, 2016, from http://www.cafebabel.co.uk/culture/article/recycle-reuse-design-eco-creativity-in-rome.html

Leachman, S. (2014). *Investing in ideas*. Retrieved August 20, 2016, from http://www.news.ucsb.edu/2014/014462/investing-ideas

Lee, V. H., Leong, L. Y., Hew, T. S., & Ooi, K. B. (2013). Knowledge management: A key determinant in advancing technological innovation? *Journal of Knowledge Management*, *17*(6), 848–872. doi:10.1108/JKM-08-2013-0315

Machiba, T. (2010). Eco-innovation for enabling resource efficiency and green growth: Development of an analytical framework and preliminary analysis of industry and policy practices. *International Economics and Economic Policy*, *7*(2-3), 357–370. doi:10.1007/s10368-010-0171-y

Marquardt, M. (2011). *Building the learning organization: Achieving strategic advantage through a commitment to learning*. Boston, MA: Nicholas Brealey.

Martins, E. C., & Terblanche, F. (2003). Building organisational culture that stimulates creativity and innovation. *European Journal of Innovation Management*, *6*(1), 64–74. doi:10.1108/14601060310456337

Mazzucato, M. (2013). Financing innovation: Creative Destruction vs. Destructive Creation. *Industrial and Corporate Change*, *22*(4), 851–867. doi:10.1093/icc/dtt025

McGrath, R. G. (2010). Business models: A discovery driven approach. *Long Range Planning*, *43*(2), 247–261. doi:10.1016/j.lrp.2009.07.005

Melville, N. P. (2010). Information Systems Innovation for Environmental Sustainability. *Management Information Systems Quarterly*, *34*(1), 1–21.

Muhammad, U. (2015). *Mass Extinction: Is the Enemy Us?* Retrieved June 19, 2016, from http://www.greattransition.org/images/GTI_publications/Muhammad-Mass-Extinction-Is-the-Enemy-Us.pdf

National Advisory Committee on Creative and Cultural Education (NACCCE). (1999). *All Our Futures: Creativity, Culture and Education*. London: Department for Education and Employment.

Nisen, M. (2013). *Robot Economy Could Cause Up To 75 Percent Unemployment*. Retrieved August 19, 2016, from http://www.businessinsider.com/50-percent-unemployment-robot-economy-2013-1

Organisation for Economic Co-Operation and Development (OECD). (2009). *Sustainable manufacturing and eco-innovation - Framework, Practices and Measurement*. Synthesis Report. Retrieved August 19, 2016, https://www.oecd.org/innovation/inno/43423689.pdf

Parjanen, S. (2012). Experiencing creativity in the organization: From individual creativity to collective creativity. *Interdisciplinary Journal of Information, Knowledge, and Management*, *7*, 109–128.

Payne, B. B. (2013). *Advantages and Disadvantages of Automation in Manufacturing*. Retrieved August 19, 2016, from http://www.vista-industrial.com/blog/advantages-and-disadvantages-of-automation-in-manufacturing/

Plucker, J. A., Beghetto, R. A., & Dow, G. T. (2004). Why isn't creativity more important to educational psychologists? Potentials, pitfalls, and future directions in creativity research. *Educational Psychologist*, *39*(2), 83–96. doi:10.1207/s15326985ep3902_1

Puccio, G. J., & Cabra, J. F. (2010). Organizational creativity: A systems approach. In J. C. Kaufman & R. J. Sternberg (Eds.), *The Cambridge handbook of creativity* (pp. 145–173). New York: Cambridge University Press.

Rodríguez, G., Soria, Á., & Campo, M. (2016). Artificial intelligence in service-oriented software design. *Engineering Applications of Artificial Intelligence*, *53*, 86–104. doi:10.1016/j.engappai.2016.03.009

Rotman, D. (2013). *How Technology Is Destroying Jobs*. Retrieved August 19, 2016, from https://www.technologyreview.com/s/515926/how-technology-is-destroying-jobs/

Runco, M. A. (2007). *Creativity. Theories and themes: Research, development and practice*. Amsterdam: Elsevier.

Scarborough, N. M., & Cornwall, J. R. (2015). *Entrepreneurship and effective small business management* (11th ed.). Boston: Pearson Education Limited.

Sherwin, C. (2011). *Creativity: missing from the sustainability jigsaw? Forum for the future*. Retrieved August 20, 2016, from https://www.forumforthefuture.org/blog/creativity-missing-sustainability-jigsaw

Smith, D. (2010). *Exploring Innovation* (2nd ed.). Berkshire, UK: McGraw-Hill Education.

Stanley, M. (2016). *Creative Capital Innovates & Sustains*. Retrieved August 20, 2016, from http://www.morganstanley.com/ideas/theme-sustainable-investing-and-creative-capital

Sung, S. Y., & Choi, J. N. (2012). Effects of team knowledge management on the creativity and financial performance of organizational teams. *Organizational Behavior and Human Decision Processes*, *118*(1), 4–13. doi:10.1016/j.obhdp.2012.01.001

The Biomimicry Institute. (2015). *Biomimicry 101*. Retrieved July 20, 2016, from https://biomimicry.org/what-is-biomimicry/#.V8XApPl97IU

United Nations Global Compact Report. (2015). *Global opportunity Report 2015*. Retrieved June 19, 2016, from https://www.unglobalcompact.org/docs/publications/Global_Opportunity_Report.pdf

Vaidyanathan, G. (2016). 10 ways climate science has advanced since An Inconvenient Truth. *Climate Wire*. Retrieved June 19, 2016, from http://www.scientificamerican.com/article/10-ways-climate-science-has-advanced-since-an-inconvenient-truth/

Vince, C. (2012). *A looming mass extinction caused by humans*. Retrieved August 20, 2016, from http://www.bbc.com/future/story/20121101-a-looming-mass-extinction

Vygotsky, L. S. (2004). Imagination and Creativity in childhood. *Journal of Russian & East European Psychology*, *42*(1), 7–97.

Wati, Y., & Koo, C. (2011, January). An Introduction to the Green IT balanced scorecard as a strategic IT management system. In *The44th Hawaii International Conference on System Sciences*. doi:10.1109/HICSS.2011.59

Yoon, S. W., Song, J. H., Lim, D. H., & Joo, B. K. (2010). Structural Determinants of Team Performance: The mutual influences of Learning culture, Creativity, and Knowledge. *Human Resource Development International*, *13*(3), 249–264. doi:10.1080/13678868.2010.483815

Zhang, A. Y., Tsui, A. S., & Wang, D. X. (2011). Leadership behaviors and group creativity in Chinese organizations: The role of group processes. *The Leadership Quarterly*, *22*(5), 851–862. doi:10.1016/j.leaqua.2011.07.007

KEY TERMS AND DEFINITIONS

Collective Creativity: Collective of creative people working as a team to create new and novel ideas and solutions.

Creativity: Creativity is about solving problems and satisfying needs by developing novel and useful solutions.

Eco-Innovation: The production, assimilation or exploitation of a novelty in products, production processes, services or in management and business methods, which aims, throughout its lifecycle, to prevent or substantially reduce environmental risk, pollution and other negative impacts of resource use.

Green Creativity: The generation of new and novel environmentally friendly and sustainable business ideas.

Innovation: The implementation and commercialisation of new and problem-solving ideas, practices or products through which change is brought about.

Chapter 2

Connecting the Dots: Bisociation, Collective Creativity, and Sustainable Business

Olajumoke Ogunsanya
University of KwaZulu-Natal, South Africa

ABSTRACT

Calls for businesses to act with concern for the environment and society create new operating scenarios in which sustainability concerns must be taken into consideration along with the primary objectives of profitability and competitiveness. These additional obligations contribute to dynamism of the marketplace and make it important for businesses to draw on creativity and innovation to find connections between the unrelated in order to establish new efficiencies that can create competitive advantage and differentiation in the environment they find themselves. The central theme of this chapter is how bisociation informs collective creativity and innovation, and influences sustainability for business organizations competing in an environment that is in a permanent state of flux. This chapter trails a series of concepts to find the relationship between the concept of bisociation, collective creativity and sustainable business practices. The aim is to show how consistent creative thinking and exploration of information in different spaces of thought can proffer innovative solutions organizations require for their long term survival and prosperity.

INTRODUCTION

A considerable level of creativity and creative capacity leading up to innovation and innovative aptitude is needed to create new approaches and skills vital to create sustainable business models and improve corporate ethics and responsibility in the current operating environment. There is a high level of uncertainty, turbulence and complexity that characterize the current business landscape. Globally, fast-paced and across-the-board change has become the norm rather than an anomaly, which makes adopting a sustainable business perspective a valuable approach for managers and organizations as a whole. The days of predictable future are over and the implication for business organizations is that they cannot be static in their bid to meet market demands. Businesses must invent their own future by developing the

DOI: 10.4018/978-1-5225-1823-5.ch002

ability to anticipate change. They must also have the kind of fluidity which supports swift and necessary adaptation to external environmental shifts while maintaining their strategic vision, identity and operations to accomplish their primary goals. Creativity and innovation are powerful elements in this regard. They have become increasingly important attributes companies need to achieve desired organizational performance, success, and long-term survival (Anderson, Potočnik & Zhou, 2014). Creativity and innovation encompass the ability to look beyond the obvious, to explore what is possible. In Fields & Bisschoff (2013), creativity is said to create new economies and social forms as solutions to some of the complex challenges in an uncertain environment. An organization able to succeed at this continuously establishes a foundation for its on-going sustainability.

It is understandable that a business' primary interests are its own viability and profitability. However, there are increasing calls for organizations to act with concern for the long-term environmental and social impact of their operations. There is mounting pressure and increasing demand for new ways of doing business to achieve equity, social change and preservation of the physical environment. These challenges present opportunities to the forward-thinking organization to devise new ways and forge new paths to create new products, new services and new processes that plug identified gaps in the market. The dynamic marketplace makes it a necessity for businesses to draw on creativity and innovation to find connections between the unrelated in order to establish new efficiencies that can create competitive advantage and differentiation in the environment they find themselves. An innovative organization will be able to invent its future, and keep up with (and sometimes possibly be ahead of) the pace of change occurring in the dynamic marketplace it finds itself. Knowing that innovation is primarily driven by creativity, it is necessary for companies to understand what drives creativity and use their strategies, people, systems and processes to facilitate it.

The objectives of this chapter are to discuss creativity in the context of need for creativity and individual creativity versus collective creativity; to present the concept of bisociation and its relationship with collective creativity; and finally, to establish a connection between collective creativity, innovation and sustainable business practices. The contribution of this chapter is that it shines light on an important model of creative thinking to promote an understanding of how finding unexpected links between seemingly unconnected information and concepts powers the processes behind creativity. The value in application of bisociative reasoning – finding new useful connections where they did not exist before – is vital in business because organizations are able to draw parallels between different domains to discover new links, new insights and new perspectives in their creative processes. Also, they will be able to see how parallels and unconventional thinking can be source of innovation to give sustainability to the organization.

Background

What is Creativity?

Creativity is the initial step in innovation. It is a precursor to innovation. One may ask, what is creativity? Robinson (2001) refers to human creativity as imaginative processes of the mind with outcomes that are original and valuable. Boden (2004) defines it as the ability to come up with new, surprising and valuable ideas or artefacts in different spheres of life. The three key words in Boden's definition: new, surprising and valuable present the context in which creativity is viewed. Firstly, creativity is said to involve newness. Most definitions of creativity agree that novelty is a key element of creativity. Amabile (1997) hinges novelty on a creative act being different from what has been done before. Fisher & Williams (2004) linked novelty to originality. To distinguish between levels of originality Boden (2004) elaborated on the context of newness by introducing two dimensions, psychological creativity (P-creativity) and historical creativity (H-creativity). P-creativity refers to originality or newness of a creative idea or act to the individual who came up with it. This means that the individual has never thought of the idea or done the act before, hence the creative outcome is new to them even though other people might have delivered same creative outcomes before. On the other hand, H-creativity is when a new idea is coming up for the first time in human history and experience. That is, the product, act or idea is new to the individual responsible for it and to all others.

The second element of creativity is the notion of surprise. A creative idea or act is surprising because it is unexpected, unfamiliar, unlikely, interesting, considered impossible and runs counter to convention (Dubitzky, Kotter, Schmidt & Berthold, 2012). The surprise caused by creative outcomes is as a result of improbable combinations of ideas occurring in a person's mind where deliberate or unconscious acts of linking familiar concepts in unfamiliar ways lead to surprising results. This reference to mental linking of concepts is further discussed in the next section of the chapter under the bisociation concept. The surprise aspect of creativity arouses a realization that a creative output does not fit into a regular, conventional or familiar mold.

The third element of creativity is that a creative idea or act must be valuable. Creativity cannot produce what is simply bizarre for the sake of generating something that has not been thought of or seen before. There must be a point to the existence of that new idea, concept, act or product, and it must be valuable in some significant way to be considered as creative. The value of a creative outcome can be determined by how suitable and appropriate it is for its purpose, how useful it is to the opportunity presented or how well it provides a solution to the problem at hand (Sternberg & Lubart, 1999). The value-element asks an important question: "to what intent and purpose is this?" as the creative process unfolds.

The Need for Creativity

The world is constantly changing. One day is not the same as the next. Change brings with it opportunities, problems, and risks. Both individuals and organizations have to deal with change that is coming from different directions. The demands of change are what make creativity a necessity. The drive to pursue opportunities, find solutions to problems and even take risks serves to explain the generation of new ideas and discovery of new ways of addressing issues brought about by change. Creativity is the way to manage change in a positive manner. Through ideas produced creativity challenges convention, routine, and tradition in the bid to discover improved and/or new ways to do things. Organizations need creativity in a business environment that is permanently in a state of flux. Creativity is needed to adapt, thrive, compete and stay relevant in a world of consistent change. It is a key factor for survival, success and excellence in light of growing sophistication of consumer demands, fierce competition and market rivalry, legislation and regulatory requirements, technological advancement, and turbulent economic atmosphere.

Bisociation and Creativity

The Bisociation Concept

Kotter, Thiel & Berthold (2010) developed the BisoNets model (Bisociative Networks) and defined bisociation as "a link that connects concepts from two or more domains, which are unconnected depending on the specific view by which the domains are defined". A concept, also referred to as a unit of knowledge, is a measure of meaning derived from reasoning or mental processes (Dubitzky et al, 2012) while a domain can be viewed as a set of concepts from the same field or knowledge area. In Kotter *et al* (2010), the theory of bisociation is credited to Arthur Koestler who originally conceived it in his work *The Act of Creation*. According to Koestler, all forms of creativity or creative acts involve bisociation, a result of series of processes in the mind that make new indirect connections between concepts and contexts which were previously unconnected or usually regarded as separate. Bisociation occurs at the point where two (or more) planes, domains or matrices of thought intersect to simultaneously share a connection.

Bisociation stimulates creativity or creative thinking by linking information from different and seemingly disparate domains to create a new, different, unusual context. According to Jursic, Cestnik, Urbancic & Lavrac (2012), three conditions are necessary for bisociation to occur: first, there must be no evident, existing or direct connection linking the concepts; second, the concepts must exist in different domains or knowledge areas so that there is a crossing of domains to find a link; and third, the bisociative link must offer new and valuable insights. So, it is the novelty, interestingness and value of the connection that makes a bisociation creative. It can be said the more remote the elements of a bisociation are seen to be the more creative the bisociative connection is. Linking remote concepts involves non-linear thinking which implies an ability to conceptualize and re-conceptualize different and possibly contradictory information and scenarios (Hitt, Keats & DeMarie, 1998).

Bisociation differs from association which is a phenomenon that establishes patterns between ideas within a given domain or matrix (Berthold, 2012). Association occurs within the boundaries of a domain guided by pre-conscious or extra-conscious processes to form patterns and connections among ideas. Skills of reasoning rely on habit and are controlled by established rules. So one can say that association follows the norm, the expected. On the other hand, bisociation traverses domains, using unfamiliar, indirect, new and interesting links to bring together independent autonomous matrices. Criss-crossing multiple domains and matrices of perception indicates a level of super-flexibility in reasoning that allows for unrestrained sub-conscious processes which may ordinarily be under restraint. This is what Segond & Borgelt (2012) refer to as a state of double-mindedness or the ability to think on several planes of thought concurrently. Koestler's work suggested that routine thinking differs from creative thinking. Routine thinking skills occur on a single plane or one matrix of thought; disciplined thinking activates only one matrix at a time. However, bisociative reasoning in creativity operates on more than one plane synthesizing diverse domains and matrices of thought to create interesting links between them where they never existed before or where they were not previously observed. Therefore, creativity or creative acts do not follow the codes of disciplined reasoning. Due to its bisociative connection, one can say that creativity is chaotic in some sense, unscripted and uninhibited, not following dogma or some prescribed rational logic. In agreement with such line of reasoning, creativity is addressed in Fields & Bisschoff

(2013) as *a successful step into the unknown* (because the creative connection has not been made before), *getting away from the main track, breaking out of the mould.... recombining ideas or seeing new relationships among ideas.*

Types of Bisociation

Bisociation, as discussed above, is the intersection of two different frames of reference or information spaces. Research has revealed many types of bisociation: some are concrete while others are found to be abstract, some are complex and others simple. Kotter & Berthold (2012) identified three distinct patterns of bisociation that have emerged over the years. These are bridging concepts, bridging graphs, and bridging by structural similarity.

Bridging Concepts

Bridging concepts is the most common type of bisociation where a single concept links two different domains. Bridging concepts fuse information from very dense, large and diverse knowledge domains using one interconnecting link to create a representation that is useful or applicable in decision-making in the relevant sphere. This type of bisociation often uses ambiguity or metaphors. Ambiguous concepts are more popular and used in humour while metaphors are applied in more serious applications considerations. Metaphors as bridging concepts have a degree of flexibility that allows a concept in one domain to be perceived and understood in terms of concepts from another entirely different frame of reference (Kotter & Berthold, 2012). More specifically, examples of bridging concepts can be found in Weeber, Vos, Klein & de Jong-van den Berg (2001), Petric, Urbancic, Cestnik & Macedoni-Luksic (2009), as well as Petric, Cestnik, Lavrac & Urbancic (2010) where actual medical and scientific discoveries were reproduced in data form to show connections made between medical conditions, diseases, chemical combinations and the human body.

Bridging Graphs

Bridging graphs are a slightly more complex pattern of bisociation where sub-graphs connect concepts from different contexts. Nagel, Thiel, Kotter, Piatek & Berthold (2012) describe bridging graphs as a group of units of information and links that provide bisociative connections between different domains. So, independent and diverse domains are linked by a subset of concepts that share some level of relatedness among them (Berthold, 2012). Also, a bridging graph can link two different and unrelated concepts from the same domain by establishing a connection through a previously unknown domain (Kotter et al, 2010).

Bridging by Structural Similarity

Bridging by structural similarity is a very complex and abstract bisociative pattern where the concept linking the domains is on the basis of similarity in the underlying structure. That is, in the different domains under observation, a bisociative connection is depicted by a similarity of structure identified in subsets of concepts or subgraphs present in the domains. In Kotter *et al* (2010) an example of structural similarity is depicted by highlighting the similarity between a prodrug that negotiates through the blood-brain barrier in the human body and the soldiers hidden in the Trojan horse to get past the gates of Troy. The bisociative connection in the two scenarios is that changing the appearance of the intruder is the means to go past the barriers (blood-brain and Troy's gates).

Bisociation and Collective Creativity

The preceding section has shown that creativity which produces innovation is achieved through operating in multiple planes or matrices of information where a creative individual integrates these domains to make new, interesting, unexpected and valuable discoveries. Individual level of creativity denotes a person's capacity to produce new or original ideas and insights which are accepted as being of value; it is an individual's ability to perceive and articulate what is hidden from others' view around an issue in order to develop novel and meaningful solutions that make for creative outputs. It also refers to a person's role and efforts in developing something new, unexpected and valuable in their sphere of human activity. So, individual creativity is about one person. The creativity potential of a person will be significantly shaped by their individual characteristics and traits, as well as social and contextual influences in their environment.

As organizations increasingly adopt a team approach to improve productivity, teams are becoming the way of life in business and industry and most creative processes involve individuals working together to solve problems they cannot solve alone. Hence, the source of creativity is no longer just individuals but progressively groups of people. While the fundamental role of individual creativity within an organization is well-emphasized it is arguable that better creative outcomes occur in social contexts rather than in isolation. The social context of creativity involves interactions with other individuals through direct collaboration or information sourcing from members of communities of practice at different stages in the creative process. Therefore, when insight, acumen and creativity ensue from these interactions, it is referred to as collective creativity (Nakakoji, Yamamoto & Ohira, 2000) where creative activity materializes from the collaboration and contribution of many individuals; where new concepts emerge from shared interactions of knowledge between individuals. *The locus of creativity in the interaction moves to the collective level when each individual's contributions not only shape the subsequent contributions of others, but, just as importantly, give new meaning to the past contributions of others* (Parjanen, Harmaakorpi, & Frantsi, 2010). The expedient role collaboration plays in creativity is in the diversity of knowledge, efforts, skill and perspectives available for stimulation of creative ideas. It is important to highlight that collective creativity cannot be arbitrarily assigned as a simple sum up of individuals' creativity. There are factors such as culture, processes, resources, leadership style that significantly influence creativity of the collective especially in an organizational setting.

As outlined, bisociative cognitive processes feature in the generation of creative ideas. When bisociation is shared by a group of people working together as a team collective creativity happens (Sanders, 2001). Because it involves more than one person, connections and movements between multiple frames of reference takes place on an increased scale to generate novel and valuable creative propositions which address emerging needs, problems and opportunities in new ways (Bilton & Cummings, 2014). The collaboration of different types of thinking and combination of ideas derived from approaching issues from different angles and views results in the discovery of what is previously unknown to come up with creative solutions. Creativity in a collaborative setting can stimulate more creativity in the individual and assuage the pressure to repeatedly come up with creative ideas which can be daunting for one person. In

Parjanen (2012), collective creativity occurs when social interactions between individuals trigger new interpretations and new discoveries of distant analogies that the individuals involved could not have generated by thinking alone.

There is a widespread shared appreciation for creativity in business. In managerial discourse the emphasis on need for creativity is not decreasing but intensifying because rapid changes in the environment create a state of constant business disruption. Disruption in this context refers to the game changing effect that intermittent change, especially technology, has on industries. In response, businesses must deftly manage the disruption as well as devise essential strategies to remain profitable, competitive and relevant. Disruption presents complex challenges, problems and opportunities. In confronting them, organizations require collaboration of diverse skills, knowledge, experience and abilities to develop with fitting solutions. This is where collective creativity comes in. The bottom line is that increasing complexity of business operations requires collective solutions to produce creative outcomes. Collective creativity is valuable and can be significant to deliver necessary and relevant outcomes. The growing use of collective creative processes is justified more so because of the pressure to produce creative ideas constantly.

COLLECTIVE CREATIVITY, INNOVATION AND SUSTAINABLE BUSINESS

United Nations and Sustainable Development

One of the goals of the United Nations (UN) in its outline of sustainable development goals is to "ensure sustainable consumption and production patterns" (www.un.org). Sustainable consumption and production is concerned with promotion of resource and energy efficiency; provision of access to basic services, green and adequate jobs and job opportunities; sustainable infrastructure, as well as an improved quality of life for all. The implementation of this goal is towards achieving overall development objectives; reduction of future economic, environmental and social costs; increased economic competitiveness and poverty reduction.

The primary purpose of sustainable consumption and production is to achieve more and better output with less inputs. This means expanding welfare gains from economic activities by reducing resource use, environmental degradation and pollution along the whole lifecycle, while improving quality of living. The achievement of sustainable business practices requires a systematic approach that will involve the cooperation of different role players and stakeholders in the lifecycle of production and consumption. This includes business, consumers, governments and policy makers, researchers, scientists, retailers, media, civic organizations and development agencies, among others (www.un.org). Current global trends in the utilization of earth's resources is identified as the cause of major environmental issues such as climate change, resource depletion, damage to biodiversity, air and water pollution (Watson, Boudreau & Chen, 2010). The existing manner of resource use in production and consumption cannot be sustained. According to a report by the UN World Commission on Environment and Development (UNWCED, 1987), also referred to as the Brundtland Report, the world needs to embrace sustainable development, which 'meets the needs of the present without compromising the ability of future generations to meet their own needs'.

Sustainable Business

Business has a key role to play in sustainable development. Putting it concisely, sustainable business is mainly about changing the way business is done. Sustainable business is changing business conduct and practices in a way where creation of new products, services or processes is achieved in a manner that alleviates negative environmental and social impacts. Sustainable business means organizations are not only focused on their own performance objective of profit maximization but also give important consideration to broader environmental and social impact of their operations. Referred to as a "triple bottom line", sustainable business is when business is done from the three-point perspective of economic profitability, environmental awareness and social consciousness; and measures of business performance are based on net impact on profit, people, and planet (Hubbard, 2009). Sustainable business requires that sustainability is not a stand-alone issue but an organizational mind-set established at core strategic level of the business and actualized in every level of operations within the organization.

The call for business practices that do not harm the environment, degrade natural resources or perpetuate societal inequality and injustice is change that presents market opportunities. Gittell, Magnusson & Merenda (2012) reckon creativity, innovation and entrepreneurship are key in implementing sustainable business practices. An entrepreneurial mindset views sustainability as an opportunity to create value from the vast and complex challenges the issue poses to business organizations. Advantages of such a problem-focus includes use of multidisciplinary teams to mobilize resources, connecting the organization with its external stakeholders because complex problems require interaction with the environments in which they occur as well as those affected by the problems (Thorp & Goldstein, 2010). In addition, with an entrepreneurial mindset, innovation becomes the rule because it enables an organization develop swift responses in form of solutions to emerging changes in the market.

Collective Creativity and Sustainable Business

Sustainable business practices require a multidisciplinary approach due to the multi-focus nature of sustainability issues. Engagements in the same circles and networks will over time yield the same kind of information, perspectives and contacts. The use of collective creativity will foster cooperation among people from different disciplines and knowledge areas working effectively together to develop solutions for identified problems. Van Kleef & Roome (2007) argued for such multi-actor collaboration in sustainable business on the basis that it is problem-focused, creates an atmosphere for joint action; provides platforms for learning and develops context-dependent knowledge. In terms of problem focus, the diversity of collaborators is valuable for the identification of specific sustainability issues affecting an organization. Such focus assists in developing appropriate sustainable solutions. Collaborations such as open innovation as well as strategic partnerships allow for new, heterogeneous and appealing inputs from stakeholders such as customers, interest groups, supply chain partners, and other external stakeholders (Antikainen, Mäkipää & Ahonen, 2010; Foster & Green, 2000). Such close collaborations provide the space to share and exchange information and knowledge with which an organization can build intelligence helpful to develop sustainable systems.

The argument for joint action in sustainability is that it ensures the consent and involvement of relevant stakeholders, those directly or indirectly involved and affected by the implementation of sustainable practices in business. Joint action is a recognition of stakeholder interest and is implemented by building collaborative linkages that span different networks an organization may have (Clark & Roome, 1995). Such networks can be intra-organizational (inside the organization), trans-organizational (between organizations in the supply chain) or supra-organizational where stakeholder relationships are with other organizations instead of individuals. In the case of learning, Boons & Berends (2001) suggested that the quality of interaction in the collective can create avenues for learning. The level of diversity of participants in collective creative processes can initiate learning in the organization and the group. Learning is important in developing knowledge; the right knowledge can elicit innovative thinking which can produce potential solutions that are able to address complex problems (Johannessen, 2008).

Roome (2001) and UNWCED (1987) acknowledge that there is a context to what may be regarded as sustainable where sustainability matters are shaped by prevalent conditions in the local area. This means that sometimes there is a context-specificity to sustainability, therefore the challenges require particular solutions and innovations that suit the context. For example, policies can be made to suit the context of a locality or region.

The concept of multi-stakeholder collaboration as enunciated in this section has its challenges. Because of the extent of diversity in the parties working together there may not be enough trust in the coalition which can create tension. When there is distrust in the coalition, ability to reach agreement is compromised and each party resorts to looking out for themselves rather than working together towards a consensus that benefits all concerned (DeFillippi, Grabher & Jones, 2007). Distrust may also result in competition between groups and individuals as well as manipulation and tussle for control of the agenda (Boons & Berends, 2001). Resource constraints around finances, legislative support and infrastructure may impede the efficiency of collective collaborations, as will differences in organizational culture and ideologies (Kale & Singh, 2009), inadequate facilitation skills to expedite group processes (Jiang, Li & Gao, 2008), lack of clarity about objective of the group collaboration (Glaister, Husan & Buckley, 2004).

Innovation and Sustainable Business

Innovation is unequivocally crucial for the long-term success of any business organization. Innovation defines most aspects of organizational creativity because it is action part of the creative process. To thrive in an environment with accelerating change and more frequent disruptions requires new ideas and ways of thinking to channel new products, new services, new markets and new processes that have market viability. Sustainability is a force of change that is altering the competitive landscape. It is making many businesses change the way they develop, manufacture and deliver their products. Also sustainability is making businesses rethink their organizational processes, technologies and business models (Nidumolu, Prahalad & Rangaswami, 2009). Innovation is a means to deliver change. Sustainable business as an economic model is also about developing a resilience and ability to withstand shocks in the environment over time. An innovative capability helps to strengthen such resilience.

So, what exactly is innovation? For companies, creative thoughts and ideas are not enough, but pointed action on developed ideas is required for impact and growth thereafter. New ideas have to be implemented to deliver value. Innovation takes creativity further by ensuring the outcomes of creativity provide value to customers and other stakeholders, and have commercial viability (Keeley, Walters, Pikkel & Quinn, 2013). Innovation is all about seeing an opportunity where creativity can make a difference. An innovative organization identifies problems that matter and systematically delivers offerings that provide solutions by linking the needs and wants of customers with the organization's creative processes necessary for achieving them. Nooteboom (2000) argued that innovation is not necessarily connected to problem solving, but is driven by technology for the purpose of improving competitiveness and profitability. In sustainable business, innovation, be it product, process, technological or business, involves changing an organization's offerings or creating new offerings that meaningfully improve the experience of a large number of stakeholders in a way that adds value economically, socially and environmentally. Innovation in sustainability is intended to align environmental and social interests with profitability objectives, to achieve change beyond the benchmarks of competitiveness and economic success (Van Kleef & Roome, 2007).

The move to sustainability must be planned and coordinated in manageable steps, with practical and viable solutions that are achievable within a realistic time frame. According to Nidumolu et al (2009), innovation in sustainable business practice is a gradual shift which can be achieved in stages. The first step is for organizations to view compliance to sustainable business practices as an opportunity. The main challenge here is ensuring that compliance with sustainability norms materialize into real innovation opportunities for the organization. Such opportunities include using compliance to stimulate experimentation with sustainable technologies, materials, and processes. An organization will need competencies to predict and influence regulations as well as skill to work with others, including rivals, to realize creative solutions.

The second step is about implementing innovations that make the entire value chain sustainable, from raw materials to the end-user. The main challenge is how to increase efficiencies throughout each link of the organization's value chain. Innovation opportunities at this stage include developing sustainable sources of raw materials and components, improving current design of operations to achieve reduction in energy usage and other natural resources, increasing the use of clean and renewable energy sources, innovative methods of waste and pollution management. Applicable organizational competencies include techniques in measuring carbon footprint and energy usage, life-cycle assessment, capacity to actively engage with suppliers and retailers to incorporate sustainability into their operations (Seuring & Müller, 2008).

In the third step the main focus is to develop new sustainable offerings or redesign existing offerings to become compliant with sustainability guidelines. Organizational competencies at this level should include ability to identify current offerings in the organization's portfolio that are most unfriendly to the environment, ability to create market acceptance and rally valid public buy-in for the organization's sustainability objectives so that new offerings are not regarded as mere green washing, collaborative capacity to build strategic partnerships that contribute to innovative ability. Opportunities to innovate exist in applying technological innovations to product and process development, and green marketing.

The next step is concerned with developing new business models. The main challenge is how to realize new ways to deliver a competitive value proposition that balances profitability with environmental and social needs (Geels, 2005). An organization will need to have a thorough understanding of consumers' current needs and wants (and possibly how those needs can evolve in the future) and find various ways to meet those customer expectations. Also, a business will need to understand how its value chain partners can boost the value of offerings and actively engage them to adopt the same sustainability philosophy. Innovation opportunities at this level include new technologies that will substantially impact value chain partnerships, technologies to empower business models to straddle digital and physical infrastructures, and innovative profit models to discover new revenue and pricing opportunities for the business' offerings. The business model of an organization should be an intermediary for innovation in the sustainability agenda, to connect production and consumption with stakeholders and their expectations (Boons & Lüdeke-Freund, 2013).

The final step by Nidumolu *et al* (2009) involves creating next- practice platforms. The main challenge is to use sustainability lens to interrogate the principal logic behind today's business practices and launch a new paradigm for the future. The competencies needed at this level include knowledge and understanding of effect of renewable and non-renewable resources on business ecosystems and industries, skills to develop sustainability business models, technologies, as well as guidelines and protocols in diverse industries. Innovation opportunities exist in building business platforms that will allow for radically new and different ways to use and manage energy. An example is increased use of smart technology to manage energy consumption.

Organizational and Managerial Implications

There is a significant amount of responsibility on organizations as a whole on what to do to encourage collective creativity, sustainability and innovation. On the basis of concepts outlined in this chapter some selected implications and/or recommendations are discussed to highlight some practical references.

Leadership

Leadership is a key influencer in collective creativity. Leading innovation will require that leadership and management create an environment where people are able and willing to do the hard work needed for innovation to thrive. Such an environment should allow for open expression of ideas, contributions and unconventional thoughts from all persons in the organization irrespective of their level in the company organogram. Leadership should promote a collaborative approach to problem solving where there is freedom to discuss, debate and advocate for ideas. Leadership must be willing to allow for errors, false starts and missteps within a reasonable and acceptable frame that does not jeopardize the company's existence. Leadership should encourage a learning culture in the organization where ideas are tested, refined and adjusted as needed. This is an experimental kind of learning or "learning-on-the-go" or "learn-as-we-discover" where learning occurs as things are discovered in the process of testing creative outcomes. Bisociation is about combining ideas that are polls apart and reconfiguring them to produce new and useful solutions that did not exist before. Leadership must be patient enough to allow all sides of the creative solution feature in decision-making, not just the aspects that seem to be the most obvious.

Development of a Networked Enterprise

The ability to communicate and exchange ideas is an important part of the collective creative process and innovation takes a "village". An organization is not an island and therefore must forge necessary internal and external networks, collaborations and partnerships to enhance its innovative capacity. Innovation is a deliberate process therefore, an organization must be intentional in engaging across domains in multi-actor collaborations and joint action. In developing innovation-oriented networks within the organization itself, in industry and market and even government using tools such as work teams, strategic alliances and partnerships, project collaborations and open innovation, a company avails itself the space to share and exchange information and knowledge with which it can build intelligence helpful to develop sustainable systems.

Enhance Sustainable Practices

A sustainable business is interested in the effects of operations on relevant aspects of the environment they are in. Therefore, to enhance and give meaning to their sustainability practices, organizations must particularly ascertain the impact and effect their operations have on the environment, then decide on the impact(s) that present the best opportunity for value creation to the company and the environment; and finally given the resources available, the business must determine the most efficient and effective ways to address such opportunities with innovative solutions. Opportunities for value creation can come through suggestion boxes in the organization, customer complaints, regulation requirements, developments in the value chain as well as standards and benchmarks in the industry.

FUTURE RESEARCH DIRECTION

Further research can be done to interrogate innovative business models adopted by organizations that have successfully imbibed sustainability into their strategic mandate. It may also be of research value to explore how creative processes in organizations have evolved over the years into the present era where knowledge has emerged as a critical element in the creation of value, and is major stimulus for economic expansion and competitiveness.

CONCLUSION

This chapter focused on the bisociation concept and its link to collective creativity and sustainable business practices. This chapter presented the bisociation concept as the outcome of reasoning processes that make new indirect connections between concepts and contexts which were previously unconnected or usually regarded as separate. The main types of bisociations - bridging concepts, bridging graphs and bridging by structural similarity – were identified and discussed. The chapter showed how bisociation is connected to collective creativity and innovation. Bisociative cognitive processes occur in the generation of creative ideas. Therefore, when bisociation is shared by a group of people working together as a team collective creativity happens. Since creativity is an antecedent to innovation, the link to collective creativity and innovation was also discussed to show that innovation takes a collective to occur. The adoption of sustainability into the business focus of competitiveness creates opportunities for capabilities and competence for innovation. This means that organizations must frequently go beyond what has worked in the past and seek new and different perspectives and connections. Using this angle, the chapter further elaborated on the link between bisociation, collective creativity, innovation and sustainable and sustainable business practices.

In this chapter a valuable model of creative thinking has been discussed to promote the understanding of how finding unexpected links between seemingly unconnected information and concepts powers the processes behind creativity. The value in application of bisociative reasoning – finding new useful connections where they did not exist before – is vital in business because organizations are able to draw parallels between different domains to discover new links, new insights and new perspectives in their creative processes. Also, they will be able to see how well such parallels hold to give sustainability to the organization. A major challenge still persists in organizations, and this is how to rationalize the performance objective of profit maximization alongside consideration for sustainability issues. Some organizations have successfully managed the balance while some others are still on the learning curve.

REFERENCES

Amabile, T. (1997). Motivating creativity in organizations: On doing what you love and loving what you do. *California Management Review*, *40*(1), 39–58. doi:10.2307/41165921

Anderson, N., Potočnik, K., & Zhou, J. (2014). Innovation and creativity in organizations: A state-of-the-science review, prospective commentary, and guiding framework. *Journal of Management*, *40*(5), 1297–1333. doi:10.1177/0149206314527128

Antikainen, M., Mäkipää, M., & Ahonen, M. (2010). Motivating and supporting collaboration in open innovation. *European Journal of Innovation Management*, *13*(1), 100–119. doi:10.1108/14601061011013258

Berthold, M. (Ed.). (2012). Bisociative knowledge discovery: An introduction to concept, algorithms, tools, and applications. Heidelberg, Germany: Springer. doi:10.1007/978-3-642-31830-6

Bilton, C., & Cummings, S. (2014). A framework for creative management and managing creativity. In C. Bilton & S. Cummings (Eds.), *Handbook of management and creativity* (pp. 1–12). Cheltenham, UK: Edward Elgar. doi:10.4337/9781781000977.00007

Boden, M. A. (2004). *The creative mind: Myths and mechanisms* (2nd ed.). London: Routledge.

Boons, F., & Berends, M. (2001). Stretching the boundary: The possibilities of flexibility as an organizational capability in industrial ecology. *Business Strategy and the Environment*, *10*(2), 115–124. doi:10.1002/bse.277

Boons, F., & Lüdeke-Freund, F. (2013). Business models for sustainable innovation: State of the art and steps towards a research agenda. *Journal of Cleaner Production*, *45*, 9–19. doi:10.1016/j.jclepro.2012.07.007

Clarke, S. F., & Roome, N. J. (1995). Managing for environmentally sensitive technology: Networks for collaboration and learning. *Technology Analysis and Strategic Management*, *7*(2), 191–216. doi:10.1080/09537329508524204

DeFillippi, R., Grabher, G., & Jones, C. (2007). Introduction to paradoxes of creativity: Managerial and organizational challenges in the cultural economy. *Journal of Organizational Behavior*, *28*(5), 511–521.

Dubitzky, W., Kotter, T., Schmidt, O., & Berthold, M. R. (2012). Towards creative information exploration based on Koestler's concept of bisociation. In Bisociative knowledge discovery: An introduction to concept, algorithms, tools, and applications (pp.11 - 32). Heidelberg, Germany: Springer.

Fields, Z., & Bisschoff, C. A. (2013). A model to measure creativity in young adults. *Journal of Social Sciences*, *37*(1), 55–67.

Fisher, R. (2004). What is creativity? In R. Fisher & M. Williams (Eds.), *Unlocking creativity: Teaching across the curriculum* (pp. 6–20). London: David Fulton Publishers.

Foster, C., & Green, K. (2000). Greening the innovation process. *Business Strategy and the Environment*, *9*(5), 287–303. doi:10.1002/1099-0836(200009/10)9:5<287::AID-BSE256>3.0.CO;2-7

Geels, F. W. (2005). *Technological transitions and system innovations: A co-evolutionary and socio-technical analysis*. Cheltenham, UK: Edward Elgar. doi:10.4337/9781845424596

Gittell, R., Magnusson, M., & Merenda, M. (2012). *Sustainable business cases*. Retrieved September 8, 2015, from: http://2012books.lardbucket.org/books/sustainable-business-cases/s07-02-business-and-government-relati.html

Glaister, K. W., Husan, R., & Buckley, P. J. (2004). *Strategic business alliances – An examination of the core dimensions*. Cheltenham, UK: Edward Elgar. doi:10.4337/9781845420543

Hitt, M. A., Keats, B. W., & DeMarie, S. M. (1998). Navigating in the new competitive landscape: Building strategic flexibility and competitive advantage in the 21st century. *The Academy of Management Executive*, *12*(4), 22–42.

Hubbard, G. (2009). Measuring organizational performance: Beyond the triple bottom line. *Business Strategy and the Environment*, *18*(3), 177–191. doi:10.1002/bse.564

Jiang, X., Li, Y., & Gao, S. (2008). The stability of strategic alliances: Characteristics, factors and stages. *Journal of International Management*, *14*(2), 173–189. doi:10.1016/j.intman.2007.09.002

Johannessen, J. (2008). Organisational innovation as part of knowledge management. *International Journal of Information Management*, *28*(5), 403–412. doi:10.1016/j.ijinfomgt.2008.04.007

Jursic, M., Cestnik, B., Urbancic, T., & Lavrac, N. (2012). Cross-domain literature mining: Finding bridging concepts with CrossBee. In *Proceedings of the International Conference on Computational Creativity* (ICCC 2012). University College Dublin.

Kale, P., & Singh, H. (2009). Managing strategic alliances: What do we know now, and where do we go from here? *The Academy of Management Perspectives*, *23*(3), 45–62. doi:10.5465/AMP.2009.43479263

Keeley, L., Walters, H., Pikkel, R., & Quinn, B. (2013). *Ten types of innovation: The discipline of building breakthroughs*. John Wiley.

Kotter, T., & Berthold, M. (2012) From information networks to bisociative information networks. In Bisociative knowledge discovery: An introduction to concept, algorithms, tools, and applications (pp. 33–50). Heidelberg, Germany: Springer. doi:10.1007/978-3-642-31830-6_3

Kotter, T., Thiel, K., & Berthold, M. R. (2010). Domain bridging associations support creativity. In *Proceedings of the International Conference on Computational Creativity - ICCC 2010* (pp. 200–204). Lisbon, Portugal: Department of Informatics Engineering, University of Coimbra

Nagel, U., Thiel, K., Kotter, T., Piątek, D., & Berthold, M. R. (2012). Towards Discovery of Subgraph Bisociations. In Bisociative knowledge discovery: An introduction to concept, algorithms, tools, and applications (pp. 263 – 284). Heidelberg, Germany: Springer. doi:10.1007/978-3-642-31830-6_18

Nakakoji, K., Yamamoto, Y., & Ohira, M. (2000). Computational support for collective creativity. *Knowledge-Based Systems*, *13*(7-8), 451–458. doi:10.1016/S0950-7051(00)00069-1

Nidumolu, R., Prahalad, C. K., & Rangaswami, M. R. (2009). Why sustainability is now the key driver of innovation. *Harvard Business Review*, (September), 57–64.

Nooteboom, B. (2000). Learning and innovation in organizations and economies. New York: Oxford.

Parjanen, S. (2012). Experiencing creativity in the organization: From individual creativity to collective creativity. *Interdisciplinary Journal of Information, Knowledge and Management*, *7*, 109–128.

Parjanen, S., Harmaakorpi, V., & Frantsi, T. (2010). Collective creativity and brokerage functions in heavily cross-disciplined innovation processes. *Interdisciplinary Journal of Information, Knowledge and Management*, *5*, 1–21.

Petric, I., Cestnik, B., Lavrac, N., & Urbancic, T. (2010). Outlier detection in cross-context link discovery for creative literature mining. *The Computer Journal*.

Petric, I., Urbancic, T., Cestnik, B., & Macedoni-Luksic, M. (2009). Literature mining method RaJoLink for uncovering relations between biomedical concepts. *Journal of Biomedical Informatics*, *42*(2), 220–232. doi:10.1016/j.jbi.2008.08.004 PMID:18771753

Robinson, K. (2001). *Out of our minds: Learning to be creative*. Oxford, UK: Capstone.

Roome, N. J. (2001). Metatextual organizations e-innovation and adaptation for global change (inaugural lecture). Centre for Sustainable Development and Management, Erasmus University Rotterdam, The Netherlands.

Sanders, L. (2001). Collective creativity. *AIGA Journal of Interaction Design Education*, *3*, 1–6.

Scott, A. J. (1998). The contribution of forums to rural sustainable development: A preliminary evaluation. *Journal of Environmental Management*, *54*(4), 291–303. doi:10.1006/jema.1998.0233

Segond, M., & Borgelt, C. B. (2012). Selecting the links in BisoNets generated from document collections. In Bisociative knowledge discovery: An introduction to concept, algorithms, tools, and applications (pp. 54 – 65). Heidelberg, Germany: Springer. doi:10.1007/978-3-642-31830-6_5

Seuring, S., & Müller, M. (2008). From a literature review to a conceptual framework for sustainable supply chain management. *Journal of Cleaner Production*, *16*(15), 1699–1710. doi:10.1016/j.jclepro.2008.04.020

Sternberg, R. J., & Lubart, T. I. (1999). The concept of creativity: Prospects and paradigms. In R. J. Sternberg (Ed.), *Handbook of creativity* (pp. 3–14). Cambridge, UK: Cambridge University Press.

Thorp, H., & Goldstein, B. (2010). *The entrepreneurial university*. Retrieved from: www.insidehighered.com/views/2010/09/27/thorp

United Nations World Commission on Environment and Development. (1987). *Our common future*. Oxford, UK: Oxford University Press.

Van Kleef, J. A. G., & Roome, N. J. (2007). Developing capabilities and competence for sustainable business management as innovation: A research agenda. *Journal of Cleaner Production*, *15*(1), 38–51. doi:10.1016/j.jclepro.2005.06.002

Watson, R. T., Boudreau, M., & Chen, A. J. (2010). Information systems and environmentally sustainable development: Energy informatics and new directions for the IS community. *Management Information Systems Quarterly*, *34*(1), 23–38.

Weeber, M., Vos, R., Klein, H., & de Jong-van den Berg, L. T. W. (2001). Using concepts in literature-based discovery: Simulating Swanson's Raynaud–fish oil and migraine–magnesium discoveries. *Journal of the American Society for Information Science and Technology*, *52*(7), 548–557. doi:10.1002/asi.1104

KEY TERMS AND DEFINITIONS

Bisociation: The outcome of cognitive processes making new and interesting connections between separate and unrelated concepts from different domains or frames of reference.

Creativity: The ability to develop new ideas.

Innovation: The implementation of new and viable creative ideas.

Sustainability: Efficient use of natural resources in the course of achieving business objectives.

Sustainable Business: A model that gives adequate consideration to the environmental and social impact of business activities while maintaining the long term profitability and competitiveness of the organization.

Chapter 3
A Need for Cyber Security Creativity

Harold Patrick
University of KwaZulu-Natal, South Africa

Ziska Fields
University of KwaZulu-Natal, South Africa

ABSTRACT

Information technology is rapidly increasing and evolving all the time in pursuit for better solutions and products for the digitized world. Technology advancement and greater connectivity has moved organizations to better economic markets for sustainability. Together with better technology and greater connectivity, cybercrime is swiftly growing on par with these developments. This chapter focuses on the cyber security landscape and threats faced by organizations. The growth and sophistication of cybercrime is stressed. Cyber security creative approaches security risk assessment, cloud collaboration and data analytics are provided. This chapter ends with propositions that security creative approaches should be used as a method of managing cybercrime and ensuring that the organization's sustainability and governance are improved.

INTRODUCTION

With the rise of the technology and digitization labelled the Fourth Industrial Revolution (World Economic Forum, 2014, p. 8) internet connectivity between countries and amongst organizations have altered the way of doing business and drives new possibilities of economic gain (Negroponte, Palmisano & Segal, 2013, p. 10). The width spread and rapid growth of the internet technology has increased better speed access to networks (NATO Cooperative Cyber Defence Centre of Excellence, 2012, p. 5) and offers better service. However, these innovations and complexity have also given rise to cybercrime actors. At the same time attacks have increased in number. It is now a priority for organizations to address cybercrime. Cybercrime requires new measures that can be costly for the organization to implement (Holtfreter & Meyers, 2015, pp. 55-61).

DOI: 10.4018/978-1-5225-1823-5.ch003

Many organizations have experienced major vulnerabilities and many prominent organizations suffered security breaches (Hardekopf, 2015, p. 1). For example, a million customers' credit and debit cards were affected and hackers stole 53 million customers' email addresses from a Home Depot store and 76 million households and seven million businesses were affected when hackers stole customers' names and email addresses from JP Morgan (Verizon, 2015, p. 1).

Traditional approaches to managing security breaches is proving to be less effective as the growth of security breaches are growing in volume, variation and velocity (Bhatti & Sami, 2015, p. 1). There are constant media headlines about new security incidents and attacks, identity theft and data breaches (Crosby, 2015, p. 1). Organizations are being bombarded with cyber-attacks and penetration threats, network intrusions and politically motivated attacks (Polancich, 2015, p. 1). Cybercrime is no more a uniqueness it has become a global reality and features in the daily operations of organizations (Symantec, 2016, p. 1).

On-going advances in the sophistication of technology, while ground breaking, bring with them a multitude of security challenges (Rogerwilco, 2015, p. 1). There is no doubt that cybercrime incidents are difficult (Zio, 2016, p. 137) and complex to manage. A new proactive approach to mitigate cyber security vulnerability and risks is needed. It is imperative that organizations understand these vulnerabilities and risks so a resilient approach is proposed (Amann & James, 2015, p. 1). Organizations will not know the type and severity of a cyber-attack until it has been a target by cybercriminals. Organizations suffer huge financial losses due to the cyber-attacks (Khan & Estay, 2015, p. 7) and some organizations may not even recover from the attacks.

Geographical location of organizations, their complex systems with increased connectivity amongst their different business operation and other organizations make cyber security efforts very challenging (Bertino, 2016, p. 13). The challenges for organizations are to demonstrate that they can adequately protect (Accenture, 2015, p. 1) and safeguard their systems and networks from new cyber security breaches thereby create a better investor confidence. Organizations must demonstrate the leadership and confidence needed to better protect the organizations systems and networks from security breaches and ensure resilience in managing these fatalities (EY, 2013, p. 2). In addition organizations must rethink their approach to meet the demands or the digitalized world (Negroponte et al., 2013, p. 4).

BACKGROUND

Importance of Cyber Security

The cyberspace ecosystem is rapidly getting bigger as a larger number of users of internet and emails increase (Jardine, 2015, p. 3). Organizations are now more globally connected in pursuit of greater sustainable economic opportunities together with this the cyber landscape is increased (Levesque, Walsh & Whyte, 2015, p. 28). Organizations need to adapt (Levesque et al., 2015, p. 32) and remain relevant to protect their systems and networks. Organizations process and store confidential information on computers and communicate across different computer networks. Continuing protection of sensitive information because of the volume and complexity is needed (University of Maryland University College, 2016, p. 1). Better security protects the organization's assets and information, maintains organization communication and ensures continuation of productivity (CISCO, 2010, p. 1).

Damballa's work (2014, p. 2) shows that this is an uneven battlefield where the balance of power favours the threat actor. The threat actor knows more about the organization or the individual than the organization or individual knows about them. They also have the resources to find out what security controls the organization has in place. Cybercriminals are well funded and are willing to use huge sums of money (Virvilis, Serrano & Dandurand, 2014, p. 1) and expertise to advance their threats and attacks to reach their goal of a breach.

These cyber actors also exploit the vulnerabilities so that they can steal information (Department of Homeland Security, 2015, p. 1). Threat actors can include persons belonging to other organization, citizens of other countries looking to secure government or organization gain an competitive advantage by stealing research development projects (Negroponte et al., 2013, p. 17) or cyber terrorism organizations (Chaturvedi, Unal, Aggarwal, Bahl & Malik, 2014, p. 2), these forms of actors are not easily identifiable and cannot identify their alliance to an organization, group or government (Retel, 2014, p. 5). Bamrara (2015, p. 1) states that an attack can take the form of:

- When an intruder gains unauthorized access.
- When the intruder destroys, alters or corrupts data.
- When an intruder impersonates a message from a certain organisation system.
- When an intruder introduces malicious processes that cause the organisations network to fail.

Threat actors can launch an attacks from any geographical locations (Wamala, 2011, p. 14) and these attacks will not appear like the same attacks (Negroponte et al., 2013, p. 4). Some threat organization offer an inclusive package of services, e.g. that includes to deploy the attack and retrieving stolen information (Ablon, Libicki & Golay, 2014, p. 4). Cyber criminals are continuously regenerating attacks and are becoming more creative in exploiting security vulnerabilities of the organization (Schober, 2016, p. 1) because they are immensely motivated by the financial gain of the attack (IBM, 2016, p. 3). Cyber criminals are multiskilled (Ablon et al., 2014, p. 4) and continuously develop their skills so that they are well equipped to deploy an attack (Retel, 2014, p. 5). Cybercriminals become masters of intelligence so that they can anonymize themselves from any detection (Bandler, 2016, p. 29). Minimizing the period of a cyber-attack reduces its cost and overall impact on the organization. Thus organizations should realize that the probability of a cyber-attack is a constant and a substantial threat (Patrick, 2016, p. 26). Traditional security measures such of detection, response and recovery are not adequately combating the cybercrime (Deloitte, 2013, p. 2). Organizations are in search of improved cyber resistance strategies because a significant number of cybercrime activities go undetected (White & Case, 2015, p. 1). This now gives rise to a need for a creative approach of dealing with cyber-security. Organizations must adopt a creative response to the challenges of decreasing cybercrime (International Cyber Security Protection Alliance, 2014, p. 8).

Cyber Security Definitions

Cyberspace can be described as an involvement of computers (hardware), networks, systems, people and their interaction with the networks (NATO Cooperative Cyber Defence Centre of Excellence, 2012, p. 8). This section will briefly highlight the broad set of terms that are used in the cyber security environment.

Cyber security is protecting the computers, programs, networks and data from unauthorized access, destruction or change (University of Maryland University College, 2016, p. 2) and cyber security is also the methods taken to protect the organization's computer and networks (Merriam-Webster, 2016, p. 1). Cybercrime is illegal activities that targets organization (KPMG, 2014, p. 2). The type of cyber-crimes are committed through the use of computer or device include creating and spreading harmful software, malware deployment, breach of computer ethics policy, distributing illegal contents of intellectual property, creating and distribution of child pornography (NATO Cooperative Cyber Defence Centre of Excellence, 2012, p. 14). Cyber espionage is when an organization or country deploys methods of spying to get unauthorized access to the organizations or country systems (InfoSec Institute, 2013, p. 1). Cyber warfare is also another crime in which countries launch offensive operations against other countries by exploiting vulnerabilities of these for the offensive countries gain. These are amongst the commonly committed cybercrimes and are by no means an exhaustive list. Retel (2014, p. 6) highlights that cybercrime destabilizes the operational functions of the organization and significantly diminishes organizations' trust in the global environment. Wamala (2011, p. 13) defines a cyber-attack is when a threat successfully breaches the organizations' or government's security existing controls for a physical or an information asset. A threat actor is a person or group that executes the attack (Wamala, 2011, p. 16).

THE SCALE OF CYBER SECURITY BREACHES

Implications of Global Threats

Organizations around the world continue to increase their business and IT infrastructure by adding more devices and increasing connectivity across their organizations. The volume of data requiring 24x7 monitoring also continues to grow (IBM, 2014a, p. 3). This increases an organization's vulnerability by making it more difficult to develop and organize effective measures to fend off cyber-attacks and breaches. The number of threats and vulnerabilities are increasing in today's dynamic business environment, and attackers are manipulating them faster than ever before and with greater complexity and stealth (IBM, 2014a, pp. 5-7). Cyber security incidents are growing in frequency as are the costs of managing and mitigating breaches (PricewaterhouseCoopers, 2014, p. 10).

Lacey (cited in Kelly, 2014, p. 4) notes that the world is more open and complex. "As more devices become connected to each with new features they become more powerful, there are benefits to society and business, but a hyper-connected world is hard to protect and secure." Security threats are very real, and the risk factors are higher than ever in today's information-centric and interconnected world. Cyber-attacks can affect and originate from any country (IBM, 2013, p. 2). These attacks are becoming more dynamic, complex and malicious. For example, a hacker from Morocco claimed responsibility for hacking the South African Social Development Department's website in response to South Africa purportedly supporting the "Sahrawi Arab Democratic Republic" which according to the hacker is an enemy of Morocco (South African Press Association, 2012, p. 1). Given the large variety of incoming cyber threats and attacks, they can be extremely challenging to detect, analyse and prevent (Wlosinski, 2015, p. 35). Today's attacks and breaches target maximum financial gain and key information, for example, for military action or extortion (Canon, 2015, p. 37).

According to Anil, Cyber defence head at NATO (cited in Ashford, 2014, p. 1), the level of cyber threats that organizations face is unlikely to decrease for at least 10 years. As a result, NATO is working with its member states and partner countries to defend themselves against the offensive cyber capabilities of other nations. The World Economic Forum (WEF) (World Economic Forum, 2014, pp. 12-13) defines a global risk as *"an occurrence that causes significant negative impact for several countries and industries over a time frame of up to 10 years."* The WEF technological risk category includes cyber-attacks, infrastructure disruptions and data loss that are ranked 29, 30 and 31, respectively. Cyber-attacks were ranked 4th in 2012 and 5th in 2014. Increased dependence on information and data ensured that this risk remained in the top five (World Economic Forum, 2014, p. 17).

Impact of Cyber Security Incidents

The drastic increase in global connectivity to organization networks has also seen a rapid growth of data volumes (Retel, 2014, p. 4). The organizations' increased dependency on these networks brings potential vulnerabilities and risks. The average organization monitored by IBM experienced more than 53 million security events in 2015 (2016, p. 4). No organization is equipped to deal with the magnitude of the potential threats on its own. Cyber security attacks in 2015 dropped to an average of 1,157 from 12,017 in 2014. IBM (2016, p. 4) reviewed those 1,157 security attacks and found that the average organization experienced 178 security incidents in 2015, 69 more than the previous year.

The 2015 Breach Level Index Report indicates that there were 1,673 data breaches and 707,509,815 records were lost or stolen worldwide (Gemalto, 2016, p. 1). The Gemalto (2016, p. 1) further cited that the frequency rate for data records was 1,938,383 million per day and almost 80,766 per hour. In 2015, the government sector was the top ranked global sector in terms of the number of data breaches, representing 43% (Gemalto, 2016, p. 1). The Verizon report for 2016 cited 100,000 security incidents and 3,141 confirmed data breaches (Verizon, 2016, p. 1). Business Insider report (2016, p. 1) estimates that during 2015 to 2020 $655 billion will be spent on cyber security initiatives. In 2015, Symantec discovered 430 million variants of malware in network vulnerabilities (Symantec, 2016, p. 5).

KEY CREATIVE INIATIVES FOR MANAGING CYBER SECURITY

Organizations information systems and networks are constantly being breached. Organizations need to contextualize their approach and decide on the level of visibility needed to manage cyber security (Kaplan, 2016, p. 1). Organizations need to understand the ramifications of cyber threat and cyber-attack and build an effective cyber security approach that will limit the impact of the cyber incident (Chartered Accountants, 2014, pp. 22-23). Preventative security systems and manual processes alone is not adequate to protect targeted attacks and malware from adversaries (Oltsik, 2013, p. 3). The work by Ahmad, Maynard & Park (2014, p. 357) shows that an organization with a creative cyber security initiative can reduce the chance of IT risks and security breaches, protect its reputation and avoid lawsuits (ISACA, 2013, pp. 141-143). Furthermore, it will save money by simplifying IT audits because risk assessments would have been included in the program (Miller, 2013, p. 3).

According to the Ponemon Institute (2014a, p. 11), a strong security position ultimately decreases the cost of data breaches. A strong security position and incident response planning decrease the per capita cost of such a breach. The Institute notes that a strong security position could reduce the average per record cost to $131.86 ($145-$14.14) because the incident management program will ensure that the incident or breach is timeously investigated and contained with minimal operational interruptions.

InfoSec is an on-going process as the threat of security incidents will increase (Ahmad et al., 2014, p. 357) with the introduction of new systems and increased network connectivity. An organization's approach to InfoSec and its security culture indicates its level of risk (Ifinedo, 2014, p. 69). A culture of security among employees is crucial (Hunt, 2014, p. 3). The Ponemon Institute (2014b, p. 20) pegs the ideal amount that an organization should invest in its security strategy at an average of $14 million over a 12-month period. However, organizations anticipate spending an average of half that amount ($7 million).

Organizations need smarter approaches (Bhatti & Sami, 2015, p. 4) that are creative in order to be effective against continuous new sophisticated threats and attacks. Creativity can be described as taking ideas and knowledge to fulfil a certain need (O'Leary & Vij, 2012, p. 3) (Lee, Olson & Trimi, 2012, p. 822). The individual and traditional security measures cannot integrate different data sets hence cannot create the context of the issues nor the measures to mitigate the risks. Cybercriminals are also becoming better at covering their threat and attack attempts (The Economist, 2014, p. 5) therefore organizations must implement safeguards that can anticipate a potential cyber threat or attack and proactively prepare (Holtfreter, 2016, p. 19). Putrus (2016, p. 46) notes that some organizations might label creative initiatives as not a profit yielding approach instead as being more concerned about prevention and mitigation of cyber threat. The next section will show that these three creative initiatives that can be taken towards developing strategic cyber security approach that could outthink threat actors and improve cyber security.

Information Security Assessment

Organizations are connected to a number of and different systems and machines, even though it encourages technology and economic growth it does exposes the organization's controls and weakness to data security (KPMG, 2014, p. 3). New technologies and commercial practices and growing cybercrime highlight the need for all organizations to conduct annual IT security assessments (California Department of Justice, 2014, p. 26). A cyber risk can be defined as the probability that a threat will exploit a weakness to breach the security of an asset (Wamala, 2011, p. 16). The Thawte report (2014, p. 8) discusses that the threat landscape is complex; thus, a risk-management approach to cyber security is crucial in assessing potential risks. InfoSec Assessment allows an organization to make informed decisions on current problem areas (Attorney-General's Department, 2013, p. 14), allocate resources and interventions to manage the cyber risks.

No security is fool proof; all organizations have an element of IT risk that is either unknown or considered to be an acceptable part of doing business (Lee, 2014, p. 6). Therefore, an IT risk and cyber security assessment approach is crucial in order to minimize risks and implement controls (for example, encryption of all email attachments). System audits (for example, an audit of users' access can be cross-referenced to users' roles and responsibilities) and penetration tests can be performed to reduce an organization's IT risk profile (Moturi & Bitta, 2013, p. 43)

Organizations tend to respond to crises rather than think proactively about IT risk, for example, running automated analysis to detect behaviour that is outside the norm (Sullivan, 2015, p. 45) in order to identify gaps that intruders will exploit. Technology, process and people are intertwined; therefore, a proactive cyber risk assessment is required to reveal deficiencies in networks and infrastructure (Patrick, 2016, p. 47). A change in cyber security is necessary in order to prepare for future challenges and the cyber risk assessment should be the first step (Yoran, 2014, p. 1).

In the current environment, many organizations use spreadsheets to perform InfoSec risk assessments (Salvi, 2013, p. 6). Thereafter, the IT security and risk team hold follow-up discussions to assess the organization's risk and recommend a mitigation strategy. However, this method does not allow for regular review of the IT risks confronting the organization. Salvi (2013, p. 6) notes that organizations need to move towards automation of the risk process by using governance, risk and compliance tools. They add that an automated process is a measurable one that can be better integrated into an overall enterprise risk management perspective and is better able to align the security strategy with the organization. James et al. (2013, p. 6) identified some of most common deficiencies in security assessments as follows:

- Inadequate digital software to conduct forensic investigation analysis; and
- Lack of threat information recording

A cyber risk assessment enables an organization to stay ahead of threats by proactively managing vulnerabilities and threats and developing the Information security strategy (Ab Rahman & Choo, 2015, p. 54). Cyber security risk assessments are an essential component that offer early warning of malicious activities that could damage the organization's infrastructure and reputation (Richards, 2014, p. 1). An InfoSec assessment enables an organization to visualize its security controls topology, calculate risk scores and review these controls (IBM, 2014, p. 1).

While many organizations have experienced a reality check when it comes to IT risks, they are still too complacent when it comes to cyber security risks levels (Lloyds, 2013, p. 11). Regular IT risk reviews ensure minimal disruption of services and operations. Thus, cyber security assessments are crucial to continuously monitor and evaluate the organization's networks for security breaches (Nolan & McFarlan, 2011, p. 101. Most organization's assessments of security controls are performed on an irregular basis (Martin, 2013, p. 3) by internal or external auditors. Martin (2013, p. 3) adds that incomplete IT assessments are no longer sufficient. Security IT controls should be measured as part of the organization's on-going capabilities.

Cyber security risk assessment forms a baseline by correlating information on cyber security exposure and identifying areas for improvement which the organization can use as a starting point (Fortinet, 2014, p. 5). The measurement of IT risks is a critical aspect of managing systemic risks and developing a cyber-security methodology. Quantification of cyber risks is essential (World Economic Forum, 2014, p. 41). The growing role of cyberspace is not only a technical and geopolitical concern but presents serious cyber risks to the economic wellbeing of the organization such as failing to manage a cyber-threat and breach and thus suffer a huge reputation damage (Lieberman, 2015, p. 47). The failure of critical infrastructure represents a systemic risk that could impact on an organization's mandate and the delivery of services and products to the economic market (World Economic Forum, 2014, p. 41).

Risks and vulnerabilities evolve over time, requiring security controls to continuously adapt. Improved controls and/or new controls should result from cyber security risk assessments (Hunt, 2014, p. 2). A lack of cyber security risk assessment increases the cyber risk exposure of the organization (Oltsik, 2014, pp. 20-21). Effective cyber security requires active IT risk management (International Cyber Security Protection Alliance, 2014, p. 5) thus organizations need to ensure that they have done a cyber-security risk assessment so that cyber risk are easily detected. The cyber assessment will result in recommendations to build and enhance such information technology management (4Di Privaca, 2014, p. 1). An organization's success can be measured by its management of cyber security risks and the deployment of security controls (Pandey & Snekkenes, 2014, p. 296). Patil (2013, p. 39) notes that cyber security controls can promote operational efficiency and reduce costs.

Organizations systems are becoming more complex due to integration of in-house systems and other organizations systems, in addition budget limitations severely impact the management of IT risk (Schmittling & Munns, 2010, p. 1). Cyber risks are shifting and becoming further complex thereby compromising the organizations systems and networks making them vulnerable to an attack (Halliday, 2015, p. 1). Threats and attacks are evolving thus gaps between the organization's risks and response are widening (EY, 2013, p. 14). Cyber security assessment would better understand the organizations risks and improve its security governance and ultimately improve an organization's performance.

As a result of the increase in cyber security threats and attacks, organizations are under severe pressure to ensure quicker and much improved response to mitigating security incidents. A cyber security assessment is a continuous creative approach that ensures that the organization's productivity disruptions is minimal, provides a quick status of the risks and thus allows speedy process of enhancing security risk controls (Schmittling & Munns, 2010, pp. 2-3). The proactive creative approach of cyber security risk assessment allows the organization to keep pace with new organization opportunities and new risk exposures (The Institute of Risk Management, 2014, pp. 9-13). Cyber security assessment can continually offer a review of the business processes so that the organization systems and networks can be protected from potential threats and attacks.

Cloud Collaboration Amongst Organizations

Collaboration is defined as bringing about a new service or process (Lee et al., 2012, p. 828). Collaboration can take different forms like inter organizational amongst multiple work groups or amongst organizations (TechTarget, 2016, p. 1) (Lee et al., 2012, p. 828). This section is thus focusing on literature only pertaining to collaboration amongst organizations. Prior to a collaboration network is formed, the organizations must ensure that its business operations are compatible to that of the prospective organization it intends to collaborate with (O'Leary & Vij, 2012, p. 6).

Cybercriminals collaborate to share new dimension information and knowledge (The Commonwealth, 2014, p. 3) to avoid detection so that their attacks are successful. Lack of collaboration amongst organizations exposes the organizations silo approach to systems (Actian, 2015, p. 1) and thereby give the threat attacks the advantage. Fostering collaboration amongst organizations leads to an intelligence approach (Attorney-General's Department, 2013, p. 8) that builds a better response to cybercrime. Organizations must foster a collaboration approach to managing cybercrime (International Cyber Security Protection Alliance, 2014, p. 6). Collaboration creates a trusting environment where expertise and capabilities (World Economic Forum, 2016, p. 61) can be shared in advancing the management of cybercrime.

Channels of communication and collaboration amongst organizations, security researchers and developers are required to promote faster and more effective mitigation, as well as regular updates on cyber security incidents or breaches (Prolexic, 2014, p. 30). Shared information can prevent financial loss and enable an organization to proactively manage cyber security threats (Wolfpack, 2013, p. 44). By sharing threat and attack information, organizations could mitigate these cyber risks (Robinson, 2014, p. 1) by putting measures in place to prevent significant damage to their systems and networks. Robinson (2014, p. 1) adds that organizations do not trust one another with threat information and that this has hindered the flow of threat information.

Lacy (cited in Kelly, 2014, p. 4) sharing cyber threat data is vital amongst organizations in order for them to stand a chance against cyber-attacks, because new threats are more sophisticated and complex. Hayes (cited in PricewaterhouseCoopers, 2014, p. 29) also argues that "in today's threat environment there is no reason for not collaborating." Heartbleed (vulnerability) has proven that organizations can protect their internal networks by sharing information on events and resources. Collaboration will also support real time responses to security incidents (Rice & Ringold, 2015, p. 23). In so doing, organizations could prepare for the next vulnerability and ensure that their employees are diligent in recognizing future security incidents (McAfee, 2014, p. 8). According to the 2012/2013 South African Threat Barometer, organizations should at least be communicating their basic InfoSec standards and approach to employees (Wolfpack, 2013, p. 44). Cho (cited in Press, 2015, p. 1) emphasizes that sharing cyber security incident information amongst organizations enables them to apply mitigating measures in order to protect their systems and networks. In addition collaboration amongst organizations empower their employees to recognize potential cyber threats and better understand the action they should take when they experience such cyber threats and attacks (Patrick, 2016, p. 72).

Collaboration develops the knowledge and solutions that can be invested (Retel, 2014, p. 6). Continued collaboration amongst organizations can create creative solutions (Mark L. Frigo, Hans Læssøe & Ramaswamy, 2015, p. 15) and initiative measures of balancing the inventions and rewards of introducing better inventions to curb cyber-attacks. Collaborative interventions amongst organizations creates better decisions (Bartnes, Moe & Heegaard, 2016, p. 35) and preparedness that can be used for responding to attacks and mitigating future threats. Collaboration amongst the organizations can ensure that there is a quicker and robust response to reinstate organizations' business processes following from a security breach (Bertino, 2016, p. 14). Through collaboration amongst organizations they are able to share capabilities and leverage creative mitigating techniques (National Institute of Standards and Technology, 2016, p. 1) and strategies to ensure improved defense against future threats. Organizations that are collaborating need to ensure the rules of information (such as threat and breaches) dissemination are taken account such as sensitivity of the information is preserved (National Institute of Standards and Technology, 2016, p. 2). Collaboration amongst organizations assists in developing new ideas (Rocha Flores, Antonsen & Ekstedt, 2014, p. 92) or implementing new policies.

Collaboration can take the form of traditional or cloud collaboration. Traditional is when organization manually share information amongst themselves. With the rise of more connectivity amongst organizations cloud collaboration is a creative process of the organization sharing real time information to ensure that their efforts of managing security incidents and threats is effective (Campbell, 2013, p. 1). With the cloud collaboration the organizations can work together on projects online to share pertinent information (TechTarget, 2016, p. 1). With cloud collaboration, ideas and solutions are speeded up because of the virtual real time access which ensures that security incidents and threats are investigated timely (Boyer, 2016, p. 3). Cyber security incident response teams in the collaborative organization have easy access so that they can work on simultaneously on the project (Campbell, 2013, p. 1). With cloud collaboration the organizations save on additional computer infrastructure and software costs. The processes of investigating cyber threats will be streamlined (Morgan & Conboy, 2013, p. 98). In addition, there is audit trail of actions performed to ensure data integrity. Han et al. (2013, p. 4) emphasize that cloud collaboration event-driven can support as a trigger of event which will require further action from the collaborate organization users.

The National Institute of Standards and Technology (2016, pp. 7-8) highlights that there are some challenges to collaboration amongst organizations, which include; establishing and maintain a trusting relations, adopting specific protocols and formats for example creating repositories to exchange threat information and ensuring that the threat information is validated prior to sharing amongst the organization. A further challenge is that an organization may be more sophisticated and well run as opposed to another organization (O'Leary & Vij, 2012, p. 4). There is a security concern about theft of data in the cloud however identity management that can counter security incidents can focus on access control (Esmaeil Mehraeen, Marjan Ghazisaeedi, Jebraeil Farzi & Mirshekari, 2016, p. 161).

Data Analytics

Data analytics is the process and activity designed to obtain and evaluate data (ISACA, 2011, p. 5) in order to extract valuable information (that is, patterns and trends). Data analytics is also termed the science of investigating raw data (Rouse, 2008, p. 1). The results of data analytics can be used to identify fraud, risks, improves business process decisions and influence organization decisions. Data analytic techniques include ad hoc data analytics, repeatable data analytics, centralized data analytics and continuous monitoring (ISACA, 2011, p. 5). Ad hoc data analytics processes include data mining or benchmarking testing. Repeatable data analytics process is predefined and same tests are performed on similar at different periods of time. Centralized data analytics is the process of creating a central data repository of repeatable data analytic tests, further scheduled analytic tests are run against the centralized data on demand (ISACA, 2011, p. 5). Continuous monitoring process is when data analytic tests are fully automated and tests are embedded into the organizations systems to run at regular intervals.

Threat actors are determined to evade any organization's detection measures, hence the real time analysis and discovery of suspicious activities is limited because threat actors are spreading their activities; data analytics would allow for more analysis and pattern correlation to avoid future hacking attempts (Virvilis et al., 2014, p. 3). Offline data analytic of captured organizations outgoing traffic can identify possible attacks and delay the future attacks (Bertino, 2016, p. 13). With the growth and complexity of data (structured and unstructured) organizations need a proactive creative analysis to monitor non-compliant and rogue activities of internal and external cyber threats (EY, 2013, p. 14). This solution allows refined analysis and which highlights similar patterns (McAfee & Brynjolfsson, 2012, p. 10) which thereby harness better decisions. A visual picture and patterns (Accenture, 2015, p. 5) of the threats and attacks optimal time of performing security analysis is reduced to allow quicker incident response time on investigating suspicious behavior across networks (Teradata, 2013, p. 11). Data analytics creates a resilient and proactive cyber defence position for the organization (Teradata, 2013, p. 13). Data analytics provides a situational awareness across the organization's systems and networks of analytical insights of exposures and thereby providing an informed planning and effective decisions (Kielman, 2015, p. 26).

Data analytics can improve the organization's security position for example network traffic can be analyzed to identify early warnings of malware threats and attacks (Durbins, 2013, p. 2). Data analytics can also be used to identify insider threats by examining email and web content activity of employees so that patterns of actions can be analyzed (Durbins, 2013, p. 2). Due the increased availability of remote access and bring your own device, the workplace allows employees easy access to the organization's systems. Data analytics could identify employees times of accessing the systems which can be analyzed against the organization's Human Resource system to identify which employees on leave are accessing the system and what actions are being performed by them (Durbins, 2013, p. 2). A text mining data analytic technique can be used for example to understand the risks posed from a prospective transaction (Accenture, 2015, p. 5) to that of the customer's needs.

US Department of Homeland Security (Kielman, 2015, p. 5) proposes some crucial questions to be harnessed by the organization:

- What part is relevant?
- What does the patterns and visual picture mean?
- How will the organisation use the results after the data analysis?
- How will the organisation convey the results after the data analysis through the organisation?

Data analytics can significantly reduce the probability of false positives where its security issues are flagged for an abnormally but in actual fact is a valid transaction (ISACA, 2011, p. 7). In addition data analytics allows for improved and better organization transparency of its systems that are being used (CaseWare, 2016, p. 5). Data analytics shifts the organization capabilities from a reactive mode to a creative proactive approach (Mohapatra, Parisa & Banerjee, 2014, p. 2). Present day cyber threats and attacks are generally forensically investigated after the security incident. With a creative automated approach like data analytics, the organization would be able to bring various data sets (that is, device activity, system log reports and vulnerability reports (Thuraisingham et al., 2016, pp. 1-2). There are some challenges to data analytic approaches which include the trustworthiness of the data (Thuraisingham et al., 2016, p. 2), quality of the data and integrating various data sets (Najafabadi et al., 2015, p. 7).

FUTURE RESEARCH DIRECTIONS

It is evident that more research and collaborative discussions need to be undertaken by researchers, academics and practitioners in respect of cloud collaboration in managing cyber security. An even more persistent issue to undertake research in understanding how better to undertake cyber security incident investigations when the cloud collaboration platform has been breached. Collaboration amongst organizations or governments to form cyber security teams and enhance cyber skills to perform cloud investigations. The best approach for cloud collaboration. What lessons learnt from creative approaches that can be applied to cyber security and cybercrime. International treaty amongst countries to collaborate on cloud security handling and how investigations should be initiated.

CONCLUSION

Connectivity in cyberspace is growing and will continue to grow due the increase on digital revolution. This development in pursuit of progress needs to be embraced for a better digitalized world. The cybercrime increase and levels should not hamper a progressive world, organizations require creative and robust approaches that can reshape cyber security and decrease cybercrime levels. Introduction of creative measures of security risk assessment, data analytic and cloud corroboration can reduce the risks of cyber-attacks and lower the costs of mitigating future attacks (Deloitte, 2013, p. 2). With the right creative approaches the organization can eradicate cyber threats (The Institute of Risk Management, 2014, p. 14) and attacks and thus create a safer and trusted environment. The organization's cyber security initiatives will ultimately demonstrate their assurance to transparency (Halliday, 2015, p. 14) and governance thereby building stakeholder confidence.

REFERENCES

Ab Rahman, N. H., & Choo, K.-K. R. (2015). A survey of information security incident handling in the cloud. *Computers & Security*, *49*, 45–69. doi:10.1016/j.cose.2014.11.006

Ablon, L., Libicki, M. C., & Golay, A. A. (2014). *Markets for Cybercrime Tools and Stolen Data*. Retrieved August 16, 2016, from United States of America: http://www.rand.org/pubs/research_reports/RR610.html

Accenture. (2015). *Fighting Financial Crime with Data*. Retrieved August 10, 2016, from United Kingdom: https://www.accenture.com/t20160519T222110__w__/us-en/_acnmedia/Accenture/Conversion-Assets/DotCom/Documents/Global/PDF/Industries_6/Accenture-Fighting-Financial-Crime-with-Data.pdf

Accountants, C. (2014). *Protecting our Cyber Future*. Retrieved August 12, 2016, from Australia: https://charteredaccountantsanz.com/~/media/FutureInc/Pdfs/2014/FutureIncCyber%20Security.ashx

Actian. (2015). *Under Siege: Combatting Cyb Analytics*. Retrieved August 8, 2016, from http://www.actian.com/about-us/blog/siege-combatting-cyber-risk-big-data-analytics/

Ahmad, A., Maynard, S., & Park, S. (2014). Information security strategies: Towards an organizational multi-strategy perspective. *Journal of Intelligent Manufacturing*, *25*(2), 357–370. doi:10.1007/s10845-012-0683-0

Amann, P., & James, J. I. (2015). Designing robustness and resilience in digital investigation laboratories. *Digital Investigation*, *12*(1), S111–S120. doi:10.1016/j.diin.2015.01.015

Ashford, W. (2014). *Alarming level of cyber threat set for a decade, says Nato*. Retrieved September 18, 2014, from http://www.computerweekly.com/news/2240230779/Alarming-level-of-cyber-set-for-a-decade-says-Nato

Attorney-General's Department. (2013). *National Plan to Combat Cybercrime*. Retrieved August 12, 2016, from Australia: https://www.ag.gov.au/CrimeAndCorruption/Cybercrime/Pages/default.aspx

Bamrara, A. (2015). Evaluating Database Security and Cyber Attacks: A Rational Approach. *Journal of Internet Banking and Commerce*, *20*(2), 1–8.

Bandler, J. (2016). Dirty Digital Dollars. *Fraud*, *31*, 28–31.

Bartnes, M., Moe, N. B., & Heegaard, P. E. (2016). The future of information security incident management training: A case study of electrical power companies. *Computers & Security*, *61*, 32–45. doi:10.1016/j.cose.2016.05.004

Bertino, E. (2016). Security Threats: Protecting the New Cyberfrontier. *Computer*, *49*(6), 11–14. doi:10.1109/MC.2016.188

Bhatti, B. M., & Sami, N. (2015). *Building adaptive defence against cybercrimes using real-time data mining*. Paper presented at the First International Conference on Anti-Cybercrime, Riyadh.

Boyer, S. (2016). *The Importance of Collaboration in the Workplace*. Retrieved August 18, 2016, from http://www.nutcache.com/blog/the-importance-of-collaboration-in-the-workplace/

BusinessDictionary. (2015). *Business Dictionary*. New York, NY: BusinessDictionary.

California Department of Justice. (2014). *California Data Breach*. Retrieved July 20, 2015, from California: http://oag.ca.gov/sites/all/files/agweb/pdfs/privacy/2014data_breach_rpt.pdf?

Campbell, B. (2013). *The Importance of Collaboration in Today's Workplace*. Retrieved August 12, 2016, from http://www.elcomcms.com/en-au/Resources/Elcom-Blog/Posts/the-importance-of-collaboration-in-todays-workplace

Canon, J. (2015). Cyberinsurance The Challenge of Transferring Failure in a Digital, Globalized World. *ISACA*, *5*, 37–42.

CaseWare. (2016). *Role of Data Analytics for Internal Fraud Detection*. Retrieved August 10, 2016, from United States of America: http://www.casewareanalytics.com/sites/default/files/whitepapers/global_benchmark.pdf

Chaturvedi, M., Unal, A., Aggarwal, P., Bahl, S., & Malik, S. (2014). *International cooperation in cyber space to combat cybercrime and terrorism*. Paper presented at the Norbert Wiener in the 21st Century IEEE Conference.

CISCO. (2010). *Cybersecurity: Everyone's Responsibility*. Retrieved August 16, 2016, from http://www.cisco.com/c/dam/en_us/solutions/industries/docs/education/C45-626825-00_Cyber_Security_Responsibility_AAG.pdf

Crosby, S. (2015). *Changing the Economics of Cybersecurity*. Retrieved December 7, 2015, from SecurityWeek website: http://www.securityweek.com/changing-economics-cybersecurity

Damballa. (2014). *Advanced Threat Detection for the 21st Century: Integrating Big Data Intelligence to Enable Breach Prevention*. Retrieved from http://forms.madisonlogic.com/FormConfirmation.aspx?pub=18&pgr=259&src=2318&cmp=13396&ast=41496&frm=446&pd=3147146-19-7-57-336-0

Deloitte. (2013). *Cybercrime fighting*. Retrieved August 5, 2016, from http://dupress.com/articles/cyber-crime-fighting/

Department of Homeland Security. (2015). *Cybersecurity Overview*. Retrieved August 16, 2016, from https://www.dhs.gov/cybersecurity-overview

Durbins, S. (2013). *Use big data to fight cybercrime*. Retrieved August 5, 2016, from http://www.techrepublic.com/blog/tech/-decision-maker/use-big-data-to-fight-cybercrime/2/

EY. (2013). *Beating cybercrime*. Retrieved August 10, 2016, from United Kingdom: http://www.ey.com/Publication/vwLUAssets/Beating_cybercrime:_Security_Program_Management_from_the_Board%E2%80%99s_perspective/$FILE/EY-Beating-Cybercrime.pdf

Fortinet. (2014). *Fortinet's Advanced Threat Protection Framework: A cohesive approach to addressing advanced targeted attacks*. Retrieved September 29, 2014, from http://www.fortinet.com/sites/default/files/whitepapers/Fortinet_ATP_2014WP.pdf

Gemalto. (2016). *Data Breach Level Index*. Retrieved August 17, 2016, from http://www.gemalto.com/brochures-site/download-site/Documents/ent-infographic-2015-Breach-Level-index.jpg

Halliday, K. (2015). *Will cyber security threaten the sustainability of returns for investors?* Retrieved August 1, 2016, from http://www.ampcapital.com.au/smsf-suite/articles/will-cyber-security-threaten-the-sustainability

Han, B. J., Jung, I.-Y., Kim, K.-H., Lee, D.-k., Rho, S., & Jeong, C.-s. (2013). Cloud-based active content collaboration platform using multimedia processing. *EURASIP Journal on Wireless Communications and Networking*, (1), 1–13. doi:10.1186/1687-1499-2013-63

Hardekopf, B. (2015). *The Big Data Breaches of 2014*. Retrieved October 22, 2015, from Forbes website: http://www.forbes.com/sites/moneybuilder/2015/01/13/the-big-data-breaches-of-2014/

Holtfreter, K., & Meyers, T. J. (2015). *Challenges for Cybercrime Theory, Research, and Policy*. Retrieved August 15, 2016, from Norwich: http://ssrn.com/abstract=2677492

Holtfreter, R. E. (2016). Immunize Your Organization. *Fraud*, *31*, 19–25.

Hunt, T. (2014). *Top Tips: 5 Security Tips to Prevent Cyber Attacks*. Retrieved September 26, 2014, from http://www.idgconnect.com/blog-abstract/8599/top-tips-security-tips-prevent-cyber-attacks

IBM. (2013). *Combat the Latest Security Attacks with Global Threat Intelligence*. Retrieved August 18, 2016, from USA: http://public.dhe.ibm.com/common/ssi/ecm/wg/en/wgw03034usen/WGW03034USEN.PDF

IBM. (2014a). *IBM Security Services 2014 Cyber Security Intelligence Index*. Retrieved August 15, 2016, from USA: http://www-03.ibm.com/security/data-breach/cyber-security-index.html

IBM. (2014b). *Managing security risks and vulnerabilities*. Retrieved September 15, 2014, from http://www.informationweek.com/whitepaper/Security/Application-Security/managing-security-risks-and-vulnerabilities-wp1398437333

IBM. (2016). *Reviewing a year of serious data breaches, major attacks and new vulnerabilities*. Retrieved August 12, 2016, from New York: http://www-01.ibm.com/common/ssi/cgi-bin/ssialias?htmlfid=SEW03133USEN

Ifinedo, P. (2014). Information systems security policy compliance: An empirical study of the effects of socialisation, influence, and cognition. *Information & Management*, *51*(1), 69–79. doi:10.1016/j.im.2013.10.001

InfoSec Institute. (2013). *Cyber Exploitation*. Retrieved August 17, 2016, from http://resources.infosecinstitute.com/cyber-exploitation/

Insider, B. (2016). *This one chart explains why cybersecurity is so important*. Retrieved August 16, 2016, from http://www.businessinsider.com/cybersecurity-report-threats-and-opportunities-2016-3

Institute of Risk Management. (2016). *Cyber risk and risk management*. Retrieved August 18, 2016, from https://www.theirm.org/knowledge-and-resources/thought-leadership/cyber-risk/

Frigo, Læssøe, & Ramaswamy, V. (2015). Integrating Strategic Risks in Managing Co-creative Enterprises. *The Journal of Enterprise Risk Management*, *1*(1), 1–15.

International Cyber Security Protection Alliance. (2014). *Project 2020 - Scenarios for the Future of Cybercrime*. Retrieved August 10, 2016, from https://www.icspa.org/uploads/media/ICSPA_Project_2020_%E2%80%93_Scenarios_for_the_Future_of_Cybercrime_01.pdf

ISACA. (2011). *Data Analytics - A Practical Approach*. Retrieved August 12, 2016, from United States of America: http://www.isaca.org/Knowledge-Center/Research/Documents/Data-Analytics_whp_Eng_0811.pdf?regnum=332054

ISACA. (2013). *CISM Review Manual 2013*. Rolling Meadows: ISACA.

Jardine, E. (2015). *Global Cyberspace is Safer than You Think: Real Trends in Cybercrime*. Retrieved August 10, 2016, from Canada: file:///C:/Users/patrick/Downloads/SSRN-id2634590.pdf

Kaplan, E. (2016). *Making Cybersecurity a Business Function Poses Challenge*. Retrieved August 18, 2016, from CFO.com website: http://ww2.cfo.com/cyber-security-technology/2016/06/making-cyber-security-business-function-poses-challenges/

Kelly, L. (2014). *Companies must act quickly to tackle cybercrime*. Retrieved December 1, 2014, from http://www.computerweekly.com/feature/Companies-must-act-quickly-to-tackle-cyber-crime

Khan, O., & Estay, D. A. S. (2015). Supply Chain Cyber-Resilience: Creating an Agenda for Future Research. *Technology Innovation Management Review*, *5*(4), 6–12.

Kielman, J. (2015). *Data Analytics: Dealing with Cyber Storms*. Retrieved August 12, 2016, from United States of America: http://www.rhsmith.umd.edu/files/Documents/SignatureEvents_Conferences_Symposiums_EventsNotSpecificToACenter/IBMWorkshop/2015/kielman.pdf

KPMG. (2014). *Cyber security: it's not just about technology*. Retrieved August 16, 2016, from https://assets.kpmg.com/content/dam/kpmg/pdf/2014/05/cyber-security-not-just-technology.pdf

Lee, M. (2014). *IT security is not an optional extra*. Retrieved September 1, 2014, from ZDNet website: http://www.zdnet.com/it-security-is-not-an-optional-extra-7000025991/

Lee, S. M., Olson, D. L., & Trimi, S. (2012). Co-innovation: Convergenomics, collaboration, and co-creation for organizational values. *Management Decision*, *50*(5), 817–831. doi:10.1108/00251741211227528

Levesque, R., Walsh, D. A., & Whyte, D. (2015). Securing Cyberspace: Towards an Agenda for Research and Practice. *Technology Innovation Management Review*, *5*(11), 26–34.

Lieberman, G. (2015). Preparing for a Cyberattack by Extending BCM Into the C-suite. *ISACA*, *5*, 47–50.

Lloyds. (2013). *Top Five Risks - Lloyds*. Retrieved October 27, 2015, from http://www.lloyds.com/~/media/files/news%20and%20insight/risk%20insight/risk%20index%202013/report/lloyds%20risk%20index%202013report100713.pdf#search='topfiverisks'

Lugabihl, J., Owen, D., Rand, T., & Tran, M. (2013). *Taking Charge of Security in a Hyperconnected World*. Retrieved August 25, 2014, from http://www.emc.com/collateral/emc-perspective/h12485-taking-charge-security-hyperconnected-world.pdf

Martin, D. (2013). *Transforming Information Security, Future-Proofing Processes*. Retrieved August 27, 2014, from http://www.emc.com/collateral/white-papers/h12622-rsa-future-proofing-processes.pdf

McAfee. (2014). *McAfee Labs Threats Report: August 2014*. Retrieved September 19, 2014, from http://www.mcafee.com/us/resources/reports/rp-quarterly-threat-q2-2014.pdf

McAfee, A., & Brynjolfsson, E. (2012). *Big Data: The Management Revolution*. Retrieved August 6, 2016, from https://hbr.org/2012/10/big-data-the-management-revolution

Mehraeen, E., Ghazisaeedi, M., Farzi, J., & Mirshekari, S. (2016). Security Challenges in Healthcare Cloud Computing: A Systematic Review. *Global Journal of Health Science*, *9*(3), 157–166. doi:10.5539/gjhs.v9n3p157

Merriam-Webster. (2016). *Definition of cybersecurity*. Retrieved August 16, 2016, from http://www.merrima-webster.com/dictionary/cybersecurity

Miller, R. (2013). *The Changing Face of Cyber-Attacks*. Retrieved September 18, 2014, from http://www.futuregov.asia/reports/e-government/changing-face-cyber-attacks-2014/

Mohapatra, B., Parisa, V., & Banerjee, J. (2014). The Value of Big Data Analytics to the Business. *ISACA*, *5*, 1–6.

Morgan, L., & Conboy, K. (2013). Key Factors Impacting Cloud Computing Adoption. *Computer*, *46*(10), 97–99. doi:10.1109/MC.2013.362

Moturi, C., & Bitta, F. (2013). Multiagent Model for System User Access Rights Audit. *ISACA*, *3*, 43–48.

Najafabadi, M. M., Villanustre, F., Khoshgoftaar, T. M., Seliya, N., Wald, R., & Muharemagic, E. (2015). Deep learning applications and challenges in big data analytics. *Journal of Big Data*, *2*(1), 1–21. doi:10.1186/s40537-014-0007-7

National Institute of Standards and Technology. (2012). *Computer Security Incident Handling Guide*. Retrieved November 10, 2014, from http://csrc.nist.gov/publications/nistpubs/800-61rev2/SP800-61rev2.pdf

National Institute of Standards and Technology. (2016). *Guide to Cyber Threat Information Sharing*. Author.

NATO Cooperative Cyber Defence Centre of Excellence. (2012). *National Cyber Security*. Retrieved August 17, 2016, from Estonia: https://ccdcoe.org/sites/default/files/multimedia/pdf/NCSFM_0.pdf

Negroponte, J. D., Palmisano, S. J., & Segal, A. (2013). *Defending an Open, Global, Secure, and Resilient Internet*. Retrieved from http://www.cfr.org/cybersecurity/defending-open-global-secure-resilient-internet/p30836

Nolan, R., & McFarlan, F. W. (2011). *Information Technology and the Board of Directors Aligning Technology with Strategy*. Boston, MA: Harvard Business School.

Norton. (2016). *Definition of Cyber Crime*. Retrieved from http://za.norton.com/cybercrime-definition

O'Leary, R., & Vij, N. (2012). Collaborative Public Management: Where Have We Been and Where Are We Going? *American Review of Public Administration*, *42*(5), 1–16. doi:10.1177/0275074012445780

Oltsik, J. (2013). *The Big Data Security Analytics Era Is Here*. Retrieved August 28, 2014, from http://southafrica.emc.com/collateral/analyst-reports/security-analytics-esg-ar.pdf?isPublic=false

Oltsik, J. (2014). *Endpoint Security Market Retools16*. Retrieved September 30, 2014, from http://searchsecurity.techtarget.com/feature/Endpoint-security-software-market-retools

Oxford Dictionaries. (2016). *Definition of Cyber Attack*. Retrieved August 18, 2-16, from http://www.oxforddictionaries.com/definition/english/cyberattack

Palo Alto. (2016). *Definition of Cyber Crime*. Retrieved August 18, 2016 from https://www.paloaltonetworks.com/documentation/glossary/what-is-cyber-security

Pandey, P., & Snekkenes, E. A. (2014). *Applicability of Prediction Markets in Information Security Risk Management*. Paper presented at the 25th International Workshop on Database and Expert Systems Applications (DEXA).

Patil, S. (2013). Information Controls and Monitoring Framework for Health Care Organisations. *ISACA*, *3*, 38–42.

Patrick, H. (2016). *Security Information Flow in the Public Sector: KZN Health & Education* (Unpublished doctoral thesis). University of KwaZulu-Natal, Durban.

Polancich, J. (2015). *The Dark Web: One Thing Always Leads to Many, Many Others*. Retrieved December 7, 2015, from SecurityWeek website: http://www.securityweek.com/dark-web-one-thing-always-leads-many-many-others

Ponemon Institute. (2014a). *2013 Global Encryption Trends Study*. Retrieved October 5, 2015, from http://img03.en25.com/Web/ThalesEsecurity/%7B3e572e03-a25c-4b78-96a2-a52f9fa4f59e%7D_Global_Encryption_Trends_Study_eng_ar_(2).pdf

Ponemon Institute. (2014b). *2014 Cost of Data Breach Study: Global Analysis*. Retrieved July 10, 2014 from www.ibm.com/services/costofbreach

Press, J. (2015). *Cyber attack at NRC kept secret from other departments*. Retrieved June 24, 2015, from http://ottawacitizen.com/news/politics/cyber-attack-at-nrc-kept-secret-from-other-departments

PricewaterhouseCoopers. (2014). *Managing cyber risks in an interconnected world*. Retrieved December 1, 2014, from USA: http://www.pwc.com/gx/en/consulting-services/information-security-survey/assets/the-global-state-of-information-security-survey-2015.pdf

4Di. Privaca. (2014). *Information Security HealthCheck*. Retrieved June 15, 2016, from http://www.4diprivaca.com/services/security-consulting-services/security-healthcheck/

Prolexic. (2014). *Prolexic Quarterly Global DDoS Attack Report*. Retrieved January 30, 2015, from USA: http://www.stateoftheinternet.com/downloads/pdfs/2014-state-of-the-internet-web-security-global-ddos-attack-report-2014-q2.pdf

Putrus, R. (2016). A Nontraditional Approach to Prioritizing and Justifying Cybersecurity Investments. *ISACA*, *2*, 46–53.

Retel, S. (2014). *Cyber Security Strategy*. Retrieved August 17, 2016, from Estonia: https://www.enisa.europa.eu/topics/national-cyber-security-strategies/ncss-map/Estonia_Cyber_security_Strategy.pdf

Rice, A., & Ringold, J. (2015). *Cybersecurity information sharing: Industries join forces*. Retrieved June 25, 2015, from http://docs.media.bitpipe.com/io_12x/io_123596/item_1139502/ISM_MAY_final.pdf

Richards, K. (2014). *High alert on cyber risk and cybersecurity preparedness*. Retrieved September 8, 2014, from http://searchsecurity.techtarget.com/opinion/High-alert-on-cyber-risk-and-cybersecurity-preparedness

Robinson, T. (2014). *Information sharing requires breaking down barriers, White House cyber guru says*. Retrieved October 23, 2015, from SC Magazine website: http://www.scmagazine.com/ari-schwartz-says-white-house-looks-to-improve-information-sharing/article/378791/2/

Rocha Flores, W., Antonsen, E., & Ekstedt, M. (2014). Information security knowledge sharing in organizations: Investigating the effect of behavioral information security governance and national culture. *Computers & Security*, *43*, 90–110. doi:10.1016/j.cose.2014.03.004

Rogerwilco. (2015). *Security in the modern age*. Retrieved April 21, 2015, from Hi Tech Security website: http://www.securitysa.com/51239n

Rouse, M. (2008). *Data analytics*. Retrieved August 10, 2016, from SearchDataManagement.com website: http://searchdatamanagement.techtarget.com/definition/data-analytics

Salvi, V. (2013). *Establish a Business-Centric Risk Assessment Process*. Retrieved August 27, 2014, from USA: http://www.emc.com/collateral/white-papers/h12622-rsa-future-proofing-processes.pdf

Schmittling, R., & Munns, A. (2010). Performing a Security Risk Assessment. *ISACA*, *1*, 1–7.

Schober, S. (2016). *How fraud and breaches of cybersecurity impact financial institutions*. Retrieved August 5, 2016, from http://www.ibmbigdatahub.com/blog/how-fraud-and-breaches-cybersecurity-impact-financial-institutions

South African Press Association. (2012). *South African websites hacked*. Retrieved November 5, 2016, from http://mybroadband.co.za/news/security/66474-south-african-websites-hacked.html

Sullivan, C. (2015). Accelerating Access Management to the Speed of Hacks. *ISACA*, *5*, 43–46.

Symantec. (2016). *Internet Security Threat Report*. Retrieved August 17, 2016, from United States of America: https://www.symantec.com/content/dam/symantec/docs/reports/istr-21-2016-en.pdf?aid=elq_&om_sem_kw=elq_9823358&om_ext_cid=biz_email_elq_&elqTrackId=283a3acdb3ff42f4a70ab5a9f236eb71&elqaid=2902&elqat=2

Techopedia. (2016). *What does Vulnerability mean?*. Retrieved August 18, 2016, from https://www.techopedia.com/definition/13484/vulnerability

TechTarget. (2016). *Collaboration*. Retrieved August 12, 2016, from http://whatis.techtarget.com/definition/collaboration

Teradata. (2013). *Cyber Security*. Retrieved August 5, 2016, from United States of America: http://assets.teradata.com/resources/ebooks/102914-CyberSecurity-eBook/FLASH/index.html

Thawte. (2014). *Top 10 Website Security Myths Revealed*. Retrieved November 12, 2015, from USA: http://www.slideee.com/slide/top-10-website-security-myths-revealed

The Commonwealth. (2014). *Report of the Commonwealth working group of experts on cybercrime*. Retrieved from United Kingdom: https://rm.coe.int/CoERMPublicCommonSearchServices/DisplayDCTMContent?documentId=09000016802f2385

The Economist. (2014). *Defending the digital frontier*. Retrieved August 15, 2016, from United Kingdom: http://www.economist.com/sites/default/files/20140712_cyber-security.pdf

The Institute of Risk Management. (2014). *Cyber Risk*. Retrieved August 12, 2016, from United Kingdom: https://www.theirm.org/media/883443/Final_IRM_Cyber-Risk_Exec-Summ_A5_low-res.pdf

Thuraisingham, B., Kantarcioglu, M., Hamlen, K., Khan, L., Finin, T., Oates, J., . . . Bertino, E. (2016). *A Data Driven Approach for the Science of Cyber Security: Challenges and Directions*. Paper presented at the IEEE Conference on Information Reuse and Integration, Pittsburgh, PA.

University of Maryland University College. (2016). *Cybersecurity*. Retrieved August 16, 2016, from http://www.umuc.edu/cybersecurity/about/cybersecurity-basics.cfm

Verizon. (2016). *Data Breach Investigation Report*. Retrieved August 15, 2016, from United States of America: http://www.verizonenterprise.com/verizon-insights-lab/dbir/2016/

Virvilis, N., Serrano, O., & Dandurand, L. (2014). Big Data Analytics for Sophisticated Attack Detection. *ISACA*, *3*, 1–5.

Wamala, F. (2011). *ITU National Cybersecurity Strategy Guide*. Retrieved August 16, 2016, from Switzerland: http://www.itu.int/ITU-D/cyb/cybersecurity/docs/ITUNationalCybersecurityStrategyGuide.pdf

WhatIs.com. (2016). *Collaboration*. Retrieved August 12, 2016, from http://whatis.techtarget.com/definition/collaboration

White & Case. (2015). *Cyber risk: Why cyber security is important*. Retrieved August 10, 2016, from http://www.whitecase.com/publications/insight/cyber-risk-why-cyber-security-important

Wlosinski, L. (2015). The Underground Threat. *ISACA*, *5*, 30–36.

Wolfpack. (2013). *The South African Cyber Threat 2012/3 Barometer*. Retrieved August 10, 2014, from http://www.wolfpackrisk.com/SA%202012%20Cyber%20Threat%20Barometer_Medium_res.pdf

World Economic Forum. (2014). *Global Risks 2014*. Retrieved September 29, 2014, from Switzerland: http://www3.weforum.org/docs/WEF_GlobalRisks_Report_2014.pdf

World Economic Forum. (2016). *The Global Risks Report 2016*. Retrieved August 12, 2016, from Switzerland: http://www3.weforum.org/docs/Media/TheGlobalRisksReport2016.pdf

Yoran, A. (2014). *How to Transform Today's Information Security Programs*. Retrieved September 30, 2014, from http://reflectionsblog.emc.com/2014/05/transform-todays-information-security-programs/

Zio, E. (2016). Challenges in the vulnerability and risk analysis of critical infrastructures. *Reliability Engineering & System Safety*, *152*, 137–150. doi:10.1016/j.ress.2016.02.009

KEY TERMS AND DEFINITIONS

Collaboration: A grouping of work groups or a number of people to achieve a certain task (WhatIs.com, 2016, p. 1).

Cyber Attack: It is an illegal act to damage a computer system (Oxford Dictionaries, 2016, p. 1).

Cyber Security Breach: A security breach is an external act that contravenes the organization's security policies or procedures (BusinessDictionary, 2015).

Cyber Security Risk: It is financial loss or damage caused by the failure of the organizations information systems (Institute of Risk Management, 2016, p. 1).

Cyber Security: It is the measures that an organization implements in order to protect its information systems (Palo Alto, 2016, p. 1).

Cybercrime: The use of computer, network or hardware to device to commit a crime (Norton, 2016, p. 1).

Incident: It is a violation or threat of the organization's computer security policies or acceptable security standards. The NIST (2012: 6) defines a incident as a "violation or imminent threat of violation of computer security policies, acceptable use policies or standard security practices." An incident is an unexpected event.

Threat Actor: A person or a group posing a threat (National Institute of Standards and Technology, 2016, p. 32).

Threat: A possible source of an adverse occurrence (National Institute of Standards and Technology, 2012: 60).

Vulnerability: Vulnerability refers to exploitation or flaw in the organization information technology system (that includes application or network (Techopedia, 2016, p. 1).

Chapter 4
Empowerment of Communities to Address Impossible Problems

Neal Shambaugh
West Virginia University, USA

ABSTRACT

The traditional view of problem solving is that experts are best addressed to solve complex but narrow problems. Intelligent novices, who have broad backgrounds and the motivation to learn and propose unique solutions, is an untapped source of experience. People increasingly want to take ownership of their lives and address problems that range from the routine (e.g., financial planning, healthcare, education) to the catastrophic (e.g., natural disasters, pandemics, terrorism). Features of human societies and traits of problem solving in humans are discussed. Examples of international problem solving are provided. The chapter describes three approaches to community problem solving, including problem solving groups, community decision support systems, and portals.

INTRODUCTION

This chapter advocates that individuals must act within collective groups to address the broad range of problems facing them, as opposed to waiting for governmental bodies to tackle these problems. The chapter first organizes human problems into three types, including routine, survival, and change. Next, the human attributes of addressing problems are summarized, including human societies and different cultural approaches, informal and formal problem solving, mental representation, and human metacognition and imagination. Inherently, humans have the ability to problem solve across a range of problem solving types (Nadler & Hibino, 1998), particularly when motivated by common concerns, such as health, safety, and well-being of the community. Historically, collective action has been the basis for social progress in the United States (Curl, 2012). International examples of cooperative activity are provided to illustrate different approaches to re-thinking governmental policies and the systems that can be developed to serve citizens.

The chapter proposes three approaches to solving community problems. The first approach is to inform citizens form problem solving groups, which take a proactive approach to addressing community

DOI: 10.4018/978-1-5225-1823-5.ch004

priorities, rather than reacting to emergencies, and also creating new bodies of knowledge and expertise (Cetina, 1999) to serve the community. Community problem solving groups could include a block of families, a small town or region, or an online community of individuals across cities, countries, or geographic regions who apply their collective creativity to directly tackle problems of common interest (Meindl, Stubbart, & Porac, 1996). A second approach to community problem solving is the development of community decision support systems, which build on open data policies. A third approach to community problem solving is to develop customized community portals to information and expertise through open source data software and networking systems. The long-term goal of these approaches is to archive the funds of knowledge, social capital, and expertise inside and outside the community, to tap this knowledge as needed, and to "grow" these resources over time.

THE RANGE OF HUMAN PROBLEMS

The cognitive research community has characterized problems as well-defined and solvable, ill-defined and resistant to solution, and wicked problems, that appear to be intractable (Churchman, 1967). Many problems that face families and communities could be characterized as ill-defined given their complexity and variability. Alternatively, this chapter labels three problem type categories, as routine, survival, and change to cover the continuum of problems facing communities in developed countries (Shambaugh, 2008).

The simplest category of problems facing middle-class families and communities can be labelled as routine, which occur throughout daily activities including jobs, family life, health and safety, education, entertainment, and well-being. Responsibilities of living in the 21st century have increased as a result of a continual and natural human demand for goods and services. "Getting and spending has been the most passionate, and often the most imaginative endeavour of modern life" (Twitchell, 2003, p. 191). Individuals now must make many important decisions related to their personal and professional lives. Increasing numbers of middle-class families from around the world are pressing the planet's resources to meet these concerns. Governmental units and business organizations find themselves unable to provide many costly services and benefits to their citizens and customers (Zakaria, 2008). While governments, institutions, and organizations will continue to serve important functions, individuals and groups have already begun to mobilize action to provide their own welfare (Stanfield, 2000).

A second category of problems can be labelled as survival problems, because of their scope, severity, and unpredictability. The citizens of the world are facing pressing, messy, and potentially disastrous problems, including disease and pandemics, natural disasters, and terrorism. In cases of floods, for example, people cannot wait for assistance. They must act. What are common citizens to do when faced with problems such as runaway diseases, destroyed communities from earthquakes or floods, or bombings from well-funded terror cells? How can people's innate abilities, collective creativity, and technological developments be leveraged to address such intractable problems?

A third category of problems, change problems, are sometimes being viewed as impossible because of their complexity over the long-term and the inability of individuals to relate or how to approach these problems. Examples include geophysical changes impacting the Earth, such as climate change, rising oceans, and drought. Another set of examples includes societal changes in ethnocentrism, xenophobia, morality, governmental structure, geography, and technology. Taking a big picture view will require humankind to adapt to changing conditions, but somehow remain aware and motivated to learn and take action steps as needed.

With the prospect of routine problems, survival threats and long-term change, informed groups of citizens can, however, initiate proactive priorities in their state and local governments as well as influence business to collectively face these potential problems. Consumers also have the power to influence innovation, which extends past the immediate needs of entertainment, self-expression, and Internet browsing to address community needs for health care, nutrition, counselling, housing, and education. Given citizens that have grown accustomed to services for routine and severe events, how will humans take responsibility for these needs? Is it possible for citizens, groups, neighborhoods, and communities to design a future in the present? The next section provides an overview of human potentials to solve problems, characterizing human societies as problem solving groups and examining several international examples of collective structures.

Human Attributes to Solve Problems

Human Societies

Despite the range and complexity of issues, humans possess the social and physical capacity to address these problems (Curl, 2012). Historically, communities managed communal needs. The tools and skills have changed over time and some of our communal needs are still tackled by family members, while others have been assigned or abdicated by voters to governmental units (McKnight & Block, 2012). Unfortunately, the functions of managing, planning, and coordination that the family or communal members used to accomplish are now less fulfilled by the governmental staff worker. Human problems now are not so much solved as studied (Nadler & Hibino, 1998).

Our propensity to live in groups and communities does imply a human-readiness to collaborate in the face of routine, survival, and change problems. In the United States, according to Zeese and Flowers (2013), "cooperation is embedded in our DNA.... From the founding of the country, community - people working together to solve common problems and make a better life for all - has been central to the national personality" (p. 1). Cultural norms, sometimes dictate the readiness or expectations to participate in rituals and events. According to Hargadon and Bechky (2006), "Collective creativity reflects a qualitative shift in the nature of the creative process, as the comprehension of a problematic situation and the generation of creative solutions draws from – and reframe – the past experiences of participants in ways that lead to new and valuable insights" (p. 484). Within community and professional learning communities and workgroups collective creativity can be tapped.

World Approaches to Community Problem Solving and Cooperation

There are numerous worldwide examples of cooperative activity between communities and workers, private enterprise, and governments. In an attempt to provide a supportive role in community revitalization, for example, the Obama presidential administration in the United States has invested $17 billions in federal funds in 1800 locations. The role of the U.S. Federal Government shifts more to leverage cross-agency expertise to support locally-defined goals and priorities (Johnson & Isaacson, 2016).

The Spanish Mondragon model of cooperation provides an example of an employer-owned enterprise that competes favourably with private corporations (Freundlich, 1998). The Mondragon Cooperative Corporation (MCC) in Spain's Basque region produces domestic appliances and machine tools and is organized not around central control, but cooperatives, which foster coordination of activities and strategic planning in autonomous working groups. Other features include an internal financing unit, an educational group, a no-layoff policy, a high enterprise survival rate, a high degree of communication between management and workers, and the use of temporary workers in non-stable markets. The Mondragon model also provides a case study of the difficulties cooperatives face in global markets and how an organization addresses not only successful, but the bankruptcy of one of its units and supporting laid-off workers with relocation and wage assistance (Alperovitz & Hanna, 2013).

Another international model with potential transfer to communities is the Kaizen philosophy of continual improvement by all participants, a small-change approach appropriate to an evolving system change to how people view problems, governments, and economic and social/cultural problems. As a business model, Kaizen was implemented by Toyota and demonstrated the value workers closest to the work to suggest improvements (Ohno, 1998). An application closer to community problem solving and a shift in culture is the application of Kaizen to health care settings (Weed, 2010) in which a continuous performance improvement (CPI) process reduced waste, processes were simplified and access to tools and resources made simpler for health care providers. The overall value of Kaizen to community problem solving is the cultural shift that occurs due to the continual involvement of everyone without undue reliance on efficiency measures alone.

The issue of limited resources, particularly financing, can be examined by other models, such as the Grameen Bank of Bangladesh (Sherraden, 1988). The concept of microcredit, small loans without collateral, provides money directly to primarily women who need the funds rather than charity. Another benefit is building on existing skills and developing initiative and creativity in individuals to become productive in ways that satisfy the debt. Underlying the Bank's approach are the Sixteen Decisions, which can be tapped and modified as needed by communities as foundational approaches. Two representative examples include "We shall collectively undertake bigger investments for higher incomes" and "we shall always be ready to help each other. If anyone is in difficulty, we shall all help him or her" (Siddiqui, 1984).

A philosophical approach to community problem solving would involve consensus on principles of action and outcomes. An international example, that addresses confrontational societies would be the Ubuntu principles from the southern Africa regions. Examples of Ubuntu principles include the value of the human being, a shift from confrontation to reconciliation, and promotion of mutual understanding, principles which can be applied to the development of community and the value of social and political groups working together over time (Equality Court, 2011).

The above examples of community-government cooperation suggests the value of understanding how specific community needs inform business and government policies rather than the other way around. While "lessons learned" may be difficult to transfer, the overarching benefit from these cases establishes starting point for dialogue, understanding, and ultimately action, depending on the needs and priorities of the community and country.

Influences on Community Cooperation

The potential for community problem solving is influenced by a complex set of interrelationships between social and cultural issues, including prevailing conditions of power, wealth and voice (Bollier, 2016), social norms, the political bias of diverse groups, and ethnicity and racial discrimination.

Within these social and cultural conditions, community, business, and governmental leaders are faced with understanding the scope of social problems and reaching consensus on priorities and approaches. An even larger issue is the degree to which leaders and support staff within community and governmental units buy into the idea of changing the current set of economic systems. For example, Alperovitz (2013) advocates an evolutionary system-change approach (Banathy, 1996) in the United States, one which democratizes wealth and also provides a big picture view of policies to manage large-scale decisions in chaotic times but at the same time support communities in ways that support their priorities. In addition to the ever present reality of limited resources, constraints on community problem solving include the depth and breadth of leadership and advocacy within the community, government regulations, relationships with international personnel, and the skill sets of the citizenry (e.g., information-seeking skills).

Humans have the capacity to plan for the future rather than just reacting, although a future-orientation is difficult to comprehend, and requires time and resources that cannot promise a solution. Humans tend to focus on routine problems and less so on the long-term problems (e.g., financial planning, healthy living and healthcare). Within social structures, ranging from ad hoc neighborhood groups to professional learning communities, humans have the ability to communicate using conversation, debate, and dialogue to collectively address common issues. The progress of the United States, for example, can be attributed to the ability of its people, not so much about individual effort, but around cooperation (Curl, 2012). In addition to language, the human abilities to problem solve, mentally represent ideas, reflect on their actions and imagine situations can be used to social advantage.

Problem Solving

Fortunately, humans possess unique problem solving tools as well as technological tools. Deep expertise and understanding requires time to develop, frequently cited as a deliberate practice of ten years (Ericsson, 1996). There are, however, some problems, which require immediate attention. Bruer (1993) used the term "intelligent novice" to describe those who can control and monitor their thought processes and make use of general strategies when necessary, even with information that is incomplete, redundant, ambiguous, and even incorrect (Lauriere, 1990). Two additional attributes to intelligent novices are that they may be intensely motivated, for example, to find a cure for the disease in a relative and that they dedicate the time and resources to stay on task (e.g.,Weiner, 2004).

Some problem solving approaches are non-rational, such as folk theory and tradition, common sense, and heuristics. Humans sometimes blend the rational and non-rational when they consciously talk through options, such as in town hall meetings and focus groups. In the case of voting, for example, some people make carefully considered options while for others a choice is based on beliefs or perceptions, and no deliberation is needed. Humans tap whatever knowledge and skills they have in the moment. Simon's (1996) idea of satisficing characterizes the human ability to make decisions with existing resources and experience. Satisficing occurs when playing games, solving problems, and making financial decisions. Designers also "satisfice" when they make decisions based on what information they can gather in the time available.

Even with everyday problems, humans can tap an array of tools. Some are rational approaches, including formal systems approaches and design thinking. Systems thinking addresses the complexities of the world before attempting to problem solve. A systems thinking language helps to address the common problem of unconsciously choosing a problem solving approach without considering options. A systems language focuses on the interdependencies of entities within a collective whole. Systems thinking may use various forms of visual tools help to reveal, clarify, and document complex issues and still retain some level of precision (e.g., data flow diagrams in software engineering).

Awareness of visual and verbal approaches provides two broad options before settling on a strategy prematurely, while many specific approaches exist, ranging from "associate" to "work backward" (McEver, 1972). The key, according to Adams (2001), is to make people aware of these strategies and provide relevant examples. Furthermore, people are rarely aware of the languages they think with, such as verbal, quantitative, visual, smells, sounds, touch and physical languages. Adams (2001) sees visual thinking as a very important alternate thinking language and consisting of perceptual imagery of the physical world, mental imagery, and graphic imagery (McKim, 1980). Other languages, according to Adam, include those of the senses, which can lead one to innovative solutions, and improve the overall clarity of one's thinking and imagery. Humans, particularly in specialized home and work settings, develop their own personal thinking languages (Waters & Gibbons, 2004). A personal thinking language consists of a mix of verbal and visual means to transform ideas and perceptions to action in social and working settings. This verbal and visual interaction of images and language is influenced by one's personal history, cultural expectations, and professional practices.

Twenty-first century humans are also capable of embodied cognition or "thinking with urban objects," such as buildings, other physical spaces, including transportation networks, and even art works as thinking objects. In addition, cities and communities become a set of networking nodes for residences to meet and socialize but also to solve problems (McCullough, 2013). Not just the information available to humans in the twenty-first century but the *richness of the context* becomes a tool for thought.

Design has taken a more "center stage" role in the popular press, being cited as a key ability or sense to cultivate for the new century (Pink, 2006). A design culture, according to Brunner, a partner of the design firm Pentagram and designer of many Apple products, provides a fundamental shift in the way we view and make change happen (Brunner & Emery, 2009). Historically, design has been situated within a specific context (e.g. interiors, curriculum, fashion, architecture) and was viewed as an activity reserved for trained professionals (Lawson, 2005; Rowe, 1987). However, twenty-first century realities call for more holistic and creative approaches to problem-solving, requiring increased participation from everyone to improve their world. The process of design supports these creative approaches, and is a human activity that all humans can participate in. However, design thinking is perceived as inaccessible to many people. Farson (2008) believes that design and design thinking are powerful tools to address our current social and economic problems. In *The Power of Design* he discusses the concept of metadesign, or "the design of design." Metadesigners include and transcend the traditional design professions, and according to Farson, have the capabilities of re-visioning major systems such as healthcare, education, and criminal justice. He sees metadesigners as leaders with the responsibility of using systems thinking to foster and manage innovation today.

Mental Representation

All humans have a unique ability to represent everyday problems using mental models, gestalt pictures, iconic images, diagrams, and metaphors and analogies. Mental models are internal constructions that form the basis for our understanding of how things work, such as electricity (Johnson-Laird, 1983). Gestalt pictures depict visually an idea or issue in a way that words cannot capture. Variations to Gestalt pictures include iconic images that provide a simple representation of a company through a logo and sign system, or internationally understood traffic signs.

Diagrams, meanwhile, provide a tool to represent complex representations in terms of analysis (e.g., picture glossaries, scale diagrams), synthesis (e.g., cutaways and cross sections), and mapping using graphs, time lines, maps, tables, and graphic design (Moline, 1995). Analogies and metaphors (Lakoff & Johnson, 1980) are perhaps the most powerful means to communicate and perhaps to problem solve with (Gentner et al, 2001; Fauconnier & Turner, 2002)). Analogies are figures of speech, which suggest that something is like something, as in "life is like an adventure," while a metaphor for life could be a ship. An analogy is an explicit verbal (written or spoken) connection between one thing and another, while a metaphor is a visual representation of that connection.

Metacognition and Imagination

Humans have an ability to think about how they think, to make judgments on this process, and to make changes, a key ability to self-improve, as well as design alternatives and to difficult, impossible problems. While metacognition is the idea that we can think about how we have thought in the past, imagination may be meta-thinking set in the future. Going beyond what we can physically see, to envision possibilities, some of which may be fanciful and based not on information but on desire, is an exemplary human ability and may be critical to facing change problems in particular. Imagination could be the one strength and the one direction that informs the motivation of citizens to tackle impossible problems as well as suggest new paths to solving them. The human capacity for curiosity, metaphoric imagination, and creative collaboration may help to discover options that escape the expert (Shambaugh, 2008). Humans possess very unique and powerful mechanisms to understand the world, the most important of which is language, the ability to communicate thoughts, feelings, and actions to others through various modes of conversation and dialogue. Humans are also aware and reflective of their metacognitive abilities to think about creative options.

In summary, the human attributes of social settings, problem solving, mental representation, and metacognition and imagination enable people to tackle a range of problems from routine to survival and even change problems. The aim of this chapter is to encourage thinking by citizens, experts, and policy-makers to collectively design in the present what a future world will look like and to tackle problems of concern rather than default to experts and governmental agents. Three approaches are suggested in the following section.

Community Problem Solving

Communities can become more proactive in terms of solving their own problems using community problem-solving groups, community-centered decision support systems, and community portals. These three approaches integrate the human problem solving potentials with the technologies of information, communication, and decision-making.

Approach 1: Community and Personal Information Problem Solving Groups

The need for problem solving by community members can be better understood by considering two general purposes for problem solving and which necessitate community involvement; namely, advocacy and education.

Problems of advocacy, for example, can involve elderly and retired persons on retirement and healthcare information. Families and community members can already tap the resources of nonprofit organizations. However, there will be a need and motivation for more proactive approaches by family members who seek more than information but who desire to have a direct hand in making decisions. Advocate needs may be short-term, addressing missing children, disaster relief, fund-raising, and annual event promotion, while long-term advocacy addresses healthcare and quality of life issues, as well as personal rights.

Community members may choose to bypass traditional educational structures, which they view as too expensive, too complicated, and not responsive to changing occupational realities. Educational needs may involve more than formal degree programs, but include a menu of self-development and home schooling options. Community leaders as well as individuals may determine that they want to develop local sources of expertise without the need for formal degrees, but still are able to provide means of certification that are accepted as evidence of proficiency and competence.

Needs for collaboration certainly can overlap with advocacy and education, but a key feature is that they directly involve people who self-organize for specific short-term or long-term purposes. Collaborative partners may be scattered across the world and there will be needs for systems and practices to structure and review the work-in-progress, as well as to archive the lessons-learned. Community needs are about the needs of people, not the needs of any organization or institution.

Whatever the identified purposes for solving problems, whether they be problems of advocacy or education or others, collaborative structures are needed. To characterize the very human challenges of working together to tap the benefits of knowledge, Bennet and Bennet (2007) use the term of collaborative entanglement. Features of such purposeful activity, according to Bennet et al. (2007) include open communications, shared understanding and decisions that support an agreed upon direction but are all based on individuals and groups who agree to share responsibility and moving beyond information sharing to tapping knowledge for the purpose of ongoing action and results.

Next, are summarized different forms of collaborative activity including action learning, action research, Conversations for Action, frame reflection, appreciative inquiry, service-learning, and knowledge to action?

- **Action Learning:** A group problem solving approach that tackles critical and complex problems, takes action, and reflects on the results and process. Action learning originated in the work of Revans (1998) who discovered the value of involving practitioners (in what were called action learning sets) who described not only their experiences as "comrades in adversity," but what they did not know; thus, creating an atmosphere of openness and an acceptance of other points of view. Because of the reflectivity component, action learning has been applied in business settings to support the professional development of workers and managers (Hale, 2012), as well as team building and development of a learning organization (Marquardt, 1999).
- **Action Research:** First described by Lewin (1946), provides a social-empowering problem solving structure, which involves all stakeholders and their experiences, tests out strategies and documents the results, and reflects on the results and proposes subsequent action steps. Action research is frequently conducted with groups who are working to build collaborative participation as opposed to solo action towards addressing problems with a progressive action approach. Outcomes from action research frequently include research-based best practices (Denscombe, 2006).

- **Appreciative Inquiry:** A form of action research (Srivastva & Cooperrider, 1990), focuses on asking questions on "What could be?" as opposed to "What is the problem?" through the use of generative images (Bushe, 2013). Dialogue is favored over analysis. Rather than analyzing causes, appreciative inquiry envisions what might be. This approach uses interviews to help people better understand the attributes and assets of a group or organization as well as to appreciate the varying motivations of individuals. One process for appreciative inquiry includes the stages of discovery, dream, design, and destiny (i.e., delivery) (Bushe, 2011).
- **Conversations for Action:** From Flores (2012) provides a framework for improving relationships in the workplace and particularly for situations where action is needed, including organizational change, life coaching, and business process design. The framework focuses largely on "language as action" and the implications of conversations for commitments and problem solving options. The priority is not viewing problem solving as tradeoffs of individual interests but "instilling a culture of commitment" in working relationships.
- **Frame Reflection:** (Schön & Rein, 1995) Provides a tool to help groups mediate the evidence behind an argument and the scope of problems. According to Gray (1996), "frames are sense-making devices that establish the parameters of a problem" (p. 576). Each person possesses a frame that views arguments and problems with different meanings. To address the conflicts that arise from people with different frames, dialogue is needed to understand these differences. Individuals "frame" problems in different ways, because they see the problems differently. Schön (1983) maintains that individuals "bound the phenomena to which they will pay attention" (p. 309). These frames dictate strategies for solutions, and the consequent policies and actions will be based on the values inherent in the frame. With frame reflection professionals first come to understand that individuals in a group will have different frames and bring to the table different options based on these frames. Furthermore, frame reflection helps people to see that policy arguments are based on value judgements, not objective measures of outcomes (Majone, 1989).
- **Service Learning:** A learning process which has been used by universities to address community needs by involving students in hands-on learning with actual clients. Students work with community group members to jointly address issues through action steps. A major challenge to this problem solving structure is identifying groups who are willing to take the time to work with students and to develop relationships, clear communications and outcome expectations. A benefit of service learning includes the integration of research-based practices with practitioner experience. Thus, the process can serve outcomes for both community needs and student learning (Jacoby, 1996).
- In terms of *knowledge to Action*, numerous terms exist for moving what we know from formal research settings to practical use (Graham et al, 2005; Lavis, 2006). Knowledge transfer is a term used in university communities, while the medical and healthcare fields refer to knowledge translation. Knowledge mobilization is a situation-based process which moves available knowledge to actual use. Participants in this process can include researchers, practitioners, community leaders, and other stakeholders and individuals (Bennet & Bennet, 2007). In the context of communities, knowledge mobilization applies research findings to critical needs (Estabrooks et al, 2008). Bennet and Bennet (2007) itemize a general approach for knowledge mobilization to include the following steps: identify situation, gather information on context, develop understanding, acknowledging theoretical knowledge and pragmatic knowledge, take action, reflect on new situation and assess

effectiveness. Knowledge mobilization is a problem solving or opportunity process that leverages what is known about the problem through information distributed across people and works.

Approach 2: Community Decision Support System (CDSS)

While citizens possess mobile devices, computers, and the Internet for information, the tools for problem solving have remained in the hands of government and business. With the advent of open data (Bollier, 2014), individuals and groups have access to citizen participation (Bollier, 2016). Stefaan Verhulst and others (2014) have reported on a proposed Internet ecosystem framework that is more collaborative, global and decentralized than current networks. Features of such a framework to support community problem solving access to networks and problem solving tools include improved coordination across institutions, improved interoperability of systems, open information sharing and evidence-based decision-making, and localized identification of expertise to aid in problem solving. Developments in both devices and networks will be necessary to support open data access to the information and expertise needed by the community.

Tools referred to as decision support systems (DSS) are integrated computer-based systems that feature databases, a problem-solving engine, and an interface to a human user. Early purposes for a DSS focused on a discrete task or decision and used existing data (Rockart & Bullen, 1986). The focus for a Community Decision Support System (CDSS) would be future-oriented and include historical data and information. The focus of individuals is rarely on the past but on the present and the near future. Although the future cannot be predicted, trends based on past and current data provide a picture of where we are in our business, career, or personal life. Making decisions on what we want our life to be for ourselves, our families, and our communities, and even "What business are we in?" necessitate a different view. The idea of a CDSS does not limit itself to individuals but is extended to helping people in communities, neighborhoods, and cities grow (Longworth, 2006).

A CDSS would involve both individual and social needs and would be a hybrid version of several DSS types (Powers, 2007). As with traditional DSS, the major components of a CDSS would include databases, reasoning models, interface, and communication options. In terms of acquiring information, databases provide a repository for information within any DSS. A CDSS would also combine local databases. The integration challenge would be initially coping with inconsistent database structures. In the long term some standardization of database structure would be required to develop an integrated database, although community-based DSS shells might be developed. A CDSS would use information and data to address specialized needs, such as healthcare, insurance, career options, and travel planning, among others. The CDSS would consist of both localized (personal computer system, mobile devices) resources and distributed (online websites and cloud storage) sources where information is stored and processed at other sites.

A model base and associated inference mechanism are used to process this information. Modeling allows knowledge to be applied across problems and facilitates analysis, explanations, and advocacy (Druzdzel & Flynn, 2000). A model base would include one or more models or representations of community expertise ranging from highly specialized (e.g., resale home value) to more general (e.g., model of a learner). Generic versions of a CDSS might include a range of common model components for financial, employment, travel, and health needs and provide simulations to help users see the implications of decisions. Integrating model bases, as with databases, will require some standardization of model structure along some common categories. Personal patterns of reasoning may also be archived to provide speed and options for new problems and additions to the model base. The inference mechanism, which processes the model base information, could include artificial intelligence types, such as scripts, rules, or frames within new generations of expert system software.

Human dialogue with databases and model bases/inference mechanisms has used a visual interface, such as a desktop metaphor. To date users have relied on the metaphor presented to them on laptops and mobile devices. Specialized interfaces could be used depending on the problem type (routine, survival, change) to facilitate queries and decision-making and construct personalized visual interfaces using different metaphors. Survival needs require that a user not be presented with too many choices, but rather customized options to fit an immediate need. These just-in-time visual views present just the information and advice as needed (Lieberman, 2002) and present to the user a limited amount of information and options to reduce mental overload.

The dissemination function of a DSS, involving the communication and sharing of information and decision options with others, represents a critical system component of a CDSS. While routine problems relate to an individual, problems of survival and change require collaboration and multi-point sharing of information facilitates decision-making. Information can be posted for everyone or particular audiences and can be edited or linked to other sources. Wireless may become an antiquated term as it becomes transparent and common in device use.

Approach 3: Community Portals

The CDSS would be connected to a human-focused front-end known as a portal. A portal provides a centralized gateway to resources as well as decision-support. Today's organizational versions are organized by top-down institutional needs and are based on explicit rules for "success," such as increasing profits and reducing costs, as well as marketing functions such as accessing new customers, recommending purchases, and improving user experience. In addition, internal portals serve to manage structured data (i.e., databases and digital files) that may be generated from a CDSS.

Cities are already tapping the power of portals with open source software and open source networks to facilitate citizen access to open data. One such example is DataLA, which began May 2014, cites one benefit as an increase in public confidence on how city government develops budgets and spends taxpayer money. With access to information, the citizenry now contributes unique ideas and approaches that fall outside existing processes and procedures. Along with the access to open data, established governments will need to work out new ways to adjust to informal networking and action (Bollier, 2016) typical of end users.

Portal development for communities can adopt the features of today's organizational portals and provide gateways, as content providers or search engines, to Internet-based content. Some portals could openly solicit customers for information to aid the user in determining problem options. Currently database and data-mining technologies develop customer profiles of purchases and preferences, while online customer sites recommend products and services. Such technologies can also be used to examine user input and suggest options, not for entertainment, electronics, or travel but for information sources and decision options for a range of problem types facing the user.

Portals provide colleges and universities with a means to attract specialty students, such as military veterans and adult learners. Traditional colleges and universities have experienced competition for student enrollment and tuition dollars from for-profit educational organizations, as well as from colleges that obtained university status and began to offer a broader range of degree programs. Higher education portals have produced some cost savings as an e-business strategy incorporating administrative and instructional functions (Jafari & Sheehan, 2003). These portals allow individuals in higher education institutions to communicate with a broad range of constituents, including new students, parents, alumni, donors, and sports enthusiasts. Internally, educational Web portals embrace many areas, such as training, staff and student services, transactions of various types, grant and development activity, learning communities, and risk and compliance needs (Burrell, 2000). Thus, Web portals for educational institutions may become a destination for human activity, rather than as a reference site of information.

Local governments developed community portals for citizens to access news on jobs, health promotion, services, and voluntary organizations. These sites provided citizens with convenient contact options using email and online pages or newsletters to communicate the availability of services and current events. Service providers for these sites could be a local governmental agency or a health-care or financial services provider. National governmental units, such as the Federal Emergency Management Agency (FEMA) and the U.S. Department of Health and Human Services, are legislatively authorized to assist citizens. The Agency for Healthcare Research and Quality, for example, is the lead agency in the Department of Health and Human Services charged with supporting research designed to improve the quality of healthcare, reduce its cost, improve patient safety, decrease medical errors, and broaden access to essential services. Governmental units, in particular, may find more resources being applied to the development of a broad-based CDSS in which consumer groups, neighborhoods, business, and governmental units address the survival challenges of natural disasters, terrorism, and pandemics. These systems build on the current use of emergency response plans and place information and options available to citizens.

Human needs cannot easily be predicted and so a major challenge for the ongoing development of a CDSS and integrated portal technologies is finding ways to continually update and improve the systems. Community systems would require frequent updating and improvement and the development of a process for an efficient iteration of the system improvements. An example of dynamic upgrading is the online value-coding systems used to identify consumer preferences in goods and services in online retailing. Cities will need to budget funds for not only technical development and support, but in liaison activity which interfaces existing government processes and community needs. Because community needs will vary considerably across a geographic or cultural area, the challenge to traditionally static government to provide responsive systems will be acute.

Recommendations for Government and Business

Both government and business have contributed to the development of technologies and systems to address the needs of citizens and customers (Hill, Brandeau, Truelove & Lineback, 2014). Now, individuals, communities, and groups are increasingly motivated to re-assume responsibility for their family and community welfare. For example, people desire more control over personal information and user-friendly access to options. Meanwhile, community groups continually face the issues of volunteer assistance and other resource needs, including information access and some means to transfer information and assistance to people. Citizens, government officials, and corporate employees can jointly contribute their resources and expertise. Specifically, the challenge is moving what we know to assist people, the focus for knowledge mobility (Bennet & Bennet, 2007). Three general recommendations are suggested for government and business.

Focus on Social Needs as Opposed to Organizational Needs

This first recommendation is based on the challenge of shifting contexts and the challenges of community groups, business, and governmental units to serve these highly changing needs. Governments have been seen as "instruments of the people," but over time bureaucracies and regulations have distanced people from governmental functions (Putnam, Feldstein, & Cohen, 2003). Businesses have seen the value of a customer-first approach and producing products and services that are needed and are easier to use. This push-strategy will require a renewed orientation of business and government towards consumer-identified priorities over an almost endless set of niche audiences. Technical features of websites have developed which aggregate consumer browsing and buying data to provide refined profiles of consumer needs. To re-assume personal and community responsibility for specific needs will require that citizens taking a more active role in determining needs, collaboratively solving problems, and developing a long view of issues, as opposed to short-term results (Schwartz, 1996). Action steps could include the following:

- Examine the philosophical stances taken by countries around the world (e.g., Grameen Bank. Ubuntu) as starting points for consensus-building activities.
- Examine the cases of cooperatives around the world to shift a business focus to human needs (Alperovitz, 2013; Freundlich, 1998).
- Develop business plans that facilitate consumer use of information and decision options.
- Discuss action steps to breaking down silos in both government and business and use open data initiatives as one way to begin this process.
- Look for ways which do not duplicate efforts across social groups, government, and commercial units.
- Revise standard request for proposal approaches and consider pilot implementations (see Bollier, 2016).
- Organize business units to act as an intermediary between people and government (Zeldin, 1994).
- Educate people on how to use business tools, such as scenario planning (Schwartz, 1996), open-space technology (Owen, 2008), dialogue mapping and breakthrough thinking (Culmsee & Awati, 2011), logic modeling (Knowlton & Phillips, 2012), and frame reflection (Schön & Rein, 1995).

Joint Problem-Solving Groups

A second recommendation involves members of neighborhoods and communities to form active problem-solving groups. These professional learning communities would enable citizens to creatively address problems as intelligent novices who are capable of seeing problems and solutions in new ways. The process of collectively facing issues would give clarity on what people really need and develop new products, services, and processes to meet these needs. Proactively viewing problems as opportunities might in time re-orient people's to reacting and short-term solutions. Action steps include the following:

- Local government solicits involvement in developing face-to-face and virtual communities on local needs (e.g., World Café communities from Brown & Isaacs, 2005).
- City government taps one or more individuals as liaisons to informal networking groups which develop access to open data.

- Local business units help to finance neighborhood systems for community use and train people to update and manage these systems.
- Community groups prioritize problems and productively work together to establish local pools of expertise (Stanfield, 2000).
- Educational units from public schools through college encourage young people to get involved and lead real community projects and tap the experiences of older workers (Putnam, Feldstein, & Cohen, 2003).

Financing Services as Including Information and Decision-Support

A third recommendation is finding new finance mechanisms to leverage governmental and business support for the development of front-end portals and decision-support systems. These financial mechanisms are needed to upgrade our current decision-making infrastructure to provide citizens directly tackle problems.

FUTURE RESEARCH DIRECTIONS

- Corporate, governmental, and educational institutions may assist the financing and development of knowledge management techniques that tie databases and Internet technology together.
- Alperovitz and Hanna (2013) cite two challenges to changing global conditions: how to include new models of cooperative structures into larger strategic plans and how to implement specific plans for underemployment and economic development with democratic or participatory features.
- Cooperative histories of regions and countries could be produced, which would provide insights as to how humans have designed unique features to solve common problems.
- Continue efforts to develop and manage open-source software and networks (Bollier, 2014).
- Study how social interaction impacts strategy and systems to share information.
- Study how knowledge moves from experts to practitioners.
- Develop portal technology that builds knowledge bases from contextual-based data and transforms this knowledge into means directly usable by people.
- The design of personal devices will continue to evolve tapping a user-centered approach and some standardization to ease user experience (Norman, 2004).
- Decision-support systems will become increasingly more personalized and provide more specialized information and decision options.
- Systems will need to include techniques to manage informal knowledge (Lenski, 2004) and develop data structures to represent this knowledge.
- Context-based data will provide groups with a new view on their data and increased emphasis on data-mining activities.
- Innovations may include new tools for collaboration and help to redefine what "community and collaboration" can be (Eichler, 2003) and contributing to new business models.

CONCLUSION

Individuals and groups will continue to become more informed and apply increased pressure on professionals, business owners, and politicians to be more responsive to their needs. Individuals and small groups will bypass any institutional impediments or obstacles and form their own problem solving groups if the need is sufficiently critical, such as matters of health or disaster, or if the professions, business and governments remain nonresponsive to personal and community needs. Tapping portals and decision-support, people will directly tackle a problem, given sufficient motivation and an awareness of context that may go unseen or viewed as unimportant by larger organizations (Gladwell, 2000). Individuals armed with context knowledge and technological tools, in conjunction with a revision of philosophies, policies, and systems by communities, government and business, will potentially address "impossible" problems.

REFERENCES

Adams, J. L. (2001). *Conceptual blockbusting: A guide to better ideas* (4th ed.). New York: Norton.

Alperovitz, G. (2013). *What then must we do? Straight talk about the next American revolution*. White River Junction, VT: Chelsea Green Publishing.

Alperovitz, G., & Hanna, T. M. (2013). Mondragon and the system problem. *Truthout*. Retrieved on June 10, 2016 at http://www.truth-out.org/news/item/19704-mondragon-and-the-system-problem

Banathy, B. H. (1996). *Designing social systems in a changing world*. New York: Plenum Press. doi:10.1007/978-1-4757-9981-1

Bennet, A., & Bennet, D. (2007). *Knowledge mobilization in the social sciences and humanities: Moving from research to action*. Frost, WV: MQI Press.

Bollier, D. (2014). *Managing digital assets: The challenge of creating and sustaining intangible value in a data-driven economy*. Washington, DC: Aspen Institute.

Bollier, D. (2016). *The city as platform: How digital networks are changing urban life and governance*. Washington, DC: Aspen Institute.

Brown, J., & Isaacs, D. (2005). *The World Café: Shaping our futures through conversations that matter*. Oakland, CA: Berrett-Koehler Publishers.

Bruer. (1993). *Schools for thought: A science of learning in the classroom*. Cambridge, MA: MIT Press.

Brunner, R., & Emery, S. (2006). *Do you matter? How great design will make people love your company*. Upper Saddle River, NJ: Pearson Education.

Burrell, S. C. (2000). *Planning and implementing an E-Business strategy: Administrative, instructional and web portal systems*. Retrieved on June 13, 2016 at http://faculty.saintleo.du/burrell/ebusiness.htm

Bushe, G. R. (2011). Appreciative inquiry: Theory and critique. In D. Boje, B. Burnes, & J. Hassard (Eds.), *The Routledge companion to organizational change* (pp. 87–103). Oxford, UK: Routledge. doi:10.4324/9780203810279.ch6

Bushe, G. R. (2013). Dialogic OD: A theory of practice. *Organization Development Practitioner*, *45*(1), 10–16.

Cetina, K. K. (1999). *Epistemic cultures: How the sciences make knowledge*. Cambridge, MA: Harvard University Press.

Churchman, C. W. (1967). Wicked problems. *Management Science, 4*(14), B-141-B-142.

Culmsee, P., & Awati, K. (Eds.). (2011). The heretic's guide to best practices: The reality of managing complex problems in organizations. Blomington, IL: iUniverse.

Curl, J. (2012). *For all the people: Uncovering the hidden history of cooperation, cooperative movements, and communalism in America* (2nd ed.). Oakland, CA: PM Press.

Denscombe, M. (2010). *Good research guide: For small-scale social research projects* (4th ed.). Berkshire, UK: Open University Press.

Druzdzel, M. J., & Flynn, R. R. (2000). Decision support systems. In A. Kent (Ed.), *Encyclopedia of library and information science* (pp. 120–133). New York: Marcel Dekker.

Eichler, G. (2003). E-Learning and communities: Supporting the circulation of knowledge pieces. In T. Bohme, G. Heyer, & H. Unger (Eds.), *Innovative Internet community systems:Third International Workshop, IICS 2003* (pp. 48-64). doi:10.1007/978-3-540-39884-4_5

Equality Court. (2011). *Afri-Forum and Another vs. Malema and others*. Retrieved on June 13, 2016 at http://www.saflii.org/za/cases/ZAEQC/2011/2.pdf

Ericsson, K. A. (1996). *The road to excellence: The acquisition of expert performance in the arts and sciences, sports and games*. Mahwah, NJ: Lawrence Erlbaum Associates, Inc.

Estabrooks, C., Derksen, L., Winther, C., Lavis, J., Scott, S., Wallin, R., & Profetto-McGrath, J. (2008). The intellectual structure and substance of the knowledge utilization field: A longitudinal author co-citation analysis, 1945 to 2004. *Implementation Science; IS*, *3*(49). PMID:19014512

Farson, R. (2008). *The power of design: A force for transforming everything*. Atlanta, GA: Greenway Communications.

Fauconnier, G., & Turner, M. (2002). *The way we think: Conceptual blending and the mind's hidden complexities*. New York: Basic Books.

Freundlich, F. (1998). *The Mondragón Cooperative Corporation (MCC): An Introduction*. Paper presented at Shared Capitalism: Mapping the Research Agenda. Conference of the National Bureau of Economic Research Madison Hotel, Washington, DC. Retrieved on June 10, 2016 at http://www.ownershipassociates.com/mcc-intro.shtm

Gentner, D., Holyoak, K. J., & Kokinov, B. N. (2001). *The analogical mind: Perspectives from cognitive science*. Cambridge, MA: MIT Press.

Gladwell, M. (2000). *The tipping point: How little things can make a big difference*. Boston: Little, Brown and Company.

Graham, I. D., Tetroe, J., Robinson, N., Grimshaw, J., & International Funders Study Research Group. (n.d.). *An international study of health research funding agencies' support and promotion of knowledge translation*. Boston, MA: Academy Health Annual Research.

Gray, B. (1996). Review of frame reflection. *Academy of Management Review*, *21*(2), 576–579.

Hale, R. (2012). Actual professional development. *Training Journal*, 39-42.

Hargadon, A. B., & Bechky, B. A. (2006). When collections of creatives become creative collectives: A field study of problem solving at work. *Organization Science*, *17*(4), 484–500. doi:10.1287/orsc.1060.0200

Hill, L., Brandeau, G., Truelove, E., & Lineback, K. (2014). *Collective genius: The art and practice of leading innovation*. Cambridge, MA: Harvard Business Review Press.

Jacoby, B. (1996). *Service-learning in higher education: Concepts and practices*. San Francisco, CA: Jossey-Bass.

Jafari, A., & Sheehan, M. (2003). *Designing portals: Opportunities and challenges*. Hershey, PA: IRM Press. doi:10.4018/978-1-59140-108-7

Johnson, B., & Isaacson, W. (2016). Moving the needle: Engaging with communities for urban innovation. *The Aspen Idea Blog*. Retrieved on June 10, 2016 at http://www.aspeninstitute.org/about/blog/moving-needle-engaging-communities-urban-innovation

Johnson-Laird, P. N. (1983). *Mental models*. Cambridge, MA: Harvard University Press.

Knowlton, L. W., & Phillips, C. C. (2012). *The logic model guidebook: Better strategies for great results* (2nd ed.). Thousand Oaks, CA: Sage Publications.

Lakeoff, G., & Johnson, M. (1980). *Metaphors we live by*. Chicago, IL: University of Chicago Press.

Lauriere, J. (1990). *Problem solving and artificial intelligence*. New York: Prentice Hall.

Lavis, J. (2006). Research, public policymaking, and knowledge-translation processes: Canadian efforts to build bridges. *The Journal of Continuing Education in the Health Professions*, *26*(1), 37–45. doi:10.1002/chp.49 PMID:16557509

Lawson, B. (2005). *How designers think: The design process demystified* (4th ed.). Philadelphia, PA: Architectural Press.

Lenski, W. (Ed.). (2004). Lecture Notes in Computer Science*Logic versus approximation: Essays dedicated to Michael M. Richter on the occasion of his 65th birthday*. New York: Springer. doi:10.1007/b98383

Lewin, K. (1946). Action research and minority problems. *The Journal of Social Issues*, *2*(4), 34–46. doi:10.1111/j.1540-4560.1946.tb02295.x

Lieberman, H. (2002). Interfaces that give and take advice. In J. M. Carroll (Ed.), *Human-computer interaction in the new millennium* (pp. 475–486). Boston, MA: Addison-Wesley.

Longworth, N. (2006). *Learning cities, learning regions, learning communities: Lifelong learning and local government*. New York: Routledge.

Majone, G. (1989). *Evidence, argument, & persuasion in the policy process*. New Haven, CT: Yale University Press.

Marquardt, M. J. (1999). *Action learning in action: Transforming problems and people for world-class organizational learning*. Palo Alto, CA: Davies-Black Publishing.

McCullough, M. (2013). *Ambient commons: Attention in the age of embodied information*. Cambridge, MA: MIT Press.

McEver, C. (1972). *The strategy notebook: A catalog of conceptual problem solving strategies*. San Francisco, CA: Interaction Associates.

McKim, R. (1980). *Experiences in visual thinking* (2nd ed.). Monterey, CA: Brooks/Cole.

McKnight, J., & Block, P. (2012). *The abundant community: Awakening the power of families and neighborhoods*. Oakland, CA: Berrett-Koehler Publishers.

Meindl, J. R., Stubbart, C., & Porac, J. F. A. (1996). *Cognition within and between organizations*. Thousand Oaks, CA: Sage Publications.

Moline, S. (1995). *I see what you mean: Children at work with visual information*. York, ME: Stenhouse Publishers.

Nadler, G., & Hibino, S. (1998). *Breakthrough thinking: The seven principles of creative problem solving*. Roseville, CA: Prima Lifestyles.

Norman, D. A. (2004). *Emotional design: Why we love (or hate) everyday things*. New York: Basic Books.

Ohno, T. (1988). *Toyota production system: Beyond large-scale production*. New York: Productivity Press.

Owen, H. (2008). *Open space technology: A user's guide*. Oakland, CA: Berrett-Koehler Publishers.

Pink, D. (2006). *A whole new mind: Why right-brainers will rule the future*. New York: Riverhead Trade. Penguin.

Powers, D. J. (2007). *A brief history of decision support systems*. Retrieved on March 10, 2007 from http://DSSResources.COM/history/dsshistory.html

Putnam, R. D., Feldstein, L., & Cohen, D. J. (2003). *Better together: Restoring the American community*. New York: Simon & Schuster.

Revans, R. W. (1998). *ABC of action learning*. London: Lemos & Crane.

Rockart, J. F., & Bullen, C. V. (1986). *The rise of managerial computing: The best of the Center for Information Systems Research, Sloan School of Management, MIT*. Homewood, IL: Dow Jones-Irwin.

Rowe, P. G. (1987). *Design thinking*. Cambridge, MA: MIT Press.

Schön, D. A. (1983). *The reflective practitioner: How professionals think in action*. New York: Basic Books.

Schön, D. A., & Rein, M. (1995). *Frame reflection: Toward the resolution of intractable policy controversies*. New York: Basic Books.

Schwartz, P. (1996). *The art of the long view: Planning for the future in an uncertain world*. New York: Currency Doubleday.

Shambaugh, N. (2008). Future design: How novices solve impossible problems. *The Journal of Design Principles & Practices*, *2*(3), 13–19. doi:10.18848/1833-1874/CGP/v02i03/37562

Sherraden, M. S. (1998). *Community economic development and social work*. Binghamton, NY: Haworth Press.

Siddiqui, K. (1984). *An evaluation of the Grameen Bank operation*. Dhaka: National Institute of Local Government.

Simon, H. A. (1996). *Sciences of the artificial* (3rd ed.). Cambridge, MA: MIT Press.

Srivastva, S., & Cooperrider, D. K. (Eds.). (1990). *Appreciative management and leadership*. San Francisco, CA: Jossey-Bass.

Stanfield, R. B. (2000). *The art of focused conversation: 100 ways to access group wisdom in the workplace*. Philadelphia, PA: New Society Publishers.

Twitchell, J. B. (2003). The liberating role of consumption and the myth of artificially created desires. In D. Doherty & A. Etzioni (Eds.), *Voluntary simplicity: Responding to consumer culture (Rights & Responsibilities)* (pp. 185–191). Lanham, MD: Rowman & Littlefield.

Verhulst, S., Noveck, B. S., Raines, J., & Declercq, A. (2014). *Innovations in global governance: Toward a distributed Internet governance ecosystem*. Retrieved on June 13, 2016 at https://www.cigionline.org/publications/innovations-global-governance-toward-distributed-internet-governance-ecosystem

Waters, S. H., & Gibbons, A. S. (2004). Design languages: Notation systems, and instructional technology: A case study. *Educational Technology Research and Development*, *52*(2), 57–68. doi:10.1007/BF02504839

Weed, J. (2010). Factory efficiency comes to the hospital. *The New York Times*. Retrieved on June 13, 2016 at http://www.nytimes.com/2010/07/11/business/11seattle.html?_r=1

Weiner, J. (2004). *His brother's keeper: A story from the edge of medicine*. New York: HarperCollins.

Zakaria, F. (2008). *The post-American world*. New York: W. W. Norton & Company.

Zeese, K., & Flowers, M. (2013). Cooperatives and community work are part of American DNA. *Truthout*. Retrieved on June 10, 2016 at http://www.truth-out.org/opinion/item/14076-cooperatives-and-community-work-are-part-of-american-dna

Zeldin, T. (1994). *An intimate history of humanity*. New York: HarperCollins.

KEY TERMS AND DEFINITIONS

Action Learning: A group problem solving approach that tackles critical and complex problems, takes action, and the results and process are reflected upon by the participants.

Action Research: A social-empowering problems solving structure, which involves all stakeholders and their experiences, testing out strategies and documenting the results, and reflecting on the results along with revising subsequent action steps.

Advocacy: One application of personal portals in which a gateway is used to support a belief, mission, or need.

Appreciative Inquiry: A form of action research, focuses on asking questions on "what could be" as opposed to "what is the problem?" through the use of interviews and generative images.

Change Problems: A type of problem with long-term consequences.

Collaborative Entanglement: A term used by Bennet and Bennet (2007) to characterize the different means in which people structure their collaborative activities.

Community Decision Support System (CDSS): A computerized decision support system, which acquires information and organizes the information so that models of reasoning can produce recommendations for further information, resources, or action, and can communicate organized information or decisions to others.

Continuous Press Improvement (CPI): An application of the Kaizen theory of continuous improvement to reduce costs, and to re-examine and simplify processes.

Conversations for Action: A framework from Flores (2012) for improving relationships in the workplace focusing lon "language as action" and the implications of conversations for commitments and problem solving options.

Decision Support System (DSS): A computerized system which assists humans to make decisions.

Embodied Cognition: The idea that tools, physical objects, and environmental settings influence human thinking.

Intelligent Novice: Those who can control and monitor their thought processes and make use of general strategies when necessary.

Kaizen Philosophy: A Japanese approach that advocates small changes on a continual basis.

Knowledge Mobilization: A situation-based process which moves available knowledge to actual use. In the context of communities, knowledge mobilization is about applying research findings to critical needs.

Open Data: Everyone has access to the information previously held by companies or governmental units.

Organizational Portal: Broad classification of portals, incorporating governmental, institutional, and corporate portals.

Personal Portals: A computerized site which provides a gateway other sites of individual interest.

Routine Problems: A type of problem faced by individuals involving complexity of choices as well as short-term and long-term implications.

Service Learning: A learning process which has been used by universities to address community needs by involving students in hands-on learning with actual clients.

Survival Problems: A type of problem characterized by extreme impacts on individuals and communities.

Chapter 5
The Role of Leadership in Cultivating a Responsible Collective Creative Work Environment

Alphonce Tavona Shiri
University of Kwazulu-Natal, South Africa

ABSTRACT

This chapter examines the concept of collective creativity in the work environment and in particular the manufacturing sector in Gweru, Zimbabwe. The chapter analyzes the role of a leader in fostering a work climate that cultivates collaborative efforts by followers in creating new ideas and for the sustainability of business operations. Literature relating to leadership role in enhancing sustainable and responsible collective creativity is reviewed. The chapter adopted a quantitative approach in which a survey questionnaire was pilot tested to assess the clarity of the questions on the questionnaire and test the internal consistency of the questions. A pilot test of the situational outlook questionnaire (SOQ) was conducted on 20 respondents in the manufacturing industry to assess the questions for clarity and internal consistency. The final survey questionnaire was distributed to 60 employees in the manufacturing sector in Gweru, Zimbabwe. The items on the questionnaire were rated on a 5 point Likert scale. Data was analysed using SPSS version 23. Data was analysed to determine the correlations between the

DOI: 10.4018/978-1-5225-1823-5.ch005

independent variables and dependent variables. Transformational leadership constructs, namely idealised influence, intellectual stimulation, inspirational motivation and individualised consideration constituted leadership independent variables. Analysis of research data reveals that high performance is related to sustainable business practices such as the creation of environmentally friendly and affordable products. Unethical business practices are found to be negatively related to business performance and collective creativity. Analysis of the data revealed a positive correlation between individualised consideration construct of transformational leadership and ideal support ($r=.527$, $p=.001$) and a positive correlation between individualised consideration and openness ($r=.343$, $p<.001$), and a positive correlation between individualised consideration and involvement ($r=.123$, $p<.001$) This means that when a leader displays support through taking into consideration the individual needs of his or her followers, subordinates feel that the leader is encouraging them to participate in company activity and increase their perception of an involving climate. Acts of leadership support also stimulate subordinate views of an open forum where they can contribute to collective creativity within the organisation.

INTRODUCTION

The manufacturing sector in Zimbabwe is hard hit by the economic crisis prevailing in the country. Most industries have scaled down on production due to the cost of operations and this has seen products from surrounding countries flooding the country as they are produced at low cost making them more attractive to consumers. It therefore requires that the manufacturing sector in Zimbabwe become creative and innovative in producing products that can compete with imported ones. Leaders and managers in the Zimbabwean manufacturing sector should play a major role in igniting collective creativity within organisations through offering guidance on the generation of new ideas in a way that embraces stakeholders' values such that new innovations become sustainable. Laszlo (2008, p. 25) states that "greater public awareness and rising societal expectations of business in terms of its impact on the environment and contribution are creating new strategic risks and opportunities". This means that stakeholders' values and perspectives on user friendly and affordable products require leadership to link them in order for business enterprises to create new products that can sustain competitive advantages. Valuing stakeholders' opinion is a management and thinking approach that sees the world from the perspective of stakeholders. Freeman & Phillips (2002) agree that stakeholder approach to managing business is a powerful lens through which managers can discover new business opportunities and manage risk. Creativity is what brings in new ideas and innovation in the business world. Collective creativity enhances organisational innovation in a way that creates competitive advantage. The objective of this chapter is to propose a framework that links leadership to collective creativity that can sustain company operations in the long run. The effects of transformational leadership on collective creativity will be examined.

BACKGROUND

In today's globalized economic environments, customers have wide access to information on the same type and range of goods and services. This access to information and range has created increased demand and appetite for more product features and higher quality such that a lot of pressure has been put on

Table 1. Evidence of innovation by manufacturing firms through recognized quality certification

	Zimbabwe	Sub-Sahara	World
Percentage of firms with an internationally recognized quality certificate	18.0	14.8	16.4
Percentage of firms using technology licensed by foreign companies	16.4	13.4	15.1

Source: Damiyano, Muchabaiwa, Mushanyuri & Chikomba (2012)

manufacturers to become more innovative and creative (Jung, Chow & Wu, 2003). The Zimbabwe manufacturing sector has not been spared by this wave of constant expectations and demands by consumers. The manufacturing sector faces a myriad of challenges and is struggling to stay afloat. The Confederation of Zimbabwe Industries (CZI) (2012) carried out a survey on the state of the manufacturing sector and concluded that the sector was in crisis. The results of the CZI (2012) survey showed that capacity utilization had declined from 57.7% to 44.2% and the GDP contribution estimate for the manufacturing sector was expected to decline from 9.4% to 5.6% by the end of year 2012. At least 60% of the manufacturers in Zimbabwe face competition from both foreign and local companies, while 14% face competition from foreign companies only (CZI, 2012). While very competitive and full of potential, the Zimbabwe manufacturing sector has been seriously affected by a depressed economy and competition from foreign firms as consumers prefer superior foreign brands over local brands (Damiyano, Muchabaiwa, Mushanyuri & Chikomba, 2012). The fact that the Zimbabwean manufacturing sector has potential is an indicator that the sector can be revived to its full potential through leadership and innovation. Evidence of high standard production processes (see Table 1) shows that the manufacturing sector can be competitive if the top management and leadership steer an innovative and creative culture to sustain a competitive edge.

Table 1 shows that the manufacturing sector in Zimbabwe has potential to produce quality products when compared to surrounding countries. However, the economic down turn being experienced in Zimbabwe since 2007 to date has had an impact on innovation efforts. It is during economic crises that companies operate on a conservative budget; effectively limiting spending on research and development. This means that the Zimbabwe manufacturing sector is affected in its endeavors to consistently produce high quality products that can compete with foreign products. Cooper (2001) asserts that the ability to consistently conceive of, create and bring to market new innovations is highly dependent on the quality of talent and the environment in which they work. Jaruzelski, Loehr & Holman (2011) agree that the work environment plays a role in influencing innovation and creativity and emphasize that leaders are responsible for creating a culture that is highly conducive to innovation and collective creativity. Homel (2009) maintains that leaders motivate creativity by inspiring followers to be innovative and energized to challenge current perspectives. This means that managers in Zimbabwe's manufacturing sector play a role in enhancing follower creativity and improving the current performance of the sector through new and competitive products. This chapter shall investigate the role played by transformational leadership in evoking collective creativity in Zimbabwe's manufacturing sector.

WHAT IS COLLECTIVE CREATIVITY?

Zhang & Bartol (2010) posit that employee creativity can significantly contribute to organizational innovation, effectiveness and survival and "Creativity refers to the production of novel and useful ideas by an individual or group of individuals working together" (p.107). Parjanem Harmaokorpi & Frantsi (2010) define creativity as the invention of a new service or product that adds value to society or the organization. Parjanen et al (2010) maintain that creativity is the outcome of a system. Hirst, Van Knippenberg and Zhou (2009) view employee creativity as an important source of workplace innovation necessary to achieve competitive advantage. Creativity may therefore be defined as the production of new ideas that replace old ways of doing things and is often the basis for altering existing ideas.

The construct of collective creativity was introduced by Hargadon & Bechky (2006) who examined collective creativity that is generated through group interaction. This means that when employees interact about a work project, they spark the development of new ideas about improving a product and solving problems. It can be argued that creativity is appropriate to problem solving and creation of new and sustainable opportunities (Sanders and Stappers, 2008). Sanders and Stappers (2008) draw a distinction between creativity and innovation by stating that creativity are ideas whereas innovation is the successful transaction of ideas into tangible products or intangible service. Therefore, creativity is one of the critical factors that influence innovation. It can be concluded that "the ability to stimulate innovation is highly dependent on the stock of creative ideas that are available for feeding innovation" (Parjen et al., 2010, p. 2).

Collective Creativity as an Exchange of Ideas

Creativity is not confined to a person's thought processes, but in the interaction between a person's thoughts and a socio-cultural context. Most creative pursuits in business and industry involve individuals working together to solve problems they cannot solve alone. Leonard & Sensiper (1998) assert that collective creativity describes the phenomenon where concepts emerge in people's minds through interacting with knowledge. This means that creative activity in the work place grows out of the relationships between an individual and his or her work, and out of ties between individuals. The focus of creativity in the interaction moves to the collective level where each individual's contributions not only shape the subsequent contributions of others, but just as importantly, give new meanings to the past contributions of others (Parjanen et al., 2010).

Hirst et al. (2009) suggest that collective creativity is a result of individuals learning from each other and the skills acquired from more experienced members of an organisation enable new comers to develop deep processing strategies necessary to facilitate accomplishment of challenging work tasks. Parjanen et al. (2010) assert that social learning theory suggests that hidden agendas, biases and inadequate understanding detract from the need to innovate products and services in a collective manner. Organisations flourish when ideas are brainstormed by a group of organisational members as opposed to individuality. This means that efforts at innovative renewal learning at the organizational level are a collaborative endeavor in which members generate new ideas by sharing their knowledge and interactions with each other. Nahapiet & Ghostal (1998) argue that the more radical and risky ideas are, the more organizational resistance and hindrance to open interaction increases. This means that management needs to encourage open communication and assist by cultivating collaborative attitudes that are necessary in innovation and collective creativity such that fellow employees are comfortable sharing ideas when high risk and radical ideas are involved.

Table 2. Leadership influence over collective creativity in the workplace

Category of Influence	Description	Collective Creative Leadership Influencing Skills
Relating	Leader's ability to relate to others in a way that brings out the best in people, groupsand organisations.	-Leader's ability to form warm, caring relationships. -Leader's ability to foster high performing teamwork. -Extent to which leader engages followers to discover common ground and work together effectively.
Self-Awareness	Leader's orientation to ongoing professional & Personal development.	-Extent to which leader's ambition paves way to creating results which serve as a common good -Leader's ability to maintain a calm, focused perspective towards conflict and high-tension situation.
Achieving	Extent to which the leader Offers visionary, authentic and high achievement Leadership	-Leader's ability to think and plan strategically to ensure long-term results. -Degree to which the leader is goal oriented and has a track record of goal achievement and high performance. -Leader's ability to make decisions

Source: Excerpts adopted from Markeviciute & Jucevicius (2013)

Linking Leadership to Collective Creativity

Rickards and Mogers (2006) maintain that top down leadership models no longer apply in today's world and have been replaced with participative leadership in which the leader empowers followers and induces an atmosphere for creativity in the work place. Ollila (2000) states that employee feedback provides an opportunity for leaders to learn and assess how best the leader can provide support and enhance followers' creative behaviours and attitudes. Politis (2004) argues that the leader is "a crucial variable contributing to the culture and climate of organisation and perception of support for creativity and innovation" (p 23). The leadership role in creating an enabling environment for collective creativity is therefore critical as highlighted in Table 2.

The excerpts adopted from Markeviciute & Jucevicius (2013) reflected in Table 2 show that a leader plays a collective creativity enabling role in the workplace. It highlights the view that the leader should be able to balance his/her involvement and support with pushing followers to collectively innovate and create new products and ways of producing that are in line with cost saving and pro-environmental protection.

Transformational and Transactional Leadership Theory

Organisational leaders are a key resource of influence on organisational culture and have a profound effect on follower creativity (Jung, Chow & Wu, 2003). Transformational leadership emphasizes long-term and vision based motivational processes while transactional leadership focuses on providing subordinates with rewards contingent on successful performance of agreed upon tasks (Si & Wei, 2012).

Transformational leadership is characterised by four dimensions, namely:

1. **Idealised Influence:** The leader models follower attitudes through self-sacrifice and portraying the values, beliefs and missions in line with organisational values that can be emulated by followers;
2. **Inspirational Motivation:** The leader inspires followers by articulating an optimistic future, emphasizing ambitions, goals and depicting ideal visions;

3. **Intellectual Stimulation:** The leader challenges followers to be creative and encourages them to think of new ways of solving old problems, and
4. **Individualised Consideration:** The leader displays concern for followers by providing support and coaching sessions (Barbuto, 2005; Paracha, Qamar, Mizra, Ul-Hassan & Waqas, 2012; Burke, Stagl, Klein, Goodwin, Salas & Haplin 2006).

Transactional leadership dimensions include:

1. **Contingent Reward:** The leader provides rewards to subordinates for completing agreed upon tasks or administers punishments for failure to fulfill contractual obligations;
2. **Active Management by Exception:** The leader monitors subordinates' work activities in search for mistakes and corrects them, and
3. **Passive Management by Exception:** The leader does not get involved in follower work activities until there are problems that have reached chronic stages (Barbuto, 2005; Paracha et al 2012; Burke et al 2006).

The above descriptions of Transformational leadership dimensions show that the leadership style exhibits behaviours that are different from those of transactional leadership. On the one hand transactional leadership seems to be more concerned with maintaining the status quo, focusing on routine and predictable ways of doing things. On the other hand, transformational leadership empowers followers to be more creative and encourages them to adopt new ways of solving problems and innovating new and creative ways of accomplishing their tasks (Si & Wei, 2012).

Transformational leadership has been conceptualized as leadership that is targeted at creativity, change, innovation and entrepreneurship (Eisenbeiss, Van Knippenberg & Boerner (2008). The link between transformational leadership and follower creativity and innovation has gained support from various leadership studies, for example Hammond, Neff, Farr, Schwall & Zhao (2011) found a positive correlation between transformational leadership and creative performance of (p. 13). In a meta-analysis Wang, Oh, Courtright & Colbert (2011) also found a positive correlation between transformational leadership and follower creative behaviours. However, transformational leadership has been criticized for lack of clarity, for example, how each dimension of transformational leadership is related to mediating processes such as communication satisfaction (Van Knippenberg & Sitking 2013). This chapter therefore focused on examining the dimensions of transformational leadership and mediating processes that induce follower creativity. The objective of the chapter was to find out how each of the dimensions specifically infuences follower creativity.

Leader Behavior and Work Climate

Sellgren, Ekvall & Tomson (2008) define organizational work climate as the conglomerate of the attitudes, feelings and behaviors which characterize life in an organization. It is how employees feel about their work environment which fosters certain attitudes, beliefs and behaviors towards their job. Sellgren et al. (2008) suggest that a creative work climate/environment is characterized by leadership support for employee's ideas/open communication, mutual trust, motivating followers and encouraging them to share information and their views. Furthermore, Sellgren et al. (2008) found a strong relationship between leader behavior and creative work climate with a correlation of .52 significance at $P< 0.001$. Isaken

& Akkermans (2011) state that organizational leaders have an influence over the climate for creativity and innovation within organizations. Organizational climate as an intervening variable between leadership and innovation was confirmed through partial correlation. Their findings support the evidence that leadership behavior plays a pivotal role in engendering a creative climate.

Leaders' Influence on Creativity

Leaders have an influence on their followers, motivation work attitudes and collaborative behavior that can be linked to creativity and innovation (Isaksen & Akkermans, 2011). They further maintain that leaders' behaviors have an influence over a wide variety of organizational outcomes. Thus leaders have an input over their followers' creativity. Isaksen & Akkermans 2011 assert that leader behaviors play a major role in encouraging idea generation (creativity) and application of those ideas in producing innovation. A leader can nurture creativity through role modeling, stimulating knowledge diffusion and providing a vision as well as company resources to enable follower collaboration and innovation. Climate is what members of the organization experience, while culture reflects what the organization values and culture are the structures of an organization that are rooted in the values, beliefs and assumptions held by its members (Isaksen & Akkermans 2011, p. 165). Climate is assessment by individual of environmental attributes in terms of acquired meaning and personal value to the individual.

Business leaderships with high integrity capacity are more likelyc, than competitors, to be aware of and more rapidly respond to stakeholder concerns and arrive at decisions that balance the needs of shareholders within those of stakeholders. Patrick and Quinn (2001) maintain that a leader may cultivate creativity and at the same time be sensitive to stakeholders needs. It is the leader's role to inspire followers toward achieving organizational goals in order to optimise shareholders value through exercising and achieving a balance within four types of micro-economic management theories, namely; rational goal theory, internal process theory, human relations theory and open systems theory. Rational goal theory focuses on the external control and stresses leadership and producers' responsibilities of:

- Goal setting.
- Taking initiative.
- Increasing productivity.
- Maximizing output by emphasizing goal clarification.
- Rational analysis and action taking.

Internal process theory focuses on internal control and stresses the monitor and coordinator role responsibilities of information management (Patrick and Quinn 2001)

- Documentation control.
- Efficient processing.
- Consolidated continuity by emphasizing process measurement.
- Smooth functioning of the organizational operations and bureaucratic order.
- Human relations focuses on: Internal flexibility and the facilitator and mentor role responsibilities of fostering.
- Openness.

- Participation.
- Team morale building and emphasizes involvement, human conflict resolution and consensus building (Isaksen & Akkermans 2011).

The Open system theory focuses on external flexibility and stresses the innovator and broker role responsibilities of cultivating organizational learning capabilities and developing the competitive power of continual creativity and negotiated external resource.

Primary Mechanisms Leaders Could Use to Enhance Creativity

1. **Challenge:** Matching the right person with the right job to play into their expertise and create thinking skills
2. **Freedom:** Intrinsic motivation and ownership are enhanced when people are free to approach their work in a way they choose.
3. **Resources:** When employees are provided with enabling resources
4. **Work Group Features:** Managers should create teams with a diversity of perspectives and backgrounds
5. **Supervisory Encouragements:** To sustain passion, people need to feel their work matters and is important
6. **Organizational Support:** Creativity is truly enhanced when the entire organization supports it.

Jung, Chow and Wu (2003) assert that while there are a basket of factors that influence creativity, in an organization, leadership has increasingly become an important determinant of organizational creativity.

How Leaders Affect Employee Creativity

Leaders define and shape the work context within which employees interact to define goals, problems and solutions. The following are ways in which leaders affect follower creativity and collective creativity:

- By articulating a vision that emphasizes long term over short-term business outcomes e.g. growth rather than quarterly profits, leaders can direct employees individual and joint efforts towards innovative work process and outcomes.
- By creating a climate that nurture follower creative efforts and facilitates diffusion of learning, leaders can significantly boost organizational creativity.
- Leaders can value and reward creative performance through compensation and awarding resources

Transformational leaders uniquely motivate followers though their behavior and components such as inspirational motivation. While transformational leaders may sometimes take a directive approach, they often seek followers' participation by highlighting the importance of cooperation in performing collective tasks, providing the opportunity to learn from shared experience and delegating to followers the authority to execute any necessary action for effective performance. Jung, Chow and Wu (2003).

Four Levels of Collective Creativity and the Role OF Leadership

Hargadon and Bechky (2006) identified four key behaviours of collective creativity, namely; help seeking, help giving, reflective reframing and reinforcing. Help seeking and help giving refer to behaviours which lead to the flow of knowledge in creative exchanges. Reflective reframing is a process of refining the question being asked and reinforcing provides a foundational context for the collective creativity process through both affirming contributions and creating the environment for this interaction to occur (Sweetman, 2010). Sanders and Stappers (2008) acknowledge that different levels of creativity exist and these levels of creativity relate to how employees operate at different levels and therefore require different leadership approaches to nurture individual creativity. Sanders and Stappers (2008) maintain that leaders need to offer relevant experiences to facilitate followers' expression of creativity at all levels. This means leading, guiding and providing scaffolds as well as clean slates to encourage people at all levels of creativity. Leadership should therefore adopt approaches that facilitate the nurturing of creativity and avoid pushing subordinates beyond their level of interest, passion and creativity.

Effective leaders are those that understand the needs of their followers and adapt styles to suit those needs. Followers' needs can be met by taping into the different levels of creativity and using the right approach for each level. Sanders and Stapper (2008) suggest the approaches for effective leadership and nurturing of creativity as follows:

- **Lead:** People who are on the doing level of creativity;
- **Guide:** Those who are at the adapting level;
- **Provide Scaffolds:** That support and serve people's need for creative expression at the 'making' level; and
- **Offer a Clean Slate:** For those at the creativity level.

Parjanen et al. (2010) posit that the centers of creativity, tend to be found at the intersections of different domains, where beliefs, life style and knowledge mingle and allow individuals to see new combinations of ideas with greater ease. This means employees can develop creative ideas through interactions with fellow employees that have similar tastes. Managers or organisational leaders should therefore create work environments that nurture and encourage cross pollination of ideas. Such homogenous grouping helps to develop new ideas and find solutions quickly. The ability to communicate and exchange ideas is an important ingredient for the creative process. Interaction is used to describe the use of language and other symbols to develop an enriched and shared understanding.

The Sustainable Value Framework

While leaders have a role to play in igniting collective creativity within organisations, they also need to guide the generation of new ideas in a way that embraces stakeholders' values such that new innovations become sustainable. This means that stakeholders' value requires managers to think from an "outside in" perspective about how their companies create and sustain competitive advantages. Valuing stakeholders' opinion is a management and thinking approach that sees the world from the perspective of stakeholders. Freeman and Phillips (2002) agree that stakeholder approach to managing business is a powerful lens through which managers can discover new business opportunities and manage risk, and state that:

The interpretation of business activity can be approached in several ways. One way is to take for granted the usefulness (others might say "truth" or "moral legitimacy" here) of a way of understanding value creation and trade (or business activity), where by individuals are presumed to be nakedly greedy, responsible to others for the effects of their action only in so far as they are caughtt doing harm, and the legitimacy of a state that pervasively regulates all aspects of value creation and trade, from rules governing the height of ladders to thousands of pages of the tax code. (p. 331).

Freeman and Phillips (2002) therefore assert that the success of any business organisation rests on its ability to manage and maintain relationships with key stakeholders such as the community, suppliers, and others in a way that reflects selfless practices and concerns for the environment and social needs of such stakeholders. This means that leaders that take into account stakeholders' concerns are better at addressing and anticipating changes in the business environment. Ultimately, stronger stakeholders' engagement allows leading companies to discover new resources of value through innovation.

Companies need to balance between shareholders' value and stakeholders' value in order to create innovative products and services that are sustainable. This can be described as two-dimensional value creation leadership styles (Laszlo 2008). Companies that deliver value of shareholders while destroying the value for other stakeholders have a fundamentally flawed business model. Those that create value for stakeholders are cultivating sources of extra value that can fuel competitive advantage for the unforeseeable future. Sustainable value occurs only when a company creates value that is positive for its shareholders and its stakeholders. This means that a balanced view of the world in which companies and businesses exist should be taken into account as managers initiate collective creativity among their followers.

Stakeholders Can Represent a Potential Source OF Hidden Business Value

When companies design manufacturing facilities that use less energy for heating and lighting, and that cost less to build and operate than conventional facilities, or when they add environmental intelligence to their products, by making them more recyclable, re-usable, biodegradable, less toxic, or otherwise healthier they are creating sustainable value through elimination of packaging waste by right sizing their products (Laszlo 2008). Sustainable value is also created when companies find ways to profitably meet unmet societal needs such as providing nutrition and clean water to the poor. Management should therefore guide collective creativity in a direction that promotes environmentally friendly products and at the same time embracing stakeholder values. Such an approach can be a source of hidden business value, which when applied can enhance competitive advantage for business enterprises.

The following six levels of strategic focus constitute an important tool to engage managers or leaders to identify how business value is created from sustainability projects.

Capturing sustainable value requires organizational leaders to see stakeholders value as essential to the growth of their companies. The primary barrier to adopting a stakeholder perspective stems from the leader's mindset, not from whether there is business value to be found. Therefore, leaders are the drivers of sustainable business environments. They influence the creation of an environment that nurtures collective creativity in a sustainable and responsible manner.

Table 3. Six levels of strategic focus towards value creation

Focus	Sources of Value
6.business context	Changing the rules of the game to provide competitive advantage for sustainability strategies
5.brand of culture	Developing a sustainability culture and brand identityamong employees
4.Market	Address new markets driven by customer and societal needs
3.Product	Creating product differentiation based on technical and environmental/societal features
2.Process	Reducing energy, waste or other process cost
1.Risk	Compliance–oriented management of risks and protecting license to operate

Source: Laszlo (2008)

Sustainable Value Creation Through Facilitative Leadership Practices

The leadership role in sustainable value creation is enabled when the leader takes an active role in inducing rather than preserving organisational structure; by departing form reliance on influencing tactics linked to power, conformity pressure and managing the inherent conflict between creativity and organisation (Mumford, Scott, Gaddis & Strange, 2002). Obstfeld (2012) agrees that it is nolonger a question of stretching and redefining the construct of work routines but adopting the appropriate leadership style that can facilitate follower creativity and unltimately lead to sustainability of operations. Hunter, Thoroughgood, Myer & Ligon (2011) also agree that leadership behaviour is the precursor for sustainable value creation. Leadership behaviours that facilitate employee creativity have been identified as leader support, leader empowerment of followers, feedback, assigning goals and monitoring the creative process (Mainemelis, Kark & Epitropaki, 2015; Sun, Zhang & Chen, 2012). Therefore, while followers may act as primary creators, their level of creative contributions are influenced by the level of leader appropriate behaviours such as leader support (Mainemelis et al 2015). This means that the role of the leader is to facilitate and create an enabling environment for followers to be intrinsically motivated toward creativity. The behavioural perspective of leadership thus argues that the leader's role in creativity is adopting behaviours that foster intrinsic motivation and employee positive moods necessary for creativity.

METHODOLOGY

This chapter adopted a quantitative approach in which a survey questionnaire was pilot tested to assess the clarity of the questions on the questionnaire and test the internal consistency of the questions. Below is a description of the procedures taken to pilot test the questionnaire.

Pilot Test

The situational outlook questionnaire (SOQ) was pilot tested on 20 respondents in the manufacturing industry to assess the questions for clarity and internal consistency. The SOQ was developed by Goran

Ekvall, an industrial psychologist, based on his observations while working for Volvo in the 1950s and later Swedish companies from 1960s to 1970s (Isaksen, Lauer, Ekvall & Britz, 2001). The items on the SOQ were pilot tested for their internal consistency using the Cronbach's alpha coefficient. The Cronbach's alpha reliability coefficient normally ranges between 0 and 1. The closer the Cronbach's alpha coefficient is to 1.0 the greater the internal consistency of the item in the scale or questionnaire. George and Mallery (2003) provide the following rules of thumb for the Cronbach's alpha: >.9 excellent, >.8 good, >.7 acceptable, >.6 questionable, >.5poor and <.5 unacceptable. The pilot test found the following:

Risk taking, conflict and ideal time were below the threshold of .7 and raised questions on internal consistency validation. All other items on the SOQ had a Cronbach's alpha above .7 and were acceptable

Table 4.

ITEM	QUESTIONS	CRONBACH'S ALPHA
INVOLVEMENT	1. Employees in my organisation are committed in contributing to the goals of the organisation. 2. Employees in my organisation are intrinsically motivated to the success of the organisation. 3. Interpersonal interactions in my organisation are dull.	.93
FREEDOM	1. In my organisation, people are given resources to define their own work. 2. In my organisation, people exercise discretion in day to day activities. 3. In my organisation, individuals are provided with the opportunity to share information about their work. 4. In my organisation, people carry out their work in prescribed ways with little room to define their tasks.	.88
OPENESS	1. In my organisation, people find it difficult to openly communicate with each other. 2. In my organisation, people count on each other for personal support. 3. In my organisation, individuals are given credit where credit is due.	.87
IDEAL TIME	1. In my organisation, time pressure makes thinking outside instructions and routines impossible. 2. In my organisation, possibilities exist to discuss suggestions not included in task assignment. 3. In my organisation, time is available to explore new ideas.	.66
PLEASANTRY	1. In my organisation, the work atmosphere is characterised by seriousness. 2. In my organisation, the work environment is easy going. 3. In my organisation, people exhibit a sense of humor.	.73
CONFLICT	1. In my organisation, groups and individuals dislike each other. 2. In my organisation, management deals effectively with diversity.	.55
DEBATES	1. In my organisation, a wide variety of viewpoints are encouraged by management. 2. In my organisation, people follow authoritarian patterns without questioning them. 3. In my organisation, people are kin on putting forward their ideas for consideration.	.91
IDEAL SUPPORT	1. In my organisation, new ideas are received in an attentive way by management. 2. In my organisation, management encourages team work. 3. In my organisation, people usually feel welcome when presenting new ideas to management.	.77
RISK TAKING	1. In my organisation, people (subordinates) tolerate uncertainty and ambiguity when making decisions. 2. In my organisation, people often venture into unknown territory. 3. In my organisation, people usually operate on the "safe side". 4. In my organisation, people tend to cover themselves in many ways.	.51

Table 5. The creative climate dimensions: Description reliabilities.

DIMENSION	DEFINITION
Challenge/ involvement	The degree to which people are involved in daily operations, long term goals and visions. High challenges involvement implies better levels of engagement, commitment and motivation
Freedom	The degree of independence shown by the people in the organization. High levels of freedom imply more perceived autonomy and ability for individual discretion.
Trust/ openness	The emotional safety in relationships. In high trust/openness situations people feel more comfortable sharing ideas and being frank and honest with each other
Ideal time	The amount of time people can and do use for elaborating new ideas. When ideal time is high, people can explore and develop new ideas that may not have been included in the original task.
Playfulness. Humor	The spontaneity and ease displayed within the workplace. Good-natured joking and laughter and a relaxed atmosphere (lower stress) are indicators of higher levels of playfulness and humor.
Conflict	The presence of personal and emotional tensions (a negative dimension in contrast to the debate dimension). When conflict is high people engage in interpersonal warfare, slander and gossip, and even plot against each other.
Idea-support	The way new ideas are treated. In a high idea support situation, people receive ideas and suggestions in an attentive and professional manner. People listen generously to each other.
Debate	The occurrence and open disagreement between viewpoints, ideas, experiences and knowledge. In the debating situation many different voices and points of view are exchanged and encouraged
Risk-taking	The tolerance of uncertainty and ambiguity. In a high risk taking climate, people can make decisions even when they do not have certainty and all the information desired. People can and do go out on a limb to put new ideas forward

Source: Isaksen, Lauer, Ekvall & Britz (2001)

for use on the questionnaire that was used for testing the link between leadership, creative and sustainable value creation in the manufacturing industries in Gweru, Zimbabwe.

The measures as used in the pilot test are explained in Table 5.

The dimensions of the SOQ have been able to discriminate between best and worst case work environment (Isaksen, Lauer, Ekvall & Britz, 2001). Isaksen & Laurer (2002) also used the SOQ dimensions to determine the most and least creative teams as well as perceived support environment for innovation (Isaksen & Lauer 2001).

Final Questionnaire Distribution AND Data Analysis Plan

After the pilot test, a survey questionnaire was distributed to 60 employees in the manufacturing sector in Gweru, Zimbabwe. The items on the questionnaire were rated on a 5 point Likert scale. Data was analysed using SPSS version 23. Data was analysed to determine the correlations between the independent variables and dependent variables. Transformational leadership constructs, namely idealised influence, intellectual stimulation, inspirational motivation and individualised consideration constituted leadership independent variables. Follower perceptions on the organisational climate such as involvement, freedom, openness and debates constituted dependent variables.

The independent variables were as follows (see Table 6).

Only the constructs with a Cronbach's alpha >.70 were assessed against the dependent variables as the internal consistent was not acceptable for the transformational leadership constructs that exhibited an alpha below .70.

RESULTS AND DISCUSSION

The age distribution of respondents is shown in Table 7 and reveals that most of the employees that responded to the questionnaire were aged between 36 and 55.

Table 6. Independent variables and their validity

ITEM	QUESTIONS	CRONBACH's ALPHA
IDEALISED INFLUENCE	1.1. My supervisor transmits a sense of mission. 1.2. My supervisor shows determination when accomplishing goals.	**.89**
INSPIRATIONAL MOTIVATION	2.1. My supervisor communicates high performance expectations. 2.2. My supervisor uses metaphors and tells organisational stories that create positive images in my mind. 2.3. My supervisor mobilises a collective sense of mission.	**.53**
INTELLECTUAL STIMULATION	3.1. My supervisor's ideas make me reconsider some of my own ideas which I had never questioned before. 3.2. My supervisor enables me to view problems from a different perspective.	**.66**
INDIVIDUALISED CONSIDERATION	4.1. My supervisor is ready to coach or instruct me whenever I need it. 4.2. My supervisor gives personal attention to those who seem neglected.	**.79**

Table 7. Age distribution of respondents

		Frequency	Percent	Valid Percent	Cumulative Percent
Valid	<31	2	3.3	3.3	3.3
	31-35	5	8.3	8.3	11.6
	36-40	11	18.3	18.3	30.0
	41-45	14	23.3	23.3	53.3
	46-50	10	16.7	16.7	70.0
	51-55	13	21.7	21.7	91.7
	56-60	4	6.7	6.7	98.3
	>60	1	1.7	1.7	100.0
	Total	60	100.0	100.0	

Source: Author compilation using respondent data

Table 8. Gender distribution of respondents

		Frequency	Percent	Valid Percent	Cumulative Percent
Valid	Female	9	15.0	15.0	15.0
	Male	51	85.0	85.0	100.0
	Total	60	100.0	100.0	

Source: Author compilation using respondent data

Table 8. shows that the respondents to the questionnaire were mostly male, comprising 85% of the respondents.

Inferential Statistics

Correlations were calculated in SPSS version 23 on the relationship between transformational leadership behaviours such as idealised influence and follower perceptions of collective creativity work climate such as ideal support.

The results show that a leader can influence collective creativity through leadership behaviours such as idealised influence and individualised consideration. The results show that Leadership has a role to play in positively influencing sustainable collective creativity within organisations. Unethical practices relate negatively to company performance.

There is a positive correlation between idealised influence construct of transformational leadership and freedom (r=.262, p=.001) and a positive correlation between transformational leadership and debates (r=.430, p<.05). This means that transformational leadership encourages an environment that allows followers to contribute meaningfully toward creativity through discussions and debates. Transformational leadership also inspires and empowers followers to be creative and think of new ways of doing things hence the significant positive relationship between transformational leadership and freedom. These results confirm Mathisen and Einarsen (2004)'s view that when employees feel that the leader is granting them the freedom to contribute novel ideas, they tend to be more innovative and creative.

There is a positive correlation between individualised consideration construct of transformational leadership and ideal support (r=.527, p=.001) and a positive correlation between individualised consideration and openness (r=.343, p<.001), and a positive correlation between individualised consideration and involvement (r=.123, p<.001) This means that when a leader displays support through taking into consideration the individual needs of his or her followers, subordinates feel that the leader is encourag-

Table 9. Correlations between idealised Influence and follower perceptions of Involvement, freedom, openness and debates

		Ideal Support	Involvement	Freedom	Openness	Debates
Idealized influence	Pearson Correlation	.099	.099	.262**	.057	.430**
	Sig. (2-tailed)	.213	.213	.001	.469	.000
	N	60	60	60	60	60

** Correlation is significant at the 0.01 level (2-tailed).

Table 10. Correlations between individualised consideration and follower perceptions of involvement, freedom, openness and debates

		Ideal Support	Involvement	Freedom	Openness	Debates
Individualised Consideration	Pearson Correlation	.527**	.123**	.089*	.343**	.149
	Sig. (2-tailed)	.000	.008	.568	.000	.058
	N	60	60	60	60	60

**. Correlation is significant at the 0.01 level (2-tailed).

ing them to participate in company activity and increase their perception of an involving climate. Acts of leadership support also stimulate subordinate views of an open forum where they can contribute to collective creativity within the organisation. These findings are in line with Mathisen & Einarsen (2004)' suggestion that organisational creativity is a result of leadership support for ideas and creation of open relationships with followers. The results therefore indicate that leadership is a key element necessary for collective creativity through the nurturing of pluralistic views, encouraging the sharing of ideas and creating an environment for knowledge transfer and sharing of experiences.

The correlations show that when leadership creates an enabling environment, it significantly influences opportunities for employees to share information and collectively generate new ideas. The results shows a positive correlation between an enabling environment and sustainable collective creativity ($r=.377$, $p<.001$), and an enabling environment is positively correlated to exploring of new ideas ($r=.512$, $p<.001$). The results therefore confirm the view point that leadership plays a major role in creating an enabling environment for collective creativity and the effect is sustainable innovation and creation of new products and services.

The results therefore enable the development of a framework that links leadership to follower collective creativity as follows in Table 12.

CONCLUSION

Collective creativity is a result of individuals learning from each other and the skills acquired from more experienced members of an organisation enable new comers to develop deep processing strategies necessary to facilitate accomplishment of challenging work tasks. Leadership in business organisations should encourage employees to interact and create new ideas that lead to new products. It is however, more important for leaders and managers to foster collective creativity that is responsible and sustainable by taking into account the needs of stakeholders and at the same time the interests of the shareholders. A balance should be reached between profit maximisation and ethical practices that engender sustainability as its main pillar.

The findings confirm that transformational leadership is instrumental in promoting creativity in the workplace. Transformational leadership is characterised by encourangement of follower debates and allowing a wide range of alternatives to be considered through giving each person a chance to contribute toward decision making and innovation. Individualised consideration behaviour of transformational leadership encourages the consideration and recognition of each member's view points and ideas. Indi-

Table 11. Various independent and dependent correlations

		2.3. My supervisor mobilises a collective sense of mission.	5.1. Collective creativity is enabled	5.2. collective ceativity in my organisationis responsible	5.3. My organisation performance is linked to sustainable collective creativity	5.4. My organisation product performance is linked to sustainable collective creativity	7.3. In my organisation, individuals are provided with the opportunity to share information about their work.	9.3. In my organisation, time is available to explore new ideas.
2.3. My supervisor mobilises a collective sense of mission.	Pearson Correlation	1	.125	.078	.059	-.069	-.104	-.039
	Sig. (2-tailed)		.347	.559	.660	.606	.432	.767
	N	59	59	59	59	59	59	59
5.1. Collective creativity is enabled	Pearson Correlation	.125	1	.381**	.390**	.377**	.433**	512**
	Sig. (2-tailed)	.347		.003	.002	.003	.001	.000
	N	59	59	59	59	59	59	59
5.2. My organisation encourages collective creativity that promotes growth	Pearson Correlation	.078	.381**	1	.556**	.480**	.017	-.224
	Sig. (2-tailed)	.559	.003		.000	.000	.897	.088
	N	59	59	59	59	59	59	59
5.3. My organisation performance is linked to sustainable collective creativity	Pearson Correlation	.059	.390**	.556**	1	.485**	.238	150
	Sig. (2-tailed)	.660	.002	.000		.000	.069	.257
	N	59	59	59	59	59	59	59
5.4. My organisation product performance is linked to sustainable collective creativity	Pearson Correlation	-.069	.377**	.480**	.485**	1	-.130	-.166
	Sig. (2-tailed)	.606	.003	.000	.000		.327	.210
	N	59	59	59	59	59	59	59
7.3. In my organisation, individuals are provided with the opportunity to share information about their work.	Pearson Correlation	-.104	-.433**	.017	-.238	-.130	1	.343**
	Sig. (2-tailed)	.432	.001	.897	.069	.327		.008
	N	59	59	59	59	59	59	59
9.3. In my organisation, time is available to explore new ideas.	Pearson Correlation	-.039	-.512**	-.224	-.150	-.166	.343**	1
	Sig. (2-tailed)	.767	.000	.088	.257	.210	.008	
	N	59	59	59	59	59	59	59

**. Correlation is significant at the 0.01 level (2-tailed).

Source: Survey research data analysis using SPSS version 23

Table 12. Framework linking leadership to collective creativity

Leader Behaviours	Climate	Outcome
a. Idealised influence b. Individualised consideration	1. Nurturing of a strong sense of Belongingness 2. Encouraging openness and contribution of ideas 3. Encouraging debates and sharing of ideas 4. Valuing individual input	1. Collective Creativity 2. Competitive Advantage 3. Collective problem solving 4. Novel idea generation 5. Less pressure on individuals

Source: Author's own compilation using results form the survey

vidualised consideration leads to an expanded source of knowledge and information for employees or group members to use in solving existing problems, thereby collectively creating new ways of operating. It is therefore recommended that leadership should foster a work environment that encourages team work and collective creativity and that management should strike a balance between maximising shareholder value and catering for stakeholders' interests.

RFERENCES

Barbuto, J. E. (2005). Motivation and transactional, charismatic and transformational leadership: A test of antecedence. *Journal of Leadership & Organizational Studies*, *2*(4), 25–40.

Burke, C. S., Stagl, K. C., Klein, C., Goodwin, G. F., Salas, E., & Halpin, S. M. (2006). What types of leadership behaviours are functional in teams? A meta-analysis. *The Leadership Quarterly*, *17*(3), 288–307. doi:10.1016/j.leaqua.2006.02.007

Cooper, R. (2001). *Winning at new products: accelerating the process from idea to launch.* New York: Harper Collins.

Damiyano, D., Muchabaiwa, L., Mushanyuri, B. E., & Chikomba, C. P. (2012). An investigation of Zimbabwe's manufacturing sector competitiveness. *International Journal of Development and Sustainability*, *1*(2), 581–598.

Eisenbeiss, S. A., van Knippenberg, D., & Boerner, S. (2008). Transformational leadershipand team innovation: Intergrating team climate principles. *The Journal of Applied Psychology*, *93*(6), 1438–1446. doi:10.1037/a0012716 PMID:19025260

Freeman, R. E., & Philips, R. A. (2000). Stakeholder theory: A libertarian defense. *Business Ethics Quarterly*, *12*(3), 331–349. doi:10.2307/3858020

George, D., & Mallery, P. (2003). *SSPS for Windows step by step: a simple guide and reference 11.0 update* (4th ed.). Boston: Allyn & Bacon.

Hammond, M. M., Neff, N. L., Farr, J. L., Schwall, A. R., & Zhao, X. (2011). Predictors of individual level innovation at work: A meta-analysis. *Psychology of Aesthetics, Creativity, and the Arts*, *5*(1), 90–105. doi:10.1037/a0018556

Hargadon, A., & Bechky, B. (2006). When collections of creative become collectives: A field study of problem solving at work. *Organization Science*, *17*(4), 484–500. doi:10.1287/orsc.1060.0200

Hirst, G., Van Knippenburg, D., & Zhou, J. (2009). A cross-level perspective on employee creativity, goal orientation, team learning behaviour and individual creativity. *Academy of Management Journal*, *52*(2), 280–293. doi:10.5465/AMJ.2009.37308035

Homel, G. (2009). Moonshots. *Harvard Business Review*, *87*(2), 91–98. PMID:19266704

Hunter, S. T., Thoroughgood, C. N., Myer, A. T., & Ligon, G. S. (2011). Paradox of leading innovative behaviours; summary, solutions and future directions. *Psychology of Aesthetics, Creativity, and the Arts*, *5*(1), 54–66. doi:10.1037/a0017776

Isaksen, S. G. II, & Akkermans, H. J. (2011). Creative Climate: A leadership lever for innovation. *The Journal of Creative Behavior*, *45*(3), 161–187. doi:10.1002/j.2162-6057.2011.tb01425.x

Isaksen, S. G., & Lauer, K. J. (2001). Convergent validity of the situational outlook questionnaire: Discriminating levels of perceived support for creatity. *North American Journal of Psychology*, *3*, 31–40.

Isaksen, S.G. & Lauer, K.J. (2002). Climate for creativity and change in teams. *Creativity and Innovation Management Journal, 11*, 74-86.

Isaksen, S. G., Lauer, K. J., Ekvall, G., & Britz, A. (2001). Perceptions of the best and worst climates for creativity: Preliminary validation evidence for the situation outlook questionnaire. *Creativity Research Journal*, *13*(2), 171–184. doi:10.1207/S15326934CRJ1302_5

Jaruzelski, B., Loehr, J., & Holman, R. (2011). The global innovation 1000: Why culture is key. *Strategy & Business*, *65*, 30–45.

Jung, D. I., Chow, C., & Wu, A. (2003). The role of transformational leadership in enhancing organisational innovation: Hypotheses and some preliminary findings. *The Leadership Quarterly*, *14*(4-5), 525–544. doi:10.1016/S1048-9843(03)00050-X

Laszlo, C. (2008). Sustainable value. *Problems of Sustainable Development*, *3*(2), 25–29.

Leonard, D., & Sensiper, S. (1998). The role of tacit knowledge in group innovation. *California Management Review*, *40*(3), 112–132. doi:10.2307/41165946

Mainemelis, C., Kark, R., & Epitropaki, O. (2015). Creative leadership: A multi-context conceptualisation. *The Academy of Management Annals*, *9*(1), 393–482. doi:10.1080/19416520.2015.1024502

Mathisen, G. E., & Einarsen, S. (2004). A review of instruments assessing creative and innovative environments within organisations. *Creativity Research Journal*, *16*(1), 119–140. doi:10.1207/s15326934crj1601_12

Morris, W. (2004). *Enhancing organisational creativity: A literature review*. Retrieved from http://www.future-edge.co.nz/Files/organisational.pdf

Mumford, M. D., Scott, G. M., Gaddis, B., & Strange, J. M. (2002). Leading creative people: Orchestrating expertise and relationships. *The Leadership Quarterly*, *13*, 705–750.

Nahapiet, J., & Ghostal, S. (1998). Social capital, intellectual capital and organisational advantage. *Academy of Management Review*, *23*(2), 242–266.

Obstfeld, D. (2012). Creative projects: A less routine approach toward getting new things done. *Organization Science*, *23*(6), 1571–1592. doi:10.1287/orsc.1110.0706

Ollila, S. (2000). Creativity and innovativeness through reflective project leadership. *Creativity and Innovation Management*, *9*(3), 195–200. doi:10.1111/1467-8691.00172

Parjanen, S., Harmaakorpi, V., & Frantsi, J. (2010). Collective creativity and brokerage functions in heavyily cross-disciplined innovation processes. *Interdisciplinary Journal of Information. Knowledge and Management*, *5*, 1–21.

Petrick, J. A., & Quinn, J. F. (2001). The challenge of leadership accountability for integrity capacity as a strategic asset. *Journal of Business Ethics*, *34*(3/4), 331–343. doi:10.1023/A:1012597201948

Politis, J. D. (2004). Transformational and transactional leadership predictors of the stimulant determinants. *Electronic Journal of Knowledge Management*, *2*(2), 23–34.

Pope, R. (2005). *Creativity, theory, history and practice*. London: Routledge.

Rickards, T., & Mogers, S. (2006). Creative leaders: A decade of contributions from creativity and innovation management journal. *Creativity and Innovation Management*, *15*(1), 4–18. doi:10.1111/j.1467-8691.2006.00365.x

Runco, M. A. (2007). *Creativity theories and themes, research development and practice*. Amsterdam: Elsevier.

Sanders, E. B. N., & Stappers, P. J. (2008). Co-creation and the new land scapes of design. *CoDesign*, *4*(1), 5–18. doi:10.1080/15710880701875068

Sellgren, S. F., Ekvall, G., & Tomson, G. (2008). Leadership behaviour of nurse managers in relation to job satisfaction and work climate. *Journal of Nursing Management*, *16*(5), 578–587. doi:10.1111/j.1365-2934.2007.00837.x PMID:18558928

Si, S., & Wei, F. (2012). Transformational and transactional leaderships, empowerment climate and innovation performance; a multilevel analysis in the Chinese context. *European Journal of Work and Organizational Psychology*, *21*(2), 299–320. doi:10.1080/1359432X.2011.570445

Sweetman, D. (2010). *Exploring the adaptive function in complexity leadership theory: An examination of shared leadership and collective creativity in innovation networks* (Dissertation). University of Nebraska, Lincoln, NE.

Wang, A., Oh, I. S., Courtright, S. H., & Colbert, A. E. (2011). Transformational leadership and performance across criteria and levels: A meta-analytic review of 25 years of research. *Group & Organization Management*, *36*(2), 223–270. doi:10.1177/1059601111401017

Zhang, X., & Bartol, K. M. (2010). Linking empowering leadership and employee creativity: The influence of psychological empowerment, intrinsic motivation and creative process engagement. *Academy of Management Journal*, *53*(1), 107–128. doi:10.5465/AMJ.2010.48037118

APPENDIX

The questionnaire used in this study contained the following questions:

SECTION A: GENERAL INFORMATION ABOUT THE RESPONDENT SUCH AS AGE, GENDER, EDUCATION AND EXPERIENCE

SECTION B: IDEALISED INFLUENCE

1.1. My supervisor transmits a sense of mission.
1.2. My supervisor shows determination when accomplishing goals.

SECTION C: INSPIRATIONAL MOTIVATION

2.1. My supervisor communicates high performance expectations.
2.2. My supervisor uses metaphors and tells organisational stories that create positive images in my mind.
2.3. My supervisor mobilises a collective sense of mission.

SECTION D: INTELLECTUAL STIMULATION

3.1. My supervisor's ideas make me reconsider some of my own ideas which I had never questioned before.
3.2. My supervisor enables me to view problems from a different perspective.

SECTION E: INDIVIDUALISED CONSIDERATION

4.1. My supervisor is ready to coach or instruct me whenever I need it.
4.2. My supervisor gives personal attention to those who seem neglected.

SECTION F: SUSTAINABLE AND RESPONSIBLE COLLECTIVE CREATIVITY

5.1. Collective creativity is enabled.
5.2. Collective creativity in my organisation is responsible.
5.3. My organisation's performance is linked to sustainable collective creativity.
5.4. My organisation product performance is not linked to sustainable collective creativity.

SECTION G: ORGANISATIONAL CLIMATE (INVOLVEMENT)

6.1. Employees in my organisation are committed in contributing to the goals of the organisation.
6.2. Employees in my organisation are intrinsically motivated to the success of the organisation.
6.3. Interpersonal interactions in my organisation are dull.

SECTION H: ORGANISATIONAL CLIMATE (FREEDOM)

7.1. In my organisation, people are given resources to define their own work.
7.2. In my organisation, people exercise discretion in day to day activities.
7.3. In my organisation, individuals are provided with the opportunity to share information about their work.
7.4. In my organisation, people carry out their work in prescribed ways with little room to define their tasks.

SECTION I: ORGANISATIONAL CLIMATE (OPENESS)

8.1. In my organisation, people find it difficult to openly communicate with each other.
8.2. In my organisation, people count on each other for personal support.
8.3. In my organisation, individuals are given credit where credit is due.

SECTION J: ORGANISATIONAL CLIMATE (IDEAL TIME)

9.1. In my organisation, time pressure makes thinking outside instructions and routines impossible.
8.2. In my organisation, possibilities exist to discuss suggestions not included in task assignment.
8.3. In my organisation, time is available to explore new ideas.

SECTION K: ORGANISATIONAL CLIMATE (PLEASANTRY)

10.1. In my organisation, the work atmosphere is characterised by seriousness.
10.2. In my organisation, the work environment is easy going.
10.3. In my organisation, people exhibit a sense of humor.

SECTION L: ORGANISATIONAL CLIMATE (CONFLICT)

11.1. In my organisation, groups and individuals dislike each other.
11.2. In my organisation, management deals effectively with diversity.

SECTION M: ORGANISATIONAL CLIMATE (DEBATES)

12.1. In my organisation, a wide variety of view points are encouraged by management.
12.2. In my organisation, people follow authoritarian patterns without questioning them.
12.3. In my organisation, people are kin on putting forward their ideas for consideration.

SECTION N: ORGANISATIONAL CLIMATE (IDEAL SUPPORT)

13.1. In my organisation, new ideas are received in an attentive way by management.
13.2. In my organisation, management encourages team work.
13.3. In my organisation, people usually feel welcome when presenting new ideas to management.

SECTION O: ORGANISATIONAL CLIMATE (RISK TAKING)

14.1. In my organisation, people (subordinates) tolerate uncertainty and ambiguity when making decisions.

14.2. In my organisation, people often venture into unknown territory.

14.3. In my organisation, people usually operate on the “safe side”.

14.4. In my organisation, people tend to cover themselves in many ways.

Chapter 6
Co-Engagement of Organisational Leadership in Collective Decision-Making:
A Case of Public Enterprise

Thea Van der Westhuizen
University of KwaZulu Natal, South Africa

Max Mkhonta
Royal Swaziland Electricity Company, South Africa

ABSTRACT

Co-engagement of organisation leadership in collective decision-making is recognised as a key modality for encouragement of collective creativity as well as responsible and sustainable business practices. In cases of public enterprise (PE) collective decision-making regarding organisational policy is necessary for organisation leadership to co-engage with key decision-makers in government to ensure responsible and sustainable execution of policy. Often policy-making and implementation allows little scope for innovation and creativity, in other words, for flexibility, with direct consequences for success or failure of collaboration. This chapter explores key inferences such as the need for creative strategic intent; need for co-engagement; need for responsible and sustainable business practices to build morale and the need for innovate approach to policy-making.

INTRODUCTION

Co-engagement of organisation leadership in collective decision-making is recognised as a key modality for encouragement of collective creativity and responsible and sustainable business practices (Van der Westhuizen, 2016). In cases of public enterprise (PE) communication and collective decision-making regarding organisational policy it is necessary for organisation leadership to co-engage with key decision-makers in government to ensure responsible and sustainable execution of policy. Often policy-making

DOI: 10.4018/978-1-5225-1823-5.ch006

and implementation allows little scope for innovation and creativity, little scope, in other words, for flexibility, with direct consequences for success or failure of collaboration (Van der Westhuizen, 2016).

Debate around the level of compensation for executive teams and senior management in PEs has reached fever pitch in recent years. Governments, shareholders, boards of directors, academics, the business community in general and employee representative bodies have all demanded a say in how senior leaders are compensated and rewarded for their performance and input in organisations (Haynie, Mossholder & Harris, 2016). The debate, according to Core et al. (1999; see also Van der Westhuizen, 2016), has centred on two key questions: who should set appropriate pay policy and how superior performance can be rewarded as organisation leadership of PEs feel they have a strong claim to co-engage in collective decision-making.

According to Filatotchev and Allcock (2010), executive compensation has recently seen a move from fixed pay structures to remuneration schemes that are predominantly linked to performance and share ownership structures, and the role of shareholders (as principals) and boards of directors in determining the structure and shape of executive compensation has become a key issue in the debate on what constitutes fair and value-adding compensation and on the need for greater accountability in responsible and sustainable business practice.

In 2010, the Swaziland government introduced new guidelines on executive remuneration for all public enterprises in Swaziland (Circular No. 3, 2010). Boards of directors and remuneration committees of government-owned entities were directed to use the new guidelines to remunerate chief executive officers, chief financial officers and executive teams of PEs. The guidelines further directed that the remuneration of the rest of the employees in PEs must be also aligned according to the same directive. In this way government sought to monitor how PEs remunerated their employees in general and their executives in particular, underpinned by the need to "establish a clear relationship between key executive performance and remuneration" (Circular 3, 2010: p2). Therefore, there was a direct link between creative and innovative business practices, collective decision-making amongst leadership, and co-engagement in business practices on the part of the organisation teams relating to key executive performance and senior leadership remuneration.

Swaziland Electricity Company Limited (SEC) is the sole electricity utility company in Swaziland, tasked with the provision of electricity services and products. It is 100% owned by the Kingdom of Swaziland government and is managed via an appointed board of directors. Research was conducted to investigate the extent to which the government pay regulations had affected performance of leaders in SEC, which is one of the largest PEs in Swaziland. From recorded perceptions of senior leaders collective insight was derived and conclusions were drawn on the existence or non-existence of a direct relationship between remuneration and performance and on the degree to which senior leadership has the flexibility to act creatively and innovatively. The performance of SEC prior to and after the introduction of the guidelines on remuneration, with particular reference both to the company's success in attracting and retaining key talent and to employee motivation, was used to give a context to the research on the success or failure of responsible and sustainable business practices.

This chapter seeks to establish a better understanding of co-engagement of organisation leadership in collective decision-making regarding the impact of remuneration on the performance of SEC since 2007 in particular, and to add to the knowledge base on PE remuneration policies in ways that would provide useful input in the development of a sustainable regulatory approach to remuneration of PEs in Swaziland and elsewhere.

Three objectives were identified in relation to the study being reported here:

1. To determine how new regulations on remuneration affect responsible and sustainable business performance in SEC;
2. To establish the effect of SEC's remuneration system on the retention of talent; and
3. To determine how SEC's remuneration system impacts on responsible and sustainable business practices in the company.

Historical Performance of Swaziland Electricity Company

As is reflected in the SEC Annual Report for 2007/8, the reasons for the transformation of SEC from parastatal to PE were two-fold. Firstly, government wished to establish a basis that would enable the company to attract private capital through equity ownership, mainly to fund its capital and expansion requirements. As a developing country, Swaziland's financial budget is hugely burdened with socioeconomic development priorities, making it necessary to explore alternative funding sources to grow the company. Secondly, through diversification of ownership, government hoped to attract strategic partners with experience in transforming public enterprises into high-performance organisations, thereby encouraging collective decision-making and co-engagement between government, PEs and private sector.

In this regard, reduced profitability of SEC in the period 2010–2014 has been a matter of considerable concern and debate for the collective leadership, but rather than company performance *per se*, the focus in this chapter is more particularly the co-engagement and collective decision-making, if any, in relation to remuneration of SEC leadership and any successes or failures in SEC performance.

Turnover Rates at Swaziland Electricity Company

SEC personnel turnover rates from 2009 to 2013 (as reflected in SEC Annual Report, 2013/14) show a spike in voluntary retirements immediately prior to Circular 3 of 2010, followed by a subsequent year-by-year acceleration in total manning turnover (excluding voluntary retirement) up to 2014. Circular 3 was itself reviewed and amended by government with the publication of Circular No.4 of 2013, in which salary caps were slightly increased to cater for inflation. The context that needs to be understood here is that between September 2010 when Circular 3 of 2010 was implemented and August 2013 when Circular 4 of 2013 was implemented, salaries for senior leadership were not reviewed to keep up with inflation, with direct consequences for responsible and sustainable business practices. Circular 4 of 2013 was therefore a welcome relief as it adjusted the 2010 rates for at least two cycles of inflation (2012 and 2013). However, a new element in the interpretation of Circular 4 of 2013 had the effect of reducing executive remuneration in that the bonus benefit which Circular 3 of 2010 had previously excluded as part of guaranteed salary was now (in terms of Circular 4) included in the salary computation.

A further provision in Circular 3 was that

where there are existing contractual arrangements which are not in line with these guidelines, there should not be an adverse effect on such obligations. At the expiry of an existing contract, the guidelines should be applied in determining the remuneration terms in the event that re-appointments occur. (Circular 3, 2010: p. 9)

The direct implication of this specific provision of Circular 3 of 2010 was that at contract renewal the majority of leaders would be subject to salary reduction so as to comply fully with the provisions of the Circular. Except where existing leaders decided to exit the organisation, remaining leaders had to be subjected to this untenable situation if they wished to stay and work for SEC. The remuneration guidelines did not have any provision for impact mitigation measures to cushion affected leaders against the resultant drop in pay. This could be regarded as an unsuccessful move in business practice because sustainability of organisation leadership is directly affected.

Co-Engagement in Organisation Leadership and Performance Rewards

According when reward management puts the emphasis on direct reward this communicates value to employees more powerfully than criteria that are regulated over time and linked to the business objectives of the organisation. Because reward occurs in the framework of an employment relationship and is intended to compensate effort, there is an unfortunate element of impetuousness in the degree to which sweat matches organisational expectations; hence the need for coherent management of performance. However, even with performance management there is still no guarantee that the choices employees make will complement the reward given. Dale-Olsen (2012), concurring broadly with Perkins and White, argues that there is generally a minimal relationship between the way a company remunerates its executives and its productivity. In his study premised on companies in Norway, Dale-Olsen found that when companies distinguished between fixed pay and productivity-based pay they paid more under performance-based pay than under fixed pay, and also that how top management were paid had more to do with choice of remuneration schemes than with the performance of the companies themselves.

In terms of the Swaziland Electricity Company Act of 2007, the company's remuneration policy is determined by the Board of Directors on the recommendation of its Remunerations Committee (effectively through co-engagement and collective decision-making). In addition, the governing board is appointed by, and represents, the shareholder, which in the case of SEC, is the government as sole shareholder. As highlighted by Circular No. 3 (2010), the Board did not have any input into the design of the remuneration guidelines as this was done by government itself and the new regulations were applicable for all PEs in Swaziland. Fels (2010) makes the point that for remuneration to be addressed more effectively the shareholders must increase their influence over the executives of the enterprise to protect the long-term sustainability of the company. But he also argues that this must be done in conjunction with other interventions, including improving overall corporate governance.

An understanding of performance management helps to explain how remuneration and performance interact. As described by Lucica (2010), performance management is a methodology which defines the key practices, attitudes, actions or approach to the enhancement of performance that are developed at the individual's point of contact with the organization and are reinforced throughout his/her tenure. Houldsworth and Jirasinghe (2006) indicate that performance management occurs in a specific organising framework that includes performance processes, reward architecture, monitoring metrics and leadership capability.

Research Approach

Problems identified for investigation in this mixed-method study were appropriate for qualitative research, and a qualitative interpretive approach enabled the researcher to acquire an initial in-depth understanding of how employees viewed the new remuneration package and its impact on their own responsible and sustainable business practices in SEC. In addition, quantitative research involving statistical measurement of data collected through questionnaires gave further comprehensiveness to this understanding, enabling the researcher to interpret findings and come up with recommendations on how the company could attract and retain (i.e. sustain) key talent and ensure employee motivation.

In its exploratory aspect, this study also sought a deeper understanding of how new pay regulations of this nature might impinge more generally on public enterprises. Qualitative research being primarily inductive, the specific questions (anchored in a case study paradigm) that were put to the SEC respondents were accordingly designed both to obtain raw data and to establish patterns that might potentially have resonance in PEs more widely.

The case study approach was also appropriate for two further reasons. It allowed the researcher to go deep in establishing how participants made meaning both of their experiences and of their roles as employees – how they viewed the new remuneration model and how they thought it ought to have been developed. It also helped to particularise the context of the new PE remuneration model (study site: SEC, in the Kingdom of Swaziland) and of the 60 SEC leaders who were the role players involved.

The target population was the entire senior leadership team of SEC, working in Operations, Customer Service, Support Services, Finance, Corporate Services and the Managing Director's Office (which incorporates the Research and Development Unit and Internal Audit). The leaders who work for SEC are deployed throughout the country and are collectively referred to here as the senior leadership of the company. All 60 leaders were included, the aim being to solicit the views of all as a full collective, rather than just of a sample, with the exception only of positions that were vacant when the investigation was conducted. Views were solicited using semi-structured questionnaires on key issues around remuneration and its impact on performance and staff retention. Insofar as this group of leaders constituted a purposefully chosen sample it allowed the researcher to focus on individuals who would provide the most information about the subject under review, with the expectation that they would provide a holistic and objective view of the key issues being canvassed – best positioned as leaders in SEC to comment on matters that affected their performance. Although they were the beneficiaries of the remuneration system, their views were not expected to be so subjective as to disqualify them from providing an honest assessment of the impact of the new remuneration guidelines.

Primary data was collected from the company's annual reports from 2007 to 2014, from the government regulations on executive remuneration, and from relevant literature on remuneration systems (particularly in public enterprises). Secondary data was gathered through the use of semi-structured questionnaires. The guiding principle in the investigation was to seek information that would be useful in the development of an alternative remuneration model for all PEs in Swaziland.

The semi-structured interview questions were determined deductively. The researcher entered the research field to collect data with a predetermined theory on reward and remuneration. The data was collected to match that theory in terms of allowing participants to respond to specific issues. This type of data collection enabled the development in turn of categories and questions which further enhanced the purpose in the data collection.

The researcher began with a pilot study to simulate the instrument to be used (i.e. questionnaire) and to verify it for obvious errors. Peer debriefing was used to verify the consistency of the findings, following the recommendation by Leedy and Ormrod (2013) that this is an appropriately creative way for researchers to improve reliability and validity of the research instrument. In the course of the pilot study the questionnaire was thoroughly evaluated for possible weaknesses and then amended to improve it.

On subsequent completion of the data-collection stage, a post-questionnaire evaluation was undertaken to test the logic of the answers given by the respondents, specifically for consistency and logic. This entailed simulating what the SEC leadership went through and assessing whether their conclusions were logical and factual. This enabled the researcher to verify the accuracy of the information given and the reliability of the responses

Results and Discussion

Response Rate and Biographical Information

Forty-five leaders participated in the study out of a total population of 54 leaders, being the entire senior leadership cohort at SEC. The initial target had been to cover 60 leaders, but there were six vacancies in leadership positions at the time of the data collection. This nonetheless constituted a response rate of 85%, which is above the acceptable threshold of 60% for an extrapolation of the statistical impact.

The majority (77.8%) of the leaders who participated in completion of the questionnaire were between the ages of 31 and 50 years, with a 78% preponderance of male participants.

More than a third of the participants (35.6%) had worked for the company for more than 10 years and almost all the participants (93.3%) had degree or postgraduate qualifications.

Analysis and Interpretation

All questionnaire statements were designed on a four-point Likert Scale in which participants were asked to either agree or disagree. The mean score can be interpreted as indicating that participants were positively disposed towards the impact of the new pay regulations.

Research Question One: To What Extent do the New Regulations on Remuneration Affect Responsible and Sustainable Business Practices in SEC?

SEC leaders were asked to respond to 10 statements regarding their co-engagement in the new remuneration regulations and 11 statements on how the regulations had affected responsible and sustainable business performance in the company. In relation to the 10 statements relating to design of the new remuneration regulations, a majority of the participants responded positively to at least eight of the statements. In relation to the 11 statements relating to design of the new remuneration regulations, responses were evenly split between positive and negative responses.

In regard to co-engagement in design of the remuneration guidelines, 86.9% of respondents agreed that PEs should be "totally independent of Government in setting remuneration systems." Although this view would seem to suggest that government as shareholder does not have a role to play in remuneration design, it is contrary to what occurs in practice. As noted by Olivia (2012), matters of executive remuneration have recently become particularly vexed and contentious owing to factors such as regulation, media scrutiny and broader stakeholder pressures. Given the perception that PEs spend public money, it is perhaps unfair (and indeed more or less inconceivable) that leaders of PEs would be immune to public scrutiny on matters related to pay.

It would therefore appear that the overwhelming vote against scrutiny in this regard may have been driven more by general frustrations on the part of the SEC leaders than by actual reality on the ground, particularly given that best practice favours more, not less, shareholder co-engagement as well as collective decision-making. An additional reason for this may be found in what Core et al. (1998) define as the general lethargy of boards of directors, given that in most instances boards tend to be controlled by the chief executive officer (CEO) and thus become ineffectual, lessening co-engagement and collective decision-making This is because board members tend to avoid confrontational positions or situations that may put them in conflict with the view of the CEO. With ineffective boards, shareholders, such as government in Swaziland, thus have no choice but to insist that remuneration policies be approved at shareholder meetings.

Eight-seven per cent of respondents agreed that the remuneration of executives in PEs must be reflective of the performance of the respective enterprise and 84.8% strongly agreed that the remuneration of leaders in PEs must in general "be reflective of the performance" of the enterprise. This finding seems to confirm what is generally reflected in the literature. Flannery et al. (1996) argue for example that employers no longer favour traditional pay systems, which they see as impeding growth and success of an organisation. They instead advocate what Niranjana and Pattanayak (2005) identify as the contemporary practice, internationally, of performance-based and variable pay strategies, particularly in the public sector.

The majority of respondents (86.6%) agreed also that any pay regulations must be designed to incentivise superior performance. Pay for performance as a way of motivating responsible and sustainable business practices has increasingly emerged as an answer to the problem of distinguishing between poor and excellent performance (WorldatWork, 2007). In this respect, SEC leaders clearly agreed to 'put their money where their mouth is' and be held accountable for performance delivery.

About two-thirds of the respondents (64.4%) disagreed with the logic of categorising PEs solely on the basis of company assets as introduced by the Circular 3 of 2010 pay guideline – subsequently superseded by Circular 4 of 2013, which latter measure was clearly vindicated in the perceptions of the SEC leaders. Both guidelines were nonetheless designed by government without any consultation with PEs either at board level or management level, which 63% of leaders felt was wrong, and 80% felt very strongly that "the management collective of PEs must be consulted in the development of pay regulations."

As has been argued by Bendix (2005), co-engagement consultation lies at the heart of good practice in employee relations. Co-engagement in employment relations is distinct from negotiation. Where collective decision-making signifies engaging another party with the intention of reaching an agreement, co-engagement relates more narrowly to the process of taking into account the views and perceptions of the other party, particularly where terms and conditions of service are concerned, in a process that may not necessarily result in agreement. Reflecting this distinction, SEC leaders felt quite strongly that the lack of co-engagement in the development of the new pay regulations undermined the intentions of government and rendered the new pay regulations ineffectual. At least 40% felt indeed that potential conflict of interest would not have detracted from the quality of their input in designing of new pay regulations. It can be assumed that the intention of government in developing the new pay regulations was to address concern with high salaries of executives set against need for PEs to deliver more value for money for the state, and more than 86% of SEC leaders did indeed confirm that management pay must be directly linked to a PE's responsible and sustainable business performance. In the face of this shared understanding it would therefore seem that the rationale for not consulting either the boards or the management of PEs is open to question.

More than two-thirds of the employees (71%) positively agreed that there is a direct correlation between financial reward systems and motivation of employees. In addition, 69% of leaders regarded the level of motivation of leaders as having "affected the performance of the rest of employees within SEC." This suggests that despite the clear link, as corroborated in the literature, between pay and performance, the way in which government introduced the new regulations on remuneration of leaders tended to undermine the otherwise commendable objectives of the regulations, resulting in unintended consequences. With clear recognition by government that the role of PEs is to drive economic growth and to create employment, it could certainly not have been government's intention to undermine performance in PEs or threaten their long-term sustainability. When at least 72% of leaders feel that the new pay regulations had been detrimental to SEC's long-term sustainability this must be taken as a regrettable unintended consequence.

Despite SEC leaders generally feeling that the design of the pay regulations had been problematic (done without appropriate creativity and innovation) and that the regulations had not impacted positively on their performance and that of the company, there was nonetheless recognition that pay alone would not influence the development of a high-performance culture. At least 78% of leaders felt that development of a high-performance organisation culture was "not solely dependent on remuneration system." This finding confirms Maslow's theory of motivation which argues that satisfaction of one need leads to the natural desire to seek satisfaction in a higher need, and also his goal setting theory which links personal satisfaction to the attainment of the overall objectives of the organisation.

The aggregate mean score on the 11 statements about regulations having affected the performance of the company was 2.41 (SD = 0.42), indicating that overall the new remuneration regulations negatively affected the performance of the SEC.

Research Question 2: To What Extent Does SEC'S Remuneration System Affect the Retention of Talent?

SEC leaders were asked to respond to seven statements regarding SEC's remuneration system and talent retention, relating directly to responsible and sustainable business practices. Eighty-nine per cent of leaders did not agree with the statement that employees are attracted to an organisation because of pay only. An overwhelming 95% did not agree that employees stay in an organisation primarily because of pay nor that the pay system is an essential tool in managing an organisation's turnover. A 78% majority felt, however, that SEC's pay system was not "perceived to be fair" and did "contribute to increased turnover" in the company (which had seen a sharp increase in turnover since the advent of the new pay regulations). If SEC leaders felt that pay alone does not attract an employee to an organisation or make him/her stay, why then did they overwhelmingly believe that the company's pay system had directly contributed to the increase in turnover? The answer may have to do with the issue of avoidability: that there are more reasons for employees to opt out of an organisation than issues of pay.

Lee (2011) suggests that the cause–effect relationship between pay and turnover is non-linear, which gives rise to its complexity. As he puts it,

> *turnover has long been a central and enduring topic in HR and management and ... unlike other issues that are really transient fads, in a worldwide knowledge-based economy where skills shortages are a constant challenge, employee turnover shows no sign of ceasing to be an important HR issue. (2011: p209).*

It is therefore understandable that on one level leaders shared the view that employees are not necessarily attracted by pay nor stay as a result of it. On another level, they argued however that SEC's turnover rate could be directly attributable to the pay system. Pay issues by their nature are complex, which explains why understanding turnover is in itself also complex. When dealing with linear issues such as pay and employee turnover it is often even more difficult for organisation leadership to exercise qualities of creativity and innovation because concrete policy allows little scope for abstract thinking.

The majority of leaders (84%) nevertheless strongly agreed that remuneration system design was "perceived to be directly linked to the goals of the company." No less than 82.6% of leaders felt that SEC's current remuneration design was "hugely influenced by skills and competency-based pay elements, given the nature of the industry and operations of the company." This finding resonates with the skills and competency-based pay approach of Armstrong and Murlis (1994), Homan (2000), Byars and Rue (2004) and Shields (2007), all of whom argue that competency-based pay inspires employees to improve their skills in line with organisational objectives and values.

Considering all the statements, the overall mean score on the statements about remuneration and retention was 3.21 (SD = 0.41) which indicated leaders' assessment that the new remuneration system negatively affected responsible and sustainable business practice in regard employee retention in the company.

Research Question 3: How does SEC's Remuneration System Impact on Responsible and Sustainable Business Practices in the Company?

Eleven statements dealt with the perceptions of the leaders on how the pay regulations had affected their own responsible and sustainable business performance and that of the company. Only 22.3% of leaders felt that the new pay regulations had positively affected leader performance at SEC, and only 13% of leaders felt that the new pay regulations had introduced clear and coherent mechanisms to reward performance. Just 6.5% affirmed that the pay regulations had impacted positively on their motivation.

Overall, 82% of leaders were of the view that the new pay regulations undermined the company's ability to create a high performance culture. The primary responsibility of leaders in organisations is to drive performance and ensure the long term sustainability of their respective organisations, and Bussin (2013) puts this point is its proper context when he opines that

high performance is a standard we strive for in all our life's activities. It implies doing a difficult thing well, whether personal or professional, and it often commands admiration and reaps rewards. The workplace is no exception and high performers often expect their achievements to be evident in their remuneration. (p. 129).

The general view among leaders on the impact of the new pay regulations on the company would seem to be that they did indeed affect the responsible and sustainable business performance of the company. In the three years during which the regulations applied (2011, 2012, 2013, 2014) profitability declined from a high of R188m in 2011 to R72m in 2013, with a slight improvement to R78m in 2014. While this may not be directly and solely attributable to the advent of the new pay regulations, it may nonetheless be reasonable to suggest that lack of motivation in the senior management team could have been a significant factor.

Key Inferences for Co-Engagement and Collective Decision-Making

Prior to introduction in 2010 of the guidelines on executive pay which affected the remuneration of senior leaders in all public enterprises in Swaziland, including SEC, and which were further amended in 2013, PEs in Swaziland determined their own remuneration policies in line with their business fundamentals. Remuneration policies generally required only the approval of the respective boards of directors and needed shareholder approval only in exceptional circumstances, limiting scope for the PE as a whole to co-engage in collective decision-making. In particular shareholder approval was only required when annual cost of living increases normally awarded to employees to compensate for the impact of inflation exceeded the annual pay-increase limit approved by the Public Enterprise Unit.

The following five key inferences may be drawn from the findings in this study on how new pay regulations have affected senior leaders at SEC.

1. **Need for Creative Strategic Intent:** None of the instruments introduced by government from 2010 to date are premised on any clear strategic intent or theoretical underpinning. The remuneration of executives is not designed to improve performance, given that the guidelines do not expressly seek to link pay and performance. While certain sections of the guidelines refer to the need for public enterprises to establish performance incentive schemes, performance incentives, where payable, would be over and above guaranteed salary. However, for the recommended pay guidelines and pay ranges to be effective and to directly influence the performance of the various PEs, clear performance parameters need to be established between the PEs and the Public Enterprise Unit. The performance contract should be in the mode of shareholder pacts, examples of which exist in private sector companies. These could be customized for the public sector, given that profit and shareholder maximisation are not fundamental to the operation of most PEs. Shareholder pacts would generally refer to key financial and qualitative ratios that organisations then use as key performance targets. Examples of financial indicators would include return on investment (ROI), return on equity (ROE), liquidity ratios, debt equity ratio, activity ratio (such as debtor and creditor days), price earnings ratio, gross and net profit margin, earnings before interest, taxes and amortisation, dividend cover ratio, net cash from operating activities, and return on net capital employed. Examples of qualitative indicators would include manpower productivity ratios, efficiency ratios and customer satisfaction index.
2. **Need for Co-Engagement:** There was no co-engagement on the new pay regulations between government and role players responsible for the running of PEs prior to their introduction in 2010 and their review in 2013. Lack of co-engagement between government and the PE boards of directors and management teams meant that a critical opportunity was lost to positively influence the performance of the country's PEs, most of which have a developmental mandate. Pay policy is a key leverage that shareholders can use to drive organisations to higher levels of performance, and while it may be true that superior performance is not driven by financial incentives alone, the absence of a clear rationale behind policy has detrimental consequences for all employees and for leaders in particular.
3. **Need for Responsible Business Practices to Build Morale:** SEC leaders in this study overwhelmingly confirmed that their emotional connection to the company had been significantly undermined by the pay regulations. In addition, they confirmed that leader morale and motivation had been eroded to a point where company performance had begun to be negatively affected. This research

substantiates the point made by WorldatWork (2007) that compensation systems are key to eliciting and reinforcing behaviours supportive of a firm's strategy and can have a substantial positive or negative effect on performance.

4. **Need for Sustainable Business Practices to Build Morale:** While SEC leaders confirmed that their performance and motivation had been affected, their responses also dispelled the myth that pay is the key driver of employee retention and loyalty. Despite criticism of the new pay regulations they nonetheless confirmed that employee retention has more to do with working conditions and environment than with an exclusive focus on pay; SEC's turnover rate has increased in recent years, but not necessarily because of the pay regulations. But emotional attachment to the organisation has been negatively affected and it is likely that leaders' loyalty and sense of belonging to SEC will be suffer going forward.
5. **Need for Innovate Approach to Policy-Making:** Employees in any work setting (leaders included) are always inward-looking in relation to matters of pay. SEC leaders in the study felt that the shareholder's involvement in the design of pay policies should be minimal, but best practice and global experience indicates otherwise. Olivia (2012) suggests that no shareholder worth his/her salt can leave the contentious and vexed issue of compensation purely to management and boards of directors. Shareholders have become very vocal and active in the determination of pay and incentives, as is apparent in their approval or rejection of pay policies at annual general meetings. It therefore is the researcher's conclusion that government was correct and within its rights to influence PE pay policy in Swaziland. Rather than focusing on the pay regulations themselves, the more important question relates to the process used to determine the pay regulations, because if left to the devices of organisations the chances are that policies may be implemented that are not in the long-term interest of shareholders.

Advancing Co-Engagement in Collective Decision-Making

Employers have come to collectively conclude that traditional pay systems impede growth and success of an organisation and that this has caused many organisations to consider new and improved compensation resolutions that support the new emphasis on values such as quality, customer service, teamwork and productivity. The study findings will hopefully offer useful input into the development of a more responsible and sustainable regulatory approach to remuneration of PEs in Swaziland. It is against this background that the following recommendations are being made:

Recommendations on co-engagement and collective decision-making in designing PE remuneration systems:

- Government as a shareholder must engage with PEs to develop clear strategic deliverables that are aligned to government's programme of action and development agenda. Pay policies work effectively when they directly promote set objectives.
- Based on this interaction, shareholder compacts or agreements with the various boards of directors must then be agreed upon and confirmed that stipulate timeframes for achievement of the set objectives and the support that will be necessary for the PEs to deliver on their mandate.
- Remuneration policies must then be developed in alignment with the shareholder agreements. In particular, and central to the remuneration policies, must be the development of a high-performance organisation culture charter.

- Performance incentives and general pay policy will then be contextualized within the parameters of the high-performance organisation culture.
- This means that government must, in principle, avoid 'one glove fits all' pay policies. PEs are different, their mandates differ as do their fundamental operating environments. Failure to take this into account will lead to policies that fail to support best practice and that hinder the achievement of important PR goals.

Recommendations on the role of boards of directors in co-engagement and collective decision-making on design of PE remuneration systems:

- Ultimately, boards of directors are appointed by the shareholder to represent its interests in running of the PE. The role of boards must be solely to create shareholder value and to continuously increase return on equity. This commercial focus is necessary if there is to be ultimate delivery on the mandate of the PE. Boards must therefore be given the necessary scope and opportunity to determine what will best enable them to deliver on the shareholder's expectations. Shareholder agreements must therefore clearly articulate this. If boards fail in their overall mandate they must be held accountable, but the mandate must not be undermined by shareholder interference.
- Pay policies lie at the heart of organisation management in that they sanction non-performance or reward superior performance. As such, the development of pay policies must be exclusive preserve of boards of directors although potentially still subject to the approval of the shareholder.

Recommendations on the types of responsible and sustainable remuneration systems suitable for PEs:

- While traditional pay systems focus on guaranteed pay, best practice explored in this research, has indicated that progressive pay policies emphasize issues like sustainability of companies and achievement of return on equity.
- Government must therefore seriously consider long-term value creation through implementing profit share schemes for senior leaders or through aggressive pay for performance schemes.
- The current trend of focusing purely on guaranteed pay negates the potential of long-term value creation, given that employees also tend to prioritise guaranteed pay at the expense of driving superior performance.
- A combination of guaranteed and variable pay must form the basket of pay policies applicable in PEs. These have worked well in private companies and thus have the potential to deliver value for public organisations if adequate checks and balances are incorporated into the design of the pay to curb excesses.

Developing remuneration levels for public enterprises must become a more refined art than it currently is and the fundamental performance and value created by the PE's, must be taken into consideration with regards to remuneration systems.

CONCLUSION

Taken together the suggestions put forward here regarding design of remuneration systems, the role of boards of directors and types remuneration systems would hopefully go a long way to support and encourage responsible and sustainable business practices of public enterprises. It is necessary for organisational leadership to co-engage and collectively make decisions both within and beyond the immediate organisational environment. Leaders need to apply abstract concepts such as creativity and innovation towards linear concepts such as policy formulation and pay regulation in order to build broad organisational morale and drive forwards-directed thinking for organisational behaviour in the twenty-first century.

REFERENCES

Armstrong, M., & Murlis, K. (1994). *Reward Management: A Handbook of Remuneration Strategy and Practice* (3rd ed.). London: Kogan.

Bendix, S. (2005). *Industrial Relations in South Africa* (4th ed.). Lansdowne: Juta.

Bussin, M. (2013). *The Performance Management Handbook for Emerging Markets*. Randburg: Knowres Publishing.

Byars & Rue. (2004). *Human Resource Management: A Practical Approach*. New York: Harcourt Brace.

Core, J., Holthausen, R., & Larcker, D. (1999). Corporate Governance, CEO Compensation, and firm performance. *Journal of Financial Economics*, *51*, 371–406. doi:10.1016/S0304-405X(98)00058-0

Dale-Olsen, H. (2012). Executive Pay Determination and Firm Performance – Empirical Evidence from a Compressed Wage Environment. *The Manchester School*, *80*(3), 355–376. doi:10.1111/j.1467-9957.2011.02225.x

Fels, A. (2010). Executive Remuneration in Australia. *Australian Accounting Review*, *20*(1), 76–82.

Filatotchev, I., & Allcock, D. (2010). Corporate Governance and Executive Compensation: A Contingency Framework. *The Academy of Management Perspectives*, *24*(1), 20–33. doi:10.5465/AMP.2010.50304414

Flannery, T. P., Hofrichter, D. A., & Platten, P. E. (1996). *People, Performance and Pay - Dynamic Compensation for Changing Organizations*. New York: Free Press.

Haynie, J. J., Mossholder, K. W., & Harris, S. G. (2016). *Justice and job engagement: The role of senior management trust*. J. Organiz. Behav. doi:10.1002/job.2082

Homan, G. (2000). Skills and Competency-Based Pay. In R. Thorpe & G. Homan (Eds.), *Strategic Reward Systems*. Essex, UK: Pearson.

Houldsworth, E., & Jirasinghe, D. (2006). *Managing & Measuring Employee Performance*. London: Kogan Page.

Lee, J. G. (2011). *HR Metrics – Strategic and Qualitative Tools for People Management*. Randburg: Knowres Publishing.

Leedy, P., & Ormrod, J. (2013). *Practical Research – Planning & Design* (10th ed.). Boston: Pearson.

Lucica, C. (2010) Performance Management. The Relationship Between Evaluation And Reward In The Pedagogical Activity Of The Romanian Secondary Education. *Managerial Challenges of the Contemporary Society. Proceedings*, 115–121.

Niranjana, P., & Pattanayak, B. (2005). Influence of Learned Optimism and Organisational Ethos on Organisational Citizenship Behaviour - A Study on Indian Corporations. *International Journal of Human Resources Development and Management*, *5*(1), 85–98. doi:10.1504/IJHRDM.2005.005987

No, C. 3 (2010). Public Enterprise Unit Guidelines on Executive Remuneration. Ministry of Finance – Government of the Kingdom of Swaziland, Government Printers.

Olivia, L. (2012). Executive Remuneration in Ireland. *International Tax Review*, *23*(5), 34–34.

Perkins, S. J., & White, G. (2011). *Reward Management: Alternatives, Consequences and Contexts* (2nd ed.). London: Chartered Institute of Personnel and Development.

Shields, J. (2007). *Managing Employee Performance and Reward: Concepts, Practices, Strategies*. Cambridge, UK: Cambridge University Press. doi:10.1017/CBO9781139168748

Swaziland Electricity Company Limited Annual Report. (2013/14). Mbabane: PrintPak.

Van der Westhuizen, T. (2016) *Developing Individual Entrepreneurial Orientation: A systemic approach through the lens of Theory U* (Doctoral thesis). University of KwaZulu-Natal, Durban.

WorldatWork. (2007). *International Remuneration. The Total Rewards Association*. Scottsdale: Northsight Boulevard.

Section 2

Strategies and Leadership for Responsible and Sustainable Business Practice

Chapter 7
The Collective Creation of Civil Commons:
The Life-Ground of Business Practice

Giorgio Baruchello
University of Akureyri, Iceland

ABSTRACT

Since the dawn of civilisation, human communities have collectively allowed for the creation, and regularly taken advantage, of concepts, social arrangements and simple as well as complex tools aimed at fulfilling life-enabling ends for their members, under remarkably diverse circumstances. Natural and artificial languages, food recipes, universal health plans, urban sewers, open paths in the countryside, sports and games, pollution controls, old-age pensions, and regulated maximum working hours and minimum wages have all been tokens of "civil commons", a term coined in the 1990s by Canadian value theorist John McMurtry, meaning the "social constructs which enable universal access to life goods". In this chapter, McMurtry's axiology is presented, explained and applied, so as to highlight its implications for responsible and sustainable business practice.

INTRODUCTION

From the long-lived monarchies by divine election of medieval Europe, down to the persisting evolutionary explanations of human cooperation within societies *qua* means of survival of the species, *via* the laws of historical development variously conceived of by Vico, Lord Kames, Hegel, Marx or Spengler, human beings have been acknowledging their collective institutions as a pivotal feature of human existence, while at the same time denying these collective institutions' creative, ultimately contingent, human origin. On the one hand, human beings have recognised that their own mortal lives would be noticeably more brutal and probably much shorter, if not even impossible, were it not for the fact that there exist such collective institutions. On the other hand, human beings have regularly believed the existence of such collective institutions to be the result of a fundamentally non-human power, e.g. God, His Divine Providence or an equally providential invisible hand, Mother Nature and her more or less

DOI: 10.4018/978-1-5225-1823-5.ch007

maternal laws, Human Nature and its attendant Rights, the cunning of Reason, of the Will to Live, of the Will to Power or, lately, of some selfish gene. Yet, as the Greek economist, philosopher, Sovietologist and psychoanalyst Cornelius Castoriadis (1982/2003) dared stating:

God does not exist, and "laws of history," in the Marxian sense, do not exist. Institutions are a creation of man. But they are, so to speak, a blind creation. People do not know that they create and that they are, in a certain sense, free to create their institutions. And they mix up the fact that there can be no society (and no human life) without institutions and laws, with the idea that there has to be some transcendent source and guarantee of the institution. (pp. 15–16)

Even a secular, sceptical and scientific—if not scientistic—age such as ours is still prone to characterise socio-historical events and the institutional changes emerging thereof in ways akin to the old ones, i.e. as natural catastrophes (e.g. financial 'tsunamis', political 'landslides', economic 'crises'), natural developments (e.g. post-communist 'transitions', industrial 'growth', bureaucratic 'sclerosis') or God-like forces (e.g. the 'will of the markets', 'market discipline', 'market miracles'). The alternative, according to Castoriadis (1982/2003), would be "collective autonomy" (p. 14), i.e. taking full responsibility for the way in which we, as potentially active members of our communities, posit and steer our own creations—or fail to do so. The proclivity to retrieve a non-human, external power upon which we can rest our case, our fears, or our hopes, is still very strong, to the point of leading the most famous American neo-pragmatist thinker of our time, Richard Rorty (2004), to speak of a "masochistic urge to submit to the nonhuman" and not "to take proper pride in our humanity" and its creative abilities (p. 13).

Whether there can be such a power or not is too big a topic to be tackled in this chapter. As a matter of intellectual history, it is a topic that has kept theologians, philosophers, social scientists, essayists and literati busy for a few thousand years. Rather, the attention here is to be set upon a specific group of collective creations, of which Canada's leading value theorist John McMurtry (2013) lists numerous examples:

[T]he nature of language[,] the air we breathe[,] the common fire[,] food recipes[,] universal health plans[,] the world wide web[,] common sewers[,] international campaigns against US war crimes[,] sidewalks and forest paths[,] sports and sports fields[,] the open science movement[,] the Chinese concept of jen[,] the Jubilee of Leviticus[,] public streetscapes[,] effective pollution controls[,] birdwatching[,] city squares and sidewalks[,] Buddha's principle of interdependent origination[,] old-age pensions[,] the rule of life-protective law[,] universal education[,] universal hygiene practices[,] footpaths and bicycle trails[,] fair elections[,] unemployment insurance[,] the global atmosphere[,] maximum work hours and minimum wages[,] public parks[,] clean water[,] the Tao[,] community fish-habitats[,] public broadcasting[,] the ancient village commons before enclosures[,] the unnamed goal of the Occupy Movement. (p. 240)

Prima facie, this list seems quite heterogeneous, to say the least. Why is McMurtry putting all these ideas, institutions and instruments into one bag? Though not immediately obvious, it can be understood that the air we breathe, the water we drink and the food we eat are, to symbolic creatures like ourselves, collective creations too. Apart from forming the corporeal World that we sense around us, they are crucial conceptual-linguistic notions for any culture to agree upon and transmit across generations for the sake of survival, which requires the members of any community to gain consciousness of them and, when necessary, take care of them (e.g. by preserving food and the sources of food). Still, what do they have in common with sidewalks, footpaths or the ancient village commons? Answering this interrogative is the first issue in the present chapter, so that McMurtry's theory of value, known as *life-value onto-axiology* [LVOA], may be introduced (cf. the following two sections), articulated (cf. the ensuing two sections) and applied[1] (cf. the final three sections), in order to assess in principle[2] the responsibility and sustainability of business practice.

The Civil Commons

Over millennia, all human communities have created, and *ipso facto* endowed themselves with, a vast array of intellectual conceptions, physical facilities, traditional practices, compassionate principles and organisations, forms of expert knowledge and disciplinary inquiry, legal and customary praxes, the chief task of which has been as simple as it has been crucial: to permit and to promote the expression and enjoyment of life capacities by all or most the members of the community at stake. Across generations, the survival and the possibly better life of entire communities, ranging from family-based clans to large multi-ethnic empires, has been prioritised and served by an immense variety of collective creations. In spite of recurrent claims of ultimate cultural relativism, imperialism, and of fundamental inscrutability of individual happiness or subjective preference, time and again there have been socially conceptualised, debated, monitored, analysed, tackled and/or managed moral notions, political conceptions of the common good, legal rights, life-expectancy measurements, hygiene standards, improved technologies for waste disposal, suicide rates, manic-depressive and bipolar pathologies, blue-collar and white-collar crime rates, literacy and numeracy levels, and a multitude of additional dimensions of individual, collective and natural existence. All of these dimensions have been the focus of attention for a corresponding plethora of human institutions, such as elders' councils, scholarly societies, tribunals, local and national registrars, hygiene and health monitoring bodies, law enforcement agencies, not to mention schools, churches, higher education centres, research institutes, legislative assemblies, etc.

Whether aware or unaware of its quintessentially life-serving purpose, and whether successful or not in every of its pursuits, a significant part of organised social agency, both physical and conceptual, has been aimed, throughout human history, at sensing, conceptualising, comprehending, and, on the one hand, promoting life-enablement or, on the other hand, inhibiting, indicating, and/or intervening against life-disablement—as these dynamic phenomena are signalled by the particular forms of standardised appraisal characterising each human institution in its specific socio-historical setting. Such forms of organised social agency are *creations* inasmuch as their coming into being introduces into a community's way of life something that did not yet exist; and they are *collective* inasmuch as more than one individual is required for their understanding, establishment and operation. None of them is inherently immune to decay, derangement or destruction. Life-disablement can also occur at the hands of elders' councils, law enforcement agencies, churches or legislative assemblies, sometimes of a dramatic magnitude. Some such collective creations are nonetheless indispensable to make civil life possible. Upon their being in place revolves civilisation itself.

John McMurtry is Guelph University's Professor Emeritus of Philosophy and a fellow of the Royal Society of Canada, as well as a noted axiologist, who has produced what is, until now, the most extensive theory of value of the 21st century, i.e. his substantial contribution as both author and Honorary Theme Editor to the vast *Encyclopedia of Life Support Systems* [EOLSS] issued by the United Nations Educational, Scientific and Cultural Organisation [UNESCO]. Concerning *all* instances of life-serving organised social agency mentioned above, he offers the concise and synthetic notion of "civil commons", which he defines as "any and all social constructs that enable universal access to life-goods" (McMurtry, 2013, p. 237).

In McMurtry's understanding, all these ideas, institutions and instruments are, *in primis*, *commons*, insofar as they typically pertain to entire communities, rather than to isolated individuals. *In secundis*, these commons are *civil*. They are not, for instance, grazing lands available to all members of the community without regulation or penalty for misappropriation and misuse. Quite the opposite, the commons at issue would be grazing lands that the community acknowledges in its symbolic system, i.e. in its frame of thought and linguistic expression, and that the community utilises in order to obtain life-enablement through time for its members at large, if possible over generational time. McMurtry's civil commons are therefore not to be confused with Garrett Hardin's (1968) textbook commons, the unregulated character and assumed tragic destiny of which provide the justification for their seizure under a regime of private ownership. In contrast, McMurtry (2013, pp. 77–79 & 237–238) is wary of such seizure and regime, because both have frequently occurred for the exclusive benefit of a restricted sub-set of community members, rather than for the benefit of the community at large (e.g. aristocratic landowners' appropriation of common lands in late-medieval and modern Britain), and/or have repeatedly converted the existing civil commons into accessories of life-disabling undertakings (e.g. human knowledge used in the profit-seeking design and manufacture of life-destructive armaments, or of financial products aimed at speculation on critical crops such as maize, rice and wheat).

Since its first appearance in the 1990s, McMurtry's notion of civil commons has been gaining widespread acceptance amongst human and social scientists across disciplinary divides. The number of researchers making use of this original notion of his has been growing steadily (e.g. Anielski, 2007; Ato, 2006; Burch, 2012; Davidson-Harden, 2013; Dickinson, Becerra, & Lewis, 2009; English & Mayo, 2012; Finlay, 2000; Florby, Shackleton, & Suhonen, 2009; Giacomini & Turner, 2015; Hodgson, 2001; Johnston, 2003; Johnston, Gismondi, & Goodman, 2006; Jordan, 2004; Kaara, 2005; Mishori, 2010; Mook & Sumner, 2008; Peekhaus, 2013; Scarfe, 2006; Shurville & Brown, 2009; Shurville, Brown, and Whitaker, 2009; Streeck, 2009; Susilowati, 2014; Suvin, 2012; Turner & Brownhill, 2004; Uzelman, 2011; Westhues, 1999), although only few of them have paid attention to the much broader, articulate, and complex new theory of value comprising it, which McMurtry himself developed fully only in the late 2000s, namely with his contribution to EOLSS (e.g. Baruchello & Johnstone, 2011; Newson, Polster & Woodhouse, 2012).[3]

Life-Value Onto-Axiology

McMurtry's theory of value pivots around the reasoned belief that, *pace* much philosophical relativism and Weberian or Paretian positivist value-neutrality, it is possible for human reason to determine a universal and objective ground of value. There exists most certainly a plurality of conceptions regarding what may be claimed to be good and what to be bad, and disagreement can be as vocal as it can be varied. Nonetheless, some preferences are, *au fond*, truly better than others, for in their absence no preference whatsoever could be expressed. Thus, as McMurtry (2009–2010) argues, we can "follow reason where it leads", namely "to recover step by step the missing life-ground of values and the ultimate meaning of how we are to live." (para. 1.16)

The first step in this process is the acknowledgment of the existence and importance of "life support systems", as these are defined by the United Nations ([UN], 2002–2010, "Definitions", para. 2):

[A]ny natural or human-engineered (constructed or made) system that furthers the life of the biosphere in a sustainable fashion. The fundamental attribute of life support systems is that together they provide all of the sustainable needs required for continuance of life. These needs go far beyond biological requirements. Thus life support systems encompass natural environmental systems as well as ancillary social systems required to foster societal harmony, safety, nutrition, medical care, economic standards, and the development of new technology. The one common thread in all of these systems is that they operate in partnership with the conservation of global natural resources.

The second step is the definition of the "life-ground" itself, upon the basis of such "life support systems": "Concretely, all that is required to take the next breath; axiologically, all the life support systems required for human life to reproduce or develop." (McMurtry, 2009–2010, Glossary) Without air, water, nourishment, spaces, rest, training in the symbolic systems of the community and socialisation therein, no value whatsoever that we may happen to appreciate will ever be experienced in reality. No value whatsoever, whether ethical, civic, mystical, artistic, cognitive, juridical or financial, can occur in reality independently of the life-ground (hence LVOA's qualifier "life-value"). Life is the indispensable prerequisite for the existence of any and every other value (hence LVOA's prefix "onto-" i.e. "regarding being"). *A fortiori*, life's ontological pre-requisites are themselves paramount and their paramount value is unavoidable in any and every other evaluation, whether we realise it or not (hence LVOA's key-noun "axiology" i.e. "value theory" or "theory of value"). Even standard epistemic values like truth and falsehood rely upon the life-ground, which is the ultimate principle of verification and falsification *qua* evaluations, even if scientists themselves do not recognise it:

The unseen flaw of scientific method as such is that it too has no internal principle of consistency with universal life support systems - "to be in accord with reality" in the deepest sense. Partial science and rationality blinker out this wider plane of coherence. What most distinguishes scientific method - openness to disconfirming evidence and resolute attention to anomalous outcomes - has thus been abdicated where these standards reach furthest and count most. Science cannot be in accord with reality until it takes this excluded baseline of all human reality into account. More exactly, scientific conclusions are not valid until tested against common life support requirements. They are false insofar as they contradict these requirements in principle or in downstream effects. (McMurtry, 2009–2010, para. 12.11.4)

In short, there can be no life as such, and even less so any good life at all, separate from the life-ground: "Life support systems… may or may not have value in themselves, but have ultimate value so far as they are that without which human or other life cannot exist or flourish." (McMurtry, 2009–2010, para. 6.2.1)

The third step is a corollary of the previous two, namely that to disaffirm the life-ground's primary importance is nothing but a performative contradiction. Whoever were to disaffirm the life-ground's primary importance would do so only after satisfying her own vital needs for the very long time required in order to develop the physical and mental faculties needed to disaffirm the life-ground's primary importance. As to sceptics and nihilists, even the legendary Pyrrho—whose friends prevented from being trampled upon by carriages or falling off cliffs because of his distrust of human senses—argued that he was willing to suspend his "judgment in all matters which do *not* refer to living and the preservation of life" (Laertius, 3rd century AD/1853; emphasis added). Suicides, pessimists and Gnostics themselves affirm it too, though by way of negation, since they do so upon the assumption of a better life that is no longer, that is fantasised or thought about, or that is expected to become reality only after one's own Earthly demise (cf. Baruchello, 2007).

From a strictly logical point of view, it still remains possible to separate life's intrinsic value from the life-ground's instrumental value. From an ontological point of view, however, such a separation is neither plausible nor possible. As McMurtry (2009–2010) observes: "All that is of worth consists in and enables life value to the extent of its experienced fields of thought, felt being and action (intrinsic value), *and* what underlies and enables these fields of life themselves, life support systems." (para. 6.1.4; emphasis added) Abstracting from the life-ground in theory still requires standing upon it in practice.

Good and Bad

The concluding passage above lays bare another step in LVOA's process of thought. McMurtry (2009–2010) takes life to manifest itself in three fundamental ways: "action" (aka "biological movement" or "motility"), "felt being" (aka "experience" or "feeling") and "thought" (para. 6.1). The plausibility of this step is supported by human experience at many levels. Nurses and physicians, for example, encounter these three fundamental ways of life-manifestation in terms of physical, affective and cognitive health (or lack thereof). Religious persons encounter them, say, in the believer's thankfulness for one's own being alive, the reassuring or stirring sense of the presence of the divine within oneself (e.g. during meditation), and the thought-provoking intricacies of theological dispute. On their part, human rights activists, lawyers, courts and legislators encounter them as constitutional provisions about "rest, leisure and reasonable limitation of working hours and periodic holidays with pay", "age limits below which the paid employment of child labor should be prohibited and punishable by law", and "the diffusion of science and culture" (ICESCR, 1966, arts. 7(d), 10 & 15). The list could go on and on, like the tokens of civil commons enumerated by McMurtry (2013). In essence, however, LVOA states that all that is intuitively acknowledged as excellence, fairness, happiness or health is—if it is genuinely good—a fruitful and comprehensive expression of life-value, in one or more of the three ways in which life is taken to manifest itself: action (e.g. physical vigour), felt being (e.g. marvel at nature's elaborate beauty) and thought (e.g. wisdom and proportionality in the verdicts of a just court of law).

Whilst logically distinguishable from one another, no ontological tri- or dualism is implicit in McMurtry's tri-partition of life-manifestation:

Although we can distinguish the cognitive and feeling capacities of any person, this does not mean dividing them into separate worlds as has occurred in the traditional divisions between mind and body, reason and the emotions. Life-value onto-axiology begins from their unity as the nature of the human organism. (McMurtry, 2009–2010, para.6.3; emphasis in the original)

As a consequence, the fundamental axioms of LVOA are:

- *X is value if and only if, and to the extent that, x consists in or enables a more coherently inclusive range of thought/feeling/action than without it*
- *X is disvalue if and only if, and to the extent that, x reduces/disables any range of thought/experience/action. (McMurtry, 2009–2010 , para.6.1; emphasis in the original)*

These axioms apply to all forms of human agency. For instance, as concerns sustainable development, McMurtry (2013) distinguishes between "zero growth" and "zero bad growth", condemning the former as negative while praising the latter as positive, since: "growth of production that serves universal human life-needs is necessary and good the more there is deprivation." (p. 42)

Basically, LVOA achieves a traditional aim of philosophical study, for it determines in principle what is good and what is bad, cutting across entrenched dualisms that, far too often, unduly polarise and *ergo* limit intellectual pursuits in many disciplines, e.g. mind *versus* body, nurture *versus* nature, laissez-faire *versus* central planning, Kantianism *versus* consequentialism, mutuality *versus* competitiveness, belief *versus* scepticism, monetary value *versus* ecological value, present well-being maximisation *versus* future generations', etc. In theory, the decisive axiological criterion is clear-cut: "good" means "comprehensively life-enabling"; "bad" means the opposite. In practice, the evaluations to be made are not always going to be as clear-cut, nor simple. Tricky cases and actual dilemmas are part and parcel of the human condition. Not even the most insightful axiology can rescue us from having to deal with them at some point. Nevertheless, if LVOA is spot-on, then any and every better option is going to be always and necessarily the outcome of appraisals of coherent life-value, insofar as no good whatsoever can be given outside the life-ground.

McMurtry's emphasis is fixed upon social forms of human activity. Nonetheless, LVOA's fundamental axioms apply also to individual forms of human activity, for these axioms discriminate between good and evil, i.e. the crucial poles of evaluation in political, moral and existential agency. As seen in the previous section of this chapter, LVOA is aimed all along at "recover[ing] step by step the missing life-ground of values and the ultimate meaning of how we are to live". Thus, life-enablement is good, and life-disablement bad, also at the level of individual agency. A good life means a life where life-enablement occurs as broadly and as deeply as possible: life-enablement ought to be as *comprehensive* as possible. Committed educators, health care professionals, real friends, conscientious leaders and devoted parents can easily grasp how this life-enablement comprehends both the initiator and the recipients of individual agency. Self-centred aesthetes and selfish individuals may find this notion more troublesome. Individuals, however, are nearly always members of communities and, as such, comprehensive life-enablement cannot but entail the notion that pursuing a good life should translate into being sources of life-enablement for others too, logically at least. Morally, instead, libertinism, nihilism, Stalinism, National Socialism, Objectivism and other ideologies rejecting the equal worth of human beings come across as perplexing, if not as blatantly unethical, precisely because the good they seek is not comprehensive. LVOA moves in the opposite direction. The more the life-capability, the better, both individually and collectively: "Against the 'red in tooth and claw' dogma… the evidence increasingly shows the 'co-operative principle' at work here confers survival and development advantage… *The more human beings subsume the requirements of their fellows' and their environment's life-capital capacities into their organizational regulation, the better off they are.*" (McMurtry, 2013, p. 310; emphasis in the original)

Needs and Wants

Understanding needs represents a pivotal further step within LVOA. As McMurtry scholars Jeff Noonan and Alison Assiter (2007) state: "N is a need, if and only if, and to the extent that, deprivation of N always leads to a reduction in organic capability" (p. 175). What truly counts as need is "*that without which life-capacities are always reduced* – the ultimate criterion of all life-goods and capital that exist." (McMurtry, 2013, p. 19; emphasis in the original) We can certainly live, and even thrive, without credit cards or breast implants, but we cannot live, not to mention thrive, without "sufficient nutriment, clean water, sewage facilities, learning of society's symbol systems, home and love, and expert care when ill" (McMurtry, 2013, p. 1). One thing is what we want; another is what we need. As Jeff Noonan (2006) observes, needs can be sharply distinguished from economic preferences or wants: "deprivation of needs always leads to harm whereas deprivation of wants is only harmful in light of revisable self-interpretation" (p. xiv); and "needs are satiable whereas wants are not" (p. 57). People may queue overnight for a new phone; some may even murder another person for a fancy watch; yet neither consumer object will ever be vital, unlike water or food.[4]

This point may seem trivial, but the fact that, in today's world, there are billions of phones and millions of fancy watches, while scores of human beings do not have access to water or food, should make the reader ponder upon what lies beyond or behind apparent triviality. This is what McMurtry (2009–2010) himself does, as he identifies the fundamental "universal life goods/necessities", i.e. "[a]ll goods *without* which human life capacities are reduced or destroyed." (Glossary) Specifically, McMurtry (2009–2010) lists seven vital goods referring to as many vital needs:

[A]tmosphere (breathable air, open space and light); organism (clean water, nourishing foods, waste disposal); home and habitat (shelter and a life-enhancing environment); care through time (love safety and healthcare); human culture (music, language, art, play and sport); human vocation (meaningful work of value to others); life justice (right to enjoy these life goods and obligation to help provide them). (Glossary)[5]

If these goods are not delivered, then vital needs are not satisfied; and if vital needs are not satisfied, then human capabilities break down, to the eventual point of individual and/or social extinction. If these needs are satisfied, instead, then human capabilities do not simply persist: they can actually blossom into the good life, individual and social. Once more, it is being argued that civilisation revolves around that which makes civil life possible, i.e. the collective creation of civil commons.

Business Practice

Given LVOA's fundamental axioms, business practice can be deemed good or bad depending on whether it comprehensively enables the provision and enjoyment of means of life to the community in which businesses operate, or disables it. Business life can be an instance of civil commons, if and only if it is conducive to comprehensive life-enablement within the community allowing for the existence and operation of businesses, and bearing their effects upon itself. Life-value assessment, i.e. the evaluation of good and bad business practice, is therefore conceptually possible at all levels, such as the likely impact of a nation's business community over the health, happiness and understanding of the population, present and future; or that of a particular company over a specific community that supplies the company with entrepreneurship, labour, customers, investors, and other stakeholders. Triple-bottom-line accounting strategies and similar forms of comprehensive evaluation of business practice are attempts to produce life-value assessments, whether fully aware of their in-built logic of value or not. So are social indicators measuring, say, literacy levels, perceived security or life-expectancy rates aimed at comparing countries, their economies, and determining which ones enjoy more 'wellbeing', 'happiness', or are more 'developed' and 'successful' (e.g. Shackman, 2006–2009).

Also, given the definitions of "civil commons" and "need" discussed above, we can grasp the intended positive function of business regulation at all levels, whether by way of hard law, soft law, voluntary programmes for social and environmental responsibility, good governance, or deontological codes. Regulation, in all or any of these forms, can be a token of civil commons, if and only if it operates as a collective creation steering business activities so that life-enabling goods may be provided through them as widely as possible, whether directly (e.g. to customers and suppliers) or indirectly (e.g. to recipients of tax money provided by fiscally compliant businesses); whilst at the same time countering life-harm, whether direct (e.g. production and sale of toxic pesticide) or indirect (e.g. reduction of life-enabling resources by tax evasion).

LVOA can help the perceptive reader not to take even the standard business aim of profitability at face value, but to discriminate in principle between good and bad forms of profitability. Consider for example the effects that the GDP-engrossing tourist industry of a country can have over the "environmental and ecological crisis" that the scientists have been denouncing for decades at their highest levels of representation (McMurtry, 2009–2010, para. 6).[6] Obvious life-harms such as impoverishment or exhaustion of fresh-water resources and increased pollution of the atmosphere by chemical contaminants can be caused, among other things, by high levels of water consumption in tropical resorts or by increased aerial traffic in popular tourist destinations. These negative additions to the ongoing environmental crisis of our age are not the consequence of any intrinsic wickedness or inattentiveness in the business sector, even if there have been cases of this ilk (e.g. hydro-intensive golf courses operating in arid regions of the planet). Instead, they are the consequence of the inability of operators in the tourism sector, which we use here as an example of businesses at large, to act in accordance with *decisive* life-grounded criteria while pursuing profitability.

Contrary to ordinary platitudes about beneficial spill-overs and trickle-down doctrines, there is no obvious and necessary connection between life-enablement and profitability *qua* defining aim of business life, whether logical or empirical. Awareness of this lack of connection can be found in the preamble of the *Global Code of Ethics for Tourism* issued by the UN World Tourism Organization ([UNWTO]) in 1999. In it, the UNWTO's (1999) experts state that "the world tourism industry as a whole has much to gain by operating in an environment that favors the market economy, private enterprise and free trade" for the sake of "the creation of wealth", which is not life-enabling as such (p. 2). Quite the reverse, in order to give rise to life-enablement, a profitability-driven "tourism industry" must accept "a number of principles and a certain number of rules" restraining its activities (UNWTO, p. 2). Devoid of these exogenous restraints, "responsible and sustainable tourism" would eventually be "*incompatible* with the growing liberalization of the conditions governing trade in services and under whose aegis the enterprises of this sector operate" (UNWTO, p. 2; emphasis added). Devoid of these exogenous restraints, businesses in the tourism sector would dedicate themselves primarily if not exclusively to seeking profit, i.e. making money, not to protecting and assisting life at large. Whilst profitability is their defining aim, protecting and assisting life at large is not. It is only thanks to criteria *external* to strict business rationality "that it is possible to reconcile in this sector economy and ecology, environment and development" (UNWTO, p. 2). Life-enablement is, in short, the pivotal function of enlightened regulation, which is then operating as civil commons.

The clash between standard business practice and what is actually needed for life-enablement lies at the core of LVOA. Gathering and analysing an immense amount of scientific literature, McMurtry's research since the 1980s offers an empirically solid demonstration of the profound difference that exists between "human and planetary life security" and "acquir[ing] ever more money" in ordinary business life

(McMurtry, 2009–2010, para. 5). Whilst their propitious coincidence is often taken for granted, typically *via* the superstitious assumption of a beneficial invisible hand, "human and planetary life security" and "acquir[ing] ever more money" have been increasingly at war with each other:

The air, soil and water cumulatively degrade; the climates and oceans destabilize; species become extinct at a spasm rate across continents; pollution cycles and volumes increase to endanger life-systems at all levels in cascade effects; a rising half of the world is destitute as inequality multiplies; the global food system produces more and more disabling and contaminated junk food without nutritional value; non-contagious diseases multiply to the world's biggest killer with only symptom cures.... the global financial system has ceased to function for productive investment in life-goods; collective-interest agencies of governments and unions are stripped while for-profit state subsidies multiply; police state laws and methods advance while belligerent wars for corporate resources increase... the academy is increasingly reduced to corporate functions; public sectors and services are non-stop defunded and privatized as tax evasion and transnational corporate funding and service by governments rise at the same time at every level. (McMurtry, 2013, p. 6; emphasis removed)

This grim picture of present-day reality may sound hyperbolic to some readers. Yet, a keen search for even one exception to these scientifically backed generalisations would show how rigorous and accurate the grim picture is (cf. IPCC, 2012; UN, 2002–2010; Weston & Bollier, 2013). Without any doubt, McMurtry is a Sartre-esque *intellectuel engagé*, a former newspaper correspondent and educator, and the *de facto* guru of Peter Joseph's (2007–2013) global *Zeitgeist* movement, hence he does not recoil from utilising strong language. Still, the grim picture portrayed above is not much a matter of oratory preference or public posturing: it is a list of casualties in the war between "human and planetary life security" and "acquir[ing] ever more money".

The Cancer Stage of Capitalism

The imagery of warfare occupies one of McMurtry's books, i.e. *Value Wars. The Global Market versus the Life Economy* (2002). However, it is not the imagery of warfare that pervades his most famous text, *The Cancer Stage of Capitalism* (1999, 2013). Therein, we find medical imagery instead. Specifically, the bio-environmental and socio-economic developments of the past decades have been so comprehensively life-disabling, that McMurtry (1995, 1999, 2013) decries them to be nothing short of cancer.

To begin, it should be noted that "the cancer stage of capitalism is not a metaphor", but "an explanatory model" (McMurtry, 2013, pp. 22–23). It is not a sheer image of resemblance. An explanatory model employs thoroughly and with methodical correspondence the carefully selected and described key-features of a cancerous pathology—in this case with reference to economic events. Additionally, McMurtry (1999, 2013) provides corroborating evidence of how his diagnosis is actually underlying or implied by a significant amount of contemporary scientific and scholarly discourses concerning the ongoing international economic crisis, as emblematically flagged by locutions such as "toxic assets", "financial contagions", "pathological *laissez-faire*", "metastasized banking", etc. (cf. Baruchello, 2014). Above all, McMurtry's oncological diagnosis arises from the determination and the assessment of the method of operation of the world's leading economic actors, i.e. national and transnational corporate businesses.

First of all, according to his study, commonplace business notions such as 'money-making', 'profits', 'return on equity', 'quarterly earning reports' and 'shareholder value' reveal the one and essential characteristic or "ruling value syntax" (McMurtry, 2009–2010, para. 1.15.5) guiding most businesses: "[T]he *subject* is money capital whose *verb* is seeking to become more without upper limit, and all *modifiers* are money-demand or its equivalents: with competing money capital subjects and the human and natural resources they purchase, exchange and dispose of always used to become *more* money capital." (McMurtry, 2009–2010: Glossary) As Chicago economist Milton Friedman (1970) eloquently put it: "The one and only responsibility of business is to make as much money for stockholders as possible" (para. 33). Friedman's iconic formulation is most revealing, for no vital needs are mentioned therein, whether past, present or future. Only making money is mentioned. Consistently with this understanding, conventional business practice refers to carcinogenic insecticides, tobacco, fat-laden fast food, pollution quotas, and even armaments as economic 'goods'. They are taken to be goods because they generate profits to businessmen and investors, even if they are bad for life, sometimes on a massive scale. *Qua* economic goods, they are duly counted in the GDP and GNP measurements of standard economics, even if they imperil the ontological preconditions for economic activity itself, i.e. living nature and living people. Such imperilments are actually commonly recognised as foreign to the inherent value-logic of ordinary business, which refers to them as 'externalities', i.e. something that is *not* internal. As McMurtry (2012) writes: "the ruling money-sequence system is in principle life-blind." (para. "Money-Value Versus Life-Value Sequences: Formalizing the Contradiction") Standard business rationality pursues unyielding self-expansion, and yet can make "no distinction between what serves organic, social and ecological life-hosts and what poisons, dismantles and loots them. All that matters is more private money-value and commodities to more" (McMurtry, 2013, p. 188; emphasis removed) In oncology, this is what cancerous cells do: *a theoretically endless process of self-replication within a host body, whose health or eventual survival is not and cannot be perceived by the self-replicating cells as an effective control response.*

The second element in McMurtry's oncological diagnosis is the recognition that the consequences of this theoretically endless self-replication are analogous in practice too. As any medical record can display, *the uncontrolled sprawling of cancerous cells leads eventually to loss of organic capacity*, causing in the end the demise of the cancer's living host. Taking stock of the bio-environmental trends recorded by scientists over decades of alleged and largely a-critical 'economic development', McMurtry (2013) concludes:

As global capitalist exploitation of the environment has advanced and advances across global life-conditions and elements, all of these global life-conditions and elements – the atmosphere, freshwaters and oceans, top soils, trees, animal habitats and species and mineral resources – degenerate in direct proportion in their life-carrying capacities and biodiversity. (p. 169; emphasis removed)

Life-blindness may not signify hostility to life on paper, but it does so in reality, especially if we consider the environmental and human costs of regular business practice's attendant processes of resource extraction (e.g. chemical pollution of underground aquifers), transformation (e.g. chemical pollution of the atmosphere), transportation (e.g. greenhouse emissions), consumption (e.g. worldwide obesity) and disposal (e.g. thyroid-impairing plastic pollution).

The third element in McMurtry's oncological diagnosis relates to the fact that, in cancerous pathologies, *the immune defences of a living organism fail to identify the cancerous cells as harbingers of death and keep facilitating their self-replication.* Analogously, societies' civil commons have been largely ineffective *vis-à-vis* the ongoing attack upon life support systems. Institutions such as national governments, central banks and sovereign parliaments have often neglected or betrayed their function as civil commons, and have actually facilitated the process of life-blind and life-destructive sprawling of money-maximising pursuits by a variety of strategies:

[R]uin of government programmes, workers' jobs and small business with the cranking up of interest rates to over 20 per cent prime in the 1980s and becoming ever more totalized after the fall of the Soviet Union and the repeal of Depression-installed regulations like Glass-Steagall. As the century turned, working-class gains had been reversed by the race to the bottom of wages, benefits and social legislation by global competition with no life-standards. The value of money was holding now not by cannibalist interest rates and debt charges, but by slashing workers' incomes and social programmes across continents. At the deepest level, life and life-support systems were being increasingly sacrificed, shock-treated and looted with plunging costs for transnational money sequences across the world. The deregulated multiplication now metastasised through nations, resources and politicians with ever fewer limits propelled by 'market reforms', trade-treaty edicts prohibiting legislation reducing 'profit opportunities', and wars on resource rich regions with social control... 'getting the fundamentals right' and 'necessary restructuring' for 'the global free market'. (McMurtry, 2013, p. 3).

Life-protective responses have been attempted as well, unquestionably, as the aforementioned *Global Code of Ethics for Tourism* illustrates in the tourism sector. Hard as well as soft regulations and voluntary programmes have been introduced over the years, so as to reduce the negative impact of daily business practice and steer it towards greener, socially responsible and truly life-enabling targets. Business people have themselves contributed with great ingenuity and good will to the ongoing efforts to change the negative trends, as exemplified by intentional schemes such as the United Nations' *Global Compact* and repeated waves of Fair Trade initiatives. Tangible episodes of local progress keep revealing that life-enabling alternatives are possible and desirable. As it happens, they can take place at all levels of standard business practice's attendant processes: extraction (e.g. national and international certifications for responsible extraction of raw materials), transformation (e.g. the cleaner production strategies promoted by the United Nations Environment Programme since 1990), transportation (e.g. Europe's zero-kilometer initiatives), consumption (e.g. growing demand for organic products) and disposal (e.g. the Zero Waste International Alliance).

However, on a global and systemic level, all these moves have been far too little—thus far. The measure of their failure is not hard to grasp, for they have neither arrested nor overturned the planetary life-harms that McMurtry (2013) highlights: chemical pollution of the atmosphere; loss of arable topsoil by desertification; depletion of fresh-water sources, tropical and boreal forests and fish stocks; rapid shrinkage of bio-diversity; increase in the unequal distribution of incomes; pro-active manufacturing, advertising, sale and intake of addictive pathogenic foodstuff; proliferation of non-contagious pathologies; ballooning of private indebtedness levels; reduction of investment in life-enabling public-sector institutions (for corroborating evidence, cf. Cecchetti, Mohanty and Zampolli, 2011; CHRP, 2013; European Commission, 2013; IPCC, 2012; HC 141, 2013; HL 48, 2013; IFS, 2013; ILO, 2013; OECD, 2011, 2013a, 2013b; TFAH, 2011; UN, 2012; WHO, 2011). Unless so-called 'economic development' swings substantially to the opposite pole and effects the regeneration of life-support systems *in lieu* of their degradation, standard business practice at large is *not* sustainable and, insofar as business actors want to be sources of real value rather than disvalue, it still is largely *irresponsible*.

CONCLUSION

The great Hungarian chemist and philosopher Michael Polanyi (1958) claimed that the way in which we think of reality determines the meaningful entities that we can retrieve therein. Thus, if we seek a cure to capitalism's "Great Sickness" (McMurtry, 2013, p. 296), we must first learn to think in a novel way. In this perspective, LVOA offers critical redefinitions of 'human', 'natural', 'knowledge' and 'social capital', as well as of 'globalisation' and 'development', such that each concept may reflect the primary importance of the life-ground. In order to do so, these economic concepts are understood in their ability to accrue to "real capital" or "life capital" i.e. "means of life that can be used to make more means of life without erosion", rather than to standard monetary capital, as expressed for instance in GDP statistics (McMurtry, 2012, para. "Money-Value Versus Life-Value Sequences: Formalizing the Contradiction"). Are non-contagious pathologies, the scourge of today's age, receding? Are the community's members enjoying longer lives? Are they reporting higher levels of perceived wellbeing? Are they reporting higher degrees of economic and employment security? Do they have easier access to healthcare when ill? Are they finding meaningful employment without difficulty, or with less difficulty, than before? Are their children enjoying better care during infancy and their early years of life? Or, as Baruchello and Johnstone (2011) discuss in their application of LVOA to human rights law, are the civil, political, economic, social and cultural rights of the nations' peoples being progressively realised?

Thus understood, real capital is increased if and only if it is positively assessed under three "universal parameters of diagnosis" of the "general determinants of social health and disease":

- Continuity of life-necessities and means to members of society...
- Functioning contribution of citizens to society's life-requirements...
- Sustaining the life-carrying capacities of the environmental life-host (McMurtry, 2013, pp. 62–63).

A tree's quality is assessed by the quality of its fruits. In a successful economy, all members of the community must have their essential needs satisfied by granting all capable members the concrete opportunity to participate in life-enabling economic undertakings, i.e. undertakings that are beneficial, not detrimental, to nature- and man-made life support systems. That way human agency can count as real, that is, life-enabling human capital, the employed natural resources as real natural capital, the shared and expressed knowledge as real knowledge capital, etc. As the increase of real capital in today's global economy is concerned, McMurtry (2013) has four specific recommendations to make:

1. "Progressive taxation" (p. 262),[7]
2. "Publicly owned resources... that can fund life-serving social investment" (p. 268),
3. "Public banking" (p. 286), and
4. "Public policy and secure funding for common life-capital advance" (p. 295).

None of the above recommendations is particularly original, since all of them, when effectively life-grounded, have been used successfully for decades in a variety of countries with remarkable life-enabling effects, e.g. Scandinavia's taxation systems since the 1940s, the effective poverty-reducing partial re-nationalisation of strategic natural assets in Latin America over the 1990s and 2000s, the public bank of North Dakota since the 1920s, Brazil's family-allowance system since 2003 and the internationally binding 1987 Montreal Ozone Protocol (cf. McMurtry, 2013).

All of the above recommendations aims at augmenting real capital, though some reader may at first notice their reliance upon the power of the State. However, McMurtry is not interested in State power *per se*. Nor, for that matter, is he seeking "equality" *qua* paramount aim, albeit he does describe it as "an appealing goal" (McMurtry, 2013, p. 300). The glaring reliance upon the power of the State is merely a practical matter in a World that, as it happens to be today, has seen its civil commons institutions blind or subservient to private money-maximisation for too many years—i.e. the third feature of the oncological diagnosis discussed in the previous section of this chapter. In recent years, for example, much public praise and considerable media attention have been bestowed on Ray Anderson's (1998, 2009) partially successful plan for a 100% sustainable industrial process of resource extraction, transformation and disposal: the green economy at its best. Who, however, or what, if not State power, would be in the position of making a 100% sustainable production system the actual standard at all levels of business activity on our planet? Who or what, if not State power, would be in the position of making the "universal parameters of diagnosis" of the "general determinants of social health and disease" the fundamental guidelines for business practice in all of its ramifications? Perhaps these are not rhetorical questions. Perhaps there are non-State-based solutions that neither McMurtry nor the author of the present chapter can envision. Superstitious belief in self-adjusting private agency is not one of them, though, as noted above. Business as usual will not do either, for the depletion of life support systems has not been halted and reversed. And the problems at issue *are* paramount. From solutions to the "Great Sickness" depends, in fact, the continuation of human existence on Earth.

REFERENCES

Anderson, R. (1998). *Mid-Course Correction: Toward a Sustainable Enterprise: The Interface Model*. White River Junction, VT: Chelsea Green Publishing.

Anderson, R. (2009). *Confessions of a Radical Industrialist: Profits, People, Purpose. Doing Business by Respecting the Earth*. New York: St. Martin's Press.

Anielski, M. (2007). *The Economics of Happiness. Building Genuine Wealth*. New Society Press.

Assiter, A., & Noonan, J. (2007). Human needs. A realist perspective. *Journal of Critical Realism*, *6*(2), 173–198. doi:10.1558/jocr.v6i2.173

Ato, S. (2006). Deferring to difference, cultivating the civil commons, honouring humanity: What's the left-universalist to do? *Humanitas*, *4*, 1–12.

Baruchello, G. (2001). Review essay of the book *The Cancer Stage of Capitalism*, by J. McMurtry. *Revue Canadienne d'Etudes du Developpement*, *22*(1), 255–269. doi:10.1080/02255189.2001.9668809

Baruchello, G. (2007). Western philosophy and the life-ground. In Encyclopedia of Life Support Systems. Paris: Eolss. Retrieved from http://www.eolss.net

Baruchello, G. (2011). Your money or your life. John McMurtry and Martha Nussbaum on the for-profit assault upon life-capabilities. *Journal of Philosophy of Life*, *1*(1), 13–48.

Baruchello, G. (2014). The presupposed oncological model of Paul Krugman's banking metastases. An introduction to John McMurtry's philosophy. *Annuaire international des droits de l'homme, 7*, 347–352.

Baruchello, G. (in press). Good versus bad tourism. *Homo viator*'s responsibility in light of life-value onto-axiology. In E. Hujibens & M. Gren (Eds.), *Tourism in the Anthropocene*. London: Routledge.

Baruchello, G., & Johnstone, R. L. (2011). Rights and value. Construing the International Covenant on Economic, Social and Cultural Rights as Civil Commons. *Studies in Social Justice*, *5*(1), 91–126.

Burch, M. A. (2012). *Educating for Simple Living*. Simplicity Institute Report.

Castoriadis, C. (2003). Psychoanalysis and society I. In *The Rising Tide of Insignificancy (The Big Sleep)*. Available from http://www.notbored.org (Original work published 1982)

Cecchetti, S. G., Mohanty, M. S., & Zampolli, F. (2011). *The real effects of debt* (BIS working papers, no. 352). Retrieved from http://www.bis.org/publ/work352.htm

Davidson-Harden, A. (2013). What is social sciences and humanities research 'worth'? Neoliberalism and the framing of social sciences and humanities work in Canada. *Policy Futures in Education*, *11*(4), 387–400. doi:10.2304/pfie.2013.11.4.387

Dickinson, T., Becerra, T. A., & Lewis, S. (Eds.). (2009). *Democracy Works. Joining Theory and Action to Foster Global Change*. Herndon: Paradigm Publishers.

Doyal, O. L., & Gough, I. (1991). *A Theory of Human Need*. London: MacMillan. doi:10.1007/978-1-349-21500-3

English, L. M., & Mayo, P. (2012). Environmental adult education. In *Learning with Adults. A Critical Pedagogical Introduction* (pp. 189–196). Rotterdam: Sense.

Finlay, L. M. (2000). All the world's a stooge? Globalization as aesthetic system. *Topia: A Canadian Journal of Cultural Studies, 4*, 39–51.

Florby, G., Shackleton, M., & Suhonen, K. (2009). Introduction to Canada: Images of a post/national society. *Canadian Studies*, *19*, 1–22.

Friedman, M. (1970, September 13). The social responsibility of business is to increase its profits. *The New York Times Magazine*. Retrieved from http://www.umich.edu/~thecore/doc/Friedman.pdf

Giacomini, T., & Turner, T. (2015). The 2014 people's climate march and flood Wall Street civil disobedience: Making the transition to a post-fossil capitalist, commoning civilization. *Capitalism, Nature, Socialism*, *26*(2), 27–45. doi:10.1080/10455752.2014.1002804

Hardin, G. (1968). The tragedy of the commons. *Science*, *162*(3859), 1243–1248. doi:10.1126/science.162.3859.1243 PMID:5699198

Hodgson, B. J. (2001). Can the beast be tamed? Reflections on John McMurtry's Unequal Freedoms: The global market as an ethical system. *Journal of Business Ethics*, *33*(1), 71–78. doi:10.1023/A:1011972421036

House of Commons' Environment, Food and Rural Affairs Committee. (2013). *Food Contamination, Vol. 1* (Fifth report of session 2013–2014, incorporating HC 1035-i-ii, session 2012-2013). London: The Stationery Office.

House of Lords' Select Committee on Economic Affairs. (2013). *Tackling Corporate Tax Avoidance in a Global Economy: Is a New Approach Needed?* (First Report of Session 2013–2014). London: The Stationery Office.

Institute for Fiscal Studies. (2013). *Food expenditure and nutritional quality over the Great Recession* (IFS Briefing Note BN143). Retrieved from http://www.ifs.org.uk/bns/bn143.pdf

Intergovernmental Panel on Climate Change. (2012). *Managing the risks of extreme events and disasters to advance climate change adaptation.* Retrieved from http://www.ipcc-wg2.gov/SREX/

International Covenant on Economic, Social and Cultural Rights. (1966). *International Covenant on Economic, Social and Cultural Rights* (Adopted 16 Dec. 1966, G.A. Res. 2200A, U.N. GAOR, 21st Sess., Supp. No. 16, at 49, U.N. Doc. A/6316 (1966). Entered into force Jan. 3, 1976). Retrieved from http://www2.ohchr.org/english/law/cescr.htm

International Labour Organization. (2013). *Public sector shock: The impact of policy retrenchment in Europe*. Geneva: ILO.

Johnston, J. (2003). Who cares about the commons? *Capitalism, Nature, Socialism, 14*(4), 1–41. doi:10.1080/10455750308565544

Johnston, J., Gismondi, M., & Goodman, J. (Eds.). (2006). *Nature's revenge: Reclaiming sustainability in an age of corporate globalization.* Toronto: Garamond Press.

Jordan, B. (2004). Growth to freedom or support to life? *Res Publica (Liverpool, England), 10*(2), 193–205. doi:10.1023/B:RESP.0000034573.80533.e5

Joseph, P. (2007–2013). *The Zeitgeist Film Series. Official website for Peter Joseph's award winning documentary trilogy.* Available from http://www.zeitgeistmovie.com/

Kaara, W. (2005). *Statement for a religious leaders' consultation on global poverty.* Retrieved from http://www.nationalcathedral.org/pdfs/050911/WahuKaara_Stmt.pdf

Laertius, D. (1853). *The Lives and Opinions of Eminent Philosophers.* (C.D. Yonge, Trans.). London: Henry G. Bohn. Retrieved from http://www.classicpersuasion.org/pw/diogenes/dlpyrrho.htm (Original work published 3rd century AD)

Lynch, D. H., Sumner, J., & Martin, R. C. (2014). Goods and services derived from organic agriculture in the Canadian context. In S. Bellon & S. Penvern (Eds.), *Organic Farming, Prototype for Sustainable Agriculture* (pp. 347–364). Dordrecht: Springer.

McMurtry, J. (1995). The social immune system and the cancer stage of capitalis. *Social Justice (San Francisco, Calif.), 22*(4), 1–25.

McMurtry, J. (1998). *Unequal Freedoms: The global market as an ethical system.* Toronto: Garamond Press.

McMurtry, J. (1999). *The Cancer Stage of Capitalism.* London: Pluto Press.

McMurtry, J. (2002). *Value Wars. The Global Market versus the Life Economy.* London: Pluto Press.

McMurtry, J. (2012). Behind global system collapse: The life-blind structure of economic rationality. *Journal of Business Ethics*, *108*(1), 49–60. doi:10.1007/s10551-011-1086-4

McMurtry, J. (2013). *The Cancer Stage of Capitalism: From Crisis to Cure*. London: Pluto Press.

McMurtry, J. (2009–2010). What is good? What is bad? The value of all values across time, place and theories. In Encyclopedia of Life Support Systems. Paris: Eolss. Retrieved from http://www.eolss.net

Mishori, D. (2010). Conceptualizing the commons: Reflections on the rhetoric of environmental rights and public ownership. In O. F. von Feigenblatt (Ed.), *Development and Conflict in the 21st Century* (pp. 104–127). Bangkok: JAPSS Press.

Mook, L., & Sumner, J. (2008). *Knowing what counts: Social accounting for sustainability* (Presentation to the Association of Co-operative Educators (ACE) conference, Ottawa, July 30, 2008). Retrieved from http://www.ace.coop/portals/0/institute/08/ACE_LaurieMook_SEC_July30_08.pdf

Newson, J., Polster, C., & Woodhouse, H. (2012). Toward an alternative future for Canada's corporatized universities. *English Studies in Canada*, *38*(1), 51–70. doi:10.1353/esc.2012.0004

Noonan, J. (2006). *Democratic Society and Human Needs*. Montreal: McGill-Quenn's University Press.

Nussbaum, M. C., & Sen, A. (Eds.). (1993). *The Quality of Life*. Oxford, UK: Clarendon Press. doi:10.1093/0198287976.001.0001

OECD. (2013a). *Addressing Base Erosion and Profit Shifting*. Retrieved from http://www.oecd-ilibrary.org/taxation/addressing-base-erosion-and-profit-shifting_9789264192744-en

OECD. (2013b). *Crisis squeezes income and puts pressure on inequality and poverty*. Retrieved from http://www.oecd.org/els/soc/OECD2013-Inequality-and-Poverty-8p.pdf

Organisation for Economic Cooperation and Development. (2011). *Divided We Stand: Why Inequality Keeps Rising*. Retrieved from http://www.oecd-ilibrary.org/social-issues-migration-health/the-causes-of-growing-inequalities-in-oecd-countries_9789264119536-en

Peekhaus, W. (2013). *Resistance is Fertile: Canadian Struggles on the BioCommons*. Vancouver: UBC Press.

Piketty, T. (2013). *Capital in the Twenty-First Century*. Cambridge, MA: Harvard University Press.

Polanyi, M. (1958). *Personal Knowledge: Towards a Post-critical Philosophy*. London: Kegan Paul.

Rorty, R. (2004). Philosophy as a transitional genre. In R. J. Bernstein, S. Benhabib, & N. Fraser (Eds.), *Pragmatism, Critique, Judgment: Essays for Richard J. Bernstein* (pp. 3–28). Cambridge, MA: MIT Press.

Scarfe, A. (2006). Global interdependence, process, and environmental *praxis*. *Revue-E-Journal*, *1*(1). Retrieved from http://www.ustpaul.ca/Philosophy/revue/articles/2006_scarfe.html

Shackman, G. (2006–2009). *Understanding the world today* (Website of the Global Social Change Research Project). Retrieved from http://gsociology.icaap.org/

Shurville, S., & Brown, H. (2009). *Developing collaborative competence in the librarians of the future* (Presentation delivered at the 2009 ALIA conference, Sydney, Australia). Retrieved from http://conferences.alia.org.au/online2009/docs/PresentationC19.ppt

Streeck, W. (2009). Four books on capitalism. *Socio-economic Review*, *7*(4), 741–754. doi:10.1093/ser/mwp019

Susilowati, S. (2014). Learning science oriented pedagogy for sustainability to build the concern for the environment. In H. Sutrisno, W.S. Brams Dwandaru, K. Prihantoso Krisnawan, D. Darmawan, E. Priyambodo, E. Yulianti, & S. Nurohman (Eds.), *International Conference on Research, Implementation and Education of Mathematics and Sciences (ICRIEMS) 2014. Conference Proceedings*. Retrieved from http://eprints.uny.ac.id/11431/

Suvin, D. (2012). Death into life: For a poetics of anti-capitalist alternative. *Socialism and Democracy*, *26*(2), 91–106. doi:10.1080/08854300.2012.686294

Trust for America's Health. (2011). *F as in Fat. How Obesity Threatens America's Future*. Retrieved from http://healthyamericans.org/reports/obesity2011/Obesity2011Report.pdf

Turner, T., & Brownhill, L. (2004). Why women are at war with Chevron: Nigerian subsistence struggles against the international oil industry. *Journal of Asian and African Studies*, *39*(1–2), 63–93. doi:10.1177/0021909604048251

UN (2012). *Political Declaration of the High-level Meeting of the General Assembly on the Prevention and Control of Non-communicable Diseases* (Adopted 24 Jan. 2012, G.A. Res. 66/2, U.N. GAOR, 66th Sess., Agenda item 117, U.N. Doc. A/RES/66/2 (2012)).

UN. (2002–2010). *Encyclopedia of life support systems*. Paris: Eolss. Available from http://www.eolss.net

Uzelman, S. (2011). Media commons and the sad decline of Vancouver Indymedia. *Communication Review*, *14*(4), 279–299. doi:10.1080/10714421.2011.624011

Westhues, K. (1999). *If the market is not god, what is?*. Retrieved from http://arts.uwaterloo.ca/~kwesthue/mcmurtry.htm

Weston, B., & Bollier, D. (2013). *Green Governance: Ecological Survival, Human Rights, and the Law of the Commons*. Cambridge, UK: Cambridge University Press.

Woodhouse, H. (2011). Your money or your life! A critical Canadian perspective on the World Bank's 'Reform Agenda' for higher education. *International Education, 40*(2), 6–21 & 92.

World Health Organization. (2011). *Noncommunicable Diseases. Country Profiles 2011*. Retrieved from www.who.int/nmh/publications/ncd_profiles_report.pdf

World Tourism Organization. (1999). *Global Code of Ethics for Tourism* (UN ref. no. A/RES/406(XIII) & A/RES/56/212). Retrieved from http://www.unwto.org/ethics/full_text/en/pdf/Codigo_Etico_Ing.pdf

ENDNOTES

1 As stated, McMurtry's theory is here introduced, articulated and applied, not subjected to critical analysis, which is something that the present author has pursued elsewhere, e.g. Baruchello (2001).

2 The present chapter is not an empirical exercise in measuring responsibility and sustainability of business practice according to a given quantitative standard, but to provide, in typical philosophical manner, an articulate rational explanation of the fundamental axiological principles presupposed by and involved in any such exercise.

3 Almost ten years later, Weston & Bollier (2013) developed a conception of "commons" that is practically identical to McMurtry's, though no reference is made therein to his work. On the one hand, such a grotesque repetition shows how compartmentalised academia can be. On the other hand, it reveals how urgent and necessary for human survival is the understanding of societies' collective creations as civil commons, especially in light of the ongoing environmental degradation of our planet's life support systems.

4 LVOA entails the universal and objective life-ground to discriminate amongst different usages of the word "need" and provide a rational foundation of genuine needs beneath and beyond cultural and individual differences, which is where the standard 'descriptive' accounts of needs by most social scientists confine themselves (e.g. Doyal & Goug, 1991).

5 McMurtry's index of vital goods contributes to the ongoing development of standards for the measurement of human wellbeing, as pursued by, e.g., Nussbaum & Sen (1993; cf. Baruchello, 2011 for a mutual comparison and analysis).

6 The case of tourism in light of LVOA is discussed in Baruchello (in press), where McMurtry's axiology is similarly introduced, articulated and applied.

7 McMurtry (2013) targets in particular the very rich not out of class-based spite or Jacobin egalitarianism, but because unrestrained income polarisation is self-fulfilling and multiplies cancerous money-sequences (cf. Piketty, 2013).

Chapter 8
Sustainable Business Model Innovation:
Using Polycentric and Creative Climate Change Governance

Job Taminiau
University of Delaware, USA

Ariella Shez Lewis
University of Delaware, USA

Joseph Nyangon
University of Delaware, USA

John Byrne
University of Delaware, USA

ABSTRACT

Establishing a sustainable energy future can justifiably be considered the next frontier in global sustainable development under the agenda laid out in the Sustainable Development Goals (SDGs). The newly adopted Paris Agreement which seeks to hold global average temperature increase to "well below 2°C" above pre-industrial levels inserts additional urgency into this agenda. To realize the commitments outlined in the agreement, implementation of innovative sustainable business models capable of producing strong mitigation and adaptation outcomes is required 'on the ground' and needs to be available for subsequent diffusion across different countries, contexts and domains. This chapter explores the value of polycentric climate change governance through an investigation of sustainable business model innovation. An example of a sustainable business model, called the Sustainable Energy Utility (SEU), is evaluated and an assessment of United Nations-based programming to aid future diffusion of such business models is conducted.

INTRODUCTION

The intergovernmental Millennium Development Goals (MDGs) effort, chartered in 2000 around eight aspirational targets for the world to achieve by 2015, has been able to realize impressive results (Galatsidas & Sheehy, 2015). Following the 2015 conclusion of the MDGs, the United Nations introduced a new and more comprehensive set of 17 aspirational goals for sustainable development. Formulated under the rubric of the Sustainable Development Goals (SDGs),[1] this effort builds on the lessons learned from the

DOI: 10.4018/978-1-5225-1823-5.ch008

MDGs and lays out targets for 2030. An important development with the new set of goals is the ambition to "ensure access to affordable, reliable, sustainable and modern energy for all". The inclusion of sustainable energy is significant as access to clean sources of energy is vital to overcome both development and climate change challenges (Kaygusuz, 2011). Indeed, establishing a sustainable energy future can justifiably be considered the next frontier in global sustainable development.

The 15-year agenda laid out in the SDGs is ambitious and will, among others, rely on a globally determined endeavor to mitigate currently ongoing global environmental change processes, particularly climate change. The recently articulated desire to hold global average temperature increase to "well below" 2°C (3.6°F) above pre-industrial levels and to "pursue efforts" to limit temperature rise to 1.5°C (2.7°F) above pre-industrial levels in the newly adopted 'Paris Agreement' inserts additional urgency into the agenda (FCCC/CP/2015/L.9). The challenge, as such, is to not only identify pragmatic, innovative, and disruptive practices but to also aid their diffusion around the world in a timely manner. The "structurally weak" and entirely voluntary Paris Agreement (Grubb, 2015), however, did not establish a strong global architecture capable of forcing such identification and diffusion as some dreamed it would earlier in the negotiations.

Therefore, to realize – and, perhaps, exceed – the commitments outlined in the Paris Agreement, innovative implementation of sustainable business models capable of producing strong mitigation and adaptation outcomes will need to take place 'on the ground' and be subsequently shared on a global platform for adoption in other contexts (Taminiau & Byrne, 2015). A strategic reconsideration is in order and, throughout this chapter, we highlight the need for ecological governance and explore the value of collective creativity. The chapter sets out the following objectives:

- Describe a proposed re-configuration of global environmental change response strategies that prioritize polycentric collective creativity over collective action (Section 2.0);
- Highlight the need for sustainable business model innovation as a key component of a polycentric collective creativity strategy (Section 3.0);
- Offer an example of a sustainable business model that could change the energy consumption paradigm (one of the key sectors contributing to climate change) (Section 4.0); and
- Assess how United Nations-based programs can be positioned to facilitate the development and diffusion of sustainable business practices in order to contribute to the UN's objectives of peace, development, *and* global sustainability as outlined in the SDGs (Section 5.0).[2]

POLYCENTRIC GOVERNANCE AS A STRATEGY TO ADDRESS GLOBAL ENVIRONMENTAL CHANGE

Guided by the success of battling ozone depletion, the theory of 'collective action' has long been positioned as the key response option to global environmental change. Essentially, the rationale is simple: local environmental complications required local solutions and, therefore, global environmental challenges require global strategies. For instance, the effort to address the issue of climate change – what can justifiably be called the most challenging environmental problem modern society has encountered – has consistently revolved around 'collective action' and has frequently been designated "inescapably global" (Depledge & Yamin, 2011).

Now more than two decades old, the global effort to address climate change through the United Nations Framework Convention on Climate Change (UNFCCC) has reached a point where the rationale of collective action has been drawn into question. Repeated shocks to the process, most notably the failure to craft the much-hoped for agreement at 'Copenhagen'[3] in 2009, has shaken the belief that a collective agreement along the configuration pursued throughout the negotiations is still feasible. In short, the climate change discourse has been a struggle (Jordan, et al., 2015).

The climate change narrative is emblematic for the state of global sustainability in our day and age. For instance, the UN Convention on Biological Diversity (CBD) failed to reach its 2010 target of 'a significant reduction of the current rate of biodiversity loss at the global, regional, and local level' and is contemplating how to move forward (Mace, et al., 2010; Secretariat of the Convention on Biological Diversity, 2010). The international community's commitment to repair the deteriorating conditions of the world's oceans (Cicin-Sain, Balgos, Appiott, Wowk, & Hamon, 2011) and coral reefs (Chin et al., 2011; Miller & Spoolman, 2012) has similarly been unable to halt degradation. Indeed, continued comprehensive assessment of the sustainability state of the world highlights that, despite substantial progress in some fields, remarkably little progress has been realized even with the deployment of significant political resources (Intergovernmental Panel on Climate Change, 2014; Worldwatch Institute, 2015). Moreover, reframing global sustainability as a 'nested' concept of environment, development, and economic progress – rather than the traditional and separate 'pillars' of sustainable development – makes clear that continued inability to substantially alleviate these environmental pressures will continue to undo progress in other areas (Griggs, et al., 2013).

Indeed, the latest evidence of 'planetary boundaries', 'tipping points', and non-linear positive feedbacks, mandates careful reconsideration of international environmental regimes, institutional governance, and regime compatibility with global sustainability trajectories (Steffen, et al., 2015). Ecological response to human-induced change is nonlinear, uncertain, and unpredictable (e.g., Schuur, et al., 2015). [4] While this "super wicked" [5] nature of global environmental challenges militates against one-shot, large-scale, top-down response frameworks (Levin, Cashore, Bernstein, & Auld, 2012), the 'collective action' thought process seeks problem resolution precisily in such forums (Hare, Stockwell, Flachsland, & Oberthur, 2011).[6]

Impatience with the "painfully slow" process (Neslen, 2015) of establishing effective, top-down regimes, [7] has prompted the research community to ask "must we wait for global agreement?" (e.g., Ostrom, 2010b; Hoffmann, 2011). Such social inquiry has produced an alternative model relying instead on 'adaptive' or 'polycentric' governance (Ostrom, 2010a; Galaz, Crona, Österblom, & Folke, 2012; Ostrom, 2014). [8] The emerging governance model can be considered 'ecological', seeking to enhance institutional 'fit' with the complexity of Earth's social-ecological systems (Ostrom, 2014).

The non-linear, uncertain, and unpredictable character of environmental degradation could thus be answered with a dynamic, non-linear, and experimental strategy organized through 'polycentric' networks of creative innovation and leadership (Taminiau, 2015; Taminiau & Byrne, 2015). Indeed, siginificant levels of sub-national and local experimentation can be observed and one of the better known examples is the promulgation of city strategies (e.g., Broto & Bulkeley, 2013). [9] Succesful implementation of such city strategies could yield substantial benefits: a recent report, for instance, put the global economic opportunity for low-carbon urban actions at $16.6 trillion over 2015-2050 (New Climate Economy, 2015).

While the international community achieved global consensus regarding climate change in the form of the recently adopted Paris Agreement, the agreement itself continues to allow for such polycentric governance as the new strategy moving forward due to its structural weaknesses and nationally determined climate change commitments. Indeed, the proposed nationally determined contributions are estimated to be insufficient to realize the international commitment (Climate Action Tracker, 2015) and successfully responding to the scale of the challenge will require more transformative innovation and change (Burch, Shaw, Dale, & Robinson, 2014, pp. 472-473). A potential pathway forward is the active identification of 'creative leadership' and to assist their further diffusion in order to scale up the response (Taminiau & Byrne, 2015). Here, the widespread diversity of polycentricity, while positioned as one of its key strengths together with iterative learning and experimentation, offers the challenge of navigating a 'chaotic' landscape of innovations and leadership examples. Innovations that stand out, due to for instance their capacity to normalize sustainability in business practices or to attract sufficient investment, need to be identified, deconstructed to their core innovative characteristics, and appropriately reconstructed in different contexts around the world keeping in mind local cultures, mind-sets, enabling capacity, and so forth.

As such, we contend that a process capable of identifying pragmatic and leading solutions is required that can subsequently deconstruct such examples of leadership into critical building blocks that can be introduced and adapted to new contexts. In effect, the evolutionary process of polycentric governance, revolving around adaptation to new circumstances and iterative problem-solving, requires the equivalent of a 'natural selection' process that can uncover the 'genetic material' of the innovation and contribute to its diffusion and further evolution. This line of argument aligns with the 'ecological' model of collective creativity as explained by, for instance, Staber (2011, p. 32): "Ecologies evolve in a process of change that populations of units undergo. In biology these units are genes, whereas in the social realm the units may be rules, skills, organizations, or any other entity that is internally cohesive and externally isolated to be able to participate in the evolutionary process". While various proposals exist for the appropriate unit for such 'social selection', Staber positions the 'idea' as a key unit for selection: "For an idea to serve as an ecological unit all that is required is that it is identifiable by the person working with the idea and that it *can* be passed on to other people. Whether it *will* be passed on depends on people's cognitive capacity and the cultural and social environment in which the idea exists" (Staber, 2011, p. 33).

Sustainable Business Model Innovation as the 'Genetic Material' for 'Social Selection'

Trillions of dollars will be injected into the economic system over the coming decades to sustain, rebuild, repair, and expand every aspect of society from the built environment, to the energy grid, to roads and highways, etc. (Dobbs, et al., 2013; Jacobsson & Jacobsson, 2012). Indeed, scaling-up (green) infrastructure investment is a key priority of developed and developing countries alike (see, e.g., Asian Development Bank, 2009; OECD, 2014). This realization positions the further development and diffusion of sustainable business models as a critical component in the polycentric approach. In turn, sustainability is an important consideration in business and investment success (e.g., Mercer, 2011). Indeed, an appropriate response to the global environmental challenge requires a fundamental re-direct of investment flows, to be implemented under sustainable business models (e.g., Jackson, 2009). For instance, several of the sustainable economy features as identified by Jackson (2009) highlight the extent of the required reconsideration of the business model:

- A sustainable economy encourages the minimization of consumption or, at least, establishes firm limitations on personal and institutional consumption of water, energy, etc.;

- A sustainable economy seeks to maximize societal *and* environmental benefit, prioritizing the accomplishment of these goals over the maximization of economic growth; and
- A sustainable economy emphasizes the delivery of function, service, and experience. This is in sharp contrast to the current focus on product ownership.

Positioning the business model as the 'genetic material', business model innovation offers options for radical change through the active reconceptualization of the purpose of the business and its value proposition. Redesign of the current business model to one of a sustainable business model could allow for integration of sustainability into the core modus operandi of the business (Stubbs & Cocklin, 2008). In particular, the *energy* infrastructure investment 'gap' is not only significant in size (e.g., Fulton & Capalino, 2014)[10] but can also, when investments take place along existing decision-making criteria that neglect sustainability, 'lock-in' the currently unsustainable trajectory (e.g., Erickson & Lazarus, 2015). As a major contributor to global environmental change, the energy sector is at the front of the challenge and ongoing discussions on energy business model evolution highlight the need to investigate sustainable business practices that allow for deviation from business-as-usual (e.g., Richter, 2012; Behrangrad, 2015).[11]

A Case Study Example of a Sustainable Business Model: The Sustainable Energy Utility (SEU)

In the U.S., the business model of the currently dominant conventional energy utility, the investor-owned utility (IOU), evolved throughout the 20th century on precepts of centralization, abundance, growth, technology, and supply (Sovacool, 2011). This evolutionary pathway was firmly supported by the 'regulatory compact' (Burr, 2007) which effectively established a 'co-dependent relationship' between the IOU and the regulator (Brooks, 2015). However, energy sustainability, operationalized through decentralization, renewable energy, and energy efficiency, conflicts with the established business model (e.g., Hess, 2015) and has spurred a lively debate regarding 'utility of the future' or 'utility 2.0' concepts (e.g., Nadel & Herndon, 2014). Regulators have developed a portfolio of responses that seek to incentivize or push the conventional utility into action. This 'carrot' and 'stick' approach has left some wondering whether entirely new business models might be more effective in scaling the sustainable energy challenge (Fox-Penner, 2010; Goldman, Satchwell, Cappers, & Hoffman, 2013).

The options for new business models can be categorized in a variety of ways. Structuring utility business models along variables of profit achievement and profit motivation, Satchwell & Cappers (2015) show that proposed regulatory repairs are not likely to bring about a fundamental reorientation of the 'utility': profit achievement largely remains commodity-based and profit motivation continues to focus on asset (e.g., ratepayer base) expansion. A similar line of thinking is offered by Richter (2012) as he identifies two basic options: utility-side and customer-side business models. While utility-side blueprints already exist, customer-side business models are emerging and are considered valuable innovation options (Richter, 2012).

The Sustainable Energy Utility (SEU) has been put forth as a model capable of moving beyond the drawing board as it offers fundamental reorientation of sustainable energy business practices (e.g., Byrne & Taminiau, 2015).[12] The next sections outline an analytical approach to the business model as a unit of 'genetic material' using Hamel's (2000) framework (Section 4.1) and apply this framework to the SEU business model (Section 4.2).

The Business Model as an Analytical Tool

The business model provides a valuable unit for analysis (Magretta, 2002) and can be applied as an analytic tool to deconstruct options for sustainable business practice innovation and subsequent diffusion (Loock, 2012; Pätäri & Sinkkonen, 2014; Richter, 2012). Indeed, core elements of business model constructs can assist in the identification of the promise of the innovation and can spur its diffusion. In terms of the energy sustainability challenge, the business model has been positioned as an analytical tool for, among others, analyzing the Energy Service Company (ESCO) sector (Pätäri & Sinkkonen, 2014), investor preference (Loock, 2012), renewable energy (Okkonen & Suhonen, 2010), micro-generation (Provance, Donnelly, & Carayannis, 2011), energy utility evolution (Richter, 2012), distributed generation (Funkhouser, Blackburn, Magee, & Rai, 2015), and energy efficiency programming (Behrangrad, 2015).

Defining 'business model', however, is complex, can be approached from many directions and has introduced confusing and overlapping terminology (Chesbrough & Rosenbloom, 2002; Pätäri & Sinkkonen, 2014, p. 266). Commonly positioned terms are value proposition, target market, value chain, revenue generation mechanisms, customer interface, value network or infrastructure, and competitive strategy (Chesbrough & Rosenbloom, 2002; Chesbrough H., 2007; Kindström, 2010; Richter, 2012). Here, we follow Pätäri & Sinkkonen's (2014) approach, relying on Hamel's (2000) comprehensive business model framework to evaluate energy sector innovation and extract core units for selection, the aforementioned 'genes' if you will, that could inform business practices around the globe.

Hamel's framework for business model analysis consists of four 'major' components (Hamel, 2000, pp. 70-113).[13] The 'core strategy' (major component 1) outlines the business' competitive decisions and is comprised of a business mission (objective of the strategy), product/market scope (field in which the business is active in terms of customers, geographies, and product segments), and a basis for differentiation (i.e. what is different compared to competitors?). Within 'customer interface' (major component 2), fulfillment and support relate to market access, information and insight cover knowledge exchange with customers, relationship dynamics describe the relationship between the business and the customers, and the pricing structure outines how customers are charged to the services. 'Strategic resources' (major component 3) refers to the competitive advantage available to the business, where core competences (business-based knowledge, skills, and capabilities), strategic assets (business-owned assets), and core processes that transform both core competences and strategic assets into customer value. The 'value network' (major component 4) represents the suppliers, partners, and coalitions that strengthen the operation of the business.

Case Study: The Sustainable Energy Utility (SEU)

The SEU originated in a set of research papers by the Center for Energy & Environmental Policy (CEEP, University of Delaware) (Byrne & McDowell, 2007; Byrne, Martinez, & Ruggero, 2009). The SEU is a community-based model of development constructed around energy conservation and community-scale renewables and has the aim to permanently lower the use of source materials, water, and energy in an effort to address concerns about climate change, rising energy prices, inequity of energy availability, and a lack of community governance of energy development (Byrne, Martinez, & Ruggero, 2009). The SEU was first implemented in the United States by the State of Delaware and the District of Columbia (Washington, DC). New versions of the model are being implemented by the Commonwealth of Pennsylvania and Sonoma County in California. International application of the model is being investigated by the City of Seoul (South Korea) [14] and the City of Thane (India) (Gopal, 2013).

Deconstructing old business models and re-constructing a new model is a critical step in transformative innovation (Hamel, 2000, pp. 69-70). In the next sub-sections, we decompose the SEU business model in order to illustrate its strategy. Critically, while the SEU shares business model innovation parameters with other innovations like the Energy Service Company (ESCO) model, the SEU model re-envisions every aspect of utility configuration. This is in line with Hamel's contention that "what is not different is not strategic" and, as such, "it is *entirely* about variety – not just in one or two areas, but in all components of the business model" (Hamel, 2000, pp. 69, emphasis in original).

Core Strategy: Return on Environment

The *business mission*, i.e. the overall objective of the SEU strategy, is the dual goal of reducing human-induced environmental pressure and improving social well-being. The importance of this fundamental goal of *satisficing* should not be understated: the essence of the SEU strategy is to redefine what is efficient. For instance, in contrast, the investor-owned utility business mission, by fiduciary responsibility, is to maximize shareholder value which is often achieved through the increase of sales. Effectively, the SEU strategy, rather than emphasizing the maximization of outputs with the same level of inputs, emphasizes the minimization of inputs for a high quality level of outputs (Byrne & Taminiau, 2015).[15] In terms of Hamel's "from" and "to", therefore, the SEU mission is to establish a business model that departs from the current high-throughput society and pursues a low-throughput world, with associated environmental improvement.

The market scope of the SEU strategy expands beyond the traditional utility perspective as the SEU strategy offers a "total solution" that *matches* performance to customer needs (in contrast to building demand by offering more). In addition, the core strategy of the SEU model differentiates itself strongly from conventional utility products as it establishes a practical and creative capitalization strategy for the *negawatt-hour*[16] as opposed to the kilowatt-hour. The dimension of differentiation, therefore, is that the SEU strategy considers "the use value of a product, instead of its exchange value, as the source of its added value, therefore selling function-based services instead of products" (Steinberger, van Niel, & Bourg, 2009, p. 368). A key component of this capitalization strategy is converting the thoroughly accepted 'energy efficiency gap' – i.e. the combined notion that not using energy is much cheaper than using energy and that the very large potential for energy use reductions is not being exploited (Gillingham & Palmer, 2014) – into an accessible value for its customers.

Strategic Resources and Opportunities: Community Utility

Hamel describes core competencies as skills and capabilities that are a) unique, b) valuable to customers, and c) transferable to new opportunities (Hamel, 2000, p. 75). The key core competency of the SEU strategy is the skill, knowledge, and capability to creatively unlock the vast energy efficiency potential that exists in a high-throughput society (Dobbs, et al., 2013; Gillingham & Palmer, 2014). The puzzle of navigating the legal, financial, and policy labyrinth to unlock existing potential for energy savings is solved, in part, by pledging monetary savings from intervention measures towards initial and high up-front investment costs (Byrne & Taminiau, 2015). A second key component of the puzzle is to raise sufficient levels of capital investment to pay for the intervention measures in the first place. The SEU strategy addresses this critical barrier – lack of sufficient capital is abundantly cited as a major obstacle to investment – by pooling together the pledged monetary savings from program participants and selling this resource on the capital markets to raise capital (Byrne & Taminiau, 2015).

As such, the community represented by the SEU is the key strategic asset available to the SEU model. In what has been described as a 'community utility' function (Byrne & Taminiau, 2015), the SEU relies on the value inherent in the community it serves, i.e. the 'commonwealth' of the community, and positions it strategically to address pressing problems (Byrne, Martinez, & Ruggero, 2009). Finally, in terms of core processes, the SEU puts in place a range of contractual engagements that raise investor confidence, *guarantee* energy and monetary savings, pre-qualify local and national ESCOs, standardize and facilitate pooled financing, and arrange detailed monitoring and verification that serves a diagnostic function. [17]

Customer Interface: Empowering Sustainable Citizens

Like other performance-based models, the SEU strategy repositions its primary target audience from *consumer* to *customer*. However, the SEU strategy expands on this configuration as it empowers customers to become *sustainable citizens*. Here, too, the difference is paradigmatic: shifting from a producer-consumer relationship to, first, a service provider-customer relationship and, second, a relationship geared towards the empowerment of customers in their pursuit of sustainability is dependent on long-term relationships built on mutual trust.[18] Sustainable citizens are provided with the capability of reducing their energy use – and, thus, environmental damage – in an absolute sense.

The SEU model fulfills and supports the transformation of consumer to sustainable citizen as it, as a community utility, positions itself as an independent representative of the community, pools community members together to gain strength in numbers (and thus a more viable financing position), processes and qualifies the companies that are to implement the energy saving measures (i.e. the ESCOs), and ensures monitoring and verification of savings and disciplines ESCOs if performance falls short of guarantees to the point where any shortfall by contract needs to be compensated. Sustainable citizens are empowered by the 'one-stop-shop' model of the SEU, delivering energy, materials, and water savings, risk reduction, and managing, for instance, solar renewable energy credit (SREC) market interaction between individual customers generating solar energy through their photovoltaic installations and the conventional energy utilities that are under public mandate to procure SRECs (for more information, see Byrne & Taminiau, 2015). In terms of pricing structure, as mentioned, energy use for sustainable citizens becomes directly tied to required services (e.g., hot water, cooling, lighting, etc.) rather than product-based interaction (i.e. selling of kilowatt-hours). Moreover, customers reap benefits in terms of energy price stabilization, after-contract (i.e. when debt is paid off) savings, and additional savings beyond the guarantee (which is estimated to be up to two times promised savings (Shonder, 2013; Larsen, Stuart, Goldman, & Gilligan, 2014)).

Value Network: Capital Market Access

Hamel sees the value network as the asset that "complements and amplifies the [business model's] own resources" (Hamel, 2000, p. 88). The key value network component of the SEU strategy is its access to the capital markets through the combined deployment of its customer interface, core strategy and strategic resources. The pioneering use of the SEU's capitalization strategy in Delaware was able to attract a $72.5 million investment that significantly amplified the SEU's capability to provide its customers with energy saving intervention measures. The pooled potential for energy saving that resides in the energy budgets of SEU customers, combined with risk reduction strategies such as guaranteed saving contracts, offers an attractive investment opportunity to investors as evidenced not only by the strong investor interest in the bond offering but also in the Standard & Poor's AA+ rating of the bond. In addition, early evidence with other models supports the hypothesis that "customer intimacy" business models like the SEU, as opposed to lowest price or best technology models, are better positioned to attract investment (Loock, 2012). By tapping into the vast pool of the capital market – the bond market is estimated at $100 trillion in outstanding debt which is significantly larger than the estimated $63 trillion equity market) (Climate Bonds Initiative, 2015) and, in 2015, so-called 'climate bonds' and 'green bonds' markets issued $41.8 billion (Climate Bonds Initiative, 2015) – the SEU is able to scale-up its offering of energy savings to infrastructure-scale change.

Overview of the SEU Business Model

Using a slightly adapted version of Hamel's framework, the customer interface, core strategy, strategic resources, and value network of the SEU business model can be outlined and factors tying the various components together can be identified (Figure 1). The relationships between the various components outline key contributions of the SEU model. First, energy price *volatility* is stabilized through long-term contracts and turned into the key 'negawatt' value proposition. Next, using a redefinition of efficiency, the model prioritizes absolute energy use reductions. Infrastructure-scale change is realized by pooled financing on the capital market. Finally, a reality of "Social Change 2.0" (Byrne & Taminiau, 2015) is established as private capital is directed towards the fulfillment of human needs rather than the maximization of consumption.

Figure 1. SEU business model along adapted version of Hamel's deconstruction

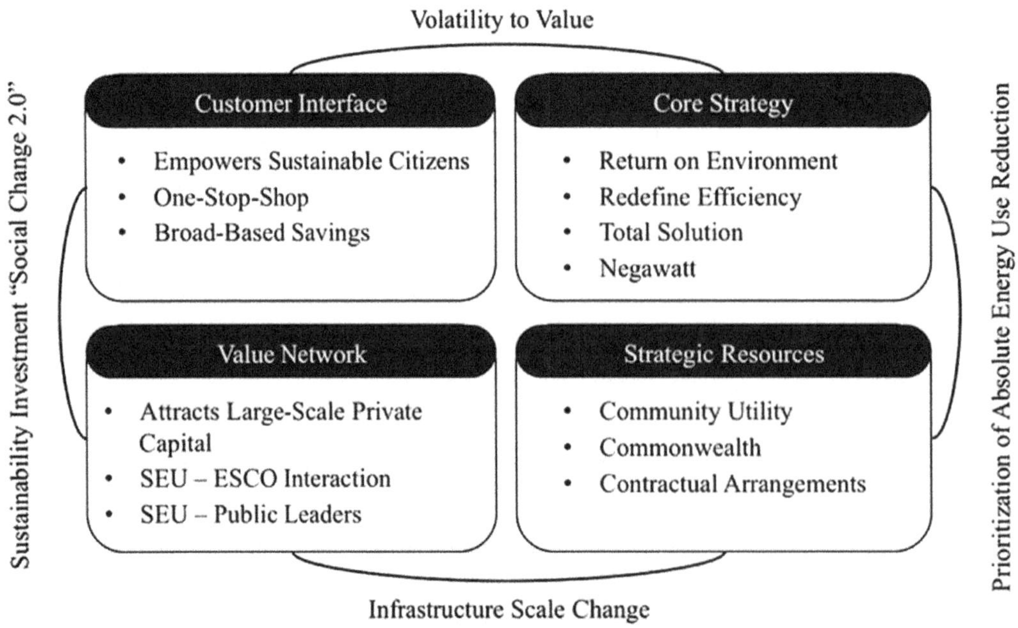

Figure 2. Overview of the SEU model and its contribution to the various archetypes (Bocken et al., 2014)

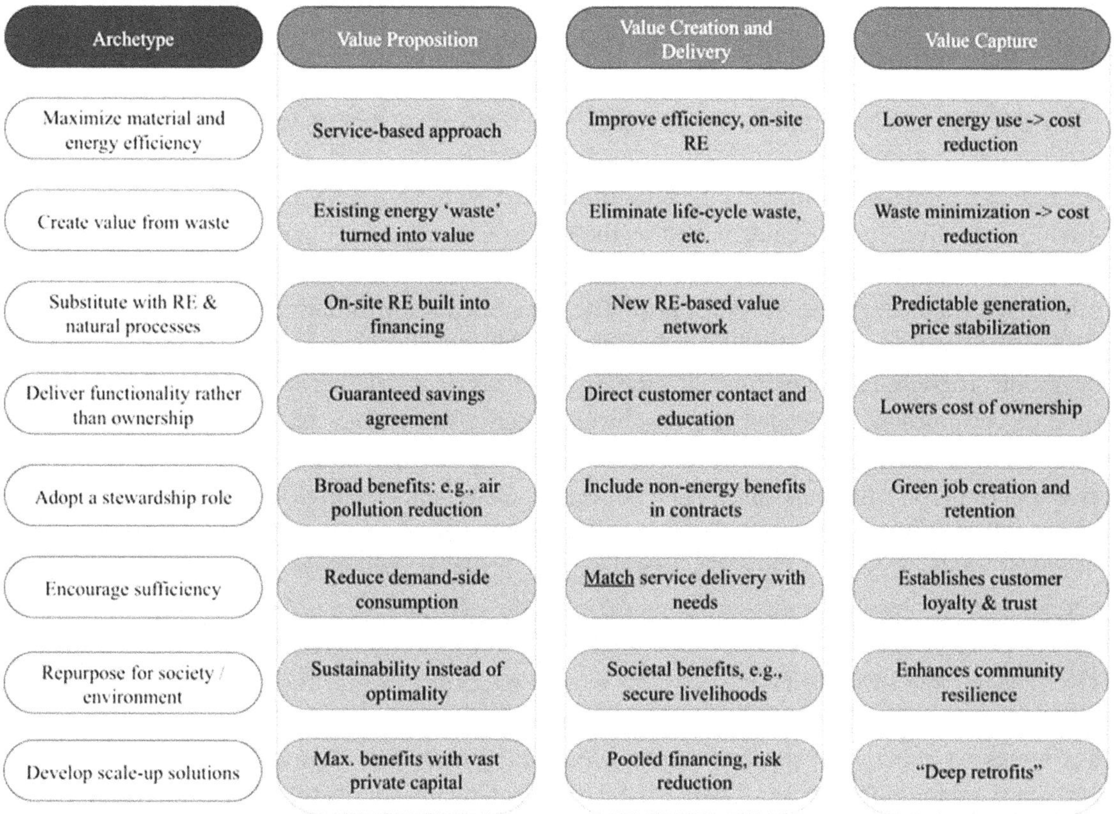

Another way to look at the SEU as a whole is to consider Bocken et al.'s (2014) concept of the sustainable business model 'archetype'. Figure 2 outlines how the SEU model relates to Bocken's (2014) eight 'archetypes':

1. To maximize material and energy efficiency,
2. To create value from waste,
3. To substitute energy use with renewable and natural processes,
4. To deliver functionality rather than ownership,
5. To adopt a stewardship role,
6. To encourage sufficiency,
7. To repurpose the business for society/environment, and
8. To develop solutions that can reach the appropriate scale.

Diffusion of Sustainable Business Model Innovations: The UN Compact

The reconfiguration of 'collective action' to 'collective creativity' and 'creative leadership' along the lines described above could benefit from another powerful modern reality. This reality is captured in Friedman's (2005) "The World is Flat", describing the changing conditions of society through globalization and establishing the reality of the 'global village' where "the world went from being small to tiny." While the process of globalization has contributed to the exportation of many negative effluents of modern society across the world, the 'global village' offers a platform for global, real-time communication and knowledge exchange that can facilitate the diffusion of selected innovations and examples of creative leadership. Importantly, international issue networks – such as various UN programs – have been constructed specifically on the notion of a 'global community' and could, as such, represent a possible candidate for retooling towards the aforementioned 'natural selection' function.

Various initiatives have been deployed by the UN to foster and facilitate sustainable business practices. For instance, the UN Green Economy Initiative assists national transitions to green economies by providing analytical and advisory support. The Green Economy Initiative joined forces with the UN South-South Cooperation program to better assist developing countries. At the core of the South-South Cooperation program is collaboration: developing countries work together on political, economic, social, cultural, environmental and technical issues by exchanging knowledge, skills, expertise and resources. The South-South Cooperation program seeks to foster developing country self-reliance by enhancing creativity and solution-finding capacity and collective self-reliance through the exchange of experiences and the pooling of technical and other resources. An important element within both these initiatives is the recognition that substantial benefits accompany a shift to a green economy in particular for proactive companies that lead their respective industries in the transition to a green economy (UNEP, 2012).

The UN Global Compact was launched in 2000 together with the MDGs and represents an attempt by UN agencies and several NGOs to directly engage the private sector (both companies and business associations) in partnerships through voluntary corporate social responsibility. The initiative was created in a context of heightened perceived gaps in global governance and a period defined by changing UN-business relations (Rasche and Kell 2010). The UN Global Compact has been well received by the business community and the private sector has responded with initiatives such as the World Business Council on Sustainable Development (WBCSD). Overall, the UN Compact's goal is to establish stable, inclusive, and sustainable markets. To reach this goal, the Compact has introduced ten principles for sustainable business practices, clustered into categories of environment, human rights, labor standards, and anti-corruption. Under these Principles for Responsible Investment (PRI), launched in April 2006, promising social, environmental, and technical innovations are nurtured and connected to broad institutional resources and responses. The PRI program is backed by the United Nations Environment Program Finance Initiative (UNEP FI) and the UN Compact.

UN Global Compact as 'Social Selection' Function for Success Story Diffusion

Relationships between the United Nations, its specialized agencies and private sector organizations is multilevel, multi-purpose and multi-issue, making it difficult to advance partnerships in the governance, design, delivery and resourcing of a particular program or cooperative initiative. The described UN initiatives – the UN Compact, the Green Economy Initiative, and the South-South Cooperation—seek to address this weakness by promoting a diversity of partnerships with the private and public sectors to deliver sustainable products and services, facilitate foreign investment, encourage sustainable and responsible business practices, and assist private sector development.

As an aspirational principle-based initiative, the UN Compact helps to establish legitimacy of the corporate responsibility agenda worldwide. As of November 10, 2015, signatories of the UN Global Compact stands at 13,235 (both companies and non-business signatories) based in 170 countries, representing nearly every industry sector and size, with equal representation from developed and developing countries. As the world's largest corporate sustainability initiative, the UN Global Compact has had noticeable, incremental impact on governments, civil society, companies, and the UN, building a strong base for continued collaboration and partnerships (Rasche and Waddock, 2014). Major and well-respected NGOs have backed it in different ways, for instance by participating in relevant working groups, by engaging in local networks, and by initiating partnerships with businesses and UN agencies (Grajew, 2010; Whelan, 2010). The Compact has developed a solid participant base for engagement.

However, while the UN Global Compact has realized incremental growth of signatories, participant numbers alone are an insufficient proxy measure for impact (Sethi & Schepers, 2014). Real transformational change "is only achieved if qualitative and quantitative growth is balanced – i.e. if more participants engage in the initiative, learn from others, and improve their performance" (Rasche & Waddock, 2014, p. 213). Business practices continue to be characterized by an overwhelming dominance of financial interests over societal and ecological priorities and ad-hoc damage control responses. Some groups have highlighted an emerging promise-performance gap: the program is a "mile wide and half an inch deep: long on promises, short on performance, and mostly silent on transparency and objective reporting" (Sethi & Schepers, 2014, p. 207).

Rasche & Waddock (2014) reject some of the strong criticism leveled against the UN Global Compact by Sethi & Schepers (2014) and position the aspirational and learning-based character of the Compact as a key element of its strategy. This open learning platform nature of the Compact could be advanced by allowing corporations to detail their *transformative* innovations on a "place where issues and ideas that are difficult for companies to deal with independently can be discussed, debated, and incorporated voluntarily" (Rasche & Waddock, 2014, p. 214). This dynamic character of the UN Global Compact offers a potential fit with the polycentric governance strategy discussed in Section 2.0 and the need to accelerate sustainable business model innovation and diffusion. Improving the Compact's capacity to motivate transformational change along financial, environmental, social, and ethical dimensions will require, at least, efforts in six inter-related issues: a) increasing effective participant engagement, b) empowering local networks, c) managing coherence of the global portfolio, d) building more uniformly engaged responsible business practices in support of UN goals, e) strengthening governance frameworks and accountability, and f) developing sustainable funding mechanisms (UNGC, 2015).

We offer that the deconstruction of business model functioning, like was done in this chapter for the SEU, could become a function of a UN-based program like the Global Compact. Such an open learning platform suitably fits with the characterization of polycentricity as an arena in which a multitude of actors and strategies co-exist in the form of a 'biodiverse' ecosystem: "the creative process evolves best in ecological systems that are open and heterogeneous and thus provide new opportunities for change" (Staber, 2011, p. 32). The UN-based Global Compact could leverage its strong and global network of participants and use its heterogeneous and open platform for the diffusion of sustainable business models. Efforts in this direction, particularly when considering cross-border interactions, would be well pressed to incorporate the lessons learned from earlier successes of knowledge and technology transfer, [19] including but not limited to:

- Complex and novel innovations are more difficult to transfer but are typically associated with a higher degree of knowledge assimilation in the host country;
- Developing country experience and institutional contexts (i.e. 'enabling environment') require capacity-building strategies that expand beyond the innovation itself;

- South-North (as opposed to North to South) and South-South opportunities should not be neglected as growth in innovation capability, particularly in China and India but also elsewhere, represents increasingly more attractive cooperation options (Tawny, Miller, & Bazilian, 2015);
- Deconstructed elements of innovations along the lines proposed above should be reconstructed in a contextually-appropriate manner where pro-poor policy approaches are prioritized over 'hard' (i.e. hardware-centric) technology transfer; and
- Certain sectoral applications – like energy efficiency innovations – appear better positioned to include knowledge and technology transfer.

Finally, to avoid the sense of UN endorsement of certain business practices over others network members fulfil the function of both innovative business model identification (through self-reporting their innovation into the platform) and business model 'social' selection by marking innovations as potentially useful for their context. Follow-up steps could include that the UN Global Compact brings together idea originators and interested parties to explore the diffusion of the model in different contexts.

CONCLUSION

Upon ratification, the Paris Agreement will become a new cornerstone of global climate change governance. Its voluntary and nationally determined character – unlike previous iterations and attempts at global climate governance which relied on stronger, top-down architectures – continues to facilitate the further development of nascent transnational, national, and sub-national networks and partnerships as a complementary and creative strategy. It appears likely that this polycentric paradigm will be the main pathway with which global climate change will be navigated (Taminiau & Byrne, 2015; Jordan, et al., 2015). The sustainable development conundrum is compounded by the urgency and scale of today's global environmental change processes. The strategy will therefore have substantial consequences for the prospects of fulfilling the SDG set of targets.

This book chapter maintains that a reliance on collective creativity, innovation, and leadership could help communities scale these challenges. A possible advancement of such a strategy is the development of a platform with strong local networks to allow global diffusion. The UN-based Global Compact is a possible candidate for such a function as it can leverage its over 13,000 signatories based in 170 countries to diffuse new, transformative ideas.

REFERENCES

Asian Development Bank. (2009). *Infrastructure for a seamless Asia*. Tokyo, Japan: Asian Development Bank and Asian Development Bank Institute.

Behrangrad, M. (2015). A review of demand side management business models in the electricity market. *Renewable & Sustainable Energy Reviews*, *47*, 270–283. doi:10.1016/j.rser.2015.03.033

Berry, D., & Ormond, A. (2015). An Unstable State: Conflict and Institutional Change in the Electric Industry. *The Electricity Journal*, *28*(2), 63–73. doi:10.1016/j.tej.2015.01.010

Bocken, N., Short, S., Rana, P., & Evans, S. (2014). A literature and practice review to develop sustainable business model archetypes. *Journal of Cleaner Production*, *65*, 42–56. doi:10.1016/j.jclepro.2013.11.039

Brooks, C. (2015). The periodic table of the electric utility landscape: A series of visual tools for enhanced policy analysis. *The Electricity Journal*, *28*(6), 82–95. doi:10.1016/j.tej.2015.06.009

Broto, V., & Bulkeley, H. (2013). A survey of urban climate change experiments in 100 cities. *Global Environmental Change*, *23*(1), 92–102. doi:10.1016/j.gloenvcha.2012.07.005 PMID:23805029

Burch, S., Shaw, A., Dale, A., & Robinson, J. (2014). Triggering transformative change: A development path approach to climate change response in communities. *Climate Policy*, *14*(4), 467–487. doi:10.1080/14693062.2014.876342

Burr, M. (2007). Razing the regulatory compact. *Public Utilities Fortnightly*, *145*(9), 18–20.

Byrne, J., Martinez, C., & Ruggero, C. (2009). Relocating Energy in the Social Commons: Ideas for a Sustainable Energy Utility. *Bulletin of Science, Technology & Society*, *2*(2), 81–94. doi:10.1177/0270467609332315

Byrne, J., & McDowell, H. (2007). *The Sustainable Energy Utility: A Delaware First*. Sustainable Energy Utility Task Force.

Byrne, J., & Taminiau, J. (2015). A review of sustainable energy utility and energy service utility concepts and applications: realizing ecological and social sustainability with a community utility. *WIREs Energy Environ*.

Chesbrough, C., & Rosenbloom, R. (2002). The role of the business model in capturing value from innovation: Evidence from Xerox corporation's technology spin-off companies. *Industrial and Corporate Change*, *11*(3), 529–555. doi:10.1093/icc/11.3.529

Chesbrough, H. (2007). Business model innovation: it's not just about technology anymore. *Strategic Leadership*, 12-17.

Cicin-Sain, B., Balgos, M., Appiott, J., Wowk, K., & Hamon, G. (2011). *Oceans at Rio+20: How well are we doing in meeting the commitments from the 1992 Earth Summit and the 2002 World Summit on Sustainable Development? Summary for decision-makers*. Global Ocean Forum.

Climate Action Tracker. (2015, November 19). *Tracking INDCs*. Retrieved April 28, 2015 from Climate Action Tracker: http://climateactiontracker.org/indcs.html

Climate Bonds Initiative. (2015). *Bonds and climate change: state of the market in 2015*. Climate Bonds Initiative.

Climate Bonds Initiative. (2015). *Year 2015 green bonds final report*. Climate Bonds Initiative.

Depledge, J., & Yamin, F. (2011). The Global Climate-change Regime: A Defence. In D. Helm & C. Hepburn (Eds.), *The Economics and Politics of Climate Change* (pp. 433–453). Oxford, UK: Oxford University Press.

Dobbs, R., Pohl, H., Lin, D.-Y., Mischke, J., Garemo, N., & Hexter, J. (2013). *Infrastructure productivity: how to save $1 trillion a year*. McKinsey Global Institute.

Erickson, P., & Lazarus, M. (2015). Global emissions: New oil investments boost carbon lock-in. *Nature*, *526*(7571), 43. doi:10.1038/526043c PMID:26432237

Fox-Penner, P. (2010). *Smart Power: climate change, the smart grid, and the future of electric utilities*. Island Press.

Fulton, M., & Capalino, R. (2014). Investing in the clean trillion: Closing the clean energy investment gap. *Ceres*.

Funkhouser, E., Blackburn, G., Magee, C., & Rai, V. (2015). Business model innovations for deploying distributed generation: The emerging landscape of community solar in the U.S. *Energy Research & Social Science*, 90–101.

Galatsidas, A., & Sheehy, F. (2015, July 6). *What have the millennium development goals achieved?* Retrieved from http://www.theguardian.com/global-development/datablog/2015/jul/06/what-millennium-development-goals-achieved-mdgs

Galaz, V., Crona, B., Österblom, P. O., & Folke, C. (2012). Polycentric systems and interacting planetary boundaries - emerging governance of climate change - ocean acidification - marine biodiversity. *Ecological Economics*, *81*, 21–32. doi:10.1016/j.ecolecon.2011.11.012

Gandenberger, C., Bodenheimer, M., Schleich, J., Orzanna, R., & Macht, L. (2015). Factors driving international technology transfer: Empirical insights from a CDM project survey. *Climate Policy*, 1–20. doi:10.1080/14693062.2015.1069176

Gillingham, K., & Palmer, K. (2014). Bridging the energy efficiency gap: Policy insights from economic theory and empirical evidence. *Review of Environmental Economics and Policy*, *8*(1), 18–38. doi:10.1093/reep/ret021

Goldman, C., Satchwell, A., Cappers, P., & Hoffman, I. (2013). *Utility business models in a low load growth/high DG future: gazing in the crystall ball? Committee on Regional Electric Power Corporation (CREPC)/State-Provincial Steering Committee*. Boise, ID: SPSC.

Gopal, S. (2013). Urban renewabilization in India through public-public partnerships: a feasibility study of applying the "sustainable energy utility" model to the city of Thane. Newark, DE: Center for Energy & Environmental Policy (CEEP), University of Delaware.

Griggs, D., Stafford-Smith, M., Gaffney, O., Rockström, J., Öhman, M., Shyamsundar, P., & Noble, I. et al. (2013). Policy: Sustainable development goals for people and planet. *Nature*, *495*(7441), 305–307. doi:10.1038/495305a PMID:23518546

Grubb, M. (2015). From Lima to Paris, Part 1: The Lima Hangover. *Climate Policy*, *15*(3), 299–301. doi:10.1080/14693062.2015.1029767

Hamel, G. (2000). *Leading the revolution*. Boston, MA: Harvard Business School Press.

Hare, W., Stockwell, C., Flachsland, C., & Oberthur, S. (2011). The architecture of the global climate regime: A top-down perspective. *Climate Policy*, *10*(6), 600–614. doi:10.3763/cpol.2010.0161

Hess, D. (2015). *The politics of niche-regime conflicts: distributed solar energy in the United States.* Environmental Innovation and Societal Transitions.

Hoffmann, M. (2011). *Climate governance at the crossroads - experimenting with a global response after Kyoto*. Oxford, UK: Oxford University Press. doi:10.1093/acprof:oso/9780195390087.001.0001

Intergovernmental Panel on Climate Change. (2014). Climate Change 2014: Impacts, Adaptation, and Vulnerability. Part A: Global and Sectoral Aspects. In Contribution of Working Group II to the Fifth Assessment Report of the Intergovernmental Panel on Climate Change. Cambridge, UK: Cambridge University Press.

Jackson, T. (2009). *Prosperity without growth: economics for a finite planet*. London, UK: Earthscan.

Jacobsson, R., & Jacobsson, S. (2012). The emerging funding gap for the European energy sector - will the financial sector deliver? *Environmental Innovation and Societal Transitions*, *5*, 49–59. doi:10.1016/j.eist.2012.10.002

Jordan, A., Huitema, D., Hilden, M., van Asselt, H., Rayner, T., Schoenefeld, J., et al. (2015). Emergence of polycentric climate governance and its future prospects. *Nature Climate Change*, 977-982.

Kaygusuz, K. (2011). Energy for sustainable development: A case of developing countries. *Renewable & Sustainable Energy Reviews*, 1116–1126.

Kindström, D. (2010). Towards a service-based business model: Key aspects for future competitive advantage. *European Management Journal*, *28*(6), 479–490. doi:10.1016/j.emj.2010.07.002

Larsen, P., Stuart, E., Goldman, C., & Gilligan, D. (2014). Current policies and practices related to the incorporation of non-energy benefits in energy saving performance contracts. Washington, DC: American Council for an Energy-Efficient Economy (ACEEE) Summer Study on Energy Efficiency in Buildings.

Levin, K., Cashore, B., Bernstein, S., & Auld, G. (2007). Playing it Forward: path dependency, progressive incrementalism, and the "Super WIcked" problem of global climate change.*International Studies Association Convention*.

Levin, K., Cashore, B., Bernstein, S., & Auld, G. (2012). Overcoming the tragedy of super wicked problems: Constraining our future selves to ameliorate global climate change. *Policy Sciences*, *45*(2), 123–152. doi:10.1007/s11077-012-9151-0

Loock, M. (2012). Going beyond best technology and lowest price: On renewable energy investors' preference for service-driven business models. *Energy Policy*, *40*, 21–27. doi:10.1016/j.enpol.2010.06.059

Lovins, A., & Lovins, H. (1982). *Brittle Power: Energy Strategy for National Security*. Andover, MA: Brick House Publishing Co., Inc.

Mace, G., Cramer, W., Diaz, S., Faith, D., Larigauderie, A., Le Prestre, P., & Mooney, H. A. et al. (2010). Biodiversity targets after 2010. *Current Opininion in Environmental Sustainability*, *2*(1-2), 3–8. doi:10.1016/j.cosust.2010.03.003

Magretta, J. (2002). Why business models matter. *Harvard Business Review*, 86–92. PMID:12024761

Mercer. (2011). *Climate change scenarios - implications for strategic asset allocation*. Mercer.

Nadel, S., & Herndon, G. (2014). The future of the utility industry and the role of energy efficiency. Washington, DC: American Council for an Energy Efficient Economy (ACEEE).

Neslen, A. (2015, August 20). *EU calls for urgency in 'seriously lagging' Paris climate talks*. Retrieved from http://www.theguardian.com/environment/2015/aug/20/paris-climate-talks-seriously-lagging-eu-calls-urgency

New Climate Economy. (2015). *Seizing the global opportunity: partnerships for better growth and a better climate*. Washington, DC: New Climate Economy.

OECD. (2014a). *Private financing and government support to promote long-term investments in infrastructure*. Paris: OECD Publishing.

Okkonen, L., & Suhonen, N. (2010). Business models of heat entrepreneurship in Finland. *Energy Policy*, *38*(7), 3443–3452. doi:10.1016/j.enpol.2010.02.018

Ostrom, E. (2010a). Beyond markets and states: Polycentric governance of complex economic systems. *The American Economic Review*, *100*(3), 641–672. doi:10.1257/aer.100.3.641

Ostrom, E. (2010b). Nested externalities and polycentric institutions: Must we wait for global solutions to climate change before taking actions at other scales? *Economic Theory*, *49*(2), 353–369. doi:10.1007/s00199-010-0558-6

Ostrom, E. (2014). A polycentric approach for coping with climate change. *Annals of Economics and Finance*, *15*(1), 97–134.

Pätäri, S., & Sinkkonen, K. (2014). Energy service companies and energy performance contracting: Is there a need to renew the business model? *Journal of Cleaner Production*, *66*(1), 264–271. doi:10.1016/j.jclepro.2013.10.017

Provance, M., Donnelly, R., & Carayannis, E. (2011). Institutional influences on business model choice by new ventures in the microgenerated energy industry. *Energy Policy*, *39*(9), 5630–5637. doi:10.1016/j.enpol.2011.04.031

Rasche, A., & Waddock, S. (2014). Global Sustainability Governance and the UN Global Compact: A Rejoinder to Critics. *Journal of Business Ethics*, *122*(2), 209–216. doi:10.1007/s10551-014-2216-6

Richter, M. (2012). Utilities' business models for renewable energy: A review. *Renewable & Sustainable Energy Reviews*, *16*(5), 2483–2493. doi:10.1016/j.rser.2012.01.072

Satchwell, A., & Cappers, P. (2015). A framework for organizing electric utility regulatory and business models. *The Electricity Journal*, *28*(8), 119–129. doi:10.1016/j.tej.2015.09.009

Schuur, E., McGuire, A., Schadel, C., Grosse, G., Harden, J., Hayes, D., & Vonk, J. E. et al. (2015). Climate change and the permafrost carbon feedback. *Nature*, *520*(7546), 171–179. doi:10.1038/nature14338 PMID:25855454

Secretariat of the Convention on Biological Diversity. (2010). Global Biodiversity Outlook 3. Montreal: Author.

Sethi, S., & Schepers, D. (2014). United Nations Global Compact: The Promise-Performance Gap. *Journal of Business Ethics*, *122*(2), 193–208. doi:10.1007/s10551-013-1629-y

Shonder, J. (2013). *Beyond guaranteed savings: Additional cost savings associated with ESPC projects*. Oak Ridge, TN: Oak Ridge National Laboratory. doi:10.2172/1086643

Sovacool, B. (2011). National energy governance in the United States. *Journal of World Energy Law and Business*, *4*(2), 97–123. doi:10.1093/jwelb/jwr005

Staber, U. (2011). The Ecological Foundations of Creativity. In F. Belussi & U. Staber (Eds.), *Managing Networks of Creativity* (pp. 30–45). New York: Routledge.

Steffen, W., Richardson, K., Rockstrom, J., Cornell, S., Fetzer, I., Bennett, E., & Sorlin, S. et al. (2015). Planetary boundaries: Guding human development on a changing planet. *Science*, *347*(6223), 1259855. doi:10.1126/science.1259855 PMID:25592418

Steinberger, J., van Niel, J., & Bourg, D. (2009). Profiting from negawatts: Reducing absolute consumption and emissions through a performance-based energy economy. *Energy Policy*, *37*(1), 361–370. doi:10.1016/j.enpol.2008.08.030

Stubbs, W., & Cocklin, C. (2008). Conceptualizing a "sustainability business model". *Organization & Environment*, *21*(2), 103–127. doi:10.1177/1086026608318042

Taminiau, J. (2015). *A paradigm analysis of ecological sustainability*. Newark, DE: University of Delaware.

Tawny, L., Miller, M., & Bazilian, C. (2015). Innovation for sustainable energy from a pro-poor perspective. *Climate Policy*, *15*(1), 146–162. doi:10.1080/14693062.2013.781456

UNEP. (2012). *The Business Case for the Green Economy: Sustainable Return on Investment*. United Nations Environment Programme.

Worldwatch Institute. (2015). *State of the World 2015: Confronting hidden threats to sustainability*. Washington, DC: Island Press.

ENDNOTES

1 The set of targets has the official title of "Transforming our World: the 2030 Agenda for Sustainable Development".

2 Arguably, the United Nations successes on overall development and peace-keeping have outpaced its capacity to attain global sustainability. It is of vital importance that similar efforts are invested in global sustainability.

3 The supreme decision-making body of the UNFCCC, called the Conference of the Parties (COP), is often referred to by the location in which the annual negotiations were held. Most recently, the 21st installment of the COP (also called COP-21) was held in Paris in December 2015. 'Copenhagen' (2009) was the 15th negotiation since the COP forum started.

4 Schuur et al. (2015) presents the dynamic relationship between climate change and organic carbon stored in the Arctic and sub-Arctic regions' permafrost; aspects of the subsequent feedback loop remain 'poorly understood.'

5 The term "super wicked" was introduced by Levin et al to introduce a new category of global environmental problems. Key features of a "super wicked" problem are: 1) the problem is urgent and requires responsive problem-solving; 2) everyone contributes to the problem of climate change and everyone is affected, but with different levels of contribution and consequences; 3) there is no central authority to address the problem or, if there is, the central authority is inept; and 4) the future is discounted beyond what the economic tool of the discount rate suggests is considered rational, delaying action. The 'super wicked' concept expands on the previously introduced 'wicked' policy problem that was characterized by: 1) the problem is symptomatic of deeper problems; 2) the problem presents unique opportunities for action that can't be easily reversed; 3) there is no clear set of alternative solutions; 4) the problem presents contradictory certitudes; 5) the problem contains redistributive implications for entrenched interests; and 6) the problem is persistent and insoluble.

6 Hare et al (2011) contends that the 'collective action problem' is contingent on 'global coordination' and the establishment of an effective system to support global coordination.

7 Major other concerns have also plagued the negotiations. For example, concerns have revolved around: a) the sustainability performance of negotiation outcomes (such as the 'Kyoto Protocol'), b) the capability to meet justice demands such as removing the existential threat to the poor and c) to ensure that those responsible for the problem of global environmental change are the ones to lead the effort. In particular, the retreat by the United States from the negotiations in the early 2000s has plagued the negotiations for the better part of the last decade.

8 The polycentric model has been developed in the 1960s but has only recently been applied to address global environmental change, particularly climate change (Ostrom, 2014).

9 While Broto & Bulkeley (2013) analyzed the rising trend of 'urban climate change experimentation' as an approach to climate governance, it is important to recognize that experimentation is occurring at all levels of government and across national and even continental borders (see, e.g., Galaz, Crona, Österblom, & Folke, 2012).

10 Fulton and Capalino (2014) discusses the gap in 'global investment in clean energy.' The report presented strategies to have the annual investment in this sector increase to the $1 trillion goal, thereby eliminating the current gap.

11 Richter (2012) argues that as renewable energy continues to be adopted, utilities must reappraise their current business model and make advantageous adjustments. To support this energy transition, Richter analyses two generic business models: utility-side business models and customer-side business models. He acknowledges the advent of customer-side business models. Similarly, Behrangrad (2015) considers the demand-side business model. Behrangrad analyzes the relationship between the demand side management ('modifications in the demand side energy consumption pattern to foster better efficiency and operations in electrical energy systems') business model and, segments of a business-as-usual electricity market.

12 The SEU model was developed through a 2007 task force study spearheaded by Dr. John Byrne (Center for Energy and Environmental Policy, University of Delaware, USA) and Delaware Senator Harris McDowell III.

13 The framework also includes three 'bridge' components and four 'factors' that are only limitedly described in this chapter in Section 4.4.5.

14 See, for instance, the archives of the 2013 Seoul International Energy Conference at: http://env.seoul.go.kr/archives/34476 (Korean source).

15 This is a simplistic explanation of a deeper discussion concerning the theoretical underpinning of 'optimality' versus 'sustainability'. For a recent publication on the optimality versus sustainability discussion, see Byrne & Taminiau (2015).

16 This is a term coined by Amory Lovins to describe the unit of energy that is not used (Lovins & Lovins, 1982).

17 For more information on the contractual arrangements of the SEU model, please see the Foundation for Renewable Energy & Environment (FREE) policy brief series, which covers the SEU model but also other topics, at http://freefutures.org/policybriefs/.

18 Trust is a critical component of the arrangement: innovations that have insufficiently established relationships on mutual trust encounter difficulty in moments of uncertainty based on, for instance, information asymmetry (Berry & Ormond, 2015). For instance, Berry & Ormond (2015) note that: "Politicization of the conflicts inherent in innovation, cost recovery, and customer options is detrimental to a long- run, open process to advance consumer and societal welfare" (p. 69).

19 For an in-depth review and empirical analysis of this topic, see for instance Gandenberger et al. (2015) or Tawny et al. (2015). Knowledge and technology transfer experiences indicate that, when thoughtfully applied, ideas and technology can be successfully disseminated across borders and sectors. For example, Gandenberger et al. (2015), analyzing the experience with the climate change mitigation-focused Clean Development Mechanism, find that about two-thirds of the evaluated projects indicated a medium to very high level of knowledge and technology transfer.

Chapter 9
Corporate Leadership and Sustainability

Neeta Baporikar
Namibia University of Science and Technology, Namibia

ABSTRACT

Due to pressures of globalization and competition, the quality of corporate leadership has come under great scrutiny as questions are being raised worldwide regarding the ability of leaders to deliver long term growth on a sustainable basis. This can be referred to as the "sustainability leadership cavity." The chapter attempts to explore: what are the evolving challenges companies faces, what are the implications on demands placed on leaders and what new leadership competencies are required to ensure sustainability goals are achieved. It also intends to provide cases of successful sustainability leadership. Through grounded theory, in-depth literature review and contextual analysis the core of this chapter is to understand the organizational elements, structure, challenges and competencies crucial and critical for sustainability leadership.

INTRODUCTION

Anticipating problems; building a team with mutual trust; maintaining self-control, common sense and energy: these are not concepts taken from the field of management science and practice. They origin from *Cyropaedia*, a treatise written by Xenophon in the fourth century B.C. describing the life of King Cyrus, who laid the ideological foundation for what would later become the empire of Alexander the Great. Following this seminal work - considered the first to analyze the foundations of "leadership" in a systematic way – numerous studies have been done on this fascinating and difficult topic. Today, once gain the focus is on this same topic 'leadership' in changed milieu. The shift is from growth and profits to – advancement, productivity, inclusivity, environment and sustainability.

According to Singer and Ricard (2015), the role of the leader in this century is different - it's to bring people together around sense of meaning, purpose, and values. In short it is empowering people. On the other hand, companies like Ford and Toyota, IKEA and Zara have been making important strides in reducing their environmental footprint. And they are getting positive press coverage for these efforts. But it's not just the global brands: corporations of all sizes and across all industries are feeling pressure to do more than create great products -- many now want to do so with greener processes and policies (Judith &

DOI: 10.4018/978-1-5225-1823-5.ch009

Pascual 2015). For the past few decades, environmental sustainability has gone from an afterthought to a critical strategic issue. Moreover, environmental variable influences companies' value creation processes and the goal of any organization strategy is to achieve sustained superior performance, which is perse dependent on the organizational positioning. In turn, the success of any given positioning depends on the sustainability of the competitive advantages on which it is based (Costa et al, 2000). Rosenberg (2015) looks at the fundamental differences between two distinct and often opposing logics: the business logic of senior management and the environmental logic of activists, journalists and legislators. The purpose of bringing these differences is not to justify or explain but to encourage a deeper understanding, so that with understanding, strategy that works for business and for the environment can be carved out and in the process of these efforts optimization both would be possible. Long-term business success depends on effectiveness in identifying opportunities and managing risks to create competitive advantage and shareholder value. Amongst other things, successful companies evaluate environmental and social issues in seeking competitive advantage, managing risk and building resilience.

Companies are increasingly recognizing that they need to address the environmental, social and broader economic impacts (terms used about these impacts and related initiatives, include: sustainability, corporate social responsibility, triple bottom line, sustainable development, ESG (environmental, social and governance), corporate sustainability and corporate citizenship) of their operations and performance in order to achieve their long term business and financial goals (CICA, 2009). The criteria that define "leadership" have evolved over time, from excellence in R&D and new product development, to operational excellence and process reengineering, to a focus on core competencies. In recent years the yardstick has been the ability to innovate. Today the framing of corporate leadership is shifting again, to a concept that encompasses the learning and best practices from all these antecedents: corporate sustainability. Most large companies acknowledge the need to be more responsive to shifting societal expectations, to be better able to establish trusting relationships with stakeholders, and to become more open and accountable. Yet there are glitches to translate good intentions into good practice. In no small way, this is due to the lack of any serious, practical guidance addressing the outmoded way in which leaders tend to be selected and developed. This can be referred to as the "sustainability leadership cavity." Sustainability is fast becoming a business megatrend, essential for organizations to address in order to maintain their competitive positions. Sustainability seeks to balance and simultaneously optimize environmental, social and financial concerns WCED (1987). Sustainability represents a particularly challenging undertaking as it necessarily encompasses the wide variety of facilities, operations and activities in any typical organization. Hence, it is closely entwined with leadership. Moreover, the subject of leadership and the role it plays in achieving more sustainable business practices is both of importance and criticality. It has become a truism among sustainability advocates that commitment needs to start at the top.

Leadership is not demonstrated when someone from the C-suite issues a set of specific edicts, but rather when those individuals develop objectives, strategies, and a disciplined plan that both guide and respond to the best people and ideas across an increasingly diverse portfolio of markets and business functions. Furthermore, as companies look to attract and develop their next generation of leaders, they will need different skill sets to be able to manage the increasingly complex sustainability factors impacting companies. Hence, effective corporate leadership at all levels of an organization - from front-line change agents to senior management - will increasingly depend on a sophisticated ability to identify, engage, and incorporate the needs and interests of a diverse range of internal and external stakeholders. Thus, the chapter attempts to fill this gap by exploring: what are the organizational elements, what is the organization structure requirements, the implications on demands placed on leaders and what new leadership competencies are required to ensure sustainability goals are achieved. Through grounded theory, in-depth literature review and contextual analysis the core of this chapter is to describe the competencies necessary corporate sustainability leadership – be it senior managers, executive teams, and boards to lead from the front.

BACKGROUND

There is a growing recognition that the way leaders lead needs to change in an increasingly economically connected, ecologically interdependent, and socially accountable world. The quality of leadership matters if companies are to play their part in making progress toward sustainability, arguably *the* challenge of our time, and prosper in doing so. While a great deal of research has been conducted over many years into leadership styles, competencies, values, and ethics, only a small fraction makes a link to sustainability. Indeed, there are remarkably few leadership models incorporating both long-established competencies and those recognizing the complexity of leading a modern, forward-looking business in a world of growing environmental and social uncertainties and opportunities. Some of the more notable recent exceptions include studies that do indeed acknowledge leadership qualities as an important aspect of a larger sustainability effort (e.g., Glen *et al* 2009; Generation Investment Management, 2012), while others go on to address competencies and executive development in some detail (e.g., Wilson *et al*, 2006; Gribben and Woudstra-van Grondelle, 2007; CPSL, 2010; Center for Tomorrow's Company, 2012; Gitsham *et al*, 2012). As useful as these studies are, few do not offer organizational approaches for making sustainable initiatives successful, nor practical guidance for leaders, senior executives and others interested in improving the quality of corporate leadership for sustainability. Leading for sustainability is challenging in large part due to the "wicked" nature of environmental and interrelated social issues. "Wickedness" – defined as where "facts are uncertain, values in conflict, stakes are high and decisions are urgent, and an extended peer community is required for the resolution of the relevant issues" (Gough et al., 1998) – applies directly to climate change, biodiversity loss, freshwater depletion, social inequity, food access and many other sustainability-related issues. Moving on a sustainable path inevitably involves wicked characteristics like stakeholder conflict, deep ethical choices, and layers of uncertainty and interconnection. These qualities require a leadership theory and practice suited to cross-boundary, systems-oriented thought and action (Shriberg, 2012).

Early leadership studies focused on the "great man" theory: leaders are born (mostly as white males), not developed, and have almost mythical qualities that ensure a bevy of followers (Gallagher, 2012). Modern leadership theory first emerged in the 1940s, following the machine-like principles of scientific management (Rost, 1997). This "rational man" model is implemented via command-and-control structures and a strict hierarchical division of labor (Dugan and Komives, 2010). In the 1950s, the transactional leadership theory emerged with the recognition that workers perform better when attention is paid to motivation. While still mechanistic and linear in its approach, transactional leadership emphasizes the role of workers in the success of an organization and a leader by offering rewards for better performance. Transformational leadership, popularized in the late 1970s and still the dominant leadership model taught in higher education (Hunt, 1999) and the popular literature, takes this evolution one step further. Charismatic "transformational" leaders transform entire organizations toward a "higher ethical purpose" through their skills in visioning, communication and building trust and loyalty (Bass and Steidlmeier, 1999). Environmental leadership as a subset of modern leadership theory is in the early developmental phase in the literature and in practice. Early environmental leaders tended to be naturalists and intellectuals (e.g., William Bartram and Ralph Waldo Emerson) or key figures in the civic reform movements of the early 20th Century (Andrews, 2012). Leadership arose organically, *Shriberg & MacDonald* based on local concerns (e.g., sanitation or the protection of a particular area), often with a charismatic figure as the public voice (e.g., John Muir). Organizing locally via loose-knit networks of individuals or fledgling organizations that eschewed hierarchy and structure, most early environmental leaders relied largely on grassroots activism and popular support to propel their agendas. There was no academic field of environmental leadership or class of environmental professionals.

As the environmental movement evolved and expanded during the late 1960s and early 1970s, a class of environmental professionals and more permanent non-profit organizations formed. Concurrently, the fledgling area of environmental leadership studies began to emerge. This form of leadership differed from that of traditional businesses – organizations and their leaders maintain a looser, non-linear structure and function (Egri and Herman, 2000). Non-profit environmental leaders tend to maintain personal values that are more "ecocentric, open to change, and self-transcendent" than traditional managers (Egri and Herman, 2000). These leaders often exhibit both transformational and transactional leadership traits. However, it is unclear how these traits emerge, as training specifically for environmental leadership is sparse and focuses more generally on non-profit management, resource management or environmental business rather than on training for the specific challenges of moving toward sustainability. Learning in part from the environmental movement and breaking with the traditional mode of leadership training, emerging leadership models with different foci and more decentralized modes of control are becoming more prevalent. For example, ecological leadership (Wielkiewicz & Stelzner, 2010), eco-leadership (Western, 2010) and deep systems leadership (Satterwhite, 2010) are based in principles of ecology and systems thinking, using an ecosystem or ecological web as the analogy for an organization. In this context, leadership is relational, context-dependent and deeply embedded in social, ecological and economic systems. However, these emerging theories have not deeply penetrated the literature and there is minimal training available. For example, Western (2010) argues that eco-leadership is a "lifestyle" more than a skill and that it "cannot be learned through skills training".

Given below in Table 1 is the Sustainability Leadership Conceptual Model. It gives the evolution of leadership theory over time, as well as the recent emergence of environmental leadership.

The concept of sustainability embodies a different, more integrative approach to leadership, visually represented as the bridge between environmental and traditional leadership theory. Given the "wicked" nature of sustainability-related problems and solutions, leadership for sustainability is more than the application of traditional leadership theory and environmental leadership to sustainability. Therefore,

Table 1. Sustainability Leadership Conceptual Model

TIME	SUSTAINABILITY LEADERSHIP	
	Leadership Theory	Environment Leadership
	Control	Dispersed
	Command	Non-Hierarchical
	Transactional	Roots of Proficiency
	Transformational	Proficient and Competent
	Systems	Ecological

organizations have a novel and difficult task to prepare managers to become sustainability leaders. This task goes far beyond defining the problem and saying "have at it" – sustainability leadership involves a specific skill set and mind set, and grooming can and should be designed to build this. While there is no currently recognized model of leadership for sustainability, or a standard set of skills for these leaders, approaches are rapidly emerging in response to the urgent call (and high interest) to develop more sustainability leaders. The chapter also attempts to fulfil that need to some extent at least. This exploratory study examines the organizational approaches for enduring successful sustainability initiatives. The hope is that by providing a better understanding of the successes and limitations of current efforts, managers in other organizations will be better able to guide their efforts.

CORPORATE SUSTAINABLE LEADERSHIP

Since the famous Brundtland Report (World Commision on Environment and Development 1987), sustainable development is defined as a development 'that meets the needs of the present without compromising the ability of future generations to meet their own needs'. Environmental and social issues are increasingly impacting the bottom line and future prospects of companies in many industries. They can present both opportunities and risks and can have important implications for strategy, competitiveness, risk management, stakeholder relations and business resilience. According to Lans *et al.* (2014), sustainability is a shared challenge with regard to economic (profit), social (people) and environmental (planet) goals for many parties in society. Sustainability is however not only something to act upon, comply with or engage in, but can also be seen as a major source for opportunities. Opportunities with regard to sustainability are more complex than business opportunities which address a one dimensional problem, remove a serious pain point, or meet a significant want or need. Sustainability opportunities have, in their rudimentary form, more the character of 'wicked' problems. Each sustainability opportunity should be approached as a new challenge. What worked in the past, does not necessarily work for the future (Lans *et al.* 2014). In the literature of strategic management, key success factors are understood as a set of essential facts that are needed in order to achieve business goals and to gain success in industry sector, to win a game of competition. To understand the nature of sustainable leadership it is needed to identify key success factors of business companies that integrate into their business model and activities the elements of sustainable leadership. Besides key success factors of sustainable enterprise, leaders must understand key success factors of specific industry of their business.

To understand nature of sustainable leadership there is need to understand sustainability. Lazos- Ruiz *et al.* (2013) provides sustainability concept that consists of: wise use of natural resources, territorial approach to rural development, local groups running the enterprise and sustainability-driven entrepreneurship. Balancing these aspects is one of key dimension of key success factors of sustainable leadership. Dentoni *et al.* (2012) have developed a framework consisting of seven competencies which are required for those who are actively involved in dealing with sustainability in their work environment. They identified the following competencies for sustainable development in a business environment (Lans *et al.* 2014):

- Systems-thinking competence: the ability to identify and analyse all relevant (sub) systems across different domains (people, planet, profit) and disciplines, including their boundaries;
- Embracing diversity and inter-disciplinarily: the ability to structure relations, spot issues and recognize the legitimacy of other viewpoints in business decision-making processes regarding envi-

ronmental, social and economic issues, to involve all stakeholders and to maximize the exchange of ideas and learning across different groups (inside and outside the organization) and different disciplines (interdisciplinary));

- Foresight-thinking competence: this capacity includes skills in creativity, opportunity recognition, innovation and balancing of local/global and short-term/long-term perspectives;
- Normative competence: the ability to map, apply and reconcile sustainability values, principles and targets;
- Action competence: the ability to actively involve oneself in responsible actions to improve the sustainability of social-ecological systems;
- Interpersonal competence: the ability to motivate, enable, and facilitate collaborative and participatory sustainability activities and research; and
- Strategic management: the ability to collectively design projects, implement interventions, transitions, and strategies towards sustainable development practices.

Secure and sustainable economic development is a complex, multifaceted process, which is being affected by an array of factors (Dudzevičiūtė 2012; Ercsey 2012; Galan – Ladero *et al.* 2013; Laužikas, Mokšeckienė 2013; Vosylius *et al.* 2013; Wahl, Prause 2013; Vasiliūnaitė 2014). Hence, in recent times, quality of corporate leadership has come under great scrutiny as many have questioned the ability of leaders to articulate and deliver a vision commanding the broad support of investors, customers, employees, and other stakeholders. Most large companies acknowledge the need to be more responsive to shifting societal expectations, to be better able to establish trusting relationships with stakeholders, and to become more open and accountable. And yet those same companies often struggle to translate good intentions into good practice. In no small way this is due to the lack of any serious, practical guidance addressing the outmoded way in which leaders tend to be selected and developed. This is generally referred to as the "sustainability leadership gap."

Organizational Elements to Support Sustainability Initiatives

Sustainability is emerging as a competitive imperative for many organizations. Lubin and Esty identify sustainability as the newest business megatrend that will transform the competitive landscape for many industries (Lubin & Esty 2010). Organizations need to embrace sustainability as a core organizational value, and consequently commit significant resources and personnel to support sustainability efforts. Nonetheless, they are significant benefits including financial from these efforts (EIU, 2008). However, there is need for key organizational elements to support sustainability initiatives and ensure their effectiveness. These are:

- Need of a champion to advocate for sustainability. A high-level champion is needed to advocate for sustainability to important stakeholders. An executive-level champion is essential in helping to define sustainability for the organizational context, securing resources for sustainability, advocating for sustainability within the organization, linking the sustainability activities to high-level strategy, and working with a sustainability coordinator who oversees day-to-day activities.
- Linking and reflecting values of the sustainability initiative in the organization's mission, vision statements. Linking to the high-level mission helps to underscore the relationship between sustainable operations and customer care. This also defines organizational norms and helps to guide

decision making. Linking sustainability to strategic values has a number of important consequences for coordinating and motivating sustainability-related activities within the organizations (Baporikar & Deshpande, 2012a). First, strategic values provide a standard for intra-organizational behavioural and cultural norms. High-level values guide employee decision making and activity prioritization. This helps to motivate activities and performance toward common goals. A mission is also public affirmation about how the organization defines itself (Baporikar, 2014a). Public promotion of an organization's sustainability must be carefully managed. On the one hand, sustainability may help to bolster the organization's brand and reputation. Research has indicated that intangible assets such as reputation may provide a more enduring competitive advantage than other business assets and support long-term success (Fombrun, 1996).

- Creating new positions or hire new people to help manage and coordinate the sustainability initiatives. These new recruits should be charged with identifying focus areas, developing sustainability-related goals, tracking performance, integrating environmental and social concerns into organizational processes, identifying significant external resources and helping to build important sustainability-related organizational capabilities.
- Professional and competent sustainability coordinators are required. These coordinators may be from and have a variety of backgrounds. Critical coordinator capabilities include familiarity with environmental management systems, communication skills, process analysis and management skills and a strong commitment to ongoing learning.
- Use variety of means to propagate sustainable leadership, based on suitability to the organization. These include best practices and processes, information technology networks, and green teams to assure flexible systems, communication, and commonality of approach at all levels. A sustainability initiative may help to attract and retain top talent. A 2009 survey by Kelly Services confirms that workers are more likely to work for socially and environmentally responsible organizations. The survey also indicated that an organization's reputation is very important to workers in all age groups (Kelly Global Workforce, 2011).
- Message and Metrics must be in place (Baporikar, 2013a; 2013b). Performance measurement systems must be in used to monitor and guide sustainability activities. The organizations need to walk the talk and regularly keep track with respect to a number of key sustainability performance indicators. These should also be monitored at the highest organizational levels. Performance management systems should also be used to align individual, department and facility level activities with strategic goals around sustainability. Sometimes, the public's perception of environmentally friendly products and services presents a quandary. A number of studies have found that the public generally perceives such products and services as inferior quality or not as effective as conventional products (Wong et al 1996) — although this perception is changing.
- At the same time, sustainability is often seen as a costly endeavour, (Natural Marketing Institute 2008) more like a "luxury". The reputational effects and public perceptions about sustainability represent a delicate balancing act for healthcare.

Sustainability balances the economic, environmental and social impacts of an organization's operations. Environmental impacts typically refer to an organization's relation to the natural earth systems, including consumption of non-renewable resources. The social component of sustainability can be more difficult to define. According to the recently crafted ISO 26000 standard on social responsibility (ISO, 2011), social sustainability addresses a business organization's relationship to the communities and societies where it operates. It includes activities around human rights, labor practices, fair operating practices, consumer support, health and safety, and community involvement and development (Baporikar, 2012c). Environmental resource management — especially energy and waste — serves as the initial and often central focus of many sustainability initiatives. Improving energy efficiency is associated with reduced operating costs, as is increasing recycling and more carefully managing all waste streams. Managing energy and waste more sustainably for organizations is critical for building organizational capabilities that could be applied to other areas, such as environmentally responsible purchasing and food management.

However, the challenge for most organizations is how to organize the wide-ranging efforts that support environmental and social sustainability, and effectively integrate them into ongoing operations. While manufacturing firms were among the first to adopt sustainability initiatives, service industries have also begun to more aggressively embrace sustainability (Baporikar, 2012b). Ray Anderson, a pioneer in business sustainability, characterizes sustainability as a journey, "a long commitment that fundamentally changes an organization." But, there is no single journey that best fits every context. There are insights that one can gain from experiences. The organizations need to develop sustainability initiatives that have reduced their organizations' environmental impact while enhancing the social impact of their activities. They have to leverage sustainability to improve efficiency or reduce costs while maintaining or improving quality of their product or service (Porter & Kramer, 2011). Signalling the strategic value of sustainability conveys a powerful message to communities and customers. A reputation for sustainability backed up by demonstrated environmentally and socially responsible behaviour and performance may convey a powerful competitive advantage (Baporikar, 2008).

Organizational Structure to Support Sustainability Initiatives

Effective organizational structures align organizational, departmental and individual activities around strategic goals. The key components of organizational structure, to support sustainability initiatives, include leadership, performance measurement and coordinating mechanisms. The salient leadership, performance measurement, and coordinating and organizing structures associated with the various sustainability initiatives organization per se needs to be understood. The three leadership characteristics that potentially affect leadership effectiveness include: the leader's background and training; leader autonomy; and position formality. Background and training refer to the leader's professional experiences, training and education. Leaders with a high degree of autonomy have a lot of discretion to make decisions about their day-to-day activities, as well as the shape the sustainability initiative. Low autonomy means that activities are closely monitored and the leader must get approval for most decisions. More autonomy is generally associated with more flexibility and creativity in problem- solving and decision making. Formality specifies the degree to which rules, policies and procedures govern a leader's activities (Tatikonda & Motoya-Weiss, 2001). High formality indicates that the leader complies with prescribed processes in carrying out their work. Mintzberg's synthesis of organizational design research identifies six basic coordinating mechanisms. These mechanisms comprise the ways that organizations integrate the work in the organization (Mintzberg, 1980). Coordination of sustainability efforts may be carried out using one or more of the following mechanisms: mutual adjustment, which is the informal communication among employees; direct supervision, or one person coordinating and monitoring the work of employees throughout the organization; training and education to standardize employee skills; standardization of routines and processes through specified rules and guidelines; standardization of output goals through performance measurement and control systems; and standardization of organizational norms and values via a common mission or vision. Coordinating mechanisms ideally promote intra-organizational collaboration and knowledge sharing. They help to guide and shape employees' interactions (Baporikar, 2014a; 2014b). Performance measurement indicates how organizations measure, analyse and review their performance. It comprises what data is collected, how metrics are identified, and how performance is tracked, reviewed, and used to improve organizational performance. The aim here is not to prescribe the optimal organizational structure choices, but to briefly examine how organizations lead, coordinate and measure the performance of their sustainability efforts and describe the leadership, performance measurement and coordinating decisions which need to be made by organizations, within their organizational contexts. There is a need to analyse and examine the specific choice in order to identify common factors and establish a framework for decision making with respect sustainability issues, as sustainability leadership and coordination will be contingent on the organizational context, e.g. type of business, history, norms, etc.

Challenges for Corporate Sustainable Leadership

Sustainability is a social objective, not a technology. It is neither an industry nor an activity. Sustainability is an objective that will become a crucial element in the strategy of companies, organizations, the financial industry, governments, municipalities, universities and think tanks (Roobeek, & De Swart, 2013). This will re-direct strategies and re-frame business, operations and consumption which will certainly throw up challenges for corporate leadership. Based on the studies of Doane, 2005; Dey & Steyaert, 2010; Eggers & Macmillan, 2013; Elkington, 1994; 2004; Fishburn & Crowd 2014; Nguyen, & Bosch, 2013, the following challenges have been identified. Some of them are still evolving and some could still emerge. In fact, the need now for corporate leaders would be to re-think on the existing business models to endure these challenges and assess the implications so as to meet the demands squarely.

Thus, in this competitive business scenario challenges particularly would include:

1. **Uncertainty and Complexity:** Leading companies tend to have a more sophisticated appreciation of complexity developed through their interest in long-term mega-trends and by engaging with a broad range of stakeholders (Baporikar, 2016b). They make a greater effort to involve a range of perspectives in risk assessment and strategy making, including from those stakeholders representing a great diversity of different and even conflicting interests, but this is becoming more complex because sustainable issues sometimes are outside the purview of specialists who are involved in the exercises of SWOT analysis, scenario building, etc.
2. **Respecting Difference:** Being able to listen to and truly hear "different voices" from inside and outside the company is a key feature for success in the future. Today, diversity has developed beyond the conventional agenda that tends to focus on gender, ethnicity, age, and so on. There is urgent need to focus on cognitive diversity that is the abilities and competencies to and of different ways of thinking, when managing talent and planning for succession and promotion (Baporikar, 2016a).
3. **Interactive Enterprise:** Organizations need to go beyond the call of duty or reporting requirements in terms of engaging with stakeholders. There is need for dialogue to ensure that the organization is seen as an interactive enterprise with both - internal or external stakeholders. This will also provide and create greater awareness of emerging risks. This would also a measure to assure stakeholders and also in turn become a hub for new ideas and innovation (Baporikar, 2015a).

4. **Moving Out of Circumference Coupled with Out-of-Box Thinking:** To ensure sustainability, leaders have challenge to move out of their comfort zone because today's recipe for success may not be tomorrow recipe. Hence the challenge is to reinvent, renovate, unlearn and relearn on a continuing basis. Merely responding to the shifting landscape will not suffice (Baporikar, 2015b). There is a dire need to be unusually active in shaping social, political, and policy environments and participate, engage in debate and deliberate on the regarding the future of their business and industry.
5. **Talent Management and Succession Planning:** With divergent knowledge oriented globalized networked structure and economic scenario, less directive, less hierarchical approach to leadership is emerging. Even strategy making is not the domain of top management only. It has become more participative process where more of those who will ultimately determine its success are involved. So the real challenge is in managing talent and succession planning (Baporikar, 2013a; 2013b; 2016a).
6. **Innovation and Corporate Entrepreneurship:** At all times, some organizations are judged to be leaders. What earns them this distinction, however, is not constant. The criteria that define "leadership" have evolved over time, from excellence in R&D and new product development, to operational excellence and process reengineering, to a focus on core competencies. In recent years the yardstick has been the ability to innovate and adopt an entrepreneurial approach to decision making (Baporikar, 2013c; 2014c; 2015a).

Today the framing of corporate leadership is shifting again, to a concept that encompasses the learning and best practices from all these antecedents: corporate sustainability. This is not surprising, given the intense competition for resources on a global scale (Baporikar, 2016b). It is quite natural for the world to look to the large institutions that control so much of the planet's physical resources and human talent to lead the way to a more sustainable future (Elkington, 2004). The move towards sustainability is not simply the pursuit of a worthy cause; rather, it is recognition that those who can make efficient and responsible use of natural resources and human capital are more likely to be global corporate leaders.

Constellation of Mechanisms Contributing to Sustainable Development Strategies for Effective Corporate Leadership

To meet the challenges of sustainable development, as discussed in the preceding paragraphs, strategic policy and planning mechanisms need to become more participatory, integrated and flexible. They also need to be recognized as learning processes, in which information about progress towards sustainability, or lack of progress, is used constructively to revise the mechanism and the means of realizing objectives. Rigid, standardized or blueprint approaches are best avoided, usually being at best irrelevant and, at worst, counter-productive. So also is the production of an 'encyclopaedia' or a long 'wish list' of unrealistic possible actions, which have little chance of being implemented.

Instead, there is a pressing need to structure a strategic approach to national sustainable development according to each individual country's own needs, priorities and resources. This in turn should shape the philosophy of how corporate sustainable leadership evolves. Different mechanisms and dialogue models exist to identify how to do evolve this philosophy that could strengthen the effectiveness of corporate sustainable leadership. A Generic model which can be adapted to individual organizations is given below in Figure 1.

Figure 1. Generic Model for Corporate Sustainable Leadership

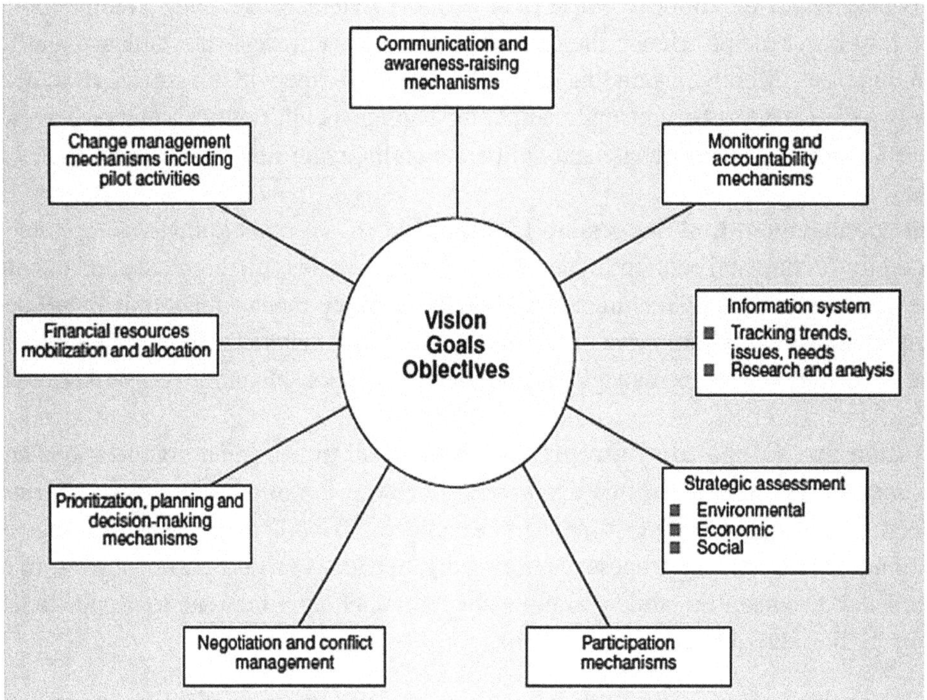

The manner in which these existing and new mechanisms and processes are implemented needs to be consistent with a set of basic strategic principles of the organization. Where these principles are successfully applied, the result will be progress towards an enhanced sustainability be it in terms of national development plans, poverty reduction strategies, national conservation strategies (OECD DAC 2000; UN DESA 2001).

Competencies for Corporate Sustainable Leadership

What new leadership competencies are required for corporate leadership to deal with sustainability on a sustainable basis? Based on the studies (Gallagher, 2012; Generation Investment Management, 2012;

Gitsham, et al 2012; Glen, 2009, Hilson & Lowitt, 2009), top comeptencies identified to meet the challenges of sustainable leadership are given below. These "competencies" are not, necessarily found in any specific frameworks. The competencies are emphasized through the attitudes, abilities, and experience necessary for leaders are to ensure stakeholder interests are protected and longer-term view is adopted. These top competencies overall identified for meeting the challenges of sustainable leadership are:

- Appreciation of trends.
- Change management.
- Ethics.
- Formulating of strategies.
- Governance.

- Integrity.
- Outer awareness.
- Risk assessment and management.
- Stakeholder engagement.
- Tractability.
- Visioning.

It is startling that these competencies identified are not all necessarily new but require significant modification from the classic definitions. Many see these as vital for business success and long-term growth prospects (Baporikar, 2016c). So, if companies are to select, develop, and promote those able to lead in an increasingly economically connected, ecologically interdependent, and socially accountable world, these competencies would be a must. That is, if the "sustainability leadership competency gap" is indeed to be bridged. Reflecting on these new competencies in the recruitment, development, and promotion of leaders will be, surely a priority over the next few years — as corporate sustainability leadership is being seen as the "the new frontier."

SOLUTIONS AND RECOMMENDATIONS

A number of organizations are moving significantly beyond cost- and efficiency- driven sustainability efforts. They are identifying opportunities to improve communities and quality of life. They extend the triple bottom line to incorporate personal values. The sustainability model that most people recognize has the social aspect, and the environmental, and the economic. Though these three are good and solid; however, there is something important missing – it is inner drive or call it learning path, spiritual and core values. That is what really guides and links well in being and doing real sustainability - its hard work. After all, learning [is] … a development of one's own understanding of the world and of oneself as a person (Saljo, 1993). People want meaning in their work. Sustainability offers a way to connect employers with their employees and communities in a powerful way. This chapter brings a fresh perspective and related "language" from the world of leadership development, and hopes to help to integrate sustainability considerations into the thinking and management practices of business leaders. With, the current loss of faith in institutions, leaders need to rebuild trust and show that multinationals have a real role to play in contributing to the solution of the world's issues. In order for that to happen, we need to see more companies developing a moral purpose of their business, or "a moral compass" (Sullivan, 2009). This goes beyond a vision being the best-rated company in the sector to [looking at the] contribution it is making to society. Here, HR has a very serious role to play in helping to develop this moral purpose, being the custodian of these shared values. This is in addition to the strong practical role HR can play in this leadership shift, to get leaders from just accepting that the world has changed to truly championing this shift, despite short-term pressures, with courage and conviction (Baporikar, 2016a). Corporate sustainable leaders are not easy to find, and there is a need to embark on a major journey revising how selecting, training, rewarding, and promoting leaders as well as redefining employer brand and corporate brand.

Furthermore, for corporate sustainable leadership to succeed it is important that:

- Alliances are formed to foster progress on targeted sustainability issues (Baporikar, 2011).
- Sustainability becomes an integral part of business strategy instead of being treated as a peripheral compliance and is integrated into the brand and client value propositions.
- Operational initiatives and related communications are focused on carefully selected themes tied to the core of the business.
- Varied and complementary, communications to key stakeholder groups are used to diffuse the sustainability priorities (Baporikar, 2011).
- Responsibility is taken for the impact of internal operations, as well as those of associated entities such as supply chain partners.
- Standards for reporting are implemented and the materiality of the issues are highlighted and well understood by both - the company and all stakeholders.

FUTURE RESEARCH DIRECTIONS

New leadership models, community engagement for sustainable practices and approaches of how to train future leaders are some of the emerging and interesting threads for study. Many of today's leaders were trained to gain power and authority, but in a rapidly changing world (including the loss of trust and confidence in institutions), leaders need to make the journey from this place to a place of alignment with the interests of society, and ultimately become passionately convinced that they and their companies have a real contribution to make to society and become "givers." This entails a real shift from, "the philosopher king" leader to a much more humble and "service to society" attitude to leadership. Many leaders will find it difficult to make this shift "leading for the ...and." This may call for new interdisciplinary approaches which need to be developed. Another new and interesting area is the focus on the relational enterprise and partnership building. Days are gone when a company can create the solutions in isolation. There is need to build strong partnerships with many partners that were unlikely a few years ago, like NGOs, government, and even competitors, how to go about doing it, without burning one's boats is crucial. Larger studies could test the associations among leadership choices, coordinating mechanisms and sustainability performance. A larger study could also evaluate the relationship between sustainability and quality performance.

CONCLUSION

Traditional development often tends to generate severe competition over resource allocation and use, and this leads invariably to conflict among stakeholders (Baporikar, 2015c). Corporate leadership and strategy development needs to address this issue for genuine partnership and participation. Thus, resolving conflicts, averting potential ones, facilitating and building capacity for negotiation, bargaining and effective inclusion must be central elements of the leadership and strategy process. Organizations that are making significant progress are those who have achieved notable environmental performance with their sustainability initiatives and efforts. Incorporating relevant sustainability activities into position descriptions throughout the organization would further legitimize the work and help to diffuse sustainability throughout the organization. Intra-organizational diffusion is cited as one of the biggest challenges facing organizations. There is opportunity to integrate sustainability with other production management approaches, such as Lean and Six Sigma. All are based on a systems view of the organization, and require analytics to continuously improve performance (Baporikar, 2015d). Managers are starting to recognize opportunities for leveraging the analytical synergies among these systems to simultaneously improve cost, quality and sustainability performance (Baporikar, 2016d). As an example, some manufacturing organizations simultaneously analyse cost, quality, waste and sustainability in their Value Stream Mapping exercises. Quality and Lean management systems rely on formal, functionally-based teams with trained employees to identify performance improvement opportunities and solve problems. Employees who know their respective processes best are empowered to innovate and improve their areas (Baporikar, 2014d; 2015a; 2016a). Training employees in problem-solving techniques with an environmental and social stewardship focus could accelerate sustainability performance. Conversely, there is enormous potential for radical improvements in the way society uses natural resources, and these improvements, cannot come only from tedious legislation but by business leading the way (Rosenberg, 2015). Top leadership in the years to come will continue to focus on the evolving demands of shareholders, employees and customers and that would certainly bring questions of business strategy and sustainability even closer together. Nevertheless, it is good to remember that sustainability extends, not redirects the leadership challenge.

REFERENCES

Andrews, R. N. L. (2012). History of environmental leadership. In D. R. Gallagher (Ed.), *Environmental leadership: A reference handbook* (Vol. 1, pp. 17–28). Los Angeles, CA: SAGE Publications. doi:10.4135/9781452218601.n3

Baporikar, N. (2008). Challenges of Global Management. *SYNERGY Management Research Journal*, *2*(1), 1–10.

Baporikar, N. (2011). Systems Thinking and Education for Sustainable Development a Conceptual Framework. In M. Sahay (Ed.), *System Thinking and System Dynamics, Macmillan Advanced Research Series, Macmillan Publishers India Ltd. ISBN No. 023 -032 – 296- 4* (pp. 48–63).

Baporikar, N., & Deshpande, M. (2012a). Sustainable Entrepreneurship - Approach of Pune Auto Components Entrepreneurs. In A. Marcus & J. J. Rayappa (Eds.), *Entrepreneurship, Youth and Inclusive Development for Brand India* (pp. 313–320). Chennai, India: Loyala Publications.

Baporikar, N. (2012b). Emerging Issues in sustainability Consulting. *Zenith International Journal of Multidisciplinary Research*, *2*(1), 77–89.

Baporikar, N. (2012c). Strategies for Sustainable Development – A Case Study of Carrefour. *JIDNYASA Research Journal*, *6*, 38–45.

Baporikar, N. (2013a). Strategic Approach to Talent Management. *JIDNYASA Research Journal*, *7*, 20–26.

Baporikar, N. (2013b). Understanding Talent Management in Borderless World. MANAGEMENT TODAY – International. *Journal of Management Studies*, *3*(4), 10–16.

Baporikar, N. (2013c). Entrepreneurship in a Modern Networked Indian Economy.[IJABIM]. *International Journal of Asian Business and Information Management*, *4*(4), 48–66.

Baporikar, N. (2014a). Strategic Management Overview and SME in Globalized World. In K. Todorov & D. Smallbone (Eds.), *Handbook of Research on Strategic Management in Small and Medium Enterprises* (pp. 22–39). Hershey, PA: Business Science Reference.

Baporikar, N. (2014b). Technology Imperative in Managerial Decision-Making. In E. Nikoi & K. Boateng (Eds.), *Collaborative Communication Processes and Decision Making in Organizations* (pp. 158–176). Hershey, PA: Business Science Reference.

Baporikar, N. (2014c). Business Research and New Technologies. In P. Ordóñez de Pablos & R. Tennyson (Eds.), *Strategic Approaches for Human Capital Management and Development in a Turbulent Economy* (pp. 166–192). Hershey, PA: Business Science Reference.

Baporikar, N. (2014d). Organizational Barriers and Facilitators in Embedding Knowledge Strategy. In M. Chilton & J. Bloodgood (Eds.), *Knowledge Management and Competitive Advantage: Issues and Potential Solutions* (pp. 149–173). Hershey, PA: Information Science Reference.

Baporikar, N. (2015a). Drivers of Innovation. In P. Ordoñez de Pablos, L. Turró, R. Tennyson, & J. Zhao (Eds.), *Knowledge Management for Competitive Advantage During Economic Crisis* (pp. 250–270). Hershey, PA: Business Science Reference.

Baporikar, N. (2015b). Framework for Social Change through Startups in India.[IJCESC]. *International Journal of Civic Engagement and Social Change*, *2*(1), 30–42.

Baporikar, N. (2015c). Knowledge Management in Small and Medium Enterprises. In J. Zhao, P. Ordóñez de Pablos, & R. Tennyson (Eds.), *Organizational Innovation and IT Governance in Emerging Economies* (pp. 1–20). Hershey, PA: Business Science Reference.

Baporikar, N. (2015d). Holistic Perspective of Standardization Strategies.[IJAMSE]. *International Journal of Applied Management Sciences and Engineering*, *2*(2), 54–65.

Baporikar, N. (2016a). Talent Management Integrated Approach for Organizational Development. In A. Casademunt (Ed.), *Strategic Labor Relations Management in Modern Organizations* (pp. 22–48). Hershey, PA: Business Science Reference.

Baporikar, N. (2016b). Strategies for Enhancing the Competitiveness of MNEs. In M. Khan (Ed.), *Multinational Enterprise Management Strategies in Developing Countries* (pp. 50–71). Hershey, PA: Business Science Reference.

Baporikar, N. (2016c). Corporate Governance and Value Creation: Indian Experience.[IJABIM]. *International Journal of Asian Business and Information Management*, *7*(2), 51–61.

Baporikar, N. (2016d). Holistic Approach for Balanced Scorecard as Managerial Decision Making Tool. [IJSDA]. *International Journal of System Dynamics Applications*, *5*(1), 31–42.

Bass, B. M., & Steidlmeier, P. (1999). Ethics, character, and authentic transformational leadership behavior. *The Leadership Quarterly*, *10*(2), 181–217. doi:10.1016/S1048-9843(99)00016-8

Brundtland, G. H. (1987). *Our Common Future, World Commission on Environment and Development*. Oxford University Press.

CICA. (2009). *Climate Change Briefing: Questions for Directors to Ask*. Toronto: Canadian Institute of Chartered Accountants.

Costa. R, Enric. J, Badal. R, Ángel. M. (2000). *Environmental strategy and value creation*. IESE, DI-408-E, 02/2000.

CPSL. (2010). *Sustainability Leadership: A Force for Change*. Cambridge, UK: University of Cambridge.

Dey, P., & Steyaert, C. (2010). The politics of narrating social entrepreneurship. *Journal of Enterprising Communities: People and Places in the Global Economy*, *4*(1), 85–108. doi:10.1108/17506201011029528

Doane, D. (2005). Beyond corporate social responsibility: Minnows, mammoths and markets. *Futures*, *37*(2-3), 215–229. doi:10.1016/j.futures.2004.03.028

Dudzevičiūtė, G. (2012). Conceptual approaches towards sustainability. *Journal of Security and Sustainability Issues*, *1*(4), 261–272. doi:10.9770/jssi.2012.1.4(3)

Dugan, J. P., & Komives, S. R. (2010). Influence on college students' capacities for socially responsible leadership. *Journal of College Student Development*, *51*(5), 525–549. doi:10.1353/csd.2010.0009

Eggers, W. D., & Macmillan, P. (2013). *The solution revolution: How business, government, and social enterprises are teaming up to solve society's toughest problems*. Boston: Harvard Business Review Press.

Egri, C. P., & Herman, S. (2000). Leadership in the North American environmental sector: Values, leadership styles, and contexts of environmental leaders and their organizations. *Academy of Management Journal*, *43*(4), 571–604. doi:10.2307/1556356

EIU. (2008). *Corporate citizenship: Profiting from a sustainable business*. Economic Intelligence Unit of the Economist.

Elkington, J. (1994). Towards the suitable corporation: Win-win-win business strategies for sustainable development. *California Management Review*, *36*(2), 90–100. doi:10.2307/41165746

Elkington, J. (2004). Enter the triple bottom line. In A. Henriques & J. Richardson (Eds.), *The Triple Bottom Line: does it all add up?* (pp. 1–16). London: Earthscan.

Ercsey, I. (2012). Perceived quality of life as sustainable development facet. *Journal of Security and Sustainability Issues*, *2*(2), 19–30. doi:10.9770/jssi.2012.2.2(2)

Fishburn & The Crowd. (2014). *The wisdom of the crowd: New business models. Leading experts share their views on the emerging generation of more sustainable business models*. London: The Crowd.

Fombrun, G. J. (1996). *Reputation: Realizing Value from the Corporate Image*. Boston: Harvard Business School Press.

Galan - Ladero, M. M., Galera - Casquet, C., Valero - Amaro, V., & Barroso - Mendez, M. J. (2013). Sustainable, socially responsible business: The cause – related marketing case, a review of the conceptual framework. *Journal of Security and Sustainability Issues*, *2*(4), 35–46. doi:10.9770/jssi.2013.2.4(4)

Gallagher, D. R. (2012). Why environmental leadership? In D. R. Gallagher (Ed.), *Environmental leadership: A reference handbook* (Vol. 1, pp. 3–10). Los Angeles, CA: SAGE Publications. doi:10.4135/9781452218601.n1

Generation Investment Management. (2012). *Sustainable Capitalism*. London: Generation Investment Management LLP.

Gitsham, M., Wackrill, J., Baxter, G., & Pegg, M. (2012). *Leadership in a Rapidly Changing World*. London: Ashridge and International Business Leaders Forum.

Glen, J., Hilson, C., & Lowitt, E. (2009). *The Emergence of Green Talent: Lessons from the Internet Revolution*. London: Accenture Institute for High Performance.

Gough, C., Castells, N., & Funtowicz, S. (1998). Integrated Assessment: An emerging methodology for complex issues. *Environmental Modeling and Assessment*, *3*, 19–29.

Gribben, C., & Woudstra-Van Grondelle, I. (2007). *A Snapshot of Executive Development of Corporate Responsibility Professionals in the UK*. London: Ashridge and Corporate Responsibility.

Group Tomorrow's Company. (2012). *The Invisible Elephant and the Pyramid Treasure*. London: Center for Tomorrow's Company.

Hunt, J. G. (1999). Transformational/charismatic leadership's transformation of the field: An historical essay. *The Leadership Quarterly*, *10*(2), 129–144. doi:10.1016/S1048-9843(99)00015-6

ISO. (2011). Retrieved 12 Dec 2015 from http://www.iso.org/management_and_leadership_standards

Judith, J. L., & Pascual, B. (2015). The Power of One to Make a Difference: How Informal and Formal CEO Power Affect Environmental Sustainability. *Journal of Business Ethics*, 1–16.

Kelly Global Workforce. (2011). *Index*. Retrieved 13 Dec 2015 from http://www.kellyservices.com

Lans, T., Blok, V., & Wesselink, R. (2014). Learning apart and together: Towards an integrated competence framework for sustainable entrepreneurship in higher education. *Journal of Cleaner Production*, *62*, 37–47. doi:10.1016/j.jclepro.2013.03.036

Laužikas, M., & Mokšeckienė, R. (2013). The role of creativity in sustainable business. *Entrepreneurship and Sustainability Issues*, *1*(1), 10–22. doi:10.9770/jesi.2013.1.1(2)

Lazos-Ruíz, A., Moreno-Casasola, P., & Galante, E. (2013). Green Rural Enterprises: Guidelines for empowering local groups towards sustainable ventures. *Journal of Environmental Planning and Management*, 1–23.

Lubin, D. A., & Esty, D. C. (2010). The Sustainability Imperative. *Harvard Business Review*, *88*(5), 42–50.

Mintzberg, H. (1980). Structure in 5's: A Synthesis of the Research on Organization Design. *Management Science*, *26*(3), 322–341. doi:10.1287/mnsc.26.3.322

Natural Marketing Institute. (2008). *2007 LOHAS Consumer Trends Database*. Natural Marketing Institute.

Nguyen, N. C., & Bosch, O. J. H. (2013). A systems thinking approach to identify leverage points for sustainability: A case study in the Cat Ba Biosphere Reserve, Vietnam. *Systems Research and Behavioral Science*, *30*(2), 104–115. doi:10.1002/sres.2145

OECD DAC. (2001). *Report on the Informal Workshop on Poverty Reduction Strategies, Comprehensive Development Framework and National Strategies for Sustainable Development: Towards Convergence*. Document DCD (2000)13. OECD.

Porter, M. E., & Kramer, M. R. (2011, January-February). Creating Shared Value. *Harvard Business Review*.

Roobeek, A., & De Swart, J. (Eds.). (2013). *Sustainable Business Modeling*. The Hague: Academic Service.

Rosenberg, M. (2015). *Strategy and Sustainability*. Palgrave Macmillan. doi:10.1007/978-1-137-50175-2

Rost, J. C. (1997). Moving from individual to relationship: A post-industrial paradigm of leadership. *The Journal of Leadership Studies*, *4*(4), 3–16. doi:10.1177/107179199700400402

Saljo, R. (1993). Learning Discourse: Qualitative Research in Education. *International Journal of Education and Research*, *19*(3), 199–203. doi:10.1016/0883-0355(93)90015-C

Satterwhite, R. (2010). Deep systems leadership: A model for the 21st century. In B. W. Redekop (Ed.), *Leadership for Environmental Sustainability* (pp. 230–242). New York, NY: Routledge.

Shriberg, M. (2012). Sustainability leadership as 21st century leadership. In D. R. Gallagher (Ed.), *Environmental leadership: A reference handbook* (Vol. 2, pp. 469–480). Los Angeles: Sage Publications. doi:10.4135/9781452218601.n50

Singer, T., & Ricard, M. (Eds.). (2015). Caring Economics: Conversations on Altruism and Compassion, Between Scientists, Economists, and the Dalai Lama. Picador USA.

Sullivan, J. D. (2009). *The Moral Compass of Companies: Business Ethics and Corporate Governance as Anti-Corruption Tools*. Global Corporate Governance Forum of the International Finance Corporation, World Bank Group.

Tatikonda, M., & Motoya-Weiss, M. (2001). Integrating Operations and Marketing Perspectives of Product Innovation: The Influence of Organizational Process Factors and Capabilities on Development Performance. *Management Science*, *4*(1), 151–172. doi:10.1287/mnsc.47.1.151.10669

UN DESA. (2001). *Indicators of Sustainable Development: Guidelines and Methodologies*. New York: Department of Economic and Social Affairs, United Nations.

Vasiliūnaitė, R. (2014). Sustainable development: Methodological approaches toward issues. *Journal of Security and Sustainability Issues*, *3*(3), 69–75. doi:10.9770/jssi.2014.3.3(6)

Vosylius, E., Rakutis, V., & Tvaronavičienė, M. (2013). Economic growth, sustainable development and energy security interrelation. *Journal of Security and Sustainability Issues*, *2*(3), 5–14. doi:10.9770/jssi.2013.2.3(1)

Wahl, M., & Prause, G. (2013). Toward understanding resources, competencies, and capabilities: Business model generation approach. *Entrepreneurship and Sustainability Issues*, *1*(2), 67–80. doi:10.9770/jesi.2013.1.2(1)

Western, S. (2010). Eco-leadership: Towards the development of a new paradigm. In B. W. Redekop (Ed.), *Leadership for Environmental Sustainability* (pp. 36–54). New York, NY: Routledge.

Wielkiewicz, R. M., & Stelzner, S. P. (2010). An ecological perspective on leadership theory, research, and practice. In B. W. Redekop (Ed.), *Leadership for Environmental Sustainability* (pp. 17–35). New York, NY: Routledge.

Wilson, A., Lenssen, G., & Hind, P. (2006). *Leadership Qualities and Management Competencies for Corporate Responsibility*. London: Ashridge and European Academy of Business in Society.

Wong, V., Turner, W., & Stoneman, P. (1996). Marketing Strategies and Market Prospects for Environmentally-Friendly Consumer Products. *British Journal of Management*, *7*(3), 263–281. doi:10.1111/j.1467-8551.1996.tb00119.x

World Commission on Environment and Development (WCED). (1987). Our Common Future. Oxford, UK: Oxford University Press.

ADDITIONAL READING

Barbier, E. B. (1987). The Concept of Sustainable Economic Development. *Environmental Conservation*, *14*(2), 101–110. doi:10.1017/S0376892900011449

Barnard, G. (1995). *Cross-cultural Communication. A Practical Guide*. London: Cassell.

Baumert, K. A., & Petkova, E. (2000). *How will the Clean Development Mechanism Ensure Transparency, Public Engagement and Accountability?* Washington, DC: World Resources Institute Climate Notes.

Carew-Reid, J. (Ed.). (1997). Strategies for Sustainability: Asia, IUCN in association with Earthscan, London

Carley, M., & Christie, I. (2000). *Managing Sustainable Development* (2nd ed.). London: Earthscan.

Chambers, N., Simmons, C., & Wackernagel, M. (2000). *Sharing Nature's Interest: Ecological Footprints as an Indicator of Sustainability*. London: Earthscan.

Creech, H., & Willard, T. (2001). *Strategic Intentions: Managing Knowledge Networks for Sustainable Development*. Winnipeg: International Institute for Sustainable Development.

Dalal-Clayton, D. B., & Bass, S. (2000). National Strategies for Sustainable Development: A Guide to Key Issues and Methods for Analysis: A Prompt for Status Reviews and Dialogues, June 2000, IIED, London (www.nssd.net)

Dalal-Clayton, D. B., & Dent, D. (2001). *Knowledge of the Land: Land Resources Information and its use in Rural Development*. Oxford University Press.

Handy, C. (1985). *Understanding Organisations*. Harmondsworth, UK: Penguin Books.

Hardy, J. E., Mitlin, D., & Satterthwaite, D. (2001). *Environmental Problems in an Urbanizing World*. London: Earthscan.

Lopez Ornat, A. (Ed.). (1997). Strategies for Sustainability: Latin America, IUCN in association with Earthscan, London

Mayers, J. (2001). *Stakeholder Power Analysis, Power Tools Series no 2*. London: IIED.

Neefjes, K. (2000). *Environments and Livelihoods: Strategies for Sustainability*. London: Oxfam Development Guidelines. doi:10.3362/9780855987152

Powell, M. (1999). *Information Management for Development Organisations*. UK: Oxfam.

Repetto, R. (1994). *The 'Second India' Revisted: Population, Poverty and Environmental Stress Over Two Decades*. Washington, DC: World Resources Institute.

Rhodes, R A W. (1997). *Understanding Governance, Politics and the State*. Basingstoke, UK: Macmillan.

Tennyson, R. (1998). *Managing Partnerships: Tools for Mobilising the Public Sector, Business and Civil Society as Partners in Development*, The Prince of Wales Business Leaders Forum, London

von Weizsacker, E. (1994). *Earth Politics*. London: Zed Books.

KEY TERMS AND DEFINITIONS

Director: Top management personnel who plays a leadership role in establishing an appropriate "tone at the top" regarding the company's dealings and relationships with its stakeholders.

Disaster Planning: Readiness for a variety of unexpected or foreseeable events (extreme weather events, floods, forest fires, ice storms, earthquakes, volcanic eruptions, environmental spills, disease outbreaks)

Ecology: The air, water, minerals, organisms, and all other externalfactors surrounding and affecting a given organism at any time.

Environment: The aggregate of surrounding things, conditions, influences; or milieu.

ISO 26000: An international standard that provides guidance on how businesses and organizations can operate in a socially responsible way.

Leader: A person who rules, guides, or inspires others; head of an organization.

Regulatory: Laws and regulations, both domestic and in foreign jurisdictions, as applicable.

Sustainability: Requirement to manage the resource base such that what we ensure ourselves can potentially be shared by future generations; more equitable, economic system.

Chapter 10
Responsible and Sustainable Management Practices in Developing and Developed Business Environments

Idahosa Igbinakhase
University of Kwazulu Natal, South Africa

ABSTRACT

This chapter focuses on responsible and sustainable management practices in business based on the 10 principles of the United Nations Global Compact (UNGC). The UNGC has been named the world's largest corporate sustainability initiative and it has already made a significant contribution to the entrenchment of globally acceptable business ethics. The UNGC identifies ethical leadership as an important organisational asset, which has also contributed to the implementation of key responsible and sustainable practices, such as anti-corruption seminars and corporate social responsibility, among others. A comparative analysis of responsible and sustainable management practices of businesses in Nigeria and the United Kingdom revealed that some practices, such as corporate social responsibility, are being practiced in both business environments, among other findings.

INTRODUCTION

Business practices in diverse operating environments are becoming increasingly socially responsible and sustainable in a bid to be ethically conscious as they gravitate towards globally acceptable business standards. Responsible and sustainable management practices in business have become the standard in today's global business environment (Baumann-Pauly & Scherer, 2013; United Nations Global Compact, 2015f). The United Nations, championing this drive and initiative through its United Nations Global Compact (UNGC) initiative has encouraged businesses to imbibe its guiding 10 principles founded around human rights, labour, the environment and anti-corruption measures in their conduct within their business environments (United Nations Global Compact, 2015f).

DOI: 10.4018/978-1-5225-1823-5.ch010

The UNGC initiative has been adopted by over 166 countries and about 8,902 businesses in these countries (United Nations Global Compact, 2016), with other businesses and countries increasingly showing interest in the United Nations' 10 principles (Rasche, 2009; United Nations Global Compact, 2015f) and carrying out activities promoting the principles (United Nations Global Compact, 2015f). In addition, some cities and stakeholders have created their own initiative from these principles (The Global Compact, 2016) with the intention of localising and adapting the principles to suit their business environments. Some of these activities and initiatives have taken the form of corporate social responsibility (CSR) (Centindamar, 2007; Rasche & Gilbert, 2012), green initiatives (environmental responsibility) (Bansal & Roth, 2000; Laroche, Bergeron, & Barbaro-Forleo, 2001), improved business ethics, seminars and workshops promoting sustainability change behaviours to protect the stakeholders and the business environment (Musari, 2016). In characterising the aforementioned socially responsible activities, businesses have adopted the CSR approach as a key mechanism that reflects their corporate social intentions in line with the United Nations global standards for business for the benefits of their business activities and their host communities (Centindamar, 2007).

Since its introduction in 2000, and its adoption by Nigeria (developing nation) in 2006 (United Nations Global Compact, 2015a) and by the United Kingdom (developed nation) in 2003 (United Nations Global Compact, 2015b) various responsible and sustainable management practices have been utilised in both indigenous environments by businesses and the outcomes are far-reaching.

This chapter provides definitions of responsible and sustainable management practices by businesses in these business environments, considering the situational issues present in these environments and businesses' responses in affiliation with the United Nations' standards. It will also present a comparison and the results of in-depth analysis with a view to highlight the considerable gains of the UNGC initiative and also the missed opportunities experienced by both countries.

From the literature reviewed, the following themes emerged:

- Background of the UNGC initiative and its role in responsible and sustainable management practices in business;
- Ethical leadership and CSR as a catalyst in responsible and sustainable management practices in business;
- Responsible and sustainable management practices in business in Nigeria's developing business environment;
- Responsible and sustainable management practices in business in the United Kingdom's developed business environment;
- A Comparative Analysis of Responsible and Sustainable Management Practices of Businesses in Nigeria and the United Kingdom; and
- An impact analysis of responsible and sustainable management practices in business in Nigeria and the United Kingdom.

Background of the UNGC Initiative and its Role in Responsible and Sustainable Management Practices in Business

The UNGC initiative may be regarded as the 'guiding principles' depicting acceptable global standards and expectations in today's business environment (Abe, 2016). According to Hale (2011), the UNGC initiative is a collaborative effort between key stakeholders in the business environment and the United

Nations to incorporate the well-defined 10 principles in terms of the environment, labour, human rights and anti-corruption measures in their business activities and conducts voluntarily.

The UNGC initiative contains four key parts and structural themes in which key principles are earmarked as the focus areas to provide an enabling business environment that is beneficial to all stakeholders in the society. These four key parts and structural themes are human rights, labour, the environment and anti-corruption measures (United Nations Global Compact, 2015f). The first part, which is dedicated to human rights, places emphasis on businesses to support and respect the internationally accepted human rights and to avoid human rights abuses (United Nations Global Compact, 2015f). Human rights are a critical aspect of our day-to-day living and existence (Farmer, 2004). According to Donnelly (2013), human rights are based on the need to preserve and maintain human dignity within various interactions in the society. Businesses play a key role in the protection of human dignity as the majority of their activities are organised around humans. A key feature of business processes is the strategic role of human inputs and outputs, which are designed to serve human beings in the form of products and services (Rosemann & Vom Brocke, 2015). The significance of human rights in our society cannot be overemphasised as it can be seen to have the potential to inform human conduct and to improve the quality of human existence. According to Donnelly (2013), human rights laws are designed to protect all within and outside business, and respecting them is ethically and morally beneficial to all. In order for businesses to be responsible and maintain quality management practices, human rights violations in any form must be avoided.

In the second part, which is labour, the UNGC initiative urges businesses to

- Eliminate discrimination with respect to employment and occupation;
- Abolish child labour;
- Eliminate all forms of forced and compulsory labour;
- Encourage freedom of association; and
- Recognise the right to collective bargaining (United Nations Global Compact, 2015f).

Labour plays a strategic role in many businesses today as it provides a pool of workers hired to meet organisational goals in the society, while also providing employment that leads to economic sustenance of the employees (Jany-Catrice & Lehndorff, 2005). Businesses and the society stand to gain when businesses adopt responsible and sustainable practices in their labour management activities, which include avoiding any form of violation with respect to local and international labour laws. This is necessary as consumers of business products and services are becoming socially conscious patronising businesses with fair labour standards (Hainmueller & Hiscox, 2015).

Focusing on the third part, which deals with the environment, the UNGC initiative emphasises that businesses should encourage a precautionary approach to environmental challenges, participate in initiatives that encourage environmental responsibility, and encourage the creation and scaling of environmentally friendly technologies (United Nations Global Compact, 2015f). Businesses cannot operate in isolation, as they must interact effectively and efficiently with their host environments for their survival and for their activities to be of value (Carroll, 2004; Garriga & Mele, 2004). The host environments for businesses are the societies and communities naturally occurring with distinct environmental features where the businesses are located and where these businesses carry out their activities (Carroll, 2004). According to Moldan, Janouskova, and Hak (2012), these environments are made up of earth's life-supporting systems, which are natural to various indigenous locations. Environmental sustainability on the part of businesses operating in various locations focuses on maintaining these systems for the benefit of all stakeholders in society. As businesses interact in their various communities, there is a need for the businesses to have it as a goal always to contribute effectively and efficiently to the maintenance of the earth's life-supporting systems to ensure unhindered business activities and a sustainable environment for everybody in society (Winn & Pogutz, 2013).

For the fourth part, which deals with anti-corruption measures, the UNGC initiative advises businesses to shun all forms of corruption, including extortion and bribery (United Nations Global Compact, 2015f). Corruption is a major problem facing business in both the developed and developing world today. Corruption is unethical behaviour exhibited for illegal and selfish gains (Osoba, 1996; Transparency International, 2015). According to Kemp (2014), cases of bribery, corruption and the encouragement of payments as inducement are rampant as reported by the Institute of Business Ethics Media Monitoring in 2013. Kemp (2014) adds that businesses still have a lot to do in terms of establishing effective anti-corruption measures in their establishment's culture and practices while the effects of corruption are negative for businesses and society. Businesses have a significant role in ending corruption, and they should utilise every opportunity to take their stand against corruption and to promote anti-corruption campaigns in every aspect of their activities in society.

It is also important to add that the 10 principles are hinged on four solid pillars, namely

- The Universal Declaration of Human Rights (Donnelly, 2013; Morsink,1999);
- The International Labour Organisation's Declaration on Fundamental Principles and Rights at Work (Alston & Heenan, 2003);
- The Rio Declaration on Environment and Development (Hens, 2005); and
- The United Nations Convention against Corruption (UNCAC) (Weilert, 2016)

These pillars give appropriate credibility to the principles and allow the UNGC initiative to bear resemblance to different operating regulations before the UNGC initiative's establishment in 2000. Some of these regulations, such as indigenous government regulations (Qu, 2007), industry standards (King & Lenox, 2000; Mann, Adebanjo, & Kehoe, 1998) and business associations guidelines (Doner & Schneider, 2000) tend to stipulate acceptable conducts and practices while making provision for penalties for any defaulters. Compared to these other regulations and guidelines, the UNGC initiative has certain similar characteristics with some of these regulations while it is also distinctive in the sense that stakeholders conform to the principles voluntarily (Rasche & Kell, 2010). It is also important to add that the UNGC initiative does not erode other established norms but serves effectively as a necessary complement to existing state and non-state laws (Rasche, 2009).

Stakeholders play significant roles in the UNGC initiative. According to Hale (2011), the initiative involves various stakeholders with transnational corporation pledging to adopt the 10 principles of the initiative. The UNGC initiative also affirms that companies and non-businesses have also adopted the initiative (The Global Compact, 2016; United Nations Global Compact, 2016). For the companies, the chief executive officers (CEOs) are the major actors, and ethical leadership (De Hoogh & Den Hartog, 2008) plays a significant role, as these CEOs are advocates of the social responsibilities of their businesses. This in turn promotes corporate citizenship (Rasche, 2009; Rasche & Kell, 2010). The social responsibilities mandated by businesses and CEOs allow for the implementation of the 10 principles in the work place while utilising ethical business processes to produce ethical products and services(Carroll, 2004). These ethical acts lead to business and leadership accountability, which is beneficial to society.

The obligation to be accountable in this context becomes the leader's social responsibility which contributes to ethical leadership (De Hoogh & Den Hartog, 2008; Zhu, Sun, & Leung, 2014). Based on the 10 principles, socially responsible leaders should be accountable in terms of issues of human rights, labour, the environment and anti-corruption measures with the intention of doing business ethically and improving society. Other stakeholders and key partners include citizens, civil societies, competitors, employees, investors, indigenous governments, and society whom businesses must consider when carrying out their business activities (Carroll, 2004; Leisinger, 2003; United Nations Global Compact, 2015c). It is important to add that, in considering these stakeholders and accepting the principles of the UNGC initiative, businesses are self-assured that their activities are universally accepted and beneficial to all stakeholders (Leisinger, 2003).

Beneficiaries of the 10 principles include businesses, other stakeholders and society. Businesses benefit from ethical leadership (Zhu et al., 2014), which sets in motion ethical processes, which eventually produce ethical goods and services (Ardichvili, Mitchell, & Jondle, 2009). Prospective employees also benefit from a recruitment process that is free, fair and ethical while being assured of well-paid employment (Ogunfowora, 2014). Other stakeholders also benefit from partnerships with ethical businesses while society benefits from thoughtful CSR initiatives (Centindamar, 2007).

Finally, in providing definitions of responsible and sustainable management practices in business in both developed and developing business environments, this chapter focuses on practices by businesses associated with the UNGC initiative structure and functions pertaining to human rights, labour, the environment and anti-corruption measures as contained in the UNGC.

Ethical leadership and CSR as a Catalyst in Responsible and Sustainable Management Practices in Business

Morally upright leaders have been known to take decisions that benefit their businesses and their host environments based on ethically guiding principles, which are the founding basis for their business operations. These leaders are often referred to as 'ethical leaders' due to their consistent regard for ethical beliefs and values that are beneficial to all. According to Stouten, Van Dijke, and De Cremer (2012), ethical leadership is an instrument to ensure that there is order in a system with an entrenched ethically compliant followership. In addition, Bello (2012) asserts that ethical leaders are leaders who consider the interests of employees objectively while disregarding any form of sentiments that may influence managers' decisions or perceptions on an issue. Gill, Haider, and Noreen (2016) opine that ethical leaders are leaders who are against the non-compliance attitude of employees to existing organisation codes of conduct and encourage employees to contribute positively for the good of the society by accepting and believing organisational values in the form of CSR. The qualities of ethical leadership include all things good and moral while excluding all things negative and amoral within and outside the internal environments of the business. The presence of ethical leadership in the organisational space consequently provides a sense of ethical movements within the private sector, which is considerate of the activities of the business and the benefits to all stakeholders. Although several ethical activities have been associated with ethically led businesses, CSR has been a prominent feature both in developing and developed business environments that tends to summarise their activities that is considerate of and beneficial to all stakeholders and the environment. According to McWilliams and Siegel (2000), CSR is defined as the actions of a firm geared towards the social good of society outside the scope of the firm's financial target gains, while Holme and Watts (1999) view CSR as a firm's duty to carry out activities in the best interests of the general society. Therefore, CSR can be seen as the motivations and actions of a firm to do that which benefits all.

In understanding the motivations and actions for the prevalence of several CSR activities in society today, it is important to understand the link between the role ethical leadership plays in the CSR policies of an organisation and the CSR practices experienced in society. According to Zhu, Sun, and Leung (2014), ethical leadership plays a significant role in the positive effects of CSR activities of the firm and that this link is indirect, while Chin, Hambrick, and Trevino (2013) affirm that the political ideologies of a firm's CEO are shown in the firm's CEO profile and the CSR activities in society. Furthermore, evidence by Du, Swaen, and Lindgreen (2013) indicates that in terms of the leadership style of a CEO, transformational CEOs are more likely to partake in institutional CSR activities than transactional leaders, and that in terms of the positive relationship between institutional CSR activities and organisational outcomes, transactional leadership improves the relationship while transformational leaders diminish it. While leadership style is important for an ethical organisation, and because ethical leadership plays a significant role in CSR activities, businesses must learn to use their CSR activities for the benefit of their leaders, for the organisation and for the benefits of all stakeholders in society.

Ethical leadership has it benefits in relation to CSR activities. Among other benefits, that ethical leadership stands to gain from doing good for the business and society, such leadership benefits from CSR activities in the form of

- An increase in employee performance based on employee trust in organisational leadership and commitment to organisational goals (Bello, 2012);
- Effective communication with stakeholders;
- Exhibition of moral courage and informed ethical decision-making (Voegtlin, 2015);
- Avoidance of infringements of any kind that could lead to the removal of the leader from the organisation; and
- Continuous involvement in fair practices.

Since ethical leadership benefits from CSR activities, there are also stakeholders who benefit from the CSR activities of these ethical organisations, including the organisation itself. It is important to note that CSR activities are also beneficial for the organisation. Aliyu (2013) observes there is a link between ethical leadership and good governance in an organisation and ethical leadership promotes good governance. In addition to the promotion of good governance in an organisation, ethical leadership enables the organisation to manage its reputation in society (Nwagbara & Reid, 2013) and improve brand image. Among other benefits, ethical leadership also leads to more loyal customers, more well-wishers (Siddique, 2014), better firm performance (Mujtaba & Cavico, 2013; Togun & Nasieku, 2015), firm value (Servaes & Tamayo, 2013), competitive advantage (Ogbo, Okechukwu, & Ukpere, 2013), risk reduction, market position enhancement and cost savings (Ugouwanyi & Ekene, 2016). While the ethical organisation benefits from its CSR activities, society as a stakeholder also benefits from CSR activities that come in various forms in both developing and developed business environments, which is very relevant, based on prevailing indigenous conditions in society. The key deliverables of CSR are:

- Poverty reduction in host communities in terms of environmentally friendly activities that preserve the host community environment and sources of sustainable livelihood (Nwagbara & Kamara, 2015);

- Preservation of the environment;
- Increased attractiveness of the business environment;
- Avoidance of human rights violation; and
- Avoiding corporate social irresponsibility (Lin-Hi & Muller, 2013).

It is a combination of ethical leaders and their CSR activities that provides the necessary entrenchment of responsible and sustainable management practices in business as initiated and encouraged by the UNGC initiative's 10 principles in various societies. This combination serves as a necessary catalyst to encourage ethical business activities that benefit both businesses and their stakeholders. It is important to add that for the CSR trend to be sustainable there should be collaborations by all stakeholders to make responsible and sustainable management practices successful and sustainable in the long term (Enuoh & Inyang, 2014).

Responsible and Sustainable Management Practices in Business in Nigeria's Developing Business Environment

Responsible and sustainable management practices in business with respect to Nigeria's business environment have been a welcome development as Nigeria launched its compliance to the UNGC initiative's 10 principles (United Nations Global Compact, 2015a). According to the United Nations Global Compact (2015a), the 10 principles are hosted within the Nigerian Economic Summit Group (NESG) (The Nigerian Economic Summit Group, 2016) and it is being managed by a steering committee with 14 members (United Nations Global Compact, 2015a). This action paved the way for Nigerian businesses in various industries and sectors to accept the 10 principles of the UNGC initiative regarding human rights, labour, environment and anti-corruption measures voluntarily in order to improve the nation's business environment.

Top business sectors with significant participants in Nigeria are banking, financial services, general industrials, mobile telecommunications and the support services (United Nations Global Compact, 2015a) and Nigeria currently boasts of over 160 participants(United Nations Global Compact, 2015a). The sectors mentioned above are key sectors of the economy, which employ a significant number of workers and interact extensively with the business environment. Some of these sectors are dominated by multinational companies (Abe, 2016; Ayoola & Olasanmi, 2013). Multinational companies in Nigeria focus on sustainable community development in the host communities (Adewuyi & Olowookere, 2010; Murthuri, Moon, & Idemudia, 2012). These communities are referred to as 'host communities' because businesses have their facilities there and they carry out their business transactions within the communities. It is also important to state that the reason for the community development strategy is based on the fact that many of these communities are underdeveloped and they lack basic amenities and key infrastructure required for proper living within the community (Eweje, 2006b). According to Eweje (2006b), multinational companies develop community projects that respond to the lack being experienced by the indigenous people in the host communities. These community projects now become part of the CSR policies of the companies which inform the business responses to prevailing issues pertaining to human rights, labour, the environment and anti-corruption measures as contained in the UNGC initiative's 10 principles that are discussed in this chapter. CSR plays a strategic role in the Nigerian business environment with the majority of firms adopting it as a policy to give back to the host community (Adewuyi & Olowookere, 2010; Amaeshi, Adegbite &Rajwani, 2016). According to Eweje (2006b), there is a great need for community development projects in developing countries, and Ite (2007) affirms that businesses are trying to meet these demands. Amaeshi and Adegbite (2014) observe that firms have developed adaptive mechanisms to carry out their CSR initiatives regardless of prevailing institutional challenges that may be present in the business environment.

CSR initiatives come in several forms to address various community issues with regard to the host environment. Adewuyi and Olowookere (2010) observe that social and environmental reporting is a key feature carried out by some companies in the Nigerian business environment. Abiodun (2015) agrees that businesses could be transformed by adopting the principles of sustainability reporting in their business functions. However, when it comes to sustainability reporting pertaining to CSR activities in respect of the environment by multinational companies in Nigeria, several environmental issues are often not reported by these companies but are experienced in various forms of environmental mishaps, which can be attributed to some kind of business activity carried out by these companies. According to Daramola and Ibem (2010) and Esan and Babatola (2015), environmental degradation is prevalent in Nigerian cities and this has drawn negative reviews in terms of Nigeria having the lowest livability index compared to other countries in the world (Esan & Babatola, 2015). Some of these degradable activities have been linked to the Niger Delta region in Nigeria (Adekola, Fischbacher-Smith, 2016), which occupies the south-south geopolitical zone of Nigeria, while other degradable activities in all six geopolitical zones in Nigeria are deforestation, desertification, the modernisation drive and the growing population (Maconachie, 2016; Omofonmwan & Osa-Edoh, 2008). The Nigerian environment has many issues when it comes to the Niger Delta region where oil exploration is ongoing (Ayanlade & Proske, 2016; Nriagu, Udofia, Ekong & Ebuk, 2016; Olobaniyi & Omo-Irabor, 2016). Environmental issues have originated from the exploration activities, and Nigeria can be seen as having a low precautionary approach to environmental challenges due to the high level of environmental degradation experienced in the Niger Delta region by multinational businesses (Emmanuel & Gordon, 2006; Kadafa, 2012). The effects of these degradable activities on the environment can be summarised to include adverse effects to human health, the ecological system and the environment (Daramola & Ibem, 2010). However, current multinational responses to these environmental degradation activities indicate that something is being done in line with the UNGC initiative principle in terms of protecting the environment (Braide, Remoue, Rat, Anozie, Vandeville, Ahiamadu, Okoroafor, Brown & Ganga, 2016; Idemudia & Osayande, 2016). According to Eweje (2006a), multinationals involved in oil production in Nigeria are now realising the importance of preventing pollution in their host community environments due to their oil exploration activities, and they are now utilising environmental impact assessments in their corporate strategy (Braide et al.,2016; Eweje, 2006a). It is also important to state that, in terms of participating in initiatives that encourage environmental responsibility, the introduction of the Petroleum Industry Bill (PIB) drafted in 2008 (De Montclos, 2014; Oyewunmi & Olujobi, 2016)tried to connect Nigeria to possible developmental solutions to its environmental challenges (Okoye, 2012;) while the establishment in 1988 (Ogbodo, 2010) of the Federal Environmental Protection Agency (FEPA) assists in controlling and managing the Nigerian environment and its resources (Omofonmwan & Osa-Edoh, 2008). The FEPA further assists in limiting the excesses that may occur from some environment-based business activities (Ogbodo, 2010). Furthermore, the creation and utilisation of environmentally friendly technologies are still very low in Nigeria as evidence by Emodi, Yusuf, and Boo (2014) suggests that Nigeria is yet to have established renewable energy standards to govern the certification and importation of renewable energy technologies.

In terms of human rights issues, evidence by Kerr (2012) affirms that human rights abuses are prevalent in the Niger Delta, and there is no adequate representation for minorities and civil society in Nigeria. This has led to various forms of agitations by civil societies (Ako & Ekhator, 2016; Ikelegbe, 2001) and youth restiveness in the Niger Delta area (Aghedo, 2015; Arowosegbe, 2009; Jike, 2004; Nwosu, 2016). Other issues of human rights abuses with respect to businesses are the negative effects of exploratory activities on the livelihood and living conditions of people of the host communities in the Niger Delta areas of Nigeria (Nriagu et al., 2016). According to Emmanuel and Gordon (2006) and Nriagu et al. (2016), the people of the Niger Delta region have been seriously affected by issues relating to their health as well as social and economic aspects of their lives due to prevalent environmental degradation (Elum,Mopipi & Henri-Ukoha, 2016). The authors further observed that crop yields have been affected greatly and negatively by the environmental degradation in the area. Economic sustenance, good health and social activities are also highly threatened (Adekola et al., 2016; Emmanuel & Gordon 2006; Nriagu et al., 2016). Kemp and Vanclay (2013) suggest that businesses should consider human rights as the main basis in their impact assessments for their business activities. They should also adequately focus on issues of human rights relating to livelihoods, the environment, health and other significant human rights focus areas. Business response to these aforementioned human rights challenges in Nigeria is the utilisation of a critical impact assessment in their prospective business conducts to limit issues of human rights violations. However, this is not always the case as evidence by Ingelson and Nwapi (2014) shows that, although environmental and impact assessment (EIA) is a regulatory requirement in Nigeria (Echefu & Akpofure, 2002), businesses are still unable to manage the effects of their activities in the environment.

Labour unions also play an active role in Nigeria and their activities have been felt by all in society (Eze & Chinwuba, 2015). With Nigeria's voluntary participation in the UNGC initiative, there has been a new awareness of the rights of workers by both employers and employees, which are in line with prevailing global labour standards (Abe, 2016). Nigeria has been witnessing incessant labour strikes in the past, such as labour strikes carried out by the Academic Staff Union of Universities (ASUU) since the 1990s and more recently in 2013 (Ugwuona, 2016), and this has been due to the Nigerian government's inability to meet their legitimate demands, which include improvement in funding, among other demands (Albert, 2014). According to Collins (2013), labour unions motivate the workers, increase productivity and protect the workers' rights and interests. Adewale, Banjo and Elumah (2013) agree that co-operation between labour unions and employers (both state and private) can boost organisation performance. Since not all labour is legal, Nigeria faces a big problem of having child labourers, which is against the UNGC initiative's labour principles. Child labour is on the increase in Nigeria due to prevalent household poverty (Nwazuoke & Igwe, 2016; Ugochukwu, Okeke, & Onubogu, 2012). According to Ugochukwu et al. (2012), children in Nnewi, a city in Anambra state in southeastern Nigeria, have taken to the streets to sell items to assist their parents in meeting the family needs. Ben-Chendo et al. (2012) also affirm that child workers are mostly utilised in palm oil processing with the children taking up roles in bunch harvesting (Bamidele, 2015), which is very risky and could lead to injuries. On a more formal level and dealing with corporations, child labour hardly exists as more organised businesses require adults (youths above 18) with other necessary requirements, such as educational qualifications for the engagement of potential employees. Another labour challenge prevalent in Nigeria is gender discrimination with respect to employment. According to Adebayo and Akanle (2014), gender imbalance is rampant in the work place and in social institutions in Nigeria. This may be due to prevalent cultural norms that limit the ability of women to domestic work at home. Although the aforementioned labour challenges are prevalent in Nigeria, business responses to these challenges in line with the UNGC initiative are:

- A non-discriminating recruitment system, such as the e-recruitment system whereby technology in the form of web based resources is utilized in the recruitment process of employees (Amusan & Oyediran, 2016; Chidi, 2013);
- Equal opportunities to both male and female prospective hires;
- The use of skilled and adult labour; and
- Respecting and encouraging the rights to freedom of association and the right to collective bargaining among other practices in line with acceptable global best practices.

Finally, on corruption and Nigeria's anti-corruption measures. Cases of corruption are prevalent in Nigeria. According to Okoosi-Simbine (2011), Nigeria has been experiencing corrupt practices for a long time and the situation has been among some of the reasons for military intervention in the country. In addition, the private sector in Nigeria has also witnessed several cases of corruption (Ufere, Perelli, Boland & Carlsson, 2012). According to Otusanya, Lauwo, and Ajibolade (2013), corruption is endemic in the private sector as the recent banking crisis in Nigeria showed that some bank executives were into corrupt practices (Sanusi, 2010;Sanusi, 2012).As in the rest of the world, the banking sector is a key service sector in Nigeria and it has also witnessed some major cases of failed banks due to instances of serious fraud, such as insider loans, which led to depositors forfeiting their funds (Brownbridge, 1998;Sanusi, 2010;Sanusi, 2012). According to Transparency International (2015), Nigeria is ranked 136 with 26% in terms of perceived levels of public sector corruption compared to 168 countries around the world. This rating is very poor and it reiterates the need for Nigeria to take the UNGC initiative principle on corruption seriously in order to reduce cases of corruption in the country. As the country's reputation is tainted with corruption (Smith, 2010), steps have been taken by Nigeria with the adoption of the UNGC initiative principles in 2006 (United Nations Global Compact, 2015a) while campaigns are being utilised to make individuals change their attitudes on the issue of corruption (Musari, 2016). Nigeria has established corporate governance regulatory institutions, such as a corporate affairs commission (CAC), the Central Bank of Nigeria, security and exchange commissions among others but their enforcement activities are not too stringent compared to developed economies (Adeoye, 2015). In addition, Nigeria has also witnessed the establishment of anti-corruption agencies like the Economic and Financial Crimes Commission (EFCC) (Raimi, Suara & Fadipe, 2013;Obuah, 2010) and the Independent Corrupt Practices and Other Related Offences Commission (ICPC) (Raimi, Suara & Fadipe, 2013) amongst many others (Ocheni & Nwankwo, 2012). Other initiatives include the establishment of codes of conduct on bribery and corruption by some organisations (Adewuyi & Olowookere, 2010) in order to fight bribery and corruption.

Responsible and Sustainable Management Practices in Business in the United Kingdom's Developed Business Environment

Responsible and sustainable management practices in the United Kingdom are highly practiced and advanced compared to what is being practiced in developing countries (Nasrullah & Rahim, 2014). These practices also take the form of CSR and have been accepted and are being used in business activities, business processes, business outputs and social interactions in the United Kingdom (Karim, Suh, Carter

& Zhang, 2015). According to Musafer (2012), CSR is a major corporate strategy among UK firms. According to Chaplier (2014), there are moves by the European Union (EU) to make it mandatory for large companies to report on environmental and social impacts. These social impacts are clearly the focus of the European Union, which the United Kingdom is a member country.

Firms in the United Kingdom are increasingly making deliberate attempts to ensure that all their business activities are sustainable and beneficial to society (Walker & Jones, 2012). Unlike what is obtainable in developing countries, the United Kingdom has been experiencing positive situations with regard to the UNGC initiative expectations and 10 principles due to high compliance levels by businesses in the United Kingdom (Anastasi, 2005; Carby-Hall, 2016). A typical example as revealed by Walker and Jones (2012) indicates sustainable supply chain management is a major strategy across the UK private sector. This is a major boost to the country's sustainability strategy while Unerman, Bebbington, and Dwyer (2007) affirm that firms also adopt sustainability accounting in their CSR activities.

Focusing on the UNGC initiative with respect to human rights, labour, environment and anti-corruption measures, there is significant evidence that the United Kingdom has done well compared to any developing country (Chen & Bouvain, 2009; Najam, 2005). However, there is a need to present situational analysis of issues and business responses which are in line with the UNGC initiative's 10 principles.

Human rights supportive policies with respect to business activities exist in the United Kingdom in line with the global business best practices (Burtler, 2016). According to Davis and Rickford (2008), the United Kingdom established the UK Company's Act in 2006 to guide business conduct in the United Kingdom. In addition, the UK Company's Act 2006 has undergone changes that required larger companies to report their outcomes in terms of human rights and the society (UK Government, 2013). Additional guidance on corporate reporting and external auditing with respect to business activities is monitored by the United Kingdom through the reporting standards described by the Financial Reporting Council (FRC) (Anders, 2015). This council mandates companies to report information that includes

- Indicators regarding human rights outcomes due to business activities;
- The monitoring of human rights outcomes;
- Communicating with the relevant stakeholders on human rights outcomes; and
- Solving issues arising from human rights outcomes among other relevant information to be reported by businesses in the United Kingdom (Financial Reporting Council, 2014; UK Government, 2013).

With these measures, cases of human rights infringement are limited and dealt with promptly according to established protocols and shareholders' decisions (Financial Reporting Council, 2014; Keay, 2012; Sarkar, 2015). Evidence by Arcot, Bruno and Faure-Grimaud (2010) and Shrives and Brennan (2015) indicate a high level of compliance by businesses in the United Kingdom.

With respect to labour, the United Kingdom operates a deregulated labour market (Bruegel & Perrons, 1998; Michie & Sheehan, 2003), has freedom of association with respect to trade unions (Wills, 2001) and encourages the right to collective bargaining (Gospel, Lockwood, & William, 2000). The country also has policies that are largely anti-discriminatory by nature (Butler, 2016; McLean, 2015). However, the United Kingdom has also had its fair share of labour strikes where its workers demanded certain rights or shown their grievances to prevailing labour conditions (Darlington, 2014). According to Lyddon (2015), the United Kingdom has experienced labour strikes between 1964 and 2014. Labour strikes in the United Kingdom have however greatly reduced since the early 1990s (Lyddon, 2015). In terms of its anti-discriminatory policy, Bruegel and Perrons (1998) affirm that the United Kingdom is an equal opportunities employer and this greatly favours women in the United Kingdom (Hope & Ross, 2010). However, Howe-Walsh and Turnbull, (2016) and Knights and Richards (2003) indicate that there is some element of gender discrimination in the United Kingdom in the academia as some women experience discrimination with respect to their contract status and career progression in the academic hierarchy. This is driven according to the male perception of success, which include active research history and having no gaps in the career history among many male-favoured requirements (Howe-Walsh & Turnbull, 2016; Knights & Richards, 2003). As an equal opportunities employer, the United Kingdom has ensured that there are minimal cases of discrimination even with its disabled citizens by supporting the disabled with legislations in every aspect of the society (Lane & Munkholm, 2015). According to Jackson and Furnham (2000), the United Kingdom made provision for the employment of disabled persons by the enactment of the 1995 Disability Discrimination Act (DDA) and employers are willing to comply based on their positive dispositions towards persons with disability and their understanding of the details of the Act (Jackson & Furnham, 2000). However, evidence by Bell and Heitmueller (2009) indicates that this has not resulted in the improvement of the employment rates of disabled persons in the United Kingdom. In the United Kingdom, labour and labour issues have been adequately addressed compared to what is being done in developing countries (Odeku & Animashaun, 2012). Some of the United Kingdom's labour practices include ensuring that workers are not discriminated against based on their labour conditions and ensuring that their rights to be gainfully employed and represented by associations are respected regardless of their disability, ethnicity, gender or religion, amongst other issues (Butler, 2016; Green, 2008).

On environmental issues, large firms and small firms engage in various environmentally sustainable environmental initiatives. According to Brammer, Hoejmose, and Marchant (2012), small firms in the United Kingdom partake in diverse ways in various environmental initiatives. This reflects a high level of adherence to sustainability issues in the United Kingdom unlike what is being done in developing countries where large firms are expected to be the major facilitators of environmental initiatives due to huge exploration activities (Abe, 2016). The United Kingdom also leads the way in recycling activities (DaCruz, Ferreira, Cabral, Simoes & Marques, 2014) and ensuring that carbon targets are defined, such as reducing emissions by 80% by 2050 and that these are met as and when due (Foxon, 2013). According to Dimireva (2012), the United Kingdom is strict on business compliance with its social and environmental rules. Dimireva (2012) affirms that the United Kingdom has programmes such as Evirowise, which is funded by the UK government to assist in the upgrade of the UK environmental performance and cost reduction alongside the Waste and Resources Action Programme (WRAP), which assists businesses and households in reducing waste and enabling them to benefit from sustainable practices. Other positives are in the area of the creation and scaling of environmentally friendly technologies. According to Caprotti (2012), there is high interest to invest in low-carbon emission technologies, while Demirel and Kesidou (2011) affirm that government and firms are seriously advocating for clean technologies, and the creation of different types of eco-innovation is on the rise in the United Kingdom. This clearly shows the United Kingdom's participation in initiatives and activities that encourage environmental responsibility that benefits all stakeholders in the society.

In considering corruption in the United Kingdom, the incidence of corrupt practices is low in the United Kingdom compared to other parts of the world and especially in developing countries (Allen,

Qian & Shen, 2015; Svensson, 2005). Cases of bribery and extortion are very rare in the United Kingdom compared to other forms of corruption (Monbiot, 2015). The prevention of corruption within the United Kingdom and by its businesses operating outside the United Kingdom is the major focus of the UK government in their fight against corruption (Mukwiri, 2015). According to Lord (2013), the United Kingdom is very strict in enforcing its anti-corruption laws and has put in place self-regulating agencies and hybrid technologies to fight corruption. This assertion is further given credibility by Transparency International (2015) in its perceived level of public sector corruption where it ranked the United Kingdom in joint 10th position with two other countries and scoring the United Kingdom 81 out of 100 indicating that its public sector is having minimal levels of corruption and corrupt activities. In addition, the United Kingdom has a corporate governance code referred to as 'the revised 2003 Combined Code on corporate governance' (Code, 2003) and large companies are complying with the guidelines of the code with a few yet to comply fully (Pass, 2006; Shrives & Brennan, 2015).

A Comparative Analysis of Responsible and Sustainable Management Practices of Businesses in Nigeria and the United Kingdom

The establishment of the UNGC initiative's 10 principles in 2000 (Rasche, 2009) has led to several responsible and sustainable management practices being designed and emulated in various environments. For ease of analysis for this chapter, the focus is on comparing responsible and sustainable management practices in both developing (Nigeria) and developed (United Kingdom) business environments with respect to situations prevalent in both countries. Table 1 reveals information on similarities of practices observed in both business environments, while Table 2 shows differences in practices in the business environments under review.

From the comparison made between the United Kingdom and Nigeria, it was found that both countries have policies and institutions set up to control and monitor activities relating to labour, human rights, environment and anti-corruption measures. However in terms of adherence to the practices of the UNGC initiative's 10 principles, the obvious differences in the situations in both countries suggest that the United Kingdom has done an excellent job in adhering to the principles of the UNGC initiative with Nigeria lagging behind. In addition, the UK situation is not yet perfect but they have made giant strides in compliance with all the principles.

Table 1. Comparative table (similarities)

Item Number	Compared Item	Responsible and Sustainable Management Practices in Business in Nigeria and the United Kingdom
1	Human rights	Both countries have institutions that deal with human rights issues.
2	Labour	Both countries have labour unions in place, which allows for collective representation and bargaining.
3	Environment	Both countries have policies to protect the environment.
4	Anti-corruption measures	Both countries conduct anti-corruption measures and have agencies that investigate and punish offenders.

Source: Author's own compilation

Table 2. Comparative table (differences)

Item Number	Compared Item	Responsible and Sustainable Management practice in Business in Nigeria	Responsible and Sustainable Management practice in Business in the United Kingdom
1	Human Rights	1.Human rights abuses high.	1.Human rights abuses low.
2	Labour	1. Discrimination with respect to gender is moderate due to cultural influences relegating many women to domestic work at their homes. • Child labour is high. • Compulsory labour is high	1. Discrimination with respect to gender is low with the equal opportunities policy, which is active in the United Kingdom. • Child labour has been abolished. • Compulsory labour has been abolished.
3	Environment	3. Precautionary approach to environmental challenges is low. 4. Creation of environmentally friendly technologies is low.	3. Precautionary approach to environmental challenges is high. 4. Creation of environmentally friendly technologies is high.
4	Anti-corruption measures	2. Anti-corruption measures are less effective.	2. Anti-corruption measures are more effective.

Source: Author's own compilation.

An Impact Analysis of Responsible and Sustainable Management Practices in Business in Nigeria and the United Kingdom

There are numerous outcomes of responsible and sustainable management practices in business with many of these positive. These outcomes have been felt by businesses, stakeholders and the society.

For businesses, the outcome has been revolutionary, changing much of the established business protocols and business processes and having a direct effect on key business associates and the business environments. According to United Nations Global Compact (2015e), its primary objective is to transform businesses and eventually to have a positive influence in the world. The United Nations Global Compact (2015d) also affirms that working with businesses will create a sustainable global economy, which will produce sustainable benefits to people, communities and markets. Since the projection of the UNGC initiative to businesses, stakeholders and societies, there have been remarkable results, such as ethical leadership (De Hoogh & Den Hartog, 2008: Zhu et al., 2014), corporate social responsibilities (Centindamar, 2007; McWilliams & Siegel, 2000), anti-corruption crusades (Musari, 2016) amongst other significant outcomes.

The rise in ethical leadership cannot be overemphasised with more firms signing up voluntarily for the UNGC initiative (United Nations Global Compact, 2016). Ethical leadership enables morally conscious leaders to lead firms and establishments in various business environments (Bello, 2012). This can be felt in the various responsible and sustainable management practices the firms adopt in their day-to-day business environments.

Another outcome is the establishment of CSR initiatives, which enable businesses to conduct their business ethically and to contribute to the overall development of the host community and the society. In addition, CSR is now a legitimate business function (McWilliams & Siegel, 2000) and businesses adopting CSR initiatives do so because it is ethical and it is improving their economic status (Centindamar, 2007). Centindamar (2007) also affirms that certain evidence has shown that CSR activities improve corporate image and enable businesses to gain network opportunities. It is also important to state that certain areas, such as the environment and workers' welfare, are among the areas with great influence that are part of the CSR reports of businesses since gaining membership of the UNGC initiative (Chen & Bouvain, 2009).

FUTURE RESEARCH DIRECTIONS

Existing literature on responsible and sustainable management practices in business shows that the UNGC initiative's 10 principles complement incomplete state and non-state laws (Rasche, 2009) and the implementation by businesses and other stakeholders of these principles is voluntary (Rasche & Kell, 2010). It is also noted that the voluntary nature of the UNGC initiative is advantageous as evidenced by Perez-Batres, Miller, and Pisani (2011) who affirm that academia and peers influence the increase of sustainable development initiatives when compared to coercive (government) regulations.

More businesses and their CSR activities are having an influence on the environment and workers' welfare with institutional arrangements in various countries influencing and promoting these activities. Based on these findings and the significance of responsible and sustainable management practices in businesses, there is need to research more outcomes which affect specifically human rights, labour, the environment and anti-corruption measures. Future research directions should focus on investigating ethical leadership in both developed and developing business environments using a comparative study focusing on various sectors of the economy. Research could investigate the effect of responsible and sustainable management practices on employee retention and employees' welfare in practicing businesses. It should also investigate the effect of responsible and sustainable management practices on alliance building and partnerships among firms such as business and contractor relationships. Research could also consider the effect of responsible and sustainable management practices on decision-making in mining and exploration of mineral resources in developing economies, and lastly, investigate the effect of responsible and sustainable management practices on lobbying activities with respect to contract bidding and public–private partnership collaborations public/private partnership collaborations.

CONCLUSION

In providing definitions of responsible and sustainable management practices in business, the adoption of the UNGC initiative's 10 principles provides a universal standardised business code for businesses to implement in their diverse business environments based on prevailing circumstances and situations. The UNGC initiative has also led to an increase in ethical leadership and the quality of responsible and sustainable management practices such as CSR by businesses for the benefit of their communities.

Other benefits include a reduction in unethical practices as experienced before the advent of global standards, which demand best practices for the benefit of all stakeholders while organisational internal ethical behaviour reflects in business outputs in the form of ethical goods and services from enshrined ethical business policies, human resource management and processes. An additional benefit to all stakeholders is the continuous awareness of ethical practices that promote good deeds in the society and preserves the environment for the benefit of all.

Finally, the UNGC initiative's 10 principles' focus on human rights, labour, the environment and anti-corruption measures creates a synergy and a cycle of opportunities for businesses and their stakeholders which could assist in creating a safe and prosperous society.

REFERENCES

Abe, O. (2016). The feasibility of implementing the United Nations guiding principles on business and human rights in the extractive industry in Nigeria. *Journal of Sustainable Development Law and Policy(The)*, *7*(1), 137–157. doi:10.4314/jsdlp.v7i1.7

Abiodun, E. (2015). *Ensuring transparent, sustainable capital market.* Retrieved from http://www.thisdaylive.com/index.php/2016/06/22/ensuring-transparent-sustainable-capital-market/

Adebayo, A. A., & Akanle, O. (2014). Gender and the academy in Nigeria. *African Journal for Psychological and Social Sciences Issues*, *17*(1), 147–154.

Adekola, J., Fischbacher-Smith, M., Fischbacher-Smith, D., & Adekola, O. A. (2016). Health risks from environmental degradation in the Niger Delta, Nigeria. *Environment and Planning. C, Government & Policy*. doi:10.1177/0263774X16661720

Adeoye, A. A. (2015). Examining corporate governance practices in Nigerian and South African firms. *European Journal of Accounting Auditing and Finance*, *3*(1), 10–29.

Adewale, O. F., Banjo, H., & Eluma, L. O. (2013). Presence of labour unions and performance of firms: A study of public and private firms in Nigeria. *Social Science Research Network*. Retrieved from http://ssrn.com/abstract=2634992

Adewuyi, A. O., & Olowookere, A. E. (2010). CSR and sustainable community development in Nigeria: WAPCO, a case study from the cement industry. *Social Responsibility Journal*, *6*(4), 522–535. doi:10.1108/17471111011083419

Aghedo, I. (2015). Sowing peace, reaping violence: Understanding the resurgence of kidnapping in post-amnesty Niger Delta, Nigeria. *Insight on Africa*, *7*(2), 137–153. doi:10.1177/0975087815580729

Ako, R., & Ekhator, E. O. (2016). The civil society and the regulation of the extractive industry in Nigeria. *Journal of Sustainable Development Law and Policy(The)*, *7*(1), 183–203. doi:10.4314/jsdlp.v7i1.9

Albert, I. O. (2014). Beyond moral panic: Negotiation theory and the university strikes in Nigeria.*Journal of Global Initiatives: Policy, Pedagogy. Perspective*, *9*(2), 81–98.

Aliyu, A. N. (2013). Ethical leadership and good governance. *European Journal of Humanities and Social Sciences*, *27*(1), 1449–1461.

Allen, F., Qian, J., & Shen, L. (2015). *Corruption and competition.* Available at SSRN 2685219

Alston, P., & Heenan, J. (2003). Shrinking the international labour code: an unintended consequences of the 1998 ILO declaration on fundamental principles and rights at work, in: N.Y.U. *Journal of International Law and Politics*, *36*, 221–264.

Amaeshi, K., Adegbite, E., & Rajwani, T. (2016). Corporate social responsibility in challenging and non-enabling institutional contexts: Do institutional voids matter? *Journal of Business Ethics*, *134*(1), 135–153. doi:10.1007/s10551-014-2420-4

Amusan, D. G., & Oyediran, M. O. (2016). Development of efficient e-recruitment system for university staff in Nigeria. *Circulation in Computer Science*, *1*(1), 10–14.

Anastasi, S. (2005). The UN Global Compact in the UK: An analysis of the achievements of the UK forum to date. *Earth and Environment*, *1*, 1–18.

Anders, S. B. (2015). Financial Reporting Council. *The CPA Journal*, *85*(7), 72–73.

Arcot, S., Bruno, V., & Faure-Grimaud, A. (2010). Corporate governance in the UK: Is the comply or explain approach working? *International Review of Law and Economics*, *30*(2), 193–201. doi:10.1016/j.irle.2010.03.002

Ardichvili, A., Mitchell, J. A., & Jondle, D. (2009). Characteristics of ethical business cultures. *Journal of Business Ethics*, *4*(4), 445–451. doi:10.1007/s10551-008-9782-4

Arowosegbe, J. O. (2009). Violence and national development in Nigeria: The political economy of youth restiveness in the Niger Delta. *Review of African Political Economy*, *36*(122), 575–594. doi:10.1080/03056240903346178

Ayanlade, A., & Proske, U. (2016). Assessing wetland degradation and loss of ecosystem services in the Niger Delta, Nigeria. *Marine & Freshwater Research*, *67*(6), 828–836. doi:10.1071/MF15066

Ayoola, T. J., & Olasanmi, O. O. (2013). Business case for integrated reporting in the Nigerian oil and gas sector. *Issues in Social and Environmental Accounting*, *7*(1), 30–54.

Bamidele, J. (2015). Occupational hazards and their effect on the health and socio-economic status of local palm oil processor in Delta state, Nigeria. *Annals of Agricultural and Environmental Medicine*, *22*(3), 483–487. doi:10.5604/12321966.1167719 PMID:26403120

Bansal, P., & Roth, K. (2000). Why companies go green: A model of ecological responsiveness. *Academy of Management Journal*, *43*(4), 717–736. doi:10.2307/1556363

Baumann-Pauly, D., & Scherer, A. G. (2013). The organizational implementation of corporate citizenship: An assessment tool and its application at UN Global Compact participants. *Journal of Business Ethics*, *117*(1), 1–17. doi:10.1007/s10551-012-1502-4

Bell, D., & Heitmueller, A. (2009). The disability discrimination ACT in the UK: Helping or hindering employment among the disabled? *Journal of Health Economics*, *28*(2), 465–480. doi:10.1016/j.jhealeco.2008.10.006 PMID:19091434

Bello, S. M. (2012). Impact of ethical leadership on employee job performance. *International Journal of Business and Social Science*, *3*(11), 228–236.

Ben-Chendo, G. N., Lemch, J. I., Ohajianya, D. O., Eze, C. C., Emeyeonu, C., & Ehirim, N. C. (2012). Household poverty and its effect on child labour use among palm oil processors in Abia state, Nigeria. *Journal of Developing Societies*, *1*(1), 27–30.

Braide, O., Remoue, C., Rat, G., Anozie, I., Vandeville, P., Ahiamadu, N., & Ganga, D. et al. (2016). Gas flaring reduction initiative Ofon phase 2 project. In *SPE International Conference and Exhibition on Health, Safety, Security, Environment, and Social Responsibility*. Society of Petroleum Engineers. doi:10.2118/179340-MS

Brammer, S., Hoejmose, S., & Marchant, K. (2012). Environment management in SMEs in the UK: Practices, pressures and perceived benefits. *Business Strategy and the Environment*, *21*(7), 423–434. doi:10.1002/bse.717

Brownbridge, M. (1998). Financial distress in local banks in Kenya, Nigeria, Uganda and Zambia: Causes and implications for regulatory policy. *Development Policy Review*, *16*(2), 173–188. doi:10.1111/1467-7679.00057

Bruegel, I., & Perrons, D. (1998). Deregulation and women's employment: The diverse experiences of women in Britain. *Feminist Economics*, *4*(1), 103–125. doi:10.1080/135457098338581

Butler, M. (2016).Equality and anti-discrimination law: the Equality Act 2010 and other anti-discrimination protections. London: Spiramus Publishing.

Caprotti, F. (2012). The cultural economy of cleantech: Environmental discourse and the emergence of a new technology sector. *Transactions of the Institute of British Geographers*, *37*(3), 370–385. doi:10.1111/j.1475-5661.2011.00485.x

Carby-Hall, J. (2016). Labour aspects of corporate social responsibility emanating from the United Nations Global Compact: The global case and that of the EU and the United Kingdom. *E-Journal of International and Comparative Labour Studies, 5*(2).

Carroll, A. B. (2004). Managing ethically with global stakeholders: A present and future challenge. *The Academy of Management Executive*, *18*(2), 114–120. doi:10.5465/AME.2004.13836269

Centindamar, D. (2007). Corporate social responsibility practice and environmental responsible behaviour: The case of the United Nations Global Impact. *Journal of Business Ethics*, *76*(2), 163–176. doi:10.1007/s10551-006-9265-4

Chaplier, J. (2014, February). EU to force large companies to report on environmental and social impacts. *The Guardian*. Retrieved from http://www.theguardian.com/sustainable-business/eu-reform-listed-companies-report-environmental-social-impact

Chen, S., & Bouvain, P. (2009). Is corporate responsibility converging? A comparison of corporate responsibility reporting in the USA, UK, Australia and Germany. *Journal of Business Ethics*, *87*(S1), 299–317. doi:10.1007/s10551-008-9794-0

Chidi, O.C. (2013). Recruitment practices and performance of unionised organisations in the food, beverage and tobacco industry in Lagos state, Nigeria. *Interdisciplinary Journal of Contemporary Research in Business, 5*(6), 359-384.

Chin, M. K., Hambrick, D. C., & Trevino, C. K. (2013). Political ideologies of CEOs: The influence of executives' values on corporate of social responsibilities. *Administrative Science Quarterly*, *58*(2), 197–232. doi:10.1177/0001839213486984

Code, C. (2003). *The combined code on corporate governance*. London: Financial Reporting Council.

Collins, E. (2013). Labour unionism and its effect on organizational productivity: A case study of Jos International Breweries(JIB) PLC, Nigeria. *African Research Review*, *7*(4), 36–48.

Da Cruz, N. F., Ferreira, S., Cabra, M., Simoes, P., & Marques, R. C. (2014). Packaging waste recycling in Europe: Is the industry paying for it? *Waste Management (New York, N.Y.)*, *34*(2), 298–308. doi:10.1016/j.wasman.2013.10.035 PMID:24262429

Daramola, A., & Ibem, E. O. (2010). Urban environmental problems in Nigeria: Implications for sustainable development. *Journal of Sustainable Development in Nigeria*, *12*(1), 124–145.

Darlington, R. (2014). Strike waves, union growth and the rank-and-file/bureaucracy interplay: Britain 1889-1890, 1910-1913 and 1919-1920. *Labour History*, *55*(1), 1–20. doi:10.1080/0023656X.2013.871476

Davis, P., & Rickford, J. (2008). An introduction to the new UK Company's Act. *European and Financial Law*, *5*(1), 48–71.

De Hoogh, A. H. B., & Den Hartog, D. N. (2008). Ethical and despotic leadership, relationships with leader's social responsibility, top management team effectiveness and subordinates' optimism: A multimethod study. *The Leadership Quarterly*, *19*(3), 297–311. doi:10.1016/j.leaqua.2008.03.002

De Montclos, M. A. P. (2014). The politics and crisis of the petroleum industry bill of Nigeria. *The Journal of Modern African Studies*, *52*(3), 403–424. doi:10.1017/S0022278X1400024X

Demirel, P., & Kesidou, E. (2011). Stimulating different types of eco-innovation in the UK. Government policies and firm innovations. *Ecological Economics*, *70*(8), 1546–1557. doi:10.1016/j.ecolecon.2011.03.019

Dimireva, I. (2012, February). Doing business in the UK: Sustainability. *EU Business*. Retrieved from http://www.eubusiness.com/europe/uk/sustainable-business

Doner, R. F., & Schneider, B. R. (2000). Business associations and economic development: Why some associations contribute more than others. *Business and Politics*, *2*(3), 261–288. doi:10.2202/1469-3569.1011

Donnelly, J. (2013). *Universal human rights in theory and practice*. Cornell University Press.

Du, S., Swaen, V., & Lindgreen, A. (2013). The roles of leadership styles in CSR. *Journal of Business Ethics*, *114*(1), 155–169. doi:10.1007/s10551-012-1333-3

Echefu, N., & Akpofure, E. (2002). *Environmental impact assessment in Nigeria: regulatory background and procedural framework. Environmental Impact Assessment (EIA)*. Training Resource Manual.

Elum, Z. A., Mopipi, K., & Henri-Ukoha, A. (2016). Oil exploitation and its socioeconomic effects on the Niger Delta region of Nigeria. *Environmental Science and Pollution Research International*, *23*(13), 12880–12889. doi:10.1007/s11356-016-6864-1 PMID:27194013

Emmanuel, O., & Gordon, D. (2006). The effect of oil spillage on crop yield and farm income in delta state in Nigeria. *Journal of Central European Agriculture*, *7*(1), 41–48.

Emodi, V. N., Yusuf, S. D., & Boo, K. J. (2014). The necessity of the development of standards for renewable energy technologies in Nigeria. *Smart Grid and Renewable Energy*, *5*(11), 259–274. doi:10.4236/sgre.2014.511024

Enuoh, R. O., & Inyang, B. J. (2014). Effective management of corporate social responsibility (CSR) for desired outcome: The Niger Delta issue in Nigeria. *Journal of Business Administration*, *5*(4), 32–38.

Esan, A. L., & Babatola, E. B. (2015). Urbanization and its environmental impacts in Nigeria: Implications for sustainable development. (A case study of Ado-Ekiti). *Pyrex Journal of Research in Environmental Studies*, *2*(3), 27–34.

Eweje, G. (2006a). Environmental cost and responsibilities resulting from oil exploitation in developing countries: The case of the Niger Delta of Nigeria. *Journal of Business Ethics*, *1*(1), 27–56. doi:10.1007/s10551-006-9067-8

Eweje, G. (2006b). The role of MNEs in community development initiative in developing countries' corporate social responsibility at work in Nigeria and South Africa. *Business & Society*, *45*(2), 93–129. doi:10.1177/0007650305285394

Eze, O. C., & Chinwuba, U. G. (2015). Organized labour, democracy and good governance in Nigeria, 1999-2007. *Journal of Politics and Law*, *8*(1), 149. doi:10.5539/jpl.v8n1p149

Farmer, P. (2004). *Pathologies of power: Health, Human rights, and the new war on the poor* (Vol. 4). Berkeley, CA: University of California Press.

Financial Reporting Council (FRC). (2014). *Guidance on the strategic report*. London: Financial Reporting Council.

Foxon, T. J. (2013). Transition pathways for a UK low carbon electricity future. *Energy Policy*, *52*, 10–24. doi:10.1016/j.enpol.2012.04.001

Garriga, E., & Mele, D. (2004). Corporate social responsibility theories: Mapping the territory. *Journal of Business Ethics*, *53*(1-2), 51–71. doi:10.1023/B:BUSI.0000039399.90587.34

Gill, S. S., Haider, S., & Noreen, S. (2016). Linking ethical leadership with organizational deviance and CSR: Empirical review. *Asian Journal of Multidisciplinary Studies*, *4*(6), 23–28.

Gospel, H., Lockwood, G., & Willman, P. (2000). British dilemma: Disclosure of information for collective bargaining and joint consultation. *Comparative Labor Law & Policy Journal*, *22*(2), 101–123.

Green, F. (2008). Temporary work and insecurity in Britain: A problem solved? *Social Indicators Research*, *88*(1), 147–160. doi:10.1007/s11205-007-9204-5

Hainmueller, J., & Hiscox, M. J. (2015). *The socially conscious consumer? Field experiment tests of consumer support for fair labour standards*. MIT Political Science Department Research Paper No. 2012-15.

Hale, T. (2011). United Nations Global Compact. In T. Hale & D. Held (Eds.), *Handbook of transnational governance: Institutions and innovations*. Cambridge, UK: Polity Press.

Hens, L. (2005). *The rio declaration on environment and development. Regional sustainable development review: Africa*. Oxford, UK: Eolss Publishers.

Holme, R., & Watts, P. (1999). *Corporate social responsibility*. Geneva: World Business Council for Sustainable Development.

Hope, C., & Ross, T. (2010). *Britain embraces positive action to abolish work place discrimination*. Retrieved from http://www.telegraph.co.uk/news/uknews/8177872/Britain-embraces-positive-action-to-abolish-workplace-discrimination.html

Howe-Walsh, L., & Turnbull, S. (2016). Barriers to women leaders in academia: Tales from science and technology. *Studies in Higher Education*, *41*(3), 415–428. doi:10.1080/03075079.2014.929102

Idemudia, U., & Osayande, N. (2016). Assessing the effect of corporate social responsibility on community development in the Niger Delta: A corporate perspective. *Community Development Journal: An International Forum*. doi:10.1093/cdj/bsw019

Ikelegbe, A. (2001). Civil society, oil and conflict in the Niger Delta region of Nigeria: Ramifications of civil society for a regional resource struggle. *The Journal of Modern African Studies*, *39*(3), 437–469. doi:10.1017/S0022278X01003676

Ingelson, A., & Nwapi, C. (2014). Environmental impact assessment process for oil, gas and mining projects in Nigeria: A critical analysis. *Law, Environment & Development Journal*, *10*(1), 35–56.

Ite, U. E. (2007). Changing times and strategies: Shell's contribution to sustainable community development in the Niger Delta, Nigeria. *Sustainable Development*, *15*(1), 1–14. doi:10.1002/sd.294

Jackson, C. J., Furnham, A., & Willen, K. (2000). Employer willingness to comply with the Disability Discrimination Act regarding staff selection in the UK. *Journal of Occupational and Organizational Psychology*, *73*(1), 119–129. doi:10.1348/096317900166912

Jany-Catrice, F., & Lehndorff, S. (2005). Work organization and the importance of labour markets in the European retail trade. Working in the service sector –a tale from different worlds. Academic Press.

Jike, V. T. (2004). Environmental degradation, social disequilibrium and the dilemma of sustainable development in Niger Delta of Nigeria. *Journal of Black Studies*, *34*(5), 686–701. doi:10.1177/0021934703261934

Kadafa, A. A. (2012). Oil exploration and spillage in the Niger Delta of Nigeria. *Civil and Environmental Research*, *2*(3), 38–51.

Karim, K., Suh, S., Carter, C., & Zhang, M. (2015). Corporate social responsibility: Evidence from the United Kingdom. *Journal of International Business Research*, *14*(1), 85–100.

Keay, A. (2014). Comply or explain in corporate governance codes: In need of greater regulatory oversight? *Legal Studies*, *34*(2), 279–304. doi:10.1111/lest.12014

Kemp, D., & Vanclay, F. (2013). Human rights and impact assessment: Clarifying the connections in practice. *Human Rights and Impact Assessment*, *31*(2), 86–96.

Kemp, H. (2014, January). The cost of corruption is a serious challenge for companies. *The Guardian*. Retrieved from http://www.theguardian.com/sustainable-business/corruption-bribery-cost-serious-challenge-business

Kerr, S. N. (2012). *A blessing in disguise? Ghana's potential to overcome Nigeria's oil curse and develop a successful model for oil production within human rights frame work. Senior Theses*. Hartford: Trinity College.

King, A. A., & Lenox, M. J. (2000). Industry self-regulation without sanctions: The chemical industry's responsible care program. *Academy of Management Journal*, *43*(4), 698–716. doi:10.2307/1556362

Knights, D., & Richards, W. (2003). Sex, discrimination in the UK academia. *Gender, Work and Organization*, *10*(2), 213–238. doi:10.1111/1468-0432.t01-1-00012

Lane, J., & Munkholm, N. V. (2015). Danish and British protection from disability discrimination at work-past, present and future. *International Journal of Comparative Labour Law and Industrial Relations*, *31*(1), 91–113.

Laroche, M., Bergeron, J., & Barbaro-Forleo, G. (2001). Targeting consumers who are willing to pay more for environmentally friendly products. *Journal of Consumer Marketing*, *18*(6), 503–520. doi:10.1108/EUM0000000006155

Leisinger, K. M. (2003). Opportunities and risks of the United Nations Global Compact. *Journal of Corporate Citizenship*, *11*(19), 113–132. doi:10.9774/GLEAF.4700.2003.au.00013

Lin-Hi, N., & Muller, K. (2013). The CSR bottom line: Preventing corporate social irresponsibility. *Journal of Business Research*, *66*(10), 1928–1936. doi:10.1016/j.jbusres.2013.02.015

Lord, N. (2013). Regulating transactional corporate bribery: Anti-bribery and corruption in the UK and Germany. *Crime, Law, and Social Change*, *60*(2), 127–145. doi:10.1007/s10611-013-9445-y

Lyddon, D. (2015). The changing pattern of UK strikes, 1964–2014. *Employee Relations*, *37*(6), 733–745.

Maconachie, R. (2016). *Urban growth and land degradation in developing cities: Change and challenges in Kano*. Routledge.

Mann, R., Adebanjo, O., & Kehoe, D. (1998). Best practices in food and drinks industry. *Benchmarking for Quality Management & Technology*, *5*(3), 184–199. doi:10.1108/14635779810226207

McLean, S. (2015). The Disability Discrimination Act(Section 3) 20 years on: Has it been successful?*Journal of Building Survey. Appraisal and Valuation*, *3*(4), 352–359.

McWilliams, A., & Siegel, D. (2000). Corporate social responsibility and financial performance:Correlation or misspecification? *Strategic Management Journal*, *21*(5), 603–609. doi:10.1002/(SICI)1097-0266(200005)21:5<603::AID-SMJ101>3.0.CO;2-3

Michie, J., & Sheehan, M. (2003). Labour market deregulation, flexibility and innovation. *Cambridge Journal of Economics*, *27*(1), 123–143. doi:10.1093/cje/27.1.123

Moldan, B., Janouskova, S., & Hak, T. (2012). How to understand and measure environmental sustainability: Indicators and targets. *Ecological Indicators*, *17*, 4–13. doi:10.1016/j.ecolind.2011.04.033

Monbiot, G. (2015, March). Let's not fool ourselves.We may not bribe, but corruption is rife in Britain. *The Guardian*. Retrieved fromhttp://www.theguardian.com/commentisfree/2015/mar/18/corruption-rife-britain

Morsink, J. (1999). *The Universal Declaration of Human Rights:origins, drafting and intent*. University of Pennsylvania Press. doi:10.9783/9780812200416

Mujtaba, B. G., & Cavico, F. J. (2013). Corporate social responsibility and sustainability model for global firms. *Journal of Leadership. Accountability and Ethics*, *1*(1), 58–75.

Mukwiri, J. (2015). British law on corporate bribery. *Journal of Financial Crime*, *22*(1), 16–27. doi:10.1108/JFC-12-2013-0072

Musafer, S. (2012, October). Corporate social responsibility: Measuring its value. *BBC News*. Retrieved from http://www.bbc.com/news/business-19876138

Musari, A. (2016). *Why anti-corruption drive is imperative for sustainable economic growth*. Retrieved from http://guardian.ng/business-services/why-anti-corruption-drive-is-imperative-for-sustainable-economic-growth/

Muthuri, J. N., Moon, J., & Idemudia, U. (2012). Corporate innovation and sustainable community development in developing countries. *Business & Society*, *51*(3), 355–381. doi:10.1177/0007650312446441

Nasrulla, N. M., & Rahim, M. M. (2014). *CSR in private enterprises in developing countries. Evidence from ready-made garments industry in Bangladesh*. New York: Springer.

Nriagu, J., Udofia, E. A., Ekong, I., & Ebuk, G. (2016). Health risks associated with oil pollution in the Niger Delta, Nigeria. *International Journal of Environmental Research and Public Health*, *13*(3), 346. doi:10.3390/ijerph13030346 PMID:27007391

Nwagbara, U., & Kamara, H. Y. (2015). Corporate social responsibility (CSR), leadership and poverty reduction: The case of Nigeria and Sierra Leone. *Economic Insights–Trends and Challenges*, *4*(67), 21–30.

Nwagbara, U.,& Reid, P. (2013). Corporate social responsibility (CSR) and management trends: Changing times and changing strategies. *Economic Insights – Trends & Challenges, 11*(65), 12–19.

Nwazuoke, A. N., & Igwe, C. A. (2016). Worst forms of child labour in Nigeria: An appraisal of international and local legal regimes. *Beijing Law Review*, *7*(01), 69–82. doi:10.4236/blr.2016.71008

Nwosu, J. E. (2016). Oil exploration and the dilemma of unemployment in the Niger Delta region of Nigeria. *Problèmes Économiques*, *1*, 6–13.

Obuah, E. (2010). Combating corruption in Nigeria: The Nigerian Economic and Financial Crimes Commission (EFCC). *African Studies Quarterly*, *12*(1), 17–44.

Ocheni, S., & Nwankwo, B. C. (2012). The effectiveness of anti-corruption agencies in enhancing good governance and sustainable development growth in Africa: The Nigeria paradox under Obasanjo administration 2003–2007. *Canadian Social Science*, *8*(3), 16–21.

Odeku, K., & Animashaun, S. (2012). Ensuring equality at the workplace by strengthening the law on prohibition against discrimination. *African Journal of Business Management*, *6*(12), 4689–4699.

Ogbo, A. I., Okechukwu, I., & Ukpere, W. I. (2013). Business ethics as a tool for competitive advantage in the banking industry in Nigeria. *Journal of Social Science*, *35*(1), 23–32.

Ogbodo, S.G. (2009). Environmental protection in Nigeria: Two decades after the Koko incident. *Annual Survey of International and Comparative Law, 15*(1).

Ogunfowora, B. (2014). The impact of ethical leadership within the recruitment context: The roles of organizational reputation, applicant personality and value congruence. *The Leadership Quarterly*, *25*(3), 528–543. doi:10.1016/j.leaqua.2013.11.013

Okoosi-Simbine, A. T. (2011). Corruption in Nigeria. In State and Economy and Society in Post-Military Nigeria. New York: Palgrave Macmillan. doi:10.1057/9780230117594_7

Okoye, A. (2012). Novel linkages for development: Corporate social responsibility, law and governance: Exploring the Nigerian Petroleum Industrial Bill. *Corporate Governance: The International Journal of Business and Society*, *12*(4), 460–471.

Olobaniyi, S. B., & Omo-Irabor, O. O. (2016). Environmental impact assessment of selected oil production facilities in parts of Niger Delta, Nigeria. *Journal of Water Resources and Protection*, *8*(2), 237–242. doi:10.4236/jwarp.2016.82020

Omofonmwan, S. I., & Osa-Edoh, G. I. (2008). The challenges of environmental problems in Nigeria. *Journal of Human Ecology (Delhi, India)*, *23*(1), 53–57.

Osoba, S. O. (1996). Corruption in Nigeria: Historical perspectives. *African Political Economy*, *23*(69), 371–386. doi:10.1080/03056249608704203

Otusanya, O. J., Lauwo, S., & Ajibolade, S. O. (2013). An investigation of corporate executive fraud by CEOs in the Nigerian banking sector. *African Journal of Accounting. Auditing and Finance*, *2*(1), 65–89. doi:10.1504/AJAAF.2013.055491

Oyewunmi, O. A., & Olujobi, O. J. (2016). Transparency in Nigeria's oil and gas industry: Is policy re-engineering the way out? *International Journal of Energy Economics and Policy*, *6*(3), 630–636.

Pass, C. (2006). The revised combined code and corporate governance: An empirical survey of 50 large UK companies. *Managerial Law*, *48*(5), 467–478. doi:10.1108/03090550610715963

Perez-Batres, L. A., Miller, V. V., & Pisani, M. J. (2011). Institutionalizing sustainability: An empirical study of corporate registration and commitment to the United Nations Global Compact guidelines. *Journal of Cleaner Production*, *19*(8), 843–851. doi:10.1016/j.jclepro.2010.06.003

Qu, R. (2007). Effects of government regulations, market orientations and ownership structure on corporate social responsibility in China: An empirical study. *International Journal of Management*, *24*(3), 582–591.

Raimi, L., Suara, I. B., & Fadipe, A. O. (2013). Role of Economic and Financial Crimes Commission(EFCC) and Independent Corrupt Practices and Other Related Offences Commission (ICPC) at ensuring accountability and corporate governance in Nigeria. *Journal of Business Administration and Education*, *3*(2), 105–122.

Rasche, A. (2009). "A necessary supplement". What the United Nations Global Compact is and is not. *Business & Society*, *48*(4), 511–537. doi:10.1177/0007650309332378

Rasche, A., & Gilbert, D. U. (2012). Institutionalizing global governance: The role of the United Nations Global Compact. *Business Ethics (Oxford, England)*, *21*(1), 100–114. doi:10.1111/j.1467-8608.2011.01642.x

Rasche, A., & Kell, G. (2010). *The United Nations Global Compact: Achievements, trends and challenges*. Cambridge, UK: Cambridge University Press. doi:10.1017/CBO9780511762642

Rosemann, M., & Vom Brocke, J. (2015). The six core elements of business process management. In *Handbook on Business Process Management 1* (pp. 105–122). Berlin: Springer. doi:10.1007/978-3-642-45100-3_5

Sanusi, L.S. (2010). *The Nigerian banking industry: what went wrong and the way forward.* Delivered at Annual Convocation Ceremony of Bayero University, Kano.

Sanusi, L. S. (2012). Banking reform and its impact on the Nigerian economy. *CBN Journal of Applied Statistics*, *2*(2), 115–122.

Sarkar, S. (2015). *The comply or explain approach for enforcing governance norms*. Retrieved fromhttp://www.igidr.ac.in/pdf/publication/WP-2015-022.pdf

Servaes, H., & Tamayo, A. (2013). The impact of corporate social responsibility on firm value: The role of customer awareness. *Management Science*, *59*(5), 1045–1061. doi:10.1287/mnsc.1120.1630

Shrives, P. J., & Brennan, N. M. (2015). A typology for exploring the quality of explanations for non-compliance with UK corporate governance regulations. *The British Accounting Review*, *47*(1), 85–99. doi:10.1016/j.bar.2014.08.002

Siddique, M. (2014). CSR practices and competitive advantages: A descriptive study. *American Journal of Trade and Policy*, *1*(3), 109–116.

Smith, D. J. (2010). *A culture of corruption: Everyday deception and popular discontent in Nigeria*. Princeton, NJ: Princeton University Press.

Stouten, J., Van Dijke, M., & De Cremer, D. (2012). Ethical leadership: An overview and future perspective. *Journal of Personnel Psychology*, *11*(1), 1–6. doi:10.1027/1866-5888/a000059

Svensson, J. (2005). Eight questions about corruption. *The Journal of Economic Perspectives*, *19*(3), 19–42. doi:10.1257/089533005774357860

The Global Compact. (2016). *Global compact cities programme*. Retrieved from http://citiesprogramme.com/aboutus/the-cities-programme

The Nigerian Economic Summit Group. (2016). *Our mission and vision.* Retrieved from http://nesgroup.org/about

Togun, O. R., & Nasieku, T. (2015). Effect of corporate social responsibility on performance of manufacturing companies in Nigeria. *International Journal of Current Advanced Research*, *4*(8), 228–233.

Transparency International. (2015). *Corruption Perceptions Index 2015*. Retrieved from https://www.transparency.org/cpi2015/

Ufere, N., Perelli, S., Boland, R., & Carlsson, B. (2012). Merchants of corruption: How entrepreneurs manufacture and supply bribes. *World Development*, *40*(12), 2440–2453. doi:10.1016/j.worlddev.2012.05.025

Ugochukwu, E.F., Okeke, K.N., Onubogu, C.U., & Edokwe, E.S. (2012). Social demographic characteristics of child street vendors in Nnewi, Nigeria. *Nigeria Journal* of *Paediatrics, 39*(4), 174-178.

Ugwunwanyi, A., & Ekene, C. (2016). Corporate social responsibility and its implementation in Nigeria: Problems and prospects. *Global Journal of Human-Management*, *4*(2), 60–69.

Ugwuona, C. N. (2016). 2013 ASSU strike discourses in Nigeria: A critical discourse analysis. *Mediterranean Journal of Social Sciences*, *7*(2), 435–444.

UK Government. (2013). *The Companies Act 2006 (Strategic Report and Directors' Report) Regulations 2013*. Retrieved from https://www.gov.uk/government/uploads/system/uploads/attachment_data/file/206241/bis-13-889-companies-act-2006-draft-strategic-and-directors-report-regulations-2013.pdf

Unerman, J., Bebbington, J., & O'Dwyer, B. (Eds.). (2007). *Sustainability accounting and accountability*. Oxon, UK: Routledge.

United Nations Global Compact. (2015a). *Act globally engage locally*. Retrieved from https://www.unglobalcompact.org/engage-locally/africa/nigeria

United Nations Global Compact. (2015b). *Act globally engage locally*. Retrieved from https://www.unglobalcompact.org/engage-locally/europe/uk

United Nations Global Compact. (2015c). *Advancing partnerships*. Retrieved from https://www.unglobalcompact.org/take-action/partnerships

United Nations Global Compact. (2015d). *Business as a force for good*. Retrieved from https://www.unglobalcompact.org/what-is-gc/mission

United Nations Global Compact. (2015e). *IMPACT: Transforming business, changing the world-The United Nations Global Compact*. Retrieved from https://www.unglobalcompact.org/library/1331

United Nations Global Compact. (2015f). *The power of principles: The ten principles of the UN Global Compact*. Retrieved from http://www.unglobalcompact.org/what-is-gc/mission/principles

United Nations Global Compact. (2016). *Let's make global goals local business*. Retrieved from https://www.unglobalcompact.org/

Voegtlin, C. (2015). What does it mean to be responsible? Addressing the missing responsibility dimension in ethical leadership research. *Leadership*, 1–29.

Walker, H., & Jones, N. (2012). Sustainable supply chain management across the UK private sector. *Supply Chain Management: An International Journal*, *17*(1), 15–28. doi:10.1108/13598541211212177

Weilert, A. K. (2016). United Nations Convention against Corruption (UNCAC)-After Ten Years of Being in Force. *Max Planck Yearbook of United Nations Law Online*, *19*(1), 216–240.

Wills, J. (2001). Community unionism and trade union renewal in the UK: Moving beyond the fragments at last? *Transactions of the Institute of British Geographers*, *26*(4), 465–483. doi:10.1111/1475-5661.00035

Winn, M. I., & Pogutz, S. (2013). Business, ecosystems, and biodiversity: New horizons for management research. *Organization & Environment*, *20*(10), 1–27.

Zhu, Y., Sun, L., & Leung, A. S. M. (2014). Corporate social responsibility, firm reputation, and firm performance: The role of ethical leadership. *Asia Pacific Journal of Management*, *31*(4), 925–947. doi:10.1007/s10490-013-9369-1

ADDITIONAL READING

Ackers, B., & Eccles, N. S. (2015). Mandatory corporate social responsibility assurance practices: The case of King III in South Africa. *Accounting, Auditing & Accountability Journal*, *28*(2), 515–550. doi:10.1108/AAAJ-12-2013-1554

Adams, C. A., & Frost, G. R. (2008). Integrating sustainability report in management practices. *Accounting Forum*, *32*(4), 288–302. doi:10.1016/j.accfor.2008.05.002

Belkaoui, A., & Karpik, P. G. (1989). Determinants of the corporate decision to disclose social information. *Accounting, Auditing & Accountability Journal*, *2*(1), 36–51. doi:10.1108/09513578910132240

Delmas, M., & Toffel, M. W. (2004). Stakeholders and environmental management practices: An institutional framework. *Business Strategy and the Environment*, *13*(4), 209–222. doi:10.1002/bse.409

Dwyer, R., Lamond, D., & Lee, K. H. (2009). Why and how to adopt green management into business organizations? The case study of Korean SMEs in manufacturing industry. *Management Decision*, *47*(7), 1101–1121. doi:10.1108/00251740910978322

Gray, R., Kouhy, R., & Lavers, S. (1995). Corporate social and environmental reporting: A review of the literature and a longitudinal study of UK disclosure. *Accounting, Auditing & Accountability Journal*, *8*(2), 47–77. doi:10.1108/09513579510146996

Mio, C., Venturelli, A., & Leopizzi, R. (2015). Management by objectives and corporate social responsibility disclosure: First result from Italy. *Accounting, Auditing & Accountability Journal*, *28*(3), 325–364. doi:10.1108/AAAJ-09-2013-1480

Rondinelli, D. A., & Berry, M. A. (2000). Environmental citizenship in multinational corporations: Social responsibility and sustainable development. *European Management Journal*, *18*(1), 70–84. doi:10.1016/S0263-2373(99)00070-5

Salzmann, O., Ionescu-Somers, A., & Steger, U. (2005). The business case for corporate sustainability: Literature review and research options. *European Management Journal*, *23*(1), 27–36. doi:10.1016/j.emj.2004.12.007

Toffel, M. W., Short, J. L., & Quellet, M. (2015). *Codes in context: How states, markets and civil society shape adherence to global labour standards*. Harvard Business School Technology and Operations Management Unit Working Paper No.13-045.UC Hasting Research Paper No.79.Retrieved from http://ssrn.com/abstract=2178540

KEY TERMS AND DEFINITIONS

Anti-Corruption Measures: Acts and practices against corruption.

Business Environment: The location and operating environment in which a business conducts its activities and thrives.

Corporate Citizenship: Entails an organisation being registered/incorporated in a defined location and contributing to the good of the location.

Corporate Social Responsibility: A practice by a business to do good deeds for the host community and for the benefit of society.

Economy: Commercial activities centred on the availability and procurement of goods and services within a business environment.

Environment: The host and immediate surroundings.

Ethics: A set of morally guiding principles.

Green: A sustainable practice that preserves the environment and protects the stakeholders.

Human Rights: Permissible freedom given to humans and allowed by law in the society.

Labour: Individuals working or available to work for an entity.

Natural Resources: Tangible and intangible resources occurring naturally within a defined location.

Social Performance: The ability to meet defined societal needs and goals.

Society: A group of people sharing similar social characteristics and adhering to the same norms and customs in a defined location.

Sustainability Reporting: A sustainability performance and monitoring reporting system.

United Nations Global Compact: Principles set and outlined by the United Nations to guide business conduct in the business environment.

United Nations: An organisation with countries/nations as members who deliberate on world issues and encourage international relations and alliances.

Chapter 11
A Systemic Approach towards Responsible and Sustainable Economic Development:
Entrepreneurship, Systems Theory, and Socio-Economic Momentum

Thea van der Westhuizen
University of KwaZulu Natal, South Africa

ABSTRACT

A possible way to increase responsible and sustainable economic development is to enhance collective innovation and entrepreneurship on various systemic levels in order to gain socio-economic developmental momentum. In an era which faces socio-economic changes on multiple systemic levels, especially within the mundosystem, collective and creative approaches towards systemic activities are necessary, not only to drive businesses forward, but to give momentum to global economies. In this chapter, the author philosophizes about entrepreneurship, systems theory and socio-economic momentum and how these play an important role to give momentum to responsible and sustainable economic growth.

INTRODUCTION

In an era which faces socio-economic changes on multiple systemic levels, especially within the mundosystem, collective creativity for responsible and sustainable economic activities are increasingly becoming of fundamental importance, not only to drive businesses forward, but to give momentum to global economies (Van der Westhuizen, 2016).

The mundo system can be referred to as global governance and relates to the bigger economic picture in national and global fields – or in other words, the Bigger Picture that's being affected by collective creative approaches for responsible and sustainable business practice (Jackson, 2003; Scharmer & Kaufer, 2013).

DOI: 10.4018/978-1-5225-1823-5.ch011

This chapter looks into a systemic approach towards responsible and sustainable economic development and how entrepreneurship, systems theory and socio-economic momentum play a role to give momentum to collective creativity within the Bigger Picture. The importance of this chapter lies within the notion of Scharmer and Kaufer (2013) that our planet is dying and humans are responsible for it.

GLOBAL NEED FOR SYSTEMIC CHANGE

The world around us consist of integrated and interrelated systems, and these systems are facing severe challenges in all aspects (van der Westhuizen, 2016). The decay in systems in the different environments around us are the cause of collective deconstructive actions of people (Scharmer & Kaufer, 2013) and only a transformation of collective consciousness towards sustainable and responsible systemic development practices will bring forward possible solutions to turn-around the decay within our systems (Gunnlaugson et al, 2013). The need for not only change, but deep systemic transformation, has come to a boiling point where global governing practices such as the United Nations, are reviewing sustainability approaches. Fitch and O'Fallon (2013) stated that systemic transformation need certain element of transformation, as well as enablers of transformation who brings forward the desired change, which will be explored further in this chapter.

Enables are people or things that makes something possible, whereas transformation can be defined as "growth in developmental maturity" (Fitch and O'Fallon, 2013). A system can be described as a complex whole whose functioning depends on its parts and the interactions between those parts (Jackson, 2003) where systemic elements affecingt the whole, rather than just parts of it, refers to the interrelatedness and integrativeness of systems (Leonard, 2010).

Scharmer (2009) distinguishes between mundo-level systems, macro-level systems, meso-level systems, and micro-level systems. In the context of this chapter, following Townsend and MacBeath (2011), *mundo system* refers to global governance, *macro system* refers to national governance or institutionalising, *meso system* refers to organisations and culture, and *micro system* refers to individuals and their thinking. Mark Edward's model of multi-level systemic wisdom (as cited in Thompson and Bevan, 2013) describes the global society in relation to the global economy as the mundo system, society at large as the macro system, organisational structure, culture and climate as the meso system, and the personal characteristics and traits of in individual as the micro system.

Waring (1999) offers the following account of systems and their components and determinants:

- A system has processes and certain outputs since a system is something.
- When components are added or removed from a system, these actions change the system.
- When any component is added to a system, there is an effect on it from being included to the system.
- When components are added to a system, it is perceived that relating hierarchical structures are formed.
- The survival of a system requires certain forms of control and communication which support system survival.
- Some of the system's properties are emergent and not easy to predict.
- The system has a boundary.
- The external environment to the boundary of the system, affects the system.

- The system is owned by someone Checkland (1999) and Jackson (2003) distinguish between physical or natural structures as hard systems, and people, organisations and their culture as soft systems. According to Leonard (2010), hard systems operate in a process that goes from extraction, to production, to distribution, to consumption and ultimately to disposal – otherwise referred to as the "materials economy". Leonard points out that the materials economy system is in crisis because it is confined to a linear sequence of hard systems which has no way of incorporating soft-systems approaches. On this point, twenty-first century scholars like Scharmer (2009), and Goleman and Senge (2014) concur that systems at all levels are in a crisis.

Soft-systems development scholars (Checkland, 1999; Jackson, 2003; Senge et al., 2008a; Senge et al., 2008b; Scharmer, 2009; Scharmer & Kaufer, 2013) propose an anthropomorphic descriptive terminology of the system – for example, that integrative systems cannot "breathe" without one another (Senge et al., 2008a).

Scharmer (2009) and Senge et al (2008a) highlights the need for collective change within systems because the impact of irresponsible and unsustainable leadership practices results into the decay of all systemic environments, whether it's a political environment, economic environment or ecological environment. These systemic challenges are evident in both developed and developing countries.

Scharmer (2009) labels interactions between systems as "breathing" or "living" and the challenges that systems may face as "beasts", going on to suggest that in interactions between hard and soft systems, "something is dying and something new is being reborn." The "something dying" is explained by Senge et al. (2008a) on a hard systemic level as the planet, its ecology and the functioning of the materials economy as it is known, and on a soft systemic level as traditional leadership and policy approaches. Therefore, these authors imply that traditional leadership and policy approaches currently used in both developed and developing countries and not sufficient to transform (change) the severe hard system challenges our different environments are facing. Leonard (2010) and Hannon et al (2013) are of opinion that a radical change is necessary to spark a remedial process within different systems.

At the 2012 Global Conference on Innovation and Entrepreneurship, Hannon et al. (Hannon et al., 2013) observed moreover that in the present era it is the micro system that takes priority, with the values, heartset and mindset of the individual shaping the integrative actions of the system as a whole. A number of authors (Senge et al., 2008a; Senge et al., 2008b; Song et al., 2010; Hermans, 2012; Hannon et al., 2013; Hoy, 2013) have noted similarly that the "spinners" of systemic development going forward are individual values and levels of self-confidence (or self-efficacy). This implies that the way forward to transform (change) global systems and steer collective creativity for responsible and sustainable business practice start with individual human beings and unless people do not change their attitudes or perspectives towards collective transformation, the desired change will not kick in.

Weinberg (2015) believes that a change in people's levels of self-confidence (self-efficacy) as well as their individual entrepreneurial orientation might lead to a transformation in their attitudes and perspective towards systemic change. On the assumption that raising levels of self-efficacy and value expectations for individuals, as definers of the microsystem, constitutes a fundamental starting point for extended development at higher systemic levels, value-centred development of individuals will, in turn, require from them deeper levels of knowledge both about themselves and about the larger system, with ability to relate on a multi-dimensional level with everything around them. Therefore, a change in an individual's attitude towards transforming different systemic levels might lead to bridging the decay within systemic development. No matter of these individuals are from developed or developing countries – collective transformation is needed.

Leonard (2010), who investigated supply chains within systems, comments that, most simply described, the world consists of interrelated and integrated systems. Scharmer (2009) distinguishes between mundo-level systems, macro-level systems, meso-level systems, and micro-level systems. In the context of this chapter, following Townsend and MacBeath (2011), a mundo system refers to global governance, a macro system refers to national governance or institutionalising, a meso system refers to organisations and culture, and a micro system refers to individuals and their thinking. Mark Edward's model of multi-level systemic wisdom (as cited in Thompson and Bevan, 2013) describes the global society in relation to the global economy as the mundo system, society at large as the macro system, organisational structure, culture and climate as the meso system, and the personal characteristics and traits of in individual as the micro system.

Systemic Levels: Mundosystems

In an era which faces socio-economic changes on multiple systemic levels, especially within the mundosystem, entrepreneurship, according to Karadeniz (2006), has become globally significant as a transformative tool for responsible and sustainable economic activities of countries, regions and businesses. Entrepreneurs potentially influence and renew socio-economic activities on various systemic levels in the contribution made by their product innovations and services innovations (Karadeniz, 2006). Therefore, contributing to the collective creativity of a country or region. Entrepreneurship in the shape of intrapreneurial input, affects socio-economic growth likewise in mundo or macro systems because it drives expansion to new markets with new products, services, or production processes, widely recognised as key factors for economic growth (Poh Kam et al., 2005; Harkema and Schout, 2008; Batabyal and Nijkamp, 2012; Galindo and Méndez-Picazo, 2013; Galindo and Méndez, 2014) but chiefly from a materials economy perspective, where the primary focus on hard-system development with less regard for soft-systems issues. The emphasis, in other words, has tended to be on economic development rather than socio-economic development.

The Global Entrepreneurship Monitor (GEM), collects worldwide data on linkage between entrepreneurship and macro-systemic or national economic development (Xavier et al., 2013). Adamson et al (2013) is of opinion that collective creativity form individuals within their nascent business practices might incept collective creativity for responsible and sustainable business practices within the Bigger Picture. Therefore, there if a need for entrepreneurs to change their attitudes and perspectives towards responsible and sustainable business practice right from incepting the nascent business idea.

In the period since the inception of GEM, the findings in terms of its conceptual model have shown a paradigm shift in national systemic output. In earlier years, emphasis was placed on the materials economy with focus on a macro-systemic economic development, but since 2013 (Figure 1) a soft-systems approach has become more evident, where final output incorporates a strong soft-systems approach to support hard-systems development for socio-economic growth (Amorós et al., 2013; Bosma, 2013; Minniti, 2013). Although Naudé (2010; 2011) regards the theoretical and empirical research needed to interpret the role of entrepreneurship in responsible and sustainable socio-economic development as still too insubstantial.

Figure 1. Entrepreneurship and socio-economic development (from GEM 2012)

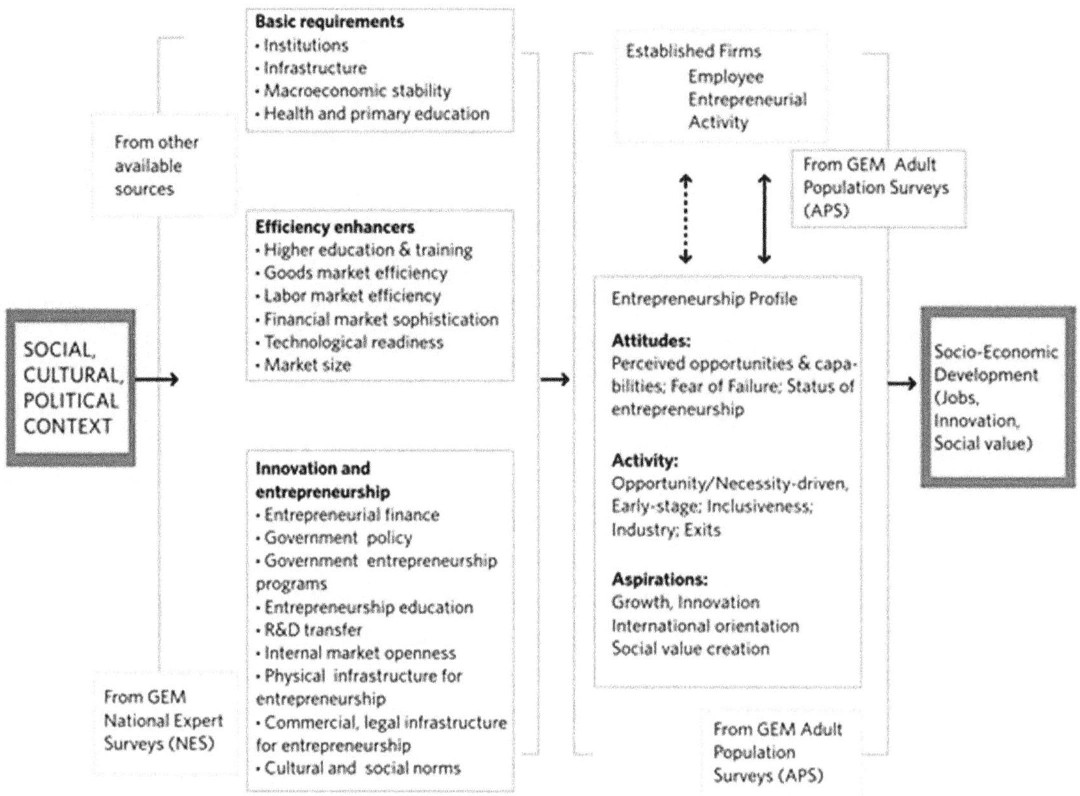

The GEM 2012 report indicates that over the past decade systematic correlation has been evident between a country's level of growth per capita GDP and the type of entrepreneurial and intrapreneurial actions in the country's meso and micro systems (Xavier et al., 2013). Therefore, the output of collective actions for responsible and sustainable business practice within the Bigger Picture is a direct outflow from those actions and processes of organisations and individuals (as representative of the meso and micro system). The 2012 emergent phase of GEM's conceptual framework of socio-economic development demonstrates the complexity of entrepreneurship within the micro system, in relation to the meso and macro system. Attitudes, activity and aspirations within the microsystem (individual entrepreneurs) in relation to the mesosystem (institutions and organisations) form the centre point of responsible and sustainable socio-economic growth in the macro system (the country) (Xavier et al., 2013). This implies driving aspects towards transformation (change) of systems, small scale and the Bigger Picture, start with the attitudes and beliefs of individuals. The key component to transformation (change) relates therefore to aspects internal to individual entrepreneurs. Further, key components to collective and sustainable business practice within systems start within the attitudes and beliefs of individuals – for example, an individual will choose to change his or her attitude or belief to support responsible and sustainable business practice.

In relation to microsystem entrepreneurship activities and macrosystem socio-economic development, Karadeniz (2006) notes that individuals and their behaviours directly affect socio-economic development on a number of different macro-systemic levels. Therefore, individual entrepreneurs have a direct impact on the collective creativity and sustainable economic activities of a region or country. Developing entrepreneurship as a driver of economic growth therefore means extending the range of systemic interactions for the individual. As set out by Karadeniz (Figure 1), entrepreneurial success hinges on a) ability to take risks within uncertain economic climate, b) ability to innovate by introducing new products and services, and c) proactive decision making. These three factors together constitute what is referred to as "Individual Entrepreneurial Orientation" (Florin et al., 2007; Bolton and Lane, 2012; Taatila & Down, 2012).

United Nations Secretary-General Ban Ki-Moon (as cited in Hannon et al., 2013) said in a 2012 address that all actors and role-players need to combine in a collective effort to address global challenges, adding that chances for not only global socio-economic development, but also survival, chances for success might be increased through system-wide partnerships and alliances, as well as through pooling comparative advantages. Viewing Moon's notion in relation to the GEM model (see figure 1) the need for change in responsible and sustainable business practice is embedded into the attitude and beliefs of individuals.

Extensive awareness raising, education and training on systemic challenges as well as possible bridging components might be necessary to bring change to Individual Entrepreneurial Orientation, as well as Entrepreneurial Self-Efficacy. Further, it is necessary to match individuals' skills with local, national and global systemic demand needs and equip individuals with the Entrepreneurial Self-Efficacy to enable the possibility to generate both solutions as well as and innovations for themselves and for their country (Hannon et al., 2013; Gruenewald and Smith, 2014; Stromquist and Monkman, 2014).

Systemic Levels: Macrosystems

The macro system (national governance) guides the policies and procedures that determine the sustainable and responsible flow of systemic interactions within various environments, whether the environment is political, socio-economic or ecological. These components will be looked into next.

Politics

National government policy and policy formulation are key elements in socio-economic development and steer directions for individuals' entrepreneurial orientation. Policy can direct influence attitudes, beliefs and actions of individuals either positively or negatively. These policies also directly determine what direction the macro system's sustainable and responsible economic growth will flow

Socio-Economic Issues and Entrepreneurship

In both developing and developed countries the gap between rich and poor continues to widen, and entrenched inequalities are a major obstacle to growth, development, and employment creation (Urban, 2012). In addition, several developing countries, such as South Arfica, has a dual-logic economy in which a highly developed economic sector exists alongside basic struggle for survival (Maas and Herrington, 2008). This wealth inequality is mirrored in many respects by the divide between and necessity-driven entrepreneurs and opportunity-driven entrepreneurs: the so-called 'push–pull' motivational dichotomy in which one would expect push factors to predominate among entrepreneurs in developing countries (Urban, 2012).

Research and policy initiatives in developing countries focus mainly on necessity-driven entrepreneurs representative of the unemployed masses. These are often mactro systemic challenges which aim to transform (change) business practice to enhance sustainable and responsible economic growth from a country. Microenterprises or survivalists, for instance, "may have entrepreneurial characteristics [but] their ability to grow and create employment is restricted by the scarcity of skills, business knowledge and resources"(Von Broembsen et al, 2005, as cited by Urban, 2012). Growth levels, if any, for these necessity-driven entrepreneurs vary significantly according to a wide range of factors that affect them (Autio, as cited by Urban, 2012). This highlights the importance of entrepreneurs within the context of responsible and sustainable economic growth of a country. Collective creativity of small-scale entrepreneurs will therefore directly influence collective creativity within the macro system.

In studies on entrepreneurship and innovation and its relation to socio-economic growth in developing countries, the emphasis is commonly on the "who", why", and "how" or entrepreneurship, coupled with the conviction that both entrepreneurship and intrapreneurship are fundamental to mundo- and macro-systemic socio-economic development, as evident over the past three decades in strongly developing economies (such as the BRIC countries) that have achieved substantial poverty alleviation (Naudé, 2013). In these countries, entrepreneurship has been supported by donors and international development agencies as means to heighten macro-systemic effectiveness and bring about more sustainable poverty alleviation and job creation (Acs et al., 2008; Block and Koellinger, 2009; Koveos, 2011; Bosma, 2013; Galindo and Méndez-Picazo, 2013; Naudé, 2013). National responsible and sustainable economic growth therefore relates directly to the collective responsible and sustainable business practice of entrepreneurs.

Sustainable and Responsible Socio-Economic Development through Entrepreneurship

Moving from the materials economy to socio-economic development, Naudé (2013) stresses the need to understand how the role of entrepreneurship resonates within development economics, pointing to what he refers to as "three 'grand ideas'" in development economics. These "grand ideas" are important to responsible and sustainable business practice because it highlights important aspects that needs to transform (change) inorder to start bridge systemic challenges and remedy systemic decay. These "grand ideas" resonate:

- That traditional approaches to the materials economy require structural transformation in the supply chain regarding "what, how and where production and consumption takes place,"
- That economic development is multi-dimensional, driven by individuals (Figure 1): to grow an economy within a macro-systemic level, development approaches require "more than just elimination of income poverty."
- That national government has an important role to play in coordinating and regulating socio-economic development and in helping to bridge prevalent market failures (Naudé, 2013).

These three "grand ideas" also appear in the GEMS 2012 conceptual model (Figure 1) where basic requirements for socio-economic development on a macro-systemic level include institutions, infrastructure, macro-economic stability and education. Therefore, a starting place to remedy systemic challenges and bring forward the needed transformation (change) for sustainable and responsible economic growth might lie within developing capacity within the meso stem (institutions, infrastructure and levels of education)

Structural Economic Transformation and Entrepreneurship

Transformation (change) to a modern economy from a low-income "traditional" economy entails radical changes in supply chain approaches (Giddens et al., 2000; Munshi & Rosenzweig, 2003; Gries & Naudé, 2010). Important enhancers of economic efficiency in such a process, as listed in the GEM 2012 model (Figure 1) are higher education and training, goods and labour market efficiencies, financial market refinement, technological readiness and market size. These enhancers might therefore equip entrepreneurs to act more creative as a collective, as well as to develop their attitudes and perspective to move towards responsible and sustainable business practice.

Naudé (2013) suggests that in this transformation process entrepreneurs are the catalysts for change that might bring forward sustainable and responsible socio-economic development, and that entrepreneurial aspects are fundamental in the provision of innovative intermediate input to the supply chain. This implies that collective creativity needs to be linked to innovation, not only regeneration of existing ideas, products or services. This allows specialisation within the supply chain as well as raising productivity and employment.

Research by Peretto (1999) indicates that long-term sustainable economic development which sees structural transformation on multiple systemic levels depends on the possibility of a shift from growth driven from within a materials economy approach to growth driven by knowledge accumulation. Peretto refers to this transition as an innovation-driven economy (Peretto, 1998; 1999). Here, the important factors for innovation and entrepreneurship, as listed in the GEM 2012 model (Figure 1) are entrepreneurial finance, government policy, government entrepreneurship programmes, entrepreneurship education, internal market openness, physical infrastructure for entrepreneurship, commercial and legal infrastructure for entrepreneurship, and cultural and social norms. Again, these aspects seem to be pertinent to responsible and sustainable business practice need scope for collective creative actions from entrepreneurs.

Multi-Dimensional Socio-Economic Development and Entrepreneurship

Research by Naudé (2013) corroborates earlier case-study findings by Leonard (2010), Scharmer (2009) and Senge et al. (2008b) that, in the relationship between entrepreneurship and development, macro-systemic focus was traditionally on the materials economy, and that development efforts have been targeted too narrowly on GDP. These authors agree that employment growth requires not only enhanced levels of productivity and growth from the microsystem, but also deeper and more multi-dimensional approaches to achieve sustainability in socio-economic development (Senge et al., 2008a; Scharmer, 2009; Leonard, 2010). With this in mind, entrepreneurial attitudes, aspirations and activity have an increasingly important role in economic growth within the socio-economic development process. Gries and Naudé (2011) make the point that the well-being and capabilities of individuals contribute to multi-dimensional development across all systems and that an individual's state of well-being directly impacts national economy, therefore internal aspects of individuals steers creative business practice as well as responsible and sustainable economic growth.

Approaching issues from the starting point of individual capabilities and orientations can bring insight to theoretical thinking and provide a useful benchmark for entrepreneurship. In this perspective, entrepreneurship is seen as an aspect of human collective creative activity that has importance as an end in itself and not just as a means to an end (Naudé, 2013). "Activities and states" which Naudé (2013) notes as "central to the human collective creative capabilities approach" include "working, resting, being literate, being healthy, being part of a community, being respected. "All of these aspects therefore are central to people's attitude towards responsible and sustainable business practice.

The Global Entrepreneurship Monitor 2012 shows evidence in data obtained in individual levels of an inverse U-shape relationship between entrepreneurship and well-being on all systemic levels. The example is often cited of the Kingdom of Bhutan in which the notion of national happiness is taken to the point where macrosystem leadership focuses on Gross National Happiness rather than a materials-driven economy – which can be seen as an example of collective creativity which resulted into responsible and sustainable economic growth of a nation (Ezechieli, 2003; Bates, 2009; Burns, 2011; Naudé, 2013). Naudé (2013) points out that entrepreneurs who are opportunity-motivated and have Entrepreneurial Self-Efficacy "may contribute to a nation's happiness but only up to a point [since] not everybody should become entrepreneurs and the happiness of a nation cannot be indefinitely increased by increasing the numbers of entrepreneurs".

Local Economic Development: A Case of South Africa as a Developing Country

South Africa's policies on socio-economic development, innovation and entrepreneurship have undergone radical changes in the post-apartheid period, therefore affective the collective creativity of the nation as a whole. An example in the eThekwini Metro Municipality, KwaZulu-Natal, is the transformation of departmental structures since 2010 in which the Supply Chain Department was branched off to form a Business Development and People Support Unit (BDPS), which in turn was branched off in 2013 to form a separate Innovation Unit responsible for innovation and entrepreneurship development in the municipal region.

In the process of building South Africa's economy, local government, parastatals and private owned businesses have been exploring responsible and sustainable employment strategies and new ways of developing soft systems (Sisk, 1995; Marais, 2001). For basic economic survival, need-driven entrepreneurship is very much evident throughout South Africa, and local communities needed to become more self-reliant in the process of living through day-to-day survival. The spread of necessity-driven entrepreneurship has seen a transformative development of the mesosystem in South Africa and is often supported by non-government organisations (Binns and Nel, 1999). This has given increasing importance to the mesosystem in South Africa, with a range of NGO and community initiatives now involved in socio-economic development (Nel, 2001a; Nel & Hill, 2001). Accelerating this trend has been the uncertainty of the global economic climate and the heightened significance of local decision making in democratic South Africa (Sisk, 1995).

The nature and purpose of local economic development (LED) – also referred to as "self-reliance, local coping [and] endogenous or bottom-up development" (Acs et al., 2008) – is given as follows by the World Bank:

The purpose of local economic development (LED) is to build up the economic capacity of a local area to improve its economic future and the quality of life for all. It is a process by which public, business and nongovernmental sector partners work collectively to create better conditions for economic growth and employment generation. (World Bank, n.d.)

In an alternative account by Abrahams (2003),

Local economic development refers to the process of creating wealth through the organised mobilisation of human, physical, capital and natural resources in a locality. The aim of LED is to produce higher standards of living, improve the quality of life, alleviate poverty, create more and better jobs, advance skills and build capacity for sustained development in the future.

From these two definitions it seems that LED encompasses multi-level systemic interactions and integrations to improve socio-economic development as a whole.

In a study of LED strategies in various parts of Africa, Nel (2001b) notes that in developing countries where the macrosystem is economically challenged and where government is not equipped to engage effectively with local communities, development processes are often top-down and locally driven, based in the host community and focused on advancing local conditions and encouraging local entrepreneurs in activities that support the LED strategy. This can be seen as a form of necessity-driven entrepreneurship (Acs et al., 2008).

Stone (cited in Nel, 2001) makes the point that joint endeavours by local agencies and people to unify their communities and businesses are necessary to improve economic and social conditions. These joint endeavours may offer tangible benefits for participating communities where the government plays a role as facilitating agent, offering support, part-financing and devolved control of the socio-economic development process.

From a survey of LED in Brazil, Peru and various Africa countries Southern Africa, Nel (2001) suggests that LED often relies on scaled-down and community-based initiatives where indigenous resources are utilised and where the foremost priority for local people is survival rather than participation in the wider economy. Nel (2001) differentiates between two broad levels of community economic participation: formal and informal. The formal level is characterised by involvement of the formal business sector as well as local or higher government structures. The informal level is characterised by actions at levels of community-based organisations and link with spontaneous self-reliance initiatives. However, as indicated above, Naudé (2013) believes self-reliance entrepreneurship is not ideal for enhancing an innovation driver economy.

Fabricius et al. (2013) in their work on community-based human capital development in Southern Africa draw attention to a "third level" of civil society where social organisation factors such as trust, norms and networks are key role-players in improving efficiency and facilitating co-ordinated socio-economic development actions. At an LED symposium held in 2014 in Durban, Dr. Shamim Bodhanya, who facilitated the symposium, pointed out that "trust" and "co-operation" are identified by community, private sector and government participants as essential elements for achieving success in community-based entrepreneurship development (personal recollection by practitoner-researcher, who attended the event).

Formal LED strategies that Nel (2001) indicates as commonly pursued by involved authorities and as identified in the GEM model (Figure 1) often include the following five elements: "financial support, land and building development, information and marketing assistance, new planning and organisational structures and training and employment."

Case-study research based on a variety of LED strategies in developing and developed countries reveals that on a practical and implementation level not all initiatives succeed (Acs et al., 2008). Case studies in South Africa and elsewhere indicate that in a project life-cycle initial enthusiasm is often followed by mediocre results and disheartenment of project managers who lack self-efficacy (McKibbin et al., 2012; Nel and Rogerson, 2013; Nel & Stevenson, 2014). Nel and Stevenson (2014) point out that as a project's life-cycle evolves it may falter or fade or change course, according to circumstances. A similar observation was also made by Bodhanya during the LED symposium referred to above.

Nel (2001) comments that not much was achieved from the application of LED in South Africa in the 1990s, and that LED is chiefly a post-1990 phenomenon. Since 2000, public-private growth coalitions are gaining increasing prominence and this approach is also advocated by government policy. Nel cites private initiatives such as valuable support and training for CBOs and NGOs provided by the National Business Initiative and the Friedrich Ebert Stiftung. Both Marais (2001) and Nel (2012) see a need to strengthen these associations along with local government LED support initiatives.

In post-apartheid South Africa, the macrosystem focus is on alleviating poverty in the meso and micro systems through promotion of entrepreneurial growth and investment. According to policy documentation (rsa, as cited in Nel, 2001), local authorities face an overriding economic challenge of inequality and poverty, tackling which should form part of all municipal objectives. Nel (2001) identifies four key variants in South African LED initiatives: "formal local government initiatives … community-based or small town initiatives … Section 21 Development Corporations, and … 'top-down' LED". These variants are of importance to this thesis as they relate to the formal Business Friendships created through the action research process of the thesis.

Formal Local Government LED Initiatives in South Africa

Nel (2001) points out that in South Africa broad-based LED strategies, with adequately staffed and funded LED units, are in place only in the four largest metropolitan areas (Johannesburg, Durban, Pretoria, Cape Town). Development activities in these centres are increasingly comprehensive, with core themes centred on poverty alleviation, entrepreneurship and global competitiveness (Rogerson, 2011; Lawrence, 2013). In return, this is aligned to the United Nation's Global Compact which aims to transform (change) business and societies and part of the GEM 2015 socio-economic development goals (van der Westhuizen, 2016).

Nel (2001) notes that is has often proved difficult to stimulate economic activity in low-income areas such as the townships. As the macro system has shifted from a materials economy approach to a socio-economic development approach (Figure 1) the KwaZulu-Natal Department of Economic Development has put more focus on support for a soft-systems development approach, leading to the establishment of separate dedicated units for Small Business and Community Economic Development, Tourism, private sector and Investment Promotion, Information, and Innovation (eThekwini Municipality, 2013). In the course of this research a Business Friendship was formed with the Small Business Development Unit.

Implicit in the set of investment opportunities in KwaZulu-Natal listed above is that the investment context in the focus area is likely to present a number of difficulties for nascent (who can be defined as individuals who are starting a new venture or entry-level entrepreneurs, to enter the market). Very few nascent entrepreneurs have start-up capital to launch a new venture in the investment areas identified. A further problem emerging from this is that nascent entrepreneurs in South Africa are mostly in the 25–34 age group – the same age group that were identified as facing severe challenges in youth entrepreneurship, in addition to high levels of unemployment (van Stel et al., 2003).

Top-Down LED

In South Africa, the principal role-player in the top-down LED approach is the national Ministry of Local Government and Economic Affairs, which Nel identifies as a key link between the meso system and the macro system. The local/national government link is an important driver in local LED-related policy formulation, leading to financial support measures such as an LED Fund to support local government projects and the Social Plan Fund to support regeneration studies in centres where there has been severe job loss (Nel, 2001). The impact is economic development that's not sustainable and irresponsible to some degree. At provincial level, strategies include very limited seed funding, actions to raise awareness of LED, and capacitating individuals with skills and education. Again, another barrier to responsible and sustainable economic growth. Nel (2001) regards these initiatives as having the potential to make a significant difference to both local communities and national socio-economic development.

It will thus be apparent that LED calls for collective creative thought from a range of stakeholders, partnerships and business friendships that will include government, community and NGO/NPO agencies. Obstacles nonetheless exist in the application and expansion of LED programmes that would help to transform need-driven entrepreneurship to innovation-driven entrepreneurship and create jobs in the process. Rogerson (Rogerson, 2010a; Rogerson, 2010b; Rogerson, 2011) notes, for example, that after almost two decades of experience and initiatives, results remain limited, and Nel (2001) points out that promising initiatives, programmes and projects have often faded out or been downscaled., with a number of possible reasons for this generally negative picture. Partly they relate to internal constraints affecting resources and skills (Nel, 2001b; Rogerson, 2010b). Other probable causes are lack of appeal to external investors in certain investment areas, and the near-absence of sustainable local government assistance from LED initiatives in South Africa (Bodhanya, 2014). These rather bleak indicators from lessons learned in the past can serve as action-evidence for accelerated backing from government and other agencies (Nel, 2001).

Systemic Levels: Mesosystems

In an innovation-driven economy, the need for collective creativity to move economies forward is now more crucial that event before (van der Westhuizen, 2016). The development of individuals' skills can only be absorbed into meso-, macro- and mundosystems if entrepreneurial stability is high, and without enabling factors for innovation and entrepreneurship, returns of hard-system and soft-system capital are low (Nelson and Pack, 1999; Nelson, 2008; Nelson, 2011). Gries and Naudé (2010) indicate that structural change on a mesosystemic level will enable organisations to deliver more complex and intermediate inputs to the macrosystem if the process is facilitated by able entrepreneurs. Such structural changes would therefore have implications for sustainable and responsible socio-economic development of entrepreneurs themselves, and are close tied to the integrative development processes between micro-, meso- and macrosystems (Naudé, 2013).

Community-Based Initiatives

While local governments in developing countries such as South Africa are constrained by legislative provisions on how funds can be utilised to engage in economic and social development activities, CBOs and NGOs have wider scope in which they can operate. These imply that initiatives for responsible and sustainable economic development are managed by community members who are keen to see change or transformation within their own community. Key change agents for local economic development in these types of initiatives are often churches, education institutions or other socially responsible organisations active in impoverished communities. The body of knowledge on LED in South Africa suggests that a critical success factor in community-based initiatives has been mesosystemic integrative collaboration, or local-level partnership development, between different organisations (Rogerson, 2010a; Khumalo, 2014; Ramukumba, 2014). Without such partnerships, or business friendships, these community-based initiatives cannot survive. Therefore, community based organisations plays an important role in development of collective creative approaches towards sustainable and responsible socio-economic development practice of a nation.

Section 21 Development Companies

Section 21 development companies (not-for-profit companies) often have an important oversight role in LED-type activity in South (Nel, 2001b; Brixiova and Kangoye, 2014). Section 21 companies often enter into partnerships with the private sector or local government in which the primary focus is to enhance business support and develop skills training (Nel, 2001). Often, because managers and leaders of these type of organisations are not driven to make a profit, they are more receptive for collective creative business approaches than counterparts who are involved in profit-driven organisations. Managers and leaders of these organisations are often more aware about the longevity of their organisation and frequently attempt to implement sustainable business practice because the lifespan of the Section 21 development company is dependent on outside party funding and financial contributions. Should sustainable and responsible business practice not be implemented, the organisation stand a chance not to survive financially.

Entrepreneurship, Systems Theory and Socio-Economic Development

Naudé's (2013) third "grand idea" in development economics concerns government and market failures on macro-, meso- and microsystemic levels. Naudé singles out the formulation of industrial policy as one role to which governments in developing and developed countries often pay particular attention in an attempt to move towards responsible and sustainable socio-economic development practice. Audretsch and Thurik (2004) distinguish three broad types of public policy – altruist policy (compensation policy), regulation, and public ownership – each of which create "red tape" for organisations functioning in the mesosystem and restrict an organisation's freedom to contract. Audrestch and Thurik suggest that whereas policy formulation was traditionally guided by a question like "how can the government withhold organisations from abusing their market power?", in the model for socio-economic development (Figure 1) a more important question is "how can the government create an environment fostering the sustainability and success of an organisation?" (Audretsch and Thurik, 2004; Thurik, 2009; Audretsch and Link, 2012). A problem that formulation of these policies often face that it includes little or no scope for collective creative contributions and these publicn policy are often the result of the brainstorm of only a selected few people. These policies are often rigid with little flexibility for creative approaches or practice.

Naudé (2013) believes that, from his "grand ideas" perspective, the two issues in relation to socio-developmental impact of entrepreneurship are enhancing quality and allocation of entrepreneurial ability (Figure 1) and alleviating the circumstances that give rise to necessity entrepreneurship. Therefore, have a direct impact on sustainable and responsible socio-economic development practice.

Also significant for socio-economic development and entrepreneurship, is the dichotomy between the formal sector and the informal sector (Maloney, 2010). According to Naudé (2013), "informal firms are often a form of 'evasive' entrepreneurship", set up to evade government regulations or taxation or to engage in illegal trade. Naudé states that the informal sector is less efficient and less able to obtain financial support from agencies and donors, and is also more susceptible to influence by less able entrepreneurs. In this way it is "much like the traditional or subsistence sector in typical dual-economy models, [where socio-economic] growth may be enhanced by encouraging entrepreneurs of high ability to migrate to the formal sector. "Again, the link between the formal and informal sector to apply sustainable and responsible socio-economic development practice face challenges in developing and developed countries. Further challenges are faced to apply collective creative approaches as a collaborative effort between the formal and informal business sectors. The impact is that the different environments (for example political, economic and environmental) in which the formal and informal business sectors continiue to face challenges due to the detachment in sustainable and responsible business practice that collectively aims towards socio-economic development.

CONCLUSION

Based on the literature, a possible way to increase responsible and sustainable socio-economic development are to promote collective innovation and entrepreneurship on various systemic levels in order to gain socio-economic developmental momentum. However, both developed and developing countries are facing severe systemic challenges throughout a spectrum of environments, including the political environment, economic environment and ecological environment – to name a few. Many of these systemic challenges relate to a lack of collective coherence amongst individuals, as well as individuals' attitudes, activities and aspirations as noted by the Global Entrepreneurship Monitor (2015).

Sustainable and responsible socio-economic development within a macro-system are challenged currently more than ever before and authors like Hannon et al (2013) believe that radical systemic transformation is necessary to remedy decay on systemic levels. Only then communities can collectively start moving towards sustainable and responsible practice for socio-economic development.

People play the most important part in sustainable and responsible socio-economic development. Individuals' entrepreneurial self-efficacy, as well as individual entrepreneurial orientation guides their attitudes, activities and aspirations towards sustainable and responsible socio-economic development – as set out by Xavier et al (2013). Systemically by developing soft systems first, therefore its people, – collective innovation might contribute to developing a country's hard systems on a meso-, macro- and mundo-scale (Scharmer, 2009; Townsend, 2011; Thompson and Bevan, 2013).

REFERENCES

Abrahams, D. (2003). Local economic development in South Africa: A useful tool for sustainable development. *Urban Forum, 2003*. Springer.

Acs, Z. J., Desai, S., & Hessels, J. (2008). Entrepreneurship, economic development and institutions. *Small Business Economics*, *31*(3), 219–234.

Amorós, J. E., Bosma, N., & Levie, J. (2013). Ten years of Global Entrepreneurship Monitor: Accomplishments and prospects. *International Journal of Entrepreneurial Venturing*, *5*(2), 120–152.

Audretsch, D. B., & Link, A. N. (2012). Entrepreneurship and innovation: Public policy frameworks. *The Journal of Technology Transfer*, *37*(1), 1–17.

Audretsch, D. B., & Thurik, A. R. (2004). *A model of the entrepreneurial economy*. Papers on entrepreneurship, growth and public policy.

Batabyal, A. A., & Nijkamp, P. (2012). A Schumpeterian Model of Entrepreneurship, Innovation, and Regional Economic Growth. *International Regional Science Review*, *35*(3), 339–361.

Bates, W. (2009). Gross national happiness. *Asian-Pacific Economic Literature*, *23*(2), 1–16.

Binns, T., & Nel, E. (1999). Beyond the development impasse: The role of local economic development and community. *The Journal of Modern African Studies*, *37*(3), 389.

Block, J., & Koellinger, P. (2009). I Can't Get No Satisfaction—Necessity Entrepreneurship and Procedural Utility. *Kyklos*, *62*(2), 191–209.

Bodhanya, S. (2014). The nexus model for local economic development. *Problems and Perspectives in Management, 12*(3).

Bolton, D. L., & Lane, M. D. (2012). Individual Entrepreneurial Orientation: Development of a Measurement Instrument. *Education + Training*, *54*(2-3), 219–233.

Bosma, N. (2013). The global entrepreneurship monitor (GEM) and its impact on entrepreneurship research. *Foundations and Trends in Entrepreneurship, 9*(2).

Brixiova, Z., & Kangoye, T. (2014). *Youth employment in Africa: new evidence and policies from Swaziland*. Springer.

Burns, G. W. (2011). *Gross National Happiness: A gift from Bhutan to the world. Positive psychology as social change*. Springer.

Checkland, P. (1999). *Systems thinking, systems practice: includes a 30-year retrospective*. Wiley.

Ethekwini Municipality. (2013). *Focus on SMMEs in eThekwini*. Available: http://www.durban.gov.za/Resource_Centre/edge/Documents/SMME's.pdf

Fabricius, C., Koch, E., Turner, S., & Magome, H. (2013). *Rights resources and rural development: Community-based natural resource management in Southern Africa*. Routledge.

Fitch, G., & O'Fallon, T. (2013). Theory U Applied in Transformation Development. In O. Gunnlaugson, C. Baron, & M. Cayer (Eds.), *Perspectives on Theory U: Insights from the Field*. Hershey, PA, USA: Business Science Reference.

Florin, J., Karri, R., & Rossiter, N. (2007). Fostering Entrepreneurial Drive in Business Education: An Attitudinal Approach. *Journal of Management Education*, *31*(1), 17–42.

Galindo, M.-Á., & Méndez, M. T. (2014). Entrepreneurship, economic growth, and innovation: Are feedback effects at work? *Journal of Business Research*, *67*(5), 825–829.

Galindo, M.-Á., & Méndez-Picazo, M.-T. (2013). Innovation, entrepreneurship and economic growth. *Management Decision*, *51*(3), 501–514.

Giddens, A., Duneier, M., Appelbaum, R. P., & Carr, D. (2000). *Introduction to sociology*. WW Norton New York.

Goleman, D., & Senge, P. (2014). Seeking the Big Picture: Systems Thinking for Schools. *Education Week*, *34*(2), 22–23.

Gries, T., & Naudé, W. (2010). Entrepreneurship and structural economic transformation. *Small Business Economics*, *34*(1), 13–29.

Gruenewald, D. A., & Smith, G. A. (2014). *Place-based education in the global age: Local diversity*. Routledge.

Gunnlaugson, O., Baron, C., & Cayer, M. (2013). *Perspectives on Theory U: Insights from the Field*. Hershey, PA: Business Science Reference.

Hannon, V., Gillinson, S., & Shanks, L. (2013). *Learning a living: radical innovation in education for work*. Dohar: Bloomsbury.

Harkema, S. J. M., & Schout, H. (2008). Incorporating Student-Centred Learning in Innovation and Entrepreneurship Education. *European Journal of Education*, *43*(4), 513–526.

Hermans, C. A. M. (2012). Towards a 'U-turn' by the Churches: How (Not) to Possibilise the Future. *Religion & Theology*, *19*(3/4), 237–264.

Jackson, M. C. (2003). *Systems thinking: Creative holism for managers*. Wiley Chichester.

Karadeniz, E. E. (2006). Entrepreneurship and Economic Development. *Kocaeli Üniversitesi Sosyal Bilimler Enstitüsü Dergisi, 11*(1).

Khumalo, P. (2014). Improving the Contribution of Cooperatives as Vehicles for Local Economic Development in South Africa. *African Studies Quarterly*, *14*(4), 61–79.

Koveos, P. (2011). Entrepreneurship and Economic Development: the Relationship Revisited. *Journal of Developmental Entrepreneurship*, *16*(2), 165–167.

Lawrence, F. (2013). The Role of Local Economic Development Agencies in the South African Local Economic Development Landscape. *Urban Forum, 24*(4), 523-541.

Leonard, A. (2010). *The story of stuff: How our obsession with stuff is trashing the planet, our communities, and our health-and a vision for change*. Simon and Schuster.

Maas, G., & Herrington, M. (2008). Global Entrepreneurship Monitor South. Cape Town: University of Cape Town Graduate School of Business.

Maloney, D. H. (2010). Solving Problems That Count. *Educational Leadership*, *68*(1), 55–58.

Marais, H. (2001). *Limits to change: The political economy of transition*. Palgrave Macmillan.

Mckibbin, J., Binns, T., & Nel, E. (2012). Uplifting small towns in post-apartheid South Africa: The experience of the Amathole Regional Economic Development Agency (Aspire). *Local Economy*, *27*(4), 388–402.

Minniti, M. (2013). *The Dynamics of Entrepreneurship: Evidence from Global Entrepreneurship Monitor Data*. Oxford University Press.

Munshi, K. D., & Rosenzweig, M. R. (2003). *Traditional institutions meet the modern world: Caste, gender and schooling choice in a globalizing economy*. Academic Press.

Naudé, W. (2010). Entrepreneurship, developing countries, and development economics: New approaches and insights. *Small Business Economics*, *34*(1), 1–12.

Naudé, W. (2011). Entrepreneurship is Not a Binding Constraint on Growth and Development in the Poorest Countries. *World Development*, *39*(1), 33–44.

Naudé, W. (2013). Entrepreneurship and economic development: Theory, evidence and policy. *Evidence and Policy. IZA Discussion Paper,* (7507).

Nel, E. (2001a). Local economic development: A review and assessment of its current status in South Africa. *Urban Studies (Edinburgh, Scotland)*, *38*(7), 1003–1024.

Nel, E. (2001b). Local Economic Development: A Review and Assessment of its Current Status in South Africa. *Urban Studies (Routledge)*, *38*(7), 1003–1024.

Nel, E., & Hill, T. (2001). De-industrialisation and Local Economic Development Alternatives in KwaZulu-Natal, South Africa. *Geography (Sheffield, England)*, *86*(4), 356.

Nel, E., & Stevenson, T. (2014). The catalysts of small town economic development in a free market economy: A case study of New Zealand. *Local Economy*, *29*(4-5), 486–502.

Nel, E. L., & Rogerson, C. M. 2013. Special economic zones in South Africa: reflections from international debates. *Urban Forum, 24*(2), 205-217.

Nelson, R. R. (2008). Economic development from the perspective of evolutionary economic theory. *Oxford Development Studies*, *36*(1), 9–21.

Nelson, R. R. (2011). Economic development as an evolutionary process. *Innovation and Development*, *1*(1), 39–49.

Nelson, R. R., & Pack, H. (1999). The Asian miracle and modern growth theory. *The Economic Journal*, *109*(457), 416–436.

Peretto, P. F. (1998). Technological change and population growth. *Journal of Economic Growth*, *3*(4), 283–311.

Peretto, P. F. (1999). Industrial development, technological change, and long-run growth. *Journal of Development Economics*, *59*(2), 389–417.

Poh Kam, W., Yuen Ping, H., & Erkko, A. (2005). Entrepreneurship, Innovation and Economic Growth: Evidence from GEM data. *Small Business Economics*, *24*(3), 335–350.

Ramukumba, T. (2014). Participatory appraisal of competitive advantage (PACA) approach in local economic development. *Development in Practice*, *24*(7), 897–907.

Rogerson, C. M. (2010a). In Search of Public Sector-Private Sector Partnerships for Local Economic Development in South Africa. *Urban Forum, 21*(4), 441-456.

Rogerson, C. M. (2010b). Local economic development in South Africa: Strategic challenges. *Development Southern Africa*, *27*(4), 481–495.

Rogerson, C. M. (2011). Tracking Local Economic Development Policy and Practice in South Africa, 1994-2009. *Urban Forum, 22*(2), 149-168.

Scharmer, C. O. (2009). *Theory U: Learning from the future as it emerges*. San Francisco: Berrett-Koehler Publishers.

Scharmer, C. O., & Kaufer, K. (2013). *Leading from the emerging future: From ego-system to eco-system economies*. Berrett-Koehler Publishers.

Senge, P., Scharmer, C. O., Jaworski, J., & Flowers, B. S. (2008a). *Presence: Human Purpose and the Field of the Future*. Broadway Business.

Senge, P., Smith, B., Kruschwitz, N., Laur, J., & Schley, S. (2008b). Anatomy of Inspiration. *T+D, 62*(8), 52-55.

Sisk, T. D. (1995). *Democratization in South Africa: The elusive social contract*. Cambridge Univ Press.

Song, L. Z., Song, M., & Parry, M. E. (2010). Perspective: Economic Conditions, Entrepreneurship, First-Product Development, and New Venture Success. *Journal of Product Innovation Management*, *27*(1), 130–135.

Stromquist, N. P., & Monkman, K. (2014). *Globalization and education: Integration and contestation across cultures*. R&L Education.

Taatila, V., & Down, S. (2012). Measuring Entrepreneurial Orientation of University Students. *Education + Training*, *54*(8-9), 744–760.

Thompson, M. J., & Bevan, D. (2013). *Wise management and organisational culture*. Palgrave MacMillan.

Thurik, A. (2009). Entreprenomics: entrepreneurship, economic growth and policy. *Entrepreneurship, growth, and public policy*, 219-249.

Townsend, D. M. J. (2011). International Handbook of Leadership for Learning. Springer.

Urban, B. (2012). Researching entrepreneurship from a cognitive perspective: A focus on necessity entrepreneurs in the Johannesburg area. *African Journal of Business Management*, *6*, 11732–11742.

Van Der Westhuizen, T. (2016). *Developing Individual Entrepreneurial Orientation: A systemic approach through the lens of Theory* (PhD Thesis). University of KwaZulu-Natal.

van Stel, A., Wennekers, S., Thurik, R., Reynolds, P., & de Wit, G. (2003). Explaining nascent entrepreneurship across countries. *Scales Research Reports,* (200301).

Weinberg, I. (2011). *Neurophysics Exploring the Multiple Dimensions of Consciousness*. Available: http://www.pninet.com/articles/Neurophysics.pdf

World Bank. (n.d.). *Local Economic Development - What is Local Economic Development (LED)?*. Available: http://go.worldbank.org/EA784ZB3F0

Xavier, S., Kelley, D., Kew, J., Herrington, M., & Vorderwülbecke, A. (2013). *Global Entrepreneurship Monitor (GEM) 2012 Global Report*. GERA/GEM.

KEY TERMS AND DEFINITIONS

Developing: The *Oxford Advanced Learner's Dictionary* (Hornby and Crowther, 1995) defines the term *develop* as "to grow gradually; to become or make larger, more advanced or more organised" and the word "developing" as " the action or process of being developed." *For the purpose of this chapter* developing implies the process that systems are going through en route to transformation.

Enablers of Transformation: *Enablers* can be defined as a person or thing that makes something possible, where transformation is defined as "A change in developmental maturity" (Fitch and O'Fallon, 2013).

Entrepreneurial Self-Efficacy: A number of authors (De Noble et al., 1999; Zhao et al., 2005; McGee et al., 2009) have given attention to the construct *Entrepreneurial Self-Efficacy*, and a definition of the term on which most would agree is that it is a "construct that measures a person's belief in their ability to successfully launch an entrepreneurial venture" (Zhao et al., 2005). *For the purpose of this chapter*, Entrepreneurial Self-Efficacy can be described as a construct that measures an individual's belief in their ability to take entrepreneurial action.

Individual Entrepreneurial Orientation: The term *entrepreneurial orientation* is commonly used in reference to performance of a business, firm or organisation (Bolton and Lane, 2012; Robinson, 2014). Individual Entrepreneurial Orientation (IEO) signifies the processes, practices and decision-making activities of an individual that lead to entrepreneurship (Lumpkin and Dess, 1996). Authors identify three distinct propensities of IEO: risk taking, innovativeness and proactivity (Callaghan, 2009; Scharmer, 2009; Bolton and Lane, 2012; Ramkissor and Cassim, 2013; Robinson and Stubberud, 2014). *For the purpose of this chapter* Individual Entrepreneurial Orientation implies the processes, practices and decision-making activities of Student Entrepreneurs in relation to raking risks, innovativeness and proactivity.

Systemic Approach: A *system* is a complex whole whose functioning depends on its parts and the interactions between those parts (Jackson, 2002) where systemic elements affect the whole, rather than just parts, and refers to the interrelatedness and integrativeness of systems (Leonard, 2010). An approach can be described as the process of going towards something. *For the purpose of this chapter*, a systemic approach implies the process of developing the whole.

Systemic Levels: Scharmer (2009) distinguishes between mundo-level systems, macro-level systems, meso-level systems, and micro-level systems. In the context of this research, following Townsend (2011), *mundo system* refers to global governance, *macro system* refers to national governance or institutionalising, *meso system* refers to organisations and culture, and *micro system* refers to individuals and their thinking. Mark Edward's model of multi-level systemic wisdom (as cited in Thompson, 2013) describes the global society in relation to the global economy as the mundo system, society at large as the macro system, organisational structure, culture and climate as the meso system, and the personal characteristics and traits of in individual as the micro system. *For the purpose of this chapters* systemic levels refers to mundo, macro, meso and micro systems.

Section 3
Responsible Management Education

Chapter 12
Principles of Responsible Management Education (PRME):
Call for Responsible Management Education

Malebo Mokoqama
University of KwaZulu-Natal, South Africa

Ziska Fields
University of KwaZulu-Natal, South Africa

ABSTRACT

Curriculums of business schools have been questioned in terms of the relevancy and practical application of real life scenarios. Business schools have a responsibility to promote and encourage responsible management education within their curricula and learning experience. Being responsible allows business schools to produce graduates who will become responsible leaders who have a lasting impact on businesses, communities, the environment, the country and the world. There is rising pressure for business schools to promote responsible management education through initiatives such as the Principals of Responsible Management Education (PRME). This chapter seeks to identify the challenges and benefits of PRME and the role that business schools play in implementing it in their curriculums.

INTRODUCTION

According to Haertle, Herzig, Godemann, and Moon (2014), there has been several business scandals and world events, such as the 2007 financial catastrophe, which has resulted in business schools being called to be more sustainable (Hasrouni, 2012). There is an urgency for educational institutions, and specifically business schools, to contribute to solving the world's social, economic and environmental problems (United Nations Global Compact, 2012). Business schools are seen as a platform to bring about change to the changing world by the adjustment in curricula, research and even teaching methods. Therefore, the objectives of this chapter are to: (1) give an overview of PRME; (2) identify the barriers

DOI: 10.4018/978-1-5225-1823-5.ch012

to the implementation of PRME;(3) identify the importance and benefits for business schools being signatories of PRME (4) The role that business schools play in the promotion of PRME.

BACKGROUND

It is suggested by Muff (2012) that the purpose and vision of business schools is to develop future business leaders who are to deal with complex challenges that society faces. Several critics further note, that the reason for the failure of business schools to adequately develop sustainable business leaders is because of the curriculum (Thomas, Thomas and Wilson, 2013). However, there are several business schools who have made claims that they are integrating sustainability in their course but a few of these business schools actually have core modules in sustainability (Barber, Wilson, Venkatachalam, Cleaves & Garnham, 2014). GSB&L is one of the business schools who do not have a core module on sustainability.

Recent statistics show that there are currently 650 PRME signatories from over 81 countries PRME2015AnnaulReport (2015). PRME, calls for business schools to not only implement sustainability issues in their curriculum but to improve their teaching and research in the aim of global exclusive growth (Ramos, Saiia, Sroufe & Sivasubramaniam, 2015). For business schools not be part of this global networks means that they forfeit the opportunity of improving their teaching and research. They also have the disadvantage of not being able to exchange innovative ideas. This is because Rasche, Unruh, Waddock & Werhane (2009), believe that PRME allows different business schools to exchange ideas that could be beneficial to each other.

Call for Responsible Business Practice

In the past years, the world has been experiencing ecological, social and environmental problems that has resulted in businesses being labelled as the key culprits responsible for such dilemmas (United Nations Global Compact, 2012). For this reason, businesses have been called to be more responsible and the common term that links businesses with being responsible is corporate social responsibility. The common perception of corporate social responsibility is the manner in which businesses conduct their operations, without disregarding the welfare of various stakeholders (Gee, 2012). Despite this concept, some businesses do not practice corporate social responsibility. This is evident from the corporate scandals that have emerged over the years. Louw (2006) points out that the Enron, WorldCom corporate scandals influenced how corporations were viewed, and a greater analysis was focused on the people that run businesses. This is when the relevance of businesses being socially responsible started to become a high priority.

Climate change is a mounting catastrophe that leads to instability, unrest and a threat to development (The United Nations Global Compact, 2015). Which is why businesses have been called to be more responsible. The results of a survey conducted on 750 business leaders within 152 countries prove that climate change is an urgent matter to that needs to be addressed (The United Nations Global Compact, 2015). The results showed that 91% believe that climate change is an urgent priority. Furthermore, 66% believed that businesses are not doing well to tackle climate change and only 34% believe that businesses are on track in fighting against climate change (The United Nations Global Compact, 2015). The business leaders were also asked what the main global challenges that could threaten business are and the results showed climate change being ranked second (Laasch & Conaway, 2015). Because of this, the importance for businesses to change resulted in the formation of global initiative called the United Nations Global Compact (UNGC). The UNGC is the largest voluntary initiative that promotes corporate social responsibility (United Nations Global Compact, 2012). The UNGC requests businesses to comply with them about how they should govern a planet, bearing in mind that they play a crucial role in global governance (Rasche, Unruh et al. 2009)

CEOs believe that education is a critical factor in the success of their business. This is proven by 766 responses from CEOS around the world in which 72% viewed education as vital in their businesses succeeding (United Nations Global Compact-Accenture CEO study, 2010). Therefore, the active engagement of Higher Education Institutions (HEI) also plays a crucial role in creating global inclusive growth (United Nations Global Compact, 2012). Furthermore, education institutions that have a positive impact on stakeholders, not only benefit stakeholders, but the institutions themselves. This is reason behind the formulation of PRME.

Role of Business Schools

Not only are corporations seen as the key problem global problems, but business schools are also seen as a cause of global problems due to the pedagogy and curriculums used (United Nations Global Compact, 2012). This has caused business schools being pressurised to conform to the changing world (Fragueiro & Thomas 2011). Therefore, focus has also been placed on business schools and the role it has to play in creating a more sustainable world. In addition, there is pressure on business schools to practice responsible management education.

According to Rasche and Gilbert (2015) responsible management education is aimed at how the business schools' educational practices can function by taking into consideration the social, environmental and ethical impact that can occur. Traditionally, business schools have been seen as a vehicle for producing individuals who are to take over the business world, become managers and conduct their organizations sustainably. However, the global financial meltdown has resulted in the questioning of the role and function of business schools. According to Thomas and Wilson (2012) organisational crashes of large corporations such as Parmalat, Enron and WorldCom, is because business schools failed to teach moral and critical thinking. This has resulted in businesses schools being questioned by various analysts about their pedagogy (Rayment and Smith, 2013). Although issues of sustainability are taught in business schools, sustainability is not deeply imbedded in the curricula (Musharbash, 2012). This shows that there is a need for business schools to take responsibility in what they teach and in the method in which they teach. Thomas et al. (2012) further allude that business schools provide 'lip service' because of the lack of reality in the concepts they teach. In addition, the results of a survey conducted by the Graduate Management Admission Council (GMAC), showed that what business schools teach does not link with how businesses are to succeed. This raises questions about the content of business school curricula (Muff, 2012). It is evident through literature that there is a need for business schools to re-evaluate their curricula and for them to align themselves with the changing world like embracing the Principles of Responsible Management Education (PRME) as part of their curricula.

As a result of global issues such as climate change, there is now a need for business schools to involve themselves in strategies that are in line with the new realities of business (Fragueiro and Thomas, 2011). Business schools are no longer just seen as institutions of higher education, but institutions that can produce business graduates who can impact the world in a positive manner (Herzig, Godemann & Moon and Powell, 2011). Solitander, Fougère, Sobczak and Herlin, (2012) further attest that indeed business schools are central in favouring the development of responsible managers. The need to operate sustainably globally has increased over the years. Hence, the response from business schools across the world to conduct education sustainably is by the formulation of an initiative called PRME. PRME is the largest global initiative that brings together business schools for the sake of promoting sustainable management education in response to the changing nature of social values (Forray & Leigh, 2012; Alcaraz & Thiruvattal, 2010).

PRME

The conception of PRME historically, started between a conversation between close friends, Manuel Escudero and David Cooperider at Western Reserve University in Cleveland, in the Weatherhead School of Management (Alcaraz & Thiruvattal, 2010). It was in the conversation that Manuel stated "what if we try to cooperate to formulate some principles to reform and to change gradually the business education toward sustainability". It was at the Center for Business as an Agent of World forum in which David Cooperider who was the director, that they first announced the concept of PRME. PRME is an initiative that was formulated by an international task force of sixty deans, university presidents and official representatives of leading business schools and follow a recommendation of all academic stakeholders of the United Nation's Global Compact (PRME, 2015). PRME encourages business schools to adapt their curricula, research and teaching methodologies in order to adapt to the changing business world (Laasch & Conaway, 2015).

The significance of the formation of PRME by a task force of people around the world, is an indication that there is no bias and one-point view about sustainability and society. PRME was formulated in collaboration with the United Nations Global Compact (UNGC), the Association to Advance Collegiate Schools of Business (AACSB), the Aspen Institute's Business and Society Program, the European Foundation for Management Development (EFMD), the Globally Responsible Leadership Initiative (GRLI), and NetImpact, a student organization with more than 13,000 members, all of which remain partners (Waddock,et al, 2009). In the year July 2007 PRME was launched in Geneva, Switzerland during the United Nations Global Compact Leaders' Summit (Waddock, et al, 2009; Alcaraz & Thiruvattal, 2010). Since its launch in 2007, the number of business schools who have signed up to PRME are over 550 from 80 different countries (Sobczak & Mukhi, 2015). The conception of PRME is also due to the notion that management education is a powerful force that is able to change the world Waddock,et al, (2009) . As well as fostering responsible management education across the planet (Sobczak & Mukhi, 2015) In addition, it was formulated in result of societal and institutional change (Forray & Leigh, 2012). PRME according to Waddock, et al, (2009) is by the UNGC principles to develop future leaders with the necessary skills, values and capabilities in order to deal with the 21st century dilemmas by following a set of voluntary guidelines. The current head of the PRME Secretariat in the UN Global Compact Office in an interview, also agrees that the purpose of PRME is to develop future responsible business leaders (Sobczak and Mukhi, 2015). Since business leaders took it upon themselves to be part of the UNGC, they then asked themselves; what are business schools currently engaged in to make sure that sustainable business leaders Waddock, et al, (2009). This question that was posed to business school resulted in the creation of PRME. A well-recognised researcher in Management, Sumantra Ghoshal, points out that what they teach in business schools should be looked because of the economic breakdown (Alcaraz & Thiruvattal, 2010). Whereas Waddock, et al (2009) and Alcaraz and Thiruvattal (2010) believe that PRME was an answer and good marker for business schools, when the economic meltdown occurred.

Alcaraz and Thiruvattal (2010) further suggest that the economic breakdown also revealed to them what they have not being teaching in business schools. In addition, they agree that they have not taught students that management is a profession that requires the manager to be aware of their future decisions.

Being a signatory of PRME does only involve just signing up and being a silent partner, but to be involved in several commitments. These commitments include more research conducted on issues pertaining to PRME; Transparency, by submitting a progress report on the implementation of PRME and lastly the adjustment of the curriculum by adding of PRME related content. Moreover, it calls for business schools to not only implement sustainability issues in their curriculum but to improve their teaching and research in the aim of global exclusive growth (Ramos, Saiia, Sroufe & Sivasubramaniam, 2015; Alcaraz & Thiruvattal, 2010). PRME is described as a new catalyst of the definition of business education (Alcaraz & Thiruvattal, 2010). PRME is an initiative that is encouraged not only by business leaders but also endorsed by two leading management education proponents, which is the body AACSB and the EFMD Waddock, et al, (2009). PRME also seeks to educate future business managers and leaders who can link profitability with sustainability, and to conduct sustainable business that will allow for inclusive global economy Waddock,vet al (2009) Alcaraz and Thiruvattal (2010) point out that PRME has three distinct characteristics, "a global call, a framework, and a learning network." This means that PRME is not only calling specific business schools to be responsible but all of them around the globe with the aim of being responsible. They further elaborate that PRME acts a framework for, curriculum change; experimenting new learning methods; research and orientation.

PRME similarly seeks to create a sense of awareness that management education courses need to educate future business leaders on how to deal with environmental, social or economic problems Waddock, et al (2009). Furthermore, they key solution to these problems is the implementation of the principles of responsible management in management curriculum. According to Waddock, et al (2009) the concept behind PRME is because the world is changing, new demands in the world require business leaders to be transparent, accountable as well as to deal with the planet more sustainably. PRME in essential, requests management schools to fully equip students with skills that will charge them to think broadly and have a global perspective on how to deal with the worlds demands (Waddock et al, 2009). It is evident through literature that there is still a gap in skills that students have in business schools to tackle 21st century problems the world at large is dealing with. Waddock et al (2009) state that "the PRME do not aim to be a compliance measurement system." Which means that the six principles are there for business schools to come up with solutions that with solutions that will fit their specific context, e.g. administrative functions. There is a term that is used by PRME organisers which is called "bluewashing." This term refers to business schools who sign up to PRME, but do not necessarily make any progress or changes in their research, teaching and learning. The organisers of PRME do not want signatories of PRME to only become members but to take the necessary steps by the changing of their curricula and research into being more sustainable. Statistics show that from the year 2007, to 2015 the number of PRME signatories has increased. The reporting showed that 46% of PRME signatories are active participants and are communicating effectively (PRME, 2015). PRME seeks to achieve transparency and accountability, which is why; signatories are obligated to have status progress reports. However, some institutions do not submit their reports that is the reason behind the 22% of these schools being deregistered.

Africa, as compared to other continents does not have many signatories of PRME. An online survey was conducted by Gibson (2011) in 2011 in which 45 respondents from 31 business schools and 9 different countries participated. The results of the survey showed that 81% believed that the values of global social and environmental responsibility are appropriate to African business schools (Gibson,

Figure 1. Reporting Status of PRME Participants Since 2007
(Source: PRME 2015 Annual Report, 2015)

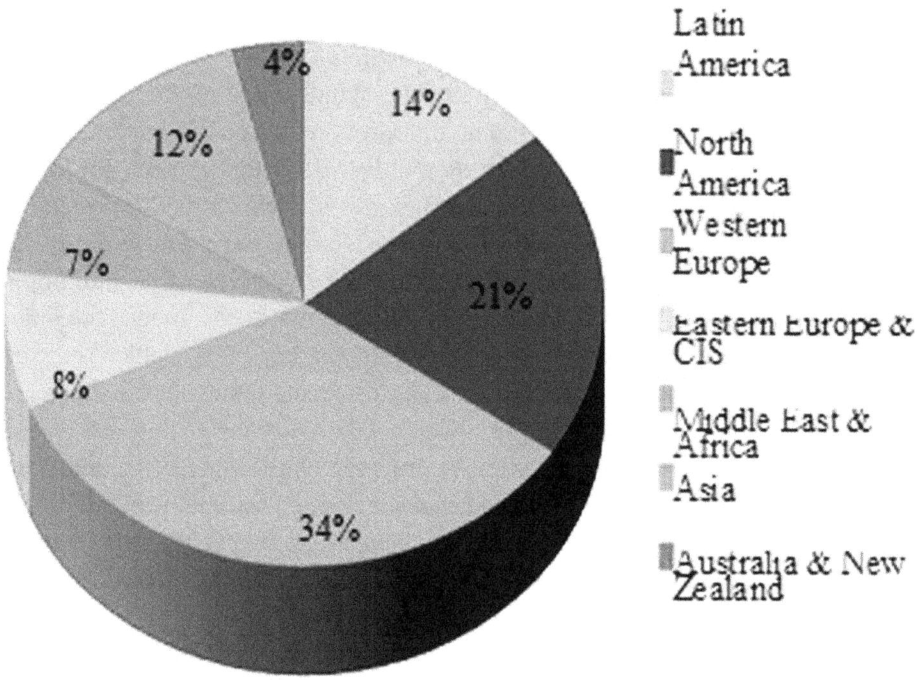

2011). These results prove that African business schools see the importance for business schools to place more emphasis on sustainability. In spite of their eagerness for sustainability, the results also showed that 55% did not receive sufficient information about PRME to inform them to participate in it, and only 26% said they had sufficient information (Gibson, 2011). This is evidence of the possible reasons for the small percentage of business schools signing up to PRME. Despite their lack of knowledge about PRME, 96% of the African businesses said they would be interested in signing up for PRME. From the PRME website, there is evidence that between 2011 to 2016, there has been an increase in the number of business schools in Africa who have signed up for PRME. Although recent stats (see Figure 1) show that by the year 2015, Middle East and Africa make up 7% of the PRME participants (PRME2015AnnualReport, 2015).

The Six Principles of Responsible Management Education (PRME)

According to Rasche and Gilbert (2015) they highlight that indeed corporate responsibility and sustainability has entered business schools but it has not gone far to the point of it being embedded in the curriculum. PRME was established in order to develop business leaders who will be able to tackle and solve challenges that the world is faced with (Laasch & Conaway, 2015) and could be faced with in future. The six principles according to Alcaraz and Thiruvattal (2010) are framed according to the values of the United Nations that seek to promote human rights; responsible labour; environmental responsibility as well as anti-corruption. Responsible management education cannot be separated from the six principles that were developed as the core focus of the initiative. This initiative seeks to achieve the following:

- **Purpose:** We will cultivate the competencies of learners in order for them to contribute to the global economy and be examples in adding sustainable value in business.
- **Values:** We will align our syllabus and academic activities in order to match up with the values that are stipulated in global initiatives such the United Nations Global Compact.
- **Method:** We will engage in operative learning processes, materials that will result in tangible learning experiences in order to achieve sustainable business leaders.
- **Research:** We will participate in experiential research that progresses our knowledge in understanding the role that corporations have in adding economic value to the society. In addition, we would consider the role of corporations in being sustainable.
- **Partnership:** We seek to communicate with owners of businesses primarily to work together in resolving issues that may arise such as corporations not being able to engage in social and environmental responsibilities.
- **Dialogue:** We are determined to facilitate and support dialogue and debate among educators, businesses, government, consumers, media, civil society organizations and other interested groups and stakeholders on critical issues related to global social responsibility and sustainability (PRME, 2015).

The first principle states that it seeks to cultivate the competencies of learners in order for them to contribute to the global economy and be examples in adding sustainable value in business (PRME, 2015). Based on the first principle outlined by PRME, it is quite evident the importance that is placed on sustainable education. The second principle, aims to align the syllabus and academic activities in order to match up with the values that are stipulated in global initiatives such the United Nations Global Compact (Louw, 2015). This principle compel business schools to re-evaluate their curriculum to make sure that it is sustainable. The third principle stipulates that business schools are called to engage in operative learning processes, materials that will result in tangible learning experiences in order to achieve sustainable business leaders (Louw, 2015). The experimental learning theory comes into play as it seeks to stimulate students by putting into practice what is being learnt in class. PRME also expects business schools to participate in experiential research that progresses knowledge in understanding the role that corporations have in adding economic value to the society (Louw, 2015). Business schools have a huge role to play collaborating with businesses. The fifth principle calls for business schools to communicate with owners of businesses primarily to work together in resolving issues that may arise such as corporations not being able to engage in social and environmental responsibilities (PMRE, 2015). Lastly, PRME envisions a business school that will facilitate and support dialogue and debate among educators, businesses, government, consumers, media, civil society organizations and other interested groups and stakeholders on critical issues related to global social responsibility and sustainability (PRME, 2015)

This initiative also shows the significant role that business schools have to play and their role in making sure that these principles are followed. The first three principles of purpose, values and methods are important, as there is a high need for them to be fulfilled. There is a huge gap in business schools where the capabilities of students in becoming sustainable leaders is not fully developed.

Opportunities of Signing up to PRME

There are several opportunities and benefits for being a signatory of PRME. Every business school according to Weybrecht (2015) has its own drivers, pressure, culture and people. Moreover, business schools differ in existing norms and values regarding education (Escudero & Rasche, 2009). Because of these differences, no single formula can work in terms of imbedding sustainability.

According to Ramos, Saiia et al. (2015), business schools who fully implement PRME have the benefit of producing responsible business graduates who are able to conceptualise the importance of sustainability and the triple bottom line. Over the past 5 years, a number of business schools recognised the role that management education is playing in advancing sustainability in order to produce sustainable business leaders (Weybrecht, 2015). Another opportunity that an institution has in implementing PRME is being able to exchange ideas and good practices with other likeminded institutions (Escudero & Rasche, 2009). This platform is given to business schools at conferences such as the Global Forum for Responsible Management Education, where business schools speak about sustainable issues. Escudero and Rasche (2009) attest that institutions that sign up to PRME enjoy the rewards of being recognised as a school that practices responsible management point it out. Business schools that do not sign up not to PRME, forfeit the opportunity to be viewed as an agent of change as a business school amongst other institutions.

Implementing PRME brings about holistic innovative change in a business school (PRME, 2012). This entails a change in the school's culture and experimental teaching and learning practices. Hence, a business school will learn to explore and utilise more innovative ways of teaching its students. This according to the Inspirational guide for the implementation of PRME (2012) will result in more partnerships and collaboration with an array of stakeholders, such the business community and Non-Governmental Organisations

From the testimonies of other institutions who have sign up for PRME, the Inspirational guide for the implementation of PRME (2012) names three internal benefits of PRME, which are that PRME:

1. Strengthens and highlights the values and mission of the school;
2. Acts as a mechanism of stimulating business schools to reframe conversations which then leads to them being relevant; and
3. Aids in terms of systematic change and improves coordination.
4. PRME calls for business schools to not only implement sustainability issues in their curricula, but to improve their teaching and research in the aim of global exclusive growth (Ramos, Saiia, Sroufe & Sivasubramaniam, 2015; Alcaraz & Thiruvattal, 2010).

Challenges to Signing up to PRME

Business schools in the past years have been under intense scrutiny (Fragueiro & Thomas 2011). Due to this scrutiny, it is evident that several business schools are now making necessary adjustments, such as making changes to their mission statements and rebranding their degrees (Weybrecht, 2015). Such changes require immense planning and careful evaluation of resources. Despite the planning that is involved, there are barriers that hinder the implementation of responsible management education within the curricula of business schools. According to (Rasche & Gilbert 2015) business schools seem to struggle when it comes to aligning their organizational practices with responsible management education. Their argument is based on a pattern that showed that 9 business schools decided to withdraw from PRME, and 43 schools were delisted from PRME. Indeed, this is clearly an indication that there are certain barriers that are prohibiting the implementation of responsible management education.

In business schools, there are powerful actors who play a significant role in attaining set goals such as organizational or academic change. In business schools, leadership usually consists of a dean, directors and even senior lecturers. According to Waddock, et al, (2009) deans of a business school play a significant role in the implementation of principles of responsible management education within the curriculum, as they are required to sign a letter as an indication of a desire to participate in PRME. That is why Alcaraz and Thiruvattal (2010) point out that the strong conviction of deans is crucial for the transformation of business schools. Deans are seen as the CEOs of business schools since they have power of setting a school's strategic direction (Fragueiro & Thomas, 2011). In addition, support is needed from upper management-the deans and directors in order for business schools to have an effective strategic approach (Weybrecht, 2015). This is a clear indication of the importance of a dean in a business school to implement change. Fragueiro and Thomas (2011) further alludes that deans may be likened to sport coaches, which are hired to improve performance at the same time having an aim of building their own careers. Despite the significance of deans in business schools, they can be a barrier in accepting to incorporate sustainable management education within the curriculum. Rasche and Gilbert, (2015) agrees that influential actors have an influence whether or not business schools adopt structural elements. In addition, Herlin, Fougère, Sobczak and Solitander (2012) believe that business schools who have signed up PRME is because they have support from the school's higher leadership.

The lecturers in business schools also play a significant role since they are the vehicle that teaches students about a series of content including responsible management education. Staff members can be a barrier by being reluctant to integrate sustainability because of the lack of knowledge and even self-confidence (Godemann et al, 2011). Furthermore, lecturers can teach aspects of the syllabus without making it practical in the actual teaching practice. (Rasche & Gilbert, 2015). This could slow down the process of implementing and making responsible management education practical. The lecturers in business schools play a significant role since they are responsible for teaching students about a series of content including responsible management education. Staff members can be a barrier by being reluctant to integrate sustainability because of the lack of knowledge and even self-confidence Godemann, Herzig et al. (2011). Furthermore, business schools tend not to receive full support from academic staff, because they feel they are changing traditional ideas Barber, Cleaves et al. (2014). Another barrier to the implementation of PRME is financial constraints. Making changes in a curriculum is not a simple and quick task, and requires time, effort and even resources. Rasche and Gilbert (2015) state that making change to existing courses or adding new ones involve financial resource commitments. Due to the current economic state there has been issues arising surrounding university budgets, and limited institutional resources (Barber et al, 2014). There seems to be not much of a difference between the business world and academia since everyone is asked to "do more for less" (Barber et al (2013).

Rakings play a crucial role in many business schools. Which is why there are three main accreditation organizations, which are: The Association of Advanced Collegiate Schools of Business (AACSB International), the European Foundation for Management Development (EFMD), and the Association of MBAs (AMBA) (Weybrecht, 2015). According to Weybrecht (2015) ranking influence a student's choice on where to study as well as many of the decisions such as curriculum change are influenced by rankings. Despite institutional pressure and limited resources, business schools still face pressure due to rankings and the obligation to practice responsible management education (Rasche & Gilbert, 2015).

Wedlin (2006) argues that business schools continuously compete with each other, this result in them having the pressure of linking up with professional organizations. The pressure and competitiveness amongst the business schools, rankings are often faced with criticism such as the lack of transparency and rigor (Weybrecht, 2015). This can influence business school's attitude towards not incorporating sustainability since they believe rankings are not clear enough.

According to Weybrecht (2015) faculty is one the biggest hindrances to the integration of sustainability in the curriculum of business school. Normally faculties have their set programs and agenda in which they adhere too. And since business schools have their own agenda some faculty may resist responsible management education because they feel it is not aligned to their agenda (Rasche & Gilbert, 2015). Furthermore, this makes it more difficult to translate sustainability into such disciplines because of the lack of understanding of the concepts of sustainability (Godemann et al, 2011). One of the problems that arise is faculties' inability to comprehend how sustainability relates to their field of study, and having limited awareness (Weybrecht, 2015). Godemann et al, (2011) argue that faculties still want to maintain their academic freedom, which explain why they may resist the implantation of the principles of responsible management education.

Implementation of PRME

There are several questions that Rasche, Unruh et al. (2009)ask themselves with regards to the implementation of PRME. These questions are:

1. What do we teach within responsible management education?
2. How do we teach responsible management?
3. What is the business school and general economic context shaping responsible management education?

Signing up to PRME is not a difficult task; there are several steps and processes that are involved in implementation. According to Rasche, Unruh et al. (2009), the most important and crucial step is getting an approval from the Dean or other authority in the business schools. Furthermore, other steps include that the business school begins to implement the principles of responsible management within research, the curriculum and operations. Therefore, the most crucial step a business school can take is approaching the Dean and seeking approval. The top-bottom approach according to Rasche, Unruh et al. (2009), is when the Dean signs up and then announces the news to the school with an expectation that change will occur. Similarly, is to involve management and those in the school by allowing for a constant dialogue as PRME is being implemented in the curriculum Rasche, Unruh et al. (2009). However, Escudero and Rasche (2009) state that it not only the top-bottom approach that is needed for the progress of PRME, but also a bottom-up strategy is needed. A bottom-up strategy is support received from staff and the school to implement PRME within research, learning and engagement (PRME). This means that the dean is not primarily the determining factor of implementing PRME but support is received from those of lower positions. Rasche, Unruh et al. (2009) further state that bottom- down approach is quickly moving in PRME into the curricula and operations while maintaining communication amongst the school.

Solutions and Recommendations

Therefore, in order to compact the lack of sustainable leaders being produced in business schools a core module on PRME would be recommendation for all business schools to incorporate in their learning programmes. This would require all students to elect this module. Business schools would implement PRME within the curricula by using the top-bottom approach. This would be achieved by the Dean of the business school being approached information about the whole concept of PRME. A PowerPoint presentation would be used in illustrating the need for PRME for all the lecturers including the Dean. Getting approval from the Dean is not complex, a letter from the Dean or a person in authority indicating the interest to sign up to PRME is what is needed Rasche, Unruh et al. (2009). Moreover, it is vital that commitments are made to implement PRME at the school from top leadership. However, top commitment is not enough but support from staff members is also important (PRME).

Future Research

The chapter explored the concept of PRME and its relevance for business schools to implement it. The literature study proved that there is still more needed to be achieved in advancing responsible management education. More awareness strategies need to put in place in order for African Business Schools, to be fully aware of the importance of PRME. More research exploring national and international implementation strategies of PRME is therefore necessary.

CONCLUSION

Business schools have been questioned about the content in their curriculum and how it trains students to be future business leaders. Literature showed that business schools need to take their position by making sure that they produce sustainable business leaders. This is because in the past, the world has experienced economic problems and business schools have been viewed as the culprits. Which is why PRME was initiated in order for business schools to have relevant content that will help future business leaders tackle current and future dilemmas.

The main objective of this chapter was to give an overview of what PRME entails. This was achieved by highlighting the various routes in which PRME could be implemented, one of them being the top-bottom approach. Moreover, the importance of PRME was highlighted by the benefits of signing up to PRME. This chapter will create an awareness for business schools about the importance of implementing PRME. The chapter will also show the challenges and opportunities of implementing PRME, this will serve as vital information for schools wanting to be signatories of PRME.

REFERENCES

Barber, N. (2014). Integrating sustainability into business curricula: University of New Hampshire case study. *International Journal of Sustainability in Higher Education*, *15*(4), 473–493. doi:10.1108/IJSHE-06-2013-0068

Conaway, O., & Laasch, N. (2015). *Principles of Responsible Management Education*. Stamford, CT: Cengage Learning.

Escudero, M., & Rasche, A. (2009). Leading Change: The Role of the Principles for Responsible Management Education. *Journal for Business, Economics and Ethics*, *10*(2), 244–250.

Fragueiro, F., & Thomas, T. (2011). *Strategic leadership in the business school:Keeping one step ahead*. New York: Cambridge University Press. doi:10.1017/CBO9780511921087

Gee, R. F. (2012). *Corporate Social Responsibility Programmes and their beneficiary Organisations: An examination of the sustainability of the relationships between corporate social responsibility programmes and their targeted beneficiary organisations*. Development Studies. Research Space, University of Kwa-Zulu Natal. Masters.

Gilbert, A., & Rasche, D. (2015). Decoupling Responsible Management Education: Why Business Schools May Not Walk Their Talk. *Journal of Management Inquiry*, *24*(3), 239–252. doi:10.1177/1056492614567315

Godemann, J. et al.. (2011). *Integrating Sustainability into Business Schools – Analysis of 100 UN PRME Sharing Information on Progress (SIP) reports J. Moon*. Nottingham University Business School.

Hasrouni, L. B. (2012). CSR in education: Cultivating values, how business schools can plant the seeds of change. *Responsible Businesses*.

Louw, M. (2006). *The relevance, importance and applicability of corporate social and environmental responsibility: South African case studies*. Academic Press.

Muff, K. (2012). Are business schools doing their job? *Journal of Management Development*, *31*(7), 648–662. doi:10.1108/02621711211243854

Musharbash, D. (2012). *CSR Education in the UAE Paving the way to sustainable change*. Academic Press.

PRME. (2015). *2015 Annual Report and 2016 Outlook*. PRME.

PRME. (2015). *Principles for Responsible Management Education*. Retrieved September 5, 2015, from http://www.unprme.org

Ramos, D. (2015). Aligning the PRME: How Study Abroad Nurtures Responsible Leadership. *Journal of Management Education*, *39*(2), 244–275. doi:10.1177/1052562914560795

Rasche, A. (2009). *The Principles for Responsible Management Education: Implications for Implementation and Assessment. Toward Assessing Business Ethics Education*. Information Age Publishing.

Rasche, A., & Gilbert, D. (2015). Decoupling Responsible Management Education: Why Business Schools May Not Walk Their Talk. *Journal of Management Enquiry*, *24*(3), 239–252.

Rayment, J., & Smith, J. (2013). The current and future role of business schools. *Education + Training*, *55*(4/5), 478–494.

Solitander, N., Fougère, M., Sobczak, A., & Herlin, H. (2012). We Are the Champions: Organizational Learning and Change for Responsible Management Education. *Journal of Management Education*, *36*(3), 337–363. doi:10.1177/1052562911431554

United Nations Global Compact. (2012). *A practical guide to the United Nations Global Compact for Higher Education Institutions: Implementing the Global Compact Principles and Communicating on Progress*. Author.

United Nations Global Compact. (2015). The United Nations Global Compact Accenture CEO study: Special Edition: A call to climate action. Author.

Waddock, . (2009). *The Principles for Responsible Management Education: Implications for Implementation and Assessment. Toward Assessing Business Ethics Education*. Information Age Publishing.

Chapter 13
Educational and Business Co-Operatives:
The Channels for Collective Creativity and Entrepreneurial Teams

Rauno Rusko
University of Lapland, Finland

Lenita Hietanen
University of Lapland, Finland

Krista Kohtakangas
University of Lapland, Finland

Riitta Kemppainen-Koivisto
University of Lapland, Finland

Katta Siltavirta
University of Lapland, Finland

Taina Järvi
Lapland Vocational College, Finland

ABSTRACT

One tendency among co-operatives is to establish co-operatives not only for the purposes of business but also for the purposes to teach collaboration practices in business education. This study investigates and compares traditional business co-operatives and educational co-operatives as the environments of entrepreneurial learning communities. The data, which consist of interviews with members of both types of co-operatives, have been analyzed using the content analysis method. The main outcomes show that in both types of co-operatives sense of community and creativity are manifested as the parts of the entrepreneurial learning process. When considering if the learning processes were manifested as single- and double-loop learning – and the development of collective creativity – some differences were observed between educational co-operatives and business co-operatives.

DOI: 10.4018/978-1-5225-1823-5.ch013

INTRODUCTION

Even today, co-operative as a business entity meets criticism and doubt. In recent years, the attitudes about co-operatives have improved because of the tendency, where the importance of creativity and innovativeness have risen in every kind of enterprises - including co-operatives. (See Kemppainen-Koivisto et al., 2015). In contrast to before, nowadays a co-operative is not only based on agrarian production or a large retail trade chain owned by the customers. Instead, it may be based on an innovative and creative group of youthful members of an entrepreneurial team. This study presents the outcomes of the publicly funded KOVI-project, which aimed to develop knowledge about co-operatives among students and people who have graduated from the universities or the universities of applied sciences. During the project process also those co-operatives without the linkages to universities were studied.

The co-operative is the form of business, which often leans on ethical and environmental basis and purposes (Hagedorn, Arzt & Peters, 2002; Troberg, 2000). Therefore, the ways, which will increase the general popularity of co-operatives, will also rise the sense of environmentalism on the general level. The contemporary business environment and business education environment has a new tendency, which emphasizes the importance of start-ups, innovation events and business venturing. The general need to have the critical mass of new business ideas, creativity and innovations have risen the popularity of cooperation structures and networks (see, e.g. Podoynitsyna et al., 2013), such as entrepreneurial teams and co-operatives in business and education.

This study focuses on the themes of business and education in the context of co-operatives and especially on the features of two kinds of co-operatives: educational co-operatives and “traditional” business co-operatives. These two types of co-operatives are related to the sense of community, collective creativity and entrepreneurial learning processes. This study constructs practical criterions to distinguish these two types of co-operatives from each other: those co-operatives, which are established because of educational credits part of the education are here defined as educational co-operatives and those co-operatives without this kind of educations context are called here as business co-operatives.

At the Finnish universities of applied sciences co-operatives have been used as a tool for entrepreneurship education since 1993 (Troberg, Ruskovaara & Seikkula-Leino, 2011). Additionally, these days there is a booming interest in the different levels of business educations to establish co-operatives for the purposes of business and team learning (Kemppainen-Koivisto et al., 2015). However, the co-operatives, established under the umbrella of educational institution, are official firms, start-ups which are doing business in the markets by the students, that is, by the members of the co-operative. At the same time, the practitioners and actors of creative industries are establishing multidisciplinary start-ups in the forms of co-operatives. So far the division of small business co-operatives between business co-operatives and educational co-operatives has been underdeveloped. One aim of the chapter is to study the similarities and differences between these two types of co-operatives, traditional business co-operatives and educational co-operatives, based on a sense of community and an entrepreneurial learning process, especially on the view of creativity. The starting points are so different between these two types of co-operatives and interesting question is what kinds of reflections these underlying differences will cause in the creativity, sense of community and learning.

Creativity has been studied in the context of teams and learning. In this sense, we will introduce later on the concepts of single-loop learning and double-loop learning (Argyris and Schön, 1974), which we see essential tools to study different forms of team learning.

The empirical material consists of 10 interviews from members of co-operatives; all of the interviewees held either management or coordinating positions in the co-operatives. The outcomes of the content analysis of these interviews reveal differences in the characteristics and development of learning between educational co-operatives and business co-operatives in terms of collective creativity. Specifically, differences were found in the sense of community felt by the members of these two types of co-operatives and in the role that single-loop and double-loop learning played during the co-operatives' development.

EDUCATIONAL AND BUSINESS CO-OPERATIVES AS CREATIVE ENTREPRENEURIAL TEAMS

Literature of business contains several alternative typologies and classifications of co-operatives, such as agricultural, livestock and fishery co-operatives and savings and credit co-operatives or: consumer co-operatives, (small) business co-operatives, health-care and social services co-operatives and educational co-operatives (Münkner, 2005). In Germany, for example, credit co-operatives are usually church-based organizations (Machauer and Schiereck, 2004).

According to literature, co-operatives are strongly associated with creativity, participation, democracy and involvement-oriented management (see, e.g. Brown, 1997; Troberg, 2000). In addition, co-operatives as a business entity are generally linked with branches such as social and health care, arts, ecology and sustainable development (Girard, 2002). Though the structure of co-operatives is institutional it might be a source of creativity (see, e.g., Kemppainen-Koivisto et al., 2015). Therefore, the organizational model of co-operatives has been noticed to be suitable for third sector organizations (Taylor, 2015).

In other words, mostly co-operatives are focused on the responsible and sustainable branches of business (Troberg, 2000, 2008), such as healthcare, social services, education, church-based organizations and art, culture and creativity (see Burton, 2005). Co-operatives also offer a mechanism for introducing demographic values (Brown, 1997; Troberg, 2000). In previous researches, there have been noticed some benefits as the consequences of cooperation in co-operatives. According to Troberg (2000) the co-operative form enhances members' motivation to and engagement in their work. Especially intrinsic motivation has clearly been recognized (Troberg, Ruskovaara & Seikkula-Leino, 2011), which is one requirement for creativity (Ryan & Deci, 2000). Co-operatives usually are flexible organisations, which offer freedom to the members and causes intrinsic motivation (Troberg & Köppä, 2011). Thus, co-operative is known as a business entity with high level corporate social responsibility and moral mission of fair trade (Fridell, 2009).

Educational and Business Co-Operatives

Also educational co-operative has been mentioned in the literature of management and education (Knox, & Castles, 1982). Often education has been linked with co-operatives in the third world and in the cases, where education is associated with production. (Knox, & Castles, 1982). Furthermore, educational co-operatives have been linked with social co-operatives basing on educational and recreational services e.g. for local families in Faenza, Emilia-Romagna, Italy, (Sacchetti & Tortia, 2014). The case study of Sacchetti and Tortia (2014) bases on CEFF (Educational Co-operative for the Faenza Families), which is a multi-stakeholder (social) co-operative. In other words, earlier educational co-operatives have been connected with social co-operatives and e.g. development projects in the third world.

In addition, one form of "educational co-operative" is the co-operative, which contains several educational units. In Dallas, for example, was a Teacher educational center, which was established by the Dallas Independent School District. Teacher educational center was an educational co-operative between the school district and eight institutions of higher learning in the North Texas area (Caldwell & Childs, 1977).

An alternative notation for "educational co-operative" is "student co-operative". However student co-operatives are often campus-based non-profit organizations designed to provide goods and services intended primarily for students, such as affordable housing and dining (see, e.g. Kusmierek & Staff, 1988). This chapter, however, uses notation educational co-operative, because we see this notation more suitable to the educational-based case study co-operatives.

Current research considers educational co-operatives differently: the social orientation of co-operatives is important theme, but not as important as it is in study of Sacchetti and Tortia (2014). This chapter do not study networks between several educational units (cf. Caldwell & Childs, 1977), but especially the business educational orientation is very important in this study. In other words, this study emphasizes in the case of educational co-operatives the learning of business and entrepreneurship skills. This emphasis is based on the educational case study co-operatives, which are mainly established to develop these business and entrepreneurship skills in the universities of applied sciences in small entrepreneurial teams consisting of students as members of co-operatives. According to Raunio (2013), co-operative-based education in the universities of applied sciences will train the skills of entrepreneurship, such as team work, management, marketing and salesmanship. In addition, student will via co-operative create his/her networks and readiness for work life. (Raunio, 2013).

Current research is focused on two different forms of co-operatives: educational co-operatives and business co-operatives. In order to study the features of educational co-operatives, it is also necessary to study "non-educational" cooperatives, in other words, ordinary business co-operatives. Both the educational and business co-operatives of the case study are from Finland, which fact increases the possibilities to compare the features between educational and business co-operatives. All the co-operatives in this research actually have business activities, but distinction is based on the underlying organization, where the co-operatives act. In this study, a co-operative that is started from or based on the support of an educational institution is defined an *educational co-operative.* The type of co-operative where the linkage with an educational institution is missing—or is very thin—is called a *business co-operative.* In an educational co-operative, the entrepreneurial team consists of students, and possibly their teacher(s), and the business activities are associated with both an educational institution and course credits. In a business co-operative, the team consists of entrepreneurs. The entrepreneurs have their own business activities, but the co-operative is a channel through which they implement their business activities. In some cases, entrepreneurs only use a co-operative as a vehicle for charging fees. In this research study, the educational co-operatives are affiliated with the institutions of higher education, especially with the universities of applied sciences because of the aims of the underlying project.

Creativity and Entrepreneurial Learning of Co-Operatives

Entrepreneurial learning has several diversified meanings. Entrepreneurial learning is possible to interpret the learning of *entrepreneurs* during their life career (Rae, 2000) or the learning in the *student-learning* environment simulating business activities (Pittaway & Cope, 2009). According to some recent studies, entrepreneurial learning should be seen as a social phenomenon and entrepreneurs viewed as practitioners who operate in social communities of practice (Pittaway & Cope, 2009). This study also emphasizes the social aspects of entrepreneurial learning.

Co-operatives as contexts for entrepreneurial learning teams have not been examined deeply. However, Troberg, Ruskovaara & Seikkula-Leino (2011) have found out that co-operatives at the Finnish universities of applied sciences have manifested themselves as innovative learning environments. Shepherd and Krueger (2002) have found linkages between entrepreneurial teams, social cognition, and collective efficiency. Also Aldrich and Kim (2007) notice the importance of social networks associated with *entrepreneurial teams*. This study sees entrepreneurial team concept important in the context of co-operatives though typically entrepreneurial teams –concept have been used associated with large firms, high turnover and large organizations (cf. Cooney, 2005)

Thus, both entrepreneurial learning and entrepreneurial teams have social dimensions, where networks and community of practices might be important. In other words, learning of business and entrepreneurship might be social (and e.g. organizational) activity. Many researchers have studied also *organizational learning* (Argyris & Schön, 1974; Senge, 1990).

One of the main themes in this study is to map the connections between entrepreneurial learning and co-operatives in a way that is based on discussions about organizational learning (Argyris & Schön, 1974) and learning organizations (Senge, 1990). Senge (1990) has defined learning organizations as communities where people continually expand their capacity to create the results they truly desire, where new and expansive patterns of thinking are nurtured, where collective aspiration is set free, and where people are continually learning to see the whole picture together. When implementing Senge's (1990) definitions widely, this chapter provides more reasons to understand co-operatives as learning organizations.

Rather than focusing on general and theoretical education as it relates to entrepreneurship, co-operatives provide a practical platform to learn about entrepreneurial activities through working in teams (Hytti & O´Gorman, 2004; Troberg, Ruskovaara & Seikkula-Leino, 2011). Compared with business co-operatives, educational co-operatives are established mainly for educational purposes, where learning—not volume and profit—is the main target. However, in current research one assumption is that members in business co-operatives go through entrepreneurial learning processes as well. One interesting theme is to study the forms and differences of organizational learning, which is also associated with single- and double-loop learning between educational co-operatives and business co-operatives.

Creativity and Single-Loop and Double-Loop Learning

The famous concepts of single-loop learning and double-loop learning consider collective creativity. Especially double-loop learning is assumed to be "creative". According to Contu et al. (2003, 935), "… general idea is that double-loop learning is the more creative, critical, innovative kind, whereas single-loop learning is the plodding, repetitious kind." In the field of management and education, learning—and especially organizational learning—we have two dimensions: theory-in-use (single-loop learning) and the espoused theory (double-loop learning) of action. Argyris and Schön (1974) firmly connected these two concepts with learning. They introduced single-loop learning and double-loop learning, where the espoused theory of action as the most general model of action, is based on single-loop learning while double-loop learning is proposed as providing feedback and enabling more effective decision-making (Argyris, 1976). Practically, in single-loop learning the students or other entities are following directly the orders of teacher or manager. In other words, they learn (or actually imitate) the instructions. Double-loop learning is a more demanding dimension, because it involves the detection and correction of errors and requires changes in the underlying assumptions and goals (Argyris, 1980), that is the entities e.g. develop the contents of instructions. In distinguishing between single-loop learning and double-loop learning, Argyris and Schön (1974; 1978) used a thermostat as an example; it is

a single-loop learner because it detects when the room is too hot or too cold. A thermostat would be a double-loop learner if it questioned why it was set at 65 degrees or why it was measuring heat. (Argyris, 1980: 291)

Double-loop learning can be connected with entrepreneurial competence development, which in the current case is seen as one purpose of the entrepreneurial learning process. According to Onstenk (2003), entrepreneurial competence are the skills that enable entrepreneurs to manage, plan, organize, and control business activities. These competence are bound to help entrepreneurs see possibilities, reflect, and make decisions, all of which Moroz and Hindle (2012) have emphasized as being essential entrepreneurial skills and competence.

STUDY DESIGN

The dilemma between theory-in-use and espoused theory poses some challenges for understanding the idea of learning in organizations. In other words, there is often a gap between what is genuinely valued (espoused theory) and what actually occurs in practice (theory-in-use) (Laiken, 2001; Argyris, 1990). Because co-operatives as organizations are based on democratic values, sustainability, flexibility, and freedom (e.g. Troberg, 2000), this study identifies some of the differences between educational co-operatives and business co-operatives that are associated with the dichotomy between theory-in-use and espoused theory. More detailed, theory-in-use and espoused theory are examined within the frame of single-loop and double-loop learning (Argyris, 1976; Romme & Van Witteloojstuin, 1999) and creativity of teams.

The research questions of this chapter are:

RQ1: How do creativity and collaboration manifest themselves in educational and business co-operatives?
RQ2: How do single-loop and double-loop learning appear in educational and business co-operatives?

Description of the Participants and the Data Collection

In some educational co-operatives, the members receive course credits, and the members used to be trainees in a co-operative where they worked 10-20 hours a week. Interviews #1, #2, #6, #7 and partly #10 consider these kinds of educational co-operatives. Interview #10 considers the case, where co-operative was established in the university course, but the activities of co-operative focused outside the university learning. The rest of the interviewees #3, #4, #5, #8 and #9 are working at business co-operatives.

The research data consist of 10 thematic interviews with members in co-operatives, including five (5) educational co-operatives and five (5) business co-operatives. Most of these interviews were held in the spring of 2014, between 23 April and 28 May. One interview was held in the autumn of 2014, on 8 September. All of the interviews were part of the activities of the KOVI project, which focuses on the

Table 1. The profiles of the 10 interviewees (in 2014)

Person	Year the co-operative was founded	Number of members	Membership year of the interviewee	Degree of education (in process or graduated)	Also employed at another workplace	Educational (E) or business (B) co-op?
# 1	2013	15	2013	polytechnic	yes	E
# 2	2013	15	2013	polytechnic		E
# 3	2011	12	2011	university		B
# 4	2007	n.a.	2013	university	yes	B
# 5	2007	24	2013	university		B
# 6	2013	15	2013	polytechnic		E
# 7	2011	33	2011	polytechnic		E
# 8	1996	200	2013	polytechnic		B
# 9	2011	18	2011	university	yes	B
# 10	2014	7	2014	university	yes	E/B

development work of co-operatives in northern Finland. The ages of the interviewees ranged from 22 to 57 years. More information about the interviewees is presented in Table 1. The duration of the interviews ranged from 17 minutes to 49 minutes.

The Method and Analysis

As a research method, the interviews and content analysis are widely known as useful tools for analyzing the features of the co-operatives (Franks, 2010). This study leans on content analysis of ten transcribed interviews. These interviews and transcriptions are based on the outcomes of the underlying research project, where some of the authors participated. The interviews were first recorded and then transcribed. These transcriptions were carefully read, analyzed and classified by authors. The empirical part of this chapter is based on the contents and found classifications of the interviews. Finally, the used citations were translated in English.

The interviews were recorded, transcribed, and analyzed by three (3) researchers affiliated with the underlying project. In addition to the interviews, the research material included an analysis of discussions from two workshops. For this study, an additional analyst, an outsider not affiliated with the project, was utilized.

Due to interviews as the most important empirical material of the analysis, the research method of this study is based on qualitative analysis. Perhaps, the most common analysis types in qualitative studies are content analysis and discourse analysis (cf. Hardy et al., 2004). Content analysis was chosen, because the aims of the study focused on the action (entrepreneurial learning) in co-operatives, not on the discourses associated with co-operatives (cf. Berg & Lune, 2004). The analysis was completed by three researchers who conducted the analysis independently in order to enable methodological triangulation through the richness in interpretations (see Silverman, 2010). Methodological triangulation was enabled when, in the first step of the analysis, each researcher had his/her own approach to the data and followed a different type of content analysis (see Krippendorff, 2004). The first researcher followed the data based content analysis by searching only for manifestations of some kind of activity. Another researcher looked for the expressions of the entrepreneurial learning process, which may be defined as theory guided analysis. The third scholar mainly used theory based content analysis by investigating how espoused theory and theory-in-use were noticed in the data. The researcher conducting the data based analysis approached the data from the leadership and psychology perspective while working with her grounded theory-based dissertation research and while also being an outsider in relation to the project. Two other analysts participated from the perspectives of management and entrepreneurship education and business administration.

THE MAIN OUTCOMES

According to the interviews, the main problem in the business co-operatives is that the members mainly use the co-operative for accounting and charging fees (Interview #3; #8). In some cases of business orientated co-operative there are no new ideas and no common development work sessions. Furthermore, the understanding and learning is an individual process and these types of co-operatives need younger members in their development work, too (Interview #5). If a co-operative is mainly based on business, the learning is connected with the practical themes like how to set the price of the products (Interview #4) or whether the co-operative is helping individual members concentrate on securing basic work and an income, while the co-operative takes care of administration, taxation, insurance, and other business-related responsibilities (Interview #8). That is to say, co-operative seems to have mainly single-loop learning. A co-operative might also be used as a common marketing institution for a group that shares common values; in this way it can create a safety net for members (Interview #9), which enables double-loop learning. Following the ideas of strategic management, business co-operatives were in the configuration phase without any challenging transformation periods (Mintzberg et al., 2005). Though steady state configuration phase, which enables strategic work, the volume of the business was not increasing significantly.

Generally, compared with business co-operatives, the interviews focused on educational co-operatives contained more optimistic and innovative perspectives. The business branches were more diversified and the members of the co-ops were still seeking the main products of the co-operatives. Though relatively low volume of business, the number of creative innovations and especially the enthusiasm for new business opportunities were high level. Typically, educational co-operatives are newer compared with business co-operatives and living their growth phases with nearly continuous transformation tendency (cf. Mintzberg, 2005).

The differences between educational and business co-operatives seem to culminate in the features of creativity, social relationships and learning. Because learning is in this case associated with business and entrepreneurship, one of the main outcomes are based on entrepreneurial learning (see Rae, 2007).

Noticed Creative Entrepreneurial Learning

In examining what kind of entrepreneurial learning occurred in the studied co-operatives, it was important to first describe how dealing with opportunities related to creativity in entrepreneurial learning process, which some scholars see important (e.g. Penaluna & Penaluna, 2009; Rae, 2007), had been manifested in the co-operatives. Second, it was also important to consider if the noticed learning processes in the teams could be defined as a single-, double-, or even triple-loop learning (Argyris & Schön, 1976; Romme & Van Witteloostuijn, 1999). In addition, it was important to determine if the noticed learning processes were collaborative learning processes or if they had manifested mainly as individual learning.

When *discovering the opportunities*, how strongly the entrepreneurs in co-operatives feel ownership of their business seems to be essential (Van Dyne & Pierce, 2004). This means that in a *business co-operative* the entrepreneurs have to discover opportunities as the basis for and the idea of the business. There are four ways in which opportunities are identified: active search, passive search, fortuitous discovery, and creation of opportunities (De Tienne & Chandler, 2004). In an *educational co-operative*, the entrepreneurs may have a bit more time to learn to discover opportunities. In some cases they even may be guided to the edge of recognizing opportunities. In educational co-operatives, the creation of opportunities seemed to first happen through the educational institution (teachers, curricula, other resources). The student entrepreneurs had noticed a need to think aloud and collaboratively evaluate the recognized opportunities. They had found that having an open mind and a willingness to share ideas and knowledge were requirements for innovativeness in and development of the co-operative (see e.g., Troberg, Ruskovaara & Seikkula-Leino, 2011). Instead, in the business co-operatives the entrepreneurs had to continuously create further opportunities, both in terms of business ideas and products. Hence, creativity seemed to have appeared in each co-operatives.

The decision-making process includes both creative problem solving and innovative thinking, among many other aspects (e.g., Gibb, 2002; Henry et al., 2005). In the educational co-operatives, the main decision focused on the form of the training enterprise, which, according to the instructions of the educational institution, had to happen collaboratively. Because of the lack of real financial responsibility, no clear decision-making processes occurred. However, according to the students' experiences in the co-operatives, they collaboratively discovered that in a business co-operative they should use both shared decision-making and, for some organizational issues, they should select some entrepreneurs to take on more responsible roles than others.

Co-Operatives as Entrepreneurial Teams

The analysis proceeded by addressing the crucial factors that were noticed in developing co-operatives as creative learning organizations. Furthermore, the general sympathy of co-operatives toward green values was noticed especially in the business co-operatives:

(Generally) in the cultural and creative branches they do not perhaps be so materialistics in their life attitudes, as usual. They are, perhaps, more collective and share their thoughts #8 (Business co-operative)

In those days we noticed the need for this – and then there were that communality, that we could – I mean- act together as entrepreneurs. #9 (Business co-operative)

In a way we have those values and we have joint ecological values and those, which we assume all to follow… #9 (Business co-operative)

Just as different ranges of students can have different needs, different co-operatives can also have different needs in the entrepreneurial learning process (see Gibb, 2008). Entrepreneurial teams, which in the current study mean co-operatives, are comprised of different individuals with various life experiences, life cycle phases, and personal career anchors (see, e.g., Schein 1974; 1996) supplementing the competence of each other. This kind of collaborative construction of different individuals might serve to strengthen the performance of the business (see Gartner *et al.*, 2006) and innovativeness (e.g. Troberg & Köppä, 2011).

The results in the current study show that the members in those business co-operatives, which were established during the student phase, see co-operatives as a place to learn about business activities and routines. Despite the lack of competence management, most of the studied elements of the entrepreneurial learning process were noticed somehow. The members found it important to learn collaboratively as is natural in co-operatives (e.g., Troberg, 2000). They wanted to benefit from the network structure of the co-operative (e.g., Gibb 2005). According to the results, the members of co-operatives think that co-operatives are not able to grow, develop, or even survive with the business without openness, networking, and a sense of community.

The initial assumption of this study was that there might be evident differences between the types of collaborative learning in the two types of co-operatives that were examined. In educational co-operatives, the learning of entrepreneurial teams proved to be a cycle in which the learning content and the activities were tightly interlinked. However, our initial assumption was that the learning would remain mainly at the single-loop level in that it was concentrated on daily tasks; in business co-operatives, the entrepreneurial team members participate in strategic planning and discussions, which will change the strategies of the co-operatives. That is, they will encounter tasks that are typical for double-loop learning and the theory-in-use perspective (cf. Argyris & Schön, 1987).

However, the outcomes of the interviews were not so self-evident. Namely, although the single-loop learning occurred in the first steps of the co-operatives' start-up in the educational co-operatives, soon the learning turned out to be double-looped. This outcome was evident: in the interviews, several of the answers given by the educational co-operative members followed the structure in which the person started explaining activities, which mainly resembles single-loop leaning, but soon the answers also contained activities, which are typical for double-loop learning. This can be seen in the interviews of the members of the studied co-operatives. Some excerpts are presented below:

Well, because of my own perspective from upper secondary (education), I think that co-operative is possible to use more purposeful for the tool of education. That YE (student) company is another alternative, but myself I have noticed here in (-) academy, that this (co-operative) is not any joke company, but real company. We are really entrepreneurs. Of course, we are students at the same time, but this IS a company, we are in the official register and it is possible to invoice us like a real company. This will develop our professional arrogance and make us more professional actors. Interview #7 (member of an educational co-operative)

Each of team (co-operative) have gone through the same circle that initially there is not any common product, nothing to sell, no professional skills, but they, however, try to get (business) contacts with customers and gradually they will find those items, what are possible to do with customers. In other words, they trust the process that each one will find something to sell. But perhaps, this start up –process is not the same process as normally. Normally, you have the business idea or product and you establish the firm in order to develop it further. Here we at first establish a firm (co-operative) and after that we wonder what we want to sell... Interview #7

Also, perhaps in our (co-operative) it that people are in different states of life that the others still studies and the others have graduated. It is clear that the studies take up the most of the time, and the own structure of the business is not clear. More it is that we are seeking the way of doing. Those who, are graduated, have the development of business as the number one. And they do not have anything else. Interview # 9 (member of business co-operative, which actually established in the educational unit without any educational purposes)

The collaborative construction of knowledge (see, e.g., Suonpää, 2013) was an important part of the learning process in both the educational co-operatives and the business co-operatives. However, in the business co-operatives the construction of knowledge might be more multifaceted because of the heterogeneous capabilities and education of the members in the co-operatives.

In other words, state of changes, management of change is challenges generally. And then we must notice that we have persons from several levels, from academic degree, and then there might be persons even with primary degree education, perhaps we have one person from primary degree and clearly better (in business) than a (typical) person with academic degree – because of plenty of practical learning and knowledge... Interview #5 (member of a business co-operative)

Though the example above shows the importance of diversity in order to achieve efficient entrepreneurial team Chowdhury (2005) has noticed that the diversity of the terms of gender, age and functional background does not contribute team-level cognitive comprehensiveness and team commitment.

In the educational co-operatives, entrepreneurship first leans on intrapreneurship; later, it leans on entrepreneurship. This personal progress of the entrepreneurial learning path has also recently been recognized in some other studies (Brixy et al., 2012). However, in the business co-operatives the learning leans more clearly on entrepreneurship from the very beginning. The remarkable result is that in business co-operatives learning in general seems to be implemented more strongly and deeply than it is in the educational co-operatives. One practical reason for this is based on the convention that membership in educational co-operatives is limited to students being in school and it ends after they have graduated, which is a fact that was also mentioned in the interviews.

Based on the empirical analysis presented above, and the experiences of the authors as members of the underlying project focused on co-operatives, the entrepreneurial learning path to educational co-operatives and business co-operatives differs in terms of single-loop and double-loop learning.

At the very beginning, the espoused theory with single-loop learning is the main driver of actions on educational co-operatives. However, gradually, during the learning process, the role of double-loop learning strengthens. The members of the co-operatives will find their own competencies and identify the main products they want to market, and the cash flow will start. The members have to cooperate in order to create turnover via network building. Because most of the educational co-operatives are temporary, lasting 3-4 years (Interviews #1, #2, and #6), the learning activities will possibly maintain their position in the double-loop level, especially because of the high sense of community due to the educational environment and the support from the educational institution. However, as the interviews showed, initially the sense of community among the members of the educational co-operative is low because of the artificial structure of the team, which is made and controlled by the educational institution (Figure 1).

Figure 1. Degree of learning and sense of community in a typical educational co-operative and in a business co-operative

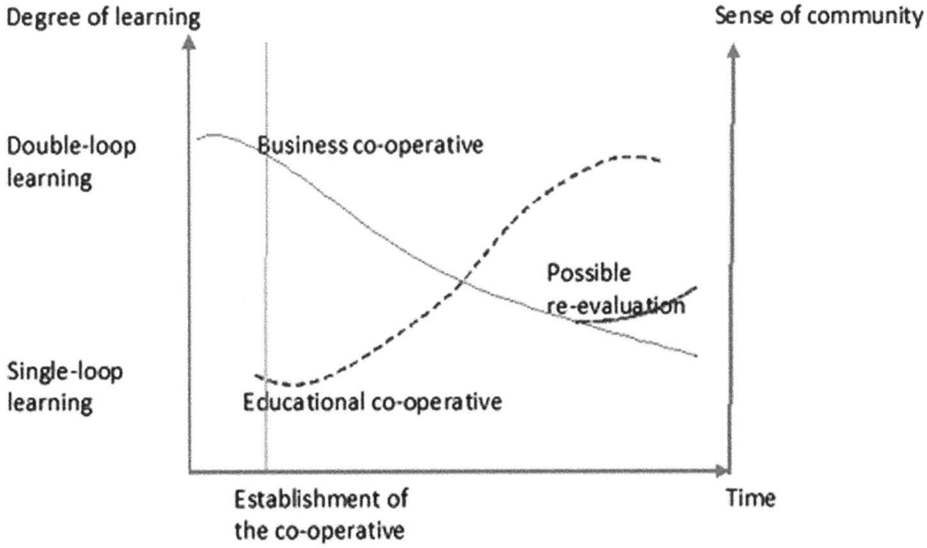

According to the empirical material of this study, in the terms of single- and double-loop learning and a sense of community, the development of a business co-operative differs remarkably from the development of an educational co-operative. In business co-operatives, the learning process of the forthcoming co-operative members is at its highest (double-loop) level at the very beginning when a person joins the co-operative, or even before the person becomes a co-operative member. This is also the case with the sense of community; in order to establish a new co-operative, the forthcoming members have to build networks with each other, which, in addition to transaction costs in the sense of the Coase theorem (Coase, 1937), also means a high sense of community, which lasts throughout the first steps of establishing the co-operative, but which easily fades gradually, in which case the main characteristic of the co-operative finally turns out to be a place to generate invoices (Interviews #8, #9). However, even a small intervention in the form of an interview might change this situation. One finding of this project was that the interviews caused changes in the routines of the business co-operatives. The members of the co-operatives re-evaluated their values and theory-in-use because of the awareness caused by the interview (Figure 1).

Furthermore, the empirical analysis revealed that, especially in educational co-operatives, opportunities are (after the confusion phase) initially identified by using active search and by the creation of opportunities via networking rather than by using passive search and fortuitous discovery (De Tienne & Chandler, 2004).

Breugst *et al.* (2015) have found two alternative developments of entrepreneurial teams: negative interaction spirals and positive interaction spirals. According to them, teams which are exposed external threats and/or internal low perceived justice might drift from positive spirals to negative spirals. This study noticed, that this kind of movement from the positive interaction spiral to the negative spiral among the examined co-operatives, especially among business co-operatives, where as in educational co-operatives the direction of movement seems to be contrary – or at least the sustainability of the positive interaction spiral (or sense of community) is on the relatively high level compared with business co-operatives.

CONCLUSION

The outcomes above showed the diverging development of educational and business co-operatives in the sense of community and in the degree of learning (single-loop and double-loop learning). Furthermore, sense of community is related to level of learning. Double-loop learning of teams seems to be linked with high sense of community and single-loop learning is typical for the teams with low level of community.

The current research increases the understanding about the opportunities to develop co-operatives as creative entrepreneurial learning organizations. Collectivity and innovation occur in a co-operative entrepreneurial team in a multi-faceted way. In the educational co-operatives, the roles of external actors, such as teachers, at the educational institutions are important, especially in the early stages of the co-operative. However, reflection, innovation, and management skills will gradually develop as well providing possibilities for double-loop learning in the future. In the business co-operatives, the business plan phase occurs before the co-operative is established; but, the educational co-operative typically does not have any business plan before the establishment phase. In addition, in business co-operatives the typical features of double-loop learning of business, such as reflection, innovation, and management skills exist at the very beginning.

Furthermore, the sense of community is an important feature in co-operatives; in an educational co-operative, the sense of community progresses from the initial low level to a higher level during the development of the co-operative. However, in a typical business co-operative the sense of community is at its highest level at the beginning and it will decrease during the development of the co-operative. Thus, although the starting point for personal and collaborative learning is lower in an educational co-operative, these types of co-operatives follow Senge's (1990) ideas about learning organizations. That is, as communities, educational co-operatives with positive interaction spirals (cf. Breugst et al., 2015) are places where people are continually expanding their capacity to create the results they truly desire, and where people are continually learning to see the whole picture together. Not only educational co-operatives, but also business co-operatives, which consist of administratively entrepreneurial teams, will be *organizations for learning*; platform which enables the members to learn business and entrepreneurship skills and collective creativity.

At the first steps, the educational co-operatives are following single-loop learning –principle: members of the co-operatives (students) are following the advices of teachers and business textbooks. They are not inventing and developing remarkable new ideas. Gradually, with the rise in the sense of community, also some activities of double-loop learning started in educational co-operatives: the students (members) of co-operatives turned to be self-guided seeking new solutions to increase turnover and to find new markets.

Furthermore, the research process has some effects, which increased the double-loop learning activities even in the business co-operatives: after the research data was collected, contacting some of the participating co-operatives revealed that double-loop learning had taken place. Reflection during the interviews resulted amongst the participants considering how they needed to develop the operations of the co-operative; for example, they started networking. The members of the largest participating co-operatives started to consider their regional possibilities for development and growth while also providing more support to their northernmost members. Other developmental meetings, such as brainstorming sessions, have been arranged in order to enable the co-operative to better meet its members' needs. These outcomes also reflect even the possibilities of triple-loop learning in the platforms of business and educational co-operatives.

The results of the comparisons between the development paths of the business co-operatives and educational co-operatives revealed the need for the business co-operatives to follow some of the ideas held by the educational co-operatives in terms of the systematic practice to activate networking and widen benefits of the entrepreneurial learning process. These actions might prevent business co-operatives from the threat of too slow reactions and the lack of agility in their everyday activities.

The results of the study show that educational co-operatives, at least in Finland, are in-between education and business. This combination seems to be fruitful for creativity and entrepreneurial learning. However, the volume of the business in educational co-operative is on the low level, at least in Finnish educational co-operatives. Internationally the studies, and obviously also the activities, of educational co-operatives are focused on e.g. social co-operatives (see, e.g. Sacchetti & Tortia, 2014). Finnish educational co-operatives are also acting for the public good (i.e. education) though they are not officially social co-operatives.

REFERENCES

Aldrich, H. E., & Kim, P. H. (2007). Small worlds, infinite possibilities? How social networks affect entrepreneurial team formation and search. *Strategic Entrepreneurship Journal*, *1*(1-2), 147–165. doi:10.1002/sej.8

Argyris, C. (1976). Single-loop and double-loop models in research on decision making. *Administrative Science Quarterly*, *21*(3), 363–375. doi:10.2307/2391848

Argyris, C. (1980). Some limitations of the case method: Experiences in a management development program. *Academy of Management Review*, *5*(2), 291–298.

Argyris, C. (1990). *Overcoming organizational defences: Facilitating organizational learning*. Boston: Allyn and Bacon.

Argyris, C., & Schön, D. (1987). Reasoning, action strategies, and defensive routines: The case of OD practitioners. In R. A. Woodman & A. A. Pasmore (Eds.), *Research in organizational change and development* (pp. 89–128). Greenwich: JAI Press.

Argyris, C., & Schön, D. A. (1974). *Theory in practice: Increasing professional effectiveness*. London: Jossey-Bass.

Argyris, C., & Schön, D. A. (1978). *Organizational Learning: A theory of action approach*. Reading, MA: Addision Wesley.

Balnave & Patmore. (in press). The outsider: lessons from the Community Co-operative Store (Nuriootpa), 1944–2010. *Business History*, 1-22.

Berg, B. L., & Lune, H. (2004). *Qualitative research methods for the social sciences* (Vol. 5). Boston: Pearson.

Bowman, B., & Stone, B. (2005). *Cooperativization as Alternative to Globalizing Capitalism*. Retrieved November 24, 2015, from http://www.geo.coop/archives/bowmanstone1104.htm

Breugst, N., Patzelt, H., & Rathgeber, P. (2015). How should we divide the pie? Equity distribution and its impact on entrepreneurial teams. *Journal of Business Venturing*, *30*(1), 66–94. doi:10.1016/j.jbusvent.2014.07.006

Brixy, U., Sternberg, R., & Stüber, H. (2012). The selectiveness of the entrepreneurial process. *Journal of Small Business Management*, *50*(1), 105–131. doi:10.1111/j.1540-627X.2011.00346.x

Brown, L. H. (1997). Organizations for the 21st Century? Co-operatives and" New" forms of organization. *Canadian Journal of Sociology/Cahiers canadiens de sociologie*, 65-93.

Burton, A. (2005). *The British Consumer Co-operative Movement and Film, 1890s-1960s*. Manchester University Press.

Caldwell, R. M., & Childs, H. (1977). *Acquisition of Specific Teaching Behaviors Through a Teacher Center Consortium*. Academic Press.

Chowdhury, S. (2005). Demographic diversity for building an effective entrepreneurial team: Is it important? *Journal of Business Venturing*, *20*(6), 727–746. doi:10.1016/j.jbusvent.2004.07.001

Coase, R. H. (1937). The nature of the firm. *Economica*, *4*(16), 386–405. doi:10.1111/j.1468-0335.1937.tb00002.x

De Tienne, D. R., & Chandler, G. N. (2004). Opportunity identification and its role in the entrepreneurial classroom: A pedagogical approach and empirical test. *Academy of Management Learning & Education*, *3*(3), 242–257. doi:10.5465/AMLE.2004.14242103

Franks, J. (2010). Boundary organizations for sustainable land management: The example of Dutch Environmental Co-operatives. *Ecological Economics*, *70*(2), 283–295. doi:10.1016/j.ecolecon.2010.08.011

Fridell, G. (2009). The co-operative and the corporation: Competing visions of the future of fair trade. *Journal of Business Ethics*, *86*(1), 81–95. doi:10.1007/s10551-008-9759-3

Gartner, W. B., Davidsson, P., & Zahra, S. (2006). Are you talking to me? The nature of community in entrepreneurship scholarship. *Entrepreneurship Theory and Practice*, *30*(3), 321–331. doi:10.1111/j.1540-6520.2006.00123.x

Gibb, A. (2002). Creating conducive environments for learning and entrepreneurship: Living with, dealing with, creating and enjoying uncertainty and complexity. *Industry and Higher Education*, *16*(3), 135–148. doi:10.5367/000000002101296234

Gibb, A. (2005). The future of entrepreneurship education—determining the basis for coherent policy and practice? In P. Kyrö & C. Carrier (Eds.), The Dynamics of Learning Entrepreneurship in a Cross-cultural University Context (pp. 44-67). Hämeenlinna: Research Centre for Vocational and Professional Education, University of Tampere.

Gibb, A. (2007). Creating the entrepreneurial university: do we need a wholly different model of entrepreneurship? In A. Fayolle (Ed.), *Handbook of research in entrepreneurship education* (Vol. 1, pp. 67–103). Cheltenham, UK: Edvard Elgar. doi:10.4337/9781847205377.00012

Gibb, A. (2008). Entrepreneurship and entrepreneurial education in schools and colleges: Insights from UK practice. *International Journal of Entrepreneurship Education*, *6*(2), 101–144.

Girard, J. P. (2002). Social Cohesion, Governance and the Development of Health and Social Care Co-operatives: Preliminary Observations. *Review of International Cooperation*, *95*(1), 58–64.

Hagedorn, K., Arzt, K., & Peters, U. (2002). Institutional arrangements for environmental co-operatives: a conceptional framework. In Environmental Co-operation and Institutional Change. Edward Elgar.

Hardy, C., Harley, B., & Phillips, N. (2004). Discourse analysis and content analysis: Two solitudes. *Qualitative Methods*, *2*(1), 19–22.

Harkema, S. J. M., & Schout, H. (2008). Incorporating student-centred learning in innovation and entrepreneurship education. *European Journal of Education*, *43*(4), 513–526. doi:10.1111/j.1465-3435.2008.00372.x

Henry, C., Hill, F., & Leitch, C. (2005). Entrepreneurship education and training: can entrepreneurship be taught? Part I. *Education + Training*, *47*(2), 98-111.

Hytti, U., & O'Gorman, C. (2004). What is enterprise education? An analysis of the objectives and methods of enterprise education programmes in four European countries. *Education + Training*, *46*(1), 11–23. doi:10.1108/00400910410518188

Kemppainen-Koivisto, R., Siltavirta, K., Rusko, R., & Särkkä, S. (2015). Creativity with Institutionalization: Co-operatives as an Alternative Way of Starting a Creative Business–Cases from Finland. In B. Christiansen & J. Koeman (Eds.), *Nationalism, Cultural Indoctrination, and Economic Prosperity in the Digital Age* (pp. 221–240). IGI Global.

Knox, D., & Castles, S. (1982). Education with production—learning from the third world. *International Journal of Educational Development*, *2*(1), 1–14. doi:10.1016/0738-0593(82)90062-1

Krippendorff, K. (2004). *Content analysis. An introduction to its methodology*. Thousand Oaks, CA: Sage.

Kusmierek, K., & Staff, L. (1988). Warch Sheds Light on University Operations, Finances and Goals. *The Lawrential*, *106*(7), 1.

Laiken, M. (2001). *Models of organizational learning: Paradoxes and best practices in the post industrial workplace.* NALL Working Paper, 25. University of Toronto. Retrieved November 24, 2015, from http://nall.oise.utoronto.ca/res/25MarilynLaiken.pdf

Machauer, A., & Schiereck, D. (2004). Church-based Credit Co-operatives in Germany. *Annals of Public and Cooperative Economics*, *75*(2), 319–337. doi:10.1111/j.1467-8292.2004.00254.x

Mintzberg, H., Ahlstrand, B., & Lampel, J. (2005). *Strategy Safari: A Guided Tour Through The Wilds of Strategic Management.* Simon and Schuster.

Moroz, P. W., & Hindle, K. (2012). Entrepreneurship as a process: Toward harmonizing multiple perspectives. *Entrepreneurship Theory and Practice, 36*(5), 781–818. doi:10.1111/j.1540-6520.2011.00452.x

Münkner, H. H. (2005). *Korea Case Study. Co-operative –Government Dialogue on Co-operative Policy and Legislation in Asia-Pacific Region.* Retrieved November 24, 2015 from: http://ica-ap.coop/sites/ica-ap.coop/files/UploadFiles/Publications/Korea%20Case%20Study%20-%20ICA%20ROAP%200905.doc

Onstenk, J. (2003). Entrepreneurship and vocational education. *European Educational Research Journal, 2*(1), 74–89. doi:10.2304/eerj.2003.2.1.12

Penaluna, A., & Penaluna, K. (2009). Assessing creativity: drawing from the experience of the UK's creative design educators. *Education + Training, 51*(8/9), 718-732.

Pittaway, L., & Cope, J. (2007). Simulating entrepreneurial learning integrating experiential and collaborative approaches to learning. *Management Learning, 38*(2), 211–233. doi:10.1177/1350507607075776

Podoynitsyna, K., Song, M., Van Der Bij, H., & Weggeman, M. (2013). Improving new technology venture performance under direct and indirect network externality conditions. *Journal of Business Venturing, 28*(2), 195–210. doi:10.1016/j.jbusvent.2012.04.004

Rae, D. (2000). Understanding entrepreneurial learning: A question of how? *International Journal of Entrepreneurial Behavior & Research, 6*(3), 145–159. doi:10.1108/13552550010346497

Rae, D. (2007). *Entrepreneurship: From Opportunity to Action.* New York: Palgrave MacMillan.

Raunio, H. (2013). Co-operative Iimproving Students' entrepreneurship. In *Finnish: Osuuskunta opiskelijayrittäjyyden edistäjänä ammattikorkeakouluissa.* Vantaa, Finland: Laurea University of Applied Sciences.

Romme, A. G. L., & Van Witteloostuijn, A. (1999). Circular organizing and triple loop learning. *Journal of Organizational Change Management, 12*(5), 439–454. doi:10.1108/09534819910289110

Ryan, R. M., & Deci, E. L. (2000). Intrinsic and extrinsic motivations: Classic definitions and new directions. *Contemporary Educational Psychology, 25*(1), 54–67. doi:10.1006/ceps.1999.1020 PMID:10620381

Sacchetti, S., & Tortia, E. C. (2014). The social value of multi-stakeholder co-operatives: the case of the CEFF system in Italy. In T. Mazzarol, S. Reboud, E. M. Liminios, & D. Clark (Eds.), *Research Handbook on Sustainable Co-operative Enterprise: Case Studies of Organisational Resilience in the Co-operative Business Model* (pp. 285–300). Cheltenham, UK: Elgar.

Schein, E. H. (1974). *Career Anchors and Career Paths: A Panel Study of Management School Graduates.* Technical Report No. 1.

Schein, E. H. (1996). Career anchors revisited: Implications for career development in the 21st century. *The Academy of Management Executive, 10*(4), 80–88.

Senge, P. M. (1990). *The Fifth Discipline: The Art and Practice of the Learning Organization.* New York: Doubleday/Currency.

Shepherd, D. A., & Krueger, N. F. (2002). An Intentions-Based Model of Entrepreneurial Teams' Social Cognition'. *Entrepreneurship Theory and Practice, 27*(2), 167–185. doi:10.1111/1540-8520.00005

Silverman, D. (2010). *Doing qualitative research. A practical handbook* (3rd ed.). London: Sage.

Suonpää, M. (2013). *Constructing an opportunity centred collaborative learning model in higher education through and for entrepreneurship* (Unpublished doctoral dissertation). Jyväskylä Studies in Business and Economics, Jyväskylä: University of Jyväskylä.

Taylor, K. (2015). Learning from the Co-operative Institutional Model: How to Enhance Organizational Robustness of Third Sector Organizations with More Pluralistic Forms of Governance. *American Scientist*, *5*(3), 148–164.

Troberg, E. (2000). The Relevance of Transaction Cost and Agency Theoretical Concepts to the Management of Knowledge Intensive Co-operatives. Turku School of Economics.

Troberg, E., & Köppä, T. (2011). The Relationship of the Co-operative Ownership Model to Knowledge Workers Levels of Innovation and Motivation. *International Journal of Co-operative Management*, *5*(2), 37–46.

Troberg, E., & Ruskovaara, E., & Seikkula-Leino, J. (2011). The State of Co-operative Entrepreneurship Education in Finland: An Explanatory Study. *International Journal of Co-operative Management*, *5*(2), 47–59.

Van Dyne, L., & Pierce, J. L. (2004). Psychological ownership and feelings of possessions: Three field studies predicting employee attitudes and organizational citizenship behavior. *Journal of Organizational Behavior*, *25*(4), 439–459. doi:10.1002/job.249

KEY TERMS AND DEFINITIONS

Business Co-Operatives: The type of co-operative where the linkage with an educational institution is missing—or is very thin.

Double Loop Learning: Learning which follows the advices and orders and also develops the new ways of doing.

Educational Co-Operative: A co-operative that is based on the support of an educational institution.

Entrepreneurial Learning: Learning, which is associated with entrepreneurship and it has to be defined within each context, which might be e.g. creativity, innovativeness, and individual's disposing towards opportunities.

Entrepreneurial Team: The team, where entrepreneurial attitudes and spirit is important feature in the working activities.

Sense of Community: Typical feature in the team or organization, where members identify themselves into the same group.

Single Loop Learning: Learning which is based directly on the advices and orders.

Section 4

Social Marketing for a Sustainable Future

Chapter 14
The Use of Social Media and Online Petitions to Achieve Collective Change for a Sustainable Future

Vannie Naidoo
University of KwaZulu-Natal, South Africa

ABSTRACT

Scandals of corruption in government and mismanagement in business and government departments has made us rethink of what the world is becoming and what should be done to steer it on the right track. Brilliant policy and law makers have tried to put in place laws and governing statutes that can assist in ethically governing businesses and governments so that they can sustain themselves and maintain a healthy respectful and transparent relationship with all their stakeholders and communities. The failure by certain governments and businesses to adhere to policy, statutes and laws has frustrated good people and their only podium left standing is social media and online petitions. On websites worldwide communities are getting together to discuss and defame businesses and governments that are perpetuating unethical behaviour. This has changed the face of marketing as marketers and the public relations departments are in change of maintain and promoting a company or governments image. The face of marketing has changed as social media has introduced itself into the mix.

INTRODUCTION

Waste and water pollution, depletion of the ozone layer and global warming affects everyone on the planet. Responsible and sustainable business practices are the only way for society to sustain itself. Business and governments have a responsibility to maintain good ethical conduct and maintain good business practice with the stakeholders and communities they do business with. It is no longer about limiting one's carbon foot print or showing solidarity towards democracy within society. Many corporates are

DOI: 10.4018/978-1-5225-1823-5.ch014

involved in shocking ethical misconduct yet they hide behind cleverly manipulated public relations and marketing campaigns that portray them as pillars of corporate society.

Corporate Social Responsibility should be the cornerstone of business practice worldwide. In order for a company to be a well-respected or good corporate citizen in the business world it needs to be socially responsible and ethical in its business practice. People in society want assurance by business and government that they will comply with the laws and regulations to maintain and sustain resources and prescribe to a body of conduct that is honest and instils confidence in society. Marketing has changed in this contemporary era. A marketer now has the responsibility to ensure their company or organisation is producing and selling products/ services that are safe, value for money and not harming the community or environment. Communities who fail to be heard by irresponsible businesses and governments are now using social media to champion their cause and be heard. Social media is a powerful tool that has grown in awareness in the business and social communities worldwide. Social media has changed the manner in which businesses and governments interact with their target audiences, distributors, suppliers, employees and communities.

In this age where resources are scarce, businesses and governments need to keep abreast of their ethical and social obligation to their customers and communities in which they reside in. Businesses and governments have an obligation to the public they serve or the services or goods they provide. The main theme in this chapter is to highlight how social media can serve as an excellent way to bring online communities together to name and shame organisations that are socially irresponsible, unethical or unsustainable.

This chapter will explore the following key themes:

1. Background into social advocacy
2. What is social media?
3. Online petitioning
4. Various theorists views on social media
5. Irresponsible behaviour by businesses
6. Cultural jamming a new concept to be taken seriously in marketing
7. A way Forward: The use of social media and online petitions to name and shame irresponsible governments and businesses.
8. Direction for future research

The chapter will start with providing a background into social advocacy and linking it to social media and online petitioning of big businesses who are corrupt and are perpetuating unethical behaviour.

Background into Social Advocacy

Activists are now using social media and on-line petitioning to gather much needed support to change the way big businesses and governments are doing things. They want to make a difference by creating awareness of the unethical practices and corruption perpetuated by big business and governments. Baron (2003) argues that through boycotts, protests, and civil suits, activists can force firms to comply with their demands or make a change to how businesses are conducting themselves. Davis, McAdam, Scott & Zald (2005) adds that neoinstitutional theorists are increasingly treating social movements as motors of institutional change.

Big businesses have an obligation to the public and its consumers. They need to take into account their behaviour before they fixate on profit margins. Research indicates that many customers in the world prefer not to purchase products from big businesses that destroy the rain forest, pollute the natural habit of animals and the environment at large and exploit poor workers. The following authors Crossley (2002); Raeburn (2004) and Schurman (2004) argue that the targeting of Nestlé, Chevron, and The Home Depot for environmental degradation, to animal rights protests against Procter & Gamble and General Motors, to the battle between gay rights proponents and opponents for sway over Disney and AT&T, activists have made corporate change a key part of broader social change agendas. While activists continue to target states and international organizations, "naming and shaming" corporations has become a signature piece in many social movement repertoires.

According to research, 30% of U.S. consumers claimed to have avoided purchasing products made by companies that pollute the environment (Cambridge Reports, 1989) and over 65% asserted that they would pay more for products that protect the environment (Pew Research Center,2003). Consumers according to surveys conducted in U.S have indicated that they would pay more in order to deter sweet-shop labour practices. According to PIPA (1999) surveys reported that consumers indicated even higher "willingness to pay" for "sweat-free" garments, with 76% of respondents in one survey asserting they would pay 25% more for a $20 garment if it were certified not to be made in a sweatshop). Respondents in another survey claiming they would pay 28% more on a $10 item and 15% more on a $100 item if they were not made in sweetshops (Elliott & Freeman, 2000).

O'Rourke (2005) argues that NGOs usually begin their campaigns by conducting an exposé on a leading firm. Campaigns are framed to challenge or undermine a company's brand reputation, targeting how it sells itself, and raising questions or highlighting hypocrisies within the brand (e.g., Nike empowering women consumers but exploiting women workers, Dell trumpeting a recycling program that turned out to involve prison labor, etc.). The media is key to these information campaigns and brand attacks. According to Sen, Gurhan-Canli & Morwitz (2001) evidence does indicate that information on firm practices and product impacts can sway consumers. Co-operative Bank (2003) added that consumers used the disclosure of negative information to help screen out and avoid socially or environmentally irresponsible companies. It is quite common now for consumers to boycott bad companies. In the UK, over 50% of respondents in a poll claimed they had punished a firm by boycotting it in the last year. Vogel (2005) argued that the "market for virtue" among individual consumers is slight but that shareholder responses to naming and shaming campaigns have sometimes proven powerful. King and Soule (2007) also indicated in their study that protest activity sends signals to shareholders regarding future market trends, stakeholder discontent or new costs for the firm.

Khondker (2011) argues that the most famous of politically-fuelled examples of online activism involved a wave of riots and demonstrations during the Arab Spring, where social media were used to organise action despite state attempts to censor the Internet. Activists can now use technology like social media and on-line petitioning to reach a broader audience in their plight to make a difference and sustain the world as we know it. According to Shellenberger (2003) NGO market campaigns first identify a specific problem that resonates with consumers (e.g., shoes made with child labor, phonebooks made out of old-growth forests, computers made with toxic chemicals) and then connect these to larger issues (e.g., labor rights, sustainable forest management, toxic use reduction). NGOs then work strategically to frame these problems in a way that supports the consumers understanding and action and places responsibility on specific corporations. Successful NGOs strategically reframe existing problems to present both specific culprits and consumer alternatives.

Since social media is relatively new in marketing the next section in this chapter will un-wrap the concept of what social media is all about.

What Is Social Media?

There are various definitions and views on social media. The definitions of social media provided by different authors contain some similarities yet each definition has a unique approach to explaining this technology. To the marketer, social media offers a different approach to traditional marketing. The marketer in today's world should understand that social media provides a platform for his business. If used correctly, social media can assist the marketer to create long lasting relationships with its consumers. Taken a step further the social media can assist marketers in getting to know how consumers feel about their product, service and brand.

The social media are electronic tools that enable communication between people in which they exchange knowledge, experience and information in virtual networks. They allow people to source and share information as well as to promote existing and new products effectively. This new technology makes it easy to convey text, photos, audio, video and information between internet users, (Thackeray *et al,* 2008).

Social media is ''a group of internet based applications that builds on the ideological and technological foundations of Web 2.0, and it allows the creation and exchange of user-generated content'' (Kaplan & Haenlein,2010).

Shettleworth (2010) mentioned that applications like social media networks permits operators to create individual web sites available and that are easily reached for conversation of individual content and message. Social media can be considered as stages, online applications and broadcasting which purpose is to enable, simplify and assist communications and interfaces to share information.

Dewing (2012) indicates that social media refers to the wide range of Internet-based and mobile services that allow users to participate in online exchanges, contribute user-created content, or join online communities".

Xie and Stevenson (2013) argues that "Social media is a means of communication through the internet that enables social interaction".

Social media is defined by Salt (2011) "as a services, tools and platforms such as Twitter, Facebook, Linkedln and others that allow users to share information with each other".

After looking at the various definitions of social media and what it means to different theorists, the next section will elaborate on on-line petition.

On-Line Petitioning

Much of the activist space today is dominated by online petitioning. An on-line petition is a petition that is signed online on a website. Another name for an on-line petition is an e-petition. People who are in support of such petitions add their names online so that they can make a difference to society.

Romano (2010) indicates that the rise in the use of social network platforms has produced a new breed of citizen or deliberative journalism, which puts the power to disseminate ideas, and to champion causes, in the hands of the public. Stassen (2010) adds that online social networks support the democratisation of knowledge sharing because they are about listening to the ideas of others and offering a response. Looking specifically at the motivations behind online protest action, Yang (2009) outlines social activism as that which is concerned with corruption, the environment, and human rights.

Briassoulis (2010) argues that "Online petitions cover all conceivable matters of interest, from the global to the local to the individual level. They are created and promoted by specialized international groups and online communities, professional or occupational organizations, special interest groups and individuals. Most petitions include some text that presents the issue at stake and the associated request for resolution. Depending on the author(s) of the petition, these texts may be very informative, offering historical documentation and facts, explanations of the issue and justification for the cause of the petition. Supporting material may be provided such as videos, photographs or important documents"

Online activism has close ties with online petitioning. According to Yang (2009) Online activism is a new form of popular contention in that is spreading worldwide. In some cases, the Internet serves to mobilize street protest. More often, protest takes place online. The most common forms include online petitions, the hosting of campaign websites, and large-scale verbal protests. The most radical is perhaps the hacking of websites. These forms of contention may be found in blogs, Internet bulletin boards, online communities, and podcast and YouTube-type web sites.

After discussing online petition, in the next section various views by different theorists on social media will be put forward and discussed. This will help to further contextual the area of social media.

Various Theorists' Views on Social Media

Perceptions by different theorists on social media are often varied. This has created a debate as some theorists advocate strongly for business's and governments' to actively use social media in the marketing and promoting of their organisations whilst other theorists believe that social media can lead to the ultimate downfall of a business or government.

If we have to look at what has occurred in industry. Companies have used social networks to support car launches for example. Chevy and Dodge were among the first to use Facebook and Twitter in their marketing objectives. Employees and target members are often used in social network campaigns. Companies are avoiding social sites and are inserting a social component to their own site. Companies have incorporated Twitter and Facebook as a means of direct interaction with their customers, these networking environments have been chosen due to their high success rate (Blakeman, 2013).

Web strategist Jordan Raynor (2013) is reported to have said "it has never been easier to be as influential as you can be today. Information is cheap. Information is easier to produce, and if you have a quality message, it's never been cheaper to get out." This surely explains the growing phenomena of social media. Through the social networking site of Twitter, 64% of its users are more likely to purchase a product from a brand they follow online, whilst Facebook users spend an average of 405 minutes per month communicating and interacting with friends and following their favourite brands, services, outlets, sport personalities, etc (Zeevi, 2013). Vinerean, Cetina, Dumitrescu & Tichindelean1 (2013) argues that in particular, peer communication through social media, a new form of consumer socialization, has profound impacts on consumer decision making and thus marketing strategies.

According to Edosomwan, Prakasan, Kouame, Watson & Seymour (2011), social media is best for the following situations:

- Promoting open communication between employees and management.
- Enabling employees to share project ideas and work in teams effectively, which helps in sharing knowledge and experiences.
- Social media also promotes better content, such as webcast and videos, than just simple text.

- Helps to communicate collaboratively between current and potential customers, in receiving feedback, product definition, product development, or any forms of customer service and support.
- Encouraging members, or part of the company's employees, to become members of a well-recognized community.
- Social media becomes a good venue for discussions and becomes a classic goal of marketing and communications, but the companies must ensure that the employees are adhering to the rules and etiquettes of social media.

Edosomwan, Prakasan, Kouame, Watson & Seymour (2011) added that many social networking sites were created in the 1990s. Some examples included Six Degrees, BlackPlanet, Asian Avenue, and MoveOn. These were, or have been, online niche social sites where people could interact, including sites for public policy advocacy and a social network based on a web of contacts model. In addition, blogging services such as Blogger and Epinions were created.

Edosomwan, Prakasan, Kouame, Watson & Seymour (2011) further added that Facebook was a social networking website launched in February 2004. In January 2009, Facebook was ranked as the most used social network worldwide. Facebook network is on the rise on a daily basis. According to Stone (2007) Facebook is also the top social network across eight individual markets in Asia—the Philippines, Australia, Indonesia, Malaysia, Singapore, New Zealand, Hong Kong and Vietnam.

Social media in marketing is a new contemporary issue being explored by theorists.

Since Facebook is so popular worldwide, the discussion below will highlight how it ties in with marketing.

Ramsaran-Fowdar & Fowdar (2013) has indicated that popular Facebook tools via which marketing objectives can be achieved are:

- **Facebook Profile:** A strong profile of the organization can be established on Facebook with its vision and mission statement stated and clearly defined.
- **Facebook Groups:** The following are the most important aspects that can be used to attract consumers: the name of the group, the group topic and image of the group.
- **Business/Fan Pages:** Fans will receive updates from the company as new information is posted. The organization can regularly post information on the business/fan page on upcoming events, articles, games, blogs, podcasts, videos and links.
- **Sharing Events:** The organization can advertise its upcoming events on Facebook.
- **Social Ads and Polls:** Social ads can be placed on Facebook according to the age, sex, location, workplaces and education level of the users. Polls can also be organized on Facebook to obtain valuable feedback from users.
- **Facebook Messages:** Can be tailored and sent to individual users.

It is interesting to note that despite its popularity social media cannot replace traditional communication methods. Carter (2012) argues that social media will not replace traditional communication methods such as print media (newspaper, magazine,), broadcast (radio and television), but believes that social media is intended to complement by creating long term relationship with current and potential customers.

It is important for marketers to bear in mind the disadvantages associated with social media. Negative feedback can be expressed and generated on-line by customers via social media. Customers here can express their disregard for the company's poor ethics or complain about its poor quality product, service or brand. Sandilands (2014) argues that unless a company has someone in charge to check their social media accounts several times a day, dissatisfied consumers can publish comments which may not always be removable. The social media application of Twitter is a public platform and companies have no control over what people say, thereon bad news can get viral as easily as good news can, doing the business irrevocable harm.

Marketers have to understand that social media can be very problematic if not understood and handled properly within the company. Sandilands (2014) also added that in June 2010, the IT governance group and Control Association released a report which revealed that brand high jacking, lack of control over content, viruses, unrealistic consumer expectation and non- compliance with record management was listed as the top five threats associated with social media that marketers need to be aware of.

Szabo and Barefoot (2010) indicated that if a company's product or service experiences negative publicity it is not wise to use social media as a tool to change that negative publicity. A good example is what happened to BP. In 2010 BP had an oil spill in the Gulf Mexico and its public relations department tried to use social media to fix its image and do damage control. This was a disaster and a media nightmare as social media just served to make the whole media debacle more talked about worldwide. The company was very hard hit by this incident. The lesson learnt by BP and other big companies is that they cannot use social media to clean up a major media disaster. Edosomwan, Prakasan, Kouame, Watson & Seymour (2011) argued that the major challenge for social media is that it should be a reliable source for communication as it is not for damage control.

Governments can and have also used social media. However Kamwaria, Kamau, Githaiga, Guantai, Mugwe, Makin & Dida (2015) cautions governments from using social media and argues that "Since social media is relatively accessible and cheaper; it is the best and versatile publicist tool that the government can utilize to engage the public on policy and development issues. However, social media is a double-edge sword; it can build as well as destroy. As such, there is need to exercise caution in its use."

According to Langley & van den Broek (2010) various internet communities have been set up by a range of individuals, social entrepreneurs, NGOs and others to stimulate the sustainable behaviour of individuals and organisations. They range from making individual CO2 footprints more transparent (e.g. MakeMeSustainable and Treemagotchi) to micro funding websites supporting entrepreneurs in third world countries (e.g. Kiva and MicroPlace). Most of these communities are part of a whole new range of internet applications, known as social media applications, in which on-line social communities with a strong bottom-up and user-friendly character play the key role and where the mobilisation (aggregation and syndication) of content generated by users is the main function.

Assaad & Gómez (2011) argues that although Social networks can help companies spread good news fast, it can also spread bad news just as quickly. Moreover, if customers want to vent their anger about your product or service, they can use your social network account. Managers need to understand how to handle those situations quickly and effectively.

After an extensive discussion on social media and how it is contextualised by various theorists the next theme seeks to explore irresponsible behaviour by businesses as activists often use social media to target such businesses.

Irresponsible Behaviour by Businesses

Over the years as watch dog organisations in society have begun to name, shame and penalise big business who have been involved in irresponsible, unethical or corrupt dealings with its various stakeholders, many companies and governments have been brought forward and in some instances charged for their poor, disgraceful and unacceptable business practices. These businesses are named, shamed and penalised because they have been guilty of crimes, corruptions or irresponsible behaviour. If we read the newspaper headline world-wide many companies have been guilty of irresponsible or unethical behaviour in recent years. Under this section irresponsible behaviour by businesses and big companies will be outlined.

In the discussion below various irresponsible and unethical companies scandals are discussed.

Enron was a company that filled the headlines of newspapers in its management's unethical behaviour and corruption scandals that rocked the business world. According to Johnson (2003), he advocated that top officials at Enron abused their power and privileges, manipulated information, engaged in inconsistent treatment of internal and external constituencies, put their own interests above those of their employees and the public, and failed to exercise proper oversight or shoulder responsibility for ethical failings.

Nestlé, maker of Kit Kat, a chocolate know by many South African's as well as Europeans was also involved in a bad scandal a few years ago. Greenpeace (2010) argued that Nestlé used palm oil from companies that were trashing the much threatened Indonesian rainforests. This resulted in threatening the livelihoods of the Indonesian local people and pushing orang-utans towards extinction.

In July 2013, labor groups protested against health and labor violations committed by Dynamic Precision Industry Corp., a Taiwanese adidas supplier with a factory in Guangzhou, China. Incidents of Benzene poisoning, hearing loss, pneumoconiosis, and hand-arm vibration syndrome (HAVS) were reported at the factory (Facing finance, 2013).

The well-known giant Anglo American was also involved in a recent scandal. Anglo American's expansion plans in the Brazilian Amazon endangered its' environment and its'

Indigenous population. The Brazilian government, motivated by the prospect of economic stimulation, had accelerated construction of necessary infrastructure (roads, railways, dams,

etc.) in the Amazon in order to make the area more suitable for mining activities. The government of Brazil had also attempted to amend certain laws to allow mining companies to operate on designated indigenous lands. Despite Anglo American receiving concessions from the federal government, Brazil's environmental regulator in northern Amapa fined Anglo American $10 million following an incident at the company's port terminal that left three people dead and three missing (Facing Finance, 2013).

South African was also rocked by a corporate scandal. In mid-November 2007 Tiger Brands was fined 98.8 million rands (roughly equivalent to US$12,8 million) by the South African Competition Commission for colluding with other bread producers to raise the price of bread by 30c and 35c per loaf (Wikipedia, 2015).

The list below developed by Global exchange (2015) was placed on-line for all the world to see which listed the top 10 corporate criminal companies. They are as follows:

1. Alpha Natural Resourcesfor pollution of rivers, streams, and groundwater; violation of the Clean Water Act; destruction of forest and wildlife habitats; and devastation of Appalachian communities.
2. Felda Global Ventures Violation of basic worker and human rights, withholding worker pay, wage manipulation, insufficient screening of work contractors company that it is affiliated with, and the use of toxic pesticides that are harmful and dangerous to both the environment and people.
3. FIFAfor forced evictions from homes and stores, damaging local business, tax evasion, labor abuse, corruption, and violating human rights including: right to adequate housing, right to free movement, right to work, right to protest, and right to labor protection.

4. Gap Inc. for refusal to sign "Accord of Fire and Building Safety in Bangladesh," refusal to compensate victims' families, workers' rights violations, and unsafe building conditions.
5. Koch Industries for thwarting public policy; forcing policies on funded politicians, judges, and organizations; working to destroy minimum wage, unions, and social security; re-segregation of public schools and toxic pollution.
6. McDonald's Corporation for limited (and relatively non-transparent) environmental policies; unethical marketing to children; and lack of willingness to reform worker wages.
7. Nissin Foods Holdings Co., LTD for weakly defined palm oil sourcing practices; compliance in conflict palm oil related human rights and environmental violations and absence of public commitment to protect the environment from unsustainable expansion of palm oil plantations.
8. The Ralph Lauren Corporation for unsustainable sourcing of raw materials in viscose fibers; deforestation; environmental damage; human rights abuses; lack of consumer transparency; increasing CO2 foot-print and cultural appropriation.
9. TransCanada for plans to construct Keystone XL Pipeline.
10. Vattenfall for destruction of the environment and communities; political manipulation and legal abuse of international treaties.

The discussion above has clearly brought to light the extent of corruption by big businesses. In the discussion that follows the theme to be explored is cultural jamming. Cultural jamming is a concept that has transformed the marketing arena. Cultural jamming and its implications on marketing is another contemporary marketing issues. In the discussion below cultural jamming would be outlined and discussed in great detail.

Cultural Jamming: A New Concept to Be Taken Seriously in Marketing

Cultural jamming is where activists seek to aggressively target businesses that are socially irresponsible or are engaging in unethical behaviour. In cultural jamming the activist/s aims to inform consumers about the reality of a company's intentions. Cultural jamming came about because activists were fed up with big companies that tried to sell the world lies about their image. These companies used the media to portray themselves as socially responsible, honest, transparent and ethical when in fact they were involved in unethical business practices to increase their market share at the risk of communities, the environment and hardworking employees. These companies cared only about profits and did not spare expense to indigenous communities, endangered animals or plant life and rain forest and poor communities who work for them under unsafe labour conditions and for very little basic wages. They disregarded human life and the environment and never once saw the error of their bad ways.

In this new age of technology, activists both human rights and consumer have taken the forefront in using social media to name and shame these unethical greedy corporate giants who have destroyed so much of the world and its natural resources. These activists work timeously to name and shame companies that say one thing and do another in their business practice. These cultural jammers often hijack unethical company's advertisements and change the context of the message. Companies like Nike were targeted as they use slave labour to produce their products. It has been brought to light that the factories used to make Nike shoes have been reported to have very poor health and safety regulations. This was not known to the international community who only saw what Nike let them see, as they were always in the media for engaging in social upliftment programs when in actually fact they were engaged in cost cut backs that lead to the use of slave labour. McDonalds is also under attack by activists who claim that the fast food restaurant is promoting an unhealthy lifestyle of obesity for its customers. Coca-Cola, another well-known international company has been cited by cultural jammers as being only profit motivated. These are but a few examples of companies who have been targeted by activists/ cultural jammers. These activists have used cultural jamming to defame companies by distorting their advertisements.

Harold (2004) argues that culture jamming is usually described as a kind of "glutting" of the system; it is an amping up of contradictory rhetorical messages in an effort to engender a qualitative change. In this sense, jamming need not be seen only as a damming, or a stopping of corporate media. Rather, it may be more useful to consider jamming as an artful proliferation of messages, a rhetorical process of intervention and invention, which challenges the ability of corporate discourses to make meaning in predictable ways.

It is interesting to note that consumers boycotted companies that were unethical or involved in corporate scandals. Becchetti and Rosati (2007) indicated that "the 2003 Corporate Social Responsibility Monitor findings revealed that more consumers looked at social responsibility in their choices of purchases. The results indicated a jump from 36 per cent in 1999 to 62 per cent in 2001 in Europe. Also, more than one in five consumers reported having either rewarded or punished companies based on their perceived social performance and more than a quarter of share-owning Americans took into account ethical considerations when buying and selling stocks. The Social Investment Forum also reported that in the US in 1999, there was more than $2 trillion worth of assets invested in portfolios that used screens linked to the environment and social responsibility."

According to Carducci (2006) to be truly effective as a cultural, media and social practice, it appears that culture jamming must be tied to a larger purpose and not be taken as an end in itself. The most effective tendencies seem to be those that link with broader social concerns about global ecology and human rights. As a result of consumer activism, Nike, to take one example, now offers PVC-free products packaged in recycled boxes and has established a code of ethics for offshore suppliers.

Harold (2004) argues that cultural jamming examples include everything from rewording conversations between popular comic strip characters, to reworking the sign on a storefront, to making subversive collages out of familiar commercial and government images.

After the discussion on cultural jamming the next section would discuss a way forward: the use of social media and on-line petitions that name and shame big businesses.

A Way Forward: The Use of Social Media and Online Petitions to Name and Shame Irresponsible Governments and Businesses

Social media has been used by activists to place online petitions or shame companies that are selling unsafe products or that are engaging in unfair or unethical business practices. Activists have a role to play in educating the public to the wrongs perpetuated by big corporates. Information is now readily available to customers and they have a right to know about the brand or company they support. According to Boulianne (2015) Social media has skyrocketed to popularity in the past few years. The Arab Spring in 2011 as well as the 2008 and 2012 Obama campaigns have fuelled interest in how social media might affect citizens' participation in civic and political life.

Political consumerism has been around for a long time. Political consumerism and its implications on marketing is very important to take note of. de Zúñiga, Copeland & Bimber (2014) have argued that political consumerism is a tool through which people can articulate social or political preference and it can take one of two forms. Firstly, people can avoid (i.e., boycott) specific products or brands to punish companies for undesirable policies or business practices. For example, people may avoid purchasing clothes and accessories made in sweatshops to promote fair labor practices. Secondly, people can purchase products from companies whose production practices or values are consistent with their own (i.e., buycott). For instance, people may purposefully buy organic fruits and vegetables because organic farms do not produce pesticide runoff that harms soil and water. The use of purchasing power to express political preferences is not new, but it is only recently that researchers have attended to consumerism.

According to Bartley and Child (2014) Wal-Mart was an early and frequent target, beginning with an exposé of child labor in its suppliers in Bangladesh, which aired on NBC's *Dateline* in early 1993. The campaign to get Wal- Mart (and to a lesser extent, Sears and Kmart) to end the employment of children, and a threatened boycott of apparel from Bangladesh, raised public awareness in the United States. Armbruster-Sandoval (2005) adds that campaigns focused on Central American factories did link local organizing with pressure on companies like The Gap, Kohl's, and Phillips-Van Heusen (PVH). UNITE, Guatemalan Unions, and international unions cooperated to build a solidarity campaign to support unionization of a PVH factory. Bartley and Child (2014) indicated that this led to demonstrations targeting PVH, as well as JC Penney, which sold many PVH goods.

Consumer activism can be seen on-line in social media across the world. Taki and Coretti (2013) posits that through the spread of information online, internet activists were able to establish networks of resistance within Egyptian political society. And, despite the relative weakness of the ties between members of these networks, it still emerged as an effective tool to facilitate collective action. Perpetual connectivity of activists enabled them to have access to an infinite number of networks of trust and multiply the impact of social protest through the creation of an insurgent community. Internet activism made political action easier, faster and more universal in Egypt.

Environmental activists such as Green peace are actively using social media to name and shame big business. They are an NGO that believes the world is worth sustaining for generations to come and companies need to be part of this or they should be taken to task for their poor business practice that can lead to the destruction of our world. Greenpeace and Friends of the Earth are two NGO's that have used social media to get their message across borders. Their message is simple the world is in trouble and it is up to all of us in the world to saved it. The hole in the Ozone layer, the devastation of the rainforests in the Amazon, the indigenous tribes of the different countries in the world, the animals, the plants and trees and the bird and insect life are humanities responsibility. They must be saved at all cost to sustain the world.

The examples below are of companies that are named and shamed by Greenpeace because they are unethical and are involved in the destruction of communities. Facing Finance (2013) indicated that a 2012 Greenpeace report accused Adidas, along with several other big garment industry names, of contaminating water systems through chemical residues left on clothing sold to consumers worldwide, even in areas where chemical use was restricted. Greenpeace appealed to the adidas Group again in a more recent report for condoning the PT Gistex Group's repeated contamination of the Citarum River in West Java, Indonesia. The region hosts several clothing factories that dye, print, and finish polyester fabrics. While adidas admits to having business ties to the factory, the company refused to reveal the extent of those ties. The factory, like many others in the region, uses the river as a dumping ground for waste.

Facing Finance (2013) posits that several of Gazprom's gas and oil projects are criticized for having serious ecological and social impacts. For example, Greenpeace and other organizations have criticized Gazprom's risky oil drilling activities in the Arctic Sea. The use of fossil fuel energy exacerbates the melting of arctic ice. Less ice makes it easier for oil and energy companies like Gazprom to operate and exploit the area's resources. Greenpeace asserts that Gazprom endangers the region's marine ecosystem because it is not prepared to handle a potential spill in such an extreme climate region. Greenpeace recently carried out several protests hoping to raise awareness for the issue of arctic drilling and to prevent Gazprom from drilling in the area.

Facing Finance (2013) Jindal a UN Global Compact participant, meaning that the company has committed to supporting, respecting, and protecting internationally proclaimed human rights. Jindal is widely criticized in Mozambique for partaking in human rights violations, environmental destruction, and corruption. In the Tete province of North-western Mozambique, Jindal Mozambique Minerals operates the Chirodzi Coal Project. Jindal is one of only three companies with mining rights in the coal-rich Moatize region located in the Tete Province. Since its arrival in the country, Jindal has been responsible for violating community rights, damaging the environment through open-pit mining, and abusing Mozambican workers. Over 2,500 people still reside near the Chirodzi Coal Project's open-pit mine. Despite the company's promise to resettle communities before mining commenced, resettlement has not taken place. Further, the communities did not receive any form of compensation or substitute land for their sacrifices. Jindal continues to extract coal from land that is vital to the survival of residents and their families. The food insecurity that has resulted from Jindal's operations makes people vulnerable to poverty and hunger.

Environmental, labor, religious and GLBT activists have waged campaigns to "name and shame" and otherwise pressure numerous firms in the United States and Europe. Firms have responded with a dizzying array of codes of conduct, "corporate social responsibility" policies and certification and labeling schemes. Among social scientists, scholars of strategy are increasingly portraying activism as a game-changing challenge for firms (Baron & Diermeier, 2007; Lenox & Eesley, 2009). The world as we know it is changing and technology can help the people of the world in their fight to sustain it.

The might of social media has grown. It is a platform that can be used by social activist to get their message across about greedy and unethical businesses. The people of the world need to be aware of the companies they buy products from. As a marketer in the new millennium it is important to understand that a good corporate image and being a social responsibility company go hand in hand in sustaining the business in the long term.

DIRECTION FOR FUTURE RESEARCH

Social media and online petitioning is an important contemporary issue in marketing. If used properly NGO's can develop marketing campaigns to expose corrupt businesses on social media. Future research needs to be done in areas that explore social media and online petitioning and its impact on big business. The impact of social movements on corporate social responsibility is another interesting area for future research since social movements can cause consumers to boycotts products that can result in affecting stock market returns.

Online petitioning of governments and its implications on sustainable can also be researched. Other areas like online petitioning of child advertising and its implications to marketers also bear future research investigation. Lastly, online petitioning on unethical business practices can be another area for future research to be explored.

CONCLUSION

Social and consumer activists have changed the landscape of marketing as activists are now using Facebook and other social media platforms to name and shame companies and large corporations that are unethical or adopting socially irresponsible business tactics. Protests can come in the form of boycotts, public demonstrations, "naming & shaming" on social media, protest tactics and forms of cultural jamming. Activists have a right to help protect the planet against big companies that want to destroy it for the sake of larger profit margins. Customers have a right to know the companies they buy from or the brands they use. In the past, big businesses hid behind their advertisements and the public was not privy to their business ethic or their social irresponsibility. Now with information being so freely available the veil has dropped on corrupt, greedy and unethical businesses do anything to increase their market share at the expense of good values or the sustainability of our world. The social media is a platform that can be used by human and consumer activists to bring about social change. The main advantage of using social media is that it offers activists a fast easy and cheap way to spread their message to millions of people worldwide. At the end of the day it is about bringing about social change.

REFERENCES

Aronczyk, M. (2013). Market(ing) Activism: Lush Cosmetics, Ethical Oil, and the Self-Mediation of Protest. *Journal Media Studies,*1-22. Available at: www.cf.ac.uk/jomecjournal

Assaad, W., & Gómez, J. M. (2011). Social Network in marketing (Social Media Marketing) Opportunities and Risks. *International Journal of Managing Public Sector Information and Communication Technologies*, *2*(1), 13–22.

Baron, D. P. (2003). Private Politics. *Journal of Economics & Management Strategy*, *12*(1), 31–66. doi:10.1162/105864003321220724

Becchetti, L., & Rosati, F. C. (2007). Global Social Preferences and the Demand for Socially Responsible Products: Empirical Evidence from a Pilot Study on Fair Trade Consumers. *World Economy*, *1*(1), 807–836. doi:10.1111/j.1467-9701.2007.01012.x

Bennett, W. L. (2008). *Civic Life Online Learning How Digital Media Can Engage Youth.* London: Mitt Press.

Blakeman, R. (2013). *Nontraditional Media in Marketing and Advertising*. SAGE Publications.

Boulianne, S. (2015). Social media use and participation: A meta-analysis of current research. *Information Communication and Society*, *18*(5), 524–538. doi:10.1080/1369118X.2015.1008542

Brennan, L., & Binney, W. (2010). Fear, guilt and shame appeals in social marketing. *Journal of Business Research*, *63*(2), 140–146. doi:10.1016/j.jbusres.2009.02.006

Briassoulis, H. (2010). Online petitions: New tools of secondary analysis? *Qualitative Research*, *10*(6), 715–727. doi:10.1177/1468794110380530

Cambridge Reports. (1989). *National omnibus survey.* Storrs, CT: Roper Center for Public Opinion Research, University of Connecticut. July.

Carducci, V. (2006). Culture Jamming A Sociological Perspective. *Journal of Consumer Culture, 6*(1), 116–138. doi:10.1177/1469540506062722

Carter, B. (2012). *The like economy: How businesses make money with facebook* (1st ed.). Indianapolis, IN: Que Publishing.

Co-Operative Bank. (2003). *The ethical consumer report.* London: Co-Operative Bank.

Crossley, N. (2002). Global Anti-corporate Struggle: A Preliminary Analysis. *The British Journal of Sociology, 53*(4), 667–691. doi:10.1080/0007131022000021542 PMID:12556289

D'Amato, A., Henderson, S., & Florence, S. (2009). *Corporate Social responsibility and sustainable business a guide to leadership tasks and functions.* Center for Creative Leadership.

Davis, G., McAdam, D., Scott, W. R., & Zald, M. (2005). *Social Movements and Organization Theory.* London: Cambridge University Press. doi:10.1017/CBO9780511791000

de Zúñiga, H. G., Copeland, L., & Bimber, B. (2014). Political consumerism: Civic engagement and the social media connection. *New Media & Society, 16*(3), 488–506. doi:10.1177/1461444813487960

Dewing, M. (2012). *Social Media: An introduction.* Library of Parliament.

Edosomwan, S., Prakasan, S. K., Kouame, D., Watson, J., & Seymour, T. (2011). The History of Social Media and its Impact on Business. *The Journal of Applied Management and Entrepreneurship, 16*(3), 1–13.

Elliott, K., & Freeman, R. (2000). *White hats or Don Quixotes? Human rights vigilantes in the global economy.* Cambridge, MA: NBER.

Erdogmus, E. I., & Cicek, M. (2012). The Impact of Social Media Marketing on brand loyalty. *Journal of Procedial Social and Behavioral Sciences, 58*(2), 1353–1360. doi:10.1016/j.sbspro.2012.09.1119

Europeana Creative Cultural Jam. (2015). Available at: https://www.google.co.za/search?q=examples+of+cultural+jamming&biw=974&bih=734&tbm=isch&tbo=u&source=univ&sa=X&sqi=2&ved=0ahUKEwig7t-wns_KAhWBQhQKHY7lDIAQsAQIOQ&dpr=1.25

Facing Finance. (2013). *Dirty Profits II: A Research Paper Prepared for Facing Finance.* Amsterdam: Facing Finance Organisation.

Globalexchange.org. (2015). Available from: http://www.globalexchange.org/corporateHRviolators

Greenpeace.org. (2010). Available from: http://www.greenpeace.org/international/en/campaigns/climate-change/kitkat/

Harold, C. (2004, September). Pranking Rhetoric: "Culture Jamming" as Media Activism. *Critical Studies in Media Communication, 21*(3), 189–211. doi:10.1080/0739318042000212693

Johnson, C. (2003). Enron's ethical collapse: Lessons for leadership educators. *Journal of Leadership Education, 2*(1), 45-56.

Kamwaria, A. N., Kamau, J. M., Githaiga, A. J., Guantai, P. M., Mugwe, R., Makin, K. R., & Dida, G. B. (2015). Socialising Government: Evaluating the Role of Social Media in Governance and Ethics in Kenya. *International Journal of Humanities and Social Science*, *5*(1), 17–122.

Kaplan, A. M., & Haenlein, M. (2010). Users of the world, unite! The challenges and opportunities of socialmedia. *Business Horizons*, *53*(1), 59–68. doi:10.1016/j.bushor.2009.09.003

King, B., & Soule, S. (2007). Social Movements as Extra-institutional Entrepreneurs: The Effect of Protest on Stock Price Returns. *Administrative Science Quarterly*, *52*(3), 413–442.

Langley, D., & van den Broek, T. (2010). *Exploring social media as a driver of sustainable behaviour: case analysis and policy implications*. Internet Politics and Policy Conference 2010, Oxford, UK.

Lenox, M., & Eesley, C. (2009). Private Environmental Activism and the Selection and Response of Firms Targets. *Journal of Economics & Management Strategy*, *18*(1), 45–73. doi:10.1111/j.1530-9134.2009.00207.x

O'Rourke, D. (2005). Nongovernmental Organization Strategies to Influence Global Production and Consumption. *Journal of Industrial Ecology*, *9*(1-2), 115–128. doi:10.1162/1088198054084608

Pew Research Center. (2003). *Values update survey. Roper Center for Public Opinion Research*. University of Connecticut.

PIPA (Program on International Policy Attitudes). (1999). *Americans & the world: International labor standards*. Available from: www.americansworld.org/digest/global issues/intertrade/laborstandards.cfm

Raeburn, N. C. (2004). *Changing Corporate America from Inside Out: Lesbian and Gay Workplace Rights*. Minneapolis, MN: University of Minnesota Press.

Ramsaran-Fowdar, R. R., & Fowder, S. (2013). The Implications of Facebook Marketing for Organizations. *Contemporary Management Research*, *9*(1), 73–84. doi:10.7903/cmr.9710

Raynor, J. (2013). *First Edelman "Last Thursday" Breakfast Seminar is a Great Success - Irish Centre for Cloud Computing and Commerce*. Available from: http://www.ic4.ie/first-edelman-last-thursday-breakfast-seminar-is-a-great-success/

Salt, S. (2011). *Social Location Marketing: Outshining Your Competitors on Foursquare, Gowalla, Yelp & Other Location Sharing Sites*. New York: Library of Congress Cataloguing.

Sandilands, T. (2014) *Advantages and Disadvantages of Social Media Marketing*. Available from: http://smallbusiness.chron.com/advantages-disadvantages-social-media-marketing-21890.html

Schurman, R. (2004). Fighting 'Frankenfoods': Industry Opportunity Structures and the Efficacy of the Anti-Biotech Movement in Western Europe. *Social Problems*, *51*(2), 243–268. doi:10.1525/sp.2004.51.2.243

Sen, S., Gurhan-Canli, Z., & Morwitz, V. (2001). Withholding consumption: A social dilemma perspective on consumer boycotts. *The Journal of Consumer Research*, *28*(3), 399–417. doi:10.1086/323729

Shellenberger, M. (2003). *Race to the top—A report on ethical business campaigns*. Portland, OR: Ethical Business Campaigns Network.

Shettleworth, S. J. (2010). Cognition, Evaluation and Behavior (2nd ed.). New York: Oxford.

Simon, B. (2011). Not going to Starbucks: Boycotts and the out-scouring of politics in the branded world. *Journal of Consumer Culture, 11*(2), 145–167. doi:10.1177/1469540511402448

Slot, M., & Frissen, V. A. J. (2007). Users In The 'Golden' Age Of The Information Society. *Observatorio Journal, 1/3*, 201–224.

Soar, M. (2002). The first things manifest to and about the politics of cultural jamming: towards a cultural economy of graphic design and advertising. *Cultural Studies, 16*(4).

Stone, B. (2007). Microsoft to Pay $240 Million for Stake in Facebook. *The New York Times*, p. 1.

Szabo, J., & Barefoot, D. (2010). *Friends with benefits: A social Media Marketing Handbook* (1st ed.). New York: William Pollock.

Taki, M., & Coretti, L. (2013). The role of social media in the Arab up-rising past and present. *Westminster Papers in Communication and Culture, 9*(2), 1-115.

Thackeray, R., Neiger, B. I., Hanson, C. L., & McKenzie, J. F. (2008). Enhancing promotional strategies within social marketing programs. Use of Web 2.0 social media. *Health Promotion Practice, 9*(4), 338–341. doi:10.1177/1524839908325335 PMID:18936268

Vinerean, S., Cetina, J., Dumitrescu, L., & Tichindelean, M. (2013). The Effects of Social Media Marketing on Online Consumer Behavior. *International Journal of Business and Management, 8*(14), 66–79. doi:10.5539/ijbm.v8n14p66

Vogel, D. (2005). *The Market for Virtue: The Potential and Limits of Corporate Social Responsibility.* Washington, DC: Brookings Institution Press.

Wikipedia . org. (2015). Available from: https://en.wikipedia.org/wiki/Tiger_Brands

Xie, I., & Stevenson, J. (2013). Social media application in digital libraries. *Online Information Review, 38*(4), 502–523. doi:10.1108/OIR-11-2013-0261

Yang, G. (2009). Online Activism. *Journal of Democracy, 20*(3), 33–36. doi:10.1353/jod.0.0094

Zeevi, D. (2013). *What Makes Social Media So Influential?* Retrieved from http://www.socialmediatoday.com/daniel-zeevi/1246736/infographic-what-makes-social-media-so-influential

KEY TERMS AND DEFINITIONS

Activists: These are people involved in transformation in society that are driven by political or social ideology.

Consumers: These are people who purchase and consume goods or services.

Cultural Jamming: A form of subvertising, used to expose questionable business practices perpetuated by big businesses and is used to name and shame them.

Government Scandals: Disgraceful, shocking behaviour perpetuated by government officials that can give the government a bad name in public.

Online Petitions: It is a petition that is a way of bringing a grievance or an issue of public concern to the attention of the public that is signed online.

Social Media: A combination of electronic tools that enables communication between different online users to exchange ideas, knowledge and information in virtual networks.

Unethical Business Practices: Where management or employees of the business are involved in irresponsible behaviour, corruption or collusion that can results in bringing the business practices name into disrepute.

Chapter 15
Using Successful Cases to Promote Environmental Sustainability:
A Social Marketing Approach

Harry Beachcroft-Shaw
University of KwaZulu-Natal, South Africa

Debbie Ellis
University of KwaZulu-Natal, South Africa

ABSTRACT

The success of encouraging environmental sustainability by means of social marketing programs is partially determined by identifying certain actions that can favourably influence people's behaviours towards a more ecologically benign lifestyle. In this chapter, such actions (remodelling businesses and the economy by means of non-market capitals, social enterprises, and economic democracy; transforming food systems; renewable energy and energy reductions and simplifying lifestyles) are gleaned from a description of Cuba's transition period, the Findhorn Ecovillage and the BedZED development where greater levels of environmental sustainability have been attained. Associating the actions to social marketing theory reveals that they are well positioned to influence behaviours towards improved levels of environmental sustainability.

INTRODUCTION

As has been uncovered in Beachcroft-Shaw and Ellis's chapter on social marketing and it's application to sustainability, social marketing is theoretically speaking a useful mechanism that, by means of collaboration and creative thinking, has the capacity to influence individual and societal behaviours towards increased levels of environmental sustainability. It is defined as an instrument to influence behaviours that is steeped in traditional marketing's theory, tools and techniques (Kotler & Lee, 2011). Based on the underlying factor that behaviours are difficult to influence (Jackson, 2005; Kilbourne, McDonagh

DOI: 10.4018/978-1-5225-1823-5.ch015

& Prothero, 1997), the applicability of social marketing to the essence of collective creativity and collaboration is summed up well by Domegan (2008: 137): [s]ocial marketing is "the co-creation of complex social and economic benefits and value 'with' customers among/throughout an entire community network of relationships". In other words, to begin with behaviours are tricky to influence and because of this require multiple and integrated ways of thinking. So, if benefits are created together with customers by developing relationships and networks of relationships with them (Eagle, Dahl, Hill, Bird, Spotswood & Tapp, 2013; Hastings & Saren, 2003; Marques & Domegan, 2011), then the complex and relationship- and behaviour-driven nature of social marketing deeply favours multiple and integrated ways to solve problems i.e. collective creativity and collaboration across several stakeholders. For example, when attempting to influence people's behaviours towards a healthier lifestyle, social marketers would likely need to involve multiple influential bodies. These could include medical practitioners such as dieticians and doctors, local businesses such as gyms, sports facilities and supermarkets, local or national government to for example pave more bicycle paths for people to cycle more frequently, groups of people who have successfully adopted a healthier lifestyle who can reflect on their changes to the broader population. Within this network of relationships, a creative and collaborative environment would be a factor of a social marketing program's success (Marques & Domegan, 2011).

In reality, some social marketing campaigns have not succeeded in the past due to the complexity of people's behaviours and the factors influencing it (Jackson, 2005; Kilbourne *et al.*, 1997). However, there have also been some cases where collaboration and creative thinking has led to successful social marketing interventions that improved environmental sustainability (e.g. Frame & Newton, 2007; French, Merritt & Reynolds, 2011; Kotler, Roberto & Lee, 2002; McKenzie-Mohr, 2000; The NSMC, 2010). Successes can be attributable to several factors, one of which is uncovering a specific set of actions[1] that can influence behaviours in the right direction (Kotler *et al.*, 2002). More specifically, actions that can act as a foundation for social marketing programs (those that dovetail well with social marketing theory) targeting people to behave in more environmentally sustainable ways are vital for social marketers. One area that social marketers can turn to for actions that could underpin social marketing interventions aimed at increasing environmental sustainability are successful cases where improvements in environmental sustainability exist in the real world.

To derive such actions that could be useful for social marketers, the chapter is divided into two sections. The main purpose of the first section is twofold: firstly, it describes three instances (Cuba, Findhorn Ecovillage & BedZED) where increases in environmental sustainability have been attained and; secondly it isolates actions common to at least two cases that can be used in social marketing programs to influence behaviours towards a more environmentally sustainable society. After drawing out actions from the three cases, the section thereafter takes these actions and collectively relates them to social marketing theory, which intrinsically represents collaboration and creativity due to its multiple-stakeholder nature.

Successful Cases of Environmental Sustainability

By examining cases in which shifts in behaviours led to a more environmentally sustainable lifestyle, social marketers can extract useful actions that could form the foundation of social marketing programs, which will likely require collaboration and creativity across multiple stakeholders such as consumers, businesses, international organisations, national governments etc. The forthcoming cases were chosen because they represent such shifts in behaviours that resulted in a greater potential of environmental sustainability. One national-level case (Cuba) discusses how an entire country shifted to more environmentally sustainable lifestyle culminating in being the only country in 2003 to be environmentally sustainable (i.e. infinitely extendable into the future) with a very high development index (Moran, Wackernagel, Kitzesa, Goldfinger & Boutaud, 2008). In the 21st century no other country has achieved this status. Reviewing one of the most successful ecovillages, the case of Findhorn Ecovillage shows how certain actions largely improved environmental sustainability at the local level that resulted in the lowest ecological footprint of the developed world (Dawson, 2009). The last case of The Beddington Zero (Fossil) Enery Development (BedZED), a planned development initiated by a non-profit organisation and developed in coordination with several organisations, exhibits how organisation-led initiatives can also lead to improvements in environmental sustainability.

Cuba's Transition Period

Perhaps the only real-life evidence of a national-scale shift to a more environmentally sustainable socio-economic system exists in Cuba's transition period. Up until Cuba's economic crisis in 1989, the country had "reached the developed world standards in life expectancy, education and social development indexes" (Boillat, Gerber & Fune-Monzote, 2012: 603). Until this point in time the country also relied heavily on imports and exports derived from monocultures: more specifically, it represented an unsustainable socio-economic system using resources in excess of local supply (Borowy, 2013; Dawn King, 2012). After the crisis, and a consequent 35% drop in Gross Domestic Product (GDP), caps on imports and exports enforced through a trade embargo compelled government to transform its policies and ordinary Cubans to change their lifestyles in order to curtail unnecessary consumption (Borowy, 2013; Dawn King, 2012). To survive, Cuba's socio-economic system had to become more environmentally (and socially) sustainable at the national level (Borowy, 2013; Dawn King, 2012). Several key factors that influenced this transformation are examined forthwith.

Since Cuba had obtained agro-chemicals and fuels through imports, the import caps on fossil fuels, fertilisers and pesticides was the catalyst for policy changes that included a shift to organic and semi-organic agricultural systems (Boillat *et al.*, 2012; Borowy, 2013; Cabello, Garcia, Sagastume, Priego, Hens and Vandecasteele, 2012). These changes equated to a smaller ecological footprint through locally produced food and the use of fewer fossil fuels and ecologically harmful substances (Boillat *et al.*, 2012; Borowy, 2013; Cabello *et al.*, 2012). Additionally, government promoted non-mechanical means of transport and farming, which also decreased the amount of fossil fuels burned (Borowy, 2013; Dawn King, 2012). For example, the government issued over 1 million bicycles, transformed vehicles to transport large amounts of people and locally manufactured buses. In the case of farming, traditional methods including animals and fewer artificial stimulants were promoted (Boillat *et al.*, 2012).

Structural changes in the agricultural sector of the economy paved the way for an increase in co-operative farming practices characterised by direct farmer-to-public trade at farmer's markets (Boillat *et al.*, 2012). Individual farmers with relatively small plots of arable land bound together to form co-operative farms, which were state owned but not state controlled i.e. farmers still maintained the means of production (Boillat *et al.*, 2012). Organic urban agriculture, which was initially a grassroots movement, was in the end also promoted and urban gardening became the norm with the aid of government laws and policies (Cabello *et al.*, 2012, Murphy and Morgan, 2013). Both structural changes (co-operative farms and urban agriculture) shortened the distance between production and consumption and therefore reduced the negative environmental effects of lengthy food distribution networks (Boillat *et al.*, 2012; Cabello *et al.*, 2012). Since these were organic and low-input operations, the ecological footprint of these agricultural methods farms was lower than conventional farming (Boillat *et al.*, 2012; Cabello *et al.*, 2012; Jawtusch, Oehen & Niggli, 2011) and increased the food production capacity of the nation (Murphy and Morgan, 2013).

A decline in oil imports from the Soviet Union also prompted government to introduce widespread measures to localise energy production and focus on energy efficiency and saving and producing renewable and decentralised energy (Cabello *et al.*, 2012; Murphy and Morgan, 2013). Large thermoelectric power plants gave way to smaller, locally distributed gas plants, which resulted in reducing greenhouse gas (GHG) emissions by 69% (Cabello *et al.*, 2012). Inefficient appliances such as old refrigerators, light bulbs, air conditioners, televisions, fans, cooking stoves and water pumps were substituted for more energy efficient appliances (Cabello *et al.*, 2012). Renewable energies such as wind energy, solar panels, small hydropower and biomass facilities were introduced (Cabello *et al.*, 2012; Morgan & Murphy, 2013). These government-led activities did not go unnoticed as in 2009 Cubans "use[d] 43 percent less energy than people in the rest of the world" (Murphy & Morgan, 2013).

On the whole, Cuba, albeit from an external resource cap, realised a shift to a more environmentally sustainable society while ensuring high levels of well-being (Boillat *et al.*, 2012: Borowy, 2013; Cabello *et al.*, 2012; Murphy and Morgan, 2013). From 1990 to 2009 the country witnessed a 25 per cent reduction in carbon dioxide (CO2) emissions (Murphy & Morgan, 2013), which in 2009 was 44 per cent less compared to the world average (Murphy & Morgan, 2013). In 2003 Cuba had "a consumption pattern that could be extended globally without entering overshoot" coupled with a very high development index – the only one of 93 countries surveyed (Moran *et al.*, 2008). As of 2006, Cuba used the equivalent resources of 1.4 planets (GFN, 2015a).

To summarise the Cuban case, it has been demonstrated that the shift to a more environmentally sustainable society was the result of changes in the broad areas of agriculture, energy production and consumption and government laws and policies. The combination of the changes influenced the everyday behaviours of people (primarily on an involuntary basis) and are thus relevant for social marketers seeking to realise environmental sustainability. This is discussed in the section that relates social marketing to certain actions.

Now that the Cuban case has been discussed, the next case looks at environmental sustainability at the local level with the similar goal to extricate actions to form the foundations of social marketing programs targeting environmental sustainability.

Findhorn Ecovillage

One of the most successful ecovillages is Findhorn Ecovillage in Scotland. The Findhorn Ecovillage began in 1985 (Findhorn Ecovillage, 2015) and "grows much of its own produce, has several renewable energy sources on site (windmills, biomass electric, passive solar), green homes, a community grocery store, a car share and community laundry facilities, and many connections to businesses in nearby towns" (Calegar, 2013, para: 2). Being a grassroots initiative, the ecovillage is governed by the resident-elected council (Findhorn Ecovillage, 2015). The ecovillage maintains an ecological footprint less than half of the United Kingdom average – "the lowest ever measured for any settlement in the industriali[s]ed world" (Dawson, 2009: 26). It is therefore seen as a highly successful means of attaining environmental sustainability. Several factors assist to achieve this status, the major ones being discussed below in no particular order.

The first factor is energy. The community's energy needs are met with a mixture of on-site renewable energies that include wind, passive solar and biomass. Energy production, on average, exceeds the community's needs by 23% with the surplus being sold back to the national grid (Tinsley and George, 2006). On-site renewable energy production and consumption represents an ecological footprint 22% of the national average (Dawson, 2009), which equates to the resources of roughly 0.7 planets. Not only is energy produced on site, primarily attributed to the four community-owned wind turbines, there is also a high degree of energy efficiency with buildings being designed and constructed with efficiency in mind (Findhorn Ecovillage, 2015). For example buildings are highly insulated, fitted with solar panels (to heat water) and are designed to be naturally heated by the sun (Findhorn Ecovillage, 2015). Additionally, residents also tend not to use much energy i.e. only when it is necessary for their well-being (Dawson, 2009).

Secondly, three local Community-Supported Agriculture (CSA[2]) farms cater to the community's local, organic, seasonal and low meat and high fruit and vegetable diets (Daswon, 2009; The Findhorn Ecovillage, 2015). A CSA farm allows the ecovillage's community to secure a portion of the farm's produce (USDA, 2016). The CSA scheme is the oldest in the United Kingdom (UK) and eliminates the long distances between production and consumption and packaging needs common to large UK retailers (The Findhorn Ecovillage, 2015). All farms combine organic techniques with the latest technology and produce a wide variety of vegetables, fruits and animal products (Findhorn Ecovillage, 2015). Harvests are sold at the ecovillage's grocery store to which all residents have access (The Findhorn Ecovillage, 2015). The ecological footprint of the ecovillage's environmentally friendly diet is 33% of the UK's median (Daswon, 2009), which equates to the resources of approximately 1 planet.

The fact that Findhorn's community consumes goods at half the rate of the average Briton (therefore equating to the resources of about 1.7 planets) is the third major reason contributing to its low ecological footprint (Dawson, 2009, Tinsley and George, 2006). Not only does the community consume less in general (Tinsley and George, 2006), they also share goods amongst themselves where possible such as televisions, washing machines and cars (Dawson, 2009). Moreover, the community does not consume many items that do not directly satisfy their needs since cultural activities and community entertainment provide them with most of their personal needs (Dawson, 2009).

When compared to the one-planet level required for environmental sustainability, Findhorn nevertheless consumed at a rate equivalent to 1.5 planets (Ewing, Goldfinger, Oursler, Reed, Moore, and Wackernagel, 2009; Tinsley and George, 2006). This is however a vast improvement from the UK's average of 3.3 planets (GFN, 2015b).

To sum up the Findhorn Ecovillage case, the presentation of literature about the community shows that it is possible to reduce the ecological footprint of those living in the developed world to one that is more sustainable. Through a combination of renewable energy, agricultural methods and consumption patterns, Findhorn Ecovillage's residents behave in a way that is more environmentally sustainable that is primarily voluntary i.e. behaviours are self-initiated. Therefore this is an important case for social marketers to take note of when targeting society to shift behaviours voluntarily to a more environmentally sustainable lifestyle.

BedZED Urban Development

Located in Hackbridge in London's Borough of Sutton, BedZED is a council-facilitated commercial development sporting a mixture of offices and living spaces (Chance, 2009; Schoon, 2016). The project is managed by several organisations including Bioregional (non-profit organisation), a housing association focusing on social housing (Peabody Trust) and architects from Bioregional and ZEDFactory (Schoon, 2016). All of these organisations focus their efforts on the benefit of the population through social or environmental means (Schoon, 2016). Construction was completed in 2002 and it is designed to encourage more sustainable lifestyles (Chance, 2009; Hodge & Haltrecht, 2009). Until 2005 it generated zero carbon emissions (Hyde, Watson, Cheshire & Thomson, 2007) – after which it's renewable energy provider closed down – and features communal gardens and car sharing options (Forrest and Wiek, 2015). The project's ecological footprint is the equivalent to 2.6 planets, which is less than the 3 planets the Borough of Sutton required in 2009 (Chance, 2009). Chance (2009) goes on to state that if residents were to further adjust their lifestyles the development could reach an average resource use of the equivalent to 1.7 planets. The factors that increase the potential for environmental sustainability at BedZED are elaborated on below.

The major aspect that offers increases in environmental sustainability is design and construction. The development is designed using passive architecture rather than technical fittings (Chance, 2009; Schoon, 2016). It is fitted with solar panels on the roof and energy efficient appliances are installed in every home (BDG, no date; Schoon, 2016). Highly insulating materials prevent large temperature fluctuations and the building's south side floor-to-ceiling windows promote natural (sun) heating (BDG, no date). Smart-energy meters are visible in the kitchens and display how much energy is being used, their total consumption and a high-use alert (Chance, 2009). Situated close to public transportation options and boasting many bicycle parking spaces, BedZED residents need not necessarily own a car (Schoon, 2016). The development's car club has an online booking system to use the hybrid car parked on site (Chance, 2009). From 2012 to 2015, these (and some other) measures reduced consumption by "53% in travel carbon footprint...36% in gas consumption...32% in CO_2 from home heating and electricity...27% in electricity consumption...[and] 23% in total carbon footprint" when compared to a conventional housing development in Sutton, London (Schoon, 2016).

Other smaller measures that were present at BedZED, for example gardening allotments and a promoted vegetable delivery scheme, have not been effectively used and therefore their impact has been minimal (Hodge & Haltrecht, 2009). It should be noted that from 2002 to 2005 BedZED was carbon neutral as a renewable distributor provided energy for all spaces (Chance, 2009). Thereafter, non-renewable sources were the predominant form of energy used to heat and power the development (Chance, 2009).

On the whole, BedZED is a reasonably successful development as it managed to maintain an ecological footprint lower than the borough's average. This achievement is primarily realised through the design and construction of the project and the direct impact it has on people's behaviours such as reduced energy use and the method of transportation used. It is therefore seen as an involuntary method of coercing people to behave in certain ways rather than promoting the voluntary adoption of behaviours.

In conclusion, from these three success stories in which improvements in environmental sustainability exist, several particular actions that could make up the foundations of social marketing programs targeted at influencing behaviours towards environmentally sustainable outcomes emerge. Two of the three cases represent one end of the social marketing spectrum with Cuba and BedZED attaining success predominantly through involuntary measures (facilitating conditions) whereas the Findhorn Ecovillage, on the other end of the spectrum, has been successful with voluntary (self-initiated) measures. Before continuing to the next section, it must be noted that these actions need not be explicitly stated in the cases. This is because they can be associated with broader/similar actions that encompass their content.

In no particular order they are remodelling businesses and the economy, transforming food systems, renewable energy and simplifying lifestyles.

Actions as Foundations for Social Marketing Programs

The following sections connect the specific actions that emerged from the previous sections to broader actions that could act as the foundations for social marketing programs seeking to achieve sustainability. Thereafter social marketing theory is brought to the forefront to which these actions are associated.

Remodelling Businesses and the Economy: Non-Market Capitals, Social Enterprises, and Economic Democracy

Non-market capitals can be seen as items (land, housing or equipment) that are controlled not by the market but by local democracies (Bruyn 1992 cited in Johanisova, Crabtree & Fraňková, 2013). Social enterprises are organisations "involved at least to some extent in the market, with a clear social, cultural and/or environmental purpose, rooted in and serving primarily the local community and ideally having a local and/or democratic ownership structure (one-member-one-vote rather than one-euro-one-vote)" (Johanisova *et al.*, 2013: 11). Economic democracy is "a system of checks and balances on economic power and support for the right of citizens to actively participate in the economy regardless of social status, race, gender, etc." (Johanisova & Wolf, 2012: 562).

A linear relationship exists between these. Non-market capitals provide the platform for social enterprises to endure (Johanisova *et al.*, 2013), which consequently provide the means for economic democracy to exist (Boillat *et al.*, 2012; Johanisova & Wolf, 2012). More specifically, democratic control of capital could enable communities to decide for themselves what best to do with such capital and could pave the way for enterprises and a type of democracy that benefits the community and environment (Deriu, 2012; Johanisova & Wolf, 2012; Johanisova *et al.*, 2013). As Boillat *et al.* (2012: 606) put it: "a voluntary reduction in material and energy consumption is only possible in an economic democracy that makes people responsible, as a community, for the environmental consequences of their own production and consumption pattern". Therefore, it is proposed that giving local democracies control of their resources such as land will in turn enable enterprises that exist to benefit and serve the local community, which will consequently bring about an active participation in the economy.

In Cuba's case, the government allowed local communities and individual farmers to take control of land to be farmed (Boillat *et al.*, 2012) thereby exhibiting non-market capitals. Seeing as non-market capitals are a prerequisite for social enterprises to exist, non-market capitals may have been the cause for social enterprises, in the form of farmer's co-operatives, to become a contributing factor in the country's transition to an environmentally sustainable period (Boillat *et al.*, 2012). Consequently, this regulated economic power because as a result farmers were allowed to sell their produce on the free market and power and economic freedom were no longer controlled by the state. At Findhorn Ecovillage, non-market capitals are controlled by the Ecovillage's democratically and member-elected council (Findhorn Ecovillage, 2015). This enables the establishment and continuation of local businesses and CSA farms as social enterprises that consequently benefit the community (Findhorn Ecovillage, 2015). This ensures that there is a balance of economic power and that local the ecovillage's residents can participate in economic activities i.e. there exists an economic democracy. At BedZED it can be argued that the land that was used for the development was handed to a form of local democracy consisting of the several organisations that spearheaded the project. Because these organisations were interested in providing positive social, cultural and environmental benefits for a community (Schoon, 2016), the organisations involved in the development can be considered similar to that of a social enterprise. An economic democracy was then partially ensured as the organisations that orchestrated the development promoted a range of population groups to be involved including low-income groups (Schoon, 2016).

Therefore, because the three case studies maintained an improvement in environmental sustainability and exhibit non-market capitals, social enterprises and economic democracy, social marketers could use this as an action to influence behaviours towards a more environmentally sustainable society. Additionally, because it will involve numerous stakeholders such as businesses, national government, consumers etc., collective creativity and collaboration will be inherently required.

Transforming Food Systems

A food system represents the complete range of variables in an entire food chain from production to consumption, including inputs and outputs at each link (FAO, 2013; Infante Amate & Gonzalez de Molina, 2013). In order to increase environmental sustainability, the way food is produced and consumed needs to be revamped.

This action is made up of more specific actions:

Localising/Regionalising Food Systems

Within food systems, large amounts of resources are exhausted by the transportation of food via lengthy national and international distribution networks (Infante Amate and Gonzalez de Molina, 2013). Localising food systems could thus shorten the distance between production and consumption (Andreoni & Galmarini, 2013), which could minimise the environmental impact of transportation, imports and packaging, and subsidiary processes thereof (Andreoni & Galmarini, 2013; EEA, 2012; Infante Amate & Gonzalez de Molina, 2013; Scherr, Uphoff & Herren, 2012; UN, 1992). Furthermore, localising/regionalising food systems would mean more seasonal and small-scale production (Infante Amate & Gonzalez de Molina, 2013; Latouche, 2010), which also maintains positive environmental outcomes (Barling, Lang & Lele, 2012).

Organic Food

"We think that only a shift towards organic farming (and corresponding changes in consumption patterns) can contribute to substantial reductions of resource use in the food system" (Infante Amate & Gonzalez de Molina, 2013: 32). Not only does organic farming promote biodiversity, provide environmental benefits and use less toxic compounds and energy (Infante Amate & Gonzalez de Molina, 2013; Jawtusch *et al.*, 2011), it can also sequester huge amounts of carbon (from fossil fuels and GHG emissions) – about 4,118 kilograms per hectare per year according to Hepperly (2003 cited in Bates & Hemenway, 2010: 51). Per acre, carbon sequestering of this magnitude equates to the GHG emissions of driving 16,000 km (EPA, 2015).

Low Meat and Dairy, High Vegetable and Fruit Diet

Due to its ecological burden, it has been said that the consumption patterns of developed nations should shift to a more vegetarian diet constituting less meat and dairy products and more vegetables and fruit – a diet that is better for the environment because it is less resource intense (Barling *et al.*, 2012; EEA, 2012; Infante Amate & Gonzalez de Molina, 2013). To illustrate this, studies from Finland and Switzerland present data indicating that households eating less meat and more (organic) vegetables have an overall lower environmental impact (EEA, 2012). This comes as no surprise considering that within the food sector meat and meat products have the highest environmental impact (Tukker, Huppes, Guinée, Heijungs, de Koning, van Oers, Suh, Geerken, Van Holderbeke, Jansen & Nielson, 2006). Additionally, according to Infante Amate and Gonzalez de Molina (2013), cooking vegetables uses up to 70 times less energy than cooking meat products.

Highlighted in the previous section, empirical evidence from research done in Cuba and at the Findhorn Ecovillage demonstrate that organic and localised food systems had a direct impact on increases in environmental sustainability. In Cuba's case, localising food production reduced imports and exports, large-scale monocultures and the extensive distribution networks previously used to transport food around the country, all of which placed a strain on natural resources (Boillat *et al.*, 2012; Borowy, 2013, Murphy and Morgan, 2013). Furthermore, the organic and semi-organic farming techniques that were used throughout the country required fewer ecologically harmful inputs (Boillat *et al.*, 2012; Borowy, 2013; Cabello *et al.*, 2012) and in return offered better yields (Murphy and Morgan, 2013). Looking at Findhorn Ecovillage, the combination of a local and organic food system and low meat and dairy and high vegetable and fruit diet directly contributed to the very low ecological footprint the ecovillage maintained (33% of national average, roughly 1 planet), and in general the ecovillage's high level of environmental sustainability (Dawson, 2009). Such a food system virtually eliminates the distance between production and consumption and reduces the amount of resources required to produce food. At the BedZED project, although gardening beds were made available and a vegetable delivery box scheme was promoted, most residents did not make use of either. Instead most residents sourced their groceries from conventional shops in the area.

Thus, because localising/regionalising food systems has in two of three cases been connected to improvements in environmental sustainability, social marketers could use this action in interventions targeting behaviours that reduce environmental harm. Special attention needs to be paid to BedZED where changes to the food system did not work. Forrest and Wiek (2015) propose the core problem was that the actual residents did not introduce organise the gardening and organic box scheme, or any other changes to the food system for that matter, and therefore the motivation to take up this initiative was difficult to create and sustain once certain driving forces had been eliminated. Keeping all three cases in mind, social marketers will need to collaborate across several territories (production, retail, consumption etc.) and creatively deliver value with customers throughout a network of relationships in order for their interventions to succeed.

Renewable Energy and Energy Reduction

Renewable energy is defined as sources of energy that quickly regenerate and do not diminish over time (EPA, 2014). "Such fuel sources include the sun, wind, moving water, organic plant and waste material (eligible biomass), and the earth's heat (geothermal)" (EPA, 2014). Non-renewable energy sources possess many negative side effects (Andreoni & Galmarini, 2013; Jackson, 2009; Moriarty & Honnery, 2012; WWF, 2014). Therefore, shifting to renewable energy sources will likely improve the chance of realising an environmentally sustainable method of energy production (Demaria, Schneider, Sekulova & Martínez-Alier, 2013; Latouche, 2010; UN, 1992). Additionally, while phasing in renewable energies, further positive effects for the environment could be obtained if (developed) nations reduce their energy consumption to only what is needed to maintain a high standard of living (R&D, 2010). This is because such actions would produce a double dividend in which both increasing renewable energy and reducing energy consumption as a whole would benefit the environment.

In all three instances described above, increasing renewable energy and decreasing energy use in general was a positive contributor to increases in environmental sustainability. Through a mixture of methods such as wind energy, solar panels, small hydropower and biomass facilities (Cabello *et al.*, 2012; Morgan & Murphy, 2013), renewable energy production in Cuba resulted in decreased fossil fuel use and thus enabled a higher level of environmental sustainability (Murphy and Morgan, 2013). Albeit out of necessity, further environmental benefits came from reducing electricity consumption as a whole (Boillat *et al.*, 2012) and exchanging inefficient appliances (televisions, refrigerators, etc.) for more efficient ones (Cabello *et al.*, 2012). Moreover, larger, inefficient plants were replaced with smaller, more efficient plants culminating in a gas reduction of 69% (Cabello *et al.*, 2012). At Findhorn Ecovillage all of the energy used is 100% renewable (predominantly wind) and comes from their community-owned wind farm (Findhorn Ecovillage, 2015). Buildings are designed and constructed to minimise energy use and are therefore oriented to make use of passive solar heating, fixed with solar panels to heat water and use extremely insulating materials. Furthermore, the district heating system is designed to be highly efficient (Findhorn Ecovillage, 2015). These were seen as essential reasons why the ecovillage preserved a high level of environmental sustainability (Dawson, 2009). The community's frugal use of energy is also seen as a contributing factor to the low level of energy use (Dawson, 2009). At BedZED, zero carbon emissions were recorded during the three years when the development's energy needs were met with renewable energy (Chance, 2009). In terms of reducing energy consumption at BedZED, its design and construction played a large role in reducing tenants' energy use, resulting in a decrease of 36% and 27% for gas and electricity consumption respectively (Schoon, 2016). Interestingly for social marketers, the installation of built-in smart-energy meters that are visible in the kitchens and display how much energy is being used, their total consumption and a high-use alert seemingly caused a 22% decrease in energy use (Chance, 2009).

Since renewable energy and reducing energy consumption will require collaboration and creative thinking across various sectors (national governments, businesses etc.) and it can increase environmental sustainability, it is seen as a promising action for social marketers to make use of when the intention is to improve environmental sustainability by influencing people's behaviours. Although wind energy was the largest producer of renewable energy at Findhorn Ecovillage, primary research will eventually determine the most appropriate renewable energy form.

Simplifying Lifestyles

Simplifying lifestyles is seen as a means to decrease material consumption by shifting away from high-consumption lifestyles (Alexander, 2011; Andrews & Urbanska, 2010). Since lower consumption means less resources used (Demaria *et al.*, 2013; Hamilton and Mail, 2003), simplifying lifestyles could benefit the environment and help achieve environmental sustainability (Videira, Schneider, Sekulova & Kallis, 2014). The three cases are discussed in relation to this action.

In Cuba's case, the lifestyle shift to a simpler one the population had to endure was not voluntary but involuntary, as the shift was forcefully imposed. The state distributed bicycles and transformed the transportation sector to reduce fuel consumption and resource use (Borowy, 2013). High-consumption lifestyles were not even possible, for example, when electricity was available only 8 hours a day, incomes were low and consumer goods were not readily available (Murphy & Morgan, 2013). In general, Cubans have smaller living spaces and as much as 90% of the population don't own a car (Morgan & Murphy, 2013). Therefore, because the ecological footprint of the country was largely reduced, Cubans make it obvious that a simpler lifestyle, albeit involuntarily, has a positive impact on environmental sustainability (Borowy, 2013; Dawn King, 2012, Morgan & Murphy, 2013). Findhorn's population decreased resource use to half the amount of the average British person (Dawson, 2009, Tinsley and George, 2006) by simplifying their lifestyle (on a voluntary basis) through purchasing less consumer goods and living a simpler life disconnected to high-consumption lifestyle (Dawson, 2009). Instead of participating in high-consumption activities the community is involved in different social and cultural activities (Dawson, 2009). Additionally, because many of the residents work on site, car travel is just 6% of the national average and is said to be even less after the introduced car pool (Dawson, 2009). Thus, without being prompted by an external source, the community at Findhorn Ecovillage demonstrates the potentially positive environmental impact of simplifying lifestyles on a voluntary basis. One feature of the BedZED development – inherent in its design – is to encourage residents to reduce the carbon dioxide emissions from personal transport (Chance, 2009; School, 2016). Its car club, close proximity to public transportation and many bicycle parking spaces, for example, are ways that BedZED's design promotes a simplified lifestyle by not having to own a car (School, 2016). Such a method to simplify lifestyles plays a large role in the 53% decrease in resident's travel carbon footprint (Schoon, 2016). Compared to Sutton's residents of which 49% travel by car to work, only 17% of BedZED residents travel to work by car (Schoon, 2016).

To promote simplifying lifestyles as an action, social marketers will likely need to collaborate with different stakeholders (e.g. businesses, consumers, etc.) and creatively attend to delivering value to all stakeholders involved with the ultimate outcome resting on decreasing consumption as it can provide environmental benefits.

The previous section has insofar described three societies that have exhibited improvements in environmental sustainability and from these extracted specific actions that could provide the means to increase environmental sustainability via creativity and collaboration fostered through social marketing programs. The forthcoming section relates these actions to elements of social marketing theory, after which the chapter is concluded.

RECOMMENDATIONS

Utilising the important theories underlying social marketing (described in more depth in Chapter 16), the actions identified and outlined above should adhere to the basic social marketing theory. In short these are that in social marketing exchanges benefits should outweigh costs, benefits and costs should be exchanged within networks of relationships and the actions should operate within a critical marketing framework. The following sections elaborate on these three important tenets of social marketing theory. Naturally, all of these theoretical insights will need to be justified by primary research to uncover the types of benefits and costs useful in exchanges, the kinds of relationships and networks the social marketer should use the way programs should be promoted to safeguard society (Eagle *et al.*, 2013; French *et al.*, 2011; Grier and Bryant, 2005; Weinreich, 2011).

Actions as Exchanges

Exchange theory refers to the basic human trait that people behave to acquire the largest benefit in exchange for the lowest cost (Grier and Bryant, 2005; Hastings and Domegan, 2014). Therefore, because social marketing programs seek to influence people's behaviours, successful programs are underwritten by exchanges that offer greater benefits than costs that fulfil real needs and wants (Hastings & Domegan, 2014; Hastings and Saren, 2003; Kotler and Lee, 2008; MacFadyen, Stead & Hastings, 2003). From a social marketing perspective, environmental sustainability is a major benefit because it has been linked to human well-being since humans depend on the planet for their prosperity (Andreoni & Galmarini, 2013; Bonaiuti, 2011; Common & Stagl, 2005; Constanza, Alperovitz, Daly, Farley, Franco, Jackson, Kubiszewski, Schor & Victor, 2013). Any costs that compete against the basic necessity humans require to exist would be seen as inferior to the benefit that would ensue. Therefore, because the actions discussed above maintain the ability to improve the chances of attaining environmental sustainability, each action maintains, as a basic premise, greater benefits than costs. Social marketers would nevertheless need to translate the benefit of environmental sustainability into target audience related benefits. For example, instead of exchanging the environmental benefits with a target audience, it might be more relevant to the target audience if exchanges focused on saving them money or their children or grandchildren's well-being.

Actions within Networks of Relationships

"Social marketing is the co-creation of complex social and economic benefits and value 'with' customers among/throughout an entire community network of relationships" (Domegan, 2008: 137). Therefore, because relationships and networks are where social marketing exchanges take place, exchanges and relationships and networks are highly interrelated. To this end, social marketers design programs to facilitate exchanges that occur within certain relationships and networks that benefit individuals, groups and/or society (Marques & Domegan, 2011). Successful social marketing interventions should thus understand how exchanges could be incorporated into different relationships and networks (Marques & Domegan, 2011). Concerning relationships and networks in which exchanges of benefits and costs occur, all actions have the capacity to be promoted via upstream and downstream measures. This is because all actions can influence behaviours via voluntary and involuntary methods respectively. For example, social marketers could target policy developers, law-makers etc. at the macro level (upstream) and the voluntary behaviours of target audiences at the micro level (downstream) when promoting simplified lifestyles for instance. When influencing behaviours at different levels using the identified actions, social marketers should develop benefits and costs for each target audience.

Actions and a Critical Marketing Framework

State of the World reports (2010, 2012, 2013) indicate that the earth's population is living at unsustainable levels and suggest that large-scale shifts are necessary. The lack of sustainability can be seen as the broad reason for actions to right the environmental degradation the world currently faces. Thus, actions that can in theory maintain large-scale environmental benefits, and therefore benefits to society, are crucial for building a critical marketing framework within which social marketing programs can successfully operate. All of the abovementioned actions could offer widespread environmental benefits and can therefore be used as the basic foundation for a critical marketing framework. Social marketers would need to explore each action in more depth to obtain a more precise critical marketing perspective i.e. to ensure that the specific action contributes positively to the population's prosperity (Andreasen, 1994; Hastings & Saren, 2003; Marques & Domegan, 2011) keeping in mind that society's well-being includes the well-being of the planet as society is dependent on the planet's well-being (Andreoni & Galmarini, 2013; Bonaiuti, 2011; Common and Stagl, 2005; Constanza *et al.*, 2013). For example, the relationship between social marketers and a network of government departments that are in charge of laws and policies to influence behaviours towards producing renewable energy should ensure that these laws and policies do not, for example, marginalise certain sections of society or provide exorbitant profits for a few companies.

To summarise this section, successful social marketing programs firstly require a set of actions that could influence behaviours towards the intended outcome (Kotler *et al.*, 2002). Secondly, successful interventions are underwritten by exchanges of benefits and costs that occur within networks of relationships that should safeguard society's well-being. Using the cases that were previously discussed, the section showed how actions could be used to establish exchanges of benefits and costs that are facilitated by networks of relationships and operate within a boundary that safeguards society. And since social marketing programs can operate at many levels i.e. between national governments, NGOs, individuals, businesses etc. and require innovative ways to address issued, it is a well-poised mechanism that intrinsically requires collective creativity and collaboration between stakeholders.

FUTURE RESEARCH DIRECTIONS

Ecovillages contain within it all the actions identified in this chapter such as renewable energy and energy reduction, transforming food systems, remodelling business and economy and simplifying lifestyles and, when combined, can have a powerful effect on environmental sustainability as witnessed in the case above. Thus, because ecovillages are a prominent candidate for realising a more environmentally sustainable future, social marketers should place emphasis on researching ecovillages and how to use them to influence behaviours to achieve more promising levels of environmental sustainability.

CONCLUSION

Behaviours are complex and therefore social marketing as a tool for influencing behaviours towards environmental sustainability demands collective creativity and collaboration across multiple sectors.

Based on the idea that social marketing programs require a set of actions that can influence behaviours towards a more environmentally sustainable society, Cuba's transition period, Findhorn Ecovillage and the BedZED development, where increases in environmental sustainability have taken place, were analysed with the aim of unearthing such actions. Specific actions that could increase the chances of realising environmental sustainability indeed surfaced: relocalising businesses and the economy, transforming food systems, renewable energy and energy reduction and simplifying lifestyles. To check whether these actions could be useful for social marketers to influence behaviours towards environmental sustainability, they were related to important theories underlying social marketing. Since the actions could be applied to social marketing theory, all actions emerged as highly favourable possibilities for social marketers targeting adherence to the resources of one planet earth. In particular, ecovillages transpired as being a highly opportune method to engender environmental sustainability as it contained within it all of the actions identified in the chapter.

REFERENCES

Alexander, S. (2011). *Property Beyond Growth: Toward A Politics Of Voluntary Simplicity* (Doctoral Dissertation).

Alexander, S., & Ussher, S. (2012). The Voluntary Simplicity Movement: A Multi-National Survey Analysis in Theoretical Context. *Journal of Consumer Culture*, *12*(1), 66–86. doi:10.1177/1469540512444019

Andreasen, A. R. (1994). Social Marketing: Its Domain and Definition. *Journal of Public Policy & Marketing*, *13*(1), 108–114.

Andreoni, V., & Galmarini, S. (2013). On the Increase of Social Capital in Degrowth Economy. *Procedia: Social and Behavioral Sciences*, *72*, 64–72. doi:10.1016/j.sbspro.2013.02.006

Andrews, C., & Urbanska, W. (2010). Inspiring People to See That Less is More. In L. Starke & L. Mastny (Eds.), *State of the World: Transforming Cultures from Consumerism to Sustainability* (pp. 3–20). Washington, DC: Island Press.

Barling, D., Lang, T., & Lele, U. (2012). Increasing Resource Efficiencies: Sustainable Production and Consumption in Food Systems. In Avoiding Future Famines: Strengthening the Ecological Foundation of Food Security through Sustainable Food Systems (pp. 29-38).

Boillat, S., Gerber, J.-F., & Funes-Monzote, F. (2012). What Economic Democracy for Degrowth? Some Comments on the Contribution of Socialist Models and Cuban Agroecology. *Futures*, *44*(6), 600–607. doi:10.1016/j.futures.2012.03.021

Bonaiuti, M. (2011). *From Bioeconomics to Degrowth: Georgescu-Roegen's "New Economics" in Eight Essays*. London: Routledge.

Borowy, I. (2013). Degrowth and Public Health in Cuba: Lessons from the Past? *Journal of Cleaner Production*, *38*, 17–26. doi:10.1016/j.jclepro.2011.11.057

Cabello, J. J., Garcia, D., Sagastume, A., Priego, R., Hens, L., & Vandecasteele, C. (2012). An Approach toSustainable Development: The Case of Cuba. *Environment, Development and Sustainability, 14*(4), 573–591. doi:10.1007/s10668-012-9338-8

Calegar, B. (2013). *Findhorn EcoVillage, Scotland*. Retrieved 16 March, 2016, from http://sd.appstate.edu/academics/study-abroad/findhorn-ecovillage-scotland

Chance, T. (2009). Towards Sustainable Residential Communities; The Beddington Zero Energy Development (BedZED) and beyond. *Environment and Urbanization, 21*(2), 527–544. doi:10.1177/0956247809339007

Common, M., & Stagl, S. (2005). *Ecological Economics: An Introduction*. Cambridge, UK: Cambridge University Press. doi:10.1017/CBO9780511805547

Constanza, R., Alperovitz, G., Daly, H., Farley, J., Franco, C., Jackson, T., & Victor, P. et al. (2013). Building a Sustainable and Desirable Economy-in-Society-in-Nature. In L. Starke (Ed.), *State of the World: Is Sustainability Still Possible?* (pp. 230–256). Washington, DC: Island Press.

Dawn King, M. (2012, March). *Cuban Sustainability: The Effects of Economic Isolation on Agriculture and Energy*. Paper presented to the Western Political Science Association, Portland, OR.

Dawson, J. (2009). Findhorn's Incredible Shrinking Footprint. *Communities, 143*, 26–71.

Demaria, F., Schneider, F., Sekulova, F., & Martinez-Alier, J. (2013). What is Degrowth? From an Activist Slogan to a Social Movement. *Environmental Values, 22*(2), 191–215. doi:10.3197/096327113X13581561725194

Deriu, M. (2012). Democracies with a Future: Degrowth and the Democratic Tradition. *Futures, 44*(6), 553–561. doi:10.1016/j.futures.2012.03.016

Domegan, C. (2008). Social Marketing: Implications for Contemporary Marketing Practices Classification Scheme. *Journal of Business and Industrial Marketing, 23*(2), 135–141. doi:10.1108/08858620810850254

Eagle, L., Dahl, S., Hill, S., Bird, S., Spotswood, F., & Tapp, A. (2013). *Social Marketing*. Harlow, UK: Pearson Education Limited.

EEA. (2012). *Consumption and the Environment — 2012 Update*. Luxembourg: Publications Office of the European Union.

EPA. (2014). *Green Power Market: Green Power Defined*. Retrieved from http://www.epa.gov/greenpower/gpmarket/

Ewing, B., Goldfinger, S., Oursler, A., Reed, A., Moore, D., & Wackernagel, M. (2009). *The Ecological Footprint Atlas 2009*. Oakland: Global Footprint Network.

FAO. (2013). *The State of Food and Agriculture*. Rome: FAO.

Forrest, N., & Wiek, A. (2015). Success Factors and Strategies for Sustainability Transitions of Small-Scale Communities – Evidence From a Cross-Case Analysis. *Environmental Innovatioan and Societal Transition, 17*, 22–40. doi:10.1016/j.eist.2015.05.005

Frame, B., & Newton, B. (2007). Promoting Sustainability Through Social Marketing: Examples from New Zealand. *International Journal of Consumer Studies*, *31*(6), 571–581. doi:10.1111/j.1470-6431.2007.00600.x

French, J., Merritt, R., & Reynolds, L. (2011). *Social Marketing Casebook*. London: Sage. doi:10.4135/9781446250877

GEN. (2014). *UN Advocacy*. Retrieved from http://gen.ecovillage.org/en/page/un-advocacy

GFN. (2015a). *Humanity Now Demanding 1.4 Earths*. Retrieved from http://www.footprintnetwork.org/de/index.php/newsletter/bv/humanity_now_demanding_1.4_earths

GFN. (2015b). *United Kingdom*. Retrieved from http://www.footprintnetwork.org/en/index.php/GFN/page/trends/united_kingdom/

Grier, S., & Bryant, C. (2005). Social Marketing in Public Health. *Annual Review of Public Health*, *26*(1), 319–339. doi:10.1146/annurev.publhealth.26.021304.144610

Hamilton, C., & Mail, E. (2003). *Downshifting in Australia: A Sea-Change in the Pursuit of Happiness*. The Australia Institute.

Hastings, G., & Domegan, C. (2014). *Social Marketing: From Tunes to Symphonies* (2nd ed.). London: Routledge.

Hastings, G., & Saren, M. (2003). The Critical Contribution of Social Marketing: Theory and Application. *Marketing Theory*, *3*(3), 305–322. doi:10.1177/147059310333005

Hyde, R., Watson, S., Cheshire, W., & Thomson, M. (2007). *The Environmental Brief: Pathways for Green Design*. Oxon, UK: Taylor & Francis.

Infante Amate, J., & Gonzalez de Molina, M. (2013). 'Sustainable De-Growth' in Agriculture and Food: An Agro-Ecological Perspective on Spain's Agri-Food System (Year 2000). *Journal of Cleaner Production*, *38*, 27–35. doi:10.1016/j.jclepro.2011.03.018

Jackson, T. (2005). *Motivating Sustainable Consumption*. Surrey, UK: University of Surrey.

Jackson, T. (2009). *Prospertiy Without Growth: Econmics for a Finite Planet*. London: Earthscan.

Jawtusch, J., Oehen, B., & Niggli, U. (2011). Environmental, Social, and Economic Impacts of Sustainability Certification in the Agricultural Sector – The Current State of Empirical Research. In H. Willer & L. Kilcher (Eds.), The World of Organic Agriculture. Statistics and Emerging Trends 2011 (pp. 88-91).

Johanisova, N., Crabtree, T., & Fraňková, E. (2013). Social Enterprises and Non-Market Capitals: A Path to Degrowth? *Journal of Cleaner Production*, *38*, 7–16. doi:10.1016/j.jclepro.2012.01.004

Johanisova, N., & Wolf, S. (2012). Economic Democracy: A Path for the Future? *Futures*, *44*(6), 562–570. doi:10.1016/j.futures.2012.03.017

Kilbourne, W., McDonagh, P., & Prothero, A. (1997). Sustainable Consumption and the Quality of Life: A macromarketing Challenge to the Dominant Social Paradigm. *Journal of Macromarketing*, *17*(1), 4–24. doi:10.1177/027614679701700103

Kotler, P., & Lee, N. (2008). *Social Marketing: Influencing Behaviours for Good* (3rd ed.). Los Angeles, CA: Sage.

Kotler, P., & Lee, N. (2011). *Social Marketing: Influencing Behaviours for Good* (4th ed.). Los Angeles, CA: Sage.

Kotler, P., Roberto, N., & Lee, N. (2002). *Social Marketing: Improving the Quality of Life* (2nd ed.). Sage.

Latouche, S. (2010). *Farewell to Growth.* Cambridge, UK: Polity.

MacFadyen, L., Stead, M., & Hastings, G. (2003). Social Marketing. In M. Baker (Ed.), *The Marketing Book* (5th ed.; pp. 694–725). Oxford, UK: Butterworth Heinemann.

Marques, S., & Domegan, C. (2011). Relationship Marketing and Social Marketing. In G. Hastings, K. Angus, & B. Carol (Eds.), *The SAGE Handbook of Social Marketing* (pp. 44–60). London: Sage. doi:10.4135/9781446201008.n4

McKenzie-Mohr, D. (2000). Promoting Sustainable Behavior: An Introduction to Community-Based Social Marketing. *The Journal of Social Issues*, *56*(3), 543–554. doi:10.1111/0022-4537.00183

Moriarty, P., & Honnery, D. (2012). Preparing for a Low-Energy Future. *Futures*, *44*(10), 883–892. doi:10.1016/j.futures.2012.08.002

Murphy, P., & Morgan, F. (2013). Cuba: Lessons from a Forced Decline. In L. Starke (Ed.), *State of the World: Is Sustainability Still Possible?* (pp. 332–342). Washington, DC: Island Press.

R&D. (2010). Degrowth Declaration of the Paris 2008 conference. *Journal of Cleaner Production*, *18*(6), 523–524. doi:10.1016/j.jclepro.2010.01.012

Scherr, S., Uphoff, N., & Herren, H. (2012). Strategies for Sustainable Agricultural Production Systems. In Avoiding Future Famines: Strengthening the Ecological Foundation of Food Security through Sustainable Food Systems (pp. 39-48).

Starke, L. (Ed.). (2010). *State of the World: Transforming Cultures from Consumerism to Sustainability.* Washington, DC: Island Press.

Starke, L. (Ed.). (2012). *State of the World: Moving Toward Sustainable Prosperity.* Washington, DC: Island Press.

Starke, L. (Ed.). (2013). *State of the World: Is Sustainability Still Possible?* Washington, DC: Island Press.

The N. S. M. C. (2010). *Case Studies.* Retrieved from http://www.thensmc.com/resources/showcase

The Findhorn Ecovillage. (no date). Retrieved 16 March, 2016, from https://www.findhorn.org/aboutus/ecovillage/ecovillage-at-findhorn/

Tinsley, S., & George, H. (2006). *Ecological Footprint of the Findhorn Foundation and Community.* Sustainable Development Research Centre.

UN. (1992, June). *Agenda 21.* Outcome of the United Nations Conference on Environment & Development, Rio de Janerio, Brazil.

UNDP. (2007). *Human Development Report 2007/2008. Fighting Climate Change: Human Solidarity in a Divided World.* New York: Palgrave Macmillan.

USDA. (2016). *Community Supported Agriculture.* Retrieved from http://afsic.nal.usda.gov/community-supported-agriculture-3

Videira, N., Schneider, F., Sekulova, F., & Kallis, G. (2014). Improving Understanding on Degrowth Pathways: An Exploratory Study Using Collaborative Causal Models. *Futures*, *55*, 58–77. doi:10.1016/j.futures.2013.11.001

WCED. (1987). *Our Common Future.* Oslo: United Nations.

Weinreich, N. (2011). *Hands-on Social Marketing: A Step-by-step Guide to Designing Change for Good.* Sage.

WWF. (2014). *Draw the Line.* Gland: WWF.

KEY TERMS AND DEFINITIONS

Economic Democracy: An economic system in which citizens are supported to actively participate regardless of their characteristics.

Food System: A food system represents the complete range of variables in an entire food chain from production to consumption, including inputs and outputs at each link (FAO, 2013; Infante Amate & Gonzalez de Molina, 2013).

Non-Market Capitals: Non-market capitals can be seen as items (land, housing or equipment) that are controlled not by the market but by local democracies (Bruyn 1992 cited in Johanisova, Crabtree & Fraňková, 2013).

Renewable Energy: Renewable energy is defined as sources of energy that quickly regenerate and do not diminish over time (EPA, 2014).

Simplifying Lifestyles: Simplifying lifestyles is seen as a means to decrease material consumption by shifting away from high-consumption lifestyles (Alexander, 2011; Andrews & Urbanska, 2010).

Social Enterprises: Social enterprises are organisations that maintain a democratic structure and aim to benefit the local community and its relationship to the environment (Johanisova *et al.*, 2013: 11).

Social Marketing: Using traditional marketing techniques and practices, social marketing is basically a means to influence a target audience's behaviours in order to benefit them and/or society (Andreasen, 1994: 111; Kotler & Lee, 2011: 26).

Social Marketing Actions: These are actions that refer to proposed activities to achieve environmental sustainability.

ENDNOTES

1 Actions refer to proposed activities to achieve environmental sustainability.

2 CSA is defined as a relationship between a farmer and a community of shareholders who invest in the farm in return produce for a share of the farm's produce (USDA, 2016).

Chapter 16
Social Marketing to Achieve Sustainability

Harry Beachcroft-Shaw
University of KwaZulu-Natal, South Africa

Debbie Ellis
University of KwaZulu-Natal, South Africa

ABSTRACT

That sustainable practices are necessary for the earth's survival, is well documented, but how to creatively balance the needs of the multiple stakeholders of society, the economy and the earth, is a major challenge. Individuals, businesses and societies require substantial changes to how they behave with regards to the earth's limited resources. Social marketing is the application of marketing principles to behaviour change and thus has the potential to guide efforts to achieve sustainability. This chapter discusses the principles and theories of social marketing and uses them to recommend actions to achieve sustainability. Exchange theory, relationship and network theory, and critical marketing theory provide guidelines to improve the success of social marketing interventions designed to achieve sustainability.

INTRODUCTION

The multiple demands of the earth, the economy and society cannot be sustained forever. There is a dire need for a more sustainable co-existence of these components (Research & Degrowth, 2010; Starke, 2013; UN, 2012). The UN World Commission on Environment and Development (WECD, 1987, p. 43) defines sustainability as "meeting the needs of current generations without limiting the ability of future generations to meet their own needs". Sustainability is however a complicated concept (Engelman, 2013; Waas, Hugé, Verbruggen & Wright, 2011) rife with interpretations and paradoxes (Jabareen, 2008). Elkington (1997) introduced the concept of the triple bottom line of sustainability with three closely interconnected dimensions: economic prosperity, social justice and environmental quality. The 'triple bottom line' conceptualisation of sustainability including profit, society and the environment, provides an important guideline for the sustainable behaviours of all members of society (Balderjahn, Buerke, Kirchgeorg, Peyer, Seegebarth & Wiedmann, 2013). Economic sustainability goals aim to achieve a fair

DOI: 10.4018/978-1-5225-1823-5.ch016

profit for producers while being affordable to consumers and at the same time meet the needs of society (social sustainability goal) and preserve the natural environment (environmental sustainability goal" (de Barcellos, Krystallis, de Melo Saab, Kügler & Grunert, 2011, p. 392).

The *State of the World* report (2013) indicates multiple benefits if sustainability can be achieved but also acknowledges that a large-scale change in the way we live, is required (Starke, 2013). However, achieving such sustainability is thought to be one of the most complex challenges of our time (Engelman, 2013; Tukker, 2013; UN, 2012; Waas, *et al.*, 2011).

Robinson (2004: 381) proposes that:

Sustainability should not be conceived of as a single concept, or even as a consistent set of concepts. Rather it is more usefully thought of as [an] approach or process of community-based thinking that indicates we need to integrate environmental, social and economic issues in a long-term perspective, while remaining open to fundamental differences about the way that is to be accomplished and even the ultimate purposes involved.

Albeit somewhat vague, Robinson's viewpoint implies that for sustainability to prevail, creativity and collaboration across multiple sectors and including multiple stakeholders is necessary. One key stakeholder in achieving sustainability, particularly environmental sustainability, is the individual consumer and members of societies. Thus a necessary component of any integrated strategy to achieve sustainability must be finding an appropriate mechanism to persuade society to live sustainably (Starke, 2010, 2012, 2013). This is where social marketing becomes important in this discussion. Social marketing has been defined as the use of commercial marketing principles to achieve *behaviour* change such that society as a whole benefits (Andreasen, 1994; Kotler, Roberto & Lee, 2002 – italics added). Social marketing uses a strategic approach to develop long-term strategies which change behaviours deemed to be problematic to society (Eagle, Dahl, Hill, Bird, Spotswood & Tapp, 2013) e.g. overuse of resources, pollution, and over consumption. However, sustainable behaviour change is not easy for social marketers to achieve (Brennan & Binney, 2008; Frame & Newton, 2007).

The aim of this chapter is to expose the reader to social marketing theory and the ways it can assist in creatively achieving sustainability. After reading this chapter, the reader will understand social marketing and how it can assist in achieving sustainability. The reader will also be able to evaluate business and marketing activities and generate creative and innovative ideas for social marketing campaigns to achieve sustainability.

SOCIAL MARKETING

This section introduces social marketing and its core principles. The section also discusses the key theories which provide a foundation to social marketing: exchange theory, relationship and network marketing theory and critical marketing theory.

Kotler and Lee (2011: 26) define social marketing as "a process that uses marketing principles and techniques to promote target-audience behaviours that will benefit society as well as the individual". Social marketing may therefore be viewed as a branch of marketing which focuses on influencing behaviours such that both the individual and society benefit (Andreasen, 1994; Kotler *et al.*, 2002).

Core Principles of Social Marketing

Social Marketing's Aim is to Influence Behaviour

While social marketing is often defined in terms of behaviour change, some social marketing efforts are designed to convince the target audience to not behave (Andreasen, 1994). For example, the goal of the 'Don't Drink and Drive' programme in South Africa, is for people *not* to drink and drive. Thus social marketing aims to stimulate the target audience to "accept a new behaviour, reject a potential behaviour, modify a current behaviour, or abandon an old behaviour" (Kotler *et al.*, 2002). To illustrate, a social marketing programme aimed at promoting a healthier lifestyle might encourage people to exercise more (accept a new behaviour), not try a new sugar-coated cereal (reject a potential behaviour), eat less fatty foods (modify a current behaviour) and completely eliminate products containing sugar (abandoning an old behaviour). Social marketing is therefore not just about providing information, educating or changing attitudes and beliefs (Andreasen, 1994). In the example above, the social marketing programme would not be deemed successful if it merely educated people about improving their eating habits or even changed people's attitudes towards certain foods and activities. Education and changed attitudes may be useful steps in the process (Kotler *et al.*, 2002) but do not constitute the aim of social marketing. Influencing behaviour is what differentiates social marketing from other marketing disciplines (Andreasen, 1994; Kotler *et al.*, 2002).

Social Marketing Efforts May Be Aimed at Voluntary or Involuntary Behaviours

Social marketing efforts may aim to encourage voluntary behaviour (known as downstream measures) or coerce involuntary behaviours (known as upstream measures). The traditional social marketing approach is to encourage voluntary behaviours (Andreasen, 1994; Hoek and Jones, 2011; Kotler *et al.*, 2002) such as communication campaigns encouraging consumers to turn off geysers in the day to reduce electricity consumption. Upstream measures on the other hand, use external factors such as laws, taxes etc. to coerce desired behaviours (Eagle *et al.*, 2013) and social marketers instead attempt to alter the environment to achieve behaviour change (Hoek and Jones, 2011). Taxes such as the new sugar tax would be an example of these upstream measures.

Often an integrated approach, combining upstream and downstream strategies, is the best strategy (Andreasen, 2006; French, Merritt, and Reynolds, 2011; Hastings and Domegan, 2014; Hoek and Jones, 2011). For example, an integrated approach to lessoning carbon emissions may be to use mass media campaigns to persuade commuters to use public transportation and bicycles (downstream) while subsidising bicycle prices and public transport tickets (upstream measures).

Beneficiaries May Be Individuals, Groups and/or Society as a Whole

Social marketing, by definition, is about influencing behaviours that benefit people (Andreasen, 1994; Kotler *et al.*, 2002) whether they are individuals in the target audience, other groups in society or society in general (Andreasen, 1994). Social marketing differs from traditional marketing in this respect as in the latter the consumer and corporate stakeholders are the beneficiaries (Kotler *et al.*, 2002).

Long- Term Perspective

Social marketing requires repeated efforts to change and maintain desired behaviours thus interventions usually require long term commitment (Eagle *et al.*, 2013). For example, in an anti-smoking intervention the individual must first stop but more importantly not return to the smoking habit.

Marketing Theory and Processes Underlie Social Marketing

This section begins with a discussion of the process of marketing strategy development as it applies to social marketing. It then goes on to look at marketing theories that have relevance for social marketing.

Social Marketing Strategy Development

As described in marketing theory, social marketing strategy is developed after a thorough analysis of the marketing environment (Eagle *et al.*, 2013; Weinreich, 2011), the process of segmenting, or dividing up, the markets to identify target markets for whom the behaviour change intervention is developed; the development of a clear positioning strategy and the use of the marketing mix to achieve this desired position. The tools and techniques used in traditional marketing theory for these analyses and strategy development processes thus also apply in social marketing albeit with some modification. These strategy development stages as they are applied to social marketing are discussed in more detail below.

Internal and external environment analyses are important to understanding the influence the environment has on behaviour (Eagle *et al.*, 2013; Kotler and Lee, 2008; Weinreich, 2011). The external marketing environment includes all factors and forces at international and national level as well as those within the industry and market which affect behaviour but which are beyond the control of the marketer (Kotler et al., 2010). For example, French *et al.* (2011) report that a campaign to encourage the use of car seats amongst a Hispanic community was successful due to the recognition of the impact of religion on behaviour, a social cultural factor. In this community people believed that car accidents were 'an act of God' and thus nothing could be done to prevent them. However, the social marketing campaign involving local religious leaders blessing the car seats, proved to be a successful strategy.

Competitor analysis is also an important component of marketing environment analysis in marketing theory. Competing behaviours are thus key elements in the social marketer's analysis (Grier and Bryant, 2005). Preferences for undesirable products (e.g. sugar-filled products), habitual behaviors, social norms in opposition to the desired behaviours and apathy are some of the behaviours that can compete with the desired behaviours (Kotler & Lee, 2008; Peattie & Peattie, 2003). While often difficult to identify, competitive behaviours are critical to identify in successful social marketing planning (Noble & Basil, 2011).

The development of marketing strategy involves segmentation and targeting and the development of positioning and marketing mix strategies (Walker and Mullins, 2014). Segmentation is "dividing a market or audience into groups based on one or more criteria" (Lotenberg, Schechter and Strand, 2011: 125). Understanding how different groups behave is crucial to the social marketer (Weinreich, 2011). Groups may differ in traditional ways e.g. geographically, demographically, psychographically and behaviourally (Kotler and Lee, 2008) but desired benefits and perceived barriers are also possible segmentation bases for social marketers (Hastings & Domegan, 2014; Kotler *et al.*, 2002).Once segments are identified, just as in traditional marketing, the social marketer must identify viable target markets (that can render the necessary results), that are accessible (can be reached with the marketing mix) and are potentially responsive (Hastings & Domegan, 2014). Different strategies may then be required for different segments. For example, TravelSmart is an initiative aimed at reducing car travel and increasing walking, cycling, and use of public transport (French *et al.*, 2011). Pioneered in Perth, Australia, three viable segments of households were identified: (1) those who required information even though they used the alternative methods of transportation; (2) those who did not require information because they had sound understanding of, and used alternative transportation; and (3) those who required information and were interested in using alternative transportation. Targeting strategies for each segment varied. Segments 1 and 3 were targeted with tailored information motivating the use (continuous) of the various alternative transportation methods while Segment 2 were encouraged to continue their use of alternative transportation by rewarding their behaviour with incentives. This social marketing initiative was deemed successful as greenhouse-gas emissions decreased due to the decrease in car use and the increase in walking, cycling and use of public transport by 26, 58 and 18 percent respectively (French *et al.*, 2011).

Positioning is about creating the desired place for the offering (in our case behaviour) in the mind of target audience so that it is distinctive relative to competing products (Kotler and Lee, 2008) and benefits are perceived t outweigh the associated costs (Hastings & Saren, 2003). The marketing mix elements then achieve this desired position (Kotler & Lee, 2011) and get consumers to choose the desired behaviour over competing ones (Peattie & Peattie, 2009).

In the social marketing marketing mix the 'product' is the benefit(s) that come from the desired behaviour (Kotler *et al.*, 2002) while price represents what the individual has to give up in order to receive these benefits (Eagle *et al.*, 2013) and may include non-monetary costs (Grier and Bryant, 2005; Weinreich, 2011) such as time, energy and effort costs (Kotler *et al.*, 2002); physical discomfort (Grier & Bryant, 2005; Kotler *et al.*, 2002) and psychological risks (Grier & Bryant, 2005; Weinreich, 2011). "Place is where and when the target market will perform the desired behaviour, acquire any related tangible objects, and receive any associated services" (Kotler *et al.*, 2002: 243) while promotion has to do with persuasively communicating the desired behaviour (product), its costs (price) and where to perform the behaviour (place) to a target audience (Kotler *et al.*, 2002).

Several marketing theories have relevance to social marketing i.e. exchange theory, relationship marketing and network marketing (Eagle *et al.*, 2013; Hastings & Saren, 2003). Critical marketing, is also of relevance to social marketing and thus will also be discussed below.

Exchange Theory

Exchange theory proposes that individuals behave so as to attain the greatest benefits for the least costs (Grier and Bryant, 2005; Hastings & Domegan, 2014). Successful social marketing interventions thus try to influence target audience behaviour through benefits which match or outweigh costs while satisfying real needs and wants (Hastings & Domegan, 2014; Hastings & Saren, 2003; Kotler and Lee, 2008; MacFadyen, Stead & Hastings, 2003). Benefits motivate the individual to act (Kotler and Lee, 2008) but are often ambiguous or difficult for the social marketer to 'sell' (Hastings & Domegan, 2014) and may benefit others but not the individual (Eagle *et al.*, 2013) e.g. blood donation. Costs or barriers may be perceived or real (Kotler & Lee, 2008; Maibach, 1993) and refer to something an individual must overcome or give up (Eagle *et al.*, 2013). These include "time, money, physical and cognitive effort … lifestyle, psychological factors … social contacts" (Lefebvre and Flora, 1988: 303). Social marketing exchanges are complex as they often involve symbolic exchanges where people exchange things for what they mean rather than only their tangible qualities (Hastings & Domegan, 2014). For example, consider a social marketing initiative aimed at curbing sexually transmitted diseases (STDs). The target audience must exchange the heightened pleasure of having unprotected sex in return for preventing STDs by using a condom (Brenkert, 2002). In this exchange, while the symbolic, intangible exchange is the positive social benefit of preventing STDs and the psychological perceived 'costs' of not having unprotected sex.

Social marketing exchanges are also complex as they may involve multiple stakeholders involved in different exchanges with other stakeholders. For example, social marketers might engage in symbolic exchanges with their target audience, while the target audience is engaged in utilitarian exchanges (exchanging money or goods for goods) with other parties (Eagle *et al.*, 2013; Hastings & Saren, 2003). These complex, multi-stakeholder exchanges require an understanding of relationships and networks.

Relationship and Network Marketing Theory

According to Domegan (2008) social marketing occurs at individual or micro level, at the inter-organisational or meso level; and at societal or macro level and as such deals with relationships and networks between the stakeholders e.g. target audience individuals, grass-roots movements, businesses, governments and international organisations. Grönroos (1994b, cited in Egan, 2004: 21) states that relationship marketing's objective is to "identify and establish [and] maintain and enhance… relationships so that the objectives of all parties involved are met; and this is done by mutual exchange and fulfilment of promises". Network marketing on the other hand, involves simultaneous relational exchanges amongst individuals and organisations (Barrutia & Echebarria, 2011). "The very core of social marketing – voluntary behavioural change and the exchange context – implicitly and explicitly embraces relationships" (Domegan, 2008: 137). Many of relationship marketing's core characteristics have applicability to social marketing: long-term inclination; dealing with complex behaviours and social structures; the importance of trust; and a focus on benefitting needy societal groups (Hastings, 2003). Relationship marketing "requires developing active partnerships and networks" (Marques & Domegan, 2011: 55) and thus network marketing is a form of relationship marketing (Lindgreen, Palmer & Vanhamme, 2004). Social marketing is "the co-creation of complex social and economic benefits and value 'with' customers among/throughout an entire community network of relationships" (Domegan, 2008: 137).

Due to social marketing's alignment with relationship marketing theory, the following section elaborates on relationship marketing's key concepts.

A key element of relationship marketing is *interaction* (Hastings, 2003; Hastings & Domegan, 2014). Interactions with customers or consumers create a collaborative environment for social marketers to create *value* with them (Marques & Domegan, 2011; Sheth & Parvatiyar, 2002) to facilitate exchanges (Domegan, 2008; Eagle *et al.*, 2013). Another key element of relationship marketing is *communications* which must be designed to support the development, maintenance and improvement of relationships with customers (Marques & Domegan, 2011). Through dialogue, established using communication, social marketers determine what needs to be exchanged through interaction and value creation (Marques & Domegan, 2011). *Trust* builds on satisfaction with the exchange and provides a foundation for the *commitment* required to sustain long-term relationships (Baron, Conway & Warnaby, 2010; Egan, 2004). As influencing behaviours through social marketing campaigns is complex and lengthy, commitment from all stakeholders (target markets, businesses, volunteers, media, local or national government, international organisations etc.) in the process is a requirement for success (Baron, *et al.*, 2010; Marques & Domegan, 2011).

Cooperation, another key construct in relationship marketing theory, involves aligning efforts to achieve mutual objectives (Morgan & Hunt, 1994). For the social marketers, cooperation is needed on many different levels (Domegan, 2008) for example, between individuals and volunteers, individuals and government and businesses and government. Project 50 per cent is an example of a social marketing initiative that applied the relationship marketing constructs to achieve more sustainable fishing in Southwest England (French *et al.*, 2011). Social marketers cooperated with fishermen, the media, national and local government and several other stakeholders to reduce fish discarding by 50 per cent. The social marketing team identified the local fishermens' sought benefits which led to trust, high perceived value and commitment. In the end the fishermen were satisfied and demonstrated higher relationship quality with the fishing authorities which had a positive influence on the communication, interaction and value creation between social marketers and fishermen.

Identification is "the perception of belonging to a group with the result that a person identifies with that group" (Marques & Domegan, 2011: 55). By identifying the groups that individuals identify with, and what relationships they have, social marketers can establish ways to overcome resistances and influence behaviour (French *et al.*, 2011). Therefore in social marketing, the target audience co-creates beneficial exchanges facilitated by the relationships and networks which the social marketer develops (Domegan, 2008; Marques & Domegan, 2011).

Critical Marketing Theory

Critical marketing theory questions the way commercial marketing influences behaviours as well as the end result (Gordon, 2011; Hastings & Saren, 2003; Saren, 2007) and acts to counteract marketing's pervasive influence (Lefebvre, 2011; Saren, 2011). When applied in social marketing contexts, critical marketing theory allows social marketers to develop a critical framework specific to a campaign/programme that safeguards society from the methods used to influence behaviours and the subsequent outcomes (Hastings & Saren, 2003). An example of the need for the application of critical marketing theory in social marketing initiatives is explained through the following example by Pfeiffer (2004). While the purpose of a social marketing programme promoting condoms was to prevent HIV/AIDS it was found to actually be detrimental to the target communities. A community belief that promiscuity causes HIV/AIDS, sparked the conviction that the social marketing campaign promoting the use of condoms, which thus was believed to increase promiscuity was therefore believed to increase HIV/AIDS. The western-style social marketing initiative espoused the benefits of cost effectiveness and fitted into the economic reform practices of the time, but disregarded the application of critical marketing theory in terms of outcomes and processes used to influence behaviours. These actions may have created further barriers to condom promotion and general distrust of western social marketing programmes (Pfeiffer, 2004). Thus social marketers must improve the well-being of the target audience rather than focus on the desires of social marketers (Gordon, 2011; Marques & Domegan, 2011).

In the above section the core principles of social marketing as well as the key underlying theories have been discussed. The next section discusses social marketing theory applied specifically to sustainability. While success in using social marketing to achieve sustainability is limited, there is some evidence of the successful application of social marketing to sustainability. These issues are discussed below with examples of successful social marketing initiatives used to achieve sustainability.

Social Marketing and Sustainability

Sustainability in its various forms: ecological, social and economic, remains one of the greatest challenges today, yet with considerable potential benefits (Starke, 2010, 2012, 2013). As social marketing is recognised as "an innovative approach to social change" (Andreasen, 2003: 293), and sustainability recognised as requiring changes to human behaviour, social marketing has been used to tackle the challenge of sustainability (Peattie & Peattie, 2011; McKenzie-Mohr, 2000). Thus social marketing initiatives aim to change behaviours which affect the environment. Social marketing has been used, albeit not overwhelmingly, to influence environmental and social behaviours in the past (e.g. Eagle *et al.*, 2013; Peattie & Peattie, 2009; Weinreich, 2011). Examples of the application of social marketing to sustainability are now discussed.

Social marketing efforts applied to sustainability in the past relied heavily on information and economic benefits (Jackson, 2005; McKenzie-Mohr, 2000). Information-intensive messages were believed to change attitudes and thus behaviour and economic benefits were believed to influence behaviour (Jackson, 2005; McKenzie-Mohr, 2000). For example, social marketing efforts focused on communicating, through mass media campaigns, the negative impact of large, polluting vehicles on the environment and it was believed that as a result of this information, consumers would seek better vehicle alternatives. Alternatively, social marketing efforts would communicate the costs of heavy, fuel-consuming vehicles in the hope that consumers would choose more efficient alternatives due to the economic benefits thereof. Campaigns such as these did not generally achieve the desired results (Burgess *et al.*, 2003 cited in Hargreaves 2011; Jackson, 2005).

There is however, some evidence that by applying the social marketing theories discussed above, social marketing interventions have been successfully used to tackle environmental and social sustainability (Frame & Newton, 2007; French *et al.*, 2011; Kotler *et al.*, 2002; The NSMC, 2010). Some examples of the positive outcomes of these initiatives are reducing waste (McKenzie-Mohr, 2000), reducing car use (French *et al.*, 2011, The NSMC, 2010), reducing electricity consumption, reducing consumption to only what is needed, increased recycling rates, (Frame and Newton, 2007, CBSM, 2010, Cole & Fieselman, 2013), and combatting salmon decline (Kotler *et al.*, 2002). As examples, Project 50 per cent and Green Pacific initiatives are briefly explained here.

The purpose of the Project 50 per cent social marketing intervention was to reduce the wasteful action of fish discarding in southwest England (French *et al.*, 2011). In this case, the current attitudes and beliefs of the fishermen that fish stocks were abundant; that declining fish stocks was a myth made up by NGOs and government and; that the assessments NGOs made were inaccurate, were all competing with the required behaviours. Fishermen were thus reluctant to use new fishing nets that could decrease discards. The social marketers developed a plan in cooperation with the fishermen, national and local government, the media and several other stakeholders, to reduce fish discarding by 50 per cent. The social marketing team developed trust with the local fishermen, which led them to be satisfied with the offering and gained their commitment. Perceived value was high because the fishermen's benefits had been identified and incorporated into the programme. By identifying the type of group the fishermen were, social marketers understood their perspective and developed the intervention around this. Cooperation was achieved because efforts from both parties maintained unidirectional objectives. Overall, fishermen were extremely satisfied and in the end demonstrated a higher relationship quality with the fishing authorities (French *et al.*, 2011).

The Green Pacific! social marketing campaign aimed to reduce paper usage, increase recycling and purchase of environmentally friendly products at a US university (Cole and Fieselman, 2013). In the research conducted on this specific initiative, the social marketing campaign strategies and materials that were found to be effective included "recycling and paper reduction prompts, a sustainable office pledge, initiating a green team and training staff leaders, and deskside recycling box distribution" (Cole & Fieselman, 2013, p. 176). In this social marketing initiative, barriers to the sustainable behaviours were identified and specific social marketing actions built into the programme to overcome these thus reducing the costs to the target audience of the desired behaviours. As a result of this social marketing initiative, use of recycled paper as well as purchase of environmentally friendly products both increased and 74 per cent of respondents reported changing their behaviour due to the social marketing initiative. For further discussion of social marketing success stories in achieving sustainability, see Chapter 15.

Despite successes such as those discussed above and the numerous social marketing actions proposed in the sustainability literature to influence behaviours to the benefit of individuals and/or society (Baker, 2006), with some exceptions, successful implementation of actions has been minimal (e.g. Castro, 2004; Engelman, 2013; Hopwood, Mellor & O'Brien, 2005; Robinson, 2004; Sneddon, Howarth & Norgaard, 2006; Waas *et al.*, 2011; Wallenborn, 2008), at least on any large scale. The changes enshrined in *Agenda 21* (UN, 1992), such as consumption practices that accept the earth's ecological limits, are a good example. Humanity's ecological footprint (the resources required to sustain a population and consume its wastes (Wackernagel & Rees, 1996)) instead of decreasing, have continued to increase with no signs of slowing (GFN, 2015; WWF, 2010). Moreover, there are still many socio-economic calamities (e.g. UN, 2012).

A lack of understanding of the complex factors relating to individual behaviour and society as a whole are often cited as reasons for these failures (Jackson, 2005; Kilbourne, McDonagh & Prothero, 1997). This supports the argument that social marketers find sustainability a complex field (Brennan & Binney, 2008; Frame & Newton, 2007).

Thus while successful social marketing campaigns do exist, as mentioned above, many fail. In the following section, recommendations are provided on how social marketing theories can be used to better achieve sustainability and improve the success of these social marketing initiatives.

RECOMMENDATIONS

Exchange Theory and Sustainability

As mentioned above, exchange theory proposes that individuals exchange benefits for costs and attempt to maximise individual benefit (Grier & Bryant, 2005; Hastings & Domegan, 2014; MacFadyen *et al.*, 2003). In the context of social marketing interventions then, exchanges where benefits outweigh costs and fulfil real needs and wants, should be more successful (Hastings & Domegan, 2014; Kotler and Lee, 2008; MacFadyen *et al.*, 2003). Thus analysing and understanding the costs/barriers and benefits in the specific social marketing exchanges is necessary (Domegan, 2008; Kotler and Lee, 2008; Lefebvre, 2011). Additionally, positioning the exchanges in ways that indicate greater benefits than costs to the target audiences, should increase the success of the social marketing programmes. The marketing mix developed to achieve the desired positioning of the proposed behaviours should taking into account the product, its costs (price), its location i.e. where the behaviours and exchanges will occur (place) and its promotion.

Benefits in Sustainability Exchanges

If we take the following social marketing activities to achieve sustainability such as transforming food systems, developing ecovillages, and promoting voluntary simplification/sustainable consumption, the ecological benefits are identifiable as a reduction of natural resource use and the ultimate outcome of ecological sustainability. Thus clear identification of the benefits is a necessary first step to successful implementation of the activities. Benefits must also be translated into specific target-audience benefits which must then be communicated in order to improve the likelihood of the social marketing activities around these actions being successful.

Exchange theory also proposes that exchanges that deliver greater benefits than costs are more likely to succeed (Hastings & Domegan, 2014; Kotler & Lee, 2008; MacFadyen *et al.*, 2003) thus if social marketing initiatives to achieve sustainability can offer both social and ecological sustainability outcomes, the social marketer is offering two sets of benefits for the same costs, an thus such initiatives will be more likely to succeed. For example, campaigns to increase renewable energy production and/or consumption or to encourage living in an ecovillage, contain both social and ecological benefits for one cost. Social marketing initiatives for sustainability that can offer, and effectively communicate multiple benefits relative to the costs, should be more successful.

Costs in Sustainability Exchanges

A cost/barrier is something an individual must forfeit or overcome in order to receive a benefit (Eagle *et al.*, 2013) thus social marketers must also understand the costs in exchanges (Domegan, 2008; Lefebvre, 2011). The sufficiency versus efficiency concepts of sustainability are used to illustrate here.

Sufficiency, which stems from the degrowth literature on sustainability, proposes that individuals and society should use only the resources necessary to provide well-being (Alcott, 2010; Kallis, 2011; Research & Degrowth, 2010). Thus with the principle of sufficiency, social marketers may be proposing that consumers actually cut back on consumption and live without certain 'non-essential' products or services. These cutbacks would represent a cost to the customer. Efficiency, a similar but subtly different construct more prominent in the sustainable development literature, suggests using resources to their maximum ability (UNEP, 2011). Efficiency as an underlying principle in social marketing activities for sustainability will impose fewer costs to the target audience as these actions will not necessarily require fundamental changes in behaviours (Robinson, 2004). Sufficiency as an underlying principle to guide social marketing activities for sustainability implies far greater costs for individuals and society as the changes are more fundamental (Demaria, Schneider, Sekulova & Martinez-Alier, 2013; Tokic, 2012; van den Bergh, 2011), but could also potentially offer greater benefits (Research & Degrowth, 2010). As actions where costs could, in the mind of the target audience, outweigh benefits are less likely to be successful, social marketers promoting actions with high costs e.g. when sufficiency is the underlying principle, must identify and communicate additional benefits to compensate for these costs. From a social marketing standpoint, fundamental changes in behaviours could be challenging to promote downstream (Kotler & Lee, 2011). It is therefore recommended that social marketers use an integrated approach (combining upstream and downstream activities) consisting of a predominantly upstream approach (e.g. encouraging the implementation of taxes that promote the efficient production and consumption of goods (Strange & Bayley, 2008; UN, 1992; UNEP, 2011) when designing social marketing programmes involving sufficiency as the guiding principle.

In summary, the application of exchange theory to social marketing activities aimed at achieving sustainability, ensures that social marketers are aware of the need for a clear understanding of the costs and benefits of actions for multiple stakeholders and the need to promote this exchange relationship such that the target audiences clearly perceive that benefits outweigh costs. Doing so will improve the chances of success of the sustainability social marketing activities. It may be necessary for such promotional campaigns to be regular and long term to maintain the perceived cost benefit ration and achieve continued behaviour change.

Relationship and Network Marketing and Sustainability

"Social marketing is the co-creation of complex social and economic benefits and value 'with' customers among/throughout an entire community network of relationships" (Domegan, 2008: 137). Social marketers develop programmes to facilitate exchanges within networks of relationships for the benefit of individuals, groups and/or society (Marques & Domegan, 2011). Thus, understanding how individuals and groups generate value among complex relationships and networks, is important to successful social marketing campaigns (Marques & Domegan, 2011). Social marketers who understand the costs and benefits of actions and manage these to facilitate exchanges and generate value for the target audience among networks of relationships, are more likely to be successful. Thus, it is important for social marketers attempting to achieve sustainability, to understand costs and benefits to develop the right relationships and networks (Domegan, 2008; Marques & Domegan, 2011). Actions that have clearly identified stakeholders, and costs and benefits identified for each of them, are more likely to succeed.

Interaction, Communication and Value Creation

For social marketing activities to be successful at increasing environmental sustainability the social marketer must communicate and creatively interact with the target audience (Hastings, 2003; Hastings & Domegan, 2014). Value for the target audience is collaboratively co-created by the individuals themselves, groups within society and the social marketer (Sheth & Parvatiyar, 2002) within an interconnected network of relationships (Domegan, 2008). It is therefore important firstly to identify the key relationship stakeholders with whom communication, interaction and co-created value should be established. For example, when using voluntary simplicity/sustainable consumption as actions to promote sustainable clothing, the social marketer must identify the stakeholders involved in production (e.g. suppliers of raw materials and manufacturers) and consumption (e.g. distributors, retailers and consumers). Furthermore, the social marketer must identify other stakeholders that could influence these target audiences, for example trade unions, governments, international organisations etc. The social marketer must then interact and communicate to collaboratively co-create sets of offerings that have value to each target audience.

Thus, through interaction and communication with multiple stakeholders and the understanding and creation of value, behaviour is influenced in a series of customised offerings (Hastings, 2003; Hastings & Domegan, 2014). For example, social marketing programmes targeting food production and consumption should use a marketing mix that facilitates several different exchanges of organic, local, seasonal foods that have been farmed using permaculture techniques or on small-scale farms and that increase vegetable consumption and decrease meat and dairy consumption. This could include, for example, eating more fresh fruit and vegetables and then, once these behaviours become habitual, decreasing imported food consumption. Multiple exchanges of co-created value products amongst various stakeholders can be identified in this example.

Perceived Value and Relationship Quality

The success of social marketing initiatives is influenced by relationship quality which is the perceived value gained from a relationship (Baron *et al.*, 2010; Gummeson, 2002), which in turn is derived from the exchange of benefits and costs (Marques & Domegan, 2011). For example, in the sustainability context of persuading people to consume less meat and dairy, exchanges facilitated among stakeholders in the network could include benefits such as cost savings and improved health for the consumers downstream but also financial savings on the health system or the number of jobs that organic food production could create, when dealing with relationships upstream with government. Thus, by offering greater benefits than costs in multiple relationships, social marketers can create high levels of perceived value and therefore better relationship quality within the network. This in turn will improve the chances of long term success for the sustainability social marketing initiative.

Trust, Cooperation, Satisfaction and Commitment

In the relationship marketing literature, trust, which is determined by perception versus performance (Baron *et al.*, 2010; Egan, 2004), leads to cooperation, relationship satisfaction and commitment to sustain the relationship, and thus ultimately the success of the social marketing programme (Baron *et al.*, 2010; Egan, 2004; Hastings, 2003). In other words, if the social marketer can develop trust, then the target audience is likely to be more willing to cooperate, more satisfied with the relationship and ultimately more committed to sustaining the desired behaviours proposed by the social marketing programme. For example, for a social marketing programme promoting ecovillages, the inclusion of an organisation such as the Global Ecovillage Network (GEN) as a key stakeholder in the programme, may improve the chances of the programme being successful because GEN is seen as a highly trustworthy stakeholder, which then facilitates cooperation, satisfaction and commitment to behaviours.

Identification

Determining what target individuals identify with can help social marketers influence behaviours (French *et al.*, 2011). For example, young consumers may identify with a celebrity that is actively involved in reducing poverty and inequality. Involving such celebrity in a social marketing programme could persuade these individuals to behave in a way that also reduces poverty and inequality.

To summarise, sustainability social marketing programmes will be more successful if they facilitate exchanges by fostering the right relationships with the key stakeholders in the network. This can be achieved by ensuring the programmes develop high quality relationships with high perceived value, earn the trust, commitment, cooperation and satisfaction of target audiences and stakeholders and identify with a target audience to motivate interaction, communication and value creation.

Critical Marketing Theory and Sustainability

By applying critical marketing theory to social marketing programmes the primary consideration is the ultimate well-being of society (Andreasen, 1994; Hastings & Saren, 2003; Marques & Domegan, 2011) where society's well-being includes the well-being of the planet because society is dependent on the planet's well-being (Andreoni & Galmarini, 2013; Constanza *et al.*, 2013). Thus, social marketers need to consider the way they implement the programmes to promote sustainability, including the relationships, tools and strategies used, and the influence the promotion of the social marketing programme itself has on society.

Using a downstream example, when promoting a pro-environmental behaviour such as the purchasing of organic produce from local farmers, it would be 'uncritical' to distribute thousands of t-shirts produced in socially unsustainable conditions using environmentally unsustainable processes and substances, as part of the promotional campaign for the organic produce. Upstream, social marketers must ensure that the relationships and networks used to achieve behaviour change are also not socially or environmentally unfavourable. For example, the relationship between the social marketer and government departments used to establish laws and policies to influence behaviours towards shifting to renewable energies should ensure that these laws and policies do not, for example, marginalise certain sections of society or provide exorbitant profits to a few companies at the same time. Ultimately it is the greater good for society that must be achieved, not benefits in one area at the expense of, or with additional cost, to another part of society.

In conclusion, social marketing actions which aim to influence behaviours that are more environmentally sustainable need to, at the same time, safeguard society's well-being as a whole, thus applying critical marketing theory

The above section has used the theories underpinning social marketing and their specific elements to provide recommendations on how to better achieve sustainability through long term behaviour change. It is acknowledged that this is not a simple recipe which will guarantee success, but it is hoped that it will provide those attempting to address sustainability through social marketing programmes with a set of guidelines which will improve their chances of achieving the desired behavioural changes required of individuals and societies.

FUTURE RESEARCH DIRECTIONS

In this chapter social marketing principles and theories have been discussed and recommendations made for how they can be applied to better achieve sustainability however, to truly test their applicability, a body of evidence supporting the theories is required. Such evidence is built through research on specific sustainability actions in specific situations. A growing body of such theory-testing cases will develop this important area of knowledge on social marketing's role in achieving sustainability.

Lessons can no doubt be learned from analysis of both the failed and successful sustainability social marketing initiatives. A meta-analysis of research literature could provide valuable evidence of the effectiveness of various social marketing initiatives.

Further research could also assess differences in social marketing initiatives to achieve sustainability across developing and developed countries. This is because developing nations would likely require different strategies to developed ones (e.g. Research & Degrowth, 2010; UN, 1992). As both developed and developing nations affect the planet's sustainability but also face unique challenges to achieving sustainability, such research will be of great value.

CONCLUSION

With social marketing being the application of traditional marketing tools and techniques to the domain of behaviour change, social marketing is a natural partner to those wishing to achieve sustainability. Sustainability requires fundamental changes to the way individuals and society behave. However, achieving sustainability is complex and examples of successful social marketing initiatives aimed at sustainability, are somewhat limited. This chapter aimed to unpack some of the key principles as well as theoretical foundations to social marketing and to explain how these might be applied better so as help social marketers choose social marketing strategies and actions most likely to succeed and also to improve the social marketing interventions through the application of sound social marketing theory.

REFERENCES

Alcott, B. (2010). Impact Caps: Why Population, Affluence And Technology Strategies Should Be Abandoned. *Journal of Cleaner Production, 18*(6), 552–560. doi:10.1016/j.jclepro.2009.08.001

Andreasen, A. R. (1994). Social Marketing: Its Domain and Definition. *Journal of Public Policy & Marketing*, *13*(1), 108–114.

Andreasen, A. R. (2003). The Life Trajectory of Social Marketing: Some Implications. *Marketing Theory*, *3*(3), 293–303. doi:10.1177/147059310333004

Andreasen, A. R. (2006). *Social Marketing in the 21st Century*. Sage.

Andreoni, V., & Galmarini, S. (2013). On the Increase of Social Capital in Degrowth Economy. *Procedia: Social and Behavioral Sciences*, *72*, 64–72. doi:10.1016/j.sbspro.2013.02.006

Baker, S. (2006). *Sustainable Development*. London: Routledge.

Balderjahn, I., Buerke, A., Kirchgeorg, M., Peyer, M., Seegebarth, B., & Wiedmann, K.-P. (2013). Consciousness for sustainable consumption: scale development and new insights in the economic dimension of consumers' sustainability. *AMS Review*, 1-12.

Baron, S., Conway, T., & Warnaby, G. (2010). *Relationship Marketing: A Consumer Experience Approach*. London: Sage.

Barrutia, J., & Echebarria, C. (2011). Networks: A Social Marketing Tool. *European Journal of Marketing*, *47*(1/2), 324–343. doi:10.1108/03090561311285574

Brenkert, G. (2002). Ethical Challenges in Social Marketing. *Journal of Public Policy & Marketing*, *21*(1), 14–25. doi:10.1509/jppm.21.1.14.17601

Brennan, L., & Binney, W. (2008). Concepts in Conflict: Social Marketing and Sustainability. *Journal of Nonprofit & Public Sector Marketing*, *20*(2), 261–281. doi:10.1080/10495140802224951

Castro, C. (2004). Sustainable Development: Mainstream and Critical Perspectives. *Organization & Environment*, *17*(2), 225. doi:10.1177/1086026604264910

CBSM. (2010). *Community-based Social Marketing: Case Studies*. Retrieved March 23, 2016 from http://www.cbsm.com/cases/search

Cole, E. J., & Fieselman, L. (2013). A community-based social marketing campaign at Pacific University Oregon: Recycling, paper reduction, and environmentally preferable purchasing. *International Journal of Sustainability in Higher Education*, *14*(2), 176–195. doi:10.1108/14676371311312888

Constanza, R., Alperovitz, G., Daly, H., Farley, J., Franco, C., Jackson, T., & Victor, P. et al. (2013). Building a Sustainable and Desirable Economy-in-Society-in-Nature. In L. Starke (Ed.), *State of the World: Is Sustainability Still Possible?* (pp. 230–256). Washington, DC: Island Press.

de Barcellos, M. D., Krystallis, A., de Melo Saab, M. S., Kügler, J. O., & Grunert, K. G. (2011). Investigating the gap between citizens' sustainability attitudes and food purchasing behaviour: Empirical evidence from Brazilian pork consumers. *International Journal of Consumer Studies*, *35*(4), 391–402. doi:10.1111/j.1470-6431.2010.00978.x

Demaria, F., Schneider, F., Sekulova, F., & Martinez-Alier, J. (2013). What is Degrowth? From an Activist Slogan to a Social Movement. *Environmental Values*, *22*(2), 191–215. doi:10.3197/096327113X13581561725194

Domegan, C. (2008). Social Marketing: Implications for Contemporary Marketing Practices Classification Scheme. *Journal of Business and Industrial Marketing*, *23*(2), 135–141. doi:10.1108/08858620810850254

Eagle, L., Dahl, S., Hill, S., Bird, S., Spotswood, F., & Tapp, A. (2013). *Social Marketing*. Harlow: Pearson Education Limited.

Egan, J. (2004). *Relationship Marketing* (2nd ed.). Harlow: Prentice Hall.

Elkington, J. (1997). *Cannibals with forks: The triple bottom line of 21st century business*. London: Capstone Publication.

Engelman, R. (2013). Beyond sustainababble. In L. Starke (Ed.), *State of the World: Is Sustainability Still Possible?* (pp. 3–16). Washington, DC: Island Press.

Frame, B., & Newton, B. (2007). Promoting Sustainability Through Social Marketing: Examples from New Zealand. *International Journal of Consumer Studies*, *31*(6), 571–581. doi:10.1111/j.1470-6431.2007.00600.x

French, J., Merritt, R., & Reynolds, L. (2011). *Social Marketing Casebook*. London: Sage. doi:10.4135/9781446250877

GFN. (2015). *World Footprint: Do We Fit on the Planet*. Retrieved from http://www.footprintnetwork.org/en/index.php/GFN/page/world_footprint/

Gordon, R. (2011). Critical Social Marketing: Definition, Application and Domain. *Journal of Social Marketing*, *1*(2), 82–99. doi:10.1108/20426761111141850

Grier, S., & Bryant, C. (2005). Social Marketing in Public Health. *Annual Review of Public Health*, *26*(1), 319–339. doi:10.1146/annurev.publhealth.26.021304.144610 PMID:15760292

Gummeson, E. (2002). Relationship Marketing in the New Economy. *Journal of Relationship Marketing*, *1*(1), 37–58. doi:10.1300/J366v01n01_04

Hargreaves, T. (2011). Practice-ing Behaviour Change: Applying Social Practice Theory to Pro-Environmental Behaviour Change. *Journal of Consumer Culture*, *11*(1), 79–99. doi:10.1177/1469540510390500

Hastings, G. (2003). Relational Paradigms in Social Marketing. *Journal of Macromarketing*, *23*(1), 6–15. doi:10.1177/0276146703023001006

Hastings, G., & Domegan, C. (2014). *Social Marketing: From Tunes to Symphonies* (2nd ed.). London: Routledge.

Hastings, G., & Saren, M. (2003). The Critical Contribution of Social Marketing: Theory and Application. *Marketing Theory*, *3*(3), 305–322. doi:10.1177/147059310333005

Hoek, J., & Jones, S. (2011). Regulation, Public Health and Social Marketing: A Behaviour Change Trinity. *Journal of Social Marketing*, *1*(1), 32–44. doi:10.1108/20426761111104419

Hopwood, B., Mellor, M., & O'Brien, G. (2005). Sustainable Development: Mapping Different Approaches. *Sustainable Development*, *13*(1), 38–52. doi:10.1002/sd.244

Jabareen, Y. (2008). A new conceptual framework for sustainable development. *Environment, Development and Sustainability*, *10*(2), 179–192. doi:10.1007/s10668-006-9058-z

Jackson, T. (2005). *Motivating Sustainable Consumption*. Surrey, UK: University of Surrey.

Kallis, G. (2011). In Defence of Degrowth. *Ecological Economics*, *70*(5), 873–880. doi:10.1016/j.ecolecon.2010.12.007

Kilbourne, W., McDonagh, P., & Prothero, A. (1997). Sustainable Consumption and the Quality of Life: A macromarketing Challenge to the Dominant Social Paradigm. *Journal of Macromarketing*, *17*(1), 4–24. doi:10.1177/027614679701700103

Kotler, P., Armstrong, G., Beneke, J., Bhowan, K., Blake, S., & Wait, M. (2010). *Principles of Marketing: Global and Southern African Perspectives*. Cape Town, South Africa: Pearson Education.

Kotler, P., & Lee, N. (2008). *Social Marketing: Influencing Behaviours for Good* (3rd ed.). Los Angeles, CA: Sage.

Kotler, P., & Lee, N. (2011). *Social Marketing: Influencing Behaviours for Good* (4th ed.). Los Angeles, CA: Sage.

Kotler, P., Roberto, N., & Lee, N. (2002). *Social Marketing: Improving the Quality of Life* (2nd ed.). Sage.

Lefebvre, C. (2011). An Integrative Model for Social Marketing. *Journal of Social Marketing*, *1*(1), 54–72. doi:10.1108/20426761111104437

Lefebvre, C., & Flora, J. (1988). Social Marketing and Public Health Intervention. *Health Education Quarterly*, *15*(3), 299–315. doi:10.1177/109019818801500305 PMID:3056876

Lindgreen, A., Palmer, R., & Vanhamme, R. (2004). Contemporary Marketing Practice: Theoretical Propositions and Practical Implications. *Marketing Intelligence & Planning, 22*(6), 673–692. doi:10.1108/02634500410559051

Lotenberg, L., Schechter, C., & Strand, J. (2011). Segmentation and Targeting. In G. Hastings, K. Angus, & B. Carol (Eds.), *The SAGE Handbook of Social Marketing* (pp. 136–151). London: Sage. doi:10.4135/9781446201008.n9

MacFadyen, L., Stead, M., & Hastings, G. (2003). Social Marketing. In M. Baker (Ed.), *The Marketing Book* (5th ed.; pp. 694–725). Oxford, UK: Butterworth Heinemann.

Maibach, E. (1993). Social Marketing for the Environment: Using Information Campaigns to Promote Environmental Awareness and Behavior Change. *Health Promotion International, 8*(3), 209–224. doi:10.1093/heapro/8.3.209

Marques, S., & Domegan, C. (2011). Relationship Marketing and Social Marketing. In G. Hastings, K. Angus, & B. Carol (Eds.), *The SAGE Handbook of Social Marketing* (pp. 44–60). London: Sage. doi:10.4135/9781446201008.n4

McKenzie-Mohr, D. (2000). Promoting Sustainable Behavior: An Introduction to Community-Based Social Marketing. *The Journal of Social Issues, 56*(3), 543–554. doi:10.1111/0022-4537.00183

Morgan, R., & Hunt, S. (1994). The Commitment-Trust Theory of Relationship Marketing. *Journal of Marketing, 58*(3), 20–38. doi:10.2307/1252308

Noble, G., & Basil, D. (2011). Competition and Positioning. In G. Hastings, K. Angus, & B. Carol (Eds.), *The SAGE Handbook of Social Marketing* (pp. 136–151). London: Sage. doi:10.4135/9781446201008.n10

Peattie, K., & Peattie, S. (2003). Ready to Fly Solo? Reducing Social Marketing's Dependence on Commercial Marketing Theory. *Marketing Theory, 3*(3), 365–385. doi:10.1177/147059310333006

Peattie, K., & Peattie, S. (2009). Social Marketing: A Pathway to Consumption Reduction? *Journal of Business Research, 62*(2), 260–269. doi:10.1016/j.jbusres.2008.01.033

Peattie, S., & Peattie, K. (2011). Social Marketing for a Sustainable Environment. In G. Hastings, K. Angus, & B. Carol (Eds.), *The SAGE Handbook of Social Marketing* (pp. 343–358). London: Sage. doi:10.4135/9781446201008.n24

Pfeiffer, J. (2004). Condom social marketing, Pentecostalism, and structural adjustment in Mozambique: A clash of AIDS prevention messages. *Medical Anthropology Quarterly, 18*(1), 77–103. doi:10.1525/maq.2004.18.1.77 PMID:15098428

Research and Degrowth. (2010). Degrowth Declaration of the Paris 2008 conference. *Journal of Cleaner Production, 18*(6), 523–524. doi:10.1016/j.jclepro.2010.01.012

Robinson, J. (2004). Squaring the Circle? Some Thoughts on the Idea of Sustainable Development. *Ecological Economics, 48*(4), 369–384. doi:10.1016/j.ecolecon.2003.10.017

Saren, M. (2007). Marketing is Everything: The View from the Street. *Marketing Intelligence & Planning, 25*(1), 11–16. doi:10.1108/02634500710722362

Saren, M. (2011). Critical Marketing: Theoretical Underpinnings. In G. Hastings, K. Angus, & B. Carol (Eds.), *The SAGE Handbook of Social Marketing* (pp. 95–106). London: Sage. doi:10.4135/9781446201008.n7

Sheth, J., & Parvatiyar, A. (2002). Evolving Relationship Marketing into a Discipline. *Journal of Relationship Marketing*, *1*(1), 3–16. doi:10.1300/J366v01n01_02

Sneddon, C., Howarth, R., & Norgaard, R. (2006). Sustainable Development in a Post-Brundtland World. *Ecological Economics*, *57*(2), 253–268. doi:10.1016/j.ecolecon.2005.04.013

Starke, L. (Ed.). (2010). *State of the World: Transforming Cultures from Consumerism to Sustainability*. Washington, DC: Island Press.

Starke, L. (Ed.). (2012). *State of the World: Moving Toward Sustainable Prosperity*. Washington, DC: Island Press.

Starke, L. (Ed.). (2013). *State of the World: Is Sustainability Still Possible?* Washington, DC: Island Press.

Strange, T., & Bayley, A. (2008). *Sustainable Development: Linking Economy, Society and Environment*. OECD. doi:10.1787/9789264055742-en

The N. S. M. C. (2010). *Case Studies*. Retrieved from http://www.thensmc.com/resources/showcase

Tokic, D. (2012). The Economic and Financial Dimensions of Degrowth. *Ecological Economics*, *84*, 49–56. doi:10.1016/j.ecolecon.2012.09.011

Tukker, A. (2013). Knowledge Collaboration and Learning by Aligning Global Sustainability Programs: Reflections in the Context of Rio.20. *Journal of Cleaner Production*, *48*, 272–279. doi:10.1016/j.jclepro.2012.12.023

UN. (1992, June). *Agenda 21*. Outcome of the United Nations Conference on Environment & Development, Rio de Janerio, Brazil.

UN. (2012, June). *Rio+20*. Outcome of the United Nations Conference on Sustainable Development, Rio de Janerio, Brazil.

UNEP. (2011). *Towards a Green Economy: Pathways to Sustainable Development and Poverty Eradication*. Geneva: UNEP.

van den Bergh, J. (2011). Environment versus Growth — A Criticism of "degrowth" and a Plea for "A-growth". *Journal of Cleaner Production*, *18*(6), 540–543. doi:10.1016/j.jclepro.2009.08.011

Waas, T., Hugé, J., Verbruggen, A., & Wright, T. (2011). Sustainable Development: A Bird's Eye View. *Sustainability*, *3*(10), 1637–1661. doi:10.3390/su3101637

Wackernagel, M., & Rees, W. (1996). *Our Ecological Footprint: Reducing Human Impact on the Earth*. Gabriola Island, BC: New Society Publishers.

Walker, O., & Mullins, J. (2014). *Marketing Strategy: A Decision-Focused Approach* (8th ed.). New York, NY: McGraw-Hill.

Wallenborn, G. (2008). *Degrowth vs.Sustainable Development: How to Open the Space of Ontological Negotiation?* Paper presented at the First International Conference on Economic De-Growth for Ecological Sustainability and Social Equity, Paris, France.

WECD. (1987). *From One Earth to One World: An Overview.* Oxford, UK: Oxford University Press.

Weinreich, N. (2011). *Hands-on Social Marketing: A Step-by-step Guide to Designing Change for Good.* Sage.

WWF. (2010). *Living Planet Report.* Gland, Switzerland: WWF International.

Compilation of References

4Di. Privaca. (2014). *Information Security HealthCheck*. Retrieved June 15, 2016, from http://www.4diprivaca.com/services/security-consulting-services/security-healthcheck/

Aarikka-Stenroos, L., & Jaakkola, E. (2012). Value co-creation in knowledge intensive business services: A dyadic perspective on the joint problem solving process. *Industrial Marketing Management*, *41*(1), 15–26. doi:10.1016/j.indmarman.2011.11.008

Ab Rahman, N. H., & Choo, K.-K. R. (2015). A survey of information security incident handling in the cloud. *Computers & Security*, *49*, 45–69. doi:10.1016/j.cose.2014.11.006

Abe, O. (2016). The feasibility of implementing the United Nations guiding principles on business and human rights in the extractive industry in Nigeria. *Journal of Sustainable Development Law and Policy(The)*, *7*(1), 137–157. doi:10.4314/jsdlp.v7i1.7

Abiodun, E. (2015). *Ensuring transparent, sustainable capital market*. Retrieved from http://www.thisdaylive.com/index.php/2016/06/22/ensuring-transparent-sustainable-capital-market/

Ablon, L., Libicki, M. C., & Golay, A. A. (2014). *Markets for Cybercrime Tools and Stolen Data*. Retrieved August 16, 2016, from United States of America: http://www.rand.org/pubs/research_reports/RR610.html

Abrahams, D. (2003). Local economic development in South Africa: A useful tool for sustainable development. *Urban Forum, 2003*. Springer.

Accenture. (2015). *Fighting Financial Crime with Data*. Retrieved August 10, 2016, from United Kingdom: https://www.accenture.com/t20160519T222110__w__/us-en/_acnmedia/Accenture/Conversion-Assets/DotCom/Documents/Global/PDF/Industries_6/Accenture-Fighting-Financial-Crime-with-Data.pdf

Accountants, C. (2014). *Protecting our Cyber Future*. Retrieved August 12, 2016, from Australia: https://charteredaccountantsanz.com/~/media/FutureInc/Pdfs/2014/FutureIncCyber%20Security.ashx

Acs, Z. J., Desai, S., & Hessels, J. (2008). Entrepreneurship, economic development and institutions. *Small Business Economics*, *31*(3), 219–234.

Actian. (2015). *Under Siege: Combatting Cyb Analytics*. Retrieved August 8, 2016, from http://www.actian.com/about-us/blog/siege-combatting-cyber-risk-big-data-analytics/

Adams, J. L. (2001). *Conceptual blockbusting: A guide to better ideas* (4th ed.). New York: Norton.

Adebayo, A. A., & Akanle, O. (2014). Gender and the academy in Nigeria. *African Journal for Psychological and Social Sciences Issues*, *17*(1), 147–154.

Adekola, J., Fischbacher-Smith, M., Fischbacher-Smith, D., & Adekola, O. A. (2016). Health risks from environmental degradation in the Niger Delta, Nigeria. *Environment and Planning. C, Government & Policy*. doi:10.1177/0263774X16661720

Adeoye, A. A. (2015). Examining corporate governance practices in Nigerian and South African firms. *European Journal of Accounting Auditing and Finance*, *3*(1), 10–29.

Adewale, O. F., Banjo, H., & Eluma, L. O. (2013). Presence of labour unions and performance of firms: A study of public and private firms in Nigeria. *Social Science Research Network*. Retrieved from http://ssrn.com/abstract=2634992

Adewuyi, A. O., & Olowookere, A. E. (2010). CSR and sustainable community development in Nigeria: WAPCO, a case study from the cement industry. *Social Responsibility Journal*, *6*(4), 522–535. doi:10.1108/17471111011083419

Afolabi, M. O., Dionne, S., & Lewis, H. (2009). *Are we there yet? A Review of Creativity Methodologies*. Retrieved May 19, 2015, http://www.cs.cornell.edu/Conferences/ASEE2006/ASEE%20Papers/Session%204/ASEE%20Final%20vs%203_Afolabi.pdf

Aghedo, I. (2015). Sowing peace, reaping violence: Understanding the resurgence of kidnapping in post-amnesty Niger Delta, Nigeria. *Insight on Africa*, *7*(2), 137–153. doi:10.1177/0975087815580729

Ahmad, A., Maynard, S., & Park, S. (2014). Information security strategies: Towards an organizational multi-strategy perspective. *Journal of Intelligent Manufacturing*, *25*(2), 357–370. doi:10.1007/s10845-012-0683-0

Ako, R., & Ekhator, E. O. (2016). The civil society and the regulation of the extractive industry in Nigeria. *Journal of Sustainable Development Law and Policy(The)*, *7*(1), 183–203. doi:10.4314/jsdlp.v7i1.9

Albert, I. O. (2014). Beyond moral panic: Negotiation theory and the university strikes in Nigeria.*Journal of Global Initiatives: Policy, Pedagogy. Perspective*, *9*(2), 81–98.

Alcott, B. (2010). Impact Caps: Why Population, Affluence And Technology Strategies Should Be Abandoned. *Journal of Cleaner Production*, *18*(6), 552–560. doi:10.1016/j.jclepro.2009.08.001

Aldrich, H. E., & Kim, P. H. (2007). Small worlds, infinite possibilities? How social networks affect entrepreneurial team formation and search. *Strategic Entrepreneurship Journal*, *1*(1-2), 147–165. doi:10.1002/sej.8

Alexander, S. (2011). *Property Beyond Growth: Toward A Politics Of Voluntary Simplicity* (Doctoral Dissertation).

Alexander, S., & Ussher, S. (2012). The Voluntary Simplicity Movement: A Multi-National Survey Analysis in Theoretical Context. *Journal of Consumer Culture*, *12*(1), 66–86. doi:10.1177/1469540512444019

Aliyu, A. N. (2013). Ethical leadership and good governance. *European Journal of Humanities and Social Sciences*, *27*(1), 1449–1461.

Allen, F., Qian, J., & Shen, L. (2015). *Corruption and competition*. Available at SSRN 2685219

Alperovitz, G., & Hanna, T. M. (2013). Mondragon and the system problem. *Truthout*. Retrieved on June 10, 2016 at http://www.truth-out.org/news/item/19704-mondragon-and-the-system-problem

Alperovitz, G. (2013). *What then must we do? Straight talk about the next American revolution*. White River Junction, VT: Chelsea Green Publishing.

Alston, P., & Heenan, J. (2003). Shrinking the international labour code: an unintended consequences of the 1998 ILO declaration on fundamental principles and rights at work, in: N.Y.U. *Journal of International Law and Politics*, *36*, 221–264.

Amabile, T. (1997). Motivating creativity in organizations: On doing what you love and loving what you do. *California Management Review*, *40*(1), 39–58. doi:10.2307/41165921

Amabile, T. M. (2011). How to kill creativity. In S. Johnson (Ed.), *The innovator's cookbook: Essentials for inventing what is next* (pp. 38–63). New York, NY: RiverheadBooks.

Amaeshi, K., Adegbite, E., & Rajwani, T. (2016). Corporate social responsibility in challenging and non-enabling institutional contexts: Do institutional voids matter? *Journal of Business Ethics*, *134*(1), 135–153. doi:10.1007/s10551-014-2420-4

Amann, P., & James, J. I. (2015). Designing robustness and resilience in digital investigation laboratories. *Digital Investigation*, *12*(1), S111–S120. doi:10.1016/j.diin.2015.01.015

Amorós, J. E., Bosma, N., & Levie, J. (2013). Ten years of Global Entrepreneurship Monitor: Accomplishments and prospects. *International Journal of Entrepreneurial Venturing*, *5*(2), 120–152.

Amusan, D. G., & Oyediran, M. O. (2016). Development of efficient e-recruitment system for university staff in Nigeria. *Circulation in Computer Science*, *1*(1), 10–14.

Anastasi, S. (2005). The UN Global Compact in the UK: An analysis of the achievements of the UK forum to date. *Earth and Environment*, *1*, 1–18.

Anderson, N., Potočnik, K., & Zhou, J. (2014). Innovation and creativity in organizations a state-of-the-science review, prospective commentary, and guiding framework. *Journal of Management*, *40*(5), 1297–1333. doi:10.1177/0149206314527128

Anderson, R. (1998). *Mid-Course Correction: Toward a Sustainable Enterprise: The Interface Model*. White River Junction, VT: Chelsea Green Publishing.

Anderson, R. (2009). *Confessions of a Radical Industrialist: Profits, People, Purpose. Doing Business by Respecting the Earth*. New York: St. Martin's Press.

Anders, S. B. (2015). Financial Reporting Council. *The CPA Journal*, *85*(7), 72–73.

Andreasen, A. R. (1994). Social Marketing: Its Domain and Definition. *Journal of Public Policy & Marketing*, *13*(1), 108–114.

Andreasen, A. R. (2003). The Life Trajectory of Social Marketing: Some Implications. *Marketing Theory*, *3*(3), 293–303. doi:10.1177/147059310333004

Andreasen, A. R. (2006). *Social Marketing in the 21st Century*. Sage.

Andreoni, V., & Galmarini, S. (2013). On the Increase of Social Capital in Degrowth Economy. *Procedia: Social and Behavioral Sciences*, *72*, 64–72. doi:10.1016/j.sbspro.2013.02.006

Andrews, C., & Urbanska, W. (2010). Inspiring People to See That Less is More. In L. Starke & L. Mastny (Eds.), *State of the World: Transforming Cultures from Consumerism to Sustainability* (pp. 3–20). Washington, DC: Island Press.

Andrews, R. N. L. (2012). History of environmental leadership. In D. R. Gallagher (Ed.), *Environmental leadership: A reference handbook* (Vol. 1, pp. 17–28). Los Angeles, CA: SAGE Publications. doi:10.4135/9781452218601.n3

Anielski, M. (2007). *The Economics of Happiness. Building Genuine Wealth*. New Society Press.

Antikainen, M., Mäkipää, M., & Ahonen, M. (2010). Motivating and supporting collaboration in open innovation. *European Journal of Innovation Management*, *13*(1), 100–119. doi:10.1108/14601061011013258

Arcot, S., Bruno, V., & Faure-Grimaud, A. (2010). Corporate governance in the UK: Is the comply or explain approach working? *International Review of Law and Economics*, *30*(2), 193–201. doi:10.1016/j.irle.2010.03.002

Ardichvili, A., Mitchell, J. A., & Jondle, D. (2009). Characteristics of ethical business cultures. *Journal of Business Ethics*, *4*(4), 445–451. doi:10.1007/s10551-008-9782-4

Argyris, C. (1976). Single-loop and double-loop models in research on decision making. *Administrative Science Quarterly*, *21*(3), 363–375. doi:10.2307/2391848

Argyris, C. (1980). Some limitations of the case method: Experiences in a management development program. *Academy of Management Review*, *5*(2), 291–298.

Argyris, C. (1990). *Overcoming organizational defences: Facilitating organizational learning*. Boston: Allyn and Bacon.

Argyris, C., & Schön, D. (1987). Reasoning, action strategies, and defensive routines: The case of OD practitioners. In R. A. Woodman & A. A. Pasmore (Eds.), *Research in organizational change and development* (pp. 89–128). Greenwich: JAI Press.

Argyris, C., & Schön, D. A. (1974). *Theory in practice: Increasing professional effectiveness*. London: Jossey-Bass.

Argyris, C., & Schön, D. A. (1978). *Organizational Learning: A theory of action approach*. Reading, MA: Addision Wesley.

Armstrong, M., & Murlis, K. (1994). *Reward Management: A Handbook of Remuneration Strategy and Practice* (3rd ed.). London: Kogan.

Aronczyk, M. (2013). Market(ing) Activism: Lush Cosmetics, Ethical Oil, and the Self-Mediation of Protest. *Journal Media Studies,*1-22. Available at: www.cf.ac.uk/jomecjournal

Arowosegbe, J. O. (2009). Violence and national development in Nigeria: The political economy of youth restiveness in the Niger Delta. *Review of African Political Economy*, *36*(122), 575–594. doi:10.1080/03056240903346178

Articles. (n.d.). *The benefits of creative workplace*. Retrieved August 18, 2016, from http://www.bestpracticeconsulting.com.au/_blog/Articles/post/Fostering_creativity_in_the_workplace/

Ashford, W. (2014). *Alarming level of cyber threat set for a decade, says Nato*. Retrieved September 18, 2014, from http://www.computerweekly.com/news/2240230779/Alarming-level-of-cyber-set-for-a-decade-says-Nato

Asian Development Bank. (2009). *Infrastructure for a seamless Asia*. Tokyo, Japan: Asian Development Bank and Asian Development Bank Institute.

Assaad, W., & Gómez, J. M. (2011). Social Network in marketing (Social Media Marketing) Opportunities and Risks. *International Journal of Managing Public Sector Information and Communication Technologies*, *2*(1), 13–22.

Assiter, A., & Noonan, J. (2007). Human needs. A realist perspective. *Journal of Critical Realism*, *6*(2), 173–198. doi:10.1558/jocr.v6i2.173

Ato, S. (2006). Deferring to difference, cultivating the civil commons, honouring humanity: What's the left-universalist to do? *Humanitas*, *4*, 1–12.

Attorney-General's Department. (2013). *National Plan to Combat Cybercrime*. Retrieved August 12, 2016, from Australia: https://www.ag.gov.au/CrimeAndCorruption/Cybercrime/Pages/default.aspx

Audretsch, D. B., & Thurik, A. R. (2004). *A model of the entrepreneurial economy*. Papers on entrepreneurship, growth and public policy.

Audretsch, D. B., & Link, A. N. (2012). Entrepreneurship and innovation: Public policy frameworks. *The Journal of Technology Transfer*, *37*(1), 1–17.

Ayanlade, A., & Proske, U. (2016). Assessing wetland degradation and loss of ecosystem services in the Niger Delta, Nigeria. *Marine & Freshwater Research*, *67*(6), 828–836. doi:10.1071/MF15066

Ayoola, T. J., & Olasanmi, O. O. (2013). Business case for integrated reporting in the Nigerian oil and gas sector. *Issues in Social and Environmental Accounting*, *7*(1), 30–54.

Baker, S. (2006). *Sustainable Development*. London: Routledge.

Balderjahn, I., Buerke, A., Kirchgeorg, M., Peyer, M., Seegebarth, B., & Wiedmann, K.-P. (2013). Consciousness for sustainable consumption: scale development and new insights in the economic dimension of consumers' sustainability. *AMS Review*, 1-12.

Balnave & Patmore. (in press). The outsider: lessons from the Community Co-operative Store (Nuriootpa), 1944–2010. *Business History*, 1-22.

Bamidele, J. (2015). Occupational hazards and their effect on the health and socio-economic status of local palm oil processor in Delta state, Nigeria. *Annals of Agricultural and Environmental Medicine*, *22*(3), 483–487. doi:10.5604/12321966.1167719 PMID:26403120

Bamrara, A. (2015). Evaluating Database Security and Cyber Attacks: A Rational Approach. *Journal of Internet Banking and Commerce*, *20*(2), 1–8.

Banathy, B. H. (1996). *Designing social systems in a changing world*. New York: Plenum Press. doi:10.1007/978-1-4757-9981-1

Bandi, N. (2007). *United Nations Global Compact: impact and its critics*. Retrieved May 25, 2016, from http://www.ethicalquote.com/docs/UnitedNationsGlobalCompact.pdf

Bandler, J. (2016). Dirty Digital Dollars. *Fraud*, *31*, 28–31.

Bansal, P., & Roth, K. (2000). Why companies go green: A model of ecological responsiveness. *Academy of Management Journal*, *43*(4), 717–736. doi:10.2307/1556363

Baporikar, N. (2008). Challenges of Global Management. *SYNERGY Management Research Journal*, *2*(1), 1–10.

Baporikar, N. (2011). Systems Thinking and Education for Sustainable Development a Conceptual Framework. In M. Sahay (Ed.), *System Thinking and System Dynamics, Macmillan Advanced Research Series, Macmillan Publishers India Ltd. ISBN No. 023 -032 – 296- 4* (pp. 48–63).

Baporikar, N. (2012b). Emerging Issues in sustainability Consulting. *Zenith International Journal of Multidisciplinary Research*, *2*(1), 77–89.

Baporikar, N. (2012c). Strategies for Sustainable Development – A Case Study of Carrefour. *JIDNYASA Research Journal*, *6*, 38–45.

Baporikar, N. (2013a). Strategic Approach to Talent Management. *JIDNYASA Research Journal*, *7*, 20–26.

Baporikar, N. (2013b). Understanding Talent Management in Borderless World. MANAGEMENT TODAY – International. *Journal of Management Studies*, *3*(4), 10–16.

Baporikar, N. (2013c). Entrepreneurship in a Modern Networked Indian Economy.[IJABIM]. *International Journal of Asian Business and Information Management*, *4*(4), 48–66.

Baporikar, N. (2014a). Strategic Management Overview and SME in Globalized World. In K. Todorov & D. Smallbone (Eds.), *Handbook of Research on Strategic Management in Small and Medium Enterprises* (pp. 22–39). Hershey, PA: Business Science Reference.

Baporikar, N. (2014b). Technology Imperative in Managerial Decision-Making. In E. Nikoi & K. Boateng (Eds.), *Collaborative Communication Processes and Decision Making in Organizations* (pp. 158–176). Hershey, PA: Business Science Reference.

Baporikar, N. (2014c). Business Research and New Technologies. In P. Ordóñez de Pablos & R. Tennyson (Eds.), *Strategic Approaches for Human Capital Management and Development in a Turbulent Economy* (pp. 166–192). Hershey, PA: Business Science Reference.

Baporikar, N. (2014d). Organizational Barriers and Facilitators in Embedding Knowledge Strategy. In M. Chilton & J. Bloodgood (Eds.), *Knowledge Management and Competitive Advantage: Issues and Potential Solutions* (pp. 149–173). Hershey, PA: Information Science Reference.

Baporikar, N. (2015a). Drivers of Innovation. In P. Ordoñez de Pablos, L. Turró, R. Tennyson, & J. Zhao (Eds.), *Knowledge Management for Competitive Advantage During Economic Crisis* (pp. 250–270). Hershey, PA: Business Science Reference.

Baporikar, N. (2015b). Framework for Social Change through Startups in India.[IJCESC]. *International Journal of Civic Engagement and Social Change*, *2*(1), 30–42.

Baporikar, N. (2015c). Knowledge Management in Small and Medium Enterprises. In J. Zhao, P. Ordóñez de Pablos, & R. Tennyson (Eds.), *Organizational Innovation and IT Governance in Emerging Economies* (pp. 1–20). Hershey, PA: Business Science Reference.

Baporikar, N. (2015d). Holistic Perspective of Standardization Strategies.[IJAMSE]. *International Journal of Applied Management Sciences and Engineering*, *2*(2), 54–65.

Baporikar, N. (2016a). Talent Management Integrated Approach for Organizational Development. In A. Casademunt (Ed.), *Strategic Labor Relations Management in Modern Organizations* (pp. 22–48). Hershey, PA: Business Science Reference.

Baporikar, N. (2016b). Strategies for Enhancing the Competitiveness of MNEs. In M. Khan (Ed.), *Multinational Enterprise Management Strategies in Developing Countries* (pp. 50–71). Hershey, PA: Business Science Reference.

Baporikar, N. (2016c). Corporate Governance and Value Creation: Indian Experience.[IJABIM]. *International Journal of Asian Business and Information Management*, *7*(2), 51–61.

Baporikar, N. (2016d). Holistic Approach for Balanced Scorecard as Managerial Decision Making Tool.[IJSDA]. *International Journal of System Dynamics Applications*, *5*(1), 31–42.

Baporikar, N., & Deshpande, M. (2012a). Sustainable Entrepreneurship - Approach of Pune Auto Components Entrepreneurs. In A. Marcus & J. J. Rayappa (Eds.), *Entrepreneurship, Youth and Inclusive Development for Brand India* (pp. 313–320). Chennai, India: Loyala Publications.

Barber, N. (2014). Integrating sustainability into business curricula: University of New Hampshire case study. *International Journal of Sustainability in Higher Education*, *15*(4), 473–493. doi:10.1108/IJSHE-06-2013-0068

Barbuto, J. E. (2005). Motivation and transactional, charismatic and transformational leadership: A test of antecedence. *Journal of Leadership & Organizational Studies*, *2*(4), 25–40.

Barling, D., Lang, T., & Lele, U. (2012). Increasing Resource Efficiencies: Sustainable Production and Consumption in Food Systems. In Avoiding Future Famines: Strengthening the Ecological Foundation of Food Security through Sustainable Food Systems (pp. 29-38).

Baron, D. P. (2003). Private Politics. *Journal of Economics & Management Strategy*, *12*(1), 31–66. doi:10.1162/105864003321220724

Baron, S., Conway, T., & Warnaby, G. (2010). *Relationship Marketing: A Consumer Experience Approach*. London: Sage.

Barrutia, J., & Echebarria, C. (2011). Networks: A Social Marketing Tool. *European Journal of Marketing*, *47*(1/2), 324–343. doi:10.1108/03090561311285574

Bartnes, M., Moe, N. B., & Heegaard, P. E. (2016). The future of information security incident management training: A case study of electrical power companies. *Computers & Security*, *61*, 32–45. doi:10.1016/j.cose.2016.05.004

Baruchello, G. (2007). Western philosophy and the life-ground. In Encyclopedia of Life Support Systems. Paris: Eolss. Retrieved from http://www.eolss.net

Baruchello, G. (2014). The presupposed oncological model of Paul Krugman's banking metastases. An introduction to John McMurtry's philosophy. *Annuaire international des droits de l'homme*, *7*, 347–352.

Baruchello, G. (2001). Review essay of the book *The Cancer Stage of Capitalism*, by J. McMurtry. *Revue Canadienne d'Etudes du Developpement*, *22*(1), 255–269. doi:10.1080/02255189.2001.9668809

Baruchello, G. (2011). Your money or your life. John McMurtry and Martha Nussbaum on the for-profit assault upon life-capabilities. *Journal of Philosophy of Life*, *1*(1), 13–48.

Baruchello, G. (in press). Good versus bad tourism. *Homo viator*'s responsibility in light of life-value onto-axiology. In E. Hujibens & M. Gren (Eds.), *Tourism in the Anthropocene*. London: Routledge.

Baruchello, G., & Johnstone, R. L. (2011). Rights and value. Construing the International Covenant on Economic, Social and Cultural Rights as Civil Commons. *Studies in Social Justice*, *5*(1), 91–126.

Bass, B. M., & Steidlmeier, P. (1999). Ethics, character, and authentic transformational leadership behavior. *The Leadership Quarterly*, *10*(2), 181–217. doi:10.1016/S1048-9843(99)00016-8

Batabyal, A. A., & Nijkamp, P. (2012). A Schumpeterian Model of Entrepreneurship, Innovation, and Regional Economic Growth. *International Regional Science Review*, *35*(3), 339–361.

Bates, W. (2009). Gross national happiness. *Asian-Pacific Economic Literature*, *23*(2), 1–16.

Baumann-Pauly, D., & Scherer, A. G. (2013). The organizational implementation of corporate citizenship: An assessment tool and its application at UN Global Compact participants. *Journal of Business Ethics*, *117*(1), 1–17. doi:10.1007/s10551-012-1502-4

Beauregard, E. (2015). *Top Ten Reasons Climate Change is a Hoax*. Retrieved May 25, 2016, from http://www.globalclimatescam.com/opinion/top-ten-reasons-climate-change-is-a-hoax/

Becchetti, L., & Rosati, F. C. (2007). Global Social Preferences and the Demand for Socially Responsible Products: Empirical Evidence from a Pilot Study on Fair Trade Consumers. *World Economy*, *1*(1), 807–836. doi:10.1111/j.1467-9701.2007.01012.x

Behrangrad, M. (2015). A review of demand side management business models in the electricity market. *Renewable & Sustainable Energy Reviews*, *47*, 270–283. doi:10.1016/j.rser.2015.03.033

Belcher, L. M. (n.d.). *Advantages and Disadvantages of Technology Advances*. Retrieved August 19, 2016, from http://smallbusiness.chron.com/advantages-disadvantages-technology-advances-12579.html

Bell, D., & Heitmueller, A. (2009). The disability discrimination ACT in the UK: Helping or hindering employment among the disabled? *Journal of Health Economics*, *28*(2), 465–480. doi:10.1016/j.jhealeco.2008.10.006 PMID:19091434

Bello, S. M. (2012). Impact of ethical leadership on employee job performance. *International Journal of Business and Social Science*, *3*(11), 228–236.

Ben-Chendo, G. N., Lemch, J. I., Ohajianya, D. O., Eze, C. C., Emeyeonu, C., & Ehirim, N. C. (2012). Household poverty and its effect on child labour use among palm oil processors in Abia state, Nigeria. *Journal of Developing Societies*, *1*(1), 27–30.

Bendix, S. (2005). *Industrial Relations in South Africa* (4th ed.). Lansdowne: Juta.

Bennet, A., & Bennet, D. (2007). *Knowledge mobilization in the social sciences and humanities: Moving from research to action*. Frost, WV: MQI Press.

Bennett, W. L. (2008). *Civic Life Online Learning How Digital Media Can Engage Youth*. London: Mitt Press.

Benyus, J. M. (2002). *Biomimicry: Innovation Inspired by Nature*. New York, NY: Perennial.

Berg, B. L., & Lune, H. (2004). *Qualitative research methods for the social sciences* (Vol. 5). Boston: Pearson.

Berry, D., & Ormond, A. (2015). An Unstable State: Conflict and Institutional Change in the Electric Industry. *The Electricity Journal*, *28*(2), 63–73. doi:10.1016/j.tej.2015.01.010

Berthold, M. (Ed.). (2012). Bisociative knowledge discovery: An introduction to concept, algorithms, tools, and applications. Heidelberg, Germany: Springer. doi:10.1007/978-3-642-31830-6

Bertino, E. (2016). Security Threats: Protecting the New Cyberfrontier. *Computer*, *49*(6), 11–14. doi:10.1109/MC.2016.188

Bhattacharya, A., Mohapatra, P., Kumar, V., Dey, P. K., Brady, M., Tiwari, M. K., & Nudurupati, S. S. (2014). Green supply chain performance measurement using fuzzy ANP-based balanced scorecard: A collaborative decision-making approach. *Production Planning and Control*, *25*(8), 698–714. doi:10.1080/09537287.2013.798088

Bhatti, B. M., & Sami, N. (2015). *Building adaptive defence against cybercrimes using real-time data mining*. Paper presented at the First International Conference on Anti-Cybercrime, Riyadh.

Bilton, C., & Cummings, S. (2014). A framework for creative management and managing creativity. In C. Bilton & S. Cummings (Eds.), *Handbook of management and creativity* (pp. 1–12). Cheltenham, UK: Edward Elgar. doi:10.4337/9781781000977.00007

Binns, T., & Nel, E. (1999). Beyond the development impasse: The role of local economic development and community. *The Journal of Modern African Studies*, *37*(3), 389.

Bissola, R., & Imperatori, B. (2011). Organizing individual and collective creativity: Flying in the face of creativity clichés. *Creativity and Innovation Management*, *20*(2), 77–89. doi:10.1111/j.1467-8691.2011.00597.x

Blakeman, R. (2013). *Nontraditional Media in Marketing and Advertising*. SAGE Publications.

Block, J., & Koellinger, P. (2009). I Can't Get No Satisfaction—Necessity Entrepreneurship and Procedural Utility. *Kyklos*, *62*(2), 191–209.

Bocken, N., Short, S., Rana, P., & Evans, S. (2014). A literature and practice review to develop sustainable business model archetypes. *Journal of Cleaner Production*, *65*, 42–56. doi:10.1016/j.jclepro.2013.11.039

Boden, M. A. (2004). *The creative mind: Myths and mechanisms* (2nd ed.). London: Routledge.

Boden, M. A. (2004). *The Creative Mind: Myths and Mechanisms*. London: Routledge.

Bodhanya, S. (2014). The nexus model for local economic development. *Problems and Perspectives in Management, 12*(3).

Boillat, S., Gerber, J.-F., & Funes-Monzote, F. (2012). What Economic Democracy for Degrowth? Some Comments on the Contribution of Socialist Models and Cuban Agroecology. *Futures, 44*(6), 600–607. doi:10.1016/j.futures.2012.03.021

Bollier, D. (2014). *Managing digital assets: The challenge of creating and sustaining intangible value in a data-driven economy*. Washington, DC: Aspen Institute.

Bollier, D. (2016). *The city as platform: How digital networks are changing urban life and governance*. Washington, DC: Aspen Institute.

Bolton, D. L., & Lane, M. D. (2012). Individual Entrepreneurial Orientation: Development of a Measurement Instrument. *Education + Training, 54*(2-3), 219–233.

Bonaiuti, M. (2011). *From Bioeconomics to Degrowth: Georgescu-Roegen's "New Economics" in Eight Essays*. London: Routledge.

Boons, F., & Berends, M. (2001). Stretching the boundary: The possibilities of flexibility as an organizational capability in industrial ecology. *Business Strategy and the Environment, 10*(2), 115–124. doi:10.1002/bse.277

Boons, F., & Lüdeke-Freund, F. (2013). Business models for sustainable innovation: State of the art and steps towards a research agenda. *Journal of Cleaner Production, 45*, 9–19. doi:10.1016/j.jclepro.2012.07.007

Borowy, I. (2013). Degrowth and Public Health in Cuba: Lessons from the Past? *Journal of Cleaner Production, 38*, 17–26. doi:10.1016/j.jclepro.2011.11.057

Bosma, N. (2013). The global entrepreneurship monitor (GEM) and its impact on entrepreneurship research. *Foundations and Trends in Entrepreneurship, 9*(2).

Boulianne, S. (2015). Social media use and participation: A meta-analysis of current research. *Information Communication and Society, 18*(5), 524–538. doi:10.1080/1369118X.2015.1008542

Bowman, B., & Stone, B. (2005). *Cooperativization as Alternative to Globalizing Capitalism*. Retrieved November 24, 2015, from http://www.geo.coop/archives/bowmanstone1104.htm

Boyer, S. (2016). *The Importance of Collaboration in the Workplace*. Retrieved August 18, 2016, from http://www.nutcache.com/blog/the-importance-of-collaboration-in-the-workplace/

Braide, O., Remoue, C., Rat, G., Anozie, I., Vandeville, P., Ahiamadu, N., & Ganga, D. et al. (2016). Gas flaring reduction initiative Ofon phase 2 project. In *SPE International Conference and Exhibition on Health, Safety, Security, Environment, and Social Responsibility*. Society of Petroleum Engineers. doi:10.2118/179340-MS

Brammer, S., Hoejmose, S., & Marchant, K. (2012). Environment management in SMEs in the UK: Practices, pressures and perceived benefits. *Business Strategy and the Environment, 21*(7), 423–434. doi:10.1002/bse.717

Brenkert, G. (2002). Ethical Challenges in Social Marketing. *Journal of Public Policy & Marketing, 21*(1), 14–25. doi:10.1509/jppm.21.1.14.17601

Brennan, L., & Binney, W. (2008). Concepts in Conflict: Social Marketing and Sustainability. *Journal of Nonprofit & Public Sector Marketing, 20*(2), 261–281. doi:10.1080/10495140802224951

Brennan, L., & Binney, W. (2010). Fear, guilt and shame appeals in social marketing. *Journal of Business Research, 63*(2), 140–146. doi:10.1016/j.jbusres.2009.02.006

Breugst, N., Patzelt, H., & Rathgeber, P. (2015). How should we divide the pie? Equity distribution and its impact on entrepreneurial teams. *Journal of Business Venturing, 30*(1), 66–94. doi:10.1016/j.jbusvent.2014.07.006

Briassoulis, H. (2010). Online petitions: New tools of secondary analysis? *Qualitative Research, 10*(6), 715–727. doi:10.1177/1468794110380530

Brixiova, Z., & Kangoye, T. (2014). *Youth employment in Africa: new evidence and policies from Swaziland*. Springer.

Brixy, U., Sternberg, R., & Stüber, H. (2012). The selectiveness of the entrepreneurial process. *Journal of Small Business Management, 50*(1), 105–131. doi:10.1111/j.1540-627X.2011.00346.x

Brooks, C. (2015). The periodic table of the electric utility landscape: A series of visual tools for enhanced policy analysis. *The Electricity Journal, 28*(6), 82–95. doi:10.1016/j.tej.2015.06.009

Broto, V., & Bulkeley, H. (2013). A survey of urban climate change experiments in 100 cities. *Global Environmental Change, 23*(1), 92–102. doi:10.1016/j.gloenvcha.2012.07.005 PMID:23805029

Brown, L. H. (1997). Organizations for the 21st Century? Co-operatives and" New" forms of organization. *Canadian Journal of Sociology/Cahiers canadiens de sociologie*, 65-93.

Brownbridge, M. (1998). Financial distress in local banks in Kenya, Nigeria, Uganda and Zambia: Causes and implications for regulatory policy. *Development Policy Review, 16*(2), 173–188. doi:10.1111/1467-7679.00057

Brown, J., & Isaacs, D. (2005). *The World Café: Shaping our futures through conversations that matter*. Oakland, CA: Berrett-Koehler Publishers.

Bruegel, I., & Perrons, D. (1998). Deregulation and women's employment: The diverse experiences of women in Britain. *Feminist Economics, 4*(1), 103–125. doi:10.1080/135457098338581

Bruer. (1993). *Schools for thought: A science of learning in the classroom*. Cambridge, MA: MIT Press.

Brundtland, G. H. (1987). *Our Common Future, World Commission on Environment and Development*. Oxford University Press.

Brunner, R., & Emery, S. (2006). *Do you matter? How great design will make people love your company*. Upper Saddle River, NJ: Pearson Education.

Burch, M. A. (2012). *Educating for Simple Living*. Simplicity Institute Report.

Burch, S., Shaw, A., Dale, A., & Robinson, J. (2014). Triggering transformative change: A development path approach to climate change response in communities. *Climate Policy, 14*(4), 467–487. doi:10.1080/14693062.2014.876342

Burke, C. S., Stagl, K. C., Klein, C., Goodwin, G. F., Salas, E., & Halpin, S. M. (2006). What types of leadership behaviours are functional in teams? A meta-analysis. *The Leadership Quarterly, 17*(3), 288–307. doi:10.1016/j.leaqua.2006.02.007

Burns, G. W. (2011). *Gross National Happiness: A gift from Bhutan to the world. Positive psychology as social change*. Springer.

Burrell, S. C. (2000). *Planning and implementing an E-Business strategy: Administrative, instructional and web portal systems*. Retrieved on June 13, 2016 at http://faculty.saintleo.du/burrell/ebusiness.htm

Burr, M. (2007). Razing the regulatory compact. *Public Utilities Fortnightly, 145*(9), 18–20.

Burton, A. (2005). *The British Consumer Co-operative Movement and Film, 1890s-1960s*. Manchester University Press.

Bushe, G. R. (2011). Appreciative inquiry: Theory and critique. In D. Boje, B. Burnes, & J. Hassard (Eds.), *The Routledge companion to organizational change* (pp. 87–103). Oxford, UK: Routledge. doi:10.4324/9780203810279.ch6

Bushe, G. R. (2013). Dialogic OD: A theory of practice. *Organization Development Practitioner*, *45*(1), 10–16.

BusinessDictionary. (2015). *Business Dictionary*. New York, NY: BusinessDictionary.

Bussin, M. (2013). *The Performance Management Handbook for Emerging Markets*. Randburg: Knowres Publishing.

Butler, M. (2016).Equality and anti-discrimination law: the Equality Act 2010 and other anti-discrimination protections. London: Spiramus Publishing.

Byars & Rue. (2004). *Human Resource Management: A Practical Approach*. New York: Harcourt Brace.

Byrne, J., & Taminiau, J. (2015). A review of sustainable energy utility and energy service utility concepts and applications: realizing ecological and social sustainability with a community utility. *WIREs Energy Environ.*

Byrne, J., Martinez, C., & Ruggero, C. (2009). Relocating Energy in the Social Commons: Ideas for a Sustainable Energy Utility. *Bulletin of Science, Technology & Society*, *2*(2), 81–94. doi:10.1177/0270467609332315

Byrne, J., & McDowell, H. (2007). *The Sustainable Energy Utility: A Delaware First*. Sustainable Energy Utility Task Force.

Cabello, J. J., Garcia, D., Sagastume, A., Priego, R., Hens, L., & Vandecasteele, C. (2012). An Approach toSustainable Development: The Case of Cuba. *Environment, Development and Sustainability*, *14*(4), 573–591. doi:10.1007/s10668-012-9338-8

Caldwell, R. M., & Childs, H. (1977). *Acquisition of Specific Teaching Behaviors Through a Teacher Center Consortium*. Academic Press.

Calegar, B. (2013). *Findhorn EcoVillage, Scotland*. Retrieved 16 March, 2016, from http://sd.appstate.edu/academics/study-abroad/findhorn-ecovillage-scotland

California Department of Justice. (2014). *California Data Breach*. Retrieved July 20, 2015, from California: http://oag.ca.gov/sites/all/files/agweb/pdfs/privacy/2014data_breach_rpt.pdf?

Cambridge Reports. (1989). *National omnibus survey*. Storrs, CT: Roper Center for Public Opinion Research, University of Connecticut. July.

Campbell, B. (2013). *The Importance of Collaboration in Today's Workplace*. Retrieved August 12, 2016, from http://www.elcomcms.com/en-au/Resources/Elcom-Blog/Posts/the-importance-of-collaboration-in-todays-workplace

Canon, J. (2015). Cyberinsurance The Challenge of Transferring Failure in a Digital, Globalized World. *ISACA*, *5*, 37–42.

Caprotti, F. (2012). The cultural economy of cleantech: Environmental discourse and the emergence of a new technology sector. *Transactions of the Institute of British Geographers*, *37*(3), 370–385. doi:10.1111/j.1475-5661.2011.00485.x

Carby-Hall, J. (2016). Labour aspects of corporate social responsibility emanating from the United Nations Global Compact: The global case and that of the EU and the United Kingdom. *E-Journal of International and Comparative Labour Studies, 5*(2).

Carducci, V. (2006). Culture Jamming A Sociological Perspective. *Journal of Consumer Culture*, *6*(1), 116–138. doi:10.1177/1469540506062722

Carroll, A. B. (2004). Managing ethically with global stakeholders: A present and future challenge. *The Academy of Management Executive*, *18*(2), 114–120. doi:10.5465/AME.2004.13836269

Carroll, A. B., & Shabana, K. M. (2010). The business case for corporate social responsibility: A review of concepts, research and practice. *International Journal of Management Reviews*, *12*(1), 85–105. doi:10.1111/j.1468-2370.2009.00275.x

Carter, B. (2012). *The like economy: How businesses make money with facebook* (1st ed.). Indianapolis, IN: Que Publishing.

CaseWare. (2016). *Role of Data Analytics for Internal Fraud Detection*. Retrieved August 10, 2016, from United States of America: http://www.casewareanalytics.com/sites/default/files/whitepapers/global_benchmark.pdf

Castoriadis, C. (2003). Psychoanalysis and society I. In *The Rising Tide of Insignificancy (The Big Sleep)*. Available from http://www.notbored.org (Original work published 1982)

Castro, C. (2004). Sustainable Development: Mainstream and Critical Perspectives. *Organization & Environment*, *17*(2), 225. doi:10.1177/1086026604264910

CBSM. (2010). *Community-based Social Marketing: Case Studies*. Retrieved March 23, 2016 from http://www.cbsm.com/cases/search

Cecchetti, S. G., Mohanty, M. S., & Zampolli, F. (2011). *The real effects of debt* (BIS working papers, no. 352). Retrieved from http://www.bis.org/publ/work352.htm

Centindamar, D. (2007). Corporate social responsibility practice and environmental responsible behaviour: The case of the United Nations Global Impact. *Journal of Business Ethics*, *76*(2), 163–176. doi:10.1007/s10551-006-9265-4

Cetina, K. K. (1999). *Epistemic cultures: How the sciences make knowledge*. Cambridge, MA: Harvard University Press.

Chance, T. (2009). Towards Sustainable Residential Communities; The Beddington Zero Energy Development (BedZED) and beyond. *Environment and Urbanization*, *21*(2), 527–544. doi:10.1177/0956247809339007

Chaplier, J. (2014, February). EU to force large companies to report on environmental and social impacts. *The Guardian*. Retrieved from http://www.theguardian.com/sustainable-business/eu-reform-listed-companies-report-environmental-social-impact

Chaturvedi, M., Unal, A., Aggarwal, P., Bahl, S., & Malik, S. (2014). *International cooperation in cyber space to combat cybercrime and terrorism*. Paper presented at the Norbert Wiener in the 21st Century IEEE Conference.

Checkland, P. (1999). *Systems thinking, systems practice: includes a 30-year retrospective*. Wiley.

Chen, S., & Bouvain, P. (2009). Is corporate responsibility converging? A comparison of corporate responsibility reporting in the USA, UK, Australia and Germany. *Journal of Business Ethics*, *87*(S1), 299–317. doi:10.1007/s10551-008-9794-0

Chen, Y. S., & Chang, C. H. (2013). The determinants of green product development performance: Green dynamic capabilities, green transformational leadership, and green creativity. *Journal of Business Ethics*, *116*(1), 107–119. doi:10.1007/s10551-012-1452-x

Chen, Y. S., Chang, C. H., Yeh, S. L., & Cheng, H. I. (2015). Green shared vision and green creativity: The mediation roles of green mindfulness and green self-efficacy. *Quality & Quantity*, *49*(3), 1169–1184. doi:10.1007/s11135-014-0041-8

Chesbrough, H. (2007). Business model innovation: it's not just about technology anymore. *Strategic Leadership*, 12-17.

Chesbrough, C., & Rosenbloom, R. (2002). The role of the business model in capturing value from innovation: Evidence from Xerox corporation's technology spin-off companies. *Industrial and Corporate Change*, *11*(3), 529–555. doi:10.1093/icc/11.3.529

Chesbrough, H. (2010). Business model innovation: Opportunities and barriers. *Long Range Planning*, *43*(2), 354–363. doi:10.1016/j.lrp.2009.07.010

Chidi, O.C. (2013). Recruitment practices and performance of unionised organisations in the food, beverage and tobacco industry in Lagos state, Nigeria. *Interdisciplinary Journal of Contemporary Research in Business, 5*(6), 359-384.

Chin, M. K., Hambrick, D. C., & Trevino, C. K. (2013). Political ideologies of CEOs: The influence of executives' values on corporate of social responsibilities. *Administrative Science Quarterly*, *58*(2), 197–232. doi:10.1177/0001839213486984

Chowdhury, S. (2005). Demographic diversity for building an effective entrepreneurial team: Is it important? *Journal of Business Venturing*, *20*(6), 727–746. doi:10.1016/j.jbusvent.2004.07.001

Churchman, C. W. (1967). Wicked problems. *Management Science, 4*(14), B-141-B-142.

CICA. (2009). *Climate Change Briefing: Questions for Directors to Ask*. Toronto: Canadian Institute of Chartered Accountants.

Cicin-Sain, B., Balgos, M., Appiott, J., Wowk, K., & Hamon, G. (2011). *Oceans at Rio+20: How well are we doing in meeting the commitments from the 1992 Earth Summit and the 2002 World Summit on Sustainable Development? Summary for decision-makers.* Global Ocean Forum.

CISCO. (2010). *Cybersecurity: Everyone's Responsibility*. Retrieved August 16, 2016, from http://www.cisco.com/c/dam/en_us/solutions/industries/docs/education/C45-626825-00_Cyber_Security_Responsibility_AAG.pdf

Clarke, S. F., & Roome, N. J. (1995). Managing for environmentally sensitive technology: Networks for collaboration and learning. *Technology Analysis and Strategic Management*, *7*(2), 191–216. doi:10.1080/09537329508524204

Climate Action Tracker. (2015, November 19). *Tracking INDCs*. Retrieved April 28, 2015 from Climate Action Tracker: http://climateactiontracker.org/indcs.html

Climate Bonds Initiative. (2015). *Bonds and climate change: state of the market in 2015*. Climate Bonds Initiative.

Climate Bonds Initiative. (2015). *Year 2015 green bonds final report*. Climate Bonds Initiative.

Coase, R. H. (1937). The nature of the firm. *Economica*, *4*(16), 386–405. doi:10.1111/j.1468-0335.1937.tb00002.x

Code, C. (2003). *The combined code on corporate governance*. London: Financial Reporting Council.

Cole, E. J., & Fieselman, L. (2013). A community-based social marketing campaign at Pacific University Oregon: Recycling, paper reduction, and environmentally preferable purchasing. *International Journal of Sustainability in Higher Education*, *14*(2), 176–195. doi:10.1108/14676371311312888

Collins, E. (2013). Labour unionism and its effect on organizational productivity: A case study of Jos International Breweries(JIB) PLC, Nigeria. *African Research Review*, *7*(4), 36–48.

Common, M., & Stagl, S. (2005). *Ecological Economics: An Introduction*. Cambridge, UK: Cambridge University Press. doi:10.1017/CBO9780511805547

Conaway, O., & Laasch, N. (2015). *Principles of Responsible Management Education*. Stamford, CT: Cengage Learning.

Constanza, R., Alperovitz, G., Daly, H., Farley, J., Franco, C., Jackson, T., & Victor, P. et al. (2013). Building a Sustainable and Desirable Economy-in-Society-in-Nature. In L. Starke (Ed.), *State of the World: Is Sustainability Still Possible?* (pp. 230–256). Washington, DC: Island Press.

Conway, S., & Steward, F. (2009). *Managing and shaping innovation*. New York, NY: Oxford University.

Co-Operative Bank. (2003). *The ethical consumer report*. London: Co-Operative Bank.

Cooper, R. (2001). *Winning at new products: accelerating the process from idea to launch*. New York: Harper Collins.

Core, J., Holthausen, R., & Larcker, D. (1999). Corporate Governance, CEO Compensation, and firm performance. *Journal of Financial Economics*, *51*, 371–406. doi:10.1016/S0304-405X(98)00058-0

Costa. R, Enric. J, Badal. R, Ángel. M. (2000). *Environmental strategy and value creation*. IESE, DI-408-E, 02/2000.

CPSL. (2010). *Sustainability Leadership: A Force for Change*. Cambridge, UK: University of Cambridge.

Cropley, D. H. (2016). Creative products: Defining and measuring novel solutions. In J. Plucker (Ed.), *Creativity and Innovation: Theory, Research, and Practice* (pp. 61–74). Austin, TX: Prufrock.

Cropley, D. H., & Cropley, A. J. (2010). Functional Creativity: Products and the generation of effective novelty. In J. C. Kaufman & R. J. Sternberg (Eds.), *Cambridge Handbook of Creativity* (pp. 301–320). New York, NY: Cambridge University. doi:10.1017/CBO9780511763205.019

Crosby, S. (2015). *Changing the Economics of Cybersecurity*. Retrieved December 7, 2015, from SecurityWeek website: http://www.securityweek.com/changing-economics-cybersecurity

Crossley, N. (2002). Global Anti-corporate Struggle: A Preliminary Analysis. *The British Journal of Sociology*, *53*(4), 667–691. doi:10.1080/0007131022000021542 PMID:12556289

Culmsee, P., & Awati, K. (Eds.). (2011). The heretic's guide to best practices: The reality of managing complex problems in organizations. Blomington, IL: iUniverse.

Curl, J. (2012). *For all the people: Uncovering the hidden history of cooperation, cooperative movements, and communalism in America* (2nd ed.). Oakland, CA: PM Press.

D'Amato, A., Henderson, S., & Florence, S. (2009). *Corporate Social responsibility and sustainable business a guide to leadership tasks and functions*. Center for Creative Leadership.

Da Cruz, N. F., Ferreira, S., Cabra, M., Simoes, P., & Marques, R. C. (2014). Packaging waste recycling in Europe: Is the industry paying for it? *Waste Management (New York, N.Y.)*, *34*(2), 298–308. doi:10.1016/j.wasman.2013.10.035 PMID:24262429

Dale-Olsen, H. (2012). Executive Pay Determination and Firm Performance – Empirical Evidence from a Compressed Wage Environment. *The Manchester School*, *80*(3), 355–376. doi:10.1111/j.1467-9957.2011.02225.x

Damballa. (2014). *Advanced Threat Detection for the 21st Century: Integrating Big Data Intelligence to Enable Breach Prevention*. Retrieved from http://forms.madisonlogic.com/FormConfirmation.aspx?pub=18&pgr=259&src=2318&cmp=13396&ast=41496&frm=446&pd=3147146-19-7-57-336-0

Damiyano, D., Muchabaiwa, L., Mushanyuri, B. E., & Chikomba, C. P. (2012). An investigation of Zimbabwe's manufacturing sector competitiveness. *International Journal of Development and Sustainability*, *1*(2), 581–598.

Daramola, A., & Ibem, E. O. (2010). Urban environmental problems in Nigeria: Implications for sustainable development. *Journal of Sustainable Development in Nigeria*, *12*(1), 124–145.

Darlington, R. (2014). Strike waves, union growth and the rank-and-file/bureaucracy interplay: Britain 1889-1890, 1910-1913 and 1919-1920. *Labour History*, *55*(1), 1–20. doi:10.1080/0023656X.2013.871476

Davidson-Harden, A. (2013). What is social sciences and humanities research 'worth'? Neoliberalism and the framing of social sciences and humanities work in Canada. *Policy Futures in Education*, *11*(4), 387–400. doi:10.2304/pfie.2013.11.4.387

Davis, G., McAdam, D., Scott, W. R., & Zald, M. (2005). *Social Movements and Organization Theory*. London: Cambridge University Press. doi:10.1017/CBO9780511791000

Davis, P., & Rickford, J. (2008). An introduction to the new UK Company's Act. *European and Financial Law*, *5*(1), 48–71.

Dawn King, M. (2012, March). *Cuban Sustainability: The Effects of Economic Isolation on Agriculture and Energy*. Paper presented to the Western Political Science Association, Portland, OR.

Dawson, J. (2009). Findhorn's Incredible Shrinking Footprint. *Communities*, *143*, 26–71.

de Barcellos, M. D., Krystallis, A., de Melo Saab, M. S., Kügler, J. O., & Grunert, K. G. (2011). Investigating the gap between citizens' sustainability attitudes and food purchasing behaviour: Empirical evidence from Brazilian pork consumers. *International Journal of Consumer Studies*, *35*(4), 391–402. doi:10.1111/j.1470-6431.2010.00978.x

De Hoogh, A. H. B., & Den Hartog, D. N. (2008). Ethical and despotic leadership, relationships with leader's social responsibility, top management team effectiveness and subordinates' optimism: A multi-method study. *The Leadership Quarterly*, *19*(3), 297–311. doi:10.1016/j.leaqua.2008.03.002

De Montclos, M. A. P. (2014). The politics and crisis of the petroleum industry bill of Nigeria. *The Journal of Modern African Studies*, *52*(3), 403–424. doi:10.1017/S0022278X1400024X

De Sousa, F. C., Pellissier, R., & Monteiro, I. P. (2012). Creativity, Innovation and Collaborative Organizations. *The International Journal of Organizational Innovation*, *5*(1), 26–64.

De Tienne, D. R., & Chandler, G. N. (2004). Opportunity identification and its role in the entrepreneurial classroom: A pedagogical approach and empirical test. *Academy of Management Learning & Education*, *3*(3), 242–257. doi:10.5465/AMLE.2004.14242103

de Zúñiga, H. G., Copeland, L., & Bimber, B. (2014). Political consumerism: Civic engagement and the social media connection. *New Media & Society*, *16*(3), 488–506. doi:10.1177/1461444813487960

Decuyper, S., Dochy, F., & Van den Bossche, P. (2010). Grasping the dynamic complexity of team learning: An integrative model for effective team learning in organisations. *Educational Research Review*, *5*(2), 111–133. doi:10.1016/j.edurev.2010.02.002

DeFillippi, R., Grabher, G., & Jones, C. (2007). Introduction to paradoxes of creativity: Managerial and organizational challenges in the cultural economy. *Journal of Organizational Behavior*, *28*(5), 511–521.

Del-Corte-Lora, V., Vallet-Bellmunt, T., & Molina-Morales, F. X. (2015). Be creative but not so much. Decreasing benefits of creativity in clustered firms. *Entrepreneurship & Regional Development*, *27*(1-2), 1–27. doi:10.1080/08985626.2014.995722

Dell'Amore, C. (2014). *Species Extinction Happening 1,000 Times Faster Because of Humans? National Geographic Reports*. Retrieved May 25, 2016, from http://news.nationalgeographic.com/news/2014/05/140529-conservation-science-animals-species-endangered-extinction/

Deloitte. (2013). *Cybercrime fighting*. Retrieved August 5, 2016, from http://dupress.com/articles/cyber-crime-fighting/

Demaria, F., Schneider, F., Sekulova, F., & Martinez-Alier, J. (2013). What is Degrowth? From an Activist Slogan to a Social Movement. *Environmental Values*, *22*(2), 191–215. doi:10.3197/096327113X13581561725194

Demirel, P., & Kesidou, E. (2011). Stimulating different types of eco-innovation in the UK. Government policies and firm innovations. *Ecological Economics*, *70*(8), 1546–1557. doi:10.1016/j.ecolecon.2011.03.019

Denscombe, M. (2010). *Good research guide: For small-scale social research projects* (4th ed.). Berkshire, UK: Open University Press.

Department of Homeland Security. (2015). *Cybersecurity Overview*. Retrieved August 16, 2016, from https://www.dhs.gov/cybersecurity-overview

Depledge, J., & Yamin, F. (2011). The Global Climate-change Regime: A Defence. In D. Helm & C. Hepburn (Eds.), *The Economics and Politics of Climate Change* (pp. 433–453). Oxford, UK: Oxford University Press.

Deriu, M. (2012). Democracies with a Future: Degrowth and the Democratic Tradition. *Futures*, *44*(6), 553–561. doi:10.1016/j.futures.2012.03.016

Dewing, M. (2012). *Social Media: An introduction*. Library of Parliament.

Dey, P., & Steyaert, C. (2010). The politics of narrating social entrepreneurship. *Journal of Enterprising Communities: People and Places in the Global Economy*, *4*(1), 85–108. doi:10.1108/17506201011029528

Dickinson, T., Becerra, T. A., & Lewis, S. (Eds.). (2009). *Democracy Works. Joining Theory and Action to Foster Global Change*. Herndon: Paradigm Publishers.

Dimireva, I. (2012, February). Doing business in the UK: Sustainability. *EU Business*. Retrieved from http://www.eubusiness.com/europe/uk/sustainable-business

Doane, D. (2005). Beyond corporate social responsibility: Minnows, mammoths and markets. *Futures*, *37*(2-3), 215–229. doi:10.1016/j.futures.2004.03.028

Dobbs, R., Pohl, H., Lin, D.-Y., Mischke, J., Garemo, N., & Hexter, J. (2013). *Infrastructure productivity: how to save $1 trillion a year*. McKinsey Global Institute.

Domegan, C. (2008). Social Marketing: Implications for Contemporary Marketing Practices Classification Scheme. *Journal of Business and Industrial Marketing*, *23*(2), 135–141. doi:10.1108/08858620810850254

Doner, R. F., & Schneider, B. R. (2000). Business associations and economic development: Why some associations contribute more than others. *Business and Politics*, *2*(3), 261–288. doi:10.2202/1469-3569.1011

Donnelly, J. (2013). *Universal human rights in theory and practice*. Cornell University Press.

Doyal, O. L., & Gough, I. (1991). *A Theory of Human Need*. London: MacMillan. doi:10.1007/978-1-349-21500-3

Druzdzel, M. J., & Flynn, R. R. (2000). Decision support systems. In A. Kent (Ed.), *Encyclopedia of library and information science* (pp. 120–133). New York: Marcel Dekker.

Dubitzky, W., Kotter, T., Schmidt, O., & Berthold, M. R. (2012). Towards creative information exploration based on Koestler's concept of bisociation. In Bisociative knowledge discovery: An introduction to concept, algorithms, tools, and applications (pp.11 - 32). Heidelberg, Germany: Springer.

Dudzevičiūtė, G. (2012). Conceptual approaches towards sustainability. *Journal of Security and Sustainability Issues*, *1*(4), 261–272. doi:10.9770/jssi.2012.1.4(3)

Dugan, J. P., & Komives, S. R. (2010). Influence on college students' capacities for socially responsible leadership. *Journal of College Student Development*, *51*(5), 525–549. doi:10.1353/csd.2010.0009

Durbins, S. (2013). *Use big data to fight cybercrime*. Retrieved August 5, 2016, from http://www.techrepublic.com/blog/tech/-decision-maker/use-big-data-to-fight-cybercrime/2/

Du, S., Swaen, V., & Lindgreen, A. (2013). The roles of leadership styles in CSR. *Journal of Business Ethics, 114*(1), 155–169. doi:10.1007/s10551-012-1333-3

Eagle, L., Dahl, S., Hill, S., Bird, S., Spotswood, F., & Tapp, A. (2013). *Social Marketing*. Harlow, UK: Pearson Education Limited.

Echefu, N., & Akpofure, E. (2002). *Environmental impact assessment in Nigeria: regulatory background and procedural framework. Environmental Impact Assessment (EIA)*. Training Resource Manual.

Edosomwan, S., Prakasan, S. K., Kouame, D., Watson, J., & Seymour, T. (2011). The History of Social Media and its Impact on Business. *The Journal of Applied Management and Entrepreneurship, 16*(3), 1–13.

EEA. (2012). *Consumption and the Environment—2012 Update*. Luxembourg: Publications Office of the European Union.

Egan, J. (2004). *Relationship Marketing* (2nd ed.). Harlow: Prentice Hall.

Eggers, W. D., & Macmillan, P. (2013). *The solution revolution: How business, government, and social enterprises are teaming up to solve society's toughest problems*. Boston: Harvard Business Review Press.

Egri, C. P., & Herman, S. (2000). Leadership in the North American environmental sector: Values, leadership styles, and contexts of environmental leaders and their organizations. *Academy of Management Journal, 43*(4), 571–604. doi:10.2307/1556356

Eichler, G. (2003). E-Learning and communities: Supporting the circulation of knowledge pieces. In T. Bohme, G. Heyer, & H. Unger (Eds.), *Innovative Internet community systems:Third International Workshop, IICS 2003* (pp. 48-64). doi:10.1007/978-3-540-39884-4_5

Eisenbeiss, S. A., van Knippenberg, D., & Boerner, S. (2008). Transformational leadershipand team innovation: Intergrating team climate principles. *The Journal of Applied Psychology, 93*(6), 1438–1446. doi:10.1037/a0012716 PMID:19025260

EIU. (2008). *Corporate citizenship: Profiting from a sustainable business*. Economic Intelligence Unit of the Economist.

Elgueta, D. (2014). *The Cassandra Syndrome - Ancient Greek Myth*. Retrieved May 25, 2016, from http://www.pseudo-paranormal.com/2014/02/the-cassandra-syndrome-ancient-greek.html

Elkington, J. (1994). Towards the suitable corporation: Win-win-win business strategies for sustainable development. *California Management Review, 36*(2), 90–100. doi:10.2307/41165746

Elkington, J. (1997). *Cannibals with forks: The triple bottom line of 21st century business*. London: Capstone Publication.

Elkington, J. (2004). Enter the triple bottom line. In A. Henriques & J. Richardson (Eds.), *The Triple Bottom Line: does it all add up?* (pp. 1–16). London: Earthscan.

Elliott, K., & Freeman, R. (2000). *White hats or Don Quixotes? Human rights vigilantes in the global economy*. Cambridge, MA: NBER.

Elum, Z. A., Mopipi, K., & Henri-Ukoha, A. (2016). Oil exploitation and its socioeconomic effects on the Niger Delta region of Nigeria. *Environmental Science and Pollution Research International, 23*(13), 12880–12889. doi:10.1007/s11356-016-6864-1 PMID:27194013

Emmanuel, O., & Gordon, D. (2006). The effect of oil spillage on crop yield and farm income in delta state in Nigeria. *Journal of Central European Agriculture, 7*(1), 41–48.

Emmott, S. (2013). Humans: the real threat to life on Earth. *The Guardian*. Retrieved June 15, 2016 from https://www.theguardian.com/environment/2013/jun/30/stephen-emmott-ten-billion

Emodi, V. N., Yusuf, S. D., & Boo, K. J. (2014). The necessity of the development of standards for renewable energy technologies in Nigeria. *Smart Grid and Renewable Energy*, *5*(11), 259–274. doi:10.4236/sgre.2014.511024

Engelman, R. (2013). Beyond sustainababble. In L. Starke (Ed.), *State of the World: Is Sustainability Still Possible?* (pp. 3–16). Washington, DC: Island Press.

English, L. M., & Mayo, P. (2012). Environmental adult education. In *Learning with Adults. A Critical Pedagogical Introduction* (pp. 189–196). Rotterdam: Sense.

Enuoh, R. O., & Inyang, B. J. (2014). Effective management of corporate social responsibility (CSR) for desired outcome: The Niger Delta issue in Nigeria. *Journal of Business Administration*, *5*(4), 32–38.

EPA. (2014). *Green Power Market: Green Power Defined.* Retrieved from http://www.epa.gov/greenpower/gpmarket/

Equality Court. (2011). *Afri-Forum and Another vs. Malema and others.* Retrieved on June 13, 2016 at http://www.saflii.org/za/cases/ZAEQC/2011/2.pdf

Ercsey, I. (2012). Perceived quality of life as sustainable development facet. *Journal of Security and Sustainability Issues*, *2*(2), 19–30. doi:10.9770/jssi.2012.2.2(2)

Erdogmus, E. I., & Cicek, M. (2012). The Impact of Social Media Marketing on brand loyalty. *Journal of Procedial Social and Behavioral Sciences*, *58*(2), 1353–1360. doi:10.1016/j.sbspro.2012.09.1119

Erickson, P., & Lazarus, M. (2015). Global emissions: New oil investments boost carbon lock-in. *Nature*, *526*(7571), 43. doi:10.1038/526043c PMID:26432237

Ericsson, K. A. (1996). *The road to excellence: The acquisition of expert performance in the arts and sciences, sports and games*. Mahwah, NJ: Lawrence Erlbaum Associates, Inc.

Esan, A. L., & Babatola, E. B. (2015). Urbanization and its environmental impacts in Nigeria: Implications for sustainable development. (A case study of Ado-Ekiti). *Pyrex Journal of Research in Environmental Studies*, *2*(3), 27–34.

Escudero, M., & Rasche, A. (2009). Leading Change: The Role of the Principles for Responsible Management Education. *Journal for Business, Economics and Ethics*, *10*(2), 244–250.

Estabrooks, C., Derksen, L., Winther, C., Lavis, J., Scott, S., Wallin, R., & Profetto-McGrath, J. (2008). The intellectual structure and substance of the knowledge utilization field: A longitudinal author co-citation analysis, 1945 to 2004. *Implementation Science; IS*, *3*(49). PMID:19014512

Ethekwini Municipality. (2013). *Focus on SMMEs in eThekwini*. Available: http://www.durban.gov.za/Resource_Centre/edge/Documents/SMME's.pdf

Europeana Creative Cultural Jam. (2015). Available at: https://www.google.co.za/search?q=examples+of+cultural+jamming&biw=974&bih=734&tbm=isch&tbo=u&source=univ&sa=X&sqi=2&ved=0ahUKEwig7t-wns_KAhWBQhQKHY7lDIAQsAQIOQ&dpr=1.25

Eweje, G. (2006a). Environmental cost and responsibilities resulting from oil exploitation in developing countries: The case of the Niger Delta of Nigeria. *Journal of Business Ethics*, *1*(1), 27–56. doi:10.1007/s10551-006-9067-8

Eweje, G. (2006b). The role of MNEs in community development initiative in developing countries' corporate social responsibility at work in Nigeria and South Africa. *Business & Society*, *45*(2), 93–129. doi:10.1177/0007650305285394

Ewing, B., Goldfinger, S., Oursler, A., Reed, A., Moore, D., & Wackernagel, M. (2009). *The Ecological Footprint Atlas 2009*. Oakland: Global Footprint Network.

EY. (2013). *Beating cybercrime*. Retrieved August 10, 2016, from United Kingdom: http://www.ey.com/Publication/vwLUAssets/Beating_cybercrime:_Security_Program_Management_from_the_Board%E2%80%99s_perspective/$FILE/EY-Beating-Cybercrime.pdf

Eze, O. C., & Chinwuba, U. G. (2015). Organized labour, democracy and good governance in Nigeria, 1999-2007. *Journal of Politics and Law*, *8*(1), 149. doi:10.5539/jpl.v8n1p149

Fabricius, C., Koch, E., Turner, S., & Magome, H. (2013). *Rights resources and rural development: Community-based natural resource management in Southern Africa*. Routledge.

Facing Finance. (2013). *Dirty Profits II: A Research Paper Prepared for Facing Finance*. Amsterdam: Facing Finance Organisation.

FAO. (2013). *The State of Food and Agriculture*. Rome: FAO.

Faraj, S., Jarvenpaa, S. L., & Majchrzak, A. (2011). Knowledge collaboration in online communities. *Organization Science*, *22*(5), 1224–1239. doi:10.1287/orsc.1100.0614

Farmer, P. (2004). *Pathologies of power: Health, Human rights, and the new war on the poor* (Vol. 4). Berkeley, CA: University of California Press.

Farson, R. (2008). *The power of design: A force for transforming everything*. Atlanta, GA: Greenway Communications.

Fauconnier, G., & Turner, M. (2002). *The way we think: Conceptual blending and the mind's hidden complexities*. New York: Basic Books.

Fels, A. (2010). Executive Remuneration in Australia. *Australian Accounting Review*, *20*(1), 76–82.

Fields, Z., & Bisschoff, C. A. (2013). A model to measure creativity in young adults. *Journal of Social Sciences*, *37*(1), 55–67.

Filatotchev, I., & Allcock, D. (2010). Corporate Governance and Executive Compensation: A Contingency Framework. *The Academy of Management Perspectives*, *24*(1), 20–33. doi:10.5465/AMP.2010.50304414

Financial Reporting Council (FRC). (2014). *Guidance on the strategic report*. London: Financial Reporting Council.

Finlay, L. M. (2000). All the world's a stooge? Globalization as aesthetic system. *Topia: A Canadian Journal of Cultural Studies*, *4*, 39–51.

Fishburn & The Crowd. (2014). *The wisdom of the crowd: New business models. Leading experts share their views on the emerging generation of more sustainable business models*. London: The Crowd.

Fisher, R. (2004). What is creativity? In R. Fisher & M. Williams (Eds.), *Unlocking creativity: Teaching across the curriculum* (pp. 6–20). London: David Fulton Publishers.

Fitch, G., & O'Fallon, T. (2013). Theory U Applied in Transformation Development. In O. Gunnlaugson, C. Baron, & M. Cayer (Eds.), *Perspectives on Theory U: Insights from the Field*. Hershey, PA, USA: Business Science Reference.

Flannery, T. P., Hofrichter, D. A., & Platten, P. E. (1996). *People, Performance and Pay - Dynamic Compensation for Changing Organizations*. New York: Free Press.

Flieschmann, K., & Hutchinson, C. (2012). Creative exchange: An evolving model of multidisciplinary collaboration. *Journal of Learning Design*, *5*(1), 23–31.

Florby, G., Shackleton, M., & Suhonen, K. (2009). Introduction to Canada: Images of a post/national society. *Canadian Studies*, *19*, 1–22.

Florida, R. (2002). *The rise of the creative class and how it's transforming work, life, community and everyday life*. New York, NY: Basic Books.

Florin, J., Karri, R., & Rossiter, N. (2007). Fostering Entrepreneurial Drive in Business Education: An Attitudinal Approach. *Journal of Management Education*, *31*(1), 17–42.

Fombrun, G. J. (1996). *Reputation: Realizing Value from the Corporate Image*. Boston: Harvard Business School Press.

Forrest, N., & Wiek, A. (2015). Success Factors and Strategies for Sustainability Transitions of Small-Scale Communities – Evidence From a Cross-Case Analysis. *Environmental Innovatioan and Societal Transition*, *17*, 22–40. doi:10.1016/j.eist.2015.05.005

Fortinet. (2014). *Fortinet's Advanced Threat Protection Framework: A cohesive approach to addressing advanced targeted attacks*. Retrieved September 29, 2014, from http://www.fortinet.com/sites/default/files/whitepapers/Fortinet_ATP_2014WP.pdf

Foster, C., & Green, K. (2000). Greening the innovation process. *Business Strategy and the Environment*, *9*(5), 287–303. doi:10.1002/1099-0836(200009/10)9:5<287::AID-BSE256>3.0.CO;2-7

Foxon, T. J. (2013). Transition pathways for a UK low carbon electricity future. *Energy Policy*, *52*, 10–24. doi:10.1016/j.enpol.2012.04.001

Fox-Penner, P. (2010). *Smart Power: climate change, the smart grid, and the future of electric utilities*. Island Press.

Fragueiro, F., & Thomas, T. (2011). *Strategic leadership in the business school:Keeping one step ahead*. New York: Cambridge University Press. doi:10.1017/CBO9780511921087

Frame, B., & Newton, B. (2007). Promoting Sustainability Through Social Marketing: Examples from New Zealand. *International Journal of Consumer Studies*, *31*(6), 571–581. doi:10.1111/j.1470-6431.2007.00600.x

Franks, J. (2010). Boundary organizations for sustainable land management: The example of Dutch Environmental Co-operatives. *Ecological Economics*, *70*(2), 283–295. doi:10.1016/j.ecolecon.2010.08.011

Freeman, R. E., & Philips, R. A. (2000). Stakeholder theory: A libertarian defense. *Business Ethics Quarterly*, *12*(3), 331–349. doi:10.2307/3858020

French, J., Merritt, R., & Reynolds, L. (2011). *Social Marketing Casebook*. London: Sage. doi:10.4135/9781446250877

Freundlich, F. (1998). *The Mondragón Cooperative Corporation (MCC): An Introduction*. Paper presented at Shared Capitalism: Mapping the Research Agenda. Conference of the National Bureau of Economic Research Madison Hotel, Washington, DC. Retrieved on June 10, 2016 at http://www.ownershipassociates.com/mcc-intro.shtm

Fridell, G. (2009). The co-operative and the corporation: Competing visions of the future of fair trade. *Journal of Business Ethics*, *86*(1), 81–95. doi:10.1007/s10551-008-9759-3

Friedman, M. (1970, September 13). The social responsibility of business is to increase its profits. *The New York Times Magazine*. Retrieved from http://www.umich.edu/~thecore/doc/Friedman.pdf

Frigo, Læssøe, & Ramaswamy, V. (2015). Integrating Strategic Risks in Managing Co-creative Enterprises. *The Journal of Enterprise Risk Management*, *1*(1), 1–15.

Fulton, M., & Capalino, R. (2014). Investing in the clean trillion: Closing the clean energy investment gap. *Ceres*.

Funkhouser, E., Blackburn, G., Magee, C., & Rai, V. (2015). Business model innovations for deploying distributed generation: The emerging landscape of community solar in the U.S. *Energy Research & Social Science*, 90–101.

Galan - Ladero, M. M., Galera - Casquet, C., Valero - Amaro, V., & Barroso - Mendez, M. J. (2013). Sustainable, socially responsible business: The cause – related marketing case, a review of the conceptual framework. *Journal of Security and Sustainability Issues*, *2*(4), 35–46. doi:10.9770/jssi.2013.2.4(4)

Galatsidas, A., & Sheehy, F. (2015, July 6). *What have the millennium development goals achieved?* Retrieved from http://www.theguardian.com/global-development/datablog/2015/jul/06/what-millennium-development-goals-achieved-mdgs

Galaz, V., Crona, B., Österblom, P. O., & Folke, C. (2012). Polycentric systems and interacting planetary boundaries - emerging governance of climate change - ocean acidification - marine biodiversity. *Ecological Economics*, *81*, 21–32. doi:10.1016/j.ecolecon.2011.11.012

Galindo, M.-Á., & Méndez, M. T. (2014). Entrepreneurship, economic growth, and innovation: Are feedback effects at work? *Journal of Business Research*, *67*(5), 825–829.

Galindo, M.-Á., & Méndez-Picazo, M.-T. (2013). Innovation, entrepreneurship and economic growth. *Management Decision*, *51*(3), 501–514.

Gallagher, D. R. (2012). Why environmental leadership? In D. R. Gallagher (Ed.), *Environmental leadership: A reference handbook* (Vol. 1, pp. 3–10). Los Angeles, CA: SAGE Publications. doi:10.4135/9781452218601.n1

Gandenberger, C., Bodenheimer, M., Schleich, J., Orzanna, R., & Macht, L. (2015). Factors driving international technology transfer: Empirical insights from a CDM project survey. *Climate Policy*, 1–20. doi:10.1080/14693062.2015.1069176

Gardner, J. W. (2015). *Quotation #2458*. Retrieved July 8, 2016 from http://www.quotationspage.com/quote/2458.html

Garriga, E., & Mele, D. (2004). Corporate social responsibility theories: Mapping the territory. *Journal of Business Ethics*, *53*(1-2), 51–71. doi:10.1023/B:BUSI.0000039399.90587.34

Gartner, W. B., Davidsson, P., & Zahra, S. (2006). Are you talking to me? The nature of community in entrepreneurship scholarship. *Entrepreneurship Theory and Practice*, *30*(3), 321–331. doi:10.1111/j.1540-6520.2006.00123.x

Geels, F. W. (2005). *Technological transitions and system innovations: A co-evolutionary and socio-technical analysis*. Cheltenham, UK: Edward Elgar. doi:10.4337/9781845424596

Gee, R. F. (2012). *Corporate Social Responsibility Programmes and their beneficiary Organisations: An examination of the sustainability of the relationships between corporate social responsibility programmes and their targeted beneficiary organisations*. Development Studies. Research Space, University of Kwa-Zulu Natal. Masters.

Gemalto. (2016). *Data Breach Level Index*. Retrieved August 17, 2016, from http://www.gemalto.com/brochures-site/download-site/Documents/ent-infographic-2015-Breach-Level-index.jpg

GEN. (2014). *UN Advocacy*. Retrieved from http://gen.ecovillage.org/en/page/un-advocacy

Generation Investment Management. (2012). *Sustainable Capitalism*. London: Generation Investment Management LLP.

Gentner, D., Holyoak, K. J., & Kokinov, B. N. (2001). *The analogical mind: Perspectives from cognitive science*. Cambridge, MA: MIT Press.

George, D., & Mallery, P. (2003). *SSPS for Windows step by step: a simple guide and reference 11.0 update* (4th ed.). Boston: Allyn & Bacon.

GFN. (2015). *World Footprint: Do We Fit on the Planet*. Retrieved from http://www.footprintnetwork.org/en/index.php/GFN/page/world_footprint/

GFN. (2015a). *Humanity Now Demanding 1.4 Earths*. Retrieved from http://www.footprintnetwork.org/de/index.php/newsletter/bv/humanity_now_demanding_1.4_earths

GFN. (2015b). *United Kingdom*. Retrieved from http://www.footprintnetwork.org/en/index.php/GFN/page/trends/united_kingdom/

Giacomini, T., & Turner, T. (2015). The 2014 people's climate march and flood Wall Street civil disobedience: Making the transition to a post-fossil capitalist, commoning civilization. *Capitalism, Nature, Socialism*, *26*(2), 27–45. doi:10.1080/10455752.2014.1002804

Gibb, A. (2005). The future of entrepreneurship education—determining the basis for coherent policy and practice? In P. Kyrö & C. Carrier (Eds.), The Dynamics of Learning Entrepreneurship in a Cross-cultural University Context (pp. 44-67). Hämeenlinna: Research Centre for Vocational and Professional Education, University of Tampere.

Gibb, A. (2002). Creating conducive environments for learning and entrepreneurship: Living with, dealing with, creating and enjoying uncertainty and complexity. *Industry and Higher Education*, *16*(3), 135–148. doi:10.5367/000000002101296234

Gibb, A. (2007). Creating the entrepreneurial university: do we need a wholly different model of entrepreneurship? In A. Fayolle (Ed.), *Handbook of research in entrepreneurship education* (Vol. 1, pp. 67–103). Cheltenham, UK: Edvard Elgar. doi:10.4337/9781847205377.00012

Gibb, A. (2008). Entrepreneurship and entrepreneurial education in schools and colleges: Insights from UK practice. *International Journal of Entrepreneurship Education*, *6*(2), 101–144.

Giddens, A., Duneier, M., Appelbaum, R. P., & Carr, D. (2000). *Introduction to sociology*. WW Norton New York.

Gilbert, A., & Rasche, D. (2015). Decoupling Responsible Management Education: Why Business Schools May Not Walk Their Talk. *Journal of Management Inquiry*, *24*(3), 239–252. doi:10.1177/1056492614567315

Gillingham, K., & Palmer, K. (2014). Bridging the energy efficiency gap: Policy insights from economic theory and empirical evidence. *Review of Environmental Economics and Policy*, *8*(1), 18–38. doi:10.1093/reep/ret021

Gill, S. S., Haider, S., & Noreen, S. (2016). Linking ethical leadership with organizational deviance and CSR: Empirical review. *Asian Journal of Multidisciplinary Studies*, *4*(6), 23–28.

Gino, F., Argote, L., Miron-Spektor, E., & Todorova, G. (2010). First, get your feet wet: The effects of learning from direct and indirect experience on team creativity. *Organizational Behavior and Human Decision Processes*, *111*(2), 102–115. doi:10.1016/j.obhdp.2009.11.002

Girard, J. P. (2002). Social Cohesion, Governance and the Development of Health and Social Care Co-operatives: Preliminary Observations. *Review of International Cooperation*, *95*(1), 58–64.

Gitsham, M., Wackrill, J., Baxter, G., & Pegg, M. (2012). *Leadership in a Rapidly Changing World*. London: Ashridge and International Business Leaders Forum.

Gittell, R., Magnusson, M., & Merenda, M. (2012). *Sustainable business cases*. Retrieved September 8, 2015, from: http://2012books.lardbucket.org/books/sustainable-business-cases/s07-02-business-and-government-relati.html

Gladwell, M. (2000). *The tipping point: How little things can make a big difference*. Boston: Little, Brown and Company.

Glaister, K. W., Husan, R., & Buckley, P. J. (2004). *Strategic business alliances – An examination of the core dimensions*. Cheltenham, UK: Edward Elgar. doi:10.4337/9781845420543

Glen, J., Hilson, C., & Lowitt, E. (2009). *The Emergence of Green Talent: Lessons from the Internet Revolution*. London: Accenture Institute for High Performance.

Global Sustainability Standards Board (GSSB). (2015). *G4 Sustainability reporting guidelines. Global reporting initiative*. Retrieved June 1, 2016, from https://www.globalreporting.org/standards/g4/Pages/default.aspx

Global, N. A. S. A. Climate Change. (2016). *Climate change: how do we know*. Retrieved June 19, 2016, from http://climate.nasa.gov/evidence/

Globalexchange.org. (2015). Available from: http://www.globalexchange.org/corporateHRviolators

Godemann, J. et al.. (2011). *Integrating Sustainability into Business Schools – Analysis of 100 UN PRME Sharing Information on Progress (SIP) reports J. Moon*. Nottingham University Business School.

Goldman, C., Satchwell, A., Cappers, P., & Hoffman, I. (2013). *Utility business models in a low load growth/high DG future: gazing in the crystall ball? Committee on Regional Electric Power Corporation (CREPC)/State-Provincial Steering Committee*. Boise, ID: SPSC.

Goleman, D., & Senge, P. (2014). Seeking the Big Picture: Systems Thinking for Schools. *Education Week*, *34*(2), 22–23.

Gong, Y., Kim, T. Y., Lee, D. R., & Zhu, J. (2013). A multilevel model of team goal orientation, information exchange, and creativity. *Academy of Management Journal*, *56*(3), 827–851. doi:10.5465/amj.2011.0177

Gopal, S. (2013). Urban renewabilization in India through public-public partnerships: a feasibility study of applying the "sustainable energy utility" model to the city of Thane. Newark, DE: Center for Energy & Environmental Policy (CEEP), University of Delaware.

Gordon, R. (2011). Critical Social Marketing: Definition, Application and Domain. *Journal of Social Marketing*, *1*(2), 82–99. doi:10.1108/20426761111141850

Gore, A. (2014). Without a Trace. *The New York Times*. Retrieved June 2, 2016, from http://www.nytimes.com/2014/02/16/books/review/the-sixth-extinction-by-elizabeth-kolbert.html?_r=0

Gospel, H., Lockwood, G., & Willman, P. (2000). British dilemma: Disclosure of information for collective bargaining and joint consultation. *Comparative Labor Law & Policy Journal*, *22*(2), 101–123.

Gough, C., Castells, N., & Funtowicz, S. (1998). Integrated Assessment: An emerging methodology for complex issues. *Environmental Modeling and Assessment*, *3*, 19–29.

Graham, I. D., Tetroe, J., Robinson, N., Grimshaw, J., & International Funders Study Research Group. (n.d.). *An international study of health research funding agencies' support and promotion of knowledge translation*. Boston, MA: Academy Health Annual Research.

Gray, B. (1996). Review of frame reflection. *Academy of Management Review*, *21*(2), 576–579.

Greek Myths & Greek Mythology. (2016). *The Myth of Cassandra*. Retrieved June 2, 2016, from http://www.greekmyths-greekmythology.com/the-myth-of-cassandra/

Green, F. (2008). Temporary work and insecurity in Britain: A problem solved? *Social Indicators Research*, *88*(1), 147–160. doi:10.1007/s11205-007-9204-5

Greenpeace.org. (2010). Available from: http://www.greenpeace.org/international/en/campaigns/climate-change/kitkat/

Gribben, C., & Woudstra-Van Grondelle, I. (2007). *A Snapshot of Executive Development of Corporate Responsibility Professionals in the UK*. London: Ashridge and Corporate Responsibility.

Grier, S., & Bryant, C. (2005). Social Marketing in Public Health. *Annual Review of Public Health*, *26*(1), 319–339. doi:10.1146/annurev.publhealth.26.021304.144610

Gries, T., & Naudé, W. (2010). Entrepreneurship and structural economic transformation. *Small Business Economics*, *34*(1), 13–29.

Griggs, D., Stafford-Smith, M., Gaffney, O., Rockström, J., Öhman, M., Shyamsundar, P., & Noble, I. et al. (2013). Policy: Sustainable development goals for people and planet. *Nature*, *495*(7441), 305–307. doi:10.1038/495305a PMID:23518546

Groenwald, D. (Ed.). (2013). *Contemporary Management Aspects*. Cape Town: Juta.

Group Tomorrow's Company. (2012). *The Invisible Elephant and the Pyramid Treasure*. London: Center for Tomorrow's Company.

Grubb, M. (2015). From Lima to Paris, Part 1: The Lima Hangover. *Climate Policy*, *15*(3), 299–301. doi:10.1080/14693062.2015.1029767

Gruenewald, D. A., & Smith, G. A. (2014). *Place-based education in the global age: Local diversity*. Routledge.

Gummeson, E. (2002). Relationship Marketing in the New Economy. *Journal of Relationship Marketing*, *1*(1), 37–58. doi:10.1300/J366v01n01_04

Gumusluoglu, L., & Ilsev, A. (2009). Transformational Leadership, Creativity, and Organizational Innovation. *Journal of Business Research*, *62*(4), 461–473. doi:10.1016/j.jbusres.2007.07.032

Gunnlaugson, O., Baron, C., & Cayer, M. (2013). *Perspectives on Theory U: Insights from the Field*. Hershey, PA: Business Science Reference.

Gurkaynak, G., Yilmaz, I., & Haksever, G. (2016). Stifling artificial Intelligence: Human perils. *Computer Law & Security Review*. Retrieved June 2, 2016, from http://www.elig.com/docs/0bc70-stifling-artificial-intelligence-human-perils.pdf

Hagedorn, K., Arzt, K., & Peters, U. (2002). Institutional arrangements for environmental co-operatives: a conceptional framework. In Environmental Co-operation and Institutional Change. Edward Elgar.

Haim, A. (2003). *The Manager's Pocket Guide to Creativity*. Mumbai: Sanman.

Hainmueller, J., & Hiscox, M. J. (2015). *The socially conscious consumer? Field experiment tests of consumer support for fair labour standards*. MIT Political Science Department Research Paper No. 2012-15.

Hale, R. (2012). Actual professional development. *Training Journal*, 39-42.

Hale, T. (2011). United Nations Global Compact. In T. Hale & D. Held (Eds.), *Handbook of transnational governance: Institutions and innovations*. Cambridge, UK: Polity Press.

Halliday, K. (2015). *Will cyber security threaten the sustainability of returns for investors?* Retrieved August 1, 2016, from http://www.ampcapital.com.au/smsf-suite/articles/will-cyber-security-threaten-the-sustainability

Hamel, G. (2000). *Leading the revolution*. Boston, MA: Harvard Business School Press.

Hamel, G., & Breen, B. (2007). *The future of management*. Boston, MA: Harvard Business School Publishing.

Hamilton, C., & Mail, E. (2003). *Downshifting in Australia: A Sea-Change in the Pursuit of Happiness*. The Australia Institute.

Hammond, M. M., Neff, N. L., Farr, J. L., Schwall, A. R., & Zhao, X. (2011). Predictors of individual level innovation at work: A meta-analysis. *Psychology of Aesthetics, Creativity, and the Arts*, *5*(1), 90–105. doi:10.1037/a0018556

Han, B. J., Jung, I.-Y., Kim, K.-H., Lee, D.-k., Rho, S., & Jeong, C.-s. (2013). Cloud-based active content collaboration platform using multimedia processing. *EURASIP Journal on Wireless Communications and Networking*, (1), 1–13. doi:10.1186/1687-1499-2013-63

Hannon, V., Gillinson, S., & Shanks, L. (2013). *Learning a living: radical innovation in education for work*. Dohar: Bloomsbury.

Hardekopf, B. (2015). *The Big Data Breaches of 2014*. Retrieved October 22, 2015, from Forbes website: http://www.forbes.com/sites/moneybuilder/2015/01/13/the-big-data-breaches-of-2014/

Hardin, G. (1968). The tragedy of the commons. *Science*, *162*(3859), 1243–1248. doi:10.1126/science.162.3859.1243 PMID:5699198

Hardy, C., Harley, B., & Phillips, N. (2004). Discourse analysis and content analysis: Two solitudes. *Qualitative Methods*, *2*(1), 19–22.

Hare, W., Stockwell, C., Flachsland, C., & Oberthur, S. (2011). The architecture of the global climate regime: A top-down perspective. *Climate Policy*, *10*(6), 600–614. doi:10.3763/cpol.2010.0161

Hargadon, A. B., & Bechky, B. A. (2006). When collections of creatives become creative collectives: A field study of problem solving at work. *Organization Science*, *17*(4), 484–500. doi:10.1287/orsc.1060.0200

Hargreaves, T. (2011). Practice-ing Behaviour Change: Applying Social Practice Theory to Pro-Environmental Behaviour Change. *Journal of Consumer Culture*, *11*(1), 79–99. doi:10.1177/1469540510390500

Harkema, S. J. M., & Schout, H. (2008). Incorporating Student-Centred Learning in Innovation and Entrepreneurship Education. *European Journal of Education*, *43*(4), 513–526.

Harkema, S. J. M., & Schout, H. (2008). Incorporating student-centred learning in innovation and entrepreneurship education. *European Journal of Education*, *43*(4), 513–526. doi:10.1111/j.1465-3435.2008.00372.x

Harold, C. (2004, September). Pranking Rhetoric: "Culture Jamming" as Media Activism. *Critical Studies in Media Communication*, *21*(3), 189–211. doi:10.1080/0739318042000212693

Hasrouni, L. B. (2012). CSR in education: Cultivating values, how business schools can plant the seeds of change. *Responsible Businesses*.

Hastings, G. (2003). Relational Paradigms in Social Marketing. *Journal of Macromarketing*, *23*(1), 6–15. doi:10.1177/0276146703023001006

Hastings, G., & Domegan, C. (2014). *Social Marketing: From Tunes to Symphonies* (2nd ed.). London: Routledge.

Hastings, G., & Saren, M. (2003). The Critical Contribution of Social Marketing: Theory and Application. *Marketing Theory*, *3*(3), 305–322. doi:10.1177/147059310333005

Haynie, J. J., Mossholder, K. W., & Harris, S. G. (2016). *Justice and job engagement: The role of senior management trust*. J. Organiz. Behav. doi:10.1002/job.2082

Henry, C., Hill, F., & Leitch, C. (2005). Entrepreneurship education and training: can entrepreneurship be taught? Part I. *Education + Training, 47*(2), 98-111.

Hens, L. (2005). *The rio declaration on environment and development. Regional sustainable development review: Africa*. Oxford, UK: Eolss Publishers.

Hermans, C. A. M. (2012). Towards a 'U-turn' by the Churches: How (Not) to Possibilise the Future. *Religion & Theology, 19*(3/4), 237–264.

Hess, D. (2015). *The politics of niche-regime conflicts: distributed solar energy in the United States*. Environmental Innovation and Societal Transitions.

Hill, L. A., Brandeau, G., Truelove, E., & Lineback, K. (2014). Collective genius. *Harvard Business Review, 92*(6), 94–102. PMID:25051858

Hill, L., Brandeau, G., Truelove, E., & Lineback, K. (2014). *Collective genius: The art and practice of leading innovation*. Cambridge, MA: Harvard Business Review Press.

Hirst, G., Van Knippenburg, D., & Zhou, J. (2009). A cross-level perspective on employee creativity, goal orientation, team learning behaviour and individual creativity. *Academy of Management Journal, 52*(2), 280–293. doi:10.5465/AMJ.2009.37308035

Hitt, M. A., Keats, B. W., & DeMarie, S. M. (1998). Navigating in the new competitive landscape: Building strategic flexibility and competitive advantage in the 21st century. *The Academy of Management Executive, 12*(4), 22–42.

Hodgson, B. J. (2001). Can the beast be tamed? Reflections on John McMurtry's Unequal Freedoms: The global market as an ethical system. *Journal of Business Ethics, 33*(1), 71–78. doi:10.1023/A:1011972421036

Hoek, J., & Jones, S. (2011). Regulation, Public Health and Social Marketing: A Behaviour Change Trinity. *Journal of Social Marketing, 1*(1), 32–44. doi:10.1108/20426761111104419

Hoffmann, M. (2011). *Climate governance at the crossroads - experimenting with a global response after Kyoto*. Oxford, UK: Oxford University Press. doi:10.1093/acprof:oso/9780195390087.001.0001

Holme, R., & Watts, P. (1999). *Corporate social responsibility*. Geneva: World Business Council for Sustainable Development.

Holtfreter, K., & Meyers, T. J. (2015). *Challenges for Cybercrime Theory, Research, and Policy*. Retrieved August 15, 2016, from Norwich: http://ssrn.com/abstract=2677492

Holtfreter, R. E. (2016). Immunize Your Organization. *Fraud, 31*, 19–25.

Holthaus. (2015). The point of no return: climate change nightmares are already here. *Rolling Stone*. Retrieved June 15, 2016 from http://www.rollingstone.com/politics/news/the-point-of-no-return-climate-change-nightmares-are-already-here-20150805

Homan, G. (2000). Skills and Competency-Based Pay. In R. Thorpe & G. Homan (Eds.), *Strategic Reward Systems*. Essex, UK: Pearson.

Homel, G. (2009). Moonshots. *Harvard Business Review, 87*(2), 91–98. PMID:19266704

Hope, C., & Ross, T. (2010). *Britain embraces positive action to abolish work place discrimination*. Retrieved from http://www.telegraph.co.uk/news/uknews/8177872/Britain-embraces-positive-action-to-abolish-workplace-discrimination.html

Hopwood, B., Mellor, M., & O'Brien, G. (2005). Sustainable Development: Mapping Different Approaches. *Sustainable Development, 13*(1), 38–52. doi:10.1002/sd.244

Houldsworth, E., & Jirasinghe, D. (2006). *Managing & Measuring Employee Performance*. London: Kogan Page.

House of Commons' Environment, Food and Rural Affairs Committee. (2013). *Food Contamination, Vol. 1* (Fifth report of session 2013–2014, incorporating HC 1035-i-ii, session 2012-2013). London: The Stationery Office.

House of Lords' Select Committee on Economic Affairs. (2013). *Tackling Corporate Tax Avoidance in a Global Economy: Is a New Approach Needed?* (First Report of Session 2013–2014). London: The Stationery Office.

Howe-Walsh, L., & Turnbull, S. (2016). Barriers to women leaders in academia: Tales from science and technology. *Studies in Higher Education*, *41*(3), 415–428. doi:10.1080/03075079.2014.929102

Hubbard, G. (2009). Measuring organizational performance: Beyond the triple bottom line. *Business Strategy and the Environment*, *18*(3), 177–191. doi:10.1002/bse.564

Hunt, T. (2014). *Top Tips: 5 Security Tips to Prevent Cyber Attacks*. Retrieved September 26, 2014, from http://www.idgconnect.com/blog-abstract/8599/top-tips-security-tips-prevent-cyber-attacks

Hunter, S. T., Thoroughgood, C. N., Myer, A. T., & Ligon, G. S. (2011). Paradox of leading innovative behaviours; summary, solutions and future directions. *Psychology of Aesthetics, Creativity, and the Arts*, *5*(1), 54–66. doi:10.1037/a0017776

Hunt, J. G. (1999). Transformational/charismatic leadership's transformation of the field: An historical essay. *The Leadership Quarterly*, *10*(2), 129–144. doi:10.1016/S1048-9843(99)00015-6

Hyde, R., Watson, S., Cheshire, W., & Thomson, M. (2007). *The Environmental Brief: Pathways for Green Design*. Oxon, UK: Taylor & Francis.

Hytti, U., & O'Gorman, C. (2004). What is enterprise education? An analysis of the objectives and methods of enterprise education programmes in four European countries. *Education + Training*, *46*(1), 11–23. doi:10.1108/00400910410518188

IBM. (2013). *Combat the Latest Security Attacks with Global Threat Intelligence*. Retrieved August 18, 2016, from USA: http://public.dhe.ibm.com/common/ssi/ecm/wg/en/wgw03034usen/WGW03034USEN.PDF

IBM. (2014a). *IBM Security Services 2014 Cyber Security Intelligence Index*. Retrieved August 15, 2016, from USA: http://www-03.ibm.com/security/data-breach/cyber-security-index.html

IBM. (2014b). *Managing security risks and vulnerabilities*. Retrieved September 15, 2014, from http://www.informationweek.com/whitepaper/Security/Application-Security/managing-security-risks-and-vulnerabilities-wp1398437333

IBM. (2016). *Reviewing a year of serious data breaches, major attacks and new vulnerabilities*. Retrieved August 12, 2016, from New York: http://www-01.ibm.com/common/ssi/cgi-bin/ssialias?htmlfid=SEW03133USEN

Idemudia, U., & Osayande, N. (2016). Assessing the effect of corporate social responsibility on community development in the Niger Delta: A corporate perspective. *Community Development Journal: An International Forum*. doi:10.1093/cdj/bsw019

Ifinedo, P. (2014). Information systems security policy compliance: An empirical study of the effects of socialisation, influence, and cognition. *Information & Management*, *51*(1), 69–79. doi:10.1016/j.im.2013.10.001

Ikelegbe, A. (2001). Civil society, oil and conflict in the Niger Delta region of Nigeria: Ramifications of civil society for a regional resource struggle. *The Journal of Modern African Studies*, *39*(3), 437–469. doi:10.1017/S0022278X01003676

Im, S., Montoya, M. M., & Workman, J. P. Jr. (2013). Antecedents and consequences of creativity in product innovation teams. *Journal of Product Innovation Management*, *30*(1), 170–185. doi:10.1111/j.1540-5885.2012.00887.x

Infante Amate, J., & Gonzalez de Molina, M. (2013). 'Sustainable De-Growth' in Agriculture and Food: An Agro-Ecological Perspective on Spain's Agri-Food System (Year 2000). *Journal of Cleaner Production*, *38*, 27–35. doi:10.1016/j.jclepro.2011.03.018

InfoSec Institute. (2013). *Cyber Exploitation*. Retrieved August 17, 2016, from http://resources.infosecinstitute.com/cyber-exploitation/

Ingelson, A., & Nwapi, C. (2014). Environmental impact assessment process for oil, gas and mining projects in Nigeria: A critical analysis. *Law, Environment & Development Journal, 10*(1), 35–56.

Insider, B. (2016). *This one chart explains why cybersecurity is so important.* Retrieved August 16, 2016, from http://www.businessinsider.com/cybersecurity-report-threats-and-opportunities-2016-3

Institute for Fiscal Studies. (2013). *Food expenditure and nutritional quality over the Great Recession* (IFS Briefing Note BN143). Retrieved from http://www.ifs.org.uk/bns/bn143.pdf

Institute of Risk Management. (2016). *Cyber risk and risk management.* Retrieved August 18, 2016, from https://www.theirm.org/knowledge-and-resources/thought-leadership/cyber-risk/

Intergovernmental Panel on Climate Change. (2012). *Managing the risks of extreme events and disasters to advance climate change adaptation.* Retrieved from http://www.ipcc-wg2.gov/SREX/

Intergovernmental Panel on Climate Change. (2014). Climate Change 2014: Impacts, Adaptation, and Vulnerability. Part A: Global and Sectoral Aspects. In Contribution of Working Group II to the Fifth Assessment Report of the Intergovernmental Panel on Climate Change. Cambridge, UK: Cambridge University Press.

International Covenant on Economic, Social and Cultural Rights. (1966). *International Covenant on Economic, Social and Cultural Rights* (Adopted 16 Dec. 1966, G.A. Res. 2200A, U.N. GAOR, 21st Sess., Supp. No. 16, at 49, U.N. Doc. A/6316 (1966). Entered into force Jan. 3, 1976). Retrieved from http://www2.ohchr.org/english/law/cescr.htm

International Cyber Security Protection Alliance. (2014). *Project 2020 - Scenarios for the Future of Cybercrime.* Retrieved August 10, 2016, from https://www.icspa.org/uploads/media/ICSPA_Project_2020_%E2%80%93_Scenarios_for_the_Future_of_Cybercrime_01.pdf

International Labour Organization. (2013). *Public sector shock: The impact of policy retrenchment in Europe.* Geneva: ILO.

ISACA. (2011). *Data Analytics - A Practical Approach.* Retrieved August 12, 2016, from United States of America: http://www.isaca.org/Knowledge-Center/Research/Documents/Data-Analytics_whp_Eng_0811.pdf?regnum=332054

ISACA. (2013). *CISM Review Manual 2013.* Rolling Meadows: ISACA.

Isaksen, S.G. & Lauer, K.J. (2002). Climate for creativity and change in teams. *Creativity and Innovation Management Journal, 11*, 74-86.

Isaksen, S. G. II, & Akkermans, H. J. (2011). Creative Climate: A leadership lever for innovation. *The Journal of Creative Behavior, 45*(3), 161–187. doi:10.1002/j.2162-6057.2011.tb01425.x

Isaksen, S. G., & Lauer, K. J. (2001). Convergent validity of the situational outlook questionnaire: Discriminating levels of perceived support for creatity. *North American Journal of Psychology, 3*, 31–40.

Isaksen, S. G., Lauer, K. J., Ekvall, G., & Britz, A. (2001). Perceptions of the best and worst climates for creativity: Preliminary validation evidence for the situation outlook questionnaire. *Creativity Research Journal, 13*(2), 171–184. doi:10.1207/S15326934CRJ1302_5

ISO. (2011). Retrieved 12 Dec 2015 from http://www.iso.org/management_and_leadership_standards

Ite, U. E. (2007). Changing times and strategies: Shell's contribution to sustainable community development in the Niger Delta, Nigeria. *Sustainable Development, 15*(1), 1–14. doi:10.1002/sd.294

Jabareen, Y. (2008). A new conceptual framework for sustainable development. *Environment, Development and Sustainability, 10*(2), 179–192. doi:10.1007/s10668-006-9058-z

Jackson, C. J., Furnham, A., & Willen, K. (2000). Employer willingness to comply with the Disability Discrimination Act regarding staff selection in the UK. *Journal of Occupational and Organizational Psychology*, *73*(1), 119–129. doi:10.1348/096317900166912

Jackson, M. C. (2003). *Systems thinking: Creative holism for managers*. Wiley Chichester.

Jackson, N. (2006). Creativity in Higher Education – creating tipping points for cultural change. *SCEPTrE Scholarly Paper*, *3*, 25.

Jackson, T. (2005). *Motivating Sustainable Consumption*. Surrey, UK: University of Surrey.

Jackson, T. (2009). *Prosperity without growth: economics for a finite planet*. London, UK: Earthscan.

Jackson, T. (2009). *Prospertiy Without Growth: Econmics for a Finite Planet*. London: Earthscan.

Jacobson, L. (2016). *Yes, Donald Trump did call climate change a Chinese hoax*. Retrieved June 15, 2016 from http://www.politifact.com/truth-o-meter/statements/2016/jun/03/hillary-clinton/yes-donald-trump-did-call-climate-change-chinese-h/

Jacobsson, R., & Jacobsson, S. (2012). The emerging funding gap for the European energy sector - will the financial sector deliver? *Environmental Innovation and Societal Transitions*, *5*, 49–59. doi:10.1016/j.eist.2012.10.002

Jacoby, B. (1996). *Service-learning in higher education: Concepts and practices*. San Francisco, CA: Jossey-Bass.

Jafari, A., & Sheehan, M. (2003). *Designing portals: Opportunities and challenges*. Hershey, PA: IRM Press. doi:10.4018/978-1-59140-108-7

Jany-Catrice, F., & Lehndorff, S. (2005). Work organization and the importance of labour markets in the European retail trade. Working in the service sector –a tale from different worlds. Academic Press.

Jardine, E. (2015). *Global Cyberspace is Safer than You Think: Real Trends in Cybercrime*. Retrieved August 10, 2016, from Canada: file:///C:/Users/patrick/Downloads/SSRN-id2634590.pdf

Jaruzelski, B., Loehr, J., & Holman, R. (2011). The global innovation 1000: Why culture is key. *Strategy & Business*, *65*, 30–45.

Jawtusch, J., Oehen, B., & Niggli, U. (2011). Environmental, Social, and Economic Impacts of Sustainability Certification in the Agricultural Sector – The Current State of Empirical Research. In H. Willer & L. Kilcher (Eds.), The World of Organic Agriculture. Statistics and Emerging Trends 2011 (pp. 88-91).

Jiang, X., Li, Y., & Gao, S. (2008). The stability of strategic alliances: Characteristics, factors and stages. *Journal of International Management*, *14*(2), 173–189. doi:10.1016/j.intman.2007.09.002

Jike, V. T. (2004). Environmental degradation, social disequilibrium and the dilemma of sustainable development in Niger Delta of Nigeria. *Journal of Black Studies*, *34*(5), 686–701. doi:10.1177/0021934703261934

Johanisova, N., Crabtree, T., & Fraňková, E. (2013). Social Enterprises and Non-Market Capitals: A Path to Degrowth? *Journal of Cleaner Production*, *38*, 7–16. doi:10.1016/j.jclepro.2012.01.004

Johanisova, N., & Wolf, S. (2012). Economic Democracy: A Path for the Future? *Futures*, *44*(6), 562–570. doi:10.1016/j.futures.2012.03.017

Johannessen, J. (2008). Organisational innovation as part of knowledge management. *International Journal of Information Management*, *28*(5), 403–412. doi:10.1016/j.ijinfomgt.2008.04.007

Johnson, B., & Isaacson, W. (2016). Moving the needle: Engaging with communities for urban innovation. *The Aspen Idea Blog*. Retrieved on June 10, 2016 at http://www.aspeninstitute.org/about/blog/moving-needle-engaging-communities-urban-innovation

Johnson, C. (2003). Enron's ethical collapse: Lessons for leadership educators. *Journal of Leadership Education, 2*(1), 45-56.

Johnson-Laird, P. N. (1983). *Mental models*. Cambridge, MA: Harvard University Press.

Johnston, J. (2003). Who cares about the commons? *Capitalism, Nature, Socialism, 14*(4), 1–41. doi:10.1080/10455750308565544

Johnston, J., Gismondi, M., & Goodman, J. (Eds.). (2006). *Nature's revenge: Reclaiming sustainability in an age of corporate globalization*. Toronto: Garamond Press.

Jones, G. R., & George, J. M. (2012). *King Report on Corporate Governance in SA*. Retrieved June 15, 2016 from http://www.iodsa.co.za/?kingIII

Jordan, A., Huitema, D., Hilden, M., van Asselt, H., Rayner, T., Schoenefeld, J., et al. (2015). Emergence of polycentric climate governance and its future prospects. *Nature Climate Change*, 977-982.

Jordan, B. (2004). Growth to freedom or support to life? *Res Publica (Liverpool, England), 10*(2), 193–205. doi:10.1023/B:RESP.0000034573.80533.e5

Joseph, P. (2007–2013). *The Zeitgeist Film Series. Official website for Peter Joseph's award winning documentary trilogy.* Available from http://www.zeitgeistmovie.com/

Judith, J. L., & Pascual, B. (2015). The Power of One to Make a Difference: How Informal and Formal CEO Power Affect Environmental Sustainability. *Journal of Business Ethics*, 1–16.

Jung, D. I., Chow, C., & Wu, A. (2003). The role of transformational leadership in enhancing organisational innovation: Hypotheses and some preliminary findings. *The Leadership Quarterly, 14*(4-5), 525–544. doi:10.1016/S1048-9843(03)00050-X

Jursic, M., Cestnik, B., Urbancic, T., & Lavrac, N. (2012). Cross-domain literature mining: Finding bridging concepts with CrossBee. In *Proceedings of the International Conference on Computational Creativity* (ICCC 2012). University College Dublin.

Kaara, W. (2005). *Statement for a religious leaders' consultation on global poverty*. Retrieved from http://www.nationalcathedral.org/pdfs/050911/WahuKaara_Stmt.pdf

Kadafa, A. A. (2012). Oil exploration and spillage in the Niger Delta of Nigeria. *Civil and Environmental Research, 2*(3), 38–51.

Kale, P., & Singh, H. (2009). Managing strategic alliances: What do we know now, and where do we go from here? *The Academy of Management Perspectives, 23*(3), 45–62. doi:10.5465/AMP.2009.43479263

Kallis, G. (2011). In Defence of Degrowth. *Ecological Economics, 70*(5), 873–880. doi:10.1016/j.ecolecon.2010.12.007

Kamwaria, A. N., Kamau, J. M., Githaiga, A. J., Guantai, P. M., Mugwe, R., Makin, K. R., & Dida, G. B. (2015). Socialising Government: Evaluating the Role of Social Media in Governance and Ethics in Kenya. *International Journal of Humanities and Social Science, 5*(1), 17–122.

Kaplan, E. (2016). *Making Cybersecurity a Business Function Poses Challenge*. Retrieved August 18, 2016, from CFO.com website: http://ww2.cfo.com/cyber-security-technology/2016/06/making-cybersecurity-business-function-poses-challenges/

Kaplan, A. M., & Haenlein, M. (2010). Users of the world, unite! The challenges and opportunities of socialmedia. *Business Horizons*, *53*(1), 59–68. doi:10.1016/j.bushor.2009.09.003

Karadeniz, E. E. (2006). Entrepreneurship and Economic Development. *Kocaeli Üniversitesi Sosyal Bilimler Enstitüsü Dergisi, 11*(1).

Karim, K., Suh, S., Carter, C., & Zhang, M. (2015). Corporate social responsibility: Evidence from the United Kingdom. *Journal of International Business Research*, *14*(1), 85–100.

Kaygusuz, K. (2011). Energy for sustainable development: A case of developing countries. *Renewable & Sustainable Energy Reviews*, 1116–1126.

Keay, A. (2014). Comply or explain in corporate governance codes: In need of greater regulatory oversight? *Legal Studies*, *34*(2), 279–304. doi:10.1111/lest.12014

Keeley, L., Walters, H., Pikkel, R., & Quinn, B. (2013). *Ten types of innovation: The discipline of building breakthroughs*. John Wiley.

Kelly Global Workforce. (2011). *Index*. Retrieved 13 Dec 2015 from http://www.kellyservices.com

Kelly, L. (2014). *Companies must act quickly to tackle cybercrime*. Retrieved December 1, 2014, from http://www.computerweekly.com/feature/Companies-must-act-quickly-to-tackle-cyber-crime

Kemp, H. (2014, January). The cost of corruption is a serious challenge for companies. *The Guardian*. Retrieved from http://www.theguardian.com/sustainable-business/corruption-bribery-cost-serious-challenge-business

Kemp, D., & Vanclay, F. (2013). Human rights and impact assessment: Clarifying the connections in practice. *Human Rights and Impact Assessment*, *31*(2), 86–96.

Kemppainen-Koivisto, R., Siltavirta, K., Rusko, R., & Särkkä, S. (2015). Creativity with Institutionalization: Co-operatives as an Alternative Way of Starting a Creative Business–Cases from Finland. In B. Christiansen & J. Koeman (Eds.), *Nationalism, Cultural Indoctrination, and Economic Prosperity in the Digital Age* (pp. 221–240). IGI Global.

Kerr, S. N. (2012). *A blessing in disguise? Ghana's potential to overcome Nigeria's oil curse and develop a successful model for oil production within human rights frame work. Senior Theses*. Hartford: Trinity College.

Khan, O., & Estay, D. A. S. (2015). Supply Chain Cyber-Resilience: Creating an Agenda for Future Research. *Technology Innovation Management Review*, *5*(4), 6–12.

Khumalo, P. (2014). Improving the Contribution of Cooperatives as Vehicles for Local Economic Development in South Africa. *African Studies Quarterly*, *14*(4), 61–79.

Kielman, J. (2015). *Data Analytics: Dealing with Cyber Storms*. Retrieved August 12, 2016, from United States of America: http://www.rhsmith.umd.edu/files/Documents/SignatureEvents_Conferences_Symposiums_EventsNotSpecific-ToACenter/IBMWorkshop/2015/kielman.pdf

Kilbourne, W., McDonagh, P., & Prothero, A. (1997). Sustainable Consumption and the Quality of Life: A macromarketing Challenge to the Dominant Social Paradigm. *Journal of Macromarketing*, *17*(1), 4–24. doi:10.1177/027614679701700103

Kindström, D. (2010). Towards a service-based business model: Key aspects for future competitive advantage. *European Management Journal*, *28*(6), 479–490. doi:10.1016/j.emj.2010.07.002

King, E. (2012). *King report on corporate governance in SA*. Retrieved June 15, 2016 from http://www.iodsa.co.za/?kingIII

King, A. A., & Lenox, M. J. (2000). Industry self-regulation without sanctions: The chemical industry's responsible care program. *Academy of Management Journal*, *43*(4), 698–716. doi:10.2307/1556362

King, B., & Soule, S. (2007). Social Movements as Extra-institutional Entrepreneurs: The Effect of Protest on Stock Price Returns. *Administrative Science Quarterly*, *52*(3), 413–442.

Kirkman, B. L., Rosen, B., Tesluk, P. E., & Gibson, C. B. (2004). The impact of team empowerment on virtual team performance: The moderating role of face-to-face interaction. *Academy of Management Journal*, *47*(2), 175–192. doi:10.2307/20159571

Kirschner, P. A., Buckingham-Shum, S. J., & Carr, C. S. (2012). *Visualizing argumentation: Software tools for collaborative and educational sense-making*. Berlin: Springer Science & Business Media.

Knights, D., & Richards, W. (2003). Sex, discrimination in the UK academia. *Gender, Work and Organization*, *10*(2), 213–238. doi:10.1111/1468-0432.t01-1-00012

Knowlton, L. W., & Phillips, C. C. (2012). *The logic model guidebook: Better strategies for great results* (2nd ed.). Thousand Oaks, CA: Sage Publications.

Knox, D., & Castles, S. (1982). Education with production—learning from the third world. *International Journal of Educational Development*, *2*(1), 1–14. doi:10.1016/0738-0593(82)90062-1

Kolberg, E. (2014). *The sixth extinction: an unnatural history*. New York: Henry Holt and Company, LLC.

Kotler, P., Armstrong, G., Beneke, J., Bhowan, K., Blake, S., & Wait, M. (2010). *Principles of Marketing: Global and Southern African Perspectives*. Cape Town, South Africa: Pearson Education.

Kotler, P., & Lee, N. (2008). *Social Marketing: Influencing Behaviours for Good* (3rd ed.). Los Angeles, CA: Sage.

Kotler, P., Roberto, N., & Lee, N. (2002). *Social Marketing: Improving the Quality of Life* (2nd ed.). Sage.

Kotter, T., & Berthold, M. (2012) From information networks to bisociative information networks. In Bisociative knowledge discovery: An introduction to concept, algorithms, tools, and applications (pp. 33–50). Heidelberg, Germany: Springer. doi:10.1007/978-3-642-31830-6_3

Kotter, T., Thiel, K., & Berthold, M. R. (2010). Domain bridging associations support creativity. In *Proceedings of the International Conference on Computational Creativity - ICCC 2010* (pp. 200–204). Lisbon, Portugal: Department of Informatics Engineering, University of Coimbra

Koveos, P. (2011). Entrepreneurship and Economic Development: the Relationship Revisited. *Journal of Developmental Entrepreneurship*, *16*(2), 165–167.

KPMG. (2014). *Cyber security: it's not just about technology*. Retrieved August 16, 2016, from https://assets.kpmg.com/content/dam/kpmg/pdf/2014/05/cyber-security-not-just-technology.pdf

Krippendorff, K. (2004). *Content analysis. An introduction to its methodology*. Thousand Oaks, CA: Sage.

Kusmierek, K., & Staff, L. (1988). Warch Sheds Light on University Operations, Finances and Goals. *The Lawrential*, *106*(7), 1.

Laertius, D. (1853). *The Lives and Opinions of Eminent Philosophers.* (C.D. Yonge, Trans.). London: Henry G. Bohn. Retrieved from http://www.classicpersuasion.org/pw/diogenes/dlpyrrho.htm (Original work published 3rd century AD)

Laiken, M. (2001). *Models of organizational learning: Paradoxes and best practices in the post industrial workplace.* NALL Working Paper, 25. University of Toronto. Retrieved November 24, 2015, from http://nall.oise.utoronto.ca/res/25MarilynLaiken.pdf

Lakeoff, G., & Johnson, M. (1980). *Metaphors we live by*. Chicago, IL: University of Chicago Press.

Lane, J., & Munkholm, N. V. (2015). Danish and British protection from disability discrimination at work-past, present and future. *International Journal of Comparative Labour Law and Industrial Relations*, *31*(1), 91–113.

Langley, D., & van den Broek, T. (2010). *Exploring social media as a driver of sustainable behaviour: case analysis and policy implications*. Internet Politics and Policy Conference 2010, Oxford, UK.

Lans, T., Blok, V., & Wesselink, R. (2014). Learning apart and together: Towards an integrated competence framework for sustainable entrepreneurship in higher education. *Journal of Cleaner Production*, *62*, 37–47. doi:10.1016/j.jclepro.2013.03.036

Lapia, R., & Knight, L. (2011). *Recycle, reuse, design: eco-creativity in Rome*. Retrieved August 20, 2016, from http://www.cafebabel.co.uk/culture/article/recycle-reuse-design-eco-creativity-in-rome.html

Laroche, M., Bergeron, J., & Barbaro-Forleo, G. (2001). Targeting consumers who are willing to pay more for environmentally friendly products. *Journal of Consumer Marketing*, *18*(6), 503–520. doi:10.1108/EUM0000000006155

Larsen, P., Stuart, E., Goldman, C., & Gilligan, D. (2014). Current policies and practices related to the incorporation of non-energy benefits in energy saving performance contracts. Washington, DC: American Council for an Energy-Efficient Economy (ACEEE) Summer Study on Energy Efficiency in Buildings.

Laszlo, C. (2008). Sustainable value. *Problems of Sustainable Development*, *3*(2), 25–29.

Latouche, S. (2010). *Farewell to Growth*. Cambridge, UK: Polity.

Lauriere, J. (1990). *Problem solving and artificial intelligence*. New York: Prentice Hall.

Laužikas, M., & Mokšeckienė, R. (2013). The role of creativity in sustainable business. *Entrepreneurship and Sustainability Issues*, *1*(1), 10–22. doi:10.9770/jesi.2013.1.1(2)

Lavis, J. (2006). Research, public policymaking, and knowledge-translation processes: Canadian efforts to build bridges. *The Journal of Continuing Education in the Health Professions*, *26*(1), 37–45. doi:10.1002/chp.49 PMID:16557509

Lawrence, F. (2013). The Role of Local Economic Development Agencies in the South African Local Economic Development Landscape. *Urban Forum, 24*(4), 523-541.

Lawson, B. (2005). *How designers think: The design process demystified* (4th ed.). Philadelphia, PA: Architectural Press.

Lazos-Ruíz, A., Moreno-Casasola, P., & Galante, E. (2013). Green Rural Enterprises: Guidelines for empowering local groups towards sustainable ventures. *Journal of Environmental Planning and Management*, 1–23.

Leachman, S. (2014). *Investing in ideas*. Retrieved August 20, 2016, from http://www.news.ucsb.edu/2014/014462/investing-ideas

Lee, M. (2014). *IT security is not an optional extra*. Retrieved September 1, 2014, from ZDNet website: http://www.zdnet.com/it-security-is-not-an-optional-extra-7000025991/

Leedy, P., & Ormrod, J. (2013). *Practical Research – Planning & Design* (10th ed.). Boston: Pearson.

Lee, J. G. (2011). *HR Metrics – Strategic and Qualitative Tools for People Management*. Randburg: Knowres Publishing.

Lee, S. M., Olson, D. L., & Trimi, S. (2012). Co-innovation: Convergenomics, collaboration, and co-creation for organizational values. *Management Decision*, *50*(5), 817–831. doi:10.1108/00251741211227528

Lee, V. H., Leong, L. Y., Hew, T. S., & Ooi, K. B. (2013). Knowledge management: A key determinant in advancing technological innovation? *Journal of Knowledge Management*, *17*(6), 848–872. doi:10.1108/JKM-08-2013-0315

Lefebvre, C. (2011). An Integrative Model for Social Marketing. *Journal of Social Marketing*, *1*(1), 54–72. doi:10.1108/20426761111104437

Lefebvre, C., & Flora, J. (1988). Social Marketing and Public Health Intervention. *Health Education Quarterly*, *15*(3), 299–315. doi:10.1177/109019818801500305 PMID:3056876

Leisinger, K. M. (2003). Opportunities and risks of the United Nations Global Compact. *Journal of Corporate Citizenship*, *11*(19), 113–132. doi:10.9774/GLEAF.4700.2003.au.00013

Lenox, M., & Eesley, C. (2009). Private Environmental Activism and the Selection and Response of Firms Targets. *Journal of Economics & Management Strategy*, *18*(1), 45–73. doi:10.1111/j.1530-9134.2009.00207.x

Lenski, W. (Ed.). (2004). Lecture Notes in Computer Science*Logic versus approximation: Essays dedicated to Michael M. Richter on the occasion of his 65th birthday*. New York: Springer. doi:10.1007/b98383

Leonard, A. (2010). *The story of stuff: How our obsession with stuff is trashing the planet, our communities, and our health-and a vision for change*. Simon and Schuster.

Leonard, D., & Sensiper, S. (1998). The role of tacit knowledge in group innovation. *California Management Review*, *40*(3), 112–132. doi:10.2307/41165946

Levesque, R., Walsh, D. A., & Whyte, D. (2015). Securing Cyberspace: Towards an Agenda for Research and Practice. *Technology Innovation Management Review*, *5*(11), 26–34.

Levin, K., Cashore, B., Bernstein, S., & Auld, G. (2007). Playing it Forward: path dependency, progressive incrementalism, and the "Super WIcked" problem of global climate change.*International Studies Association Convention*.

Levin, K., Cashore, B., Bernstein, S., & Auld, G. (2012). Overcoming the tragedy of super wicked problems: Constraining our future selves to ameliorate global climate change. *Policy Sciences*, *45*(2), 123–152. doi:10.1007/s11077-012-9151-0

Lewin, K. (1946). Action research and minority problems. *The Journal of Social Issues*, *2*(4), 34–46. doi:10.1111/j.1540-4560.1946.tb02295.x

Lieberman, G. (2015). Preparing for a Cyberattack by Extending BCM Into the C-suite. *ISACA*, *5*, 47–50.

Lieberman, H. (2002). Interfaces that give and take advice. In J. M. Carroll (Ed.), *Human-computer interaction in the new millennium* (pp. 475–486). Boston, MA: Addison-Wesley.

Lindgreen, A., Palmer, R., & Vanhamme, R. (2004). Contemporary Marketing Practice: Theoretical Propositions and Practical Implications. *Marketing Intelligence & Planning*, *22*(6), 673–692. doi:10.1108/02634500410559051

Lin-Hi, N., & Muller, K. (2013). The CSR bottom line: Preventing corporate social irresponsibility. *Journal of Business Research*, *66*(10), 1928–1936. doi:10.1016/j.jbusres.2013.02.015

Lloyds. (2013). *Top Five Risks - Lloyds*. Retrieved October 27, 2015, from http://www.lloyds.com/~/media/files/news%20and%20insight/risk%20insight/risk%20index%202013/report/lloyds%20risk%20index%202013report100713.pdf#search='topfiverisks'

Longworth, N. (2006). *Learning cities, learning regions, learning communities: Lifelong learning and local government*. New York: Routledge.

Loock, M. (2012). Going beyond best technology and lowest price: On renewable energy investors' preference for service-driven business models. *Energy Policy*, *40*, 21–27. doi:10.1016/j.enpol.2010.06.059

Lord, N. (2013). Regulating transactional corporate bribery: Anti-bribery and corruption in the UK and Germany. *Crime, Law, and Social Change*, *60*(2), 127–145. doi:10.1007/s10611-013-9445-y

Lotenberg, L., Schechter, C., & Strand, J. (2011). Segmentation and Targeting. In G. Hastings, K. Angus, & B. Carol (Eds.), *The SAGE Handbook of Social Marketing* (pp. 136–151). London: Sage. doi:10.4135/9781446201008.n9

Louw, M. (2006). *The relevance, importance and applicability of corporate social and environmental responsibility: South African case studies*. Academic Press.

Lovins, A., & Lovins, H. (1982). *Brittle Power: Energy Strategy for National Security*. Andover, MA: Brick House Publishing Co., Inc.

Lubin, D. A., & Esty, D. C. (2010). The Sustainability Imperative. *Harvard Business Review*, *88*(5), 42–50.

Lucica, C. (2010) Performance Management. The Relationship Between Evaluation And Reward In The Pedagogical Activity Of The Romanian Secondary Education. *Managerial Challenges of the Contemporary Society. Proceedings*, 115–121.

Lugabihl, J., Owen, D., Rand, T., & Tran, M. (2013). *Taking Charge of Security in a Hyperconnected World*. Retrieved August 25, 2014, from http://www.emc.com/collateral/emc-perspective/h12485-taking-charge-security-hyperconnected-world.pdf

Lyddon, D. (2015). The changing pattern of UK strikes, 1964–2014. *Employee Relations*, *37*(6), 733–745.

Lynch, D. H., Sumner, J., & Martin, R. C. (2014). Goods and services derived from organic agriculture in the Canadian context. In S. Bellon & S. Penvern (Eds.), *Organic Farming, Prototype for Sustainable Agriculture* (pp. 347–364). Dordrecht: Springer.

Maas, G., & Herrington, M. (2008). Global Entrepreneurship Monitor South. Cape Town: University of Cape Town Graduate School of Business.

Mace, G., Cramer, W., Diaz, S., Faith, D., Larigauderie, A., Le Prestre, P., & Mooney, H. A. et al. (2010). Biodiversity targets after 2010. *Current Opininion in Environmental Sustainability*, *2*(1-2), 3–8. doi:10.1016/j.cosust.2010.03.003

MacFadyen, L., Stead, M., & Hastings, G. (2003). Social Marketing. In M. Baker (Ed.), *The Marketing Book* (5th ed.; pp. 694–725). Oxford, UK: Butterworth Heinemann.

Machauer, A., & Schiereck, D. (2004). Church-based Credit Co-operatives in Germany. *Annals of Public and Cooperative Economics*, *75*(2), 319–337. doi:10.1111/j.1467-8292.2004.00254.x

Machiba, T. (2010). Eco-innovation for enabling resource efficiency and green growth: Development of an analytical framework and preliminary analysis of industry and policy practices. *International Economics and Economic Policy*, *7*(2-3), 357–370. doi:10.1007/s10368-010-0171-y

Maconachie, R. (2016). *Urban growth and land degradation in developing cities: Change and challenges in Kano*. Routledge.

Magretta, J. (2002). Why business models matter. *Harvard Business Review*, 86–92. PMID:12024761

Maibach, E. (1993). Social Marketing for the Environment: Using Information Campaigns to Promote Environmental Awareness and Behavior Change. *Health Promotion International*, *8*(3), 209–224. doi:10.1093/heapro/8.3.209

Mainemelis, C., Kark, R., & Epitropaki, O. (2015). Creative leadership: A multi-context conceptualisation. *The Academy of Management Annals*, *9*(1), 393–482. doi:10.1080/19416520.2015.1024502

Majone, G. (1989). *Evidence, argument, & persuasion in the policy process*. New Haven, CT: Yale University Press.

Maloney, D. H. (2010). Solving Problems That Count. *Educational Leadership*, *68*(1), 55–58.

Mann, R., Adebanjo, O., & Kehoe, D. (1998). Best practices in food and drinks industry. *Benchmarking for Quality Management & Technology*, *5*(3), 184–199. doi:10.1108/14635779810226207

Marais, H. (2001). *Limits to change: The political economy of transition*. Palgrave Macmillan.

Marquardt, M. (2011). *Building the learning organization: Achieving strategic advantage through a commitment to learning*. Boston, MA: Nicholas Brealey.

Marquardt, M. J. (1999). *Action learning in action: Transforming problems and people for world-class organizational learning*. Palo Alto, CA: Davies-Black Publishing.

Marques, S., & Domegan, C. (2011). Relationship Marketing and Social Marketing. In G. Hastings, K. Angus, & B. Carol (Eds.), *The SAGE Handbook of Social Marketing* (pp. 44–60). London: Sage. doi:10.4135/9781446201008.n4

Martin, D. (2013). *Transforming Information Security, Future-Proofing Processes*. Retrieved August 27, 2014, from http://www.emc.com/collateral/white-papers/h12622-rsa-future-proofing-processes.pdf

Martins, E. C., & Terblanche, F. (2003). Building organisational culture that stimulates creativity and innovation. *European Journal of Innovation Management*, *6*(1), 64–74. doi:10.1108/14601060310456337

Mathisen, G. E., & Einarsen, S. (2004). A review of instruments assessing creative and innovative environments within organisations. *Creativity Research Journal*, *16*(1), 119–140. doi:10.1207/s15326934crj1601_12

Mazzucato, M. (2013). Financing innovation: Creative Destruction vs. Destructive Creation. *Industrial and Corporate Change*, *22*(4), 851–867. doi:10.1093/icc/dtt025

McAfee, A., & Brynjolfsson, E. (2012). *Big Data: The Management Revolution*. Retrieved August 6, 2016, from https://hbr.org/2012/10/big-data-the-management-revolution

McAfee. (2014). *McAfee Labs Threats Report: August 2014*. Retrieved September 19, 2014, from http://www.mcafee.com/us/resources/reports/rp-quarterly-threat-q2-2014.pdf

McCullough, M. (2013). *Ambient commons: Attention in the age of embodied information*. Cambridge, MA: MIT Press.

McEver, C. (1972). *The strategy notebook: A catalog of conceptual problem solving strategies*. San Francisco, CA: Interaction Associates.

McGrath, R. G. (2010). Business models: A discovery driven approach. *Long Range Planning*, *43*(2), 247–261. doi:10.1016/j.lrp.2009.07.005

McKenzie-Mohr, D. (2000). Promoting Sustainable Behavior: An Introduction to Community-Based Social Marketing. *The Journal of Social Issues*, *56*(3), 543–554. doi:10.1111/0022-4537.00183

Mckibbin, J., Binns, T., & Nel, E. (2012). Uplifting small towns in post-apartheid South Africa: The experience of the Amathole Regional Economic Development Agency (Aspire). *Local Economy*, *27*(4), 388–402.

McKim, R. (1980). *Experiences in visual thinking* (2nd ed.). Monterey, CA: Brooks/Cole.

McKnight, J., & Block, P. (2012). *The abundant community: Awakening the power of families and neighborhoods*. Oakland, CA: Berrett-Koehler Publishers.

McLean, S. (2015). The Disability Discrimination Act(Section 3) 20 years on: Has it been successful?*Journal of Building Survey. Appraisal and Valuation*, *3*(4), 352–359.

McMurtry, J. (2009–2010). What is good? What is bad? The value of all values across time, place and theories. In Encyclopedia of Life Support Systems. Paris: Eolss. Retrieved from http://www.eolss.net

McMurtry, J. (1995). The social immune system and the cancer stage of capitalis. *Social Justice (San Francisco, Calif.)*, *22*(4), 1–25.

McMurtry, J. (1998). *Unequal Freedoms: The global market as an ethical system*. Toronto: Garamond Press.

McMurtry, J. (1999). *The Cancer Stage of Capitalism*. London: Pluto Press.

McMurtry, J. (2002). *Value Wars. The Global Market versus the Life Economy*. London: Pluto Press.

McMurtry, J. (2012). Behind global system collapse: The life-blind structure of economic rationality. *Journal of Business Ethics*, *108*(1), 49–60. doi:10.1007/s10551-011-1086-4

McMurtry, J. (2013). *The Cancer Stage of Capitalism: From Crisis to Cure*. London: Pluto Press.

McWilliams, A., & Siegel, D. (2000). Corporate social responsibility and financial performance:Correlation or misspecification? *Strategic Management Journal*, *21*(5), 603–609. doi:10.1002/(SICI)1097-0266(200005)21:5<603::AID-SMJ101>3.0.CO;2-3

Mehraeen, E., Ghazisaeedi, M., Farzi, J., & Mirshekari, S. (2016). Security Challenges in Healthcare Cloud Computing: A Systematic Review. *Global Journal of Health Science*, *9*(3), 157–166. doi:10.5539/gjhs.v9n3p157

Meindl, J. R., Stubbart, C., & Porac, J. F. A. (1996). *Cognition within and between organizations*. Thousand Oaks, CA: Sage Publications.

Melville, N. P. (2010). Information Systems Innovation for Environmental Sustainability. *Management Information Systems Quarterly*, *34*(1), 1–21.

Mercer. (2011). *Climate change scenarios - implications for strategic asset allocation*. Mercer.

Merriam-Webster. (2016). *Definition of cybersecurity*. Retrieved August 16, 2016, from http://www.merrima-webster.com/dictionary/cybersecurity

Michie, J., & Sheehan, M. (2003). Labour market deregulation, flexibility and innovation. *Cambridge Journal of Economics*, *27*(1), 123–143. doi:10.1093/cje/27.1.123

Miller, R. (2013). *The Changing Face of Cyber-Attacks*. Retrieved September 18, 2014, from http://www.futuregov.asia/reports/e-government/changing-face-cyber-attacks-2014/

Minniti, M. (2013). *The Dynamics of Entrepreneurship: Evidence from Global Entrepreneurship Monitor Data*. Oxford University Press.

Mintzberg, H. (1980). Structure in 5's: A Synthesis of the Research on Organization Design. *Management Science*, *26*(3), 322–341. doi:10.1287/mnsc.26.3.322

Mintzberg, H., Ahlstrand, B., & Lampel, J. (2005). *Strategy Safari: A Guided Tour Through The Wilds of Strategic Management*. Simon and Schuster.

Mishori, D. (2010). Conceptualizing the commons: Reflections on the rhetoric of environmental rights and public ownership. In O. F. von Feigenblatt (Ed.), *Development and Conflict in the 21st Century* (pp. 104–127). Bangkok: JAPSS Press.

Mohapatra, B., Parisa, V., & Banerjee, J. (2014). The Value of Big Data Analytics to the Business. *ISACA*, *5*, 1–6.

Moldan, B., Janouskova, S., & Hak, T. (2012). How to understand and measure environmental sustainability: Indicators and targets. *Ecological Indicators*, *17*, 4–13. doi:10.1016/j.ecolind.2011.04.033

Moline, S. (1995). *I see what you mean: Children at work with visual information*. York, ME: Stenhouse Publishers.

Monbiot, G. (2015, March). Let's not fool ourselves.We may not bribe, but corruption is rife in Britain. *The Guardian*. Retrieved fromhttp://www.theguardian.com/commentisfree/2015/mar/18/corruption-rife-britain

Mook, L., & Sumner, J. (2008). *Knowing what counts: Social accounting for sustainability* (Presentation to the Association of Co-operative Educators (ACE) conference, Ottawa, July 30, 2008). Retrieved from http://www.ace.coop/portals/0/institute/08/ACE_LaurieMook_SEC_July30_08.pdf

Morgan, L., & Conboy, K. (2013). Key Factors Impacting Cloud Computing Adoption. *Computer*, *46*(10), 97–99. doi:10.1109/MC.2013.362

Morgan, R., & Hunt, S. (1994). The Commitment-Trust Theory of Relationship Marketing. *Journal of Marketing*, *58*(3), 20–38. doi:10.2307/1252308

Moriarty, P., & Honnery, D. (2012). Preparing for a Low-Energy Future. *Futures*, *44*(10), 883–892. doi:10.1016/j.futures.2012.08.002

Moroz, P. W., & Hindle, K. (2012). Entrepreneurship as a process: Toward harmonizing multiple perspectives. *Entrepreneurship Theory and Practice*, *36*(5), 781–818. doi:10.1111/j.1540-6520.2011.00452.x

Morris, W. (2004). *Enhancing organisational creativity: A literature review*. Retrieved from http://www.future-edge.co.nz/Files/organisational.pdf

Morsink, J. (1999). *The Universal Declaration of Human Rights:origins, drafting and intent*. University of Pennsylvania Press. doi:10.9783/9780812200416

Moturi, C., & Bitta, F. (2013). Multiagent Model for System User Access Rights Audit. *ISACA*, *3*, 43–48.

Muff, K. (2012). Are business schools doing their job? *Journal of Management Development*, *31*(7), 648–662. doi:10.1108/02621711211243854

Muhammad, U. (2015). *Mass Extinction: Is the Enemy Us?* Retrieved June 19, 2016, from http://www.greattransition.org/images/GTI_publications/Muhammad-Mass-Extinction-Is-the-Enemy-Us.pdf

Mujtaba, B. G., & Cavico, F. J. (2013). Corporate social responsibility and sustainability model for global firms. *Journal of Leadership. Accountability and Ethics*, *1*(1), 58–75.

Mukwiri, J. (2015). British law on corporate bribery. *Journal of Financial Crime*, *22*(1), 16–27. doi:10.1108/JFC-12-2013-0072

Mumford, M. D., Scott, G. M., Gaddis, B., & Strange, J. M. (2002). Leading creative people: Orchestrating expertise and relationships. *The Leadership Quarterly*, *13*, 705–750.

Münkner, H. H. (2005). *Korea Case Study. Co-operative –Government Dialogue on Co-operative Policy and Legislation in Asia-Pacific Region.* Retrieved November 24, 2015 from: http://ica-ap.coop/sites/ica-ap.coop/files/UploadFiles/Publications/Korea%20Case%20Study%20-%20ICA%20ROAP%200905.doc

Munshi, K. D., & Rosenzweig, M. R. (2003). *Traditional institutions meet the modern world: Caste, gender and schooling choice in a globalizing economy.* Academic Press.

Murphy, P., & Morgan, F. (2013). Cuba: Lessons from a Forced Decline. In L. Starke (Ed.), *State of the World: Is Sustainability Still Possible?* (pp. 332–342). Washington, DC: Island Press.

Musafer, S. (2012, October). Corporate social responsibility: Measuring its value. *BBC News.* Retrieved from http://www.bbc.com/news/business-19876138

Musari, A. (2016). *Why anti-corruption drive is imperative for sustainable economic growth.* Retrieved from http://guardian.ng/business-services/why-anti-corruption-drive-is-imperative-for-sustainable-economic-growth/

Musharbash, D. (2012). *CSR Education in the UAE Paving the way to sustainable change.* Academic Press.

Muthuri, J. N., Moon, J., & Idemudia, U. (2012). Corporate innovation and sustainable community development in developing countries. *Business & Society, 51*(3), 355–381. doi:10.1177/0007650312446441

Nadel, S., & Herndon, G. (2014). The future of the utility industry and the role of energy efficiency. Washington, DC: American Council for an Energy Efficient Economy (ACEEE).

Nadler, G., & Hibino, S. (1998). *Breakthrough thinking: The seven principles of creative problem solving.* Roseville, CA: Prima Lifestyles.

Nagel, U., Thiel, K., Kotter, T., Piątek, D., & Berthold, M. R. (2012). Towards Discovery of Subgraph Bisociations. In Bisociative knowledge discovery: An introduction to concept, algorithms, tools, and applications (pp. 263 – 284). Heidelberg, Germany: Springer. doi:10.1007/978-3-642-31830-6_18

Nahapiet, J., & Ghostal, S. (1998). Social capital, intellectual capital and organisational advantage. *Academy of Management Review, 23*(2), 242–266.

Najafabadi, M. M., Villanustre, F., Khoshgoftaar, T. M., Seliya, N., Wald, R., & Muharemagic, E. (2015). Deep learning applications and challenges in big data analytics. *Journal of Big Data, 2*(1), 1–21. doi:10.1186/s40537-014-0007-7

Nakakoji, K., Yamamoto, Y., & Ohira, M. (2000). Computational support for collective creativity. *Knowledge-Based Systems, 13*(7-8), 451–458. doi:10.1016/S0950-7051(00)00069-1

Nasrulla, N. M., & Rahim, M. M. (2014). *CSR in private enterprises in developing countries. Evidence from ready-made garments industry in Bangladesh.* New York: Springer.

National Advisory Committee on Creative and Cultural Education (NACCCE). (1999). *All Our Futures: Creativity, Culture and Education.* London: Department for Education and Employment.

National Institute of Standards and Technology. (2012). *Computer Security Incident Handling Guide.* Retrieved November 10, 2014, from http://csrc.nist.gov/publications/nistpubs/800-61rev2/SP800-61rev2.pdf

National Institute of Standards and Technology. (2016). *Guide to Cyber Threat Information Sharing.* Author.

NATO Cooperative Cyber Defence Centre of Excellence. (2012). *National Cyber Security.* Retrieved August 17, 2016, from Estonia: https://ccdcoe.org/sites/default/files/multimedia/pdf/NCSFM_0.pdf

Natural Marketing Institute. (2008). *2007 LOHAS Consumer Trends Database.* Natural Marketing Institute.

Naudé, W. (2013). Entrepreneurship and economic development: Theory, evidence and policy. *Evidence and Policy. IZA Discussion Paper,* (7507).

Naudé, W. (2010). Entrepreneurship, developing countries, and development economics: New approaches and insights. *Small Business Economics*, *34*(1), 1–12.

Naudé, W. (2011). Entrepreneurship is Not a Binding Constraint on Growth and Development in the Poorest Countries. *World Development*, *39*(1), 33–44.

Negroponte, J. D., Palmisano, S. J., & Segal, A. (2013). *Defending an Open, Global, Secure, and Resilient Internet.* Retrieved from http://www.cfr.org/cybersecurity/defending-open-global-secure-resilient-internet/p30836

Nel, E. L., & Rogerson, C. M. 2013. Special economic zones in South Africa: reflections from international debates. *Urban Forum, 24*(2), 205-217.

Nel, E. (2001a). Local economic development: A review and assessment of its current status in South Africa. *Urban Studies (Edinburgh, Scotland)*, *38*(7), 1003–1024.

Nel, E. (2001b). Local Economic Development: A Review and Assessment of its Current Status in South Africa. *Urban Studies (Routledge)*, *38*(7), 1003–1024.

Nel, E., & Hill, T. (2001). De-industrialisation and Local Economic Development Alternatives in KwaZulu-Natal, South Africa. *Geography (Sheffield, England)*, *86*(4), 356.

Nel, E., & Stevenson, T. (2014). The catalysts of small town economic development in a free market economy: A case study of New Zealand. *Local Economy*, *29*(4-5), 486–502.

Nelson, R. R. (2008). Economic development from the perspective of evolutionary economic theory. *Oxford Development Studies*, *36*(1), 9–21.

Nelson, R. R. (2011). Economic development as an evolutionary process. *Innovation and Development*, *1*(1), 39–49.

Nelson, R. R., & Pack, H. (1999). The Asian miracle and modern growth theory. *The Economic Journal*, *109*(457), 416–436.

Neslen, A. (2015, August 20). *EU calls for urgency in 'seriously lagging' Paris climate talks.* Retrieved from http://www.theguardian.com/environment/2015/aug/20/paris-climate-talks-seriously-lagging-eu-calls-urgency

New Climate Economy. (2015). *Seizing the global opportunity: partnerships for better growth and a better climate.* Washington, DC: New Climate Economy.

Newson, J., Polster, C., & Woodhouse, H. (2012). Toward an alternative future for Canada's corporatized universities. *English Studies in Canada*, *38*(1), 51–70. doi:10.1353/esc.2012.0004

Nguyen, N. C., & Bosch, O. J. H. (2013). A systems thinking approach to identify leverage points for sustainability: A case study in the Cat Ba Biosphere Reserve, Vietnam. *Systems Research and Behavioral Science*, *30*(2), 104–115. doi:10.1002/sres.2145

Nidumolu, R., Prahalad, C. K., & Rangaswami, M. R. (2009). Why sustainability is now the key driver of innovation. *Harvard Business Review*, (September), 57–64.

Niranjana, P., & Pattanayak, B. (2005). Influence of Learned Optimism and Organisational Ethos on Organisational Citizenship Behaviour - A Study on Indian Corporations. *International Journal of Human Resources Development and Management*, *5*(1), 85–98. doi:10.1504/IJHRDM.2005.005987

Nisen, M. (2013). *Robot Economy Could Cause Up To 75 Percent Unemployment*. Retrieved August 19, 2016, from http://www.businessinsider.com/50-percent-unemployment-robot-economy-2013-1

No, C. 3 (2010). Public Enterprise Unit Guidelines on Executive Remuneration. Ministry of Finance – Government of the Kingdom of Swaziland, Government Printers.

Noble, G., & Basil, D. (2011). Competition and Positioning. In G. Hastings, K. Angus, & B. Carol (Eds.), *The SAGE Handbook of Social Marketing* (pp. 136–151). London: Sage. doi:10.4135/9781446201008.n10

Nolan, R., & McFarlan, F. W. (2011). *Information Technology and the Board of Directors Aligning Technology with Strategy*. Boston, MA: Harvard Business School.

Noonan, J. (2006). *Democratic Society and Human Needs*. Montreal: McGill-Quenn's University Press.

Nooteboom, B. (2000). Learning and innovation in organizations and economies. New York: Oxford.

Norman, D. A. (2004). *Emotional design: Why we love (or hate) everyday things*. New York: Basic Books.

Norton. (2016). *Definition of Cyber Crime*. Retrieved from http://za.norton.com/cybercrime-definition

Nriagu, J., Udofia, E. A., Ekong, I., & Ebuk, G. (2016). Health risks associated with oil pollution in the Niger Delta, Nigeria. *International Journal of Environmental Research and Public Health*, *13*(3), 346. doi:10.3390/ijerph13030346 PMID:27007391

Nussbaum, M. C., & Sen, A. (Eds.). (1993). *The Quality of Life*. Oxford, UK: Clarendon Press. doi:10.1093/0198287976.001.0001

Nwagbara, U.,& Reid, P. (2013). Corporate social responsibility (CSR) and management trends: Changing times and changing strategies. *Economic Insights – Trends & Challenges*, *11*(65), 12–19.

Nwagbara, U., & Kamara, H. Y. (2015). Corporate social responsibility (CSR), leadership and poverty reduction: The case of Nigeria and Sierra Leone. *Economic Insights–Trends and Challenges*, *4*(67), 21–30.

Nwazuoke, A. N., & Igwe, C. A. (2016). Worst forms of child labour in Nigeria: An appraisal of international and local legal regimes. *Beijing Law Review*, *7*(01), 69–82. doi:10.4236/blr.2016.71008

Nwosu, J. E. (2016). Oil exploration and the dilemma of unemployment in the Niger Delta region of Nigeria. *Problèmes Économiques*, *1*, 6–13.

O'Rourke, D. (2005). Nongovernmental Organization Strategies to Influence Global Production and Consumption. *Journal of Industrial Ecology*, *9*(1-2), 115–128. doi:10.1162/1088198054084608

Obstfeld, D. (2012). Creative projects: A less routine approach toward getting new things done. *Organization Science*, *23*(6), 1571–1592. doi:10.1287/orsc.1110.0706

Obuah, E. (2010). Combating corruption in Nigeria: The Nigerian Economic and Financial Crimes Commission (EFCC). *African Studies Quarterly*, *12*(1), 17–44.

Ocheni, S., & Nwankwo, B. C. (2012). The effectiveness of anti-corruption agencies in enhancing good governance and sustainable development growth in Africa: The Nigeria paradox under Obasanjo administration 2003–2007. *Canadian Social Science*, *8*(3), 16–21.

Odeku, K., & Animashaun, S. (2012). Ensuring equality at the workplace by strengthening the law on prohibition against discrimination. *African Journal of Business Management*, *6*(12), 4689–4699.

OECD DAC. (2001). *Report on the Informal Workshop on Poverty Reduction Strategies, Comprehensive Development Framework and National Strategies for Sustainable Development: Towards Convergence*. Document DCD (2000)13. OECD.

OECD. (2013a). *Addressing Base Erosion and Profit Shifting*. Retrieved from http://www.oecd-ilibrary.org/taxation/addressing-base-erosion-and-profit-shifting_9789264192744-en

OECD. (2013b). *Crisis squeezes income and puts pressure on inequality and poverty*. Retrieved from http://www.oecd.org/els/soc/OECD2013-Inequality-and-Poverty-8p.pdf

OECD. (2014a). *Private financing and government support to promote long-term investments in infrastructure*. Paris: OECD Publishing.

Ogbo, A. I., Okechukwu, I., & Ukpere, W. I. (2013). Business ethics as a tool for competitive advantage in the banking industry in Nigeria. *Journal of Social Science*, *35*(1), 23–32.

Ogbodo, S.G. (2009). Environmental protection in Nigeria: Two decades after the Koko incident. *Annual Survey of International and Comparative Law, 15*(1).

Ogunfowora, B. (2014). The impact of ethical leadership within the recruitment context: The roles of organizational reputation, applicant personality and value congruence. *The Leadership Quarterly*, *25*(3), 528–543. doi:10.1016/j.leaqua.2013.11.013

Ohno, T. (1988). *Toyota production system: Beyond large-scale production*. New York: Productivity Press.

Okkonen, L., & Suhonen, N. (2010). Business models of heat entrepreneurship in Finland. *Energy Policy*, *38*(7), 3443–3452. doi:10.1016/j.enpol.2010.02.018

Okoosi-Simbine, A. T. (2011). Corruption in Nigeria. In State and Economy and Society in Post-Military Nigeria. New York: Palgrave Macmillan. doi:10.1057/9780230117594_7

Okoye, A. (2012). Novel linkages for development: Corporate social responsibility, law and governance: Exploring the Nigerian Petroleum Industrial Bill. *Corporate Governance: The International Journal of Business and Society*, *12*(4), 460–471.

O'Leary, R., & Vij, N. (2012). Collaborative Public Management: Where Have We Been and Where Are We Going? *American Review of Public Administration*, *42*(5), 1–16. doi:10.1177/0275074012445780

Olivia, L. (2012). Executive Remuneration in Ireland. *International Tax Review*, *23*(5), 34–34.

Ollila, S. (2000). Creativity and innovativeness through reflective project leadership. *Creativity and Innovation Management*, *9*(3), 195–200. doi:10.1111/1467-8691.00172

Olobaniyi, S. B., & Omo-Irabor, O. O. (2016). Environmental impact assessment of selected oil production facilities in parts of Niger Delta, Nigeria. *Journal of Water Resources and Protection*, *8*(2), 237–242. doi:10.4236/jwarp.2016.82020

Oltsik, J. (2013). *The Big Data Security Analytics Era Is Here*. Retrieved August 28, 2014, from http://southafrica.emc.com/collateral/analyst-reports/security-analytics-esg-ar.pdf?isPublic=false

Oltsik, J. (2014). *Endpoint Security Market Retools16*. Retrieved September 30, 2014, from http://searchsecurity.techtarget.com/feature/Endpoint-security-software-market-retools

Omofonmwan, S. I., & Osa-Edoh, G. I. (2008). The challenges of environmental problems in Nigeria. *Journal of Human Ecology (Delhi, India)*, *23*(1), 53–57.

Onstenk, J. (2003). Entrepreneurship and vocational education. *European Educational Research Journal*, *2*(1), 74–89. doi:10.2304/eerj.2003.2.1.12

Organisation for Economic Co-Operation and Development (OECD). (2009). *Sustainable manufacturing and eco-innovation - Framework, Practices and Measurement.* Synthesis Report. Retrieved August 19, 2016, https://www.oecd.org/innovation/inno/43423689.pdf

Organisation for Economic Cooperation and Development. (2011). *Divided We Stand: Why Inequality Keeps Rising.* Retrieved from http://www.oecd-ilibrary.org/social-issues-migration-health/the-causes-of-growing-inequalities-in-oecd-countries_9789264119536-en

Osoba, S. O. (1996). Corruption in Nigeria: Historical perspectives. *African Political Economy, 23*(69), 371–386. doi:10.1080/03056249608704203

Ostrom, E. (2010a). Beyond markets and states: Polycentric governance of complex economic systems. *The American Economic Review, 100*(3), 641–672. doi:10.1257/aer.100.3.641

Ostrom, E. (2010b). Nested externalities and polycentric institutions: Must we wait for global solutions to climate change before taking actions at other scales? *Economic Theory, 49*(2), 353–369. doi:10.1007/s00199-010-0558-6

Ostrom, E. (2014). A polycentric approach for coping with climate change. *Annals of Economics and Finance, 15*(1), 97–134.

Otusanya, O. J., Lauwo, S., & Ajibolade, S. O. (2013). An investigation of corporate executive fraud by CEOs in the Nigerian banking sector. *African Journal of Accounting. Auditing and Finance, 2*(1), 65–89. doi:10.1504/AJAAF.2013.055491

Owen, H. (2008). *Open space technology: A user's guide.* Oakland, CA: Berrett-Koehler Publishers.

Oxford Dictionaries. (2016). *Definition of Cyber Attack.* Retrieved August 18, 2-16, from http://www.oxforddictionaries.com/definition/english/cyberattack

Oyewunmi, O. A., & Olujobi, O. J. (2016). Transparency in Nigeria's oil and gas industry: Is policy re-engineering the way out? *International Journal of Energy Economics and Policy, 6*(3), 630–636.

Palo Alto. (2016). *Definition of Cyber Crime.* Retrieved August 18, 2016 from https://www.paloaltonetworks.com/documentation/glossary/what-is-cyber-security

Pandey, P., & Snekkenes, E. A. (2014). *Applicability of Prediction Markets in Information Security Risk Management.* Paper presented at the 25th International Workshop on Database and Expert Systems Applications (DEXA).

Parjanen, S. (2012). Experiencing creativity in the organization: From individual creativity to collective creativity. *Interdisciplinary Journal of Information, Knowledge and Management, 7*, 109–128.

Parjanen, S. (2012). Experiencing creativity in the organization: From individual creativity to collective creativity. *Interdisciplinary Journal of Information, Knowledge, and Management, 7*, 109–128.

Parjanen, S., Harmaakorpi, V., & Frantsi, J. (2010). Collective creativity and brokerage functions in heavyily cross-disciplined innovation processes. *Interdisciplinary Journal of Information. Knowledge and Management, 5*, 1–21.

Parjanen, S., Harmaakorpi, V., & Frantsi, T. (2010). Collective creativity and brokerage functions in heavily cross-disciplined innovation processes. *Interdisciplinary Journal of Information, Knowledge and Management, 5*, 1–21.

Pass, C. (2006). The revised combined code and corporate governance: An empirical survey of 50 large UK companies. *Managerial Law, 48*(5), 467–478. doi:10.1108/03090550610715963

Pätäri, S., & Sinkkonen, K. (2014). Energy service companies and energy performance contracting: Is there a need to renew the business model? *Journal of Cleaner Production, 66*(1), 264–271. doi:10.1016/j.jclepro.2013.10.017

Patil, S. (2013). Information Controls and Monitoring Framework for Health Care Organisations. *ISACA*, *3*, 38–42.

Patrick, H. (2016). *Security Information Flow in the Public Sector: KZN Health & Education* (Unpublished doctoral thesis). University of KwaZulu-Natal, Durban.

Payne, B. B. (2013). *Advantages and Disadvantages of Automation in Manufacturing.* Retrieved August 19, 2016, from http://www.vista-industrial.com/blog/advantages-and-disadvantages-of-automation-in-manufacturing/

Peattie, K., & Peattie, S. (2003). Ready to Fly Solo? Reducing Social Marketing's Dependence on Commercial Marketing Theory. *Marketing Theory*, *3*(3), 365–385. doi:10.1177/147059310333006

Peattie, K., & Peattie, S. (2009). Social Marketing: A Pathway to Consumption Reduction? *Journal of Business Research*, *62*(2), 260–269. doi:10.1016/j.jbusres.2008.01.033

Peattie, S., & Peattie, K. (2011). Social Marketing for a Sustainable Environment. In G. Hastings, K. Angus, & B. Carol (Eds.), *The SAGE Handbook of Social Marketing* (pp. 343–358). London: Sage. doi:10.4135/9781446201008.n24

Peekhaus, W. (2013). *Resistance is Fertile: Canadian Struggles on the BioCommons*. Vancouver: UBC Press.

Penaluna, A., & Penaluna, K. (2009). Assessing creativity: drawing from the experience of the UK's creative design educators. *Education + Training, 51*(8/9), 718-732.

Peretto, P. F. (1998). Technological change and population growth. *Journal of Economic Growth*, *3*(4), 283–311.

Peretto, P. F. (1999). Industrial development, technological change, and long-run growth. *Journal of Development Economics*, *59*(2), 389–417.

Perez-Batres, L. A., Miller, V. V., & Pisani, M. J. (2011). Institutionalizing sustainability: An empirical study of corporate registration and commitment to the United Nations Global Compact guidelines. *Journal of Cleaner Production*, *19*(8), 843–851. doi:10.1016/j.jclepro.2010.06.003

Perkins, S. J., & White, G. (2011). *Reward Management: Alternatives, Consequences and Contexts* (2nd ed.). London: Chartered Institute of Personnel and Development.

Petric, I., Cestnik, B., Lavrac, N., & Urbancic, T. (2010). Outlier detection in cross-context link discovery for creative literature mining. *The Computer Journal.*

Petric, I., Urbancic, T., Cestnik, B., & Macedoni-Luksic, M. (2009). Literature mining method RaJoLink for uncovering relations between biomedical concepts. *Journal of Biomedical Informatics*, *42*(2), 220–232. doi:10.1016/j.jbi.2008.08.004 PMID:18771753

Petrick, J. A., & Quinn, J. F. (2001). The challenge of leadership accountability for integrity capacity as a strategic asset. *Journal of Business Ethics*, *34*(3/4), 331–343. doi:10.1023/A:1012597201948

Pew Research Center. (2003). *Values update survey. Roper Center for Public Opinion Research.* University of Connecticut.

Pfeiffer, J. (2004). Condom social marketing, Pentecostalism, and structural adjustment in Mozambique: A clash of AIDS prevention messages. *Medical Anthropology Quarterly*, *18*(1), 77–103. doi:10.1525/maq.2004.18.1.77 PMID:15098428

Piketty, T. (2013). *Capital in the Twenty-First Century*. Cambridge, MA: Harvard University Press.

Pink, D. (2006). *A whole new mind: Why right-brainers will rule the future*. New York: Riverhead Trade. Penguin.

PIPA (Program on International Policy Attitudes). (1999). *Americans & the world: International labor standards.* Available from: www.americansworld.org/digest/global issues/intertrade/laborstandards.cfm

Pittaway, L., & Cope, J. (2007). Simulating entrepreneurial learning integrating experiential and collaborative approaches to learning. *Management Learning*, *38*(2), 211–233. doi:10.1177/1350507607075776

Plucker, J. A., Beghetto, R. A., & Dow, G. T. (2004). Why isn't creativity more important to educational psychologists? Potentials, pitfalls, and future directions in creativity research. *Educational Psychologist*, *39*(2), 83–96. doi:10.1207/s15326985ep3902_1

Podoynitsyna, K., Song, M., Van Der Bij, H., & Weggeman, M. (2013). Improving new technology venture performance under direct and indirect network externality conditions. *Journal of Business Venturing*, *28*(2), 195–210. doi:10.1016/j.jbusvent.2012.04.004

Poh Kam, W., Yuen Ping, H., & Erkko, A. (2005). Entrepreneurship, Innovation and Economic Growth: Evidence from GEM data. *Small Business Economics*, *24*(3), 335–350.

Polancich, J. (2015). *The Dark Web: One Thing Always Leads to Many, Many Others*. Retrieved December 7, 2015, from SecurityWeek website: http://www.securityweek.com/dark-web-one-thing-always-leads-many-many-others

Polanyi, M. (1958). *Personal Knowledge: Towards a Post-critical Philosophy*. London: Kegan Paul.

Politis, J. D. (2004). Transformational and transactional leadership predictors of the stimulant determinants. *Electronic Journal of Knowledge Management*, *2*(2), 23–34.

Ponemon Institute. (2014a). *2013 Global Encryption Trends Study*. Retrieved October 5, 2015, from http://img03.en25.com/Web/ThalesEsecurity/%7B3e572e03-a25c-4b78-96a2-a52f9fa4f59e%7D_Global_Encryption_Trends_Study_eng_ar_(2).pdf

Ponemon Institute. (2014b). *2014 Cost of Data Breach Study: Global Analysis*. Retrieved July 10, 2014 from www.ibm.com/services/costofbreach

Pope, R. (2005). *Creativity, theory, history and practice*. London: Routledge.

Porter, M. E., & Kramer, M. R. (2011, January-February). Creating Shared Value. *Harvard Business Review*.

Powers, D. J. (2007). *A brief history of decision support systems*. Retrieved on March 10, 2007 from http://DSSResources.COM/history/dsshistory.html

Press, J. (2015). *Cyber attack at NRC kept secret from other departments*. Retrieved June 24, 2015, from http://ottawacitizen.com/news/politics/cyber-attack-at-nrc-kept-secret-from-other-departments

PricewaterhouseCoopers. (2014). *Managing cyber risks in an interconnected world*. Retrieved December 1, 2014, from USA: http://www.pwc.com/gx/en/consulting-services/information-security-survey/assets/the-global-state-of-information-security-survey-2015.pdf

PRME. (2015). *2015 Annual Report and 2016 Outlook*. PRME.

PRME. (2015). *Principles for Responsible Management Education*. Retrieved September 5, 2015, from http://www.unprme.org

Prolexic. (2014). *Prolexic Quarterly Global DDoS Attack Report*. Retrieved January 30, 2015, from USA: http://www.stateoftheinternet.com/downloads/pdfs/2014-state-of-the-internet-web-security-global-ddos-attack-report-2014-q2.pdf

Provance, M., Donnelly, R., & Carayannis, E. (2011). Institutional influences on business model choice by new ventures in the microgenerated energy industry. *Energy Policy*, *39*(9), 5630–5637. doi:10.1016/j.enpol.2011.04.031

Puccio, G. J., & Cabra, J. F. (2010). Organizational creativity: A systems approach. In J. C. Kaufman & R. J. Sternberg (Eds.), *The Cambridge handbook of creativity* (pp. 145–173). New York: Cambridge University Press.

Putnam, R. D., Feldstein, L., & Cohen, D. J. (2003). *Better together: Restoring the American community*. New York: Simon & Schuster.

Putrus, R. (2016). A Nontraditional Approach to Prioritizing and Justifying Cybersecurity Investments. *ISACA*, *2*, 46–53.

Qu, R. (2007). Effects of government regulations, market orientations and ownership structure on corporate social responsibility in China: An empirical study. *International Journal of Management*, *24*(3), 582–591.

R&D. (2010). Degrowth Declaration of the Paris 2008 conference. *Journal of Cleaner Production*, *18*(6), 523–524. doi:10.1016/j.jclepro.2010.01.012

Raeburn, N. C. (2004). *Changing Corporate America from Inside Out: Lesbian and Gay Workplace Rights*. Minneapolis, MN: University of Minnesota Press.

Rae, D. (2000). Understanding entrepreneurial learning: A question of how? *International Journal of Entrepreneurial Behavior & Research*, *6*(3), 145–159. doi:10.1108/13552550010346497

Rae, D. (2007). *Entrepreneurship: From Opportunity to Action*. New York: Palgrave MacMillan.

Raimi, L., Suara, I. B., & Fadipe, A. O. (2013). Role of Economic and Financial Crimes Commission(EFCC) and Independent Corrupt Practices and Other Related Offences Commission (ICPC) at ensuring accountability and corporate governance in Nigeria. *Journal of Business Administration and Education*, *3*(2), 105–122.

Ramos, D. (2015). Aligning the PRME: How Study Abroad Nurtures Responsible Leadership. *Journal of Management Education*, *39*(2), 244–275. doi:10.1177/1052562914560795

Ramsaran-Fowdar, R. R., & Fowder, S. (2013). The Implications of Facebook Marketing for Organizations. *Contemporary Management Research*, *9*(1), 73–84. doi:10.7903/cmr.9710

Ramukumba, T. (2014). Participatory appraisal of competitive advantage (PACA) approach in local economic development. *Development in Practice*, *24*(7), 897–907.

Rasche, A. (2009). "A necessary supplement". What the United Nations Global Compact is and is not. *Business & Society*, *48*(4), 511–537. doi:10.1177/0007650309332378

Rasche, A. (2009). *The Principles for Responsible Management Education: Implications for Implementation and Assessment. Toward Assessing Business Ethics Education*. Information Age Publishing.

Rasche, A., & Gilbert, D. (2015). Decoupling Responsible Management Education: Why Business Schools May Not Walk Their Talk. *Journal of Management Enquiry*, *24*(3), 239–252.

Rasche, A., & Gilbert, D. U. (2012). Institutionalizing global governance: The role of the United Nations Global Compact. *Business Ethics (Oxford, England)*, *21*(1), 100–114. doi:10.1111/j.1467-8608.2011.01642.x

Rasche, A., & Kell, G. (2010). *The United Nations Global Compact: Achievements, trends and challenges*. Cambridge, UK: Cambridge University Press. doi:10.1017/CBO9780511762642

Rasche, A., & Waddock, S. (2014). Global Sustainability Governance and the UN Global Compact: A Rejoinder to Critics. *Journal of Business Ethics*, *122*(2), 209–216. doi:10.1007/s10551-014-2216-6

Raunio, H. (2013). Co-operative Iimproving Students' entrepreneurship. In *Finnish: Osuuskunta opiskelijayrittäjyyden edistäjänä ammattikorkeakouluissa*. Vantaa, Finland: Laurea University of Applied Sciences.

Rayment, J., & Smith, J. (2013). The current and future role of business schools. *Education + Training*, *55*(4/5), 478–494.

Raynor, J. (2013). *First Edelman "Last Thursday" Breakfast Seminar is a Great Success - Irish Centre for Cloud Computing and Commerce*. Available from: http://www.ic4.ie/first-edelman-last-thursday-breakfast-seminar-is-a-great-success/

Retel, S. (2014). *Cyber Security Strategy*. Retrieved August 17, 2016, from Estonia: https://www.enisa.europa.eu/topics/national-cyber-security-strategies/ncss-map/Estonia_Cyber_security_Strategy.pdf

Revans, R. W. (1998). *ABC of action learning*. London: Lemos & Crane.

Rice, A., & Ringold, J. (2015). *Cybersecurity information sharing: Industries join forces*. Retrieved June 25, 2015, from http://docs.media.bitpipe.com/io_12x/io_123596/item_1139502/ISM_MAY_final.pdf

Richards, K. (2014). *High alert on cyber risk and cybersecurity preparedness*. Retrieved September 8, 2014, from http://searchsecurity.techtarget.com/opinion/High-alert-on-cyber-risk-and-cybersecurity-preparedness

Richter, M. (2012). Utilities' business models for renewable energy: A review. *Renewable & Sustainable Energy Reviews*, *16*(5), 2483–2493. doi:10.1016/j.rser.2012.01.072

Rickards, T., & Mogers, S. (2006). Creative leaders: A decade of contributions from creativity and innovation management journal. *Creativity and Innovation Management*, *15*(1), 4–18. doi:10.1111/j.1467-8691.2006.00365.x

Robinson, T. (2014). *Information sharing requires breaking down barriers, White House cyber guru says*. Retrieved October 23, 2015, from SC Magazine website: http://www.scmagazine.com/ari-schwartz-says-white-house-looks-to-improve-information-sharing/article/378791/2/

Robinson, J. (2004). Squaring the Circle? Some Thoughts on the Idea of Sustainable Development. *Ecological Economics*, *48*(4), 369–384. doi:10.1016/j.ecolecon.2003.10.017

Robinson, K. (2001). *Out of our minds: Learning to be creative*. Oxford, UK: Capstone.

Rocha Flores, W., Antonsen, E., & Ekstedt, M. (2014). Information security knowledge sharing in organizations: Investigating the effect of behavioral information security governance and national culture. *Computers & Security*, *43*, 90–110. doi:10.1016/j.cose.2014.03.004

Rockart, J. F., & Bullen, C. V. (1986). *The rise of managerial computing: The best of the Center for Information Systems Research, Sloan School of Management, MIT*. Homewood, IL: Dow Jones-Irwin.

Rodríguez, G., Soria, Á., & Campo, M. (2016). Artificial intelligence in service-oriented software design. *Engineering Applications of Artificial Intelligence*, *53*, 86–104. doi:10.1016/j.engappai.2016.03.009

Rogerson, C. M. (2010a). In Search of Public Sector-Private Sector Partnerships for Local Economic Development in South Africa. *Urban Forum, 21*(4), 441-456.

Rogerson, C. M. (2011). Tracking Local Economic Development Policy and Practice in South Africa, 1994-2009. *Urban Forum, 22*(2), 149-168.

Rogerson, C. M. (2010b). Local economic development in South Africa: Strategic challenges. *Development Southern Africa*, *27*(4), 481–495.

Rogerwilco. (2015). *Security in the modern age*. Retrieved April 21, 2015, from Hi Tech Security website: http://www.securitysa.com/51239n

Romme, A. G. L., & Van Witteloostuijn, A. (1999). Circular organizing and triple loop learning. *Journal of Organizational Change Management*, *12*(5), 439–454. doi:10.1108/09534819910289110

Roobeek, A., & De Swart, J. (Eds.). (2013). *Sustainable Business Modeling*. The Hague: Academic Service.

Roome, N. J. (2001). Metatextual organizations e-innovation and adaptation for global change (inaugural lecture). Centre for Sustainable Development and Management, Erasmus University Rotterdam, The Netherlands.

Rorty, R. (2004). Philosophy as a transitional genre. In R. J. Bernstein, S. Benhabib, & N. Fraser (Eds.), *Pragmatism, Critique, Judgment: Essays for Richard J. Bernstein* (pp. 3–28). Cambridge, MA: MIT Press.

Rosemann, M., & Vom Brocke, J. (2015). The six core elements of business process management. In *Handbook on Business Process Management 1* (pp. 105–122). Berlin: Springer. doi:10.1007/978-3-642-45100-3_5

Rosenberg, M. (2015). *Strategy and Sustainability*. Palgrave Macmillan. doi:10.1007/978-1-137-50175-2

Rost, J. C. (1997). Moving from individual to relationship: A post-industrial paradigm of leadership. *The Journal of Leadership Studies*, *4*(4), 3–16. doi:10.1177/107179199700400402

Rotman, D. (2013). *How Technology Is Destroying Jobs*. Retrieved August 19, 2016, from https://www.technologyreview.com/s/515926/how-technology-is-destroying-jobs/

Rouse, M. (2008). *Data analytics*. Retrieved August 10, 2016, from SearchDataManagement.com website: http://searchdatamanagement.techtarget.com/definition/data-analytics

Rowe, P. G. (1987). *Design thinking*. Cambridge, MA: MIT Press.

Runco, M. A. (2007). *Creativity theories and themes, research development and practice*. Amsterdam: Elsevier.

Runco, M. A. (2007). *Creativity. Theories and themes: Research, development and practice*. Amsterdam: Elsevier.

Ryan, R. M., & Deci, E. L. (2000). Intrinsic and extrinsic motivations: Classic definitions and new directions. *Contemporary Educational Psychology*, *25*(1), 54–67. doi:10.1006/ceps.1999.1020 PMID:10620381

Sacchetti, S., & Tortia, E. C. (2014). The social value of multi-stakeholder co-operatives: the case of the CEFF system in Italy. In T. Mazzarol, S. Reboud, E. M. Liminios, & D. Clark (Eds.), *Research Handbook on Sustainable Co-operative Enterprise: Case Studies of Organisational Resilience in the Co-operative Business Model* (pp. 285–300). Cheltenham, UK: Elgar.

Saljo, R. (1993). Learning Discourse: Qualitative Research in Education. *International Journal of Education and Research*, *19*(3), 199–203. doi:10.1016/0883-0355(93)90015-C

Salt, S. (2011). *Social Location Marketing: Outshining Your Competitors on Foursquare, Gowalla, Yelp & Other Location Sharing Sites*. New York: Library of Congress Cataloguing.

Salvi, V. (2013). *Establish a Business-Centric Risk Assessment Process*. Retrieved August 27, 2014, from USA: http://www.emc.com/collateral/white-papers/h12622-rsa-future-proofing-processes.pdf

Sanders, E. B. N., & Stappers, P. J. (2008). Co-creation and the new land scapes of design. *CoDesign*, *4*(1), 5–18. doi:10.1080/15710880701875068

Sanders, L. (2001). Collective creativity. *AIGA Journal of Interaction Design Education*, *3*, 1–6.

Sandilands, T. (2014) *Advantages and Disadvantages of Social Media Marketing*. Available from: http://smallbusiness.chron.com/advantages-disadvantages-social-media-marketing-21890.html

Sanusi, L.S. (2010). *The Nigerian banking industry: what went wrong and the way forward.* Delivered at Annual Convocation Ceremony of Bayero University, Kano.

Sanusi, L. S. (2012). Banking reform and its impact on the Nigerian economy. *CBN Journal of Applied Statistics*, *2*(2), 115–122.

Saren, M. (2007). Marketing is Everything: The View from the Street. *Marketing Intelligence & Planning*, *25*(1), 11–16. doi:10.1108/02634500710722362

Saren, M. (2011). Critical Marketing: Theoretical Underpinnings. In G. Hastings, K. Angus, & B. Carol (Eds.), *The SAGE Handbook of Social Marketing* (pp. 95–106). London: Sage. doi:10.4135/9781446201008.n7

Sarkar, S. (2015). *The comply or explain approach for enforcing governance norms*. Retrieved fromhttp://www.igidr.ac.in/pdf/publication/WP-2015-022.pdf

Satchwell, A., & Cappers, P. (2015). A framework for organizing electric utility regulatory and business models. *The Electricity Journal*, *28*(8), 119–129. doi:10.1016/j.tej.2015.09.009

Satterwhite, R. (2010). Deep systems leadership: A model for the 21st century. In B. W. Redekop (Ed.), *Leadership for Environmental Sustainability* (pp. 230–242). New York, NY: Routledge.

Scarborough, N. M., & Cornwall, J. R. (2015). *Entrepreneurship and effective small business management* (11th ed.). Boston: Pearson Education Limited.

Scarfe, A. (2006). Global interdependence, process, and environmental *praxis*. *Revue-E-Journal*, *1*(1). Retrieved from http://www.ustpaul.ca/Philosophy/revue/articles/2006_scarfe.html

Scharmer, C. O. (2009). *Theory U: Learning from the future as it emerges*. San Francisco: Berrett-Koehler Publishers.

Scharmer, C. O., & Kaufer, K. (2013). *Leading from the emerging future: From ego-system to eco-system economies*. Berrett-Koehler Publishers.

Schein, E. H. (1974). *Career Anchors and Career Paths: A Panel Study of Management School Graduates*. Technical Report No. 1.

Schein, E. H. (1996). Career anchors revisited: Implications for career development in the 21st century. *The Academy of Management Executive*, *10*(4), 80–88.

Scherr, S., Uphoff, N., & Herren, H. (2012). Strategies for Sustainable Agricultural Production Systems. In Avoiding Future Famines: Strengthening the Ecological Foundation of Food Security through Sustainable Food Systems (pp. 39-48).

Schmittling, R., & Munns, A. (2010). Performing a Security Risk Assessment. *ISACA*, *1*, 1–7.

Schober, S. (2016). *How fraud and breaches of cybersecurity impact financial institutions*. Retrieved August 5, 2016, from http://www.ibmbigdatahub.com/blog/how-fraud-and-breaches-cybersecurity-impact-financial-institutions

Schön, D. A. (1983). *The reflective practitioner: How professionals think in action*. New York: Basic Books.

Schön, D. A., & Rein, M. (1995). *Frame reflection: Toward the resolution of intractable policy controversies*. New York: Basic Books.

Schurman, R. (2004). Fighting 'Frankenfoods': Industry Opportunity Structures and the Efficacy of the Anti-Biotech Movement in Western Europe. *Social Problems*, *51*(2), 243–268. doi:10.1525/sp.2004.51.2.243

Schuur, E., McGuire, A., Schadel, C., Grosse, G., Harden, J., Hayes, D., & Vonk, J. E. et al. (2015). Climate change and the permafrost carbon feedback. *Nature*, *520*(7546), 171–179. doi:10.1038/nature14338 PMID:25855454

Schwartz, P. (1996). *The art of the long view: Planning for the future in an uncertain world*. New York: Currency Doubleday.

Scott, A. J. (1998). The contribution of forums to rural sustainable development: A preliminary evaluation. *Journal of Environmental Management*, *54*(4), 291–303. doi:10.1006/jema.1998.0233

Secretariat of the Convention on Biological Diversity. (2010). Global Biodiversity Outlook 3. Montreal: Author.

Segond, M., & Borgelt, C. B. (2012). Selecting the links in BisoNets generated from document collections. In Bisociative knowledge discovery: An introduction to concept, algorithms, tools, and applications (pp. 54 – 65). Heidelberg, Germany: Springer. doi:10.1007/978-3-642-31830-6_5

Sellgren, S. F., Ekvall, G., & Tomson, G. (2008). Leadership behaviour of nurse managers in relation to job satisfaction and work climate. *Journal of Nursing Management*, *16*(5), 578–587. doi:10.1111/j.1365-2934.2007.00837.x PMID:18558928

Senge, P., Smith, B., Kruschwitz, N., Laur, J., & Schley, S. (2008b). Anatomy of Inspiration. *T+D, 62*(8), 52-55.

Senge, P. M. (1990). *The Fifth Discipline: The Art and Practice of the Learning Organization*. New York: Doubleday/Currency.

Senge, P., Scharmer, C. O., Jaworski, J., & Flowers, B. S. (2008a). *Presence: Human Purpose and the Field of the Future*. Broadway Business.

Sen, S., Gurhan-Canli, Z., & Morwitz, V. (2001). Withholding consumption: A social dilemma perspective on consumer boycotts. *The Journal of Consumer Research*, *28*(3), 399–417. doi:10.1086/323729

Servaes, H., & Tamayo, A. (2013). The impact of corporate social responsibility on firm value: The role of customer awareness. *Management Science*, *59*(5), 1045–1061. doi:10.1287/mnsc.1120.1630

Sethi, S., & Schepers, D. (2014). United Nations Global Compact: The Promise-Performance Gap. *Journal of Business Ethics*, *122*(2), 193–208. doi:10.1007/s10551-013-1629-y

Seuring, S., & Müller, M. (2008). From a literature review to a conceptual framework for sustainable supply chain management. *Journal of Cleaner Production*, *16*(15), 1699–1710. doi:10.1016/j.jclepro.2008.04.020

Shackman, G. (2006–2009). *Understanding the world today* (Website of the Global Social Change Research Project). Retrieved from http://gsociology.icaap.org/

Shambaugh, N. (2008). Future design: How novices solve impossible problems. *The Journal of Design Principles & Practices*, *2*(3), 13–19. doi:10.18848/1833-1874/CGP/v02i03/37562

Shellenberger, M. (2003). *Race to the top—A report on ethical business campaigns*. Portland, OR: Ethical Business Campaigns Network.

Shepherd, D. A., & Krueger, N. F. (2002). An Intentions-Based Model of Entrepreneurial Teams' Social Cognition'. *Entrepreneurship Theory and Practice*, *27*(2), 167–185. doi:10.1111/1540-8520.00005

Sherraden, M. S. (1998). *Community economic development and social work*. Binghamton, NY: Haworth Press.

Sherwin, C. (2011). *Creativity: missing from the sustainability jigsaw? Forum for the future*. Retrieved August 20, 2016, from https://www.forumforthefuture.org/blog/creativity-missing-sustainability-jigsaw

Sheth, J., & Parvatiyar, A. (2002). Evolving Relationship Marketing into a Discipline. *Journal of Relationship Marketing*, *1*(1), 3–16. doi:10.1300/J366v01n01_02

Shettleworth, S. J. (2010). Cognition, Evaluation and Behavior (2nd ed.). New York: Oxford.

Shields, J. (2007). *Managing Employee Performance and Reward: Concepts, Practices, Strategies*. Cambridge, UK: Cambridge University Press. doi:10.1017/CBO9781139168748

Shonder, J. (2013). *Beyond guaranteed savings: Additional cost savings associated with ESPC projects*. Oak Ridge, TN: Oak Ridge National Laboratory. doi:10.2172/1086643

Shriberg, M. (2012). Sustainability leadership as 21st century leadership. In D. R. Gallagher (Ed.), *Environmental leadership: A reference handbook* (Vol. 2, pp. 469–480). Los Angeles: Sage Publications. doi:10.4135/9781452218601.n50

Shrives, P. J., & Brennan, N. M. (2015). A typology for exploring the quality of explanations for non-compliance with UK corporate governance regulations. *The British Accounting Review*, *47*(1), 85–99. doi:10.1016/j.bar.2014.08.002

Shurville, S., & Brown, H. (2009). *Developing collaborative competence in the librarians of the future* (Presentation delivered at the 2009 ALIA conference, Sydney, Australia). Retrieved from http://conferences.alia.org.au/online2009/docs/PresentationC19.ppt

Siddique, M. (2014). CSR practices and competitive advantages: A descriptive study. *American Journal of Trade and Policy*, *1*(3), 109–116.

Siddiqui, K. (1984). *An evaluation of the Grameen Bank operation*. Dhaka: National Institute of Local Government.

Silverman, D. (2010). *Doing qualitative research. A practical handbook* (3rd ed.). London: Sage.

Simon, B. (2011). Not going to Starbucks: Boycotts and the out-scouring of politics in the branded world. *Journal of Consumer Culture*, *11*(2), 145–167. doi:10.1177/1469540511402448

Simon, H. A. (1996). *Sciences of the artificial* (3rd ed.). Cambridge, MA: MIT Press.

Singer, T., & Ricard, M. (Eds.). (2015). Caring Economics: Conversations on Altruism and Compassion, Between Scientists, Economists, and the Dalai Lama. Picador USA.

Si, S., & Wei, F. (2012). Transformational and transactional leaderships, empowerment climate and innovation performance; a multilevel analysis in the Chinese context. *European Journal of Work and Organizational Psychology*, *21*(2), 299–320. doi:10.1080/1359432X.2011.570445

Sisk, T. D. (1995). *Democratization in South Africa: The elusive social contract*. Cambridge Univ Press.

Slot, M., & Frissen, V. A. J. (2007). Users In The 'Golden' Age Of The Information Society. *Observatorio Journal*, *1/3*, 201–224.

Smith, D. (2010). *Exploring Innovation* (2nd ed.). Berkshire, UK: McGraw-Hill Education.

Smith, D. J. (2010). *A culture of corruption: Everyday deception and popular discontent in Nigeria*. Princeton, NJ: Princeton University Press.

Sneddon, C., Howarth, R., & Norgaard, R. (2006). Sustainable Development in a Post-Brundtland World. *Ecological Economics*, *57*(2), 253–268. doi:10.1016/j.ecolecon.2005.04.013

Soar, M. (2002). The first things manifest to and about the politics of cultural jamming: towards a cultural economy of graphic design and advertising. *Cultural Studies, 16*(4).

Solitander, N., Fougère, M., Sobczak, A., & Herlin, H. (2012). We Are the Champions: Organizational Learning and Change for Responsible Management Education. *Journal of Management Education*, *36*(3), 337–363. doi:10.1177/1052562911431554

Song, L. Z., Song, M., & Parry, M. E. (2010). Perspective: Economic Conditions, Entrepreneurship, First-Product Development, and New Venture Success. *Journal of Product Innovation Management*, *27*(1), 130–135.

South African Press Association. (2012). *South African websites hacked.* Retrieved November 5, 2016, from http://mybroadband.co.za/news/security/66474-south-african-websites-hacked.html

Sovacool, B. (2011). National energy governance in the United States. *Journal of World Energy Law and Business*, *4*(2), 97–123. doi:10.1093/jwelb/jwr005

Srivastva, S., & Cooperrider, D. K. (Eds.). (1990). *Appreciative management and leadership.* San Francisco, CA: Jossey-Bass.

Staber, U. (2011). The Ecological Foundations of Creativity. In F. Belussi & U. Staber (Eds.), *Managing Networks of Creativity* (pp. 30–45). New York: Routledge.

Stanfield, R. B. (2000). *The art of focused conversation: 100 ways to access group wisdom in the workplace.* Philadelphia, PA: New Society Publishers.

Stanley, M. (2016). *Creative Capital Innovates & Sustains.* Retrieved August 20, 2016, from http://www.morganstanley.com/ideas/theme-sustainable-investing-and-creative-capital

Starke, L. (Ed.). (2010). *State of the World: Transforming Cultures from Consumerism to Sustainability.* Washington, DC: Island Press.

Starke, L. (Ed.). (2012). *State of the World: Moving Toward Sustainable Prosperity.* Washington, DC: Island Press.

Starke, L. (Ed.). (2013). *State of the World: Is Sustainability Still Possible?* Washington, DC: Island Press.

Steffen, W., Richardson, K., Rockstrom, J., Cornell, S., Fetzer, I., Bennett, E., & Sorlin, S. et al. (2015). Planetary boundaries: Guding human development on a changing planet. *Science*, *347*(6223), 1259855. doi:10.1126/science.1259855 PMID:25592418

Steinberger, J., van Niel, J., & Bourg, D. (2009). Profiting from negawatts: Reducing absolute consumption and emissions through a performance-based energy economy. *Energy Policy*, *37*(1), 361–370. doi:10.1016/j.enpol.2008.08.030

Sternberg, R. J., & Lubart, T. I. (1999). The concept of creativity: Prospects and paradigms. In R. J. Sternberg (Ed.), *Handbook of creativity* (pp. 3–14). Cambridge, UK: Cambridge University Press.

Stone, B. (2007). Microsoft to Pay $240 Million for Stake in Facebook. *The New York Times*, p. 1.

Stouten, J., Van Dijke, M., & De Cremer, D. (2012). Ethical leadership: An overview and future perspective. *Journal of Personnel Psychology*, *11*(1), 1–6. doi:10.1027/1866-5888/a000059

Strange, T., & Bayley, A. (2008). *Sustainable Development: Linking Economy, Society and Environment.* OECD. doi:10.1787/9789264055742-en

Streeck, W. (2009). Four books on capitalism. *Socio-economic Review*, *7*(4), 741–754. doi:10.1093/ser/mwp019

Stromquist, N. P., & Monkman, K. (2014). *Globalization and education: Integration and contestation across cultures.* R&L Education.

Stubbs, W., & Cocklin, C. (2008). Conceptualizing a "sustainability business model". *Organization & Environment*, *21*(2), 103–127. doi:10.1177/1086026608318042

Sullivan, J. D. (2009). *The Moral Compass of Companies: Business Ethics and Corporate Governance as Anti-Corruption Tools.* Global Corporate Governance Forum of the International Finance Corporation, World Bank Group.

Sullivan, C. (2015). Accelerating Access Management to the Speed of Hacks. *ISACA*, *5*, 43–46.

Sung, S. Y., & Choi, J. N. (2012). Effects of team knowledge management on the creativity and financial performance of organizational teams. *Organizational Behavior and Human Decision Processes*, *118*(1), 4–13. doi:10.1016/j.obhdp.2012.01.001

Suonpää, M. (2013). *Constructing an opportunity centred collaborative learning model in higher education through and for entrepreneurship* (Unpublished doctoral dissertation). Jyväskylä Studies in Business and Economics, Jyväskylä: University of Jyväskylä.

Susilowati, S. (2014). Learning science oriented pedagogy for sustainability to build the concern for the environment. In H. Sutrisno, W.S. Brams Dwandaru, K. Prihantoso Krisnawan, D. Darmawan, E. Priyambodo, E. Yulianti, & S. Nurohman (Eds.), *International Conference on Research, Implementation and Education of Mathematics and Sciences (ICRIEMS) 2014. Conference Proceedings*. Retrieved from http://eprints.uny.ac.id/11431/

Suvin, D. (2012). Death into life: For a poetics of anti-capitalist alternative. *Socialism and Democracy*, *26*(2), 91–106. doi:10.1080/08854300.2012.686294

Svensson, J. (2005). Eight questions about corruption. *The Journal of Economic Perspectives*, *19*(3), 19–42. doi:10.1257/089533005774357860

Swaziland Electricity Company Limited Annual Report. (2013/14). Mbabane: PrintPak.

Sweetman, D. (2010). *Exploring the adaptive function in complexity leadership theory: An examination of shared leadership and collective creativity in innovation networks* (Dissertation). University of Nebraska, Lincoln, NE.

Symantec. (2016). *Internet Security Threat Report*. Retrieved August 17, 2016, from United States of America: https://www.symantec.com/content/dam/symantec/docs/reports/istr-21-2016-en.pdf?aid=elq_&om_sem_kw=elq_9823358&om_ext_cid=biz_email_elq_&elqTrackId=283a3acdb3ff42f4a70ab5a9f236eb71&elqaid=2902&elqat=2

Szabo, J., & Barefoot, D. (2010). *Friends with benefits: A social Media Marketing Handbook* (1st ed.). New York: William Pollock.

Taatila, V., & Down, S. (2012). Measuring Entrepreneurial Orientation of University Students. *Education + Training*, *54*(8-9), 744–760.

Taki, M., & Coretti, L. (2013). The role of social media in the Arab up-rising past and present. *Westminster Papers in Communication and Culture*, *9*(2), 1-115.

Taminiau, J. (2015). *A paradigm analysis of ecological sustainability*. Newark, DE: University of Delaware.

Tatikonda, M., & Motoya-Weiss, M. (2001). Integrating Operations and Marketing Perspectives of Product Innovation: The Influence of Organizational Process Factors and Capabilities on Development Performance. *Management Science*, *4*(1), 151–172. doi:10.1287/mnsc.47.1.151.10669

Tawny, L., Miller, M., & Bazilian, C. (2015). Innovation for sustainable energy from a pro-poor perspective. *Climate Policy*, *15*(1), 146–162. doi:10.1080/14693062.2013.781456

Taylor, K. (2015). Learning from the Co-operative Institutional Model: How to Enhance Organizational Robustness of Third Sector Organizations with More Pluralistic Forms of Governance. *American Scientist*, *5*(3), 148–164.

Techopedia. (2016). *What does Vulnerability mean?*. Retrieved August 18, 2016, from https://www.techopedia.com/definition/13484/vulnerability

TechTarget. (2016). *Collaboration*. Retrieved August 12, 2016, from http://whatis.techtarget.com/definition/collaboration

Teradata. (2013). *Cyber Security*. Retrieved August 5, 2016, from United States of America: http://assets.teradata.com/resources/ebooks/102914-CyberSecurity-eBook/FLASH/index.html

Thackeray, R., Neiger, B. I., Hanson, C. L., & McKenzie, J. F. (2008). Enhancing promotional strategies within social marketing programs. Use of Web 2.0 social media. *Health Promotion Practice*, *9*(4), 338–341. doi:10.1177/1524839908325335 PMID:18936268

Thawte. (2014). *Top 10 Website Security Myths Revealed*. Retrieved November 12, 2015, from USA: http://www.slideee.com/slide/top-10-website-security-myths-revealed

The Biomimicry Institute. (2015). *Biomimicry 101*. Retrieved July 20, 2016, from https://biomimicry.org/what-is-biomimicry/#.V8XApPl97IU

The Commonwealth. (2014). *Report of the Commonwealth working group of experts on cybercrime*. Retrieved from United Kingdom: https://rm.coe.int/CoERMPublicCommonSearchServices/DisplayDCTMContent?documentId=09000016802f2385

The Economist. (2014). *Defending the digital frontier*. Retrieved August 15, 2016, from United Kingdom: http://www.economist.com/sites/default/files/20140712_cyber-security.pdf

The Findhorn Ecovillage. (no date). Retrieved 16 March, 2016, from https://www.findhorn.org/aboutus/ecovillage/ecovillage-at-findhorn/

The Global Compact. (2016). *Global compact cities programme*. Retrieved from http://citiesprogramme.com/aboutus/the-cities-programme

The Institute of Risk Management. (2014). *Cyber Risk*. Retrieved August 12, 2016, from United Kingdom: https://www.theirm.org/media/883443/Final_IRM_Cyber-Risk_Exec-Summ_A5_low-res.pdf

The N. S. M. C. (2010). *Case Studies*. Retrieved from http://www.thensmc.com/resources/showcase

The Nigerian Economic Summit Group. (2016). *Our mission and vision*. Retrieved from http://nesgroup.org/about

Thompson, M. J., & Bevan, D. (2013). *Wise management and organisational culture*. Palgrave MacMillan.

Thorp, H., & Goldstein, B. (2010). *The entrepreneurial university*. Retrieved from: www.insidehighered.com/views/2010/09/27/thorp

Thuraisingham, B., Kantarcioglu, M., Hamlen, K., Khan, L., Finin, T., Oates, J., . . . Bertino, E. (2016). *A Data Driven Approach for the Science of Cyber Security: Challenges and Directions*. Paper presented at the IEEE Conference on Information Reuse and Integration, Pittsburgh, PA.

Thurik, A. (2009). Entreprenomics: entrepreneurship, economic growth and policy. *Entrepreneurship, growth, and public policy*, 219-249.

Tinsley, S., & George, H. (2006). *Ecological Footprint of the Findhorn Foundation and Community*. Sustainable Development Research Centre.

Togun, O. R., & Nasieku, T. (2015). Effect of corporate social responsibility on performance of manufacturing companies in Nigeria. *International Journal of Current Advanced Research*, *4*(8), 228–233.

Tokic, D. (2012). The Economic and Financial Dimensions of Degrowth. *Ecological Economics*, *84*, 49–56. doi:10.1016/j.ecolecon.2012.09.011

Townsend, D. M. J. (2011). International Handbook of Leadership for Learning. Springer.

Transparency International. (2015). *Corruption Perceptions Index 2015*. Retrieved from https://www.transparency.org/cpi2015/

Troberg, E. (2000). The Relevance of Transaction Cost and Agency Theoretical Concepts to the Management of Knowledge Intensive Co-operatives. Turku School of Economics.

Troberg, E., & Köppä, T. (2011). The Relationship of the Co-operative Ownership Model to Knowledge Workers Levels of Innovation and Motivation. *International Journal of Co-operative Management*, *5*(2), 37–46.

Troberg, E., & Ruskovaara, E., & Seikkula-Leino, J. (2011). The State of Co-operative Entrepreneurship Education in Finland: An Explanatory Study. *International Journal of Co-operative Management*, *5*(2), 47–59.

Trust for America's Health. (2011). *F as in Fat. How Obesity Threatens America's Future*. Retrieved from http://healthyamericans.org/reports/obesity2011/Obesity2011Report.pdf

Tukker, A. (2013). Knowledge Collaboration and Learning by Aligning Global Sustainability Programs: Reflections in the Context of Rio.20. *Journal of Cleaner Production*, *48*, 272–279. doi:10.1016/j.jclepro.2012.12.023

Turner, T., & Brownhill, L. (2004). Why women are at war with Chevron: Nigerian subsistence struggles against the international oil industry. *Journal of Asian and African Studies*, *39*(1–2), 63–93. doi:10.1177/0021909604048251

Twitchell, J. B. (2003). The liberating role of consumption and the myth of artificially created desires. In D. Doherty & A. Etzioni (Eds.), *Voluntary simplicity: Responding to consumer culture (Rights & Responsibilities)* (pp. 185–191). Lanham, MD: Rowman & Littlefield.

Ufere, N., Perelli, S., Boland, R., & Carlsson, B. (2012). Merchants of corruption: How entrepreneurs manufacture and supply bribes. *World Development*, *40*(12), 2440–2453. doi:10.1016/j.worlddev.2012.05.025

Ugochukwu, E.F., Okeke, K.N., Onubogu, C.U., & Edokwe, E.S. (2012). Social demographic characteristics of child street vendors in Nnewi, Nigeria. *Nigeria Journal* of *Paediatrics, 39*(4), 174-178.

Ugwunwanyi, A., & Ekene, C. (2016). Corporate social responsibility and its implementation in Nigeria: Problems and prospects. *Global Journal of Human-Management*, *4*(2), 60–69.

Ugwuona, C. N. (2016). 2013 ASSU strike discourses in Nigeria: A critical discourse analysis. *Mediterranean Journal of Social Sciences*, *7*(2), 435–444.

UK Government. (2013). *The Companies Act 2006 (Strategic Report and Directors' Report) Regulations 2013*. Retrieved from https://www.gov.uk/government/uploads/system/uploads/attachment_data/file/206241/bis-13-889-companies-act-2006-draft-strategic-and-directors-report-regulations-2013.pdf

UN (2012). *Political Declaration of the High-level Meeting of the General Assembly on the Prevention and Control of Non-communicable Diseases* (Adopted 24 Jan. 2012, G.A. Res. 66/2, U.N. GAOR, 66th Sess., Agenda item 117, U.N. Doc. A/RES/66/2 (2012)).

UN DESA. (2001). *Indicators of Sustainable Development: Guidelines and Methodologies*. New York: Department of Economic and Social Affairs, United Nations.

UN. (1992, June). *Agenda 21*. Outcome of the United Nations Conference on Environment & Development, Rio de Janerio, Brazil.

UN. (2002–2010). *Encyclopedia of life support systems*. Paris: Eolss. Available from http://www.eolss.net

UN. (2012, June). *Rio+20*. Outcome of the United Nations Conference on Sustainable Development, Rio de Janerio, Brazil.

UNDP. (2007). *Human Development Report 2007/2008. Fighting Climate Change: Human Solidarity in a Divided World.* New York: Palgrave Macmillan.

UNEP. (2011). *Towards a Green Economy: Pathways to Sustainable Development and Poverty Eradication.* Geneva: UNEP.

UNEP. (2012). *The Business Case for the Green Economy: Sustainable Return on Investment.* United Nations Environment Programme.

Unerman, J., Bebbington, J., & O'Dwyer, B. (Eds.). (2007). *Sustainability accounting and accountability.* Oxon, UK: Routledge.

United Nations Global Compact Report. (2015). *Global opportunity Report 2015.* Retrieved June 19, 2016, from https://www.unglobalcompact.org/docs/publications/Global_Opportunity_Report.pdf

United Nations Global Compact. (2012). *A practical guide to the United Nations Global Compact for Higher Education Institutions: Implementing the Global Compact Principles and Communicating on Progress.* Author.

United Nations Global Compact. (2015). The United Nations Global Compact Accenture CEO study: Special Edition: A call to climate action. Author.

United Nations Global Compact. (2015a). *Act globally engage locally.* Retrieved from https://www.unglobalcompact.org/engage-locally/africa/nigeria

United Nations Global Compact. (2015b). *Act globally engage locally.* Retrieved from https://www.unglobalcompact.org/engage-locally/europe/uk

United Nations Global Compact. (2015c). *Advancing partnerships.* Retrieved from https://www.unglobalcompact.org/take-action/partnerships

United Nations Global Compact. (2015d). *Business as a force for good.* Retrieved from https://www.unglobalcompact.org/what-is-gc/mission

United Nations Global Compact. (2015e). *IMPACT: Transforming business, changing the world-The United Nations Global Compact.* Retrieved from https://www.unglobalcompact.org/library/1331

United Nations Global Compact. (2015f). *The power of principles: The ten principles of the UN Global Compact.* Retrieved from http://www.unglobalcompact.org/what-is-gc/mission/principles

United Nations Global Compact. (2016). *Let's make global goals local business.* Retrieved from https://www.unglobalcompact.org/

United Nations World Commission on Environment and Development. (1987). *Our common future.* Oxford, UK: Oxford University Press.

University of Maryland University College. (2016). *Cybersecurity.* Retrieved August 16, 2016, from http://www.umuc.edu/cybersecurity/about/cybersecurity-basics.cfm

Urban, B. (2012). Researching entrepreneurship from a cognitive perspective: A focus on necessity entrepreneurs in the Johannesburg area. *African Journal of Business Management*, *6*, 11732–11742.

USDA. (2016). *Community Supported Agriculture.* Retrieved from http://afsic.nal.usda.gov/community-supported-agriculture-3

Uzelman, S. (2011). Media commons and the sad decline of Vancouver Indymedia. *Communication Review*, *14*(4), 279–299. doi:10.1080/10714421.2011.624011

Vaidyanathan, G. (2016). 10 ways climate science has advanced since An Inconvenient Truth. *Climate Wire*. Retrieved June 19, 2016, from http://www.scientificamerican.com/article/10-ways-climate-science-has-advanced-since-an-inconvenient-truth/

van den Bergh, J. (2011). Environment versus Growth — A Criticism of "degrowth" and a Plea for "A-growth". *Journal of Cleaner Production, 18*(6), 540–543. doi:10.1016/j.jclepro.2009.08.011

Van der Westhuizen, T. (2016) *Developing Individual Entrepreneurial Orientation: A systemic approach through the lens of Theory U* (Doctoral thesis). University of KwaZulu-Natal, Durban.

Van Der Westhuizen, T. (2016). *Developing Individual Entrepreneurial Orientation: A systemic approach through the lens of Theory* (PhD Thesis). University of KwaZulu-Natal.

Van Dyne, L., & Pierce, J. L. (2004). Psychological ownership and feelings of possessions: Three field studies predicting employee attitudes and organizational citizenship behavior. *Journal of Organizational Behavior, 25*(4), 439–459. doi:10.1002/job.249

Van Kleef, J. A. G., & Roome, N. J. (2007). Developing capabilities and competence for sustainable business management as innovation: A research agenda. *Journal of Cleaner Production, 15*(1), 38–51. doi:10.1016/j.jclepro.2005.06.002

van Stel, A., Wennekers, S., Thurik, R., Reynolds, P., & de Wit, G. (2003). Explaining nascent entrepreneurship across countries. *Scales Research Reports,* (200301).

Vasiliūnaitė, R. (2014). Sustainable development: Methodological approaches toward issues. *Journal of Security and Sustainability Issues, 3*(3), 69–75. doi:10.9770/jssi.2014.3.3(6)

Verhulst, S., Noveck, B. S., Raines, J., & Declercq, A. (2014). *Innovations in global governance: Toward a distributed Internet governance ecosystem.* Retrieved on June 13, 2016 at https://www.cigionline.org/publications/innovations-global-governance-toward-distributed-internet-governance-ecosystem

Verizon. (2016). *Data Breach Investigation Report.* Retrieved August 15, 2016, from United States of America: http://www.verizonenterprise.com/verizon-insights-lab/dbir/2016/

Videira, N., Schneider, F., Sekulova, F., & Kallis, G. (2014). Improving Understanding on Degrowth Pathways: An Exploratory Study Using Collaborative Causal Models. *Futures, 55*, 58–77. doi:10.1016/j.futures.2013.11.001

Vince, C. (2012). *A looming mass extinction caused by humans.* Retrieved August 20, 2016, from http://www.bbc.com/future/story/20121101-a-looming-mass-extinction

Vinerean, S., Cetina, J., Dumitrescu, L., & Tichindelean, M. (2013). The Effects of Social Media Marketing on Online Consumer Behavior. *International Journal of Business and Management, 8*(14), 66–79. doi:10.5539/ijbm.v8n14p66

Virvilis, N., Serrano, O., & Dandurand, L. (2014). Big Data Analytics for Sophisticated Attack Detection. *ISACA, 3*, 1–5.

Voegtlin, C. (2015). What does it mean to be responsible? Addressing the missing responsibility dimension in ethical leadership research. *Leadership*, 1–29.

Vogel, D. (2005). *The Market for Virtue: The Potential and Limits of Corporate Social Responsibility.* Washington, DC: Brookings Institution Press.

Vosylius, E., Rakutis, V., & Tvaronavičienė, M. (2013). Economic growth, sustainable development and energy security interrelation. *Journal of Security and Sustainability Issues, 2*(3), 5–14. doi:10.9770/jssi.2013.2.3(1)

Vygotsky, L. S. (2004). Imagination and Creativity in childhood. *Journal of Russian & East European Psychology, 42*(1), 7–97.

Waas, T., Hugé, J., Verbruggen, A., & Wright, T. (2011). Sustainable Development: A Bird's Eye View. *Sustainability*, *3*(10), 1637–1661. doi:10.3390/su3101637

Wackernagel, M., & Rees, W. (1996). *Our Ecological Footprint: Reducing Human Impact on the Earth*. Gabriola Island, BC: New Society Publishers.

Wahl, M., & Prause, G. (2013). Toward understanding resources, competencies, and capabilities: Business model generation approach. *Entrepreneurship and Sustainability Issues*, *1*(2), 67–80. doi:10.9770/jesi.2013.1.2(1)

Walker, H., & Jones, N. (2012). Sustainable supply chain management across the UK private sector. *Supply Chain Management: An International Journal*, *17*(1), 15–28. doi:10.1108/13598541211212177

Walker, O., & Mullins, J. (2014). *Marketing Strategy: A Decision-Focused Approach* (8th ed.). New York, NY: McGraw-Hill.

Wallenborn, G. (2008). *Degrowth vs.Sustainable Development: How to Open the Space of Ontological Negotiation?* Paper presented at the First International Conference on Economic De-Growth for Ecological Sustainability and Social Equity, Paris, France.

Wamala, F. (2011). *ITU National Cybersecurity Strategy Guide*. Retrieved August 16, 2016, from Switzerland: http://www.itu.int/ITU-D/cyb/cybersecurity/docs/ITUNationalCybersecurityStrategyGuide.pdf

Wang, A., Oh, I. S., Courtright, S. H., & Colbert, A. E. (2011). Transformational leadership and performance across criteria and levels: A meta-analytic review of 25 years of research. *Group & Organization Management*, *36*(2), 223–270. doi:10.1177/1059601111401017

Waters, S. H., & Gibbons, A. S. (2004). Design languages: Notation systems, and instructional technology: A case study. *Educational Technology Research and Development*, *52*(2), 57–68. doi:10.1007/BF02504839

Wati, Y., & Koo, C. (2011, January). An Introduction to the Green IT balanced scorecard as a strategic IT management system. In *The44th Hawaii International Conference on System Sciences*. doi:10.1109/HICSS.2011.59

Watson, R. T., Boudreau, M., & Chen, A. J. (2010). Information systems and environmentally sustainable development: Energy informatics and new directions for the IS community. *Management Information Systems Quarterly*, *34*(1), 23–38.

WCED. (1987). *Our Common Future*. Oslo: United Nations.

WECD. (1987). *From One Earth to One World: An Overview*. Oxford, UK: Oxford University Press.

Weeber, M., Vos, R., Klein, H., & de Jong-van den Berg, L. T. W. (2001). Using concepts in literature-based discovery: Simulating Swanson's Raynaud–fish oil and migraine–magnesium discoveries. *Journal of the American Society for Information Science and Technology*, *52*(7), 548–557. doi:10.1002/asi.1104

Weed, J. (2010). Factory efficiency comes to the hospital. *The New York Times*. Retrieved on June 13, 2016 at http://www.nytimes.com/2010/07/11/business/11seattle.html?_r=1

Weilert, A. K. (2016). United Nations Convention against Corruption (UNCAC)-After Ten Years of Being in Force. *Max Planck Yearbook of United Nations Law Online*, *19*(1), 216–240.

Weinberg, I. (2011). *Neurophysics Exploring the Multiple Dimensions of Consciousness*. Available: http://www.pninet.com/articles/Neurophysics.pdf

Weiner, J. (2004). *His brother's keeper: A story from the edge of medicine*. New York: HarperCollins.

Weinreich, N. (2011). *Hands-on Social Marketing: A Step-by-step Guide to Designing Change for Good*. Sage.

Western, S. (2010). Eco-leadership: Towards the development of a new paradigm. In B. W. Redekop (Ed.), *Leadership for Environmental Sustainability* (pp. 36–54). New York, NY: Routledge.

Westhues, K. (1999). *If the market is not god, what is?*. Retrieved from http://arts.uwaterloo.ca/~kwesthue/mcmurtry.htm

Weston, B., & Bollier, D. (2013). *Green Governance: Ecological Survival, Human Rights, and the Law of the Commons*. Cambridge, UK: Cambridge University Press.

WhatIs.com. (2016). *Collaboration*. Retrieved August 12, 2016, from http://whatis.techtarget.com/definition/collaboration

White & Case. (2015). *Cyber risk: Why cyber security is important*. Retrieved August 10, 2016, from http://www.whitecase.com/publications/insight/cyber-risk-why-cyber-security-important

Wielkiewicz, R. M., & Stelzner, S. P. (2010). An ecological perspective on leadership theory, research, and practice. In B. W. Redekop (Ed.), *Leadership for Environmental Sustainability* (pp. 17–35). New York, NY: Routledge.

Wikipedia . org. (2015). Available from: https://en.wikipedia.org/wiki/Tiger_Brands

Wills, J. (2001). Community unionism and trade union renewal in the UK: Moving beyond the fragments at last? *Transactions of the Institute of British Geographers*, *26*(4), 465–483. doi:10.1111/1475-5661.00035

Wilson, A., Lenssen, G., & Hind, P. (2006). *Leadership Qualities and Management Competencies for Corporate Responsibility*. London: Ashridge and European Academy of Business in Society.

Winn, M. I., & Pogutz, S. (2013). Business, ecosystems, and biodiversity: New horizons for management research. *Organization & Environment*, *20*(10), 1–27.

Wlosinski, L. (2015). The Underground Threat. *ISACA*, *5*, 30–36.

Wolfpack. (2013). *The South African Cyber Threat 2012/3 Barometer*. Retrieved August 10, 2014, from http://www.wolfpackrisk.com/SA%202012%20Cyber%20Threat%20Barometer_Medium_res.pdf

Wong, V., Turner, W., & Stoneman, P. (1996). Marketing Strategies and Market Prospects for Environmentally-Friendly Consumer Products. *British Journal of Management*, *7*(3), 263–281. doi:10.1111/j.1467-8551.1996.tb00119.x

Woodhouse, H. (2011). Your money or your life! A critical Canadian perspective on the World Bank's 'Reform Agenda' for higher education. *International Education, 40*(2), 6–21 & 92.

World Bank. (n.d.). *Local Economic Development - What is Local Economic Development (LED)?*. Available: http://go.worldbank.org/EA784ZB3F0

World Commission on Environment and Development (WCED). (1987). Our Common Future. Oxford, UK: Oxford University Press.

World Economic Forum. (2014). *Global Risks 2014*. Retrieved September 29, 2014, from Switzerland: http://www3.weforum.org/docs/WEF_GlobalRisks_Report_2014.pdf

World Economic Forum. (2016). *The Global Risks Report 2016*. Retrieved August 12, 2016, from Switzerland: http://www3.weforum.org/docs/Media/TheGlobalRisksReport2016.pdf

World Health Organization. (2011). *Noncommunicable Diseases. Country Profiles 2011*. Retrieved from www.who.int/nmh/publications/ncd_profiles_report.pdf

World Tourism Organization. (1999). *Global Code of Ethics for Tourism* (UN ref. no. A/RES/406(XIII) & A/RES/56/212). Retrieved from http://www.unwto.org/ethics/full_text/en/pdf/Codigo_Etico_Ing.pdf

WorldatWork. (2007). *International Remuneration. The Total Rewards Association*. Scottsdale: Northsight Boulevard.

Worldwatch Institute. (2015). *State of the World 2015: Confronting hidden threats to sustainability*. Washington, DC: Island Press.

WWF. (2010). *Living Planet Report*. Gland, Switzerland: WWF International.

WWF. (2014). *Draw the Line*. Gland: WWF.

Xavier, S., Kelley, D., Kew, J., Herrington, M., & Vorderwülbecke, A. (2013). *Global Entrepreneurship Monitor (GEM) 2012 Global Report*. GERA/GEM.

Xie, I., & Stevenson, J. (2013). Social media application in digital libraries. *Online Information Review*, *38*(4), 502–523. doi:10.1108/OIR-11-2013-0261

Yang, G. (2009). Online Activism. *Journal of Democracy*, *20*(3), 33–36. doi:10.1353/jod.0.0094

Yoon, S. W., Song, J. H., Lim, D. H., & Joo, B. K. (2010). Structural Determinants of Team Performance: The mutual influences of Learning culture, Creativity, and Knowledge. *Human Resource Development International*, *13*(3), 249–264. doi:10.1080/13678868.2010.483815

Yoran, A. (2014). *How to Transform Today's Information Security Programs*. Retrieved September 30, 2014, from http://reflectionsblog.emc.com/2014/05/transform-todays-information-security-programs/

Zakaria, F. (2008). *The post-American world*. New York: W. W. Norton & Company.

Zeese, K., & Flowers, M. (2013). Cooperatives and community work are part of American DNA. *Truthout*. Retrieved on June 10, 2016 at http://www.truth-out.org/opinion/item/14076-cooperatives-and-community-work-are-part-of-american-dna

Zeevi, D. (2013). *What Makes Social Media So Influential?* Retrieved from http://www.socialmediatoday.com/daniel-zeevi/1246736/infographic-what-makes-social-media-so-influential

Zeldin, T. (1994). *An intimate history of humanity*. New York: HarperCollins.

Zhang, A. Y., Tsui, A. S., & Wang, D. X. (2011). Leadership behaviors and group creativity in Chinese organizations: The role of group processes. *The Leadership Quarterly*, *22*(5), 851–862. doi:10.1016/j.leaqua.2011.07.007

Zhang, X., & Bartol, K. M. (2010). Linking empowering leadership and employee creativity: The influence of psychological empowerment, intrinsic motivation and creative process engagement. *Academy of Management Journal*, *53*(1), 107–128. doi:10.5465/AMJ.2010.48037118

Zhu, Y., Sun, L., & Leung, A. S. M. (2014). Corporate social responsibility, firm reputation, and firm performance: The role of ethical leadership. *Asia Pacific Journal of Management*, *31*(4), 925–947. doi:10.1007/s10490-013-9369-1

Zio, E. (2016). Challenges in the vulnerability and risk analysis of critical infrastructures. *Reliability Engineering & System Safety*, *152*, 137–150. doi:10.1016/j.ress.2016.02.009

About the Contributors

Ziska Fields is currently an Academic Leader and Associate Professor at the University of KwaZulu-Natal, South Africa. Her research interests focus on creativity and innovation specifically in tertiary education, business environments, entrepreneurship, responsible and sustainable business education, and research. She also developed two theoretical models to measure creativity in South Africa, focusing on the youth and tertiary education specifically. She has published in international recognised journals such as the Journal of Social Sciences. Recent publications have looked at measuring creativity in various contexts. Prof. Fields is also a member of the South African Institute of Management (SAIM), the Ethics Institute of South Africa (Ethics SA), and the Institute of People Management (IPM).

* * *

Sulaiman Olusegun Atiku is currently a postdoctoral fellow in Management and Entrepreneurship discipline at the University of KwaZulu-Natal. He is a pragmatic researcher specialising on contemporary issues in Human Resource Management, Industrial Relations and Organisational Behaviour. He has over 8 years' experience in Higher education. A native of Lagos, Sulaiman graduated from the University of KwaZulu-Natal with a PhD degree in Human Resource Management. The author acquired his Masters of Science degree in Human Resource Management and Industrial Relations at the Lagos State University, Nigeria. His Bachelor of Science (Honours) degree was also awarded at the Lagos State University in the field of Industrial Relations and Personnel Management. He has lectured several courses in his field home/abroad and published many scholarly articles in international journals. He is a member of the Nigerian Institute of Management (NIM), Certified Institute of Warehousing and Materials Management (CIWM), and Institute of People Management (IPM) South Africa.

Neeta Baporikar is currently Director/Professor (Business Management) at Harold Pupkewitz Graduate School of Business (HP-GSB), Namibia University of Science and Technology, Namibia. Prior to this she was Head-Scientific Research, with Ministry of Higher Education CAS-Salalah, Sultanate of Oman, Professor (Strategic Management and Entrepreneurship) at IIIT Pune and BITS India. With more than a decade of experience in industry, consultancy and training, she made a lateral switch to research and academics in 1995. Dr. Baporikar holds D.Sc. (Management Studies) USA, PhD in Management, University of Pune INDIA with MBA (Distinction) and Law (Hons.) degrees. Apart from this, she is also an External Reviewer, Oman Academic Accreditation Authority, Accredited Management Teacher, Qualified Trainer, Doctoral Guide and Board Member of Academics and Advisory Committee in accredited B-Schools. Reviewer for international journals, she has to her credit 5 conferred doctorates, several refereed research papers, and authored books in the area of Entrepreneurship, Strategy, Management and Higher Education.

Giorgio Baruchello was born in Genoa, Italy. He is an Icelandic citizen and serves as Full Professor of Philosophy at the School of Humanities and Social Sciences of the University of Akureyri, Iceland. He read philosophy in Genoa and Reykjavík, Iceland, and holds a Ph.D. in philosophy from the University of Guelph, Canada. His publications encompass several different areas, including socio-political philosophy, theory of value and philosophy of science. Since 2005 he edits Nordicum-Mediterraneum, Iceland's scholarly journal in Nordic and Mediterranean studies.

Harry Beachcroft-Shaw is a PhD candidate at the University of KwaZulu-Natal in South Africa majoring in Marketing. His doctoral thesis focuses on identifying certain actions that can be used in social marketing interventions to influence behaviours towards a sustainable society.

John Byrne is the Chairman and President of the Foundation for Renewable Energy & Environment (FREE). The Foundation was created in 2011 to promote a better future based on energy, water and materials conservation, renewable energy use, environmental resilience, and sustainable livelihoods. Dr. Byrne has contributed since 1992 to Working Group III of the Intergovernmental Panel on Climate Change (IPCC). The 2007 Nobel Peace Prize was awarded to the Panel. He is the architect of the Sustainable Energy Utility (SEU) model and its innovative energy efficiency finance program, which received U.S. White House recognition as part of the nation's Be tter Buildings Challenge. The Asian Development Bank has also recommended the model to its member countries. From 2007 to 2012, he co-chaired the Delaware Sustainable Energy Utility Oversight Board. Delaware was the first jurisdiction to create an SEU modeled on Dr. Byrne's work. He presently leads FREE's efforts to diffuse this model, with initiatives in Pennsylvania (the Pennsylvania Sustainable Energy Finance Program or PennSEF – a partnership with Pennsylvania Treasury, Drinker, Biddle, Becker Capital, and West Penn Power Sustainable Energy Fund), California (the Sonoma County Efficienc Finance Program or SCEF), Maryland (assisting sustainable energy outreach ef-forts of the Maryland Port Administration), Washington, DC (advising the District's Sustainable Energy Utility), South Korea (the Seoul Metropolitan Government recently signed an MOU with FREE), and others. Dr. Byrne is Distinguished Professor and Director of the Center for Energy and Environmental Policy (CEEP) at the University of Delaware. CEEP's graduate program is ranked among the three best in the field. He holds an appointment as Distinguished Professor of Sustainable Energy at the Daegu Gyeongbuk Institu e of Science and Technology in South Korea and has worked extensively with South Korea and China. Dr. Byrne is a founding member of and serves on the board of the International Solar Cities Initiative – a pioneering program to assist cities around the world in building sustainable futures. He has served on the National Council for Science and the Environment (U.S.) and advised the Interagency Working Group on Environmental Justice, coordinated by the U.S. EPA. He has published 17 books and over 160 research articles.

Debbie Ellis is an Associate Professor in Marketing in the School of Management, IT and Governance, UKZN. She has a PhD from KTH Royal Institute of Technology, Sweden. Debbie has 25 years of teaching and research experience. Her work has been published in Business Horizons, the International Journal of Wine Business Research, the South African Journal of Business Management, South African Journal of Economic and Management Sciences, and the International Journal of Consumer Studies among others. Her primary areas of research interest include eco-consumption, social marketing, young consumers, consumer knowledge, wine marketing, sports marketing and positioning.

Lenita Hietanen, PhD, is a University Lecturer in Music Education in the Faculty of Education at the University of Lapland, Rovaniemi, Finland. Before her university career, Hietanen has worked as a music teacher for roughly 20 years in comprehensive and upper secondary schools. Dr Hietanen is The President of the Scientific Association for Entrepreneurship Education years 2016-2017. Additionally, she is a member of the European Council for Small Business (ECSB), and a member of the Finnish Educational Research Association (FERA). Hietanen's research interests are social and societal equality, entrepreneurship and entrepreneurship education, music education, and teaching, learning and curriculum.

Idahosa Igbinakhase received his MSc in Management from The Robert Gordon University, Aberdeen (United Kingdom) and received his BSc in Technical Education(Mechanical Technology Option) from Rivers State university of Science and Technology, Port Harcourt (Nigeria) in 2004. In 2011 he was hired by the Federal Ministry of Education Nigeria to teach Technical Subjects in Federal Unity Colleges in Nigeria. He is currently a Doctoral student at the University of KwaZulu Natal carrying out a study on social entrepreneurship in Nigeria. His other research interests include family entrepreneurship, technology management, strategic management, resource management and sustainable development. He is very passionate about management research and strongly believes that sound management practices holds the key to a sustainable society.

Ariella Lewis is a Ph.D. student in energy and environmental policy at the Center for Energy and Environmental Policy, University of Delaware. Her research interests focus on governance for sustainable development, climate and energy policy, and animal rights.

Max Mkhonta (MCom in Leadership Studies) was appointed at Royal Swaziland Sugar Corporation as Group Human Resources Manager in April 2015 and has over 23 years' experience in Human Resource Management having worked in a variety of industries including pulp & paper, textile, communication, services and energy. Max serves on several Boards in Swaziland, including the Sincephetelo Motor Vehicle Fund (SMVAF) where he chairs the Board's Sub-Committee on Remuneration.

Malebo Mokoqama completed her Bachelor's degree in Bachelor of Social Science in Management and Communication and proceeded to complete her Bachelor of Commerce honours in Management. She currently works as a tutor for the School of Management, Information Technology and Governance at the University of Kwa-Zulu Natal. Malebo is currently a Masters student at the Graduate School of Business and Leadership, University of Kwa-Zulu Natal. What keeps her going in life is her faith. She aspires in the near future to work in academia as she is passionate about working and helping students.

Vannie Naidoo lectures in the School of Management, Information technology and Governance (MIG). She has presented local and international papers on various themes in management, education and marketing. She is actively involved in teaching undergrad and post-graduate students in the discipline of management and entrepreneurship. she is actively involved in supervision of Masters and PHD students in the school of MIG and the Business School. Dr Naidoo has published chapters and journal articles on areas of strategy, project management, service quality, technology and education, social media, gender issues and contemporary issues in marketing.

Joseph Nyangon is a PhD candidate at the Center for Energy and Environmental Policy (CEEP), University of Delaware, USA, where he is researching utility business model innovation in U.S. electricity market, including the impact of natural gas and renewable energy resources and the transition towards low-carbon power systems. He holds a BSc (Engineering) from the College of Architecture and Engineering, University of Nairobi where he was Chief Editor of Student Engineer Journal and President of Engineering Student Council. He has a M.Sc. in Computing Systems and Engineering from the School of Computing and Mathematical Sciences, University of Greenwich (U.K.) and an M.P.A in Environmental Science and Policy from Columbia University's School of International and Public Affairs (SIPA). He has led research on the transformative impact of carbon-free energy on sustainability, climate finance, infrastructure-scale green bonds market, and new business models for sustainable energy innovation. He is a member of the following professional and academic associations: the Institute of Electrical and Electronics Engineers (IEEE), the International Association for Energy Economics (IAEE), the United States Association for Energy Economics (USAEE), the New York Academy of Sciences (NYAS), Chartered Financial Analysts (CFA) Institute, American Society of Civil Engineers (2005), the Institution of Engineering and Technology, U.K. (IET) (2004), and Project Management Institute (PMI). His practice centers on electricity markets, regulation and competition issues; energy finance and economics; sustainable business model innovation; and energy policy.

Olajumoke Ogunsanya has a Master of Commerce degree in Management from the University of KwaZulu Natal in South Africa. Her research interests are in management innovation and entrepreneurship.

Harold Patrick is a Forensic Investigation Specialist at the University of KwaZulu-Natal, South Africa. His research interests include Information Security, Information Security Incident Management, Information Security Collaboration, Information Security Information Flow, Cybercrime and Forensics. He received his MCom and PhD in Information Technology from the University of KwaZulu-Natal, South Africa. He is a Certified Fraud Examiner. He is one of the founding members of the Durban Information Security Interest Group. A voluntary group that promotes the Information Security profession, collaborates and advances Information security amongst Information Security Professionals.

Rauno Rusko is a lecturer of management at the University of Lapland. His research interests are in the cooperative, competitive and coopetitive features of business and management, especially in the branches of ICT, forest industry and tourism. His works have been published e.g. in the Forest Policy and Economics, the International Journal of Business Environment, International Journal of Technoentrepreneurship, the International Journal of Tourism Research, Industrial Marketing Management, Managing Leisure, European Management Journal, International Journal of Innovation in the Digital Economy, Global Business and Management Research: An International Journal and in the forms of several book chapters.

Neal Shambaugh is a Professor of Learning Sciences and Human Development. He is a former Associate Dean of Academic Affairs and a Graduate Programs Coordinator of Instructional Design and Technology (IDT) in the College of Education and Human Services at West Virginia University. The master's IDT program has been 100% online delivered since 2010, and he teaches courses in IDT and Educational Psychology. He has been a university liaison to an elementary/middle public school for a dual-degree, five-year teacher education program. Prior to academia, his work experiences included radio station ownership, engineering, announcing, and sales; training program consultant, and an audio and video producer.

Alphonce Tavona Shiri received his Master's degree in Business Administration (MBA) from Bellevue University in Nebraska in 2003. He worked as a Medicare Auditor at Mutual of Omaha and an IRA Specialist at Ameritrade, among other jobs while living in Nebraska. Alphonce moved back to Zimbabwe in 2005 where he was hired by Zimbabwe Open University as a Lecturer in the Faculty of Commerce and Law. Alphonce is currently studying toward a PhD in Management with the University of KwaZulu-Natal in Durban of South Africa and has published articles in the area of management and leadership.

Job Taminiau is a Postdoctoral Research Fellow at the Center for Energy and Environmental Policy, University of Delaware and a Research Principal at the New York-based Foundation for Renewable Energy and Environment (FREE). Dr. Taminiau leads FREE projects on 'best practice' energy efficiency policy, green technology investment, climate-sensitive economic development, and energy conservation awareness for public sector clients in and beyond the U.S. He completed his doctorate on climate change policy and economics at the Center for Energy and Environmental Policy (CEEP). He regularly publishes peer-reviewed papers and book chapters on a wide range of energy and environmental topics. For his work, he was rewarded with a first place climate policy thesis award from CE Delft (Netherlands), a second place in the MIT Climate CoLab contest, two University of Delaware Graduate Fellowships, and a FREE Minds Award.

Thea van der Westhuizen developed an eye for entrepreneurial trends as early as he primary school years where she was selling several novelty items for a profit to peers. She graduated from the North West University with a Master's Degree, cum laude and co-authored a book soon thereafter called "Guesthouse Management in South Africa" where her contribution was strategic planning and business development aspects. Thea relocated to Mossel Bay at age 23 where she opened two businesses. Tesen Tourism Planning provided strategic planning and business development services to the Garden Route Municipality and several other private clients. Its biggest business success was to develop a 4 story beachfront building owned by Petroleum South Africa into a Arts and Craft centre, which is still standing. The other business was Garden Route Tourism Academy which provided training to several hundreds of people within the tourism industry in the Garden Route. Dr Thea van der Westhuizen decided to further her career internationally and relocated to the Middle East, where some of her early professional achievements included: Innovating and developing a Human Resource performance appraisal system for one of the world's largest private owned education systems, Sabis International; Appointed as business development manager for a large property development group, Al Masah International where she was responsible for developing the Abu Dhabi branch from scratch, to a profitable business dealing with multi-million dollar accounts After the global resection hit Dubai, Thea perused a career in Higher Education, where her professional achievements included several innovations: Appointed by Sheigh Hamdan as the best Business Lecturer within the Western Region of Abu Dhabi for her innovative approaches to take learning outside the classroom into the field of action; Part of a core team who innovated the first ever watersport festival within the Western region of Abu Dhabi, (a watersports festival in the desert!) attracting over 76 thousands visitors over a period of 2 weeks. The Al Gharbia Watersports festival still sustain up to this day; Innovated the first ever shopping festival within the Western Region of Abu Dhabi hosted by women for women, which is still happening once a year; Innovated the first ever Entrepreneurship conference held within the Western Region of Abu Dhabi; Awarded by the British Ambassador together with her students as winners of the Lion's Den Business Plan competition After all these corporate action and visiting to 22 countries over a period of 10 years, Thea felt "tired" and decided to take a break from business, relocated back to South Africa where she chose Durban to "settle down" . Currently Dr van der Westhuizen is involved with: Permanent Academic Staff Member at UKZN; Founded a social entrepreneurship program (SHAPE – Shifting Hope, Activating Potential Entrepreneurship); Owns an international recognised Not for Profit Organisation, Paddle For the Planet, with presence in over 38 countries and formally supported by the International Canoe Federation Thea's advice to prospective entrepreneurs is: Follow your heart, act with passion and associate yourself with like-heated people. Be softly persistent and treat everybody, absolute everybody, with respect. People and their hearts are the cornerstones on which an economy is build.

Index

A

B

C

D

E

F

G

H

I

K

L

M

N

O

P

R

S

T

U

V

www.ingramcontent.com/pod-product-compliance
Lightning Source LLC
LaVergne TN
LVHW060405300926
849162LV00006B/1350